Introduction to
MEASUREMENT
IN PHYSICAL EDUCATION AND EXERCISE SCIENCE

Introduction to
MEASUREMENT
IN PHYSICAL EDUCATION AND EXERCISE SCIENCE

Margaret J. Safrit, Ph.D.

Professor
Department of Health and Fitness
The American University
Washington, D.C.

Terry M. Wood, Ph.D.

Department of Exercise and Sport Science
Oregon State University
Corvallis, Oregon

.

THIRD EDITION

with 244 illustrations

WCB
McGraw-Hill

Boston, Massachusetts   Burr Ridge, Illinois   Dubuque, Iowa
Madison, Wisconsin   New York, New York   San Francisco, California   St. Louis, Missouri

WCB/McGraw-Hill

*A Division of The **McGraw·Hill** Companies*

INTRODUCTION TO MEASUREMENT IN PHYSICAL EDUCATION AND EXERCISE SCIENCE

Publisher: James M. Smith
Senior Acquisitions Editor: Vicki Malinee
Developmental Editor: Christy Wells
Project Manager: Linda Clarke
Senior Production Editor: Patricia C. Walter
Interior Designer: Nancy McDonald
Cover Illustration: Bruce Dean
Manufacturing Manager: Betty Richmond

Printed in the United States of America
Composition by Progressive Information Technologies
Printing/binding by RR Donnelley—Crawfordsville

Library of Congress Cataloging in Publication Data
Safrit, Margaret J., 1935 –
     Introduction to measurement in physical education and exercise
science / Margaret J. Safrit, Terry M. Wood.—3rd ed.
       p.   cm.
     Includes bibliographical references and index.
     ISBN: 0-8016-7849-8
     1.   Physical fitness—Testing.   I. Wood, Terry M., 1949–
II. Title.
GV436.S223   1995
613.7—dc20   94-48271
                                             CIP

567890 DOC DOC 01987654321

http://www.mhcollege.com

In memory of our fathers, Ernest C. Safrit, Sr. and Gordon A. Wood

&

In honor of our mothers, Margaret C. Safrit and Mary L. Wood

FOCUS

In the fields of physical education, exercise science, and kinesiology, two concepts assume universal significance: measurement of various forms of physical activity, and evaluation of the performance of physical skills and the effectiveness of programs. Teachers of physical education should be able to select good tests, administer them properly, and use the results to improve student achievement. Although tests of motor behavior are of predominant interest to the teacher, tests of knowledge and of affective behavior—such as sportsmanship—are also used. Evaluation of instruction, curricula, and programs should also be implemented. Specialists in fitness, sports, and wellness centers have similar needs. The status of incoming clients should be evaluated. The effectiveness of the center, both programmatically and financially, must be assessed. Indeed, without the tools of measurement, indicators of attainment would be limited to totally subjective judgments.

Many changes have taken place in the area of physical fitness testing. Two organizations, the American Alliance for Health, Physical Education, Recreation, and Dance (AAHPERD) and the Cooper Institute for Aerobics Research, have formed an alliance for the purpose of promoting youth fitness testing and programming. The Prudential *FITNESS*GRAM is used for testing, reporting, and promotion. AAHPERD is the major source of program material development for youth fitness.

Overall, the purpose of this textbook is to prepare undergraduate students in physical education, exercise science, and kinesiology to use measurement and evaluation techniques effectively. However, the material in this book is also relevant for students majoring in recreation, physical therapy, and occupational therapy. The basic principles are exemplified in both school and nonschool settings, because many students prepare for careers in nonschool settings. Numerous examples of tests are provided throughout the book.

ORGANIZATION

This book is divided into ten parts. Part One presents an overview of measurement and evaluation, including up-to-date coverage of the importance of these concepts in school and nonschool settings. In Part Two, statistical techniques that can be used to describe test scores are presented in a straightforward manner, with step-by-step examples and problems and answers. The material is written in a simplified manner for those who have only the most basic arithmetic skills. Part Three includes a new and an expanded chapter on microcomputers. Part Four focuses on concepts in measurement and is presented in understandable and accurate terminology. Both norm-referenced and criterion-referenced measurement are covered. The latter approach to measurement has become even more important, since the Prudential *FITNESS*GRAM (now used by AAHPERD) has adopted criterion-referenced standards. Part Five discusses the problems in testing in the schools, and includes a treatise on grading. In Part Six, the use of tests in nonschool settings is described. A variety of unique measurement concerns in the field are covered in Part Seven, including the measurement of children, measurement of special populations, and affective measurement. Part Eight gives a detailed description of test construction techniques for both sports skills and knowledge tests. Parts Nine and Ten present and analyze many examples of physical performance tests. These include tests of sports skills, health-related physical fitness, performance-related physical fitness, muscular strength and endurance, and balance and flexibility. The appendices include statistical tables and sources for a wide variety of sports skills tests.

NEW AND SUCCESSFUL FEATURES

The third edition of this textbook features a new co-author, Dr. Terry M. Wood, a measurement and evaluation specialist from Oregon State University. Dr. Wood's contributions provide welcome expertise in all aspects of measurement and evaluation, but especially in the use of computers.

One of the prominent features of this book is its straightforward presentation of measurement and evaluation concepts. It is based on the authors' accumulated experience of 40 years in teaching measurement to undergraduate students majoring in physical education, exercise science, and kinesiology and provides a clear, accurate discussion of issues appropriate to this level of instruction.

An important feature of this book is that it is timely—it represents the field of physical education, exercise science, and kinesiology as it exists today. No longer are all students majoring in these fields preparing to teach or coach physical education; many are interested in alternative careers in a nonschool setting, such as fitness centers, therapy clinics, or recreation sites. A practical approach to testing in these settings is included.

Another strong point is the major chapter on the use of microcomputers, replacing two chapters from the second edition. Knowledge of what programs are available and how to obtain them is critical for any student working in the field of physical education whether it be in the private, corporate, or educational arenas.

The organization of the book provides a practical presentation for learning. After a general introduction to measurement and evaluation in the field, the technical section of the book is introduced by an overview of basic statistics, microcomputers, and measurement concepts. The next section of the book encompasses easy-to-locate material on testing and types of tests. The last portion of the book deals with typical problems associated with the measurement of physical skills and abilities.

Award strategies differ according to the new beliefs about motivating children to engage in exercise behavior leading to fitness. All criterion-referenced standards have been updated. Chapter 17 has been revised substantially to include this new information.

Chapter 10 on testing in a nonschool setting has been expanded to include a description of a government worksite health promotion program. Chapter 13 has been modified to include more recent information about the legal and practical implications of testing special populations.

A new chapter on inferential statistics has been added as Chapter 4. It provides students with a solid foundation and a review of statistical analyses, including analysis of variance (ANOVA).

PEDAGOGICAL FEATURES

The extensive experience of the authors in teaching undergraduate students in measurement and evaluation has been used to design a book that is a genuine aid to student learning.

- *Key words:* Each chapter begins with a list of the most important terms, which the student should learn when reading the chapter.
- *Introduction:* A description of the purpose of the chapter prepares the student for each chapter's application of information to many fields, including physical education and exercise science.
- *Tables, drawings, and photographs:* The tables and illustrations used throughout provide the student with additional information and clarify concepts and activities.
- *Summary:* A summary closes each chapter and carefully reiterates the major points of content.
- *References:* Presenting the most complete and up-to-date documentation, the references provide sources for further study.
- *Annotated readings:* Selected resources are provided with annotations to enhance the learning process.
- *Learning experiences:* A set of learning experiences concludes each chapter and provides the student with exercises to reinforce the material in the text. Answers are provided when appropriate.
- *Glossary:* The text concludes with a comprehensive glossary in which the key words shown at the beginning of each chapter are listed and defined.

ANCILLARIES

An instructor's manual and test bank are available for instructors using the textbook. Included in the manual are chapter objectives; chapter overviews; additional learning experiences; additional sample tests; transparency masters of important drawings, tables, and charts; and over 660 multiple-choice, true-false, matching, and essay test questions. Separate answer keys are provided.

Two new software programs are available to qualified adopters. *Statistics with Finesse* by Dr. James Bolding of the University of Arkansas is a comprehensive statistical program that includes file management and spreadsheet capabilities. Statistical options include nonparametric tests, multivariate techniques, cluster analysis, *t*-tests, and many ANOVAs, including Latin square and MANOVA (multivariate analyses of variance). The software may also be networked with suggested laboratory activities for student practice. Students may purchase the program shrink-wrapped with the text for a nominal additional charge. This program may also be networked for use at a computer laboratory facility.

Also available to qualified adopters is *Mosby's Laboratory Activity Software*. This easy-to-use program includes more than 100 fitness and health activities from Mosby texts. Students can assess their own performance and behaviors as well as input data for others. Please contact your Mosby sales representative for more information concerning these two outstanding software programs.

ACKNOWLEDGMENTS

No textbook can be completed without the assistance of many individuals, and that is certainly true for this book. The support of everyone involved is gratefully acknowledged.

Many authors and publishers granted their permission to reproduce material in this text. The American Alliance for Health, Physical Education, Recreation, and Dance was especially generous. Several colleagues—Michael Pollack, Timothy Lohman, Janet Seaman, and Dale Ulrich—kindly granted permission to reproduce several of their photographs.

Sincere appreciation is expressed to Linda Spraker for the artwork and Jerry M. Capps for many of the photographs. Thanks are extended to the National Center for Health Fitness for granting permission to take photographs at the Army Materiel Center in Virginia.

Reviewers were selected by the publisher to evaluate the second edition of the textbook. Their reviews were extremely helpful in revising the text and, without question, contributed to improvements on the original version. A very special debt of gratitude is conveyed to the following individuals for their thorough and conscientious analysis of the book: Anne Garcia, University of Michigan; Stephen Langendorfer, Kent State University; Beth McManis, Ithaca College; and Arthur Miller, University of Montana.

Finally, well-deserved recognition is extended to the Mosby staff for supplying sound direction during the preparation of the text. We especially thank Christy Wells for her assistance and support throughout the development of the third edition.

Margaret J. Safrit
Terry M. Wood

contents

Part six

MEASUREMENT IN A NONSCHOOL SETTING

Part seven

MEASURING SPECIAL POPULATIONS AND ABILITIES

Part eight

PRINCIPLES OF TEST CONSTRUCTION

Part nine
MEASURES OF PHYSICAL FITNESS

Part ten
OTHER MEASUREMENTS OF PHYSICAL FITNESS

Introduction to MEASUREMENT

IN PHYSICAL EDUCATION AND EXERCISE SCIENCE

An Overview of Measurement and Evaluation

The Value of Measurement and Evaluation

Watch for these words as you read the following chapter

Achievement
Competency-based
  evaluation
Criterion-referenced
  test
Evaluation
Formative evaluation
Improvement
Mastery test
Measure

Measurement
Norm-referenced test
Qualitative
  measurement
Quantitative
  measurement
Summative evaluation
Test
Test user
Title IX

The field of physical education has changed dramatically during the past two decades. From its inception to the early 1970s, the majority of students majoring in physical education planned to teach physical education in a school and perhaps coach one or two sports. During the 1970s the interests of some students began to change. As knowledge about health and fitness mushroomed in the United States, careers other than teaching in schools became available to physical education majors. For instance, as fitness centers sprang up around the country, managers and instructors trained in physical education were sought. How has this changed the field of physical education? Even though many physical education principles are relevant for those with other career options in the motor behavior area, the application of these principles may vary. Thus, every area of specialization in physical education is affected, including the measurement and evaluation area. For example, tests are sometimes used to motivate students in a school setting. Some students may be motivated because they realize their test scores will be used in determining unit grades. In nonschool settings, such as private fitness centers, private sports clubs, corporate fitness centers, the Young Women's Christian Association (YWCA), and the Young Men's Christian Association (YMCA), tests will not be motivating because of grades, at least in the traditional sense. On the other hand, a test may stimulate some individuals to improve their performance in both school and nonschool settings. The underlying principles of measurement are the same in both settings, but the application of these principles may differ depending on the clientele and the objectives.

Measurement and evaluation are vital aspects of instruction. The importance of these processes is not diminished if the instruction takes place in a nonschool setting. This book focuses on the use of measurement and evaluation of motor behavior in school and nonschool settings, because instruction in physical education takes place in both of these environments. The basic measurement principles are equally applicable no matter where a test is administered. However, the way in which test scores are used may vary, depending on the setting.

Suppose an individual joins a fitness center. Before prescribing an exercise program for the client, a staff member administers a battery of fitness tests. These tests might be similar to those used in physical education classes in local high schools. Yet in the private club context, the constraints surrounding the measurement process can be quite different from the public school situation. In the private club, testing is often individualized. The age and needs of the client may differ from those of the high-school student. Attention must be paid to

Measuring long jump performance.

appropriate motivational strategies. Techniques that are effective in the fitness center may not have the same impact in the high school, and vice versa. The importance of prior medical approval is magnified in the older population (AAHPERD, 1989). Since private clubs are often able to administer tests on a one-to-one basis, the use of laboratory-type testing procedures is more feasible in this setting than in the schools.

Most students reading this textbook will have already spent many years in physical education classes in the school system. Can you recall whether tests were used in these classes? If so, when were tests usually administered during a unit of instruction? Did testing seem important to your physical education teacher? How were the test scores used? Were test results used for any purpose other than determining grades? The use of tests probably varied from unit to unit. The same situation exists in nonschool settings. In some instances no tests are used at all, and in others the testing program is of high quality. In subsequent chapters several of these testing programs are described. Measurement practices in both school and nonschool settings are included, with material directed to the budding exercise specialist or private sports club instructor as well as the future teacher of physical education. Since the nonschool and school settings encompass so many potential career options, each with a different title, the term **test user** will be used in a generic sense throughout this textbook to refer to a person who selects and administers a test, regardless of his or her job title.

MEASUREMENT AND EVALUATION DEFINED

Measurement and evaluation are closely related processes. From a practical standpoint, **measurement** takes place when a test is administered and a score is obtained. If the test is **quantitative,** the score is a number. If the test is **qualitative,** the score may be a phrase or a word such as "excellent"; or it may be a number representing a phrase or word. A more precise definition of measurement is the process of assigning a number to an attribute of a person or object. By this definition, measurement is a quantitative and not a qualitative process. If body fatness is the attribute of interest, it can be measured by determining skinfold thickness. The number assigned to this attribute represents skinfold thickness reported in millimeters (mm). This score would fit the universal definition of the term *measurement*. Throughout this textbook, however, measurement is interpreted in the broadest sense as encompassing both quantitative and qualitative indicators.

The process of **evaluation** involves the interpretation of a score. Once skinfold thickness has been measured, what does the score mean? If the sum of triceps plus calf skinfolds is 18 mm for a 10-year-old boy, is this a reflection of a desirable body composition? The score must be interpreted for it to have true meaning. In the strictest sense of the word, measurement is an objective, nonjudgmental process, whereas evaluation requires that judgments be made.

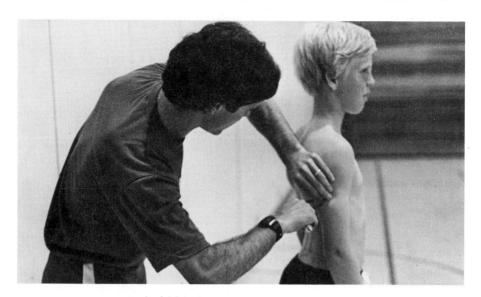

Measuring skinfold thickness.

USE OF TESTS

Throughout this textbook **test** will be used synonymously with **measure.** For example, a **measure** of maximal oxygen uptake has the same meaning as a **test** of maximal oxygen uptake. Tests have many uses in school and nonschool settings. A test may be administered for one purpose or for multiple purposes, as determined by the test user. Usually, the rationale for using a test encompasses more than one purpose. The following are a few of the uses of tests in the physical education field.

Motivation

Tests are frequently administered for motivational purposes. A skills test might be administered in a physical education class to encourage students to improve their skills further. In a corporate fitness center, skinfold measures might be used to motivate overweight employees to lose weight. When a performance standard must be met in a public service setting, examinees are sometimes motivated to work toward meeting the standard by taking a test. The advance knowledge of an upcoming test can motivate students to practice a skill with greater intensity. When a test is administered more than once, students are usually interested in the extent to which they have improved. They like to compare their current score with a previous score, which, in itself, can be a motivational factor. The use of tests for motivation is most effective if scores are viewed in the context of areas needing improvement rather than in a punitive sense. In other words, the test should be used as a positive factor in performance before, during, and after the test's administration.

Achievement

One of the most common uses of tests is the assessment of achievement. How much has an individual achieved during a specified period of time? If most of the clients in a center are below average in their levels of fitness after a year of participation in a fitness program, this points to insufficient achievement by the participants. Do students achieve a higher level of skill in several sports after participating in a physical education program year after year? Do employees in a corporate fitness center achieve the targeted amount of weight loss? **Achievement** should not be confused with **improvement.** Improvement is the difference in performance from one point in time to another. These points may or may not coincide with the beginning and end of the course. Achievement in and of itself encompasses only the final ability level at a designated point in time and is often relative to a standard or criterion.

Improvement

The idea of measuring improvement is near and dear to the hearts of many test users and understandably so. An often-held belief is that individuals lacking in skill cannot be expected to achieve the level a highly skilled group can attain; thus, the beginning ability level of each participant should be considered and the extent to which the individual improved beyond that point should be assessed. Similarly, individuals with initial low levels of fitness are not expected to achieve the same level of fitness upon completion of a training program as those who are highly fit. These are valid concerns. Nonetheless, a number of factors make the desired amount of improvement difficult to obtain when dealing with sports and other forms of physical activity. One, units of instruction are often too short to bring about the desired level of improvement. Two, the background of the student or client can also affect the amount of improvement during a unit. Those who have an adequate understanding of the underlying principles of movement can sometimes learn new skills in a shorter period than those without this knowledge. Three, although a more highly skilled group may meet a standard of performance faster than a low-skilled group, the high-skill group will probably show less overall improvement than the low-skill group. On the surface, measuring improvement seems to be a reasonable solution to the problems associated with fairly assessing individuals with varying skill levels. However, inherent problems do exist in the measurement of improvement and they are discussed in Chapter 9.

Diagnosis

One of the most important uses of measurement in physical education is to diagnose weaknesses in performance. What is wrong with a student's tennis serve? Why does a racquetball club member have an ineffective backhand? Why has an individual's running performance failed to improve? In other words, the diagnostic process helps the participant learn more efficiently. Furthermore, the teacher is able to teach more effectively. Diagnostic procedures can be particularly potent when dealing with knowledge in our field. In this case, errors in responding to individual items or clusters of items can pinpoint gaps in the examinee's knowledge of specific content. For example, a student in a badminton class may answer incorrectly many of the test items dealing with rules specific to the singles game in badminton. This suggests a need to review that particular section of the rules book. Of course, tests are not the only means of diagnosing weaknesses, but they are extremely useful in this respect. Some diagnostic tests can be self-administered, allowing the instructor to spend more time meeting other instructional needs.

Prescription

Once weaknesses have been diagnosed, the test user formulates a prescription for correcting these weaknesses. **Exercise prescription** is a widely used term for prescribing the appropriate exercise program for an individual. Of course, teachers frequently prescribe corrective activities for students even though the term *prescription* might not be used. This usage of tests is not limited to exercise programs. When an area needing improvement has been identified on the basis of test results, a prescription for improvement is appropriate regardless of the form of sport or physical activity. Sometimes students can generate their own prescription for improving performance, based on test results.

Grading

Grading is a practice that occurs in almost all physical education programs throughout the United States. Sound grading practices are based on the use of objective tests, since grades represent symbols of achievement. Moreover, once a teacher makes the decision on grades for a given unit, the impact on students is immediate, long-lasting, and usually irreversible. However, grades are not always determined on the basis of tests. The stark reality is that grades are still determined subjectively by many physical education teachers and are frequently based on behavioral assessments such as wearing proper uniforms, effort, and sportsmanship, rather than physical performance. The use of measurement to determine grades is certainly appropriate, but to administer tests solely for the purpose of determining grades suggests a limited view of the value of measurement.

Evaluation of Unit of Instruction

In planning a unit of instruction, a set of objectives is typically set forth. At the end of the unit, an effort is usually made to determine whether the objectives have been met. Making this judgment is difficult without administering tests, especially if the evidence must be submitted to someone else such as the school principal, club manager, or corporation president. Test data can also be used to demonstrate the effectiveness of programs in a nonschool setting to potential members.

Evaluation of Program

The evaluation of individual units of instruction, along with an assessment of the overall program, provides evidence of the effectiveness of a total program.

One or two teachers in a school might have met the predetermined objectives in their classes, but overall the school might have fallen short in this respect. A system-wide program evaluation can include the evidence from this unit as well as broader evaluation procedures encompassing the program in the entire system. All of the franchises for a fitness corporation might be evaluated on the ability of the corporation as a whole to meet program objectives and financial goals. Program evaluation forces examination of the total picture rather than narrowly focusing on an isolated unit in a single location.

Classification

Over the years tests have been frequently used to place individuals into groups on the basis of their ability level in motor performance, allowing those with the same or similar classifications to be grouped for purposes of instruction. The underlying assumption is that both learning and instruction are more efficient if the learners have similar ability levels.

Prediction

One way in which tests have been used with increasing frequency is as predictors of various aspects of motor behavior. Coaches have, for many years, been interested in tests that would predict success in their sport. Since sport psychology has blossomed as an area of specialization in physical education, there has been considerable interest in attempting to predict success in a variety of physical activities using measures of psychological and physiological parameters. In some instances the prediction involved Olympic athletes; other efforts were directed to the college athlete. Efforts have also been directed to predicting long-term involvement in physical activity. In exercise physiology, scores on a fitness test might be used to estimate maximal oxygen uptake. The percentage of one's body fat can be predicted using indicators such as skinfold thickness tests. These are merely a few examples of the widespread use of tests as predictors in physical education and exercise science.

NORM-REFERENCED AND CRITERION-REFERENCED MEASUREMENT

Just as a test can be used for various purposes, it can be designed by the test developer to perform different functions. One of these functions is to measure individual differences. For many years sport psychologists have been interested in studying an athlete's traits, such as self-motivation. To be able to study self-motivation, it must be possible to measure it. Thus, if a sport psychologist plans an experiment on self-motivation, a test would be administered to the athletes at some point during the experiment. If all athletes obtained the same score on the test, how would the results be interpreted? It would be logical to suggest that all athletes participating in the experiment had the same level of self-motivation, yet this outcome is not very likely. A group of athletes—in fact, any group of individuals—would be expected to detect **individual differences** in the trait. In the early part of the twentieth century, most of the advances in measurement were made by people interested in this approach.

Educators have also been interested in this function of measurement. One way of knowing how much a student has achieved is to examine his or her score in relation to the scores of others on the same test. In essence, a student's score is compared with other students' scores. Here again, individual differences are anticipated because some students are expected to perform better than others. This function identifies the test as a **norm-referenced** test. The score is compared with a set of norms. For example, scores on the President's Challenge, a youth fitness test published by the President's Council on Physical Fitness and Sport, are usually compared with the national norms for the participant's gender and age group. A teacher who is interested in norm-referenced standards is usually interested in the performance of students in relation to other students.

Although educators are aware that students differ in many ways, they are, however, sometimes unconcerned about individual differences. Suppose, for example, a physical education teacher identifies a cardiorespiratory function objective for his or her classes and plans to use a test of the mile run to measure this objective. A standard that reflects a satisfactory level of cardiorespiratory endurance is also set for the test. For example, a standard of 7 minutes and 30 seconds is set for 16-year-old boys. In other words, the goal for each 16-year-old boy in all classes is to run the mile in 7:30 by the end of the school year. This type of test is called a **criterion-referenced** test. A standard of performance is set that all or most students are expected to meet. The standard assumes importance because it is *referenced to a criterion behavior.* In the above example, the criterion behavior is a satisfactory level of cardiorespiratory function. Students who meet the standard are labeled *masters* and those who do not are labeled *non-masters.* Another name for a test performing this type of function is a **mastery test.** There are no restrictions on the number of students who master the test. The question of interest is whether or not the student was able to meet the predetermined standard. In a norm-referenced context, the question of interest concerns how the student's score compares with the scores of others. Several of the recently revised national physical fitness tests use criterion-referenced rather than norm-referenced standards. Examples of these standards are presented in Chapter 17. Competency examinations, such as those used by the American College of Sports Medicine to certify exercise specialists, represent a prime example of criterion-referenced tests.

Each of these types of measurement, norm-referenced and criterion-referenced, provides a valuable approach to testing. To suggest that one function is better than another is not meaningful, because one approach may be more desirable in a specific context. Most of the published tests in physical education are norm-referenced measures; however, interest in criterion-referenced testing has increased in recent years, especially in the schools. This is particularly true of FITNESSGRAM. This interest should lead to an increase in the development of new mastery tests.

FORMATIVE AND SUMMATIVE EVALUATION

A number of new terms are being introduced in this chapter that will be used throughout this textbook. The term **evaluation** was defined in a previous section as the interpretation of a score. The process of evaluation can take place at any time during a program or unit of instruction. In an aerobic dance class, for instance, an informal self-evaluation often takes place several times during each session of an instructional unit. The participant engages in vigorous physical activity, stopping to measure heart rate at periodic intervals. Evaluation of the heart rate is accomplished by judging whether the rate is high enough to provide the desired physiological benefits. When evaluation occurs *during* the training period or instructional unit, it is known as **formative evaluation.** This type of evaluation is not uncommon in physical fitness units, where performance is often monitored on a daily basis. Formative evaluation is also appropriate for other aspects of the physical education curriculum in the schools but has been used less frequently in this setting. More typically, tests are administered at the end of the unit. When evaluation takes place solely at the end of a unit, it is referred to as **summative evaluation.** For example, the last 2 days of a tennis unit might be devoted to administering one or two skills tests, a written test, and a test of playing ability. The test scores are usually used to evaluate achievement. In a physical education class this may be translated to a unit grade. In a private tennis club, and perhaps in a school setting, these test scores might be used as an indicator of the effectiveness of instruction.

When only summative evaluation takes place, it is often too late to correct problems that have been identified. In a school setting students move to another unit of instruction; thus if the objectives of the previous unit were not met, it is too late to remedy the situation. Had evaluation taken place during the unit of instruction, deficiencies could have been addressed in a more positive way. The teacher could have prescribed activities to correct these deficiencies. Should formative evaluation be used in a nonschool setting? Yes, the provision of feedback to clients on an ongoing basis helps them understand their strengths and weaknesses. In fact, when exercise is the primary mode of physical activity, it is only through regular evaluation that the instructor can monitor the appropriateness of the exercise. When the physical activity involves a sport, private clubs are less likely to engage in formal evaluation, either formative or summative.

Although formative evaluation has been emphasized in this section of the book, one should not assume it is superior to summative evaluation. Sometimes one approach is more appropriate than the other, depending upon the reasons for evaluation. Formative evaluation is stressed here simply because it has been neglected in the past. Using either approach exclusively is not necessary. To maximize the effectiveness of evaluation procedures, both formative and summative evaluations should be used.

A BRIEF HISTORY OF MEASUREMENT

In the late 1880s a number of prominent physical educators were also medical doctors. They were primarily interested in body symmetry and proportion and prescribed exercise to modify body size. Thus anthropometric measures were used extensively during this period. In 1861 Edward Hitchcock of Amherst, Massachusetts, developed standards of age, height, and weight; chest, arm, and forearm girths; and strength of the upper arm. He was the leading authority in anthropometry between 1860 and 1880. Because of his contributions in the area, Hitchcock is often called the father of measurement in physical education. In 1878 Dudley Sargent of Harvard University developed similar tables of standards. Strength tests were also used during this early period. Sargent was an active contributor in this area as well as in anthropometry, developing the Intercollegiate Strength Test in the 1870s.

Widespread usage of both strength and anthropometric measurement lagged in the early 1900s. Although interest in the measurement of strength subsequently resumed, anthropometric measures have never regained the prominence they received in the early days. Nonetheless, this type of measure still holds an important place in the physical education field in measuring growth, body composition, and body types. At the turn of the century, there was considerable interest in measuring cardiorespiratory function because of the development of measures of endurance and of heart and lung tests. At that time there was also the general perception that individuals became musclebound by strength exercises, and thus hindered in athletic performance. The first test of cardiac function, the Blood Ptosis Test, was developed by C. Ward Crampton in 1905. Crampton noted changes in cardiac rate and arterial pressure on assuming the erect position from a supine position. In the 1920s more sophisticated work was published on the measurement of physical efficiency. E. C. Schneider designed a test used in aviation in World War II to determine fatigue and physical condition for flying. The relationship between pulse rate and blood pressure in the reclining position and the standing position was determined, as well as the ability to recover to normal standing values after a measured bout of exercise. In 1931 W. W. Tuttle modified a block-stepping test similar to a step test measuring endurance and general state of training called the Tuttle Pulse-Ratio Test, a forerunner of the Harvard Step Test developed in 1943. The efficiency of the circulatory system was indicated by the increase in heart rate during exercise and the speed with which the heart rate returned to normal after exercise. Work in this area became increasingly sophisticated with the development of the Balke Treadmill Test in 1954 and other similar measures. These latter tests still represent the standard for measuring cardiorespiratory function in a laboratory setting.

The earliest tests of sports skills were developed as part of athletic perform-ance batteries. For example, in 1913 the Athletic Badge Tests were published by the Playground and Recreation Association of America. David Brace at the Uni-versity of Texas first attempted to measure a group of fundamental skills for a specific sport, basketball, in 1924. He also worked on the development of tests for indoor baseball and soccer. In a 1930 measurement textbook, Bovard and Cozens noted that the area of skill testing was relatively untouched (Bovard and Cozens, 1930). They identified 1916 as the approximate year that the physical education curriculum was broadened to include game activities. Therefore, they noted, physical educators ought to be prepared to measure sports skills as well as other aspects of physical activity. Although tests were being developed during this time, many were not published. Several outstanding measurement specialists in physical education emerged during this period, including Ruth Glassow at the University of Wisconsin. Skills test development was empha-sized at Wisconsin, and Glassow and Broer published a measurement book in 1938, which was almost entirely devoted to skills tests and batteries. Charles McCloy at the University of Iowa was a strong critic of subjective measures of skill in his 1942 textbook; similarly, Harrison Clarke at the University of Oregon was a critic in his 1945 textbook. Subsequently Gladys Scott and her students at the University of Iowa made many contributions to the development of skills tests in the field of physical education. A number of these tests were described in the 1959 textbook by Scott and French.

After a temporary lag in the use of strength tests, interest was restored with the development of new tests in this area, such as the Strength Index and Physi-cal Fitness Index developed by Frederick Rand Rogers in 1925. This type of measurement became much more precise with the development of the cable tensiometer tests by Harrison Clarke. Clarke's innovative thinking led to the design of equipment allowing an investigator to measure the strength of many different body parts. As more sophisticated equipment such as dynamometers and weight-training machines became available to the physical educator, other approaches to testing strength were feasible.

The history of physical fitness testing is described in Chapters 17 and 18. Up to the 1950s physical fitness was typically emphasized when the United States was at war. In 1954 the results of administering the Kraus-Weber Test of Mini-mum Strength to American and English children were published. For the first time, fitness was stressed as important to the individual's health rather than solely as an indicator of readiness for combat (see Chapters 17 and 18 for de-tails).

Up to this point, one type of testing in the physical education field has been ignored—the measurement of general motor ability. "Motor ability" is an ex-pression that was already familiar to physical educators in the early 1900s. Actually, as early as 1894 the Normal School of Gymnastics in Milwaukee and the Gymnastics Societies in Cleveland administered batteries of tests that measured ability in events such as jumping, climbing, shot-putting, lifting, and so forth. As time passed, many schools began to institute testing programs, including basic events from track and field. Most of the test batteries developed then had many similarities, and none of the original batteries was based on sound test development as we know it today. In the 1930–1940 era, a number of test batteries purporting to measure basic motor ability were published, based on a much stronger scientific rationale. However, the overall validity of these batteries was never firmly established. Yet the popularity of the concept of motor ability continued into the late 1950s. At that time the concept began to be questioned in light of emerging research evidence. Suffice it to say that the idea of general motor ability, while intuitively appealing, has never been verified scientifically.

In conclusion, the development of tests in physical education has occurred despite the absence of a strategy for systematically adding to various categories of tests and modifying tests when necessary. More attention has been paid to field and laboratory tests of various physiological attributes largely because of the existence of exercise physiology laboratories in departments of physical education throughout the United States. These laboratories provide a mechanism for systematic work on test development. No similar environment exists for the development of skills tests and tests of basic movement. As a result, there is a significant void in the availability of tests, in particular for preschool and elementary school-age children in physical education. This deficit points to the pressing need for a test service to provide the impetus for the development of tests of all aspects of motor behavior.

RECENT CHANGES IN MEASUREMENT PRACTICES

Measurement and evaluation courses have been taught for many years in physical education programs throughout the United States. Tests of sport skills, fitness, and motor ability, for example, have been advocated in these courses. Presumably, some testing has taken place in physical education programs as well as in exercise and sports programs in nonschool settings. Have measurement practices in the fields changed in recent years? Although judging the extent to which changes have taken place is difficult, events transpiring over the past two decades point to the need for certain changes to occur. The most prominent events include a new recommendation on physical activity, the use of competency-based tests in the public schools, the accessibility of microcomputers, the passage of Title IX, and a concern for the development of health-related physical fitness.

New Recommendation on Physical Activity

In 1993 a new recommendation on physical activity was published by the Centers for Disease Control and the American College of Sports Medicine. In previous years, adults in America had been encouraged to engage in continuous exercise for 20 or more minutes on 3 or more days a week. However, few adults were meeting this standard. Only 22% of American adults participated in the recommended amount of physical activity. Almost one fourth were completely sedentary (Casperson and Merritt, 1992). The reason so few adults were participating in physical activity was that high-intensity exercise had been overemphasized. In addition, epidemiologic studies showed that men who participated in moderate physical activity had a lower death rate than those who remained inactive (Paffenbarger et al., 1993). Thus, the following recommendation was put forth: "Every American should accumulate 30 minutes or more of moderate intensity physical activity over the course of most days of the week" (CDC and ACSM, 1993, p.2).

This recommendation will have a major impact on physical fitness testing over time. Fitness behaviors rather than fitness performance will be emphasized. For example, FITNESSGRAM is already incorporating a program called "It's Your Move," in which the exercise behavior of children is monitored. Fitness programs may continue to use physical fitness tests, but the emphasis on awards is likely to be reduced. Rather than rewarding performance, participation will be the more important factor.

Competency-Based Evaluation

Competency-based evaluation is based on the premise that there are certain competencies identifiable for a group of examinees that ought to be mastered. A test is developed for each competency, and a test score is selected as the standard representing the criterion behavior—the behavior representing mastery of the competency. Those who meet or exceed the standards pass the competency-based evaluation; all others fail. Decisions made on the basis of this type of evaluation can have a tremendous impact on the individuals involved. For example, some states have developed a competency-based program for their high-school students. Students who fail to meet the standards expected for a high-school graduate are sometimes denied a high-school diploma. These programs are highly controversial, since the decisions about those who are competent and those who are not will never be error-free. In other words, the decisions will sometimes be wrong. The most serious consequence of an incorrect decision is the classification of a student as unsuccessful in meeting the standard, when, in reality, the student is competent. At best, the student must undertake remedial work to obtain a diploma that should have been awarded in the first place. In some states competency-based evaluation is applied in the certification of teachers. A standardized test of knowledge about teaching and content areas is administered to prospective teachers. If the predetermined standard for prospective teachers in a specified area (e.g., art, physical education, mathematics) is not met, the student will not be certified to teach in that state. As you might suspect, these programs also promote controversy because 100% accuracy is not possible when decisions are made. Criterion-referenced tests are

Testing the badminton short serve.

generally used in competency-based programs, and these tests must be rigorously developed.

Authentic Assessment

Authentic assessment refers to assessment that takes place in a natural environment (Wiggins, 1989; Maeroff, 1991). Emphasis on this type of assessment sprang from a dissatisfaction with testing in artificial settings. For example, rather than administer a fitness test battery to a child in a gymnasium setting, use a heart monitor to assess the amount of physical activity of the child throughout the day to determine if the heart rate is sufficient to maintain a desirable level of physical fitness. Rather than administer a volleyball pass test to a student, observe the student executing the pass in a game and rate this performance. In other words, the true test of skill or ability depends upon performance in a real-life setting. In addition, evaluation is viewed as most accurate when the person being tested has an opportunity to display his or her skills in a variety of natural settings (Wiggins, 1989). Performance may be above average in most settings but below average in one or two. When sufficient samples of performance are obtained, below-average performances may be seen as rare.

The impact of this approach to testing may be significant for physical education instruction. Although many teachers currently use subjective ratings in measuring students in physical education, many times the observations are made in an artificial setting. The movement education approach in elementary school physical education may come closer to meeting the definition of authentic assessment. If done well, this approach to assessment should be developed more thoroughly; for instance, rating scales should include meaningful descriptors judged to be valid by experts in the sport or physical activity. Authentic assessment is not necessarily a faster method of evaluating students. It may even require more time than the administration of skills tests. Nonetheless, the approach should appeal to teachers who oppose the skills testing approach.

Microcomputers

In the early 1970s it was unusual for a student in a measurement class in physical education to own a minicalculator. Analyzing a set of test scores was accomplished either by hand or by using a large desk calculator, if available. Although the small, hand calculators were being sold, they were expensive and capable of only a few basic arithmetic operations. By the end of the decade, the cost of the minicalculator had dropped to an affordable price and the capability of the instrument had markedly expanded, allowing many physical education majors in measurement classes to use their own minicalculators. Vast improvements in the microchip have resulted in the development of desktop computers, which are gradually becoming more affordable. Several brands of microcomputers are available at relatively modest prices. Many college students now own microcomputers. The notebook computer can be carried into the classroom, although the pocket computer will probably be the tool most appropriate to classroom use. The pocket computer is the latest innovation to be introduced on the market. Because of its small size (it literally can fit into a pocket), it will be easy to transport around campus. The impact of microcomputers on measurement and evaluation in physical education and exercise science has been significant; Chapter 5 is devoted to this topic. Certainly these technological advances have facilitated measurement and evaluation practices in the field.

Reassessment of Physical Performance Standards for Girls and Women

When physical education programs were first promoted in the United States, providing separate programs for boys and girls was not uncommon. Many colleges and universities even established separate physical education departments for men and women. Almost all activities were taught in separate classes for males and females. In 1975 a set of regulations known as Title IX of the Education Amendments of 1972 became effective. This legislation required fair and equal opportunities in all phases of education, including evaluation. It pointed to the need for greater attention to ability grouping and performance standards. Three subparagraphs in the Title IX legislation are directed specifically to physical education.

Subparagraph 86.34(b) provides that ability grouping in physical education classes is permissible provided that the composition of the groups is determined objectively with regard to individual performance rather than on the basis of sex. Subparagraph 86.34(c) allows separation by sex within physical education classes during competition in wrestling, boxing, ice hockey, football, basketball, and other sports, the purpose or major activity of which involves bodily contact. Subparagraph 86.34(d), requiring the use of standards for measuring skill or progress in physical education which do not impact adversely on members of one sex, is intended to eliminate the problem that when a goal-oriented standard is used to assess skill or progress, women almost invariably score lower than men. For example, if progress is measured by determining whether an individual can perform 25 pushups, the standard may be out of reach for many more women than men because of the sex differences in strength. Accordingly, the appropriate standard might be an individual progress chart based on the number of pushups that might be expected of that individual (DHEW, 1975).

More research needs to be conducted on sex differences in motor performance. Some of these differences may be caused by differences in basic physiological factors; others may be culturally induced. As opportunities increase for women to participate in athletics, their physical abilities and skills are, presumably, also increasing. These changes should be monitored on an annual basis.

In the summer of 1981 the Illinois State Board of Education sponsored a Physical Education Ability Grouping and Performance Evaluation Symposium. The purpose of the symposium was to identify guidelines that physical education teachers could use to develop their own objective, sex-fair standards of measures for grouping and evaluating students. An outgrowth of the symposium was a useful publication including tips and techniques for the teacher (Illinois State Board of Education, 1982).

The New Wave of Physical Fitness Tests

Historically, Americans have been concerned about physical fitness in times of war. This is not surprising because many young men who had been inducted into the services during previous wars were not physically fit. This emphasis on fitness was also felt in the schools, especially in physical education classes. Between wars interest waned, despite the stress placed on fitness by presidents such as Eisenhower and Kennedy. This pattern began to change in the 1970s when Americans became concerned about their own fitness for health-related reasons. The fitness explosion has led to a proliferation of fitness clubs and health spas throughout the country.

Physical fitness testing has taken on a health-related focus. Far more dramatic is the expansion of physical fitness programming and the emphasis on programs rather than tests (e.g., Osness, 1985). Physical fitness tests are viewed as only a small part of physical fitness programs. More curricular materials associated with fitness have become available in recent years. For example, the

Chrysler Fund–AAU fitness program includes a nutrition curriculum and a home fitness package (Chrysler Fund–AAU, 1987). Computer software for fitness tests continues to become more sophisticated. The new recommendation on physical activity, mentioned in a previous section, will affect the future use of fitness tests. The philosophical approach to fitness testing as well as the tests themselves will be closely scrutinized in the future.

The most recent surveillance study of American children and youth was conducted by the U.S. Department of Health and Human Services (1985). In this study three major questions were asked: (1) How fit are American boys and girls in grades 5 through 12? (2) What are the physical activity patterns of children and youth in these grades? (3) How do differences in physical activity patterns affect measured fitness? As a result of this investigation, a new set of fitness norms was formulated. These norms are presented in Appendix E.

SUMMARY

Measurement and evaluation represent essential aspects of most careers in physical education and exercise science. Tests are used for many purposes and can range from simple field measures to highly sophisticated laboratory measures. In the next decade, changes in the measurement of motor behavior will result from the new recommendation on physical activity, the widespread use of competency-based measurement, the availability of notebook and pocket computers, an increased emphasis on authentic testing, the enforcement of Title IX legislation, and an increased emphasis on health-related fitness, in particular fitness programming.

Learning Experiences
1. Try to remember when tests were used in your high school physical education program. What types of tests were used? Were they administered at the end of each unit or throughout the unit? How were the test results used?
2. Familiarize yourself with one of the tests of motor skill or physical fitness included in this textbook. Think of ways of which the test could be used (a) in a school setting and (b) in a nonschool setting. Write a brief paper summarizing your thoughts.
3. Interview a physical education teacher who teaches in a public or private school in your area, or invite one to visit one of your measurement classes. Ask the teacher about the tests used in his or her classes. Ask about the major problems a physical education teacher faces in implementing a sound testing program.

References
American Alliance for Health, Physical Education, Recreation and Dance (AAHPERD). 1988. Physical Best: a physical fitness education & assessment program. Reston, VA: American Alliance for Health, Physical Education, Recreation and Dance.

American Alliance for Health, Physical Education, Recreation and Dance (AAHPERD). 1989. Fitness test for older adults. Reston, VA: American Alliance for Health, Physical Education, Recreation and Dance.

Bovard JF, Cozens FW. 1930. Tests and measurements in physical education. Philadelphia: W.B. Saunders Co.

Casperson CJ, Merritt RK. 1992. Trends in physical activity patterns among older adults: the Behavioral Risk Factor Surveillance System, 1986–1990. Medicine and Science in Sport and Exercise, **24**(suppl), 26.

Centers for Disease Control and American College of Sports Medicine (CDC-ACSM). 1993. Summary statement: workshop on physical activity and public health. Atlanta and Indianapolis: Centers for Disease Control and American College of Sports Medicine.

Chrysler Fund–Amateur Athletic Union (AAU). 1987. Physical fitness program. Bloomington, Ind. Chrysler Fund–Amateur Athletic Union.

Clarke HH. 1976. Application of measurement to health and physical education, ed. 5. Englewood Cliffs, NJ: Prentice-Hall, Inc.

Illinois State Board of Education. 1982. Tips and techniques: ability grouping and performance evaluation in physical education. Springfield: Illinois State Board of Education.

Maeroff GI. 1991. Assessing alternative assessment. Phi Delta Kappan, December, pp. 273-281.

McCloy CH. 1942. Tests and measurements in health and physical education. New York: Appleton-Century-Crofts.

Osness WH. 1985. Physical assessment procedures: the use of functional profiles. Journal of Physical Education, Recreation and Dance, **57**(1), 22–24.

Paffenbarger RS, Hyde RT, Wing AL, Lee IM, Dexter LJ, and Kempert JB. 1993. The association of changes in physical-activity level and other lifestyle characteristics with mortality among men. New England Journal of Medicine, **328**, 538–545.

Rogers FR. 1925. Physical capacity tests in the administration of physical education. New York: Teachers College Contribution to Education.

Scott MG, French E. 1959. Measurement and evaluation in physical education. Dubuque, IA: Wm. C. Brown Group.

U.S. Department of Health and Human Services. 1985. Summary of findings from the National Children and Youth Fitness Study. Journal of Physical Education, Recreation and Dance, **56**(1):43–90.

U.S. Department of Health, Education, and Welfare (DHEW). 1975. Federal Register, 40 (June 4) 108.

Wiggins G. 1989. A true test: toward more authentic and equitable assessment. Phi Delta Kappan, May, pp. 703–713.

Annotated Readings

Daves CW. 1984. The uses and misuses of tests. San Francisco: Jossey-Bass Inc., Publishers.

Addresses several major issues associated with the use of tests: the public stake in proper test use, professional standards for proper test use, issues in test use in schools, and test use and the law: written by experts in measurement, but in readable, nontechnical language.

Disch JG. 1983. The measurement of basic stuff. Journal of Physical Education, Recreation, and Dance, **54**(8):17–29.

A series of articles on the measurement of the body of knowledge in physical education as presented in the Basic Stuff Series, published by the American Alliance for Health, Physical Education, Recreation and Dance; includes articles on measurement in exercise physiology, motor development, biomechanics, humanities in physical education, psychosocial aspects of physical education, and motor learning.

Perkins MR. 1982. Minimum competency in testing: what? why? why not? Educational Measurement, **1**(4):5–9, 26.

Presents various definitions of minimum competency testing; describes the perceived benefits of this use of tests; discusses the perceived costs of minimum competency testing; valuable reading for teachers involved in competency-based testing.

Ross JG, Gilbert GG. 1985. A summary of findings. Journal of Physical Education, Recreation and Dance, **56**(1):45–53.

A description of the National Children and Youth Fitness Study, which was designed to determine the fitness status and activity levels of students in grades 5 through 12; includes a brief overview of the data collection procedures, new fitness standards, and a summary of other results.

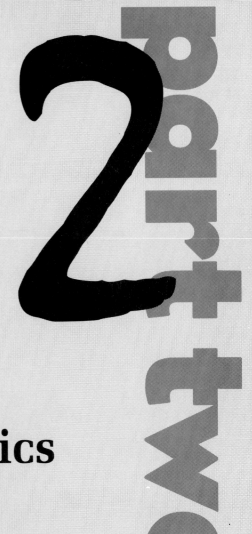

Simplified Statistics

Summarizing a Set of Test Scores

Watch for these words as you read the following chapter

Cumulative frequency (cf)
Cumulative percent (c%)
Descriptive statistics
Frequency (f)
Frequency distribution
Frequency polygon
Histogram
Interval (i)

Measurement
Median
Percentile
Percentile rank
Range (R)
Real limits
Score limits
Statistics
Tally

It is not uncommon for the terms *measurement* and *statistics* to be used interchangeably by students. Although both disciplines deal with sets of scores, **measurement** encompasses the process of obtaining test scores and **statistics** provides the methodology for analyzing the scores. In Chapter 1 *measurement* was defined as the process of assigning numbers to an object or a person according to some rule. Statistics, on the other hand, is defined as a method of analyzing a set of scores to enhance its interpretation. While an extensive coverage of statistics is not necessary in a measurement textbook, a few basic concepts must be covered to provide an understanding of certain measurement practices described later in the book. The type of statistics primarily covered in this book is **descriptive statistics,** which can be used to describe a data set. Basically, statistics will be used in the following ways in this book:

Testing elementary school children.

1. *To describe a set of test scores.* Having obtained a set of test scores, what kind of information can be derived from these scores? The scores can be ordered in *frequency distribution* form, and a measure of the *center* and *spread* of the distribution can be calculated. (These terms are defined later in this chapter.)

2. *To standardize a test score.* Sometimes standardizing a person's score on a test is useful so that the score can be compared with those of other people. This can be accomplished by transforming scores to a different scale such as a *z*-score or a **percentile** scale.

3. *To estimate the validity and reliability of a test.* In measurement theory a test has certain characteristics such as *reliability* and *validity*. These test characteristics are often estimated using a statistic known as the *correlation coefficient.*

Another branch of statistics is known as *inferential* statistics. When a data set is obtained from a sample that is assumed to be representative of the population from which the sample is drawn, it is appropriate to use inferential statistics to analyze the data. Two examples of inferential statistics, the *t*-test and analysis of variance (ANOVA), are described in Chapter 4.

Numerous statistics software packages are now available for microcomputers. Some are relatively inexpensive and easy to use. Refer to Chapter 5 for more information on microcomputers.

MEASUREMENT SCALES

Whenever a measurement instrument is used, some type of score is obtained. To interpret the score, knowing the rule underlying the score is helpful. An accurate interpretation depends in part on the type of scale the score reflects. Four types of scales are commonly described: *nominal, ordinal, interval,* and *ratio.*

A **nominal** scale is a set of mutually exclusive categories. Each category represents one aspect of the attribute being measured. If a score can legitimately be placed in more than one category, the categories are not mutually exclusive. In a properly developed nominal scale, a score can fit one and only one category. There is, however, no meaningful order to the categorization. Classifying football players by number is an example of nominal scaling. A player who is assigned number 42 is not necessarily better than a player assigned number 12. Another example of a nominal scale is gender, that is, male or female.

An **ordinal** scale is determined by ranking a set of objects with regard to some specific characteristic. A basketball coach might be asked to rank the basketball teams in a league on the basis of predicted success at the end of the season. If 10 teams are in the league, a rank of 1 is assigned to the team predicted to win the league title and a rank of 10 to the team expected to be at the bottom of the league. Since a rank of 1 is better than a rank of 2, the order of the numbers is important. However, the top-ranked team might be considerably better than the teams ranked 2, 3, and 4, while the latter three teams might be similar in ability. These differences are not reflected in the differences between ranks. Ordinal scales can also characterize scores that are not in the form of actual ranks. For example, when all-star teams are selected by the national press, sportswriters are asked to vote for the player of their choice. Suppose player F receives 232 votes; player R, 190 votes; and player N, 93 votes. Clearly, player F is considered outstanding by the largest number of sportswriters, but the number of votes does not disclose how much better player F is than player R. Because the distance between numbers does not have a meaningful interpretation, the scores represent ordinal data. Although the actual number of votes may be reported by the press, future reference to the all-star players generally centers on the ranks of the players.

In the **interval** scale the scores have a meaningful order, and units of measurement are an equal distance apart on the scale. On a test of motor behavior the distance between 93 and 90 represents the same range of ability as the difference between 53 and 50. If an interval scale contains a score of 0, the 0 score does not reflect total absence of the attribute being measured.

In contrast, the **ratio** scale uses a 0 score that represents absence of the attribute. For example, a score of 0 on a vertical jump would be interpreted as the total lack of ability to execute a jump vertically. The ordering of numbers is meaningful (larger numbers represent higher jumps), the distance between numbers is equal (the difference between 15 and 12 inches is equal to the difference between 10 and 7 inches), and the ratio of numbers is meaningful (12 inches is twice as long as 6 inches). Although a 3-inch difference represents the same distance on the scale wherever it is located, in a sport, setting a 3-inch difference at the upper end of the scale represents a greater performance increment than 3 inches at lower heights. Ratio scales include measures of length, weight, and time, which are frequently used in measuring motor skills.

Table 2-1   Four Types of Scales
Nominal scale: numbers representing a set of mutually exclusive categories
Ordinal scale: numbers reflecting a ranking of objects on some special characteristic
Interval scale: numbers with a meaningful order and units of measurement an equal distance apart on the scale
Ratio scale: a set of numbers with zero representing the absence of an attribute; also has both features of the interval scale

A summary of the four types of scales is presented in Table 2-1.

Why is it important to understand measurement scales? Certain descriptive statistics are designed specifically for a designated scale. For example, the Spearman rank-difference (rho) correlation coefficient (described in Chapter 3) was developed to be used with ordinal data. Of greater importance is that the properties of the measurement scale should reflect the underlying characteristics of the attribute being measured. For example, if the numbers have no meaningful order and are merely used for classification purposes, the nominal scale best reflects the characteristic being measured. Scales are used in an effort to describe data as accurately as possible.

DISCRETE AND CONTINUOUS VARIABLES

A variable may be classified as either *continuous* or *discrete*. A continuous variable is one that, in theory, can be measured to continuing finer degrees. Many physical measures—such as distance, time, and weight or mass—are examples of continuous variables. A long jump, for example, can be measured to the nearest foot, the nearest inch, the nearest half-inch, and so on. Variables that are not continuous are known as discrete variables, since these variables can assume values only at distinct or discrete points on a scale. A baseball team might score 8 runs during a game, but never 8½ or 8¼ runs. Other examples of discrete variables are the number of students in a class, the number of teams in a league, and the number of books in a library.

FREQUENCY DISTRIBUTION

Suppose, as the instructor of a newly formed health and fitness class, you administer several tests to the class members before beginning instruction. These tests include body composition measures, a test of physical work capacity, and a measure of flexibility. Close examination of each data set is essential before beginning work with this group. A simple way of making sense of the data sets is to develop a **frequency distribution** for each set. A frequency distribution is a method of organizing data and has two basic characteristics. First, the test scores must have a meaningful order. For instance, assume that you have drawn two test scores out of one of the data sets and that each score has a different value. If the score with the higher value represents a greater amount of the attribute being measured, the scores in this set meet the criterion of having a meaningful order. Using the triceps skinfold as an example, it is obvious that a skinfold of 9 mm represents a thicker skinfold than a skinfold of 6 mm. On the surface all numbers may seem to have a meaningful order, but sometimes objects are given numerical labels merely for convenience. This is almost always the case with lockers in gymnasium dressing rooms, for example, since numbers are frequently used for identification. A locker with a higher number does not represent a better locker than one with a lower number. Thus it would be inappropriate to build a frequency distribution of locker numbers.

However, in many instances, categorical data *can* be summarized using a frequency table. Note that frequency "table" is used rather than frequency "distribution" when the numbers do not represent a distribution of scores. For example, assume a volleyball coach wanted to inventory volleyball equipment. The following frequency table might be formed:

Equipment	f
Practice balls	50
Game balls	20
Nets	10
Standards	12
Ball air pumps	2

The second characteristic is that categories in a frequency distribution must be *mutually exclusive*. Assigning a score to more than one category should not be possible. The scores in one category, then, should never overlap with those in other categories.

Frequency Distribution with Interval Size of 1

Now let us turn to the task of actually building a frequency distribution. When the number of scores is small, the procedure is very simple. As the number of scores increases, the procedure becomes more complex, although it is certainly not difficult.

Ordered Scores Not in Frequency Distribution Form

When a test is administered to a small number of people, a frequency distribution is probably not needed. However, no matter how small the data set, the test user should interpret the test scores. Administering a test and failing to use the data in any way is a waste of time for the examinee as well as the test user. Thus with a small data set the scores might simply be ordered from highest to lowest. Consider the following set of scores, representing subscapular skinfold thicknesses for 9-year-old girls:

Data set of 10 scores (in mm): 6, 9, 7, 10, 2, 4, 9, 5, 3, 6

Listing these scores from highest to lowest would yield the following order:

10-9-9-7-6-6-5-4-3-2

Such an ordering can be useful, but this is *not* a frequency distribution. If the characteristics of a frequency distribution in the previous section are reviewed, the reason this representation of the data is not a frequency distribution should be clear. The numbers have a meaningful order, but there are no mutually exclusive categories. To convert this data set into a frequency distribution, every possible score from 10 to 2 would be listed once; thus each score would form a category.

Construction of Frequency Distribution

Suppose we administered a test of throwing accuracy to 24 elementary school children:

Data set of 24 scores (in points): 6, 1, 8, 7, 5, 5, 9, 6, 4, 10, 3, 6, 6, 5, 4, 7, 7, 8, 6, 4, 6, 5, 7, 5

The symbol for the number of test scores (or the number of people obtaining scores on a test) is N. In this example, N = 24. Note that the range is still small (10 − 1 + 1 = 10); thus it would be appropriate to use intervals of size 1 to form a frequency distribution. Of course, listing each possible score in the data set, from highest to lowest, is possible; however, the data would not be in frequency-distribution form. With 24 scores, building a frequency distribution would be simpler. In addition, the description of the data would be more concise.

Score	Tally	f	cf	c%
10	x	1	24	100.0
9	x	1	23	95.8
8	xx	2	22	91.7
7	xxxx	4	20	83.3
6	xxxxxx	6	16	66.7
5	xxxxx	5	10	41.7
4	xxx	3	5	20.8
3	x	1	2	8.3
2		0	1	4.2
1	x	1	1	4.2

Note the columns in the above distribution. One is labeled **tally,** which represents the recording of a score in the appropriate interval. Each *x* designates one score in an interval. The next column, *f*, consists of the **frequency** of scores in each interval. This can be more simply expressed as the number of scores in each interval and is obtained by summing the tallies in each interval. The next column is labeled *cf*, the symbol for **cumulative frequency.** The numbers in this column are obtained by summing the frequencies from the bottom interval to the top. In the above example the *cf* for the interval 6 is *16*. This indicates that 16 out of 24 people obtained scores of 6 or below on this measure. The c%, or **cumulative percent,** column displays the conversion of the cf column to percentages. Take another look at interval 6. A cf of 16 is converted to a c% of 66.7% by dividing 16 by the total number (N) of test scores, in this case, 24. The result must then be multiplied by 100. Thus, c% = cf/N × 100, or cf divided by N times 100. Referring to the interval 6, it would be appropriate to say that 66.7% of the group of 24 obtained scores of 6 or below. The percentages in this column are similar to *percentiles,* which are described later in this chapter.

With a larger range of score values, using intervals of size 1 would become very cumbersome. For instance, if the highest score in a data set is 80 and the lowest is 21, the range would be 60 (80 − 21 + 1). It would be tedious and very time-consuming to list 60 intervals of size 1 in forming a frequency distribution. Developing intervals larger than size 1 would be more expedient. This is sometimes referred to as a *group frequency distribution.* The major purpose of forming a frequency distribution is to summarize the data for easier interpretation. If too many intervals are used, the original purpose may be defeated. A large number of intervals often spreads the data too much to be interpretable, while a very small number of intervals can mask important trends in the data. The **range** (R) is determined by subtracting the lowest score from the highest score and adding 1 as symbolized in Formula 2-1:

$$R = (\text{highest score} - \text{lowest score}) + 1 \qquad \text{Formula 2-1}$$

Adding 1 to (highest score − lowest score) provides a more accurate indicator of the range as it reflects all possible scores in the distribution. Consider a small data set consisting of four scores: 7, 6, 5, 4. If 7 − 4 is used to calculate the range, the result is 3. Yet it is evident that there are four scores in the data set. The addition of 1 would yield a range of 4. Not all textbooks recommend adding 1 to determine the range. From a practical point of view, the difference between the two versions of the range is relatively minor.

The formula for the range is modified slightly if the score is recorded to one or more decimal places. For example, if a score is recorded to one decimal place, the range is equal to (highest score − lowest score) + .1.

Frequency Distribution with Interval Sizes Larger Than 1

When a set of test scores is distributed over a wider range, grouping the data into intervals larger than size 1 is preferred. As noted previously this is sometimes referred to as a group frequency distribution. Additional steps must be followed when the interval size exceeds 1, such as the determination of an appropriate interval size and a suitable number of intervals.

Description of Procedure

Consider a data set of 22 scores on a physical fitness knowledge test, with the scores ranging from 80 to 99. The range of this set is 99 − 80 + 1 = 20. It would be more efficient and provide a better representation of the data if a frequency distribution with intervals larger than 1 were used. How many intervals should be formed? The general rule is to use *no fewer than 10 and no more than 20 intervals.* How large should the interval size be? Many interval sizes are legitimate possibilities, but the most widely used options are 2, 3, 5, 7, 10, and multiples of 5 thereafter. Since it has been determined that the range of this set of scores is 20 and that no fewer than 10 intervals should be used, the best interval size for this data set is 20/10 = 2.

Data set of 22 scores (Fitness Knowledge Test): 89, 86, 91, 82, 80, 93, 96, 87, 82, 98, 96, 99, 95, 90, 89, 91, 88, 92, 93, 87, 89, 91

$$N = 22; \quad R = 99 - 80 + 1 = 20$$

Intervals	Tally	f	cf	c%
98-99	xx	2	22	100.0
96-97	xx	2	20	91.0
94-95	x	1	18	81.8
92-93	xxx	3	17	77.3
90-91	xxxx	4	14	63.6
88-89	xxxx	4	10	45.5
86-87	xxx	3	6	27.2
84-85		0	3	13.6
82-83	xx	2	3	13.6
80-81	x	1	1	4.5

Traditionally, frequency distributions are constructed so that the highest scores are at the top of the column and the lowest scores are at the bottom. Displaying an interval with the lowest score in the interval placed to the left of the interval and the highest score to the right is customary. The reason higher scores are usually placed at the top of the **interval** (i) column is that higher scores typically represent better performances. However, this is not always true in measuring motor behavior, especially when the score is recorded in time. When measuring running speed, for example, faster times (smaller scores) represent better performances. In these cases building the frequency distributions with the smaller scores at the top of the interval column would be appropriate (see example, p. 36). Keep in mind that the purpose of a frequency distribution is to present a meaningful summary of the data.

Summary of Steps

The following steps are taken in constructing a frequency distribution with intervals of size 1. (Other equally effective approaches may be used to accomplish the same purpose.)

1. Calculate the range of the set of scores (highest score − lowest score + 1). List all possible scores in the range, regardless of whether the score actually occurs in the data set. The score representing the best performance should be placed at the top of the list, and the score reflecting the poorest performance should be at the bottom of the list.

2. Tally each of the scores in the data set, using *x*'s or *1*'s as tallies.
3. Develop the frequency (*f*) column by summing the tallies for each interval.
4. Generate the cumulative frequency (*cf*) column by adding the frequencies, beginning with the bottom interval.
5. Develop the cumulative percent (*c%*) column by dividing *cf* by *N* and multiplying by 100.

If the frequency distribution includes intervals larger than size 1, two additional steps, *1a* and *1b*, must be taken between steps *1* and *2* above.

1a. Select an appropriate number of intervals to ensure that the distribution will contain no more than 20 intervals and no fewer than 10.
1b. Select an appropriate interval size. Remember that typical interval sizes are 2, 3, 5, 7, and 10. To determine the interval size, the number of intervals can be divided into the range.

Another way to approach the development of a frequency distribution with intervals larger than size 1 is to estimate the interval size first, taking into account the range, then divide the range by the interval size to obtain the number of intervals. Let's contrast the two approaches. If the number of intervals is determined first, even a cursory examination of the frequency distribution data on p. 32 would show that the number will be relatively small. This is evident, since the range (20) itself is small. Thus a reasonable estimate of an appropriate number of intervals is 10, and 20/10 = 2. The distribution, then, would have 10 intervals with an interval size of 2. To take the other approach, determining the interval size first, simply reverse your thought process as follows. Since the range is small, the number of intervals can be maximized by keeping the interval size small. As this example deals with intervals larger than size 1, the smallest possible interval size is 2. Dividing the range (20) by 2 yields 10 intervals. This is basically a trial-and-error process. The interval size and the number of intervals are adjusted until both numbers are acceptable.

Graphing Distributions

Although the frequency distribution is a simple method of summarizing a set of scores, it may not be the most effective way of displaying the summary to others. Graphical representations are sometimes more powerful when presenting your data to principals, club managers, laboratory directors, clients, parents, and so forth. Two popular types of graphs are the **frequency polygon** and the **histogram.**

In Figure 2-1 the frequency distribution on p. 32 is shown in frequency polygon form. Since the intervals in this distribution are larger than size 1, the points used to plot the frequency polygon are the midpoints of the intervals shown on the horizontal axis. On the vertical axis of the graph, the frequency of cases (number of test scores) is depicted.

The histogram is a type of bar graph. The width of the bar represents the width of the interval displayed on the horizontal axis of the graph. As with the

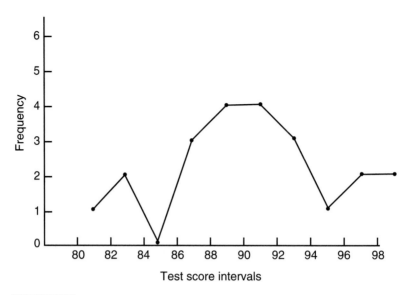

Figure 2-1   Frequency polygon of scores on Physical Fitness Knowledge
Test.

frequency polygon, the frequency of cases is shown on the vertical axis. Figure
2-2 depicts the distribution on p. 32 in histogram form. The choice between
using a histogram or a frequency polygon is largely a matter of personal preference.

Earlier in this chapter, we discussed graphing categorical data. A frequency
table was developed to represent the volleyball equipment in a school. These
frequencies could be developed in histogram form, although the bars should not
touch one another. This would suggest the numbers form a distribution, but in
this case they do not. See Figure 2-3 for an example of a histogram representing
the data on p. 29.

Special Case of Frequency Distribution

In situations where lower scores represent better performances, such as golf
and running events, the frequency distribution may be modified accordingly.
When a frequency distribution or a graph of the distribution is of primary interest, the lowest scores can be placed at the top of the distribution. This provides a
clear presentation of the set of scores, since people generally expect to see better
scores at the top of a frequency distribution. The percentile and percentile rank
formulas (presented later in this chapter) must be modified to be used with this
type of distribution of scores. Consider the following set of time scores on a
shuttle run test, where test performance is timed to the nearest tenth of a second.

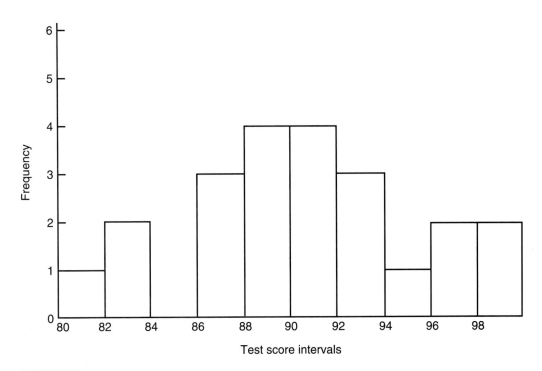

Figure 2-2   Histogram of scores on Physical Fitness Knowledge Test.

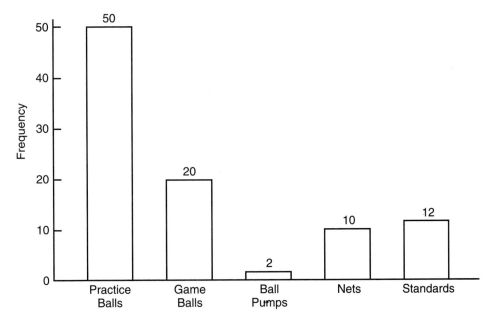

Figure 2-3   Frequency table of equipment inventory.

Data set of 20 scores (in seconds): 9.2, 11.1, 9.7, 10.3, 10.5, 9.8, 10.9, 11.6, 11.3, 9.0, 10.0, 10.3, 10.0, 9.8, 9.8, 10.3, 9.7, 10.5, 10.0, 10.1

$N = 20$; $R = 11.6 - 9.0 + 0.1 = 2.7$ or 27 scores recorded to the nearest tenth of a second

Interval	Tally	f
9.1-9.0	x	1
9.3-9.2	x	1
9.5-9.4		0
9.7-9.6	xx	2
9.9-9.8	xxx	3
10.1-10.0	xxxx	4
10.3-10.2	xxx	3
10.5-10.4	xx	2
10.7-10.6		0
10.9-10.8	x	1
11.1-11.0	x	1
11.3-11.2	x	1
11.5-11.4		0
11.7-11.6	x	1

Even though these scores are recorded to the nearest tenth of a second, each tenth can be considered as a score to determine the interval size. Thus the range for this set of scores is 27 (116 − 90 + 1). If an interval size of 3 were selected, the number of intervals would be 9, which would not fit the rule of thumb of 10 to 20 intervals. If an interval size of 2 were chosen, the number of intervals would be 14 (27/2 = 13.5, rounded to 14). Note that the lower scores represent better performances on the shuttle run test. Therefore these scores are placed at the top of the *Interval* column. Furthermore, within each interval the lower (better) score is placed at the top of the interval (to the right) and the higher (poorer) score is placed at the bottom (to the left). If the data were presented in graph form, the scores would be plotted in the same manner, with the lower scores placed to the right of the horizontal axis and the higher values to the left. Remember, however, that the formulas described in the remaining sections of this chapter are not appropriate to use with this distribution unless they are modified.

CALCULATION OF PERCENTILES

After a test has been administered and a frequency distribution has been developed for a set of scores, using the distribution to calculate one or more percentiles is often helpful. For example, the **median** is frequently of interest because it represents the center of the distribution of scores. The median is the 50th **percentile,** often expressed by the symbol $X_{.50}$. The median is the score that

Testing soccer kick.

divides the distribution so that 50% of the scores fall above this point and 50% fall below. Of course, other percentiles also provide useful information, especially when standards of performance are needed to interpret a set of scores. In the following sections the format followed in describing the development of a frequency distribution is used. First, the calculation of percentiles for ordered scores (not in frequency distribution form) is described. Then, the procedures for calculating percentiles are presented for the simple frequency distribution (intervals of size 1) and the group frequency distribution (intervals larger than size 1).

Calculation from Ordered Scores

Using ordered scores (not in frequency distribution form), calculating the median or any other percentile is simple, especially if the number of cases is small. Consider, for example, scores on a pull-up test.

Data set of 17 scores (no. of pull-ups): 7, 4, 10, 1, 6, 6, 4, 3, 7, 10, 1, 7, 4, 10, 7, 4, 8

These scores can simply be ordered from highest to lowest, not in frequency distribution form:

10-10-10-8-7-7-7-7-6-6-4-4-4-4-3-1-1

There are 17 scores in this data set. By definition, the median will be represented by the score dividing the distribution into equal halves. The median, then, will be the ninth score, since this score divides the distribution in halves of 8 scores each. Counting up from the bottom (or down from the top), the ninth score is a score of 6. Thus the median is *6* in this example. Let's identify another percentile—the 75th percentile, or $X_{.75}$. This is the score separating the top one fourth of the distribution from the bottom three fourths. Four scores fall above this point and 12 fall below; thus, the 75th percentile is 7.

Calculation from Frequency Distribution with Interval Size of 1

This same set of 17 scores can also be displayed in simple frequency distribution form, with intervals of size 1.

Interval	Tally	f	cf
10	xxx	3	17
9		0	14
8	x	1	14
7	xxxx	4	13
6	xx	2	9
5		0	7
4	xxxx	4	7
3	x	1	3
2		0	2
1	xx	2	2
		17	

Score Limits

Up to this point, the numbers used to represent intervals have been the scores an examinee might actually obtain on a test. These numbers are called the **score limits** of the interval. For example, the top two intervals in the above distribution can be displayed as follows:

[————] [————]
  9   10

Conceptually, a set of test scores is viewed as a distribution of scores. The shape of the distribution is determined by the way the scores are spread throughout the possible range of scores. If most of the scores are grouped in the center of the distribution with a smaller number of scores at each end, the distribution will resemble a normal curve. The only point to keep in mind now is that the space under the curve is the area represented by the test scores. When score limits are used to represent a data set, the representation is incomplete because a small amount of area is left out between the score limits of the intervals. Note in the above display of score limits that all scores in the interval of 9 are considered to be in the middle of the interval. The same is true for the interval 10. These scores represent the score limits of the two intervals. A small amount of space is unaccounted for between the intervals. In this case the space between the two midpoints of each interval, 9 and 10, is unaccounted for. For this reason *real limits* must be used to calculate percentiles more precisely.

Real Limits

To obtain **real limits,** first examine the score limits for any two adjacent intervals. A real limit is determined by taking half the distance between any two adjacent score limits representing the upper score limit of one interval and the lower score limit of the adjacent interval. In this case (intervals of size 1) the upper score limit and the lower score limit are the same for each interval. Look back to the two score limits in this section. The distance between the score limits is 1. By taking half of 1 and adding to and subtracting from the score limits, real limits of 8.5 to 9.5 and 9.5 to 10.5 are obtained. (Real limits are not used for purposes of tallying; only score limits are used for the placement of tallies.) Compare this representation with the one for score limits:

$$
\begin{array}{ccc}
[\rule{2cm}{0.4pt}] & [\rule{2cm}{0.4pt}] \\
8.5 \quad\quad 9.5 \quad\quad 10.5
\end{array}
$$

When real limits are determined for every interval in a distribution, the entire area under the curve is taken into account. Real limits are also used in calculating percentiles using a group frequency distribution (intervals larger than 1) as well as in calculating percentile ranks.

Percentile Formula

To use the following percentile (%ile) formula, Formula 2-2, the data must be in frequency distribution form.

$$\%\text{ile} = \text{lrl} + \frac{.x(N) - \Sigma fb}{fw}(i)$$
Formula 2-2

where %ile = percentile; for example, $X_{.50}$ = 50th percentile or median
  lrl = *lower real limit* of interval containing the score representing the desired percentile
  .x = *percentile* displayed as a proportion; for example, the 50th percentile is displayed as .50
  N = total *number* of scores; total frequency in data set
  Σfb = sum of *frequencies* below the interval containing the score representing the desired percentile
  fw = *frequency within* this interval
  i = size (width) of the *interval*

Now Formula 2-2 is used below with the frequency distribution on p. 38 to calculate the 75th percentile.

Be certain you are working in the correct interval before you begin calculating. In this case, the correct interval is identified by determining 75%N or .75(17), which equals 12.75. This is the calculation for .x(N) in Formula 2-2. The 12.75th score is the 75th percentile in this set of scores. Checking the *cf* column of the frequency distribution, the 12.75th score is located in the interval 7, since 12.75 is larger than 9 but not greater than 13. Although the interval has now been identified, the score must still be calculated. The formula is completed as follows:

$$75\text{th \%ile} = 6.5 + \frac{12.75 - 9}{4} \quad (1)$$

$$= 7.4375$$

Calculation from Frequency Distribution with Interval Sizes Larger than 1

When calculating percentiles using frequency distributions with intervals larger than size 1 (group frequency distribution), Formula 2-2 *must* be used. When data are grouped in this way, some information on the original data set is lost. However, the data are portrayed in a more concise form and thus are more easily interpreted. The value of the percentile calculated from a group frequency distribution will be slightly different from the value calculated from ordered data, again due to the loss of information brought about by grouping. The frequency distribution presented below is used to demonstrate this calculation. The data represent scores (in inches) on the standing long jump for a group of 14-year-old boys, where N = 60.

Interval	f	cf
80-82	1	60
77-79	3	59
74-76	5	56
71-73	6	51
68-70	9	45
65-67	12	36
62-64	9	24
59-61	6	15
56-58	5	9
53-55	3	4
50-52	1	1

Before describing the steps in this calculation, a review of the concept of real limits is appropriate, since larger (wider) intervals are being used. The score limits for the top two intervals in the above distribution can be displayed as follows:

```
[————] [————]
77    79 80    82
```

When score limits are used to represent the data set, the distribution of the scores is not completely displayed. A small amount of area is left out between the score limits of adjacent intervals. Note in the above display of score limits that the area between 79 and 80 is not represented. To be precise in calculating percentiles, *all* of the area must be taken into account.

In this case the lower score limit of the top interval of the above example is 80, and the upper score limit of the lower interval is 79. The distance or area between these limits is 1. Taking half of 1 and adding to and subtracting from the upper and lower score limits, real limits of 76.5 to 79.5 and 79.5 to 82.5 are obtained. The real limits are depicted as follows:

$$[\underline{\hspace{2cm}}] \, [\underline{\hspace{2cm}}]$$
$$76.5 \quad 79.5 \quad 82.5$$

The median and other percentiles can be calculated using Formula 2-2. Since the median is frequently of interest to a test user, let's calculate this value first.

$$X_{.50} = 64.5 + \frac{30 - 24}{12}\,(3)$$
$$= 66$$

Be certain you are working in the correct interval before you begin calculating. In this case, the correct interval is identified by determining 50%N or .5(60), which is 30. Thus, the 30th case is the median in this set of scores. Checking the *cf* column of the frequency distribution, the 30th score is located in the interval 65 and 67 (30 is larger than 24 but less than 36). Now that the interval has been identified, the score must be calculated. Since the range of scores in the interval equals 3, the score representing the median is unknown. To determine the interval size, subtract the lower score limit from the upper score limit and add 1 to the result. For instance, if 65 were subtracted from 67, the result would equal 2. However, it is clear that the interval 65–67 contains *three* scores—65, 66, and 67. By adding 1 to the result, an interval size of 3 is obtained, which is correct. Of course, the correct size could also be obtained by subtracting the lower real limit from the upper real limit.

As another example, let's calculate the 80th percentile, or $X_{.80}$. To identify the correct interval, find 80%N or .8(60), which equals 48. Since 48 is larger than 45 in the *cf* column but not greater than 51, the interval 71–73 contains the 48th case, which in turn includes the 80th percentile. Now the percentile formula can be used to calculate the score representing the 80th percentile.

$$X_{.80} = 70.5 + \frac{48 - 45}{6}\,(3)$$
$$= 70.5 + 1.5$$
$$= 72$$

Summary of Steps

The following steps summarize the procedure for calculating percentiles:

1. Identify the interval containing the percentile by determining x%(N) or .x(N). Use the *cf* column to locate this number, then mark the corresponding interval.
2. Determine the lower real limit (lrl) of the interval identified in step *1*.
3. Find Σfb, the sum of the frequencies below this interval by referring to the *cf* column immediately below the interval.
4. Find *f*w, the frequency within the interval, by noting the number of cases in the *f* column for this interval.
5. Determine i, the interval size, by subtracting the lower real limit from the upper real limit.
6. Use Formula 2-2 to calculate the percentile.

Calculating Percentiles When Lower Scores Represent Better Performance

On p. 36 a special case of the frequency distribution was described. The special case is appropriate when lower scores represent better performance, a common occurrence in our field. The formula for calculating percentiles must be modified under these circumstances. Consider the following frequency distribution of time scores (recorded to the nearest tenth of a second) for an agility run test:

X	Tally	f	cf
10.1	x	1	20
10.2	xx	2	19
10.3	xx	2	17
10.4	xxx	3	15
10.5	xxxx	4	12
10.6	xxx	3	8
10.7	xx	2	5
10.8	xx	2	3
10.9		0	1
11.0	x	1	1

Calculate the 50th percentile:

$$\%tile = lrl + \frac{\Sigma fb - .xN}{fw} \text{ (i)} \qquad \text{Formula 2-3}$$

where lrl (in this case only) = X + ½ unit of measurement (½ of .1 = .05)

$$X_{.50} = 10.55 + \frac{8 - .5(20)}{4}(.1)$$

$$= 10.55 + \frac{-2}{4}(.1)$$

$$= 10.55 - .05 = 10.5$$

CALCULATION OF PERCENTILE RANKS

The answer to the question, "What is the nth percentile?" is always a test score. A teacher may wish to provide summary information on students' test performances for review by the principal. The manager of a fitness club may ask for information on specific *percentiles* for certain measures of fitness administered to clients at some point in their program. On the other hand, from the standpoint of the client or the student, the most useful information might be the **percentile rank** representing his or her own score. Here the known factor is the student's score, and the unknown factor is the percentage, now called the **percentile rank.** Now the question is, "What is the percentile rank for a score of X?" The score is known and the percentile rank is unknown; in the previous section the percentile was known and the score was unknown. Keep in mind that percentiles and percentile ranks are reciprocal concepts.

Calculations from Ordered Scores

You will recall that it was possible to calculate a percentile without forming a frequency distribution at all. The scores were simply ordered from highest to lowest, which is reasonable if the number of scores in the data set is small. Let us use the example on p. 38 to show how percentile ranks can also be calculated from an ordered set of scores. Consider a score of 8; what percentile rank does this score represent? By counting from the lowest score upward, we find that the score of 8 is the 14th score in the data set. Since N = 17, the percentile rank can be calculated by dividing 14 by 17, which equals 82%. Therefore a score of 8 reflects a percentile rank of 82%, meaning that 82% of the examinees in this sample obtained scores of 8 or below on this test. Only 18% of the examinees scored higher than 8; thus 8 is a very good score. Using the same set of ordered scores, calculate the percentile rank for a score of 3. The answer you should have obtained is 18%. A score of 3 is the third score in the ordered data set, and the percentile rank is 3/17 = 18%. Percentile ranks can also be calculated from frequency distributions, either with intervals of size 1 or intervals larger than size 1.

Calculation for Frequency Distribution with Interval Sizes Larger than 1

Formula 2-4 is used to calculate more precise estimates of the percentile rank. This formula, as well as Formula 2-2 on p. 39, has many variations that will yield the same answer. Although the calculation will be exemplified using a frequency distribution with intervals larger than size 1, the formula is equally applicable when the intervals are of size 1.

$$\text{PR for } X = \frac{\Sigma fb + \dfrac{X - |rl|}{i}\,(fw)}{N}\,(100) \qquad\qquad \text{Formula 2-4}$$

where PR = percentile rank
X = score
lrl = lower real limit
i = interval size
f = frequency

It is not necessary to perform any calculation to locate the interval, since the examinee's score is provided, which automatically locates the interval. Let's calculate the percentile rank for a score of 69, using the distribution on p. 40.

$$\text{PR for } 69 = \frac{36 + \dfrac{69 - 67.5}{3}(9)}{60}(100)$$

$$= \frac{36 + \dfrac{1.5}{3}(9)}{60}(100)$$

$$= 67.5\%$$

A score of 69 has a percentile rank of 67.5.

Note that the real limits must be used in calculating this statistic. A table of percentiles and scores can easily be set up for a test, and then either the percentile or the percentile rank can be read from the table. If a test is used frequently, such a table is useful. Sample tables of percentiles are included in several chapters of this textbook. When the distribution of scores forms an approximate normal curve (see Chapter 3), the mean and standard deviation of the set of scores are used to calculate percentiles. These calculations are shown in Table 2-2. Once the mean and standard deviation have been determined, this table can be set up by hand, although using a computer program is far easier.

Table 2-2   Development of Table of Percentiles using Mean and Standard Deviation

PR	%	PR	%
99.9	$\overline{X} + 3.00s$	45.0	$\overline{X} - .13s$
95.0	$\overline{X} + 1.64s$	40.0	$\overline{X} - .25s$
90.0	$\overline{X} + 1.28s$	35.0	$\overline{X} - .39s$
85.0	$\overline{X} + 1.04s$	30.0	$\overline{X} - .52s$
80.0	$\overline{X} + .84s$	25.0	$\overline{X} - .67s$
75.0	$\overline{X} + .67s$	20.0	$\overline{X} - .84s$
70.0	$\overline{X} + .52s$	15.0	$\overline{X} - 1.04s$
65.0	$\overline{X} + .39s$	10.0	$\overline{X} - 1.28s$
60.0	$\overline{X} + .25s$	5.0	$\overline{X} - 1.64s$
55.0	$\overline{X} + .13s$	0.1	$\overline{X} - 3.00s$
50.0	$\overline{X} + .00s$		

Summary of Steps

The steps for calculating percentile ranks are summarized below:

1. Identify the interval containing the score of interest.
2. Find Σcf, the cumulative frequency of scores, just below the interval identified in step *1*.
3. Determine lrl, the lower real limit, by subtracting half of the unit of measurement from the lowest score in the interval.
4. Find i, the interval size, and fw, the frequency.
5. Calculate the percentile rank.

Calculating PR When Lower Scores Represent Better Performance

The percentile rank formula must be modified when lower scores represent better performance.

$$\text{PR for X} = \frac{\Sigma fb + \dfrac{\text{lrl} - X}{i}(fw)}{N}(100) \qquad\qquad \text{Formula 2.5}$$

The data from the frequency distribution on p. 42 will be used to exemplify this calculation:

$$\text{PR for 10.3} = \frac{15 + \dfrac{10.35 - 10.3}{.1}(2)}{20}(100)$$

$$= \frac{15 + .05/.1(2)}{20}(100)$$

$$= \frac{15 + 1}{20}(100)$$

$$= .80 \text{ or } 80\%$$

SUMMARY

Once a test has been administered to a group of examinees, the test scores can be interpreted. Several types of questions might be of interest. How are the test scores distributed for the entire group? To answer this question, a frequency distribution can be constructed and graphed for easier analysis. For example, what is the 50th percentile? For any percentile, the corresponding test score can be calculated. How good is a score of X? The percentile rank of any score in the distribution can be determined. At the very least, a frequency distribution should be formed for each set of test scores unless the number of scores is small; then a simple ordering of scores will often suffice. Test information should not be wasted. If administering the test is important enough, analyzing the scores properly is certainly worthwhile.

References

Glass GV, Stanley JC. 1980. Statistical methods in education and psychology. Englewood Cliffs, NJ: Prentice-Hall.

Hopkins KD, Stanley JC. 1981. Educational and psychological measurement and evaluation. Englewood Cliffs, NJ: Prentice-Hall.

Mattson DE. 1981. Statistics: difficult concepts, understandable explanations. St Louis: Mosby.

Stahl SM, Hennes JD. 1980. Reading and understanding applied statistics: a self-learning approach, ed 2, St Louis: Mosby.

Vincent WJ. 1995. Statistics in kinesiology. Champaign, IL: Human Kinetics.

Annotated Readings

Gutnam A. 1984. Computerized instruction in statistics. Lavallette, NJ: Holt, Rinehart & Winston.

Consists of comprehensive courseware package; explains and illustrates the major concepts found in introductory statistics textbooks; class-tested for user-friendliness and ease of operation; eight tutorial disks cover statistical concepts; interactive exercises; eight stat-paks; available for Apple II + or IIe.

Hills JR. 1983. Interpreting percentile scores. Educational Measurement, 2(2):24.

Ten true-false items on the interpretation of percentile scores; provides correct answers and brief explanations for all items; useful way to review the concept of percentiles.

Spatz C, Johnston JO. 1984. Basic statistics: tales of distribution, ed 3, Belmont, Calif.: Brooks/Cole.

Designed for use in a one-term introductory course; emphasizes conceptualization and interpretation of statistical results; uses distinctive pedagogical devices to stimulate interest and facilitate understanding; covers both descriptive and inferential statistics; presents problems and answers with all necessary steps and explanations.

Weinbery SL, Goldberg KP. 1979. Basic statistics for education and the behavioral sciences. Boston: Houghton Mifflin.

Written for beginning students; presents case studies from education and the behavioral sciences at the end of each chapter; provides realistic examples of each concept; reviews basic mathematics in an appendix; instructor's manual includes eight sample examinations with complete solutions.

Wike EL. 1985. Numbers: a primer of data analysis. Columbus, Ohio: Charles E Merrill.

Lays the foundation for the underlying concepts of statistics; designed for the beginning student; avoids the characteristic dryness of many statistics texts; includes a computer addendum at the end of each chapter, relating material to the MINITAB computer program; uses practical examples and problems.

Problems

1. Answer the following questions *without* forming a frequency distribution:

Data set of 15 scores (on push-ups test):
28, 19, 30, 15, 19, 9, 20, 28, 33, 10, 14, 32, 27, 24, 19

  a. Order the scores from highest to lowest.
  b. Calculate the median.
  c. Calculate the 66⅔ (round to 67th) percentile.
  d. What is the percentile rank for a score of 15?
2. Use the following data set to form a frequency distribution:

Data set of 15 scores (on sit-ups test):
62, 60, 59, 66, 60, 57, 61, 65, 58, 59, 65, 60, 64, 61, 60

  a. Form a frequency distribution with intervals of size 1. Include columns
   for tally, f, cf, and c%.
  b. Calculate the median.
  c. Calculate the 75th percentile.
  d. What is the percentile rank of a score of 58?
3. Use the following data set to build a frequency distribution:

Data set of 30 scores (on tennis serve test):
63, 59, 76, 60, 44, 41, 59, 68, 64, 55, 79, 65, 65, 58, 48, 65, 40, 72, 68, 70, 59, 46, 66, 51,
52, 69, 75, 46, 59, 58

  a. Form a frequency distribution with intervals of size 4. Include columns
   for real limits, tally, f, cf, and c%.
  b. Calculate the median.
  c. Calculate the 25th percentile.
  d. What is the percentile rank for a score of 66?
4. Use the following data to form a frequency distribution:

Data set of 20 scores (on the 50-yard dash):
7.4, 7.5, 6.8, 8.1, 8.7, 7.2, 9.1, 8.4, 7.2, 6.5, 8.2, 7.5, 8.1, 9.4, 8.0, 6.9, 7.5, 9.0, 6.7, 7.0

Form a frequency distribution with intervals of size 3 (actually .3, since the
data are recorded in tenths of seconds). Remember that you are working with
time scores and lower scores represent better performances. Include columns
for real limits, tally, f, cf, and c%.
5. Use the following data set to form a frequency distribution:

Data set of 20 scores on 50-yard dash: (unit = seconds)
7.0, 7.8, 7.5, 7.2, 7.3, 7.4, 7.4, 7.2, 7.5, 7.6, 7.7, 8.0, 7.7, 7.5, 7.8, 7.6, 7.5, 7.7, 7.5, 7.4.

  a. Form a frequency distribution with intervals of size .1. Include columns
   for real limits, tally, f, cf, and c%.
  b. Calculate the median.
  c. Calculate the 60th percentile.
  d. What is the percentile rank of a score of 7.4 seconds?
6. Use the following data set to build a frequency distribution:

Data set of 45 scores on standing long jump: (unit = cm)
226 267 232 243 258 238 239 238 240 241 247 250 257 248 240 231 222 254 243 243
238 232 236 235 259 240 264 244 251 245 217 248 253 260 234 250 224 246 226 245
247 230 252 235 242

a. Form a frequency distribution with intervals of size 5. Include columns for real limits, tally, *f*, *cf*, and c%.
b. Calculate the median.
c. Calculate the 90th percentile.
d. What is the percentile rank for a score of 248 cm?
e. What is the percentile rank for a score of 229 cm?

Answers to Problems

1. a. 33-32-30-28-28-27-24-20-19-19-19-15-14-10-9
   b. $X_{.50} = 20$
   c. $X_{.67} = 27.5$
   d. PR for score of 15 = 26.67%

2. a.

Interval	Tally	f	cf	c%
66	x	1	15	100.0
65	xx	2	14	93.3
64	x	1	12	80.0
63		0	11	73.3
62	x	1	11	73.3
61	xx	2	10	66.7
60	xxxx	4	8	53.3
59	xx	2	4	26.7
58	x	1	2	13.3
57	x	1	1	6.7

   b. $X_{.50} = 60$
   c. $X_{.75} = 64$
   d. PR for score of 58 = 13.3%

3. a.

Interval	Real limits	Tally	f	cf	c%
76-79	75.5-79.5	xx	2	30	100.0
72-75	71.5-75.5	xx	2	28	93.3
68-71	67.5-71.5	xxxx	4	26	86.7
64-67	63.5-67.5	xxxxx	5	22	73.3
60-63	59.5-63.5	xx	2	17	56.7
56-59	55.5-59.5	xxxxxx	6	15	50.0
52-55	51.5-59.5	xx	2	9	30.0
48-51	47.5-51.5	xx	2	7	23.3
44-47	43.5-47.4	xxx	3	5	16.7
40-43	39.5-43.5	xx	2	2	6.7

   b.
$$X_{.50} = 55.5 + \frac{15 - 9}{6}(4) = 55.5 + \frac{6}{6}(4)$$
$$= 59.5$$

c.
$$X_{.25} = 51.5 + \frac{7.5 - 7}{2}(4) = 51.5 + \frac{.5}{2}(4)$$

$$= 52.5$$

d.

$$\text{PR for 66} = \frac{17 + \frac{66 - 63.5}{4}(5)}{30}(100)$$

$$= 67.1\%$$

4.

Interval	Real limits	Tally	f	cf	c%
6.7-6.5	6.75-6.55	xx	2	20	100.0
7.0-6.8	7.05-6.75	xxx	3	18	90.0
7.3-7.1	7.35-7.05	xx	2	15	75.0
7.6-7.4	7.65-7.35	xxxx	4	13	65.0
7.9-7.7	7.95-7.65		0	9	45.0
8.2-8.0	8.25-7.95	xxxx	4	9	45.0
8.5-8.3	8.55-8.25	x	1	5	25.0
8.8-8.6	8.85-8.55	x	1	4	20.0
9.1-8.9	9.15-8.85	xx	2	3	15.0
9.4-9.2	9.45-9.15	x	1	1	5.0

5. a.

Interval	Real limits	Tally	f	cf	c%
7.0	7.05-6.95	x	1	20	100
7.1	7.15-7.05		0	19	95
7.2	7.25-7.15	xx	2	19	95
7.3	7.35-7.25	x	1	17	85
7.4	7.45-7.35	xxx	3	16	80
7.5	7.55-7.45	xxxxx	5	13	65
7.6	7.65-7.55	xx	2	8	40
7.7	7.75-7.65	xxx	3	6	30
7.8	7.85-7.75	xx	2	3	15
7.9	7.95-7.85		0	1	5
8.0	8.05-7.95	x	1	1	5

b.
$$X_{.50} = 7.55 - \frac{0.50(20) - 8}{5}(0.1)$$

$$= 7.55 - 0.04$$
$$= 7.51$$

c.
$$X_{.60} = 7.55 - \frac{0.60(20) - 8}{5}(0.1)$$

$$= 7.55 - 0.08$$
$$= 7.47$$

d.

$$\text{PR for } 7.4 = \frac{13 + \dfrac{7.45 - 7.4}{0.1}(3)}{20}(100)$$

$$= \frac{13 + 1.5}{20}(100)$$

$$= 72.5\%$$

6. a.

Interval	Real limits	Tally	f	cf	c%
263-267	262.5-267.5	xx	2	45	100.0
258-262	257.5-262.5	xxx	3	43	95.6
253-257	252.5-257.5	xxx	3	40	88.9
248-252	247.5-252.5	xxxxxx	6	37	82.2
243-247	242.5-247.5	xxxxxxxxx	9	31	68.9
238-242	237.5-242.5	xxxxxxxxx	9	22	48.9
233-237	232.5-237.5	xxxx	4	13	28.9
228-232	227.5-232.5	xxxx	4	9	20.0
223-227	222.5-227.5	xxx	3	5	11.1
218-222	217.5-222.5	x	1	2	4.4
213-217	212.5-217.5	x	1	1	2.2

b.

$$X_{.50} = 242.5 + \frac{0.50(45) - 22}{9}(5)$$

$$= 242.5 + 0.278$$
$$= 242.778$$

c.

$$X_{.90} = 257.5 + \frac{0.90(45) - 40}{3}(5)$$

$$= 257.5 + 0.833$$
$$= 258.333$$

d.

$$\text{PR for } 248 = \frac{31 + \dfrac{248 - 247.5}{5}(6)}{45}(100)$$

$$= \frac{31 + 0.6}{45}(100)$$

$$= 70.2\%$$

e.

$$\text{PR for } 229 = \frac{5 + \dfrac{229 - 227.5}{5}(4)}{45}(100)$$

$$= \frac{5 + 1.2}{45}(100)$$

$$= 13.78\%$$

Describing a Distribution of Test Scores

Watch for these words as you read the following chapter

Central tendency
Correlation
Correlation coefficient
  (r)
Interpercentile range
Interquartile range
Mean
Median
Mode

Normal curve
Raw score
Skewness
Standard deviation
Standard scores
T-Scores
Variability
Variance
z-Scores

In the previous chapter a detailed description of the process of building a frequency distribution to summarize a data set in an orderly manner was emphasized. Procedures were also set forth for calculating percentiles and percentile ranks with or without a frequency distribution. Test users and test developers frequently use two other pieces of information: a measure of **central tendency** and a measure of **variability.** The focus of the first section of this chapter is on measures of central tendency. This material is followed by a discussion of standard scores, correlation, and the use of norms. At its best, test development includes the generation of norms. Although you may not develop these norms yourself, be certain that the normative information is appropriate for the examinees.

MEASURES OF CENTRAL TENDENCY

A measure of central tendency provides information about the center of a distribution of test scores. Three measures of central tendency are commonly used to describe a set of test scores—the **mean,** the **median,** and the **mode.** Remember from Chapter 2 that the *median,* or 50th percentile, is the score dividing the distribution into equal halves. The *mode* is the score occurring most frequently in a distribution. Consider the following set of test scores.

Data set of 12 scores: 39, 33, 31, 29, 27, 26, 26, 26, 24, 23, 23, 21

In this case, the mode is *26,* the most frequently occurring score. The *mean* is the arithmetic average of a set of scores. The mean is emphasized in this section, since the calculation of the median has already been described and the mode can be determined in a straightforward manner.

Recall that the median could be calculated for a data set that was ordered from highest to lowest scores, even when the data were not in frequency-distribution form. Neither developing a frequency distribution to compute the mean nor ordering the scores is necessary. Examine the five test scores below.

Data set of 5 scores: 20, 10, 14, 18, 15

Obtaining scores on throwing ability.

By using elementary arithmetic a simple average can be determined by summing the scores and dividing by N. This is represented by Formula 3-1:

$$\overline{X} = \frac{\Sigma X}{N}$$ Formula 3-1

where $\overline{X}$ = the *mean* (referred to as *X-bar*)
Σ = *sum* of
X = *score* for one examinee
ΣX = *sum* of all *scores* in data set (20 + 10 + 14 + 18 + 15)

For the data set given on p. 52:

$$\overline{X} = \frac{77}{5} = 15.4$$

Sometimes it is more convenient to calculate the mean from a set of scores in frequency-distribution form, especially when the raw scores for the test are not available. A **raw score** is the actual score an examinee obtains on the test. Usually these scores are available; therefore, only the simplest case of a frequency distribution is described here. This is the frequency distribution with interval sizes equal to 1. To keep the example simple a frequency distribution of only 6 intervals is used. (Keep in mind, however, that a proper distribution should have no fewer than 10 and no more than 20 intervals.)

X	f	fX
10	2	20
9	3	27
8	4	32
7	6	42
6	3	18
5	1	5
	N = 19	144

With the data in this form, Formula 3-1 must be modified slightly to take into account that more than one person obtained a score in most of the above intervals. If all of the scores in the X column were merely added and the sum were divided by N, the answer would be incorrect. The frequency column, as shown in Formula 3-2, must also be considered.

$$\overline{X} = \frac{\Sigma fX}{N}$$ Formula 3-2

where X = *score* in a frequency distribution
f = *frequency* of scores in interval of frequency distribution
fX = *frequency multiplied* by score representing interval [e.g., for top interval, fX = 2(10) = 20]
ΣfX = *sum of frequency multiplied* by score for all intervals [2(10) + 3(9) + . . . + 1(5) = 144]

By multiplying the X column by the f column, a score for each person is included in the calculation. In this case:

$$\overline{X} = \frac{144}{19} = 7.58$$

The calculation of the mean for data sets in frequency distribution form with intervals larger than size 1 is omitted from this chapter. This calculation is not difficult, but it is cumbersome. With the ready availability of hand-calculators, punching in the raw scores and computing the mean are simple transactions. A discussion of more complex procedures is unnecessary at this level; the formulas presented in this section should be adequate. Although information about the center of a distribution is useful in itself, a more accurate interpretation of the data set is possible by obtaining information on the *spread* of the scores.

MEASURES OF VARIABILITY

Suppose two friends, Jim and Paul, bowled five lines apiece and obtained the following scores:

Jim: 138 142 140 139 141
Paul: 120 140 160 100 180

Let's order these scores to compare them more easily.

Jim: 138 139 140 141 142
Paul: 100 120 140 160 180

Which score represents the center of Jim's set of scores? Which represents Paul's set of scores? In this example both the mean and the median of each set of scores equal 140. Does the fact that these measures of central tendency are the same for both boys suggest that they have similar levels of ability in bowling?

If only the means and medians were available, this conclusion might be drawn. Since all five scores are available for each boy, let's look at them more closely in their ordered form. Jim's raw scores are similar, but Paul's vary to a great degree. One might say Paul is a more erratic bowler than Jim. Thus even though the sets of scores have one characteristic in common—their centrality—they are quite different in another way—their variability.

Range and Interpercentile Range

Three measures of variability are described in this section. The first is the **range** (highest score − lowest score + 1). The second measure is the **interpercentile range,** which provides an indication of how scores vary around the median, the 50th percentile. The most frequently used interpercentile range is the absolute value of $X_{.75} - X_{.25}$, known as the **interquartile range.** The method for obtaining interpercentile ranges involves removing a small percentage of scores from both ends of the distribution. As a result the most extreme scores are not allowed to affect the indicators of variability. If $X_{.75} = 50$ and $X_{.25} = 27$, the interquartile range is $50 - 27 = 23$. The number 23 is expressed in raw score units. Smaller numbers represent smaller ranges, with more scores clustering around the center of the distribution. Many other interpercentile ranges may be used, such as $X_{.90} - X_{.10}$ or $X_{.85} - X_{.15}$, as long as equal portions of the distribution are deleted from both ends.

Standard Deviation

When the mean is used as the measure of the center of the distribution, variability is estimated using the **standard deviation.** This statistic provides information about the extent to which scores deviate from the mean. In statistics Greek lowercase sigma, σ, is sometimes used to represent the standard deviation of a population of examinees, and s is used to represent the standard deviation of a sample of examinees drawn from the population. For convenience and simplicity the symbol s is used in this chapter.

Conceptual Formula

Earlier in this chapter, Formula 3-1 was used to calculate the mean of 15.4 for a set of five scores. The same set of five scores is listed below, this time from highest to lowest.

X	$X - \overline{X}$	$(X - \overline{X})^2$
20	4.6	21.16
18	2.6	6.76
15	$-.4$	.16
14	-1.4	1.96
10	-5.4	29.16
	0	59.20
	$[\Sigma(X - \overline{X})]$	$[\Sigma(X - \overline{X})^2]$

Since the standard deviation reflects the deviation of scores from the mean, it seems logical to calculate this statistic by subtracting the mean from each score and summing the deviations. This calculation is demonstrated in the second column in the above example. Note the result of obtaining the deviations and summing them. The answer of 0 would be obtained regardless of the data set used. The mean, as you know, represents the average of a set of scores. If we subtract each raw score from the mean, the deviations below the mean equal the deviations above the mean. This concept should be easy to understand if you think of the mean as the balancing point at the center of the distribution. When the deviations on both sides of the mean equal 0, the mean perfectly balances the distribution. Look back and examine the individual deviations from the mean. Although an answer of 0 indicates no variability in the data set, this is obviously not true for this set of scores. An answer of 0 would only *accurately* reflect no variability in a data set if all scores were identical. Thus, to obtain a deviation score that provides an accurate indication of the deviation of scores from the mean, these deviations are squared. The squared deviations are shown in the third column of the above example. The sum of these deviations is 59.20.

Now that we are working with *squared* deviations, the statistic being calculated is s^2, which is known as the **variance**. Once the variance is known, the standard deviation can be calculated by taking the square root of the variance. Formula 3-3 for the variance follows:

$$s^2 = \frac{\Sigma(X - \bar{X})^2}{N}$$

Formula 3-3

The sum of the squared deviations is divided by N to determine the average of the deviations. The numerator of this formula has already been determined for the set of five scores and, of course, $N = 5$. Thus,

$$s^2 = \frac{59.20}{5} = 11.84$$

Although calculating the variance to obtain the standard deviation is necessary, the numerical value for the variance is not as easily interpreted as the standard deviation. The variance is not expressed in the original raw score units of the test. The square root of this value, the standard deviation, is more useful in describing a set of test scores, since it is expressed in the actual score units of the test. Formula 3-4 for calculating the standard deviation follows:

$$s = \sqrt{\frac{\Sigma(X - \bar{X})^2}{N}}$$

Formula 3-4

A variance of 11.84 yields a standard deviation of 3.44. To summarize for the set of five scores, the mean is 15.4 and the standard deviation is 3.44. Assume that the five scores were obtained by administering an agility test to five students. The scores are expressed in seconds. A small standard deviation means that the scores tend to cluster around the mean. In this case the standard deviation indicates that the scores are spread out on both sides of the mean rather than clustered. Since the time scores are for a test of short duration, a deviation of 3 seconds or greater is considerable. In a measure of much longer duration, such as a long-distance run, a deviation of 3 seconds would have much less significance. The standard deviation must be interpreted in light of the actual score units of the test. In the previous example the examinees would not have similar abilities on the attribute being measured. If the standard deviation were smaller (e.g., 1.1 seconds), the scores would be clustered much more closely around the mean. In this case the ability levels of the examinees would be similar. Formula 3-4 is known as a conceptual formula rather than a computational formula. In other words, it depicts in a clear-cut manner the meaning and deviation of the standard deviation. (Do not use Formula 3-4 in the actual calculation of the standard deviation.)

If you have previously taken an elementary statistics course, you might have used a formula for the standard deviation with $N - 1$ in the denominator rather than N, as shown in Formulas 3-4 and 3-5. When $N - 1$ is used, the test user wishes to use a set of test scores to estimate the standard deviation of a population of individuals like those in the group being tested. For example, a teacher might administer a standing long jump test to a group of fourth-grade girls randomly selected from the entire school district. The mean and standard deviation calculated for the set of test scores could be interpreted as representative of all fourth-grade girls in the district. Under these circumstances the standard deviation formula should be used with $N - 1$ in the denominator so that the estimate of the standard deviation will be unbiased. In contrast, the more typical situation encountered in test administration is the use of a test with a specific group. Of greatest interest is the mean and standard deviation for this specific group. Generalizing to a population of individuals may not be important or, more often, may not be feasible. In this case the standard deviation formula with N in the denominator is appropriate. Thus, throughout this text, any version of the standard deviation formula will include N in the denominator. If you use a hand-calculator that is programmed to calculate the standard deviation, determine which term is used in the denominator. Many calculators provide two estimates of s, one calculated using N in the denominator and the other using $N - 1$ in the denominator.

Computational Formula

The standard deviation can be easily calculated from a set of raw scores by using many of the inexpensive calculators now on the market. In some cases, after the scores have been entered, the standard deviation can be calculated with the push of a button. In others the sum of squares needed in the computational formula is automatically calculated. The computational formula for the standard deviation used in this textbook is Formula 3-5. (A number of equivalent formulas that are equally appropriate may be used.)

$$s = \sqrt{\frac{N\Sigma X^2 - (\Sigma X)^2}{N(N)}} \qquad \text{Formula 3-5}$$

where ΣX^2 = the *sum* of each *number squared;* for the data set of five scores this
would be $20^2 + 18^2 + \ldots + 10^2$
$(\Sigma X)^2$ = the *square* of the *sum* of all *scores;* in this example $(20 + 18 + \ldots + 10)^2$

Let's apply Formula 3-5 to the small data set on p. 52.

$$s = \sqrt{\frac{5(1245) - (77)^2}{5(5)}}$$

$$= \sqrt{\frac{6225 - 5929}{25}}$$

$$= \sqrt{11.84}$$

$$= 3.44$$

To summarize, the standard deviation is the square root of the variance. The variance must be calculated first because the sum of the deviations of scores from the mean is *always 0.* However, the standard deviation is the statistic of greater interest, since it is expressed in raw score units. Now both the mean and standard deviation of this small set of five scores have been calculated. Interpreting these values is easier if the normal curve and its characteristics are clarified.

SCORE DISTRIBUTIONS

When data obtained from a test administration are graphed in the form of a curve, the shape of the curve will depend on the way in which the scores are distributed. The most common types of curves represented in data sets at this level are the normal curve and the skewed curve.

Normal Curve

In the previous chapter test scores were graphed in frequency polygon or histogram form. If it were possible to administer a test to a large number of examinees, perhaps several thousand, and the test scores were graphed, the resultant curve would approach the **normal curve** for most physical performance tests.

The normal curve (Figure 3-1) has several characteristics that can be of assistance in interpreting a set of scores. First, the curve is symmetrical. If the curve were lifted at one tail and folded over on top of the other side, the two halves of the curve would match precisely. In this case the mean, median, and mode would be identical. Second, the area under the curve represents 100%. It is possible to calculate the area for any portion of the curve. On the baseline of the curve, a mark is placed in the center to represent the center of the distribution. In addition, three marks are placed equidistant from one another above the center (in this context, the mean), and three marks are placed below the mean.

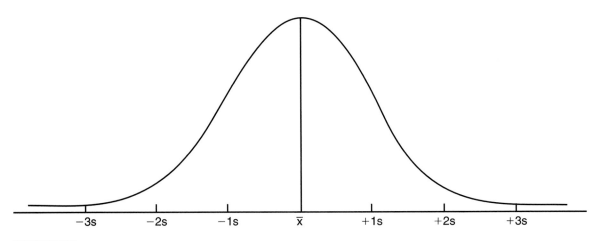

Figure 3-1   Normal curve.

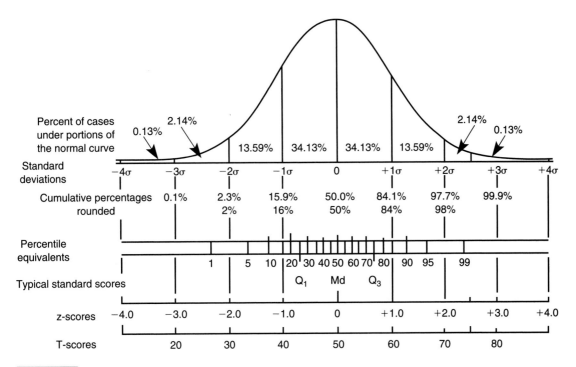

Figure 3-2   Areas under normal curve.

These marks, representing 3 standard deviations both above and below the mean, divide the normal curve into six portions. The percentage of area between these points is calculated and provides useful information for test users and developers. These portions and the percentage of area in each are displayed in Figure 3-2. Note that the tails of the curve do not touch the baseline. Obtaining scores representing 4 or more standard deviations above or below the mean is possible. For example, a genius might have an IQ that is greater than 5 or 6 standard deviations above the mean of the distribution of IQ scores. However, the likelihood of obtaining extreme scores is remote; thus the normal curve is usually described as being characterized by ± 3 standard deviations.

What kind of information can be obtained from Figure 3-2? Look at the point designated as + 1s, or 1 standard deviation above the mean. If an examinee's score falls at exactly this point, approximately 84% of the group taking the test scored below this point. The 84% was approximated by adding the percentages in each section to the left of + 1s.

A distribution of scores for a sit-ups test is depicted in Figure 3-3. The mean for this set of scores is 40, and the standard deviation is 7. One standard deviation above the mean is a score of 47 (40 + 7). One standard deviation below the mean is a score of 33 (40 − 7). Thus 84% of the group of examinees received scores at or below 47, while scores for approximately 16% of the group were at or below a score of 33. Of course, many scores fall between standard deviations expressed as whole numbers (e.g., + 2, − 1). For example, how should a score of

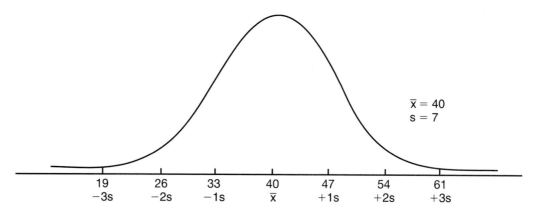

Figure 3-3   Normal curve with standard deviations expressed in score units (number of sit-ups).

35 be interpreted? Certainly this score is below average, falling between the mean and 1 standard deviation below the mean. However, the score cannot be interpreted with precision unless it is converted to standard score form.

Skewed Distributions

The bell shape typically associated with the normal curve shows that most of the examinees obtained scores in the middle of the distribution, with a few people scoring at each end. The two ends of the distribution are referred to as *tails* of the distribution. In short, the majority of the examinees represented under the normal curve obtained scores surrounding the average, while a smaller number received high and low scores. However, in real-life testing situations the test scores do not always approximate the normal curve. Sometimes most of the examinees will do well on a test, or sometimes most will perform poorly. Then these scores formed **skewed** distributions, with most of the area clustered at one end of the distribution.

When most of the examinees receive low scores on the test, the distribution is positively skewed. As shown in Figure 3-4, the majority of scores fall in the lower portion of the distribution, with a small number of high scores occurring in the long tail stretching out to the right. The *skewed* end of the distribution is the one with the long tail. If the skewness is located to the right, as in Figure 3-4, the distribution is labeled positively skewed. If the skewed end is located to the left, the distribution is labeled negatively skewed, as depicted in Figure 3-5. In this case a large portion of the examinees received high scores on the test, and only a few scored at the lower end of the distribution. When mastery tests are used, a negatively skewed distribution is often a desirable result. If most examinees master the material, they will do well on the test.

Consider the best way to describe these distributions. Should the mean and standard deviation be used as measure of central tendency and variability, or should the median be used? How is this decision made? First, a set of test scores should be summarized in frequency distribution form and graphed as a fre-

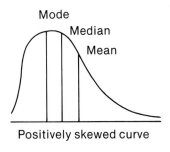

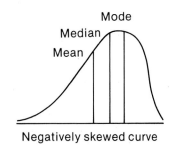

Figure 3-4   Positively skewed distribution.

Figure 3-5   Negatively skewed distribution.

quency polygon. Next, the graph (frequency polygon) should be examined. If the distribution of scores appears to approximate the normal curve, the mean and standard deviation should be used, since these values have stronger mathematical properties than the median and *interpercentile range.* If the distribution of scores is skewed, the mean will be closer to the skewed tail of the distribution than the median because the mean is affected by the extreme scores in the tail. Therefore, the median is a better representation of the center of the distribution when it is skewed. Since the median is a percentile, the corresponding measure of variability is one of the interpercentile ranges.

STANDARD SCORES

In Chapter 2 you learned how to convert test scores to percentile ranks. Two rules of thumb apply when transforming scores to standard scores. First, the median and the interpercentile range are used together. If these statistics are used to describe the center and spread of the distribution, percentile ranks should be used to convert scores. Second, the mean and the standard deviation are used together. When these statistics are used to describe a data set, a standard score transformation should be used.

The z-Score Transformation

Standard scores may take many forms, but all are based on the **z-score transformation,** which is the basic standard score transformation. Another term for this unit of transformation is the *standard deviation unit.* Formula 3-6 converts test scores to z-scores.

$$z\text{-score} = \frac{X - \bar{X}}{s} \qquad \text{Formula 3-6}$$

All the symbols in Formula 3-6 should look familiar. Refer back to the data from the sit-ups test. The mean of 40, the standard deviation of 7, and the precise interpretation of a score of 35 were of interest. The z-score transformation is one way of providing greater precision. Let's apply the data to Formula 3-6 and calculate the z-score for a score of 35.

$$z\text{-score} = \frac{35 - 40}{7} = -.71$$

The z-scores form a distribution with fixed parameters—a mean of 0 and a standard deviation of 1. Examine the z-score distribution in Figure 3-6. The mean of the distribution is 0, and 1 standard deviation above the mean is +1. One standard deviation below the mean is −1. The z-score values above the mean are all positive; those below the mean are all negative. Whatever the metric of the test score, the z-score formula converts it to the standard z-score metric. In other words, across a wide variety of distributions the mean of each distribution is converted to a z-score mean of 0. One of these tests might be scored in feet and inches, and another may be scored in minutes and seconds; yet the z-score means of the two tests will both be 0. The standard deviations are standardized in the same way.

Certain raw scores can be easily determined without the use of Formula 3-6, if the score is equal to 1 or more standard deviations above or below the mean. In the previous example it is apparent that a z-score of +1 equals 47 and a z-score of −1 equals 33. Both a z-score of +1 and a raw score of 47 equal 1 standard deviation above the mean. A z-score of −1 and a raw score of 33 both equal 1 standard deviation below the mean.

Refer to the interpretations of a score of 35 on the sit-ups test; the z-score for this score is −.71. The negative sign indicates that the score falls below the mean, and the size of the z-score (.71) indicates that almost three fourths of a standard deviation is represented. Thus a score of 35 is approximately three fourths of 1 standard deviation below the mean.

When interpreting only a few test scores from a single data set, it is possible to interpret the scores without converting them to z-scores if the mean and standard deviation of the data set are known. However, in exercise science several tests are often administered to a group of examinees during a single testing session. Each of the tests may be scored in different units. For example, a set of tests might include a test of skinfold thickness, a 1-mile run, and a sit-

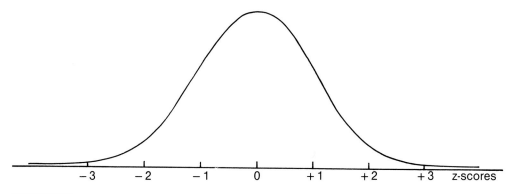

Figure 3-6   Graph of z-score distribution.

and-reach test of flexibility. The first measure is scored in millimeters; the second, in minutes and seconds; and the third, in centimeters (cm). How can an examinee's score on these three tests be compared? For this purpose the z-score transformation is a very useful tool. Assume that the examinee who performed 35 sit-ups in the previous example also took the sit-and-reach test and obtained a score of 25 cm. The mean and standard deviation of the group on the test was 23 cm and 2 cm, respectively. It is rather cumbersome to graph a distribution and mark the mean and standard deviations for the sit-ups test and sit-and-reach test so that the two test scores could be compared. If the score transformations of many examinees are needed, then the graphing approach is totally inefficient. What is the z-score for a sit-and-reach score of 25 cm?

$$\text{z-score} = \frac{25 - 23}{2} = +1$$

Now the score on the sit-ups test can be compared with the score on the sit-and-reach test. The score of 35 on the sit-ups test is represented by a z-score of $-.71$ and the sit-and-reach score of 25 by a z-score of $+1$. Referring to any other information about either of the two data sets is not necessary when comparing the two z-scores. This particular examinee is below average in abdominal strength and above average in low-back flexibility. This same procedure could be used to compare the scores of two or more individuals on the same test.

The T-Score Transformation

A practical reason for converting test scores to standard scores is to inform others of the examinee's performance on a test. For instance, a comparison of scores on different tests is information that is often requested by parents of a child in a physical education class, by the principal of a school, or by the manager of a fitness club. While z-scores provide a logical means of comparison, the z-score scale itself is not the easiest standard score to explain. This difficulty is primarily because the negative scores occur below the mean and the scores with decimal points can be found both above and below the mean. Most test developers resolve this problem by transforming the z-scores to another standard score that is easier for the layperson to interpret. Generally these transformations remove the negative sign and the decimal point from the z-scores. All these transformations, however, are based on the z-score distribution.

The **T-score distribution** is a popular conversion with developers of sport skills and basic motor abilities tests. The T-score distribution has a mean of 50 and a standard deviation of 10. To convert z-scores to T-scores, Formula 3-7 is used.

$$\text{T-score} = 10z + 50 \qquad \text{Formula 3-7}$$

Since two z-scores were calculated in the previous section, let's use these to calculate T-scores.

$$\text{T-score (for sit-ups score)} = 10(-.71) + 50 = 42.9$$
$$\text{T-score (for sit-and-reach score)} = 10(1) + 50 = 60$$

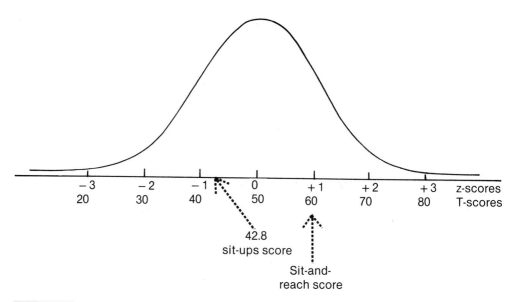

42.8
sit-ups score

Sit-and-
reach score

Figure 3-7   Comparison of scores using T-score distribution.

Compare these scores using the T-score distribution presented in Figure 3-7. Note that no T-score begins with a negative sign or a decimal. At the same time the information obtained from the T-score calculations does not conceal anything previously secured from the z-scores themselves. However, T-scores have a few inherent qualities that allow this distribution to be explained more easily to the public. In general, the scores range between 0 and 100. Although scores exceeding a − 3 or + 3 standard deviation (exceeding T-scores of 20 or 80) are rare, a range of scores from 0 to 100 seems plausible. Furthermore, the mean of the T-score distribution is 50, which seems like a reasonable average for a test to many people.

Constant-Value Method

Frequently a test user is more interested in determining the T-scores for an entire set of test scores than in calculating individual T-scores. If so, the *constant-value method* can be used to construct a T-score table for the data set. This table can be used to convert raw scores to T-scores, not only for this year's examinees but also for those who take the test in future years. Of course, these types of tables must be recalculated periodically so that they remain updated. The following steps are used in the constant-value method.

1. Calculate the mean and standard deviation for a set of test scores. For the sit-ups test the mean was 40 and the standard deviation was 7.
2. Calculate $s/10$. In our example, $7/10 = .7$. This is the constant used to add and subtract from the mean.

3. List each possible T-score from 20 to 80.
4. Add the constant to the mean (40) to obtain the raw score for a T-score of 51. In this case, $40 + .7 = 40.7$. Proceed in the same manner for T-scores 52–80. Note that the addition is cumulative. For example, to calculate the raw score for a T-score of 52, add the constant (.7) to the raw score for a T-score of 51 (40.7). The raw score for a T-score of 52 is 41.4.
5. For all T-scores below the mean, subtract the constant. For a T-score of 49, subtract the constant (.7) from the mean (40) to obtain an equivalent raw score. The raw score for a T-score of 49 is 39.3. Proceed in the same manner for T-scores of 48 down to 20.
6. Round off the raw scores to correspond with the actual test scores. In this case the actual test scores are in whole numbers (number of sit-ups); there-fore, the raw scores should be rounded to the nearest whole number.

As an example, the use of the constant-value method is exemplified for T-scores of 45 to 55.

T-score	Corresponding raw score	Rounded raw score
55	43.5	44
54	42.8	43
53	42.1	42
52	41.4	41
51	40.7	41
50	40.0	40
49	39.3	39
48	38.6	39
47	37.9	38
46	37.2	37
45	36.5	37

To complete the table of T-scores, raw score values must be calculated for all T-scores from 20 to 80. Note that several T-score values have the same raw score values. This is not unusual, especially when the standard deviation is a small number. Once the completed T-score table has been developed, it can be used to convert all scores in a data set, assuming the test examinees are similar to those whose scores were used to prepare the table. This method is much simpler than calculating T-scores for each raw score in a set of test scores.

Lower Scores, Better Performances

For certain measures of motor behavior, higher scores reflect poorer perform-ance. If the data set consists of scores on a shuttle run test, lower times are faster times and thus reflect better performance. When a z-score is calculated for a time score that is actually better than the mean in a performance context but lower than the mean in a numerical context, the result may be confusing. As an example, the mean of a set of shuttle run test scores is 11.2 seconds and the standard deviation is 0.4 second. What is the z-score for a raw score of 11.8? Use Formula 3-6 to solve this problem.

$$\text{z-score} = \frac{11.8 - 11.2}{4} = +1.5$$

The result is a $+1.5$ z-score, which indicates that the score is above the mean. This, of course, implies above-average performance. Yet in a performance context this is not true. A shuttle run score of 11.8 is slower than the average score for the group; it is a below-average score. The formula for calculating z-scores, as with any other statistical formulas, only deals with numbers and not with their interpretations. Therefore whenever lower scores equal better perform-ances, change the sign of the z-score to the opposite; the result will then repre-sent the correct *interpretation* of the score. Instead of obtaining a $+1.5$ z-score for a shuttle run score of 11.8, the answer would be -1.5. When the z-score is transformed to a T-score, it will also be correct in an interpretive sense. A z-score of -1.5 is equal to a T-score of 35, a below-average score.

When lower scores represent better performances, an easier method of calcu-lating the z-score is to use a variation of Formula 3-6 shown in Formula 3-8.

$$\text{z-score} = \frac{\overline{X} - X}{s} \qquad\qquad \text{Formula 3-8}$$

This formula is a special case of the usual z-score formula.

When using Formula 3-8, the resulting answer corresponds with the inter-pretation of the score in a performance context. In other words, a time score larger than the mean actually represents poorer performance; thus, the negative z-score provides the correct interpretation.

CORRELATION

To be able to analyze a test, a basic understanding of test reliability and validity is necessary. To estimate these two test characteristics, a statistic known as the **correlation coefficient** is often used. The term **correlation** refers to the *rela-tionship between two variables, x and y.* The symbol x already represents a score on a test; now y will be used to represent a score on another test. Is the ability to perform one skill related to the ability to perform a second skill? To gain insight into this type of question, a correlation coefficient can be calcu-lated.

Pearson Product-Moment Correlation Coefficient

The *Pearson product-moment correlation coefficient,* the most commonly used correlation coefficient, is symbolized as r_{xy}. Correlation coefficients can range from $+1.00$ to -1.00. These extremes are depicted in the data sets below.

	Data set A		Data set B	
	Leg strength	Standing long jump	Leg strength	Arm strength
A	42	7 ft, 5 in	42	8
B	40	7 ft, 0 in	40	10
C	38	6 ft, 5 in	38	12
D	36	6 ft, 0 in	36	14
E	34	5 ft, 5 in	34	16

In both data sets the leg strength measure (X) is an indicator of leg extensor strength measured in foot-pounds. In Data set A the second variable (Y) is the standing long jump, and in Data set B arm strength is measured by a test of pull-ups. All these data sets are formed hypothetically to demonstrate the extreme range of correlation coefficients, $r_{xy} = +1.00$ and $r_{xy} = -1.00$. In Data set A the first examinee, A, has the highest scores on both tests, and the fifth examinee, E, has the lowest scores. This pattern can be observed across all examinees. Thus it is intuitively obvious that a high relationship exists between leg strength and the ability to perform the standing long jump (i.e., those with greater leg strength are able to jump longer distances). If r_{xy}, the Pearson product-moment correlation coefficient, were calculated for this data set, it would equal $+1.00$. A correlation coefficient of $+1.00$ represents a *perfect positive correlation*.

Now examine the two sets of scores in Data set B. Note that precisely the reverse trend is evident in the arm strength and leg strength scores. As the leg strength scores decrease, the arm strength scores increase. The correlation between these two sets of scores is negative. In fact, in this example, the correlation coefficient is -1.00, a perfect negative correlation. Normally, it is not appropriate to calculate the correlation coefficients for such small data sets. With only five examinees the resultant coefficients may not be an accurate indicator of the relationship between two variables, since the idiosyncrasies of one person could drastically affect the coefficient. Even in the next example, the number of cases is too small; 30 or more examinees would be desirable. However, a small data set is convenient for demonstrating the calculation of the correlation coefficient. In this example the correlation coefficient for scores of eight examinees on two variables, pull-ups and push-ups, will be determined.

Examinee	Pull-ups(x)	Push-ups(y)	X²	Y²	XY
A	10	15	100	225	150
B	2	5	4	25	10
C	5	11	25	121	55
D	6	10	36	100	60
E	7	14	49	196	98
F	1	3	1	3	3
G	9	16	81	256	144
H	5	8	25	64	40
	45	82	321	996	560

The Pearson product-moment correlation coefficient, r_{xy}, is calculated using Formula 3-9.

$$r_{xy} = \frac{N\Sigma XY - (\Sigma X)(\Sigma Y)}{\sqrt{[N\Sigma X^2 - (\Sigma X)^2][N\Sigma Y^2 - (\Sigma Y)^2]}}$$

Formula 3-9

where ΣXY = the *sum* of the products of XY for each examinee; in this example, $(10)(15) + (2)(5) + \ldots + (5)(8) = 560$

$(\Sigma X)(\Sigma Y)$ = the *product* of the *sum* of the X-scores and the *sum* of the Y-scores; in this example, $(45)(82) = 3690$

ΣX^2 = the *sum* of each X-value *squared*; in this example, $(10^2 + \ldots + 5^2) = 321$; use the same concept for Y^2

$(\Sigma X)^2$ = the *square* of the *sum* of all X-values; in this example, $(10 + 2 + \ldots + 5)^2 = 2025$; use the same concept for $(\Sigma Y)^2$

Now Formula 3-9 will be used with the pull-ups and push-ups data.

$$r_{xy} = \frac{8(560) - (45)(82)}{\sqrt{[8(321) - (45)^2][8(996) - (82)^2]}} = .96$$

A coefficient of .96 represents a high positive relationship between push-ups and pull-ups, suggesting that performance of each measure is dependent to a large extent on a similar type of arm and shoulder girdle strength.

Spearman Rank Correlation Coefficient

Ranking the scores in each data set on p. 52 is also possible. The highest scores in each data set would be given ranks of 1, and so forth. In the pull-ups data set, Examinees C and H received the same score of 5. The scores represent two rank positions, yet the ranks for the two scores should be identical. These ranks are calculated by *averaging* the two rank positions, in this case *5* and *6*, and assigning the average rank of 5.5 to each score of 5. Without performing any type of calculation on the ranks, it is possible to obtain a general idea about the degree of relationship between two variables from a visual examination of the ranks. For example, Examinee A would be assigned ranks of 1 on pull-ups and 2 on push-ups; Examinee F would be assigned ranks of 8 and 8, respectively. Although the ranks are not identical for each person, they are similar; this points to a substantial relationship between the two variables. Of course it is known that the relationship is high, since r_{xy} has already been calculated using the raw scores. Calculating a correlation coefficient using ranks only is also possible; it requires a different statistic known as the **Spearman rank correlation coefficient** (ρ). Formula 3-10 is used to calculate the ρ.

$$\rho = 1 - \frac{6(\Sigma D^2)}{N(N^2 - 1)}$$

Formula 3-10

where D = the *difference* between the two ranks for each subject

D^2 = *square* of the *difference* between ranks for an examinee

ΣD^2 = *sum* of D^2 for all examinees

The push-ups and pull-ups data will be used again, and for purposes of convenience the raw scores will be reproduced as well as ranked. Note that ΣD equals 0. This is always true, regardless of the data set. This calculation is a convenient way to check the numbers in the D column.

X	Rank(X)	Y	Rank(Y)	D	D²
10	1	15	2	−1	1
2	7	5	7	0	0
5	5.5	11	4	1.5	2.25
6	4	10	5	−1	1
7	3	14	3	0	0
1	8	3	8	0	0
9	2	16	1	1	1
5	5.5	8	6	−0.5	0.25
				0	5.50
				ΣD	(ΣD^2)

$$\rho = 1 - \frac{6(5.50)}{8(8^2 - 1)} = .935$$

Note that the result of the rank difference method is not the same as the result obtained using r_{xy}, although the values are similar. This is expected, since the process of converting raw scores to ranks leads to a loss of information about the original data sets.

To summarize, when two sets of scores are available for the same set of examinees, the relationship between the two variables can be estimated using a correlation coefficient. When the raw scores are continuous or discrete data (not initially in rank form), the Pearson product-moment correlation coefficient (r_{xy}) is appropriate under most circumstances. When the scores are converted to ranks, or obtained as ranks initially, the Spearman rank correlation coefficient (ρ) may be used. The rank difference formula is easier to use, but its result is not as accurate as r_{xy}. For all practical purposes, however, the discrepancy between estimates is not serious.

Graph of Relationship Between Two Variables

Correlational information is often presented in graphic form by plotting the *coordinates* of the X- and Y-scores, with the Y-scores represented on the *vertical* axis and the X-scores represented on the *horizontal* axis. Lower or poorer scores are located on the lower portion of the Y axis and higher or better scores on the upper portion. On the X-axis lower or poorer scores are placed to the left; higher or better scores are to the right. A coordinate is a point on the graph representing the paired X- and Y-scores for each examinee. The push-ups and pull-ups scores for eight examinees are presented in graph form in Figure 3-8.

Each point on the graph represents two scores for an examinee. If the X- and Y-scores increase proportionally, that is, as the X-scores increase, the Y-scores

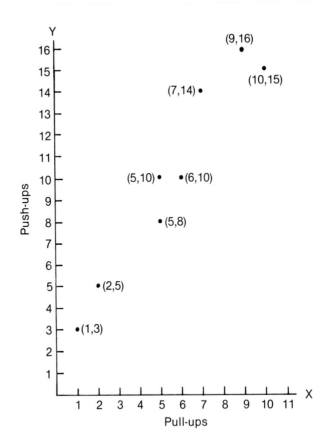

Figure 3-8   Graph of relationship between push-ups and pull-ups scores.

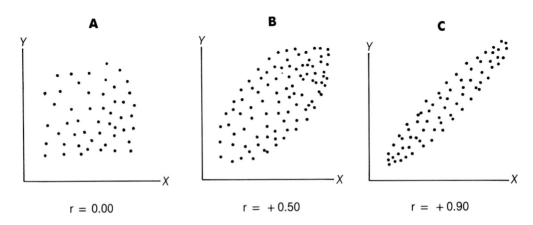

Figure 3-9   Graph of various sizes of correlation coefficients. **A,** No relationship between X and Y. **B,** Moderate relationship. **C,** High relationship.

also increase by the same proportion, the coordinates will fall on or close to a straight line that slants from the lower-left corner of the graph to the upper-right corner. While the increase in X- and Y-scores is not precisely proportional in Figure 3-8, the tendency can be observed. This is an example of a high positive correlation represented in graph form. Examples of other sizes of correlation coefficients are displayed in graph form in Figure 3-9. A negative relationship is represented by XY coordinates that fall on or close to a straight line that slants from the upper right-hand corner of the graph to the lower left-hand corner.

Interpretation of Correlation Coefficients

Opinions vary about how the size of a correlation coefficient should be interpreted. How high should a coefficient be to be classified as high? Moderate? Low? A general rule of thumb is presented below, but under certain circumstances the interpretation may vary even from this general rule.

$\pm.80-1.00$	High
$\pm.60-0.79$	Moderately high
$\pm.40-0.59$	Moderate
$\pm.20-0.39$	Low
$\pm.00-0.19$	No relationship

Measuring form and skill in throwing.

Another way of interpreting the coefficient is to square it. This statistic, r_{xy}^2, is known as the *coefficient of determination.* As an example, assume the correlation between two measures of arm strength is .80. The square of the correlation is an indication of the *shared variance between two variables.* In other words, this is the variance the two variables share. For the two measures of arm strength, the shared variance is .64. This means that 64% of the variance between these two measures taps a common element, which can be assumed to be arm strength. With higher correlation coefficients the shared variance is substantial. However, with correlation coefficients of moderate and small sizes, the coefficient of determination is affected to a greater extent. For example, if r_{xy} = .50, the square of the coefficient equals .25. Another advantage of using the squared correlation coefficient in interpreting r_{xy} is that squared coefficients can be compared as ratios, unlike the regular correlation coefficient. For example, a coefficient of .90 does not represent twice as much of a relationship as a coefficient of .45. However, when r_{xy} is squared, coefficients can legitimately be compared in this manner. For example, a coefficient of determination of .50 represents twice as much variance as a coefficient of .25.

USE OF NORMS

Raw Scores and Derived Scores

A raw score is the score an individual obtains on a test. If the only information available about an examinee's test performance is the raw score, interpreting it meaningfully can be difficult. For instance, if Mary runs the 50-yard dash in 7.8 seconds, is the score good? To answer this question the score can be transformed to another scale, yielding a *derived score.* In Chapter 2 and in this chapter procedures are described for developing both percentile and standard score norms. Even better, the raw scores can be compared to a table in which derived scores have already been calculated for the raw scores.

Types of Norms

Norms are derived scores determined from the raw scores obtained by a specific group on a specific test. Whenever percentile norms are determined for a group of examinees, half will score above the middle of the distribution and half will score below. No inherent value is attached to any given norm score. The norm describes an examinee in relation to a large sample of people who have taken the test. Any judgment made about the norm is made by the test user. Several types of norms might be used, including grade norms, age norms, percentiles, and standard scores.

Grade Norms

Grade norms are calculated by determining the average of the raw scores for a grade and using the grade equivalent in place of that average. For example, if the average distance that a class of fifth-grade boys could throw a softball were 96 feet, a score of 96 feet would represent a grade norm of 5. However, scores on measures of physical performance are rarely transformed to grade norms because each grade includes children of different ages; the older children, more advanced in physical growth and development, have a natural advantage in many motor skills.

The use of grade norms has several other limitations. The units from one grade to another are not equal over different parts of the scale. Thus achievement from grade 2 to grade 3 may be greater or less than achievement from grade 8 to grade 9. Performance on physical fitness items, for instance, usually increases consistently from grade to grade for elementary school girls. However, this performance increment may level off before entrance into high school. Thus the significance of a grade norm of 11 for a ninth-grade student is not nearly as great as a grade norm of 4 for a second-grade student.

Furthermore, grade units may be unequal from test to test. A seventh-grade student with grade norms of 11 on the distance run and 9 on the sit-and-reach test would appear to have more cardiorespiratory endurance than flexibility. However, there may be a greater range of distance-run scores than flexibility scores for the sixth grade, and the student might actually have high percentile ranks on both tests.

Grade norms are useful for reporting growth in basic skills at the elementary school level. Since this type of norm can be misinterpreted so easily, other types are often preferred.

Age Norms

Age norms are determined by calculating the average score for a given age. A raw score is then interpreted in terms of an age equivalent. If the average performance by 17-year-old boys on the standing long jump is 7 feet 2 inches, then a raw score of 7 feet 2 inches is used to represent an age norm of 17. Although this type of norm has been used with tests of physical performance, in reality skeletal maturation may play a more significant role than age. In growth and development scales a form of age norms is sometimes used to describe sequences of motor behavior.

Percentile Rank Norms

Get Fit!, published by the President's Council on Physical Fitness and Sports (1991), and the Chrysler Fund–AAU physical fitness program (1993), include tables of norms based on percentile ranks. Norms are presented by age and gender. Grouping by age or grade should not be confused with age norms and grade norms. In the latter case ages or grades represent the norms; in the former case, percentiles represent the norms. Other publishers of physical fitness tests do not follow this precedent. As you will learn later, several tests now use standards that are based on the normal curve.

In Chapter 2 you learned how to calculate percentile ranks. The *percentile rank norm* is based on the position of the person's score relative to others in the group. Whatever the range of raw scores, the percentiles can only range from 1

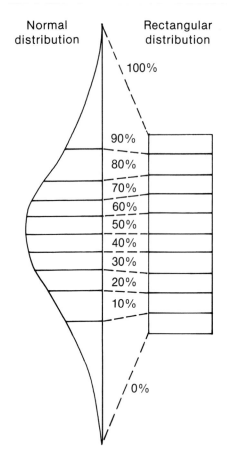

Figure 3-10 Relationship between normal and rectangular distributions.

to 99. Percentiles divide a distribution of scores into 100 groups of equal size. Although a set of raw scores often forms a bell-shaped distribution, percentiles form a rectangular one, as shown in Figure 3-10. Percentiles are not equally spaced throughout the distribution because more people are clustered at the middle of the distribution than at the extremes. Only if the same number of examinees obtains each score are the percentiles equally spaced. However, such a distribution is not likely. Therefore, although percentiles seem simple to interpret, it is easy to overemphasize differences near the median and underemphasize differences near the extremes.

Sometimes averaging percentile ranks for several tests is desirable. To do so, the percentiles must first be converted to z-scores. This conversion can be made using tables that are available in most statistics textbooks. The z-scores are then averaged, and this average is converted back to a percentile rank using the same table. The raw score distribution is assumed to be normal for each set of raw scores. Also, the same norm group should be used to generate the percentiles.

Standard Score Norms

Standard score norms, like percentile norms, are widely used for measures of physical performance, although they have typically not been used to determine national norms in the physical education field. Figure 3-2 represents the relationship between percentiles and standard scores. All standard scores are based on the z-score distribution, which was described earlier in this chapter. Most test users prefer to use a transformation of the z-score because this score is expressed in decimal places and, in some instances, is a negative number. The most widely used transformation in the field is the T-score, also described earlier in this chapter.

Local and National Norms

National norms, if properly developed, can be useful for certain purposes. A physical education teacher may wish to compare students' test scores with a national sample as partial evidence of a successful program. If the test scores match high norms, the program is obviously achieving satisfactory results in the area tested. If the norms are low, perhaps certain aspects of the program need to be improved. National norms are also useful for comparisons among distinct subpopulations within an area. For example, in a large metropolitan area comparisons of performance level of "inner city," "fringe-area," and suburban students with national norms could yield interesting results.

On the other hand, national norms are limited in the type of information they can provide. In a school with a good physical education program, all the students may score above the middle of the distribution using a table of national norms. Although this information may be useful in justifying a physical education program, the individual student receives little feedback on personal performance relative to other students in the same school. *Local norms* would provide more useful information in this case. A student who is above average using national norms may be average or even below average compared with local norms. Teachers within a school district can develop local norms by collecting test scores over a period of several years to obtain adequate data; these norms should also be revised periodically so that they remain up-to-date.

SUMMARY

Measures of central tendency and variability provide essential information for a concise interpretation of a set of test scores. If the test scores are distributed so that they approximate the normal curve, the mean and standard deviation are preferred measures. When the distribution is skewed, the median is a more accurate representation of the center of the distribution. In this case the interpercentile range would be used as the measure of variability. Because tests of motor skill and physical fitness are scored in different metrics, scores are frequently transformed to a common scale using percentiles, z-score transformations, or T-score transformations. In this way scores recorded in minutes and seconds can be compared with scores recorded in feet and inches.

Sometimes it is of interest to know whether two variables bear a relationship to each other. This can be examined by calculating a correlation coefficient using the two variables. The Pearson product-moment procedure can be used to calculate this statistic; if the scores are ranked, the rank difference method can be used. These coefficients may be interpreted on both practical and statistical grounds.

The scores of normative groups should be taken into account in interpreting scores on tests of motor behavior. Information on local and national norms is useful in obtaining an overall perspective of the ability of individual examinees in relation to others.

Learning Experiences

1. Ten students were given the long jump test and the 50-yard dash test. Their scores were:

Student	Long jump (inches) (Test A)	50-yard dash (unit-second) (Test B)
1	72	8.0
2	69	8.0
3	51	9.7
4	69	7.6
5	63	8.3
6	81	7.3
7	66	8.2
8	78	7.5
9	72	7.4
10	75	7.8

  a. Calculate the mean, median, and mode for Test A and Test B.

  b. Calculate the range and interquartile range for Test A and Test B.

  c. Calculate the standard deviation for Test A and Test B.

  d. Calculate z-scores and T-scores for each score on Test A.

  e. Calculate z-scores and T-scores for each score on Test B.

  f. Calculate the correlation coefficient between Test A and Test B using the Pearson product-moment method. Interpret the correlation coefficient.

  g. Calculate the percentage of variance that Test A and Test B share.

  h. Rank the Test A scores.

  i. Rank the Test B scores.

  j. Calculate the rank-difference correlation coefficient.

References

American Association for Health, Physical Education and Recreation (AAHPER). 1967. AAHPER sports skills tests. Washington, DC: American Association for Health, Physical Education and Recreation.

American Psychological Association (APA). 1985. Standards for educational and psychological tests. Washington, DC: American Psychological Association.

Chrysler Fund–Amateur Athletic Union (AAU). (1993). Physical fitness program. Bloomington, Ind: Chrysler Fund–Amateur Athletic Union.

Downing D, Clark J. 1983. Statistics the easy way. Woodbury, NY: Barron's Educational Series.

Lyman HB. 1978. Test scores and what they mean, ed 3, Englewood Cliffs, NJ: Prentice-Hall.

Mosteller F, Fienberg SE, Rourke REK. 1983. Beginning statistics with data analysis. Reading, Mass: Addison-Wesley.

President's Council on Physical Fitness and Sports (1991). *Get fit! A handbook for youth ages 6–17.* Washington, DC: President's Council on Physical Fitness and Sports.

Rothstein AL. 1985. Research design and statistics for physical education. Englewood Cliffs, NJ: Prentice-Hall.

Sprinthall RC. 1982. Basic statistical analysis. Reading, Mass: Addison-Wesley.

Annotated Readings

Glasnapp DR, Pogglo JP. 1985. Essentials of statistical analysis for the behavioral sciences. Columbus, Ohio: Charles E Merrill.

Introductory statistics text tailored to students with little mathematics background and no experience studying statistics; focuses on applied statistics; problems use data reflecting children in actual situations—the "Sesame Street" database; includes enough theory to lay a firm foundation and enough application to be genuinely practical; emphasizes key concepts.

Hinkle DE, Wiersma W, Jurs SG. 1979. Applied statistics for the behavioral sciences. Boston: Houghton Mifflin.

Emphasizes conceptual understanding of basic statistical procedures; helps students achieve computational skills needed for statistical procedures in practical settings; examples taken from actual settings (40% from education); begins with elementary descriptive statistics and progresses to more sophisticated procedures.

Jaeger R. 1983. Statistics: a spectator sport. Beverly Hills, Calif: Sage.

Designed to help anyone who wants to understand statistics; includes clear explanations that enable readers to learn what statistics are, what they mean, and how they are used and interpreted; does not include any equations; provides applications to a wide range of research and evaluation problems, giving particular attention to studies in the computerized files of Educational Resources Information Center (ERIC).

Kirk RE. 1984. Elementary statistics, ed 2, Florence, Ky: Brooks/Cole.

Introduction to statistics for students in education and behavioral sciences; emphasizes verbal rather than mathematical problems; includes in-depth treatments of individual concepts and their interrelationships; develops the underpinnings of statistics through the use of high-school mathematics; contains a concise review of elementary mathematics in an appendix; incorporates real-life examples in the review exercises; provides an interesting introduction to the history of statistics, as well as extensive references on important topics.

Witte RS. 1984. Statistics, ed 2. Lavallette, NJ: Holt, Rinehart & Winston. Emphasizes concepts rather than just computations; covers a wide range of topics in descriptive and inferential statistics without overwhelming students with mathematics; includes extensive problem sets in each chapter, ranging from simple computational tasks to questions of interpretation, with step-by-step progressions to problem solving.

Problems

1. Use the data set below to calculate the mean and the standard deviation.

   Data set of 30 $\dot{V}O_2$ max (maximum oxygen consumption) scores: 54, 49, 53, 56, 55, 50, 47, 60, 53, 41, 58, 53, 48, 37, 55, 62, 54, 51, 39, 54, 53, 47, 57, 55, 42, 57, 54, 45, 49, 53

2. a. Use the above data set of 30 $\dot{V}O_2$ max scores to form a frequency distribution with intervals of size 2. Include columns for tally, f, cf, and $c\%$.
   b. Calculate the interquartile range for this distribution, using the frequency distribution in a.

3. The mean of a set of basketball scores is 32 and the standard deviation is 3. Calculate z-scores and T-scores for the following test scores: 31, 39, 29, 27, 33, 25.

4. Using the Pearson product-moment method, calculate the correlation coefficient for the scores on the first (X) and second (Y) examinations given in an undergraduate course on measurement in physical education.

Student	Test 1 (X)	Test 2 (Y)
1	47	33
2	54	49
3	48	40
4	47	44
5	50	48
6	45	36
7	50	35
8	56	50
9	54	46
10	48	37
11	53	40
12	47	39
13	38	32
14	47	42
15	48	39
16	49	37
17	53	42
18	53	40
19	49	40
20	52	47

   a. Draw a graph of the relationship between X and Y. Plot the coordinates and record their numerical values at each point, as in Figure 3-8.
5. Thought question: Interpret the relationship between the scores on the two measurement examinations that were correlated in 4. Consider both the size and sign of the correlation coefficient. What does this mean in terms of the students' abilities on the two tests?
6. Use the data set below to calculate the mean and standard deviation.

   Data set of nine 100-meter dash scores: (unit = second) 12.9, 13.1, 13.5, 13.8, 14.0, 14.2, 14.5, 14.7, 15.4

7. The mean of a set of 400-meter run scores is 70.5 seconds and the standard deviation is 6.0 seconds. Calculate z-scores and T-scores for the following scores:

   58.7, 64.5, 70.5, 76.5, 88.0

8. The mean of a set of standing long jump scores is 100.5 inches and the standard deviation is 4.47 inches. Calculate z-scores and T-scores for the following test scores:

   89, 92, 100.5, 105, 112

9. a. Using the Pearson product-moment method, calculate the correlation coefficient for the scores on 100-meter dash (X) scores and the average length of steps in dash (Y) collected from 12 male athletes in competition.

Athlete no.	100-Meter time X (sec)	Average length of steps Y (m)
1	9.98	2.23
2	9.90	2.13
3	10.22	2.15
4	10.11	2.13
5	10.25	2.11
6	10.41	2.29
7	10.00	2.00
8	10.30	2.04
9	10.30	2.00
10	10.30	1.95
11	10.30	2.04
12	10.70	1.98

   b. Draw a graph of the relationship between X and Y. Plot the coordinates and record their numerical values at each point, as in Figure 3-8.
10. The data set below is the scoring rate of spikes (X) and the winning order (Y) of the first eight winning teams in a volleyball competition.

Team no.	Scoring rate of spikes X (%)	Winning order Y
1	44.0	1
2	40.3	2
3	40.6	3
4	46.1	4
5	37.4	5
6	43.5	6
7	37.4	7
8	38.9	8

Calculate the rank difference correlation coefficient for the scoring rate of spikes (X) and the winning order (Y) of the volleyball teams.

Answers to Problems

1. $\bar{X} = \dfrac{1541}{30} = 51.37$; $s = \sqrt{\dfrac{(30)(80211) - (1541)^2}{(30)(30)}} = 5.93$

2. a.

Intervals	Tally	f	cf	c%
61-62	x	1	30	100.0
59-60	x	1	29	96.7
57-58	xxx	3	28	93.3
55-56	xxxx	4	25	83.3
53-54	xxxxxxxxx	9	21	70.0
51-52	x	1	12	40.0
49-50	xxx	3	11	36.7
47-48	xxx	3	8	26.7
45-46	x	1	5	16.7
43-44		0	4	13.3
41-42	xx	2	4	13.3
39-40	x	1	2	6.7
37-38	x	1	1	3.3

b. $X_{.75} = 55.25$; $X_{.25} = 48.17$
Interquartile range $= 55.25 - 48.17 = 7.08$

3.

Score	z-score	T-score
31	$-.33$	46.7
39	2.33	73.3
29	-1.00	40.0
27	-1.67	33.3
33	.33	53.3
25	-2.33	26.7

4. a. $r_{xy} = \dfrac{20(40593) - 988(816)}{\sqrt{[20(49118) - 976144][20(33808) - 665856]}} = 0.706$

   b. Answer is depicted in the figure below.

6. $\bar{X} = \dfrac{\Sigma X}{N} = \dfrac{126.1}{9} = 14.01$

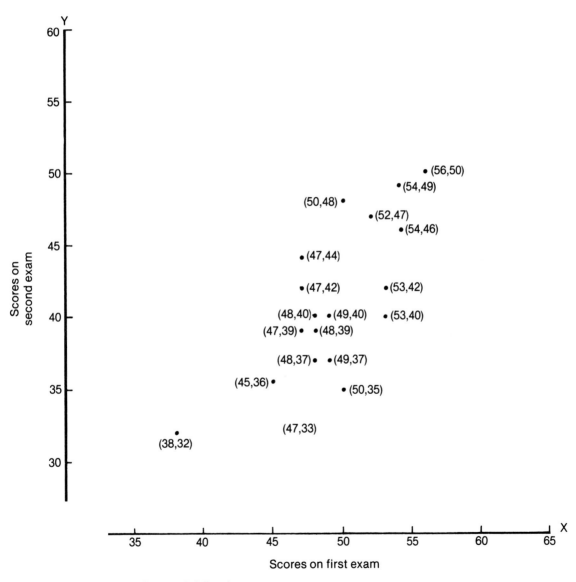

Measuring form and skill in throwing.

$$S = \sqrt{\frac{N\Sigma X^2 - (\Sigma X)^2}{N(N)}}$$

$$= \sqrt{\frac{9(1771.85) - (126.1)^2}{9(9)}}$$

$$= \sqrt{\frac{45.44}{81}}$$

$$= \sqrt{0.561}$$

$$= .75$$

7.
Raw score	z-score	T-score
58.7	1.97	69.7
64.5	1.00	60.0
70.5	0.00	50.0
76.5	− 1.00	40.0
88.0	− 2.92	20.8

8.
Raw score	z-score	T-score
112	2.57	75.7
105	1.01	60.1
100.5	0.00	50.0
92	− 1.90	30.9
89	− 2.57	24.3

9. a.
$$r_{xy} = \frac{12(256.2111) - (122.77)(25.05)}{\sqrt{[12(1256.5515) - (122.77)^2][12(52.4115) - (25.05)^2]}}$$

$$= \frac{-0.8553}{2.9701}$$

$$= -.288$$

10.
Team no.	X	Rank (X)	Y	Rank (Y)	D	D^2
1	44.0	2	1	1	1	1
2	40.3	5	2	2	3	9
3	40.6	4	3	3	1	1
4	46.1	1	4	4	− 3	9
5	37.4	7.5	5	5	2.5	6.25
6	43.5	3	6	6	− 3	9
7	37.4	7.5	7	7	0.5	0.25
8	38.9	6	8	8	− 2	4
					$\Sigma D^2 =$	39.5

$$P = 1 - \frac{6(39.5)}{8(8 - 1)}$$

$$= 1 - .47$$

$$= .53$$

Inferential Statistics

Suppose we want to divide a class of students into basketball teams. Preferably, no team should be appreciably taller than the others. We could measure the height of each student and calculate the mean height of each team. We would not expect the mean height of all teams to be exactly the same. That is, we expect some sampling error (i.e., there is a small chance that a few of the shorter students were selected to the same team, thus lowering the team's average height). However, the differences in average team height should be quite small. What if we find that the mean height of one team is larger than the means of the other teams? Is the difference large enough to consider forming new teams? In other words, is the difference in height due to expected sampling error (i.e., due to chance) or is there really a height difference? Statistical procedures are available to examine the mean differences. If the differences are statistically significant, we are not likely to get these differences merely by sampling error alone. If statistical significance is not obtained, the mean heights may not be different enough to matter.

Two statistical techniques to test the difference between group means are the **t-test** and the **analysis of variance (ANOVA).** Both methods use an indirect method to determine if means are significantly different. For example, let's say that one of the teams had an average height of 7 feet. If you learn that due to sampling error alone, the chances of forming a team with a mean height of 7 feet was 1 chance out of a million, you might suspect that this team is significantly taller than the other teams. In contrast, if the team was only 2 inches taller on the average than the other teams, the chances of this happening because of sampling error might be about 50 times out of a hundred. Then you would probably conclude that the team is not significantly taller than the other teams. To make such statistical decisions, knowledge of **z-scores** and the normal curve is essential. As noted in the previous chapter, the normal curve is a bell-shaped curve with defined areas under the curve. Review the section on standard scores in Chapter 3. The z-score in particular will be important in our discussion of the normal curve. The normal curve is a mathematical function. Actually, there is a family of normal curves, depending on the value of the population mean and standard deviation. We will be working with the unit normal curve, with a mean of 0 and a standard deviation of 1.

Recall from the previous chapter that the area under the curve is 1 when using the unit normal curve. The mean divides the curve into two equal halves. Therefore, .50 or 50% of the area under the curve is to the left of the mean and 50% is to the right. We have also discussed other percentages representing areas under the curve. The area between z-scores of -1 and $+1$ is about 68%; between z-scores of -2 and $+2$, 95%; and between z-scores of $\pm$, 99%. Values of z-scores typically range from -3.00 to $+3.00$. All but a very small percentage of the area under the curve falls within this range.

FINDING AREAS AND z-SCORES

To conduct a t-test or ANOVA, knowledge of the *region of rejection* under the curve is essential. The larger the region of rejection, the easier it is to get a significant t- or F-value (variance ratio), and vice versa. Therefore, we must be able to answer questions such as "What is the size of the area under the curve between the mean and a z-score of 1.33?" Or "How much of the area under the curve lies between a z-score of $-.51$ and $+1.12$?" If you can answer questions like these, you will understand how to identify the region of rejection for t- and F-tests.

A table is available to help answer these questions. The table is in Appendix G. Let's first solve the problem of finding the area falling below a specified z-score. Use a z of 1.33. Referring to Appendix G, take the absolute value (ignore the sign) of the z-score. Note the column of z-values and find 1.33. The area is .4082. However, this number represents **only** the area between **the mean** and **a z-score of 1.33.** The other half of the curve represents .50 of the area under the curve. Thus, the area below a z of 1.33 is .4082 + .50 = .9082, as shown in Figure 4-1.

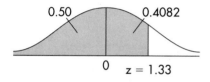

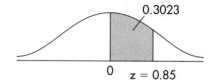

Figure 4-1   Area below z-score of 1.33.

Figure 4-2   Z-Score for area of 0.85.

We also could use Appendix G in the opposite way. If we know the area under the curve, we can look up the z-score. For example, if the area under the curve is .3023, the z-score for this area is .85 (Figure 4-2).

Before you continue, work this problem. Find the area falling below a z-score of 1.69. First, look in Appendix G for the tabled value for this area. The correct answer is .4535. However, this represents the area between the mean and a z of 1.69. Add this area to the area below the mean. We already know this is half of the area under the curve, or .50. Thus the total area is .4535 + .50 = .9535 (Figure 4-3).

Other Examples of Finding the Area

How could we find the area **above** a z of 1.69? We know that the area between the mean and a z of 1.69 is .4535. We also know that the total area above the mean is .50. To determine the area **above** a z of 1.69, subtract .4535 from .50. The answer is .50 − .4535 = .0465 (Figure 4-4).

Next let's consider the area between two z-scores, one below the mean and one above the mean. For example, use a − 1.20 and a + 2.31 z-score. For a z of − 1.20, the area is .3849. For a z of 2.31, the area is .4896. Find the total area by adding the two areas, .3849 + .4896 = .8745 (Figure 4-5).

What if the area under the curve is between two z-scores on the same side of the mean? For example, use z-scores of − .56 and − 2.44. The corresponding areas are .2123 and .4927. The area between the two z-scores is determined by subtracting the smaller area from the larger one, or .4927 − .2123 = .2804 (Figure 4-6).

Finding the z-Score

When we already know the area, we can determine the z-score using Appendix G. For example, how do you find the z-scores that are the boundaries of the middle 95% of the distribution? We know that the middle 95% spans both sides of the mean. One half of this area is on each side of the mean. Thus, ½(95%) = 47.5% of the area lies on each side of the mean. Using Appendix G, find the

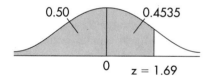

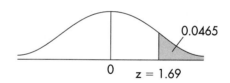

Figure 4-3   Area below z-score of 1.69.

Figure 4-4   Areas above z-score of 1.69.

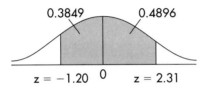

0.3849   0.4896

z = −1.20   0   z = 2.31

Figure 4-5   Area between z of − 1.20
and z of 2.31.

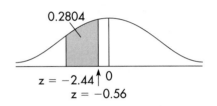

0.2804

z = −2.44   0
z = −0.56

Figure 4-6   Area between z of − 0.56
and z of − 2.44.

z-score for .475. The z is 1.96. Thus, the area is bounded by z-scores of − 1.96 and + 1.96 (Figure 4-7).

We also might want to find the z-score representing a percentile. Recall from Chapter 2 that a percentile is a point below which lies a specified percentage of the distribution. For example, what is the z-score corresponding to the 78th percentile? We know that 28% of this area lies above the mean (78 − 50 = 28). Using Appendix G, we find that an area of 28% is equal to a z-score of .77. (Note that the exact value of 28 is not shown in the table. Use the value closest to 28.) Thus the 78th percentile is equivalent to a z-score of .77 (Figure 4-8).

The procedure varies a little when the percentile is below the mean. For example, find the z-score for the 40th percentile. This represents 10 percentile points below the mean (50 − 40 = 10). Find the area of 10% in Appendix G. Using the number closest to 10% (.0987), we find z equals .25. Since we are working with a percentile below the mean, the corresponding z-score is negative (− .25) (Figure 4-9).

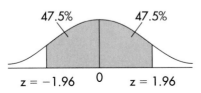

47.5%   47.5%

z = −1.96   0   z = 1.96

Figure 4-7   z-Scores around middle
95% of distribution.

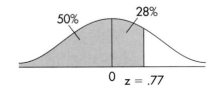

50%   28%

0   z = .77

Figure 4-8   z-Score corresponding to
78th percentile.

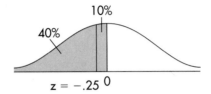

10%

40%

z = −.25   0

Figure 4-9   z-Score corresponding to
40th percentile.

EXAMPLES IN EXERCISE SCIENCE

A person with a serum cholesterol level higher than 200 mg/dL falls in a high-risk category for cardiac disease. What percentage of the population would not be in the high-risk category? If $\overline{X} = 180$ and $s = 20$, the z-score would be

$$z = \frac{X - \mu}{s} = \frac{200 - 180}{20} = \frac{20}{20} = 1.0$$

Referring to Appendix G, the area for a z-score of 1.0 is equal to .3413. Since we are working above the mean, we must add the area below the mean to get the percentile. Thus, .3413 + .5000 = .8413. Therefore, 84.13% of the population would not be at risk. By subtracting .8413 from 1.00, we learn that 15.87% of the population is at risk. Assume the VO_2 max (maximum oxygen consumption) mean for 30-year old women is 42 ml · kg/min and the standard deviation is 5 ml · kg/min. What is the percentage of the population falling between 30 ml and 50 ml? First we must calculate the z-scores for these values.

$$z = \frac{30 - 42}{5} = \frac{-12}{5} = -2.4$$

$$z = \frac{50 - 42}{5} = \frac{8}{5} = 1.6$$

Referring to Appendix G, the area associated with $z = -2.4$ is .4918 and with $z = 1.6$, .4452. Since we want to find the area **between** the two z-scores, we add the two areas (.4918 + .4452) and find that the total area is .937. Thus, 93.7% of the total population of 30-year-old women have VO_2 max values between 30 and 50 ml.

t-TEST

Suppose we administered a sit-ups test to two classes of sixth-grade boys at Jefferson Elementary School. In class A, the average number of sit-ups performed was 30; in class B, the average number was 31. Would you conclude there was a real difference in the average number of sit-ups the two classes could perform or was the difference due to expected sampling error? What if $\overline{X} = 30$ for a sixth-grade class and $\overline{X} = 36$ for an eighth-grade class? Would you judge these two averages to be meaningfully different? We can test the differences with a statistical procedure called the *t*-test. Sometimes small differences between means can be statistically significant and, in other cases, larger differences might not be significant. Statistical significance is influenced by sample size and the variability of group scores.

   In conducting a *t*-test, the difference between two means is compared. However, examining the mean difference is not enough. This difference must be considered in light of the variability of scores. The mean difference, then, is interpreted relative to the standard error of the difference between means. Calculate the standard error ($S_{d\bar{x}}$) using the standard deviations of the samples. Formula 4.1 is used:

$$S_{d\bar{x}} = \sqrt{\frac{N_1 s_1^2 + N_2 s_2^2}{N_1 + N_2 - 2} \left(\frac{1}{N_1} + \frac{1}{N_2} \right)}$$ Formula 4-1

where s_1 equals the standard deviation of the first sample
s_2 equals the standard deviation of the second sample
N_1 is the size of the first sample
N_2 is the size of the second sample

The *t*-test is a test of the hypothesis that $\mu_1 - \mu_2 = 0$. In other words, we make the assumption (termed the **null hypothesis**) that there is no difference between the two means and then ask the following question: Under the assumption of no difference between the means, what are the chances of obtaining an actual mean difference $\bar{X}_1 - \bar{X}_2$ or greater due to sampling error alone? If the chance of obtaining the actual mean difference is very small (e.g., 5 out of 100), then we would be reasonably safe in concluding that our assumption of no difference between the groups was incorrect (i.e., we reject the null hypothesis). There most likely is a statistically significant difference. The following assumptions must be met for the test to be valid:

1. Random samples
2. Independence of populations
3. Normally distributed populations
4. Equality of variances: $\sigma_1^2 = \sigma_2^2 = \sigma^2$

The *degrees of freedom (df)* are determined by adding the two sample sizes and subtracting 2 ($df = N_1 + N_2 - 2$).

The *t*-test for comparing two independent means is calculated using Formula 4-2.

$$t = \frac{\bar{X}_1 - \bar{X}_2}{S_{d\bar{x}}}$$ Formula 4-2

where $\bar{X}_1$ = mean of group 1
$\bar{X}_2$ = mean of group 2
$S_{d\bar{x}}$ = standard error of difference between means

Referring to Appendix C and assuming a *two-tailed* test and $\alpha = .05$, look up the *t*-value for $\alpha = .05/2 = .025$ and $df = N_1 + N_2 - 2$. If the obtained *t*-value (obtained from Formula 4-2) is equal to or greater than the *t*-value in the table (regardless of the sign of the *t*-value), reject the hypothesis that the two means are equal. Conclude with $\alpha \leq .05$ (Type I error) that the difference between the two sample means is statistically significant. If the obtained *t*-value does not fall within the critical region, do not reject H_0 and conclude there is no evidence that the samples differ significantly from each other.

Example

Now the *t*-test will be used in an example of two groups performing pull-ups. One group (Trained) participated in a weight-training program involving the upper body. The other group (Untrained) participated in aerobic activity but did not use weights. The following data were obtained:

Trained	Untrained
9	3
15	6
4	2
11	3
5	6
7	5
5	2
8	4
10	9
8	2

$$\Sigma X \quad 82 \qquad\qquad 42$$
$$\bar{X}_1 = 8.2 \quad \bar{X}_2 = 4.2$$

To conduct the *t*-test, we first calculate $S_{d\bar{x}}$:

$$S_{d\bar{x}} = \sqrt{\frac{(10)(3.124)^2 + 10(2.182)^2}{10 + 10 - 2}\left(\frac{1}{10} + \frac{1}{10}\right)}$$

$$= \sqrt{1.3166} = 1.1474$$

$$t = \frac{8.2 - 4.2}{1.1474} = 3.4861$$

The computed value of *t*, 3.4861, is greater than the critical value of *t*, 2.101. Thus, we conclude that the group trained on the weight-training machines was able to perform significantly more pull-ups than the untrained group.

ANALYSIS OF VARIANCE

The *t*-test is a useful statistical method for testing the significance of the difference between two groups. However, if we have tested three or more groups, it is no longer appropriate to use the *t*-test. Instead we can use a statistical technique known as the analysis of variance (ANOVA).

Let's assume a study has been conducted in a fitness center to examine three methods of managing stress. These methods include group interactions, independent self-study, and sessions with a personal trainer. A group is assigned to each of the three methods. Which method is most effective in reducing stress? To answer this question, compare the means of the three groups. ANOVA can be used to compare these means.

> **TOTAL VARIANCE**
> The variability between all scores from the three groups
>
> **VARIANCE BETWEEN GROUPS**
> The variability between the means of the three groups
>
> **VARIANCE WITHIN GROUPS**
> The variability of scores within groups, averaged across the three groups

Administer a stress reduction inventory to each person in each group. Use the score on this inventory to compare the groups. One of the advantages of using ANOVA is that this statistical technique uses variance to analyze the data. Recall that the variance is the square of the standard deviation, and the standard deviation represents the deviation of scores from the mean. Variance can be partitioned or broken up in many ways. In our study of stress management methods, we can break up the variance as shown in the box above.

The total variance consists of the variance between groups plus the variance within groups, or:

Total variance = variance between groups + variance within groups

To calculate these variances, we first determine their numerators. The numerators of the variances are known as the sums of squares.

Sums of Squares

To calculate the sums of squares, deviations of scores from means are determined. However, the mean used for this calculation must be appropriate for the sum of squares of interest. To find the **total sum of squares,** each score is subtracted from the mean of **all** scores. To find the **between-groups sum of squares,** the mean of **each** group is subtracted from the mean of all scores. To find the **within-groups sum of squares,** each score is subtracted from the mean of the group *in which it falls.*

Total Sum of Squares (SS_t)

The **total sum of squares** is calculated by subtracting each score (X) from the mean of *all* scores ($\overline{X}_t$), which we will call the total mean: $\Sigma(X - \overline{X}_t)^2$. If we use three groups with four people in each group, each of the 12 scores is subtracted from the total mean and the difference is squared and summed.

$$SS_t = \Sigma(X - \overline{X}_t)^2 = (X_1 - \overline{X}_t)^2 + (X_2 - \overline{X}_t)^2 + (X_3 - \overline{X}_t)^2 + \ldots + (X_{12} - \overline{X}_t)^2$$

Formula 4-3

Between-Groups Sum of Squares (SS_b)

The **between**-groups sum of squares is calculated by subtracting the mean for **each** group ($\overline{X}_g$) from the total mean ($\overline{X}_t$): $\Sigma N_g(\overline{X}_g - \overline{X}_t)^2$. The deviation of the group mean from the total mean is multiplied by the sample size for that group.

In other words, each group mean is weighted by N. Again using three groups with four persons in each group:

$$SS_b = \Sigma N_g(\bar{X}_g - \bar{X}_t)^2 = N_1(\bar{X}_1 - \bar{X}_t)^2 + N_2(\bar{X}_2 - \bar{X}_t)^2 + N_3(\bar{X}_3 - \bar{X}_t)^2 \quad \text{Formula 4-4}$$

Within-Groups Sum of Squares (SS_w)

The **within**-groups sum of squares is calculated by subtracting the score for each group member (X) from the group mean ($\bar{X}_g$): $\Sigma\Sigma(X - \bar{X}_g)^2$. Within each group, individual scores are subtracted from the group mean and these differences are squared and summed. When these calculations are completed for all groups the sums for all groups are added.

$$SS_w = \Sigma\Sigma(X - \bar{X}_g)^2 = (X_1 - \bar{X}_1)^2 + (X_2 - \bar{X}_1)^2 + (X_3 - \bar{X}_1)^2 + (X_4 - \bar{X}_1)^2 +$$
$$(X_1 - \bar{X}_2)^2 + (X_2 - \bar{X}_2)^2 + (X_3 - \bar{X}_2)^2 + (X_4 - \bar{X}_2)^2 +$$
$$(X_1 - \bar{X}_3)^2 + (X_2 - \bar{X}_3)^2 + (X_3 - \bar{X}_3)^2 + (X_4 - \bar{X}_3)^2$$

Formula 4-5

Group 1	Group 2	Group 3
5	2	9
3	5	7
4	2	8
4	3	8
16	12	32
$\bar{X}_1 = 4$	$\bar{X}_2 = 3$	$\bar{X}_3 = 8$

$$\bar{X}_t = \frac{\Sigma X_t}{N_t} = \frac{16 + 12 + 32}{12} = \frac{60}{12} = 5$$

SS_t:

$$\Sigma(X - \bar{X}_t)^2 = (5 - 5)^2 + (3 - 5)^2 + (4 - 5)^2 + (4 - 5)^2 + (2 - 5)^2 + (5 - 5)^2 +$$
$$(2 - 5)^2 + (3 - 5)^2 + (9 - 5)^2 + (7 - 5)^2 + (8 - 5)^2 + (8 - 5)^2 = \mathbf{66}$$

SS_b:

$$\Sigma N_g(\bar{X}_g - \bar{X}_t)^2 = 4(4 - 5)^2 + 4(3 - 5)^2 + 4(8 - 5)^2$$
$$= 4 + 16 + 36$$
$$= \mathbf{56}$$

SS_w:

$$\Sigma\Sigma(X - \bar{X}_g)^2 = (5 - 4)^2 + (3 - 4)^2 + (4 - 4)^2 + (4 - 4)^2$$
$$(2 - 3)^2 + (5 - 3)^2 + (2 - 3)^2 + (3 - 3)^2$$
$$(9 - 8)^2 + (7 - 8)^2 + (8 - 8)^2 + (8 - 8)^2$$
$$= 1 + 1 + 0 + 0 = 2$$
$$1 + 4 + 1 + 0 = 6$$
$$1 + 1 + 0 + 0 = 2$$
$$= 2 + 6 + 2 = \mathbf{10}$$

$SS_t = SS_b + SS_w$
$66 = 56 + 10$

Mean Squares

Once the sums of squares are calculated, the variances can be calculated by dividing the sums of squares for between groups and within groups by their respective degrees of freedom. The concept of **degrees of freedom** can be difficult for the novice to understand. Degrees of freedom are the number of observations that are "free to vary." For example, assume we are working with three observations or scores: 4, 4, 7. Once we calculate the mean to be 5, then only two of the three scores can vary. Once these two scores are determined, then the third score is fixed. Using the scores in our example, once we know the mean is 5 and two of the scores are 4 and 7, the third score must be 4. It cannot be other than 4.

Recall that we used $N - 1$ in the denominator of the variance formula for an unbiased estimate of the variance. In an ANOVA setting, the degrees of freedom for the variance of the total group is $N_t - 1$. Once the mean is known for the total number of observations and deviations of scores from the mean are determined, $N_t - 1$ scores are "free to vary."

The degrees of freedom for the between-groups variance equal $k - 1$, where k equals the number of groups. The degrees of freedom for the within-group variance is equal to $N_t - k$, equivalent to determining $N - 1$ for each group.

In our example using three groups, the following degrees of freedom are appropriate:

$$df_t = N_t - 1 = 12 - 1 = 11$$
$$df_b = k - 1 = 3 - 1 = 2$$
$$df_w = N_t - k = 12 - 3 = 9$$

Just as the sums of squares are additive, so are the degrees of freedom:

$$df_t = df_b + df_w$$
$$11 = 2 + 9$$

Formulas for Mean Squares

The mean squares are used to calculate the *F*-ratio (or *F*-test). To conduct this test, divide the mean square for between-groups variance by the mean square for within-groups variance. A mean square for the total variance is of no interest to us, because mean squares are not additive.

The formulas for calculating these mean squares estimates are

$$MS_b = \frac{SS_b}{k - 1} \hspace{4cm} \text{Formula 4-6}$$

$$MS_w = \frac{SS_w}{N_t - k} \hspace{4cm} \text{Formula 4-7}$$

In our example,

$$MS_b = \frac{56}{3-1} = 28.00$$

$$MS_w = \frac{10}{12-3} = 1.111$$

The mean squares between groups represents the three groups in our management example.

Calculation of F-Ratio

To conduct the F-test, divide the mean square for between-groups by the within-groups mean square. If the null hypothesis is true, we would expect this ratio to be approximately 1.0. That is, we expect the variance between groups to be similar to the variance within groups. If the between-groups variance is larger than the within-groups variance, the difference between groups might be statistically significant. To determine whether the difference is significant, conduct the F-test:

$$F = \frac{MS_b}{MS_w}$$

Formula 4-8

Using our example,

$$F = \frac{28.00}{1.111} = 25.2$$

To determine whether $F = 25.2$ is significant, turn to Appendix C. Remember that for MS_b, $df = 2$; for MS_w, $df = 9$. Using 2 and 9 df, the tabled value of F for $\alpha = .05$ is 4.26. Since 25.2 is greater than 4.26, the F-ratio is significant. It is important at this point to clarify a few terms. The *critical value* of F is the F-ratio found in the table. The *actual value* of F is the value we calculated. If the critical value of F exceeds the actual value, the mean differences are not significant (or we fail to reject the null hypothesis). If the actual value of F is greater than the critical value, the null hypothesis is rejected. The results of an ANOVA are typically presented in table form.

Table 4-1 gives you all of the information you need to interpret the results of the F-test used in the stress management study. We now know that the differences between the means were statistically significant. However, we do not know **which** mean differences resulted in statistical significance. Is group 1 (group interaction) different from group 2 (independent self-study)? Is group 2 (independent self-study) different from group 3 (personal trainer)?, and so on.

Post-hoc Testing for Differences Between Means

If we obtain a significant F-ratio when comparing the differences between three or more groups, a follow-up statistical test should be used to locate the group

Table 4-1   ANOVA Summary Table

Source of Variance	df	SS	MS	F
Between-groups	2	56	28.00	25.2*
Within-groups	9	10	1.111	
Total	11	66		

*$P < .05$

means that are significantly different. If the *F*-ratio is not significant, do not use a follow-up. If only two groups are tested and the *F*-ratio is significant, no follow-up test is needed. It is evident that the statistical significance is due to the differences between the two means. In our example, the *F*-ratio was significant and three groups were tested. Thus, we should proceed with a follow-up test. Several tests could be used for this purpose; however, in this text we will use only one test, **Tukey's** HSD (honestly significant difference) **test.**

The follow-up test is known as a **multiple comparison test** or a **post hoc test.** To conduct the HSD test, the differences between all combinations of three means is determined. The size of each difference is compared with the HSD value. The formula for computing the HSD value is

$$HSD = q(\alpha, k, N - k) \sqrt{\frac{MS_w}{n}}$$ Formula 4-8

where q = value obtained from the table in Appendix H, α = significance level (.05 in our case), k = number of groups (three in our case), N = total number of observations, MS_w = within mean square error, and n = the number of observations for each group.

In our example,

$$\overline{X}_1 - \overline{X}_2 = 4 - 3 = 1$$

$$\overline{X}_2 - \overline{X}_3 = 3 - 8 = -5$$

$$\overline{X}_1 - \overline{X}_3 = 4 - 8 = -4$$

We are only interested in the absolute value of the differences. Ignore the minus signs. We have already calculated the within−mean square (1.111) and we know n is 4. The only unknown is q. To find q, refer to Appendix H. Using $\alpha = 0.05$, k = 3, and N − k = 12 − 3 = 9, we find q to be 3.95. Now the HSD formula can be used:

$$HSD = 3.95 \sqrt{\frac{1.111}{4}} = 2.081$$

Note that both $\overline{X}_2 - \overline{X}_3$ and $\overline{X}_1 - \overline{X}_3$ are greater than 2.081. Thus, we conclude there is a significant difference between these groups but not between groups 1 and 2. Managing stress through sessions with a personal trainer is more effective than the use of group interactions or independent self-study. There is no difference in the effectiveness of using group interactions or independent self-study.

If the group sample sizes are not equal, the Tukey Method for Unequal N's is the appropriate test to use. The HSD test is only one of the methods your instructor may choose to conduct a multiple comparison test.

Assumptions Underlying the Use of ANOVA

Use the F-test only when the appropriate assumptions have been met. These assumptions are:

1. The samples are randomly drawn.
2. The samples are drawn from a population that is normally distributed.
3. The samples have equality of variances.

SUMMARY

The analysis of variance is a useful statistical test in that it permits the partitioning of the total variance. The variance can be broken up in many ways depending on the design of the study. In this chapter, a simple one-way ANOVA was described. Refer to statistics books for more complex ANOVA designs. One final point of interest is that the ANOVA is equivalent to the t-test when using only two groups. In fact, $F = t^2$ in this case.

Examples

1. Suppose a physical education teacher administers a basketball skill test to two groups of physical education students. One group received instruction for 2 months, and the other did not. Test the mean difference for significance at the .05 level using the following data:

	Trained	Untrained
	9	3
	15	6
	4	2
	11	3
	5	6
	7	5
	5	2
	8	4
	10	9
	8	2
ΣX	82	42
ΣX^2	770	224

Answer

$$\overline{X}_1 = 82/10 = 8.2 \qquad \overline{X}_2 = 42/10 = 4.2$$

$$S_1 = \sqrt{\frac{10(770) - (82)^2}{10(10)}} = 3.124 \qquad S_2 = \sqrt{\frac{10(224) - (42)^2}{10(10)}} = 2.182$$

$$t = \frac{8.2 - 4.2}{\sqrt{\dfrac{3.124^2}{10} + \dfrac{2.182^2}{10}}} = \frac{4}{\sqrt{1.4520}} = \frac{4}{1.2050} = 3.320$$

The critical value for $\alpha = 0.05$ and 18 df $(10 + 10 - 2)$ is ± 2.101 (from t-table). For a more precise estimate of s, use $N(N - 1)$ in the denominator.

Since the computed value is 3.320 and is greater than $+ 2.101$, we conclude that there is a significant difference between the trained and untrained group. The trained group displayed superior performance.

2. A physical education teacher gave a bowling test on the last day of class. There were 20 boys and 20 girls in the class. The teacher wanted to find out if boys differ from girls in their performance. The number of pins knocked down when the first ball was bowled for each of 10 frames was recorded. A trial performance standard of 8 was used to classify students as master or nonmaster.

Based on the following data that are the number of times that each student was classified as master (in 10 trials), test whether the boys' performance is different from the girls' performance.

	Boys		Girls	
	Subject Numbers			
	1-4	11-8	1-2	11-6
	Scores			
	2-3	12-4	2-4	12-5
	3-6	13-5	3-6	13-4
	4-7	14-9	4-5	14-5
	5-3	15-3	5-6	15-4
	6-6	16-1	6-3	16-5
	7-4	17-7	7-3	17-3
	8-6	18-6	8-3	18-5
	9-3	19-6	9-4	19-5
	10-10	20-8	10-4	20-7

Answer

$$\Sigma X_{boys} = 109 \qquad\qquad \Sigma X_{girls} = 89$$
$$\overline{X}_{boys} = 109/20 = 5.45 \qquad \overline{X}_{girls} = 89/20 = 4.45$$
$$\Sigma X^2_{boys} = 697 \qquad\qquad \Sigma X^2_{girls} = 427$$

$$S_{boys} = \sqrt{\frac{20(697) - (109)^2}{20(20)}} = 2.27 \qquad S_{girls} = \sqrt{\frac{20(427) - (89)^2}{20(20)}} = 1.24$$

$$t = \frac{5.45 - 4.45}{\sqrt{\frac{2.27^2}{20} + \frac{1.24^2}{20}}} = \frac{1}{\sqrt{0.3345}} = \frac{1}{0.5784} = 1.729$$

The critical value for $\alpha = 0.05$ and 38 df is ± 2.03.

Since the obtained t-value, 1.729, is not greater than 2.03, there is no evidence to suggest that the performance of girls is significantly different from the performance of boys in this particular class.

Problems

1. Two groups of students were trained on their vertical jump ability. After the sample period of training, the descriptive statistics of the vertical jump test for both groups are as follows:

$$\text{Group 1:} \quad \bar{X}_1 = 7.6 \quad S_1 = 3.90 \quad n_1 = 17$$
$$\text{Group 2:} \quad \bar{X}_2 = 4.8 \quad S_2 = 3.29 \quad n_2 = 15$$

Test the significance of the mean difference between two groups at the .05 level. (Assume the vertical jump scores are normally distributed.)

2. The data below represent the heart rate of male and female athletes measured from a maximum exercise test between the 60th and 70th second.

Male: $\bar{X}_1 = 27.52$ beats/10 sec. $S_1 = 2.87$ beats/10 sec. $n_1 = 32$
Female: $\bar{X}_2 = 28.78$ beats/10 sec. $S_2 = 2.42$ beats/10 sec. $n_2 = 28$

Test the significance of the difference between the mean heart rate of male and female athletes at the .05 level. (Assume the distribution of heart rate during maximum exercise is normal.)

3. Assume you have two samples from two normal populations. Your sample values are as follows:

$$\text{Sample 1:} \quad \bar{X}_1 = 36 \quad S_1 = 4.00 \quad n_1 = 15$$
$$\text{Sample 2:} \quad \bar{X}_2 = 30 \quad S_2 = 6.00 \quad n_2 = 16$$

4. Use a t-test to determine the significance of the difference between means. Use $\alpha = .05$. Ten hypertensive patients participated in a physical therapy program. The diastolic blood pressure values of the patients measured before and after the program are given below. Test the significance of the mean difference between the pre- and post-test blood pressure values.

Patient	Pre-test	Post-test
1	100	94
2	113	98
3	134	118
4	95	84
5	122	116
6	117	119

Patient	Pre-test	Post-test
7	92	85
8	120	96
9	114	104
10	138	120

Answers to Problems

1. $t = \dfrac{|7.6 - 4.8|}{\sqrt{\dfrac{3.90^2}{17} + \dfrac{3.29^2}{15}}} = \dfrac{2.8}{\sqrt{1.6163}} = \dfrac{2.8}{1.2713} = 2.2025$

   $df = 17 + 15 - 2 = 30 \qquad t_{.05(30)} = 2.042$

   $t = 2.2025 > t_{.05(30)} = 2.042$. Therefore, there is a significant difference between two means ($p < .05$).

2. $t = \dfrac{|28.78 - 27.52|}{\sqrt{\dfrac{2.87^2}{32} + \dfrac{2.42^2}{28}}} = \dfrac{1.26}{\sqrt{.4666}} = \dfrac{1.26}{.6831} = 1.8445$

   $df = 32 + 28 - 2 = 58 \qquad t_{.05(58)} = 2.000.$

   $t = 1.8445 < t_{.05(58)} = 2.000$. Therefore, there is no significant difference between two means ($p > .05$).

3. $t = \dfrac{|30 - 36|}{\sqrt{\dfrac{4^2}{15} + \dfrac{6^2}{16}}} = \dfrac{6}{\sqrt{3.3167}} = \dfrac{6}{1.8212} = 3.2945$

   $df = 15 + 16 - 2 = 29 \qquad t_{.05(29)} = 2.045$

   $t = 3.2945 > t_{.05(29)} = 2.045$. Therefore, there is a significant difference between two means ($p < .05$).

4.

Patient	Pre-test	Post-test	d	d²
1	100	94	6	36
2	113	98	15	225
3	134	118	16	256
4	95	84	11	121
5	122	116	6	36
6	117	119	−2	4
7	92	85	7	49
8	120	96	24	576
9	114	104	10	100
10	138	120	18	324

$\Sigma d = 111 \qquad \Sigma d^2 = 1727 \qquad \bar{d} = 11.1 \qquad S_d = 7.0349 \qquad N = 10$

$t = \dfrac{\bar{d}}{S_d/\sqrt{N}} = \dfrac{11.1}{7.0349/\sqrt{10}} = \dfrac{11.1}{2.3450} = 4.7335$

$df = 10 - 1 = 9 \qquad t_{.05(9)} = 2.262$

$t = 4.7335 > t_{.05(9)} = 2.262$. Therefore, there is a significant difference between the blood pressure values of pre-test and post-test ($p < .05$).

5. $t = \dfrac{|103.4 - 114.5|}{\sqrt{\dfrac{14.5757^2}{10} + \dfrac{13.3357^2}{10}}} = \dfrac{11.1}{\sqrt{39.0292}}$

$$= \frac{11.1}{6.2473}$$

$$= 1.7768$$

$df = 10 + 10 - 2 = 18 \qquad t_{.05(18)} = 2.101$

$t = 1.7768 < t_{.05(18)} = 2.101$. Therefore, there is no significant difference between two means ($p > .05$).

Microcomputers

Computers in Measurement and Evaluation

Watch for these words as you read the following chapter

Applications program	Integrated software
Bits	Interface card
Bus	Keyboard
Bytes	Kilobyte (K)
Central processing unit (CPU)	Laptop
	Laser printer
Compact disk–read-only memory (CD-ROM)	Megabyte
	Microcomputer
	Modem
Computer program	Mouse
Database	Network
Desktop	Operating system
Disk	Palmtop
Disk drive	Parallel communication
Disk operating system (DOS)	Random access memory (RAM)
Dot-matrix printer	
Electronic bulletin board	Read-only memory (ROM)
Electronic mail (e-mail)	Serial communication
Formatting	Shareware
Freeware	Software
Gigabyte	Spreadsheet
Graphical user interface (GUI)	User-friendly
	Virus
Hard disk	Windows
Hardware	Word processor
Ink-jet printer	

I do not fear computers. I fear the lack of them.

—Isaac Asimov

The invention and advancement of computer technology is perhaps the single most important technological development of the twentieth century. Computers affect almost every facet of our lives. Computers are indispensable for telecommunications, the stock market, banking, scientific research, meteorology, engineering, graphic design, commercial aviation, the space program, and in the manufacture and design of such common consumer goods as watches, automobiles, stereos, and kitchen appliances. Without computers large organizations such as hospitals and government agencies would have great difficulty keeping track of client records, while advanced technology such as laser technology and robotics would be impossible without computers. The impact of computer technology is being felt in exercise science and physical education. Exercise physiologists are becoming dependent on computers to monitor and record stress tests, compute body composition parameters from hydrostatic weighing and bioelectric impedance techniques, and to determine bone mineral density. Biomechanists rely on computers to estimate the kinetic and kinematic parameters of body movement, while sport psychologists are beginning to explore the use of sophisticated statistical techniques to model the factors that contribute to exercise adherence and motivation to participate in physical activity. Athletic trainers and exercise specialists share the need for efficient record keeping and the means of providing information to clients on their health and physical status—tasks well suited for computers. Physical educators are finding computer technology to be useful in determining grades; constructing, scoring, and analyzing tests; managing student records; and enhancing the teaching and learning environment through computer-assisted instruction. The use of computers in measurement and evaluation has unlimited potential. Computers can administer, score, analyze, and develop tests; summarize, analyze, and transform test scores; and compare scores with norms. Data banks consisting of tests, test questions, and test scores can be constructed on computers and made available to professionals interested in developing their own tests and test batteries.

Microcomputers are here to stay. They will be part of your life, both professionally and personally. Whether you plan to teach, do research, or become an athletic trainer, physical therapist, or exercise specialist, you will require a basic understanding of computers and their application in exercise science and physical education. This chapter is organized into two parts: *Computer Basics* and *Computing in Measurement and Evaluation*. *Computer Basics* is designed as a user-friendly introduction to computers and computing for readers with little or no experience with computers. Experienced computer users will find *Computer Basics* to be a useful review of computer concepts. *Computing in Measurement and Evaluation* focuses on the application of computers in measurement and evaluation with particular emphasis on using generic applications software such as word processing, spreadsheets, and databases to facilitate test construction, test administration, and evaluation.

COMPUTER BASICS

You do not need to know all the parts of a computer system in order to use a computer any more than you need to know all the parts of a car to drive one. However, your effectiveness in using a computer will be greatly enhanced if you know the basic components of a computer system and understand how a computer works. The objective of *Computer Basics* is to familiarize the novice user with the structure and function of a computer. After reading this section plus a little practice, you should feel comfortable with accessing the computer to enhance your measurement and evaluation practices.

Hardware and Software

A computer system consists of **hardware** and **software.** Hardware is the plastic, wire, metal, and silicon that make up the machinery. The computer circuitry, screen, keyboard, printer, and disk drives are classified as hardware. In contrast, software consists of three parts:

1. The instructions (also known as a **computer program**) which run the computer
2. The media on which the instructions are stored (e.g., a **disk**)
3. The manual that explains how to use the software

For example, if you purchase statistics software from a computer store you will receive one or more manuals describing how to use the software and one or more disks on which the program is stored.

Hardware Basics

A computer is simply an electronic machine that accepts instructions and data from a user, stores the information electronically in a place called "memory," processes the instructions and data from memory at incredibly fast speeds, and then provides the results in a usable form.

Basic Components of a Computer

Computers come in many sizes, shapes, and price ranges. However, all computers have four basic components (see Figure 5-1)—one or more input devices (e.g., keyboard, mouse) used to convey information to the computer, **memory** for storage of information conveyed to the computer, a **central processing unit (CPU)** for processing information stored in memory, and one or more output devices (e.g., printer, monitor) for viewing the results of the computer's processing.

INPUT DEVICES

Input devices transmit information to the computer. Input devices come in many forms and several types can be attached to a computer. The most common input devices are the keyboard, mouse, disk drive, and modem. The **keyboard** is similar to the keyboard on a typewriter. However, there are notable differences. For example, many computer keyboards have special function keys labeled F1 to F12 that can be programmed to perform user-defined tasks. In addition, on

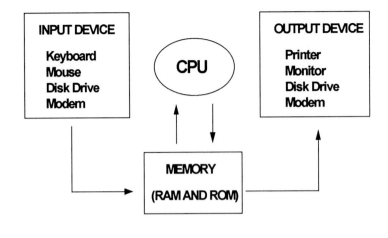

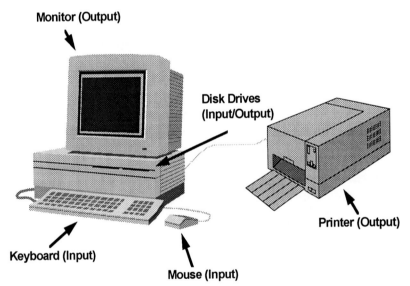

Figure 5-1   Basic hardware components of a computer system. *CPU* = central processing unit; *RAM* = random access memory; *ROM* = read-only memory.

computer keyboards there are several unique keys such as the "control" (CTRL) and "escape" (ESC) keys which are used in combination with other keys to perform special functions. A numerical keypad for the input of numerical data is another common feature of computer keyboards. It is important to note that computers are very particular and exact when interpreting keyboard input. For example, a computer distinguishes between the number *one* (1) and the lowercase letter *el* (l) and between zero (0) and uppercase letter O.

A **mouse** is a handheld input device which allows the user to direct the movement of a pointer on the computer screen. As you move the mouse across your desktop a ball housed in the mouse moves and sends signals to the computer to move the screen pointer in the same direction. Undue pressure on the mouse can result in damage to the ball; therefore, a foam "mouse pad" should be placed under the mouse. The mouse also contains one or more buttons for executing commands. The Apple Macintosh microcomputer popularized the use of the mouse; however, the mouse is becoming an integral input device on most modern computers. Other pointing devices that can be used on a computer are trackballs (essentially an inverted stationary mouse on which you move the ball with your fingers), joysticks, and light pens.

Disk drives are both input and output devices. Computer programs magnetically stored on disks can be transmitted to computer memory via the disk drive. Similarly, information stored in the computer's memory can be output to more permanent storage on a disk via the disk drive. Several types of disk drives, categorized by the type of disk accessed, can be attached or built into a computer. Floppy disk drives come in 3.5-inch or 5.25-inch varieties according to whether they can store and retrieve information from 3.5-inch or 5.25-inch disks. Microcomputers commonly have one or two floppy drives built in, although an external floppy drive can be attached to the machine. **Hard disks** consist of rigid metal platters sealed in an airtight case. Magnetic information is stored and retrieved from the platters. Hard disks are commonly built in to microcomputers, but external hard disks can be attached to the machine. The advantages of hard disks over floppy disks are greater storage capacity and speed of information storage and retrieval.

A **modem** (i.e., **mod**ulate-**dem**odulate) is a device that permits computers to communicate across telephone lines. In Figure 5-2 a modem attached to a computer at location *A* translates the electronic digital signal from the computer to the analog tonal signal of a telephone (modulation). The analog signal is transmitted across the telephone line to the receiving modem at location *B* which translates the analog signal back to an electronic digital signal (demodulation) for the receiving computer. Because modems transmit and receive information,

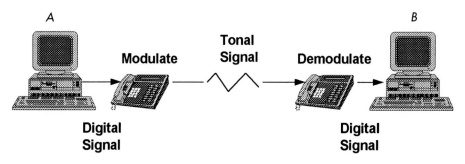

Figure 5-2   Communicating across telephone lines with a modem.

they are both input and output devices. Modems can be classified as direct-connect or acoustic coupler modems. Acoustic coupler modems consist of two cups in which the telephone's handset fits. These types of modems are becoming less popular due to their slower transmission speeds, high error rates, and manual mode of operation. In contrast, direct-connect modems have cables which attach directly to the telephone line and to the computer, allowing faster transmission rates and lower error rates than acoustic modems. Direct-connect modems come in stand-alone versions or on an interface card which can be plugged into an expansion slot on the computer's circuit board. Sophisticated communications software (e.g., PROCOMM PLUS, PC-Talk) can be purchased for direct-connect modems to take advantage of such features as automatic dialing and automatic redial from your computer to the receiving computer.

It is not uncommon for microcomputers to include the keyboard, mouse, floppy disk drives, hard disk drive, and modem as standard equipment. Other input devices that can be attached to your computer are optical disk drives such as **compact disk–read-only memory (CD-ROM) drives** and write-once read-many (WORM) drives. CD-ROM drives read information from disks similar to the CDs used in home entertainment centers. Because CD-ROM disks can store a large amount of information (typically more than the amount of information that can be stored on thousands of floppy disks), they are used to store reference works such as encyclopedias, almanacs, and dictionaries and to store bibliographic databases commonly used in libraries. Search-and-retrieve software can be purchased to quickly and efficiently look for required information. CD-ROM disks are purchased prerecorded; you cannot save your own data to them. WORM disks overcome this disadvantage, allowing users to save their own information to the disk. Unfortunately, data cannot be erased once written to the disk (hence "write-once read-many") and the disk will eventually fill up.

MEMORY

Computer memory can be classified as *primary memory* and *secondary memory*. Primary memory is memory that is contained on the computer's circuit board in the form of integrated circuits or chips (Figure 5-3). Primary memory can be further classified as **random access memory (RAM)** and **read-only memory (ROM).** ROM chips contain information preprogrammed by the computer manufacturer. The information is "burned" permanently onto the chip and cannot be changed by the user. Therefore ROM is viewed as static, unchanging, or nonvolatile memory. ROM chips contain instructions that are necessary to operate the computer, although some ROM chips contain complete software programs such as word-processing and spreadsheet applications. When the computer is turned on, electricity flows through the ROM chips and activates the instructions. When the computer is turned off the instructions are unchanged. Hence "read-only memory."

RAM chips provide memory space for storage of data and programs transmitted by the user. When you use a program you must first load it into RAM. Similarly when you input data from the keyboard it is stored in RAM.

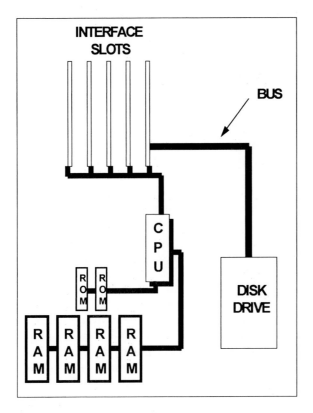

Figure 5-3   Diagram of a computer circuit board.

You can read information from RAM and overwrite information in RAM; thus data storage in RAM is temporary or volatile. In fact, when you turn the computer off, RAM is erased and any data or programs you have stored in RAM are lost. Thus computers must have a means for saving information in RAM to a more permanent location. This more permanent storage location is known as secondary (external or auxiliary) memory. Secondary memory is usually in the form of devices attached externally or internally to the machine. Floppy disks and hard disks are two common secondary memory devices. Electronic signals from RAM are translated via the disk drives to a magnetic format on the disks. Information on the disks can then be reloaded at your convenience from the disks back into RAM via the disk drives. Other secondary storage devices are magnetic tape, CD-ROM, and WORM drives.

CENTRAL PROCESSING UNIT (CPU)

The CPU or microprocessor is the heart or brain of the computer. It controls and coordinates the flow of information through the computer and is the location for mathematical calculations and logical functions. Physically the CPU is hundreds of thousands of transistors packed onto a single wafer-thin silicon microchip about the size of a postage stamp. The CPU is encased in plastic and can be found plugged into the computer's main circuit board (see Figure 5-3). Information stored in memory is processed through the CPU at incredibly fast speed. Because the power of a CPU determines the power of a computer system, it is important to consider the CPU when purchasing a computer. CPU power is influenced by two factors: the amount of information that can be cycled through the CPU and the speed at which information can be cycled. CPU speed or clock speed is measured in megahertz (MHz)—millions of cycles per second. Early microcomputers ran at speeds of around 4.77 MHz. Today it is common for microcomputers to run at 33 to 60 MHz. The amount of information that can be processed in a single cycle is given as the number of bits (for an explanation of the term *bit*, see Representing Information in Memory on p. 114), usually as multiples of 8 bits. Early CPUs were 8-bit processors, while today's microcomputers can process 32 bits at a time—a fourfold increase! CPUs that process 32 bits at clock speeds exceeding 50 MHz can thus process more information at faster speeds than their 8-bit, 4.77-MHz predecessors.

There are many brands of CPUs in today's computer market. Two popular microcomputer CPUs are manufactured by Intel and Motorola. The Intel CPU is found in IBM and IBM-compatible computers while the Motorola chip is used in the Apple Macintosh series. Advances in CPU technology have resulted in microprocessors that can process larger pieces of information at faster speeds. To distinguish advanced microprocessors from their less powerful predecessors, CPU manufacturers have employed a numerical labeling system. For example in 1978 Intel labeled its first commercially available microprocessor the 8086. The 8086 was used by IBM in its first personal computer. Since that time Intel has developed the 8088, 80286, 80386, 80486, and Pentium (80586) (Figure 5-4) microprocessors, each with a significant increase in the amount and speed of processing (e.g., the 80386 CPU is a 32-bit processor that can process about four times the amount of information four times faster than the 8-bit 8086 CPU). Such increases in CPU power are necessary to run the complex software available today.

OUTPUT DEVICES
Output devices are used to display data and results from a computer. Common output devices are the computer monitor, printer, and disk drives (remember that disk drives are both input and output devices). The computer's monitor, or display screen, is the primary output device. Display screens come in several varieties: cathode ray tubes (CRTs) function similarly to television screens and are found on most desktop computers; liquid crystal displays (LCDs), light-emitting diodes (LEDs), and gas plasma displays are found on laptop and palm-top computers because they are less bulky and use less power than CRTs. CRTs, however, offer better resolution and color output.

Because you spend most of your time on a computer looking at the monitor it is important to consider the monitor's resolution, screen color, and physical

Figure 5-4   Intel's highest performance Pentium processor.

size. Resolution refers to the density of the dots which make up the computer screen (Figure 5-5). Each dot is referred to as a pixel. The more pixels contained on a screen the greater the resolution and hence the sharper and clearer the image presented on the screen. High-resolution monitors have a pixel array of 1,074 rows by 768 columns (i.e., 768,432 pixels), in contrast to the more common array of 640 rows by 350 pixels (i.e., 224,000 pixels) found on most computer systems. As for color, monitors come in two varieties: color displays or

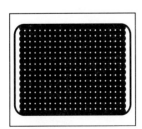
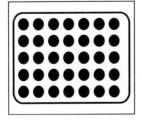

High Resolution   Low Resolution

Figure 5-5   Monitor resolution depends on density of pixels.

monochrome displays. Monochrome displays show one color (usually green or amber) on a black background, while color graphics monitors can display many colors depending on the type of monitor purchased. Color graphics monitors require the installation of a graphics interface card onto the computer's main circuit board. Three major types of graphics cards are available: color graphics adapters (CGA), which show four colors with 320-by-200 resolution; enhanced color adapters (EGA), which show up to 16 colors in 640-by-480 resolution; and video graphics adapters (VGA), which show up to 16 colors with 640-by-480 resolution. More recently, the development of super VGA (SVGA) cards has greatly enhanced the resolution and color capability of computer monitors. Monitor display screens come in various sizes ranging from a few inches on palmtops to the large projection screens which permit many users to view the output. However, common screen sizes for desktop computers range from 13- to 15-inch diagonal screens. The size of screen you purchase depends on how close you will be sitting to the screen and the software you will be using. For close-up work a smaller screen will be easier on your eyes. If you plan to use your computer for generating drawings, charts, and other graphics, a larger screen will be advantageous.

Printers provide output printed on paper. Today, three technologies have

Figure 5-6   The Hewlett-Packard LaserJet 4MP printer for the Macintosh offers 600-dots-per-inch printing.

captured the lion's share of the printer market—laser printers, dot-matrix printers, and ink-jet printers. Laser printers offer the best resolution and speed of printing of the three, but are more expensive (starting at around $800). **Laser printers** (Figure 5-6) operate much like a photocopy machine. The typed image is etched by laser onto a treated metal drum. A plastic toner that is attracted to the laser-exposed areas of the drum is applied to the drum. The drum rolls over paper which is heated to seal the toner to the paper. **Dot-matrix printers** work on the principle that any typed character can be represented by an array of dots. Imagine a playing card (e.g., the ace of spades) with three rows of three dots (i.e., a 3 × 3 array) cut into the card. Also imagine that behind each hole is a spring-loaded pin. In front of the card is a typewriter ribbon. If we were to place a piece of paper on top of the typewriter ribbon, and then push the middle column of pins through the holes to strike the ribbon onto the paper we could form the lowercase letter *l* on the paper. Dot-matrix printers use a similar technology. The number of dots included on the printhead determines the resolution (the greater number of dots, the greater the resolution). Dot-matrix printers are relatively inexpensive and can be used for both text and graphics output; however, they are comparably noisy, slower, and do not have the print quality of laser printers. **Ink-jet printers** (Figure 5-7) also use an array of dots to form the printed image; however, instead of firing pins against a ribbon, ink is sprayed through nozzles, directly onto the paper.

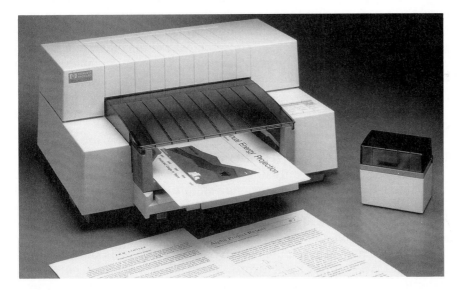

Figure 5-7   The DeskJet 500C printer from Hewlett-Packard uses ink-jet technology to produce both black and white and color output for personal computers.

BUS

The communications links between the components of a computer system are given the term **bus.** There is a bus linking each component of a system as illustrated by the arrowed lines in Figure 5-1. For example, there must be a bus to link each input and output device to the main circuit board. A bus typically consists of (a) an **interface card,** which provides the communication between the component and the computer circuit board, and (b) a wire connecting the device to the interface card. Many computers can be purchased with interface cards built in. For example Macintosh computers have printer, mouse, and keyboard interfaces built in. You simply plug the mouse, printer, and keyboard cables into the appropriate plugs in back of the computer. Other computers require that you purchase interface cards and plug them into slots provided on the main circuit board (see Figure 5-3). For example, if you wanted to buy a graphics monitor you would have to buy an EGA or VGA interface card, plug it into the main circuit board, and plug your monitor directly into the card. Similarly, if you added an external hard drive to your system you would first install the appropriate hard disk controller card onto the main circuit board and then plug the external drive into the card. When purchasing a computer determine how many empty slots the computer has available. If there are no slots, then you will not be able to add extra components to your computer. For example, the Macintosh SE/30 has only a single slot available, whereas the Macintosh II series offers more versatility with several empty slots.

Lastly, the communication between the computer and its various input and output devices can be classified as **serial** or **parallel communication.** Devices that communicate serially send or receive information in a stream of information one bit at a time. A good analogy for serial communication is a single-lane highway on which vehicles must follow one behind the other. In contrast, devices which use parallel communication receive information much like a multilane freeway (Figure 5-8).

How a Computer Works

REPRESENTING INFORMATION IN MEMORY

At the most basic level the only thing a computer recognizes is if electricity is flowing through a circuit or not. Imagine a simple light switch that can be either on or off (Figure 5-9). To symbolize this two-state system we can label on *1* and off *0*. Next, imagine eight of these switches placed beside one another. If the first three switches are on and the rest are off we can symbolize this sequence by 11100000. In computer terminology each of these switches is known as a **bit,** or binary digit, the smallest amount of information a computer can recognize. Eight of these bits (i.e., eight circuits) grouped together are known as a **byte.** A computer uses a byte to represent a single typed character. For example if you type the lowercase letter *a* it is stored in RAM as a series of eight circuits or bits (i.e., 1 byte) with the sequence 01100001, while the number *1* is represented as eight circuits with the sequence 00110001. How many cir-

Serial Communication

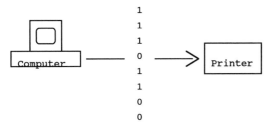

Parallel Communication

Figure 5-8   Parallel and serial communication between a computer and a printer.

cuits (i.e., bits) and bytes would it take to store the word "fitness" in RAM? If you answered 56 circuits (i.e., 7 characters × 8 bits) and seven bytes (i.e., 7 characters) you're correct! If the computer power is switched off, RAM is erased because all the circuits are set to zero. Each letter of the alphabet, number, and special symbol (e.g., !@#) on the keyboard has its own unique 8-bit code. To

= 1 circuit = 1 binary digit (bit)

= on = 1

= off = 0

= 8 circuits = 1 byte = 1 typed character

For example, the letter "t" is 1 byte stored in memory as

0 1 1 1 0 1 0 0

1024 bytes = 1 kilobyte (k)
1 million bytes = 1 megabyte (MB)
1 billion bytes = 1 gigabyte (GB)

Figure 5-9   Storing information in computer memory.

standardize the codes so that computers can communicate using the same binary code for each character, the American Standard Code for Information Interchange (ASCII) was developed. For example the ASCII representation for 7 is 01010111 and the representation of the uppercase letter *E* is 10100101. Computers that recognize ASCII can thus readily exchange information.

By now you can see that a computer needs thousands of circuits to store the information we input via the keyboard, mouse, disk drives, or modem. The capacity of a computer to store information in RAM is expressed in **kilobytes (K).** One K is 1,024 bytes or the capacity to store 1,024 typed characters. Thus a RAM of size 640K has the capacity to store $640 \times 1024 = 655,360$ bytes or typed characters (which translates to $8 \times 655,360 = 5,242,880$ circuits!). Other measures of memory capacity are the **megabyte (MB)** which represents approximately 1 million bytes and the **gigabyte (GB)** which is approximately 1 billion bytes. There are two significant reasons for knowing the memory capacity of your computer. First, the size of RAM limits the size of the computer programs and the amount of data you can input. For example, if you have a computer with 256K of RAM and you desire to run a complex computer program that requires 400K of RAM, the amount of RAM in your computer must be increased before the program can be loaded. Moreover, if there is just enough RAM to load a program such as a word processor, little space will remain to store the text created using the program. To effectively run the large programs found in today's market, RAM exceeding 4MB is recommended. Second, the memory capacity of disk drives is represented in values of K, MB, or GB. For example hard disks have a memory capacity ranging from 10MB up to several GB, although it is most common to find hard disk sizes of 60MB to 250MB on most microcomputers. Floppy disks commonly come in sizes ranging from 320K to almost 3MB.

PROCESSING INFORMATION IN THE CPU

The CPU is a very complex microminiaturized combination of transistors and silicon, yet conceptually its function is quite simple. We first input a computer program into RAM via the keyboard or most commonly by loading it from a disk drive. The program resides in RAM in the form of bits and bytes as described in the preceding section. When we command the computer to run the program the CPU takes control and executes the program one line at a time using two cycles for each line—an instruction cycle and an execution cycle. During the instruction cycle the CPU accesses the first line of the program and decodes the instruction so that the proper action will be taken. During the execution cycle the CPU executes the desired task (e.g., data is collected from the appropriate location or an arithmetic operation is completed). The cycling process of the CPU is very orderly, logical, and extremely fast. Thousands of lines of programming can be executed each second.

Types of Computers

Computers can be categorized according to size, memory capacity, processing speed, and cost. At the top of the list are mainframe computers. These computers derive their name from the metal frames which support the hardware. Commonly found in large businesses and universities, mainframes are expensive and powerful large-scale computers requiring a full-time professional staff for their operation. Supercomputers (e.g., the Cray computer), used primarily for scientific research, are the most powerful of the mainframe computers. A step down from the mainframes are the minicomputers (e.g., Sun computers) which derive their name from the fact that they are much smaller than the mainframes. Minicomputers offer powerful processing coupled with moderate memory storage and desktop size at a price affordable by medium-size businesses and research laboratories. **Microcomputers,** which derive their name from the microprocessor used as a CPU, were introduced in the mid-1970s and are currently the most popular type of computer owing to the combination of reasonable processing speed, moderate memory size, small physical size, and affordable price. Microcomputers are further categorized as desktop, laptop, and palmtop computers. **Desktop computers** (e.g., IBM PS/2 series and the Macintosh II series) typically consist of a CRT, keyboard, floppy disk drive, built-in hard disk, and optional printer which fit comfortably on a desk (Figure 5-10). **Laptop** (e.g., Macintosh PowerBook series and Hewlett-Packard Omnibook 300) (Figure 5-11) and **palmtop** (Figure 5-12) computers are designed for users wanting portability. Employing a built-in keyboard and trackball, disk drives, and flip-up LCD or gas plasma monitor, laptop computers provide powerful portable computing that can fit into a briefcase. Also available are lighter and smaller laptop computers called notebooks (e.g., Macintosh PowerBook series). Palmtop computers are a recent addition to the computer market. Not much bigger than a hand-calculator, palmtops typically come with small RAM, reduced processing speed, and very small keyboards and display screens. Because current palmtops are not as powerful as other microcomputers and because they use unique technology for inputting data, their success in the computer market is a question mark.

Although microcomputers are manufactured under many different company names, Apple Macintosh and IBM and IBM-compatible computers have captured most of the consumer market. IBM introduced the IBM PC (personal computer) in 1981. The PC employed an Intel CPU and used an operating system called PC-DOS (PC–disk operating system) developed by Microsoft Corporation. IBM subsequently introduced in 1984 the IBM AT (advanced technology) which employed the Intel 80286 CPU, and the PS/2 series in 1987. The PS/2 series incorporated the Intel 80386 processor and introduced a multitasking bus known as Micro Channel Architecture (MCA). IBM-compatible computers employ the Intel CPU and thus are able to run the same software as an IBM computer. Such computers are manufactured by many different companies (e.g., Zenith, Packard Bell, AST, Compaq, Dell, Hewlett-Packard).

The Apple Macintosh computer was introduced in 1984 as the "people's computer." Designed with a graphics interface that permitted the user to perform tasks by pointing to graphics images (i.e., icons) on the screen with a mouse, the Macintosh has revolutionized how people communicate with computers. The Macintosh utilizes a Motorola CPU and an operating system known

Figure 5-10   The HP Vectra 486/66XM personal computer from Hewlett-Packard offers enhanced graphics performance, networking capabilities, and the first desktop implementations of infrared communications technology.

as the System. Like the IBM computer, the Macintosh has evolved into several models. Currently Apple offers lower-end (i.e., lower-priced and less power) Macintosh computers such as the Classic and LC, higher-end computers such as the Quadra, Proforma, and Mac II series, and a popular laptop known as the PowerBook.

Until recently, there was little compatibility between IBM software and Macintosh software. Software developers programmed both IBM and Macintosh versions of their applications (e.g., Microsoft offers both IBM and Macintosh versions of its Works, Word, and Excel programs) and users could not easily exchange information between the two computer brands. One solution for bridging the IBM-Macintosh compatibility gap are programs such as SoftPC (Insignia Solutions, Mountain View, Calif.) which permit users to run IBM software on Macintosh computers. However, IBM and Apple Computer have contracted with Motorola to develop a new CPU, the PowerPC, to compete with

Figure 5-11   The Hewlett-Packard Omnibook 300 superportable personal computer weighs just 2.9 lb and fits easily into a briefcase.

Intel's Pentium processor. New computer models using the PowerPC processor are capable of running both IBM and Macintosh software.

Purchasing a Microcomputer

Purchasing a microcomputer can be a daunting task for novices and experts alike. Perhaps the best advice is do your homework before making a purchase! Kubiszyn and Borich (1987) outline four steps in selecting a microcomputer:

1. Identify objectives.
2. Identify software.
3. Identify special features.
4. Make comparisons.

When identifying your objectives consider the present and future uses for the computer. Will word processing be your primary use, or do you plan to perform complex statistical analyses on large data sets which require a powerful CPU and large memory? Once your objectives have been identified you should next

Figure 5-12   The Hewlett-Packard 100LX palmtop personal computer features built-in electronic mail and personal computer software compatibility.

consider the specific software you will require. Remember that each brand of software has its unique hardware requirements. For example, the popular spreadsheet Microsoft Excel for the IBM and IBM-compatibles needs a computer with at least an 80386 CPU, 2MB of memory, and an EGA monitor. To further complicate the issue, some software requires the purchase of additional software. Excel requires that your computer run the Microsoft DOS (MS-DOS) operating system and the Microsoft Windows graphics interface, each purchased separately. Special hardware features that you should consider are memory, keyboard, monitor, graphics card (e.g., EGA or VGA), disk drives (5.25-inch or 3.5-inch drives, hard disk size), power and speed of the CPU, and the additional hardware you want to add such as printer, modem, and CD-ROM drive. In addition, you should also consider the length and services offered in the warranty that accompanies the hardware. The last step before purchase is the comparison step. A good place to start is popular computer magazines such as *Personal Computing, MacWorld,* and *PC Magazine.* Such sources offer expert reviews and comparisons of selected brands of desktop, laptop, and palmtop computers and other hardware. Once you have narrowed your choices to meet your objectives and your pocketbook, a test drive of the final choices is highly recommended. Most computer stores have on display for your use the computers they sell. In addition, most of the best-selling software is available for you to try out. Don't be afraid to spend a half-hour or more getting a feel for the keyboard, the computer's speed, and the ease of using the machine.

Computer Networking

Two or more computers communicating with one another and sharing resources is known as a computer **network.** Computers can communicate across large geographical areas (wide area network, or WAN) using telephone lines, telecommunications satellites, or microwave technology. They can also connect directly to one another via cable (e.g., fiberoptic cable) or infrared light, in one office, building, or group of buildings (local area network, or LAN). Networks allow computers to share software resources such as applications programs and data files and hardware resources such as printers and hard drives. For example, a physical education teacher connected to a LAN could have access to student records stored in the school's administrative computer, or several computers connected to a network could share a single laser printer. Applications programs such as word processors and spreadsheets stored on the network are accessible to computers linked to the network and files can be transferred among network users. Thus fitness data collected at several sites can be electronically transmitted across a network to a central location for analysis and interpretation, or a teacher can develop an examination on the word processor, send it to a colleague for review, and then transmit the file to clerical staff for final editing and printing. Networks in the workplace are accessible from home computers via a modem, therefore providing working parents with the option of working at home.

The connectivity allowed by networking provides users with several means of electronic communication. **Electronic mail (e-mail)** permits network users to send messages to one another. Messages are transmitted along the network and stored in the recipient's electronic mailbox until the recipient accesses the network and reads his or her mail. E-mail can be accessed nationally and internationally over worldwide networks such as Internet. E-mail is relatively inexpensive, faster than the postal service, reduces the amount of paper used in memos and letters, and all but eliminates the aggravation of playing "telephone tag." Two other popular forms of electronic communication are facsimilie (fax) technology and bulletin boards. Computerized fax technology permits users to transmit and receive computerized text and graphics over telephone lines. **Electronic bulletin boards** are computerized public access message systems analogous to the message boards seen in laundromats, offices, and elsewhere. A common method of accessing an electronic bulletin board is through a modem. The user simply dials the telephone number of the bulletin board and connects to the bulletin board's modem. Bulletin boards are useful sources for inexpensive software that can be copied from the bulletin board computer to a disk in your computer.

Software Basics

Without instructions to tell it what to do, a computer is simply a mass of plastic, silicon, and metal with electricity humming through it. Every function of a computer, from reading a disk in a disk drive to performing complex mathematical operations, requires instructions. The instructions we give to the computer (i.e., a computer program), the media on which the instructions are stored (e.g., a floppy disk), and the manuals that describe how the instructions work are known as computer software. In this section we describe types of computer programs, trends in software development, and how programs are stored on disks.

Types of Computer Programs

Computer programs can be categorized as private programs, applications programs, or operating systems. Private programs are written in one of many available computer programming languages (e.g., Fortran, BASIC, C + +, APL) by an individual for private use. For example, a technician in an exercise physiology laboratory writes a program to sample data from a Beckman gas analyzer, or a physical education teacher writes a program to compute percent body fat from input of skinfold measures. Private programs are often accessible through electronic bulletin boards or by word of mouth.

Many people have no desire to learn a computer language and develop their own programs. Fortunately, computer programmers have developed sophisticated programs called **applications programs** that can be purchased to solve a wide variety of problems. Applications programs typically consist of one or more disks on which the program is stored and one or more manuals that describe how to use the program. Although there is an almost unlimited choice of application software in today's market, five general categories of applications software can be described:

1. **Word processors** (e.g., Microsoft Word, WordPerfect) for composing written documents such as letters, memos, etc.
2. **Spreadsheets** (e.g., Microsoft Excel, Borland's Quattro Pro) for analyzing numerical data
3. **Databases** (e.g., Borland's Paradox, Microsoft Access) for organizing, manipulating, and retrieving information
4. Graphics programs (e.g., MacDraw, Cricket Draw, Microsoft PowerPoint) for designing and drawing
5. Communications programs (e.g., Procomm Plus) for allowing computers to communicate over phone lines.

An **operating system** is an organized collection of programs that is used to control the overall operation of the computer. It provides an interface between the hardware and applications programs. Operating system programs control such tasks as saving information from RAM to a disk, loading programs from disk into RAM, copying files from one disk to another, routing print requests to the printer, and preparing disks for use with the computer.

Each time a computer is powered on, its operating system must be loaded into RAM (known as "booting" the operating system). Without first loading the operating system, application programs cannot be accessed. The operating system can be loaded from a floppy disk drive or from a hard drive. Booting from the hard drive is automatic every time the computer is powered on.

The operating system for microcomputers is called a **disk operating system (DOS)** because many of the operating system programs manage disk drive functions. Typically, the operating system is packaged with a new computer; however, alternative operating systems can be purchased. For example, IBM-compatible computers have traditionally employed the popular MS-DOS. New competitors to MS-DOS are OS/2 and Dr.DOS (Digital Research). The operating system for Macintosh computers goes by the name SYSTEM. To maintain a competitive edge, operating systems are continually upgraded. Traditionally, new versions of operating systems are identified by a version number, with higher numbers reflecting most recent versions (e.g., MS-DOS v. 6 is a more recent version than v.5, and SYSTEM 7.5 is an enhanced version of SYSTEM 6).

Software Trends

Software is increasing in complexity, size, speed, and usefulness. Several trends in software development are integrated software, user-friendly software, the use of graphical-user interface (GUI), freeware and shareware, and the proliferation of computer viruses.

User-friendly software is software that is easy to use and self-instructing. If a program can be used simply by loading it into RAM and following menus and pictures on the screen, then it would be considered to be user-friendly. User-friendliness is enhanced by the inclusion of a **graphical-user interface** or **GUI** (pronounced "gooey"). Pioneered by Macintosh computers, a GUI is characterized by a device such as a mouse which is used to point at pictures (i.e., icons) on the screen resulting in visual communication between the user and the computer. A popular GUI for IBM-compatible computers is Microsoft **Windows.** Windows is loaded into RAM after the operating system is loaded, providing pictorial communication between the user and the computer as shown in Figure 5-13.

Integrated software (e.g. Microsoft Works, Claris Works, Lotus 1-2-3) combines two or more applications into a single computer program. For example, Microsoft Works includes word-processing, database, spreadsheet, and communications modules in one single package. The advantages of integrated software are a shared set of commands and an identical file structure so that data from one application can be integrated easily into another (e.g., a budget developed with a spreadsheet can be easily integrated into a word-processed report concerning the budget). On the negative side, integrated software requires a large RAM and each application is usually not as powerful as a stand-alone application (e.g., the Microsoft Works word processor is not as powerful as the stand-alone word processor Microsoft Word).

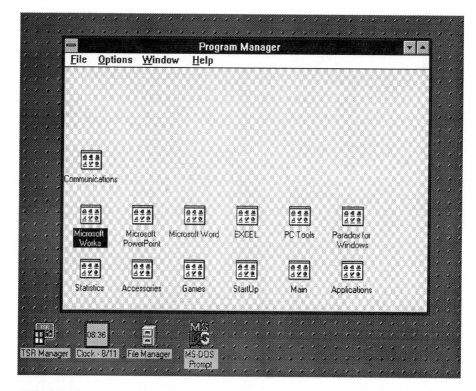

Figure 5-13 A typical Microsoft Windows screen display.

Software can range in price from several dollars to several thousands of dollars. However, accessing freeware and shareware can reduce the cost. **Freeware** are privately developed programs made available free of charge. Commonly, freeware is found on electronic bulletin boards and can be copied onto your hard disk. Freeware carries no guarantee of accuracy and no technical support. **Shareware** is also found on electronic bulletin boards. With shareware, however, you are expected to donate a small fee to the software developer if you decide to use the program. Shareware is often upgraded and may provide technical support. A popular applications program known as ProComm began as shareware, becoming so popular that it is now commercially marketed as one of the leading communications packages.

An excellent source of freeware and shareware for physical education and exercise science is SOFTSHARE. Based at California State University at Fresno, SOFTSHARE provides a repository of inexpensive software for IBM-compatible, Macintosh, and Apple IIe computers. SOFTSHARE holdings range from activity aids, exercise physiology, fitness testing, and grading programs to statistics, test construction, and writing aids.

A computer **virus** is a computer program designed by its developer to be annoying at best and destructive at worst. As the name implies, computer viruses invade or "infect" a computer system by attaching to normal programs. The virus quickly spreads to other software and to other computers as software is copied from computer to computer or shared over computer networks. Once inside the computer, viruses often lie dormant until a predetermined time on the computer's internal clock. Presently, hundreds of viruses torment the computer world causing symptoms ranging from annoying messages on the screen to sudden hardware crashes and destruction of data on a hard drive. For example, in 1992 the notorious Michelangelo virus infected thousands of computers worldwide. Designed to detonate on March 6, the virus virtually wiped out information stored on the infected computer's hard drive.

Prevention of virus infection is no easy task. However the following tips can reduce the chances of infection or serious damage from infection:

- Know the source of the software you use. Pirated software or software copied from computer bulletin boards or student computer laboratories are potential sources of computer viruses.
- Use a virus detection program regularly. The proliferation of computer viruses has spawned a new software industry—antivirus software. Antivirus software scans computer memory, disk drives, and hard drives for viruses and disinfects files. All computer programs acquired, including those purchased in shrink-wrap from computer stores, should be scanned before installing software on your system. In addition, frequent scans of your hard disk are recommended. Many virus detection programs are available including commercial products such as Anti-Virus by Central Point Software (Beaverton, Ore.), shareware such as F-Prot (Frisk Software International, Reykjavik, Iceland), and freeware such as GateKeeper for the Macintosh.
- Scan and backup your important files regularly. If a computer virus damages your system, the backup files can be used to restore necessary files.

Evaluating Software

Because software can be a significant financial investment, it is important to choose your software carefully. Listed below are 14 factors to consider when purchasing software:

- What is the cost?
- Will it run on your computer? (e.g., does it require an IBM-compatible or Macintosh, a hard disk, a mouse, a specific type of printer, a minimal size RAM?)
- How fast does it process data?
- Is it easy to install?
- What is the quality of the manuals that come with it?
- Is it user-friendly?
- Can a backup copy be made?
- Can it be upgraded at low cost?
- Will it do what you require?

- Can you preview it?
- Does it have adequate technical support?
- Amount of training required?
- Can it be stored on a hard disk?

Storing Programs on Disks

Suppose you have been working for several hours on an application such as a word-processing document or a spreadsheet and it is time to power down the computer. Since the information stored in RAM is volatile, shutting off the computer will erase all of your work. A place for more permanent storage, such as a disk, is needed. Using DOS we can instruct the computer to place a copy of the information in RAM on a disk. The space reserved on the disk for the information is called a file. We give the file a name and DOS labels the file and records on the disk the file's location and name. We can view a disk as a file drawer. Several files can be stored on a disk, so many in fact that DOS provides methods such as directory structures and folders for organizing disk files.

FORMATTING DISKS

Contrary to the cartoon shown above there is nothing magical about how information is stored on a disk. When a floppy disk is purchased its surface is a blank magnetized field, unusable by the computer. How can we store electronic information (i.e., bits) from RAM on such a surface? First the disk must be prepared for storing information by a process known as **formatting** or "initializing." Formatting is accomplished by one of the DOS programs and must be performed on every blank disk in order for the computer to store information on it, although preformatted disks can be purchased. Because disk formatting is a DOS procedure, disks formatted under the Macintosh DOS are not directly readable by IBM-compatible machines and vice versa (with the exception of PowerPC computers). The formatting process accomplishes four tasks (Figure 5-14):

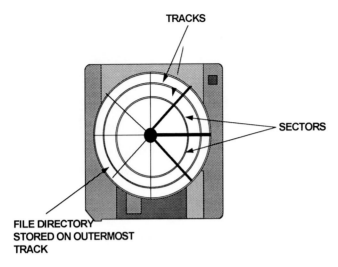

Figure 5-14   Formatting a disk.

1. The surface of the disk is logically broken up into a grid of concentric circles or tracks and pie-shaped sectors.
2. Each segment of the grid is labeled with a unique address so it can be identified by the computer
3. The outermost track is reserved as a "directory" for storing information such as filenames, file size, creation date, and location of file on the disk
4. Optionally a copy of DOS can be stored on the disk making the disk a bootable or "system" disk.

When a user directs the computer to save information from RAM to a file on the disk, the bits stored electronically in RAM are stored as polarized areas on the disk. The file name and location (i.e., the addresses of the segments on the disk in which bits are stored) are stored in the disk's directory so that the computer can locate the file at a future date. To read a disk's directory, execute the appropriate DOS command. Under MS-DOS the command is DIR. Double-clicking on a disk icon will reveal the contents of a disk under the Macintosh DOS.

TYPES OF FLOPPY DISKS

Floppy disks are constructed of Mylar plastic-coated with a magnetic oxide and are encased in a protective covering. They are classified according to their physical dimensions and to the amount of information they are capable of storing. Figure 5-15 shows the two most common sizes — 5.25-inch disks encased in a flexible or "floppy" protective covering and the newer 3.5-inch disks encased in a hard plastic covering. Both varieties come in single-density, double-density, and high-density capacities (density refers to the number of bits that can be

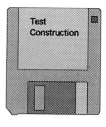

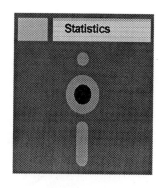

3.5" Disk   **5.25" Disk**

Figure 5-15   Common types of floppy disks.

stored in a given area of the disk); however, 3.5-inch disks can store more information at each capacity. Single-density disks store approximately 160K of information while double-density disks can store approximately 360K to 800K. High-density disks with storage capacities of almost 3MB are available. It is important to know the disk size and capacity of your disk drives. For example, high-density drives are required for reading high-density disks and, of course, 3.5-inch drives are incapable of reading 5.25-inch disks!

CARING FOR FLOPPY DISKS

Information stored on disks is relatively safe if disks are properly cared for. Curtin (1989) provides the following tips for protecting your disks:

- Keep disks away from magnets.
- Keep disks away from extremes in temperature (50–150°F).
- Store disks in protective jackets.
- Use a felt-tip pen to label a disk.
- Don't expose disks to static electricity.
- Keep disks away from moisture.
- Make backup copies of your important disks.
- Don't touch the disk's recording surface.
- Don't insert or remove a disk from a disk drive while drive is operating.

Putting It Together

A computer is an electronic device that inputs instructions and data into memory, manipulates instructions at incredible speed, and outputs results in a usable form. To reinforce your understanding of how a computer works, consider the following scenario. Mary Jo has collected scores from 20 students in her physical education class and wants to use her microcomputer to compute descriptive statistics. Her computer has two 3.5-inch disk drives and no hard drive. Before she loads her statistics application program into RAM, Mary Jo must first load the operating system. She places her DOS disk in one of the disk drives and turns the machine's power switch on. One of the computer's ROM chips has instructions that tell the computer to immediately access one of the disk drives and look for DOS as soon as the computer is powered on. Therefore, DOS is automatically copied from the DOS disk into RAM. Now that DOS is loaded, Mary Jo can load her statistics program into RAM. She inserts her application disk into the empty disk drive and then types a DOS command directing the computer to run the statistics program on her applications disk. Once the statistics program is up and running, she inputs her scores from the keyboard and directs the program to compute and print the results. Of course Mary Jo remembers that every command she gives to the computer and every program she runs is processed by the CPU in a matter of microseconds. She appreciates that every character typed on the keyboard and every character loaded from the disk drive is stored in RAM as a series of circuits which are either on or off (i.e., 1 or 0). Last, Mary Jo realizes that computers can facilitate her measurement and evaluation practices, the topic of the next section.

COMPUTING IN MEASUREMENT AND EVALUATION

Computers make it easier to do a lot of things, but most of the things they make it easier to do don't need to be done.

—Andy Rooney

It is misleading to state that computers are necessary for measurement and evaluation. Given plenty of paper, a sharp pencil, a hand-calculator, typewriter, and lots of time, practitioners can calculate statistics, draw graphs, and type reports by hand. Computers, however, greatly enhance measurement and evaluation practices, providing, in many instances, superior data analysis and reporting (e.g., computerized graphics, individualized sport or physical fitness profiles, statistical analysis) with little additional investment in time and energy.

In this section we explore the use of computers in enhancing measurement and evaluation practices. For each computer application in measurement and evaluation, examples of applicable generic (i.e., word-processing, database, spreadsheet, or graphics) and speciality software are provided.

Constructing, Administering, and Analyzing Written Tests

Consider the plight of Jim, a newly hired middle-school physical education teacher, faced with developing a written test of basketball rules. With grim determination, Jim sits down in front of a desktop computer and pulls out his secret weapon: test construction software. Using menus and graphics the software guides Jim through the steps of written test construction including outlining instructional objectives, choosing the type of test (multiple choice, true/false, fill in the blanks, or essay), writing questions, assembling the final product (e.g., providing space for a title, the student's name, instructions), and printing the test. In addition, the software allows Jim to save test questions sorted by content area in a test item bank on a disk, so they can be used in future tests.

Let's assume that Jim's school has a computer laboratory with 30 microcomputers. Instead of printing his test and administering a paper copy to students, Jim employs test administration software to administer the multiple choice and true/false portion of the test on the computer. Such software records answers for each question, determines total scores for each student, and reports scores for each question and for the test. Moreover, Jim's program administers test questions in random order for each student, decreasing the opportunities for cheating.

Enthused by the usefulness of computers in testing his students, Jim decides to employ test analysis software to determine statistically the effectiveness of his test questions in testing basketball rules (see Chapter 16). Using data from the test administration program, Jim computes statistics that indicate the level of question difficulty, items that discriminated between students who scored high and low on the test, and the internal-consistency reliability of the test. Such information gives Jim valuable evidence for retaining, revising, or deleting questions from the test, allowing him to increase the effectiveness of future test versions.

Specialty Software

Assessment Systems Corporation (ASC) (St. Paul, Minn.) offers a relatively expensive but very complete set of products for constructing, administering, and analyzing written tests. Aimed at the professional test developer is MicroCAT, a collection of 16 programs for creating test banks, developing written and computer-administered tests, and analyzing test scores. MicroCAT offers both traditional and item response test administration and analysis. For those interested in test construction only, ASC offers the Assessment Systems Topical Exam Creation System (ASTEC), a menu-driven program which includes powerful test item banking and test formatting components.

At the more affordable end of the spectrum is Diploma II (Brownstone Research Group, Denver) a combination gradebook, datebook, test construction, and test administration program with IBM-compatible and Apple IIe versions. Diploma II comes with a readable manual and includes the basic functions required by teachers for developing and administering written tests. Teachers interested in constructing unique "fun" quizzes such as crossword puzzles and word recognition tests are urged to preview Crossword Magic (Mindscape, Inc., 3444 Dundee Road, Northbrook, IL 60062).

Statistics programs often include test analysis modules. An example of an affordable package is Statistics with Finesse (Bolding, 1989) which provides basic item statistics, reliability, and summary statistics for both the total test and for subtests. Also available on the market are several affordable test analysis packages which analyze multiple-choice test data input from an optical mark reader such as the Scantron. Test Analysis Program (Bertamax, Inc., Seattle) and Test Analysis (Classroom Consortia Media, Inc., Staten Island, N.Y.) programmed for IBM-compatibles are representative of this type of software.

SOFTSHARE is a valuable source for affordable test construction and administration software. Cross Master for the Macintosh and Word Hunt for IBM-compatibles are reasonably priced crossword puzzle and word-search test makers while Besttest and Testwriter for IBM-compatibles offer low-cost test construction packages.

Generic Software

Specialty software can be expensive, complex, and require unavailable hardware. Fortunately, test construction and analysis can be accomplished using word-processing, spreadsheet, and database software. A word-processing program is ideal for constructing written tests. The automatic numbering function available on most word processors allows users to add or delete questions without the frustration of renumbering questions. The graphics capabilities of today's word-processing software enlivens tests with boxes, lines, and clip art graphics such as drawings of sporting equipment and diagrams of sport strategies. Additionally word-processing software can be used for developing a test blueprint or table of specifications to aid in determining content validity of a test (see Chapter 6).

Database software is a useful alternative to test item banking software. Test questions developed on a word processor can be imported to a database, coded for content, and sorted and retrieved at a future date. Sophisticated database programs such as Paradox (Borland) can save graphic images along with text, offering a powerful item banking option.

Test analysis is easily accomplished via spreadsheet software. At a minimum, item difficulty and discrimination statistics along with test score descriptive statistics such as mean, median, standard deviation, range, and minimum and maximum scores can be computed by the spreadsheet. More experienced spreadsheet users can tackle computation of internal consistency reliability. Figure 5-16 illustrates a simple test analysis spreadsheet using Microsoft Excel for a five multiple-choice question quiz administered to 12 students.

Reporting Results of Tests

The medium used to report test scores is an important consideration. Test results in public school physical education provide an important teaching tool and a valuable communication link between teachers, students, parents, and administrators. In clinical settings choice of report format can make a difference between results that are ignored by clients and results that are easily interpreted and used.

Specialty Software

Recognizing the importance of reporting test results several national fitness tests such as FITNESSGRAM (Institute for Aerobics Research), Physical Best

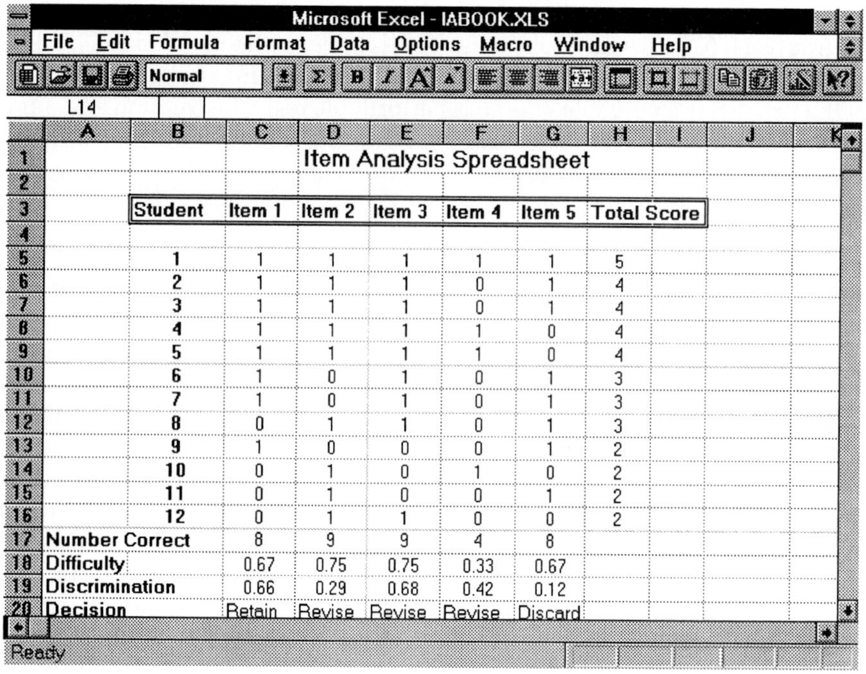

Item Analysis Spreadsheet

Student	Item 1	Item 2	Item 3	Item 4	Item 5	Total Score
1	1	1	1	1	1	5
2	1	1	1	0	1	4
3	1	1	1	0	1	4
4	1	1	1	1	0	4
5	1	1	1	1	0	4
6	1	0	1	0	1	3
7	1	0	1	0	1	3
8	0	1	1	0	1	3
9	1	0	0	0	1	2
10	0	1	0	1	0	2
11	0	1	0	0	1	2
12	0	1	1	0	0	2
Number Correct	8	9	9	4	8	
Difficulty	0.67	0.75	0.75	0.33	0.67	
Discrimination	0.66	0.29	0.68	0.42	0.12	
Decision	Retain	Revise	Revise	Revise	Discard	

Figure 5-16 A customized Microsoft Excel item analysis spreadsheet.

(American Association for Health, Physical Education, Recreation, and Dance, AAHPERD), and the Chrysler Fund–AAU Physical Fitness Program have developed Macintosh and IBM-compatible software for tabulating results and generating individualized physical fitness profiles. Typically, fitness profiles include the respondent's test scores and percentile rank, a graph of the scores compared to norm-referenced or criterion-referenced standards, an interpretation of scores, and an exercise prescription.

Generic Software

With planning and a little creativity, word-processing, database, and spreadsheet software can be effectively used to report test results. A simple, yet attractive report card can be developed on a word processor. Taking advantage of the mail-merge function available on many word processors, student scores stored in a database are "merged" into the report card "template," automatically producing individualized report cards. Alternatively, the report generator in a database could be used to generate the report card template. Data stored in the database are processed through the report generator to produce individualized report cards.

Spreadsheets are ideal for developing sport and fitness profiles. Figure 5-17 shows a sport profile developed using Microsoft Excel. To use the profile, the teacher types in test scores, the mean and the standard deviation for each test,

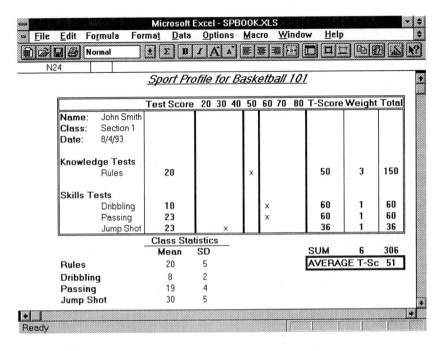

Figure 5-17   A customized Microsoft Excel sport profile.

and the X's representing the T-score for each test. The spreadsheet computes T-scores, weighted scores, and the final weighted average for the unit of instruction.

Grading

Formulating final grades is an important task for teachers of physical education. However, combining several skills tests, cognitive tests, projects, and homework assignments into a single-letter grade representing overall class performance for several classes numbering 30 or more students is time-consuming and computationally complex. Since most teachers have a limited amount of time at the end of a term to compute and submit grades, it is little wonder that grading is a task that many teachers love to hate. Luckily, grading software can minimize the burden of mathematical computations and reporting grades. Reasonably priced programs such as Grade Quick (Compu-Teach, Inc., New Haven, Conn.) offer sophisticated grading strategies, graphing, reporting, statistical analysis, and data management functions that reduce the mechanics of grading to inputting scores for each test and instructing the program to output the grade list. Additionally, effective use of grading programs can enhance the instructional process through identification of trends such as grade inflation or decline in fundamental knowledge and skill, and immediate feedback to students concerning their current status in meeting course objectives and the timely prescription of remedial work.

Let's consider important design, computation, and reporting features of grading software. Most grading programs use either a database or spreadsheet design. Spreadsheet designs tend to be more efficient for data entry, data editing, and screen output. Computationally, grading programs differ widely and it is important to determine exactly how the program computes grades. For example, some programs use a point system which simply totals the obtained scores for each test and divides by the total of the maximum scores for each test to obtain an overall percent, while other programs convert each obtained score to a common metric such as a z-score or percent and then take the simple average of the derived scores. More sophisticated programs offer a choice of computational alternatives. Before using a grading program, compute the grades for several students by hand and then compare these grades with the program's calculations. Most grading programs print class lists which include student names, identification numbers, scores for each test, final percent, and a letter grade. Additional features to look for are:

- Ability to sort students by name, identification number, and final letter grade
- Confidentiality in posting grades, the ability to print class lists using the identification number instead of student names
- Ability to report basic descriptive statistics (e.g., mean, standard deviation, minimum and maximum score) for each test and the final grade
- Ability to weight individual tests and categories of tests (e.g., quizzes vs. examinations) to reflect their importance in the grade
- Ability to graph score distributions for individual tests and overall grades
- Ability to choose one of several grading schemes (e.g., A–F, pass-fail)
- Ability to set norm-referenced or criterion-referenced grading standards
- Ability to print class reports, test reports, and reports for individual students.

Specialty Software

Of the grading programs available, many are developed for Apple II and IIe computers. Popular commercial programs for the Apple IIe are "Report Card" (Sensible Software), "GradeCalc" (Tamarack Software, Inc.), "Gradebook" (Scholastic Software), and "Teacher's Gradebook" (Dynacomp, Inc.); however, less expensive freeware and shareware programs can be obtained through SOFTSHARE.

For IBM-compatibles, "Diploma II" (which also offers a version for the Apple IIe) and "GradeQuick" are useful programs. "Diploma II" (Brownstone Research Group) employs a database design and provides basic input, computational, and reporting functions at a reasonable cost. "GradeQuick" (CompuTech) is a powerful and flexible grading program. Using a spreadsheet design, it features superior reporting, including 17 statistics; easy data input; standard or user-assigned grading schemes; attendance records and missing work lists; weighting of each assignment, assignment category, and grading period; detailed graphs and charts; and the ability to import, export, and merge data files (Figure 5-18).

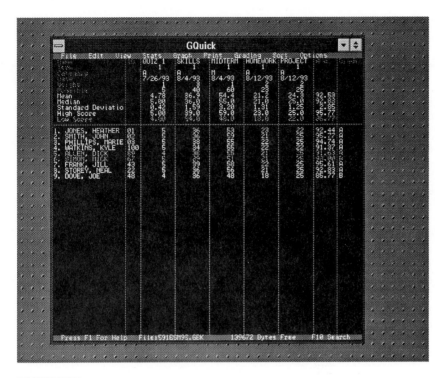

Figure 5-18   A "GradeQuick" gradesheet.

The SOFTSHARE catalog presents over 20 affordable grading programs for Macintosh, Apple, and IBM-compatible computers. These programs range from the rather sophisticated program "Super Duper Gradebook" for the Macintosh to the specialty program, "Weight Lifting Grading," for the IBM.

Generic Software

Developing a personal grading program using spreadsheet software is a relatively easy task. Figure 5-19 illustrates a simple grading program developed using Microsoft Excel. The teacher inputs student names, identification numbers, test information such as maximum obtainable score and weight, and scores on each test for each student. The program computes the final weighted grade and letter grade for each student and descriptive statistics for each test. In addition a three-dimensional (3-D) bar graph of the final grade distribution is printed out.

Clinical and Research Settings

Technological advances in measuring clinical parameters such as dynamic strength, oxygen consumption, body composition, dynamic balance, and the kinetics and kinematics of humans in motion have depended in large part on the integration of computer technology with sophisticated electronic measure-

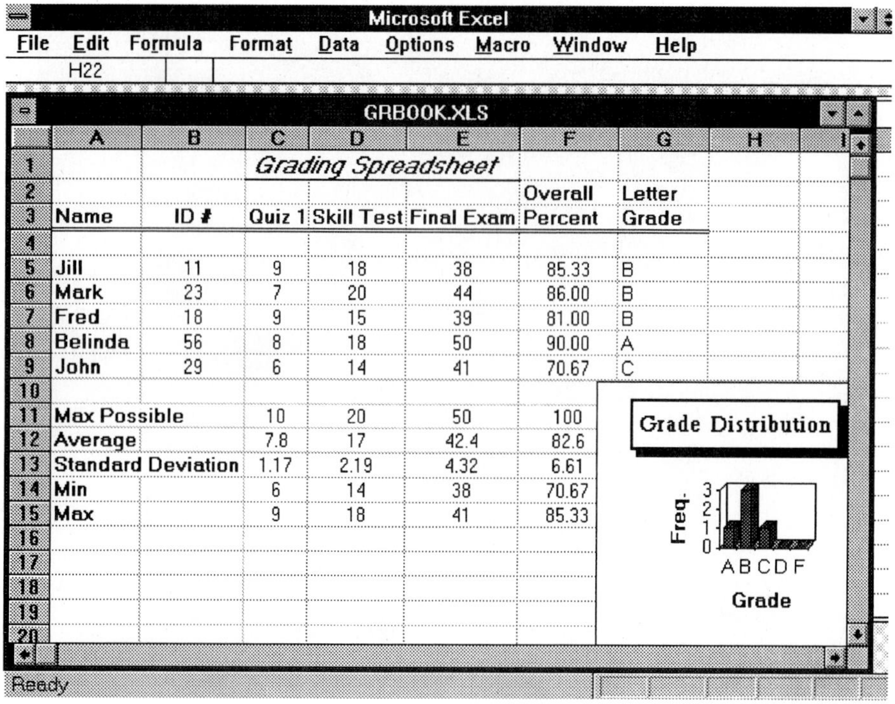

Microsoft Excel — GRBOOK.XLS

Name	ID #	Quiz 1	Skill Test	Final Exam	Overall Percent	Letter Grade
Jill	11	9	18	38	85.33	B
Mark	23	7	20	44	86.00	B
Fred	18	9	15	39	81.00	B
Belinda	56	8	18	50	90.00	A
John	29	6	14	41	70.67	C
Max Possible		10	20	50	100	
Average		7.8	17	42.4	82.6	
Standard Deviation		1.17	2.19	4.32	6.61	
Min		6	14	38	70.67	
Max		9	18	41	85.33	

Figure 5-19 Microsoft Excel customized grading program.

ment instruments. Interfacing computers with measurement devices offers the following advantages:

- Increased data collection speed and data storage. Computers can record thousands of samples per second and store the data on disks. Additionally, client demographic and clinical histories can be stored with test data.
- Increased accuracy of data collection and data reduction. Reducing thousands of data points to meaningful statistics can be accomplished quickly and accurately with a computer.
- Increased control over the measurement protocol. Computers can be used to control the timing of data collection and to control such devices as treadmills and video recorders.
- Reduced cost of data collection. Effective use of computers can reduce costs associated with personnel.

Examples of computers interfaced with measurement devices in the clinical setting include:

1. KIN-COM (Chattanooga Group, Inc., Hixson, Tenn.) muscle testing and training system. The KIN-COM shown in Figure 5-20 uses a computer to

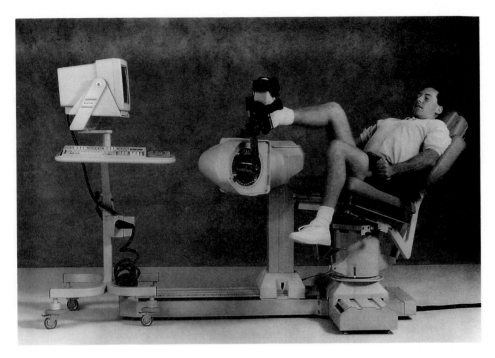

Figure 5-20   The KIN-COM muscle testing and training system.

monitor speed, velocity, range of motion, and muscle tension generated by a specified movement (e.g., knee extension) as well as to control user-defined training programs for isokinetic, isometric, and isotonic contractions.

2. PEAK system (Peak Performance Technologies, Inc., Englewood, Colo.) is used extensively in biomechanics for analyzing the kinetics and kinematics of movement. Digitized data obtained from frame-by-frame analysis of videotaped performance are entered and analyzed by the PEAK system to create 3-D computer simulations of movement on a computer screen. For example, to analyze the performance of a cross-country skier, videotape from three cameras shooting simultaneously from three different angles are digitized frame by frame and the data entered into the PEAK system. Figure 5-21 shows the screen output for such an analysis of skiers at the 1992 Winter Olympic Games.

3. Pro Balance Master (Neurocom International, Inc., Clackamas, Ore.) provides quantitative assessment and training for static and dynamic balance rehabilitation (see Chapter 21).

4. Metabolic Measurement Cart (SENSORMEDICS, Yorba Linda, Calif.) is a complete cardiopulmonary assessment device which analyzes inhaled and exhaled respiratory gases in determining anaerobic threshold and maximum oxygen consumption ($\dot{V}O_2$ max).

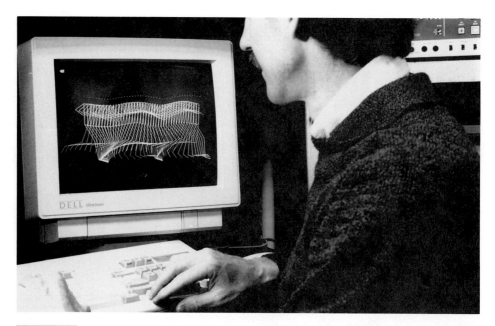

Figure 5-21   Digitized data of an Olympic cross-country skier analyzed on the PEAK system.

5. Hologic QDR 1000/W Bone Densitometer (Hologic, Waltham, Mass.) is used for estimating bone mineral density via low-level radiation scanning.
6. SMI (Sport Medicine Industries, Inc., St. Cloud, Minn.) measures anaerobic power of clients on ergometric devices.
7. Bio-Resistance Body Composition Analyzer (Valhalla Scientific, San Diego) uses a computer to determine body composition using bioelectrical impedance techniques. A low-level electric current is passed through the client's body between electrodes fixed to the ankle and the wrist. The computer estimates body composition using complex formulas based on the relationship between electrical resistance and body water which is related to fat-free weight.
8. LFT3000 Pulmonary Function Testing Laboratory (GO MI INC., San Anselmo, Calif.) analyzes inspired and expired gases and provides a complete analysis of pulmonary function useful in research and diagnostic settings.

In addition, computers are being used extensively in fitness program management. Health clubs are recognizing the advantages of computer technology for fitness assessment and prescription, health-risk appraisal, dietary analysis, managing daily fitness activities, and record management. Baun and Baun (1985) describe such a management program instituted at Tenneco Corporation in Houston. The Tenneco program consists of four functions: (1) an employee membership program for storage and retrieval of client data; (2) the participant check-in and check-out program for identifying eligible clients and monitoring their frequency and duration of facility use; (3) a fitness and medical testing program for recording fitness and medical data, and (4) a unique exercise logging program which allows clients to record their physical activity on conveniently located computer terminals. The exercise logging module provides immediate feedback regarding caloric expenditure and is the basis for monthly and yearly activity reports.

Statistics

Statistics software takes the tedium out of summarizing test scores and evaluating tests for validity and reliability. A wide range of statistics software is available in today's market.

Specialty Software

For sophisticated applications with large data sets (e.g., the research setting) mainframe packages such as MINITAB, SPSS/X, BMDP, and SAS provide up-to-date statistical procedures coupled with powerful data manipulation, graphics, and reporting features. However, the appearance of powerful desktop computers has been matched by the development of MINITAB, SPSS, BMDP and SAS desktop computer versions. While the desktop versions handle less data and are relatively slower than their mainframe counterparts, they tend to be more interactive and user-friendly than the mainframe versions. For example, SPSS offers a highly interactive Windows desktop version. IBM and Macintosh versions of MINITAB and SPSS are currently available, while BMDP and SAS are available for IBM-compatibles only.

Two major trends in statistics software development are the use of sophisticated graphics and spreadsheet technology. "Systat" (Systat) and "StatView" (Abacus Concepts) for the Macintosh provide excellent examples of such software. Both programs employ a user-friendly spreadsheet interface and take advantage of the Macintosh's graphics capabilities to create 3-D high-resolution graphics. Abacus Concepts also markets for the Macintosh a powerful analysis of variance (ANOVA) program called "SuperANOVA."

A myriad of affordable statistics desktop computer programs are available through SOFTSHARE. "Epitstat" and "Arcus Professional" for IBM-compatibles provide reasonable sophistication and compute a wide variety of statistics, while Easy-Stats is aimed at the novice user. Another useful program for novices is "Statistics with Finesse" (Bolding, 1989) for the Apple IIe and IBM-compatibles. This program presents basic statistical functions and an easy-to-use menu-driven interface for a reasonable price.

Generic Software

Another approach to statistical computing is developing your own statistical functions on a spreadsheet. Most commercial spreadsheets incorporate built-in functions for statistics such as mean, standard deviation, correlation, regression, and ANOVA, easily accessible with a few key strokes or the click of a mouse. More complex routines can be programmed into the spreadsheet by the

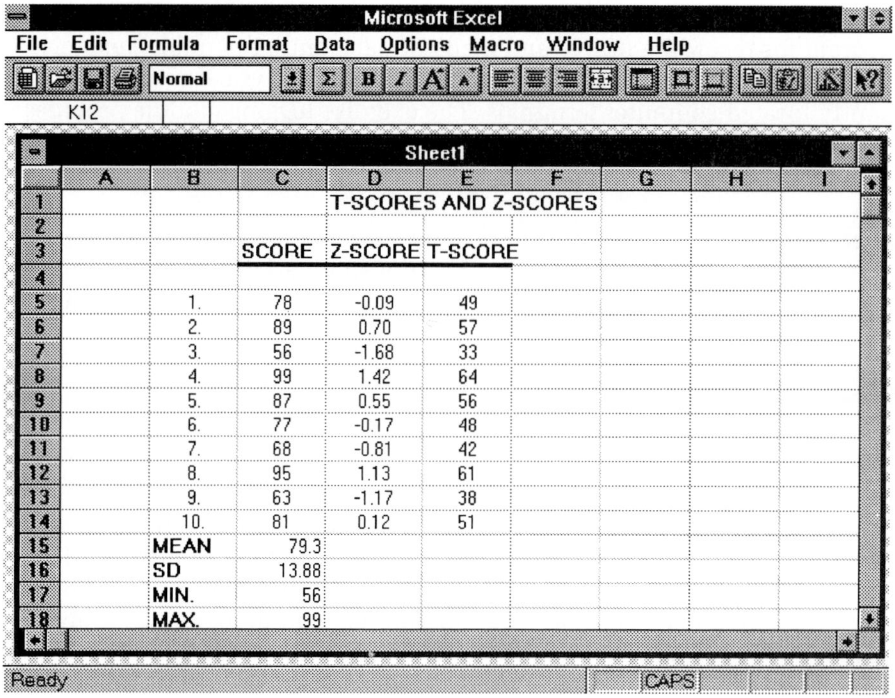

| | Microsoft Excel | | | | | | | | |
| File | Edit | Formula | Format | Data | Options | Macro | Window | Help | |

```
K12
```

	Sheet1								
	A	B	C	D	E	F	G	H	I
1				T-SCORES AND Z-SCORES					
2									
3			SCORE	Z-SCORE	T-SCORE				
4									
5		1.	78	-0.09	49				
6		2.	89	0.70	57				
7		3.	56	-1.68	33				
8		4.	99	1.42	64				
9		5.	87	0.55	56				
10		6.	77	-0.17	48				
11		7.	68	-0.81	42				
12		8.	95	1.13	61				
13		9.	63	-1.17	38				
14		10.	81	0.12	51				
15		MEAN	79.3						
16		SD	13.88						
17		MIN.	56						
18		MAX.	99						

Ready   CAPS

Figure 5-22   Customized Microsoft Excel z-score and T-score program.

user. Figure 5-22 presents a Microsoft Excel spreadsheet for determining z- and T-scores for a set of numbers. Once the raw scores are entered, the program automatically computes the mean, standard deviation, minimum and maximum scores, and the T and z-score equivalents for each raw score.

SUMMARY

Effective use of computer technology greatly enhances measurement and evaluation practices. Software for collecting, analyzing, and reporting test scores and for evaluating tests can be obtained commercially; through shareware programs; or by developing custom applications on spreadsheets, databases, and word processors. Understanding basic concepts of computer hardware and software will help maximize the impact of computers in measurement and evaluation. Concepts such as the components of a computer system, how information is stored and processed by a computer, types of computer programs, and trends in software development provide a springboard to effective computer utilization.

Learning Experiences

1. One of the easiest ways of learning to use a microcomputer is to try out the computer's demonstration disk. The demonstration disk provides a graphic

tutorial that explains how to use the computer and its components. Visit the computer center or one of the microcomputer laboratories on your campus. Alternatively, stop by a computer retail outlet. Ask for the demonstration disk for the type of computer you wish to use. Computer laboratory supervisors and retail salespeople are usually very helpful, so don't hesitate to ask for assistance in using the demonstration disk.

2. Popular computer magazines provide a wealth of information concerning hardware, software, and how to use computers effectively. Find a computer magazine (e.g., *MacWorld, Personal Computing*) on the magazine rack of a bookstore, pharmacy, or grocery. Find an article that provides a review of software and one that reviews hardware. For each article write a short paragraph which summarizes the main points of the article.

3. Visit a computer store and find the software section. Choose one of the generic software packages (e.g., word processor, spreadsheet, graphics, or communications) and find the following information by reading the package: name and version of the software, publisher, price, required hardware such as RAM, type of computer, type of disk drives, graphics card, etc.

4. Visit a computer retail store and inquire about a computer brand that interests you. Ask about the amount of RAM, type of CPU, availability and size of the hard disk, number and type of floppy disk drives, warranty, repair service, type of monitor and graphics interface card, software which comes with the computer, and price. Write a description of your experience and your feelings about it. Would you feel confident purchasing this computer?

5. Visit a fitness club operator or a schoolteacher and write a description of how computers are used in the workplace. If computers are not used extensively, make suggestions about how computers could be used effectively.

References

Baun WB, Baun M. 1985. A corporate health and fitness program: Motivation and management by computers. In Cundiff DE, ed. Implementation of health fitness exercise programs. Reston, Va: American Association for Health, Physical Education, Recreation, and Dance, pp 86–89.

Bolding J. 1989. Statistics with finesse. Fayetteville, Ark: Author.

Curtin DP. 1989. Microcomputers: Applications and software, ed 2. Englewood Cliffs, NJ: Prentice-Hall.

Capron HL. 1990. Computers: Tools for an information age. Redwood City, Calif: Benjamin/Cummings.

Fuori WM, Aufiero LJ. 1989. Computers and information processing, ed 2. Englewood Cliffs, NJ: Prentice Hall.

Kubiszyn T, Borich G. 1987. Educational testing and measurement: Classroom application and practice, ed 2. Glenview, Ill: Scott, Foresman.

Annotated Readings

Abernethy K, Nanney T, Porter H. 1989. Exploring Macintosh: Concepts in visually oriented computing. New York: Wiley.

Provides a step-by-step tutorial in learning to use applications on the Macintosh computer. Covers the basics of word processing, database management, spreadsheeting, and communications using the Microsoft Works program.

Davis WS. 1991. Computing fundamentals: Concepts. Reading, Mass: Addison-Wesley.

An excellent short course in the fundamentals of computer hardware and software. Recommended for novice users.

Donnelly J, ed. 1987. Using microcomputers in physical education and the sport sciences. Champaign, Ill: Human Kinetics.

One of the few books in exercise science that focuses on computers and computing. Various authors provide descriptions of microcomputer applications ranging from applications in the school setting to applications in biomechanics, motor behavior, and exercise physiology.

Madron T, Tate C, Brookshire RG. 1985. Using microcomputers in research. Beverly Hills, Calif: Sage.

Although written for those interested in research, this volume provides an engaging approach to describing how computers can be used in collecting data and in statistical analysis.

Shelly G, Cashman T. 1994. Learning to use Windows applications: Microsoft Works 2.0 for Windows. Danvers, Mass: Boyd & Fraser.

For users interested in learning how to use the Windows interface and the integrated software package Microsoft Works. Provides excellent instruction with step-by-step tutorials.

Characteristics of a Good Test

Validity and Reliability of Norm-Referenced Tests

Watch for these words as you read the following chapter

Concurrent validity
Construct-related evidence of validity
Content-related evidence of validity
Contingency table
Convergent validity
Criterion-related evidence of validity
Discriminant validity
Intraclass correlation coefficient
Logical validity

Objective test
Objectivity
Predictors
Predictive validity
Reliability
Split-half reliability
Standard error of measurement
Subjective test
Test-retest

n Chapter 1 the concept of norm-referenced measurement was introduced. This type of test, in which the score is interpreted by comparing it to a norm, is used when both the test user and the examinee want to know who has the most ability, who has the least, and so forth. Before placing any faith in the test results, one must be certain that the test is a good one: the test should measure what it is supposed to measure (validity) with consistency (reliability), using an accurate scoring system (objectivity). (For a discussion of these characteristics in a criterion-referenced measurement framework, see Chapter 7.) In this chapter the concept of validity is covered first, because a test can be reliable but not necessarily valid. Validity is the most important element of test theory.

Distance run testing in elementary school children.

More practical attributes of a test—such as cost, ease of administration, and appropriateness—are discussed in other chapters.

VALIDITY

Assume you are a student who has just completed a fitness unit. Mr. Miller, your teacher, announces that he will give a written test on short-term effects of physical activity, long-term effects of physical activity, and the components of an exercise prescription (frequency, intensity, duration, and type), which he taught during the unit. You carefully study all three areas and feel well prepared to take the test. When the test is administered, you skim through it quickly and find that all the items deal with the long-term effects of physical activity. No questions on short-term effects or exercise prescriptions are included. After completing the test, you might comment to the teacher or a classmate that this was not a good test because it did not measure what it was supposed to measure. In other words, the test lacked **validity.**

A *valid test* can be loosely defined as a measure that is sound in terms of the purpose of the test and that meets satisfactory criteria for test construction. More broadly, validity is the soundness of the interpretation of the test. It is the closeness of agreement between what the test measures and the behavior it is intended to measure. Furthermore, to be valid a test must also have acceptable reliability, or consistency of measurement, which is discussed more thoroughly later in this chapter.

How does one evaluate the validity of a test? First, it is important to recognize that a test can have many validities. Therefore to describe a test as "valid" is

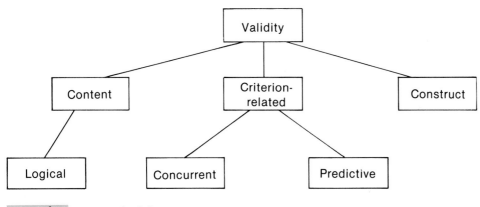

Figure 6-1   Types of validity.

really not accurate; rather, a test should be designated as "valid for a given purpose." For example, a test might be valid for 5-year-old girls but not for 25-year-old women. It might be valid for measuring an individual skill but not game-playing ability. The first step in interpreting test validity is to think through how you plan to use the test. Then the type of validity of greatest interest must be determined. The most common types of evidence of validity are content, criterion-related, and construct. In the physical education field, logical validity, a special case of content validity, is frequently used (Figure 6-1).

Types of Validity

Because many definitions of validity have been proposed, the concept can be confusing to the test user. In an effort to alleviate this confusion several national measurement organizations have developed a set of standards for educational and psychological tests. These standards include the categorization of validity into three types of evidence—content-related, criterion-related, and construct-related (APA, 1985). The most important point to keep in mind is that validity, no matter what type, is the single most important concept in evaluating a test.

Content-Related Evidence of Validity

The content validity of a test is "the degree to which the sample of items, tasks, or questions on a test are representative of some defined universe or 'domain' of content" (APA, 1985). More simply stated, when a test developer demonstrates that the items in a test adequately represent all important areas of content, the test has content validity. This type of validity is appropriate for written tests. How is the content-related evidence of validity of a test evaluated? This process can be demonstrated by analyzing a classroom test of badminton rules (Wood, 1989). This test was developed according to a table of specifications, sometimes referred to as a test blueprint. Table 6-1 shows the specifications for college-age players in a beginning badminton class. The content areas are listed on the left side of the table and represent the content judged to be important for

Table 6-1   Test Blueprint for a Classroom Test of Badminton Rules

	BEHAVIORS			
Content	**Knowledge**	**Comprehension**	**Application**	**%**
Playing surface	1, 2, 3			7.5
Equipment	8			2.5
General rules				
Scoring	4		6	5.0
Serving	12	22, 19	10	10.0
Receiving	13	15	16	7.5
Playing	20, 23, 39, 37	18, 17	21	17.5
Singles rules				
Scoring	9, 11			5.0
Serving			14	2.5
Doubles rules				
Scoring	25, 27, 36	34		10.0
Serving	32, 36	24		7.5
Receiving	30, 29, 31	28	33	12.5
Playing	35		38, 40	7.5
Etiquette	5, 7			5.0
	60.0%	20.0%	20.0%	

students in physical education classes. Across the top of the table are levels of cognitive behavior, which will be described in Chapter 16. The cells under the heading reflecting cognitive behaviors contain one or more numbers. These numbers represent the actual test question numbers. For example, *11* represents item 11 on the test. For each cell in the table, the test developer writes a predetermined number of test items. The percentage of items is determined by the educational importance attached to each category of content and cognitive behavior. Refer to the percentages listed along the bottom and right side of the table. These percentages provide the weighting or relative importance of each content and behavioral category. The largest percentage of items for a content area in the badminton test is 17.5%. This suggests that the test developer viewed the rules associated with playing as the most important content area. Now look at the percentages at the bottom of the page. The largest number of items for an area of cognitive behavior is 60, placing the greatest weight on knowledge of the content.

Begin analyzing the test itself by evaluating its content validity. Copies of the test and the table of specifications are needed. First, take the test just as a student would be required to do. Then arbitrarily select several items from the test and find them in the table of specifications. Answer the following question about each item: Does the item properly fit the cell designated by the test publisher? Suppose one of the items in Table 6-1 that you have chosen to analyze is *29*. This item is written as follows:

Item 29. Player X serves to player Y and wins the ensuing rally. Before the next serve, player Y and partner decide to change receiving courts so that player Y is again the receiver for player X's serve.

The receiving team wins the next rally before the error is discovered. What is the correct ruling?

    A. A let is awarded for the last point only.
    B. The serving team is awarded the point.
    C. The receiving team's victory in the rally is upheld.
    D. The receiving team is given a warning.

                                                    (Wood, 1989)

According to its placement, item 29 is a measure of knowledge about the rules for service reception in doubles play. The knowledge is factual and could be learned by memorization, a low level of cognitive behavior. Reread the test item. Does it measure what it is supposed to measure? If so, the item contributes to the content validity of the test. If not, it is not a valid item. Obviously this is a demanding job, but a test user is obligated to at least spot-check the test developer's decisions.

Another important aspect of content validity is whether the content areas are important in terms of the test user's educational goals. Should an area be emphasized more, deemphasized, added, or eliminated? These are judgments the test user must make. In the preceding paragraph a substantial number of items measuring the acute effects of physical activity were noted. One might question whether the degree of emphasis on this content area is warranted. The relative importance of various areas of content might differ markedly across school districts, depending on the curricular objectives of the particular physical education program. Including a substantial number of test items in a fitness test on the short-term and long-term effects of physical activity might be desirable in a program where physical fitness is an important part of the curriculum. In a program where skill development is stressed in the curricular objectives, a strong emphasis on exercise physiology might be unacceptable. Is it appropriate to use a standardized test to judge the outcomes of a physical education program, when the content taught in the curriculum receives a different emphasis from that provided in the test? The test may not be useful for judging program outcomes, but it can still provide valuable information to the physical education staff in a school system. For example, the test might be administered to determine the status of student knowledge in three content areas, without making a judgment on the quality of their physical education program. The test results might then be used to reexamine the current physical education curriculum. Standardized tests of this type should never be used to determine grades. They can be used appropriately as a part of program evaluation or simply to determine how well students can perform on a nationally standardized test.

To summarize, the following steps are recommended for reviewing a published test to determine its content validity:

1. Answer the test items and score your responses. This step should be standard procedure for any teacher with any test. If this step is taken seriously, detecting weaknesses in a test, including one's own test, is much easier.
2. Review the publisher's statement on content validity.
3. Examine the table of specifications.
4. Assess the appropriateness of the placement of items in the content and behavior categories.
5. Examine the universe (content and behavior categories) and respond to the following four questions:
   a. Are important elements of a content area omitted from the universe?
   b. Are unimportant elements of the content area erroneously included?
   c. Are any categories included in the content and behavior areas weighted improperly? (Weighting is reflected in the number of items included in a category.)
   d. Are all elements of the content and behavior areas educationally important?

Now that the procedure for evaluating the content validity of a published test has been described, let us examine the approach to be used when planning to develop your own test. Perhaps you are interested in developing a test of basketball rules. Obviously, including questions on all the rules in the rule book is not possible; therefore a representative sample of rules must be selected. The rules should be categorized in a table of specifications. Two of the categories might be offensive and defensive rules. If there are more offensive rules than defensive, the proportions of test items should reflect this difference. Levels of cognitive behavior can also be considered. When students are first learning the rules, the test might primarily measure a low level of cognitive behavior. If the rules test is intended for experienced players, you may be more interested in the degree to which students can apply the rules and thus design items measuring higher levels of cognitive behavior. Many tests include items reflecting several levels of cognitive behavior. Whatever the case, the identification of items should follow a systematic plan. To summarize, the following steps should be taken to demonstrate content validity when you have developed the test yourself:

1. Develop a table of specifications for the test. Determine the number of items that should be written for each cell of the table. Write the appropriate number of items for each cell.
2. Prepare the test items in the format you plan to use with your students.
3. Take the test and score your responses. This step should be taken even if the test is your own!
4. Select 25% of the test items and reexamine the appropriateness of their placement in the content and behavior categories of the table of specifica-

tions. Revise the items if necessary. If more than 5% (of the 25% selected) of the items are inappropriately placed, reexamine the placement of the remaining 75% of the items.

5. Determine whether the content and behavior categories should be altered in any way. Additions? Deletions? Increased emphasis? Decreased emphasis?

Often a test is developed by writing down item after item as each one comes to mind, until enough items have been written to fill the testing period. Such an approach may lead to haphazard results. The test may be heavily weighted with items in one or two categories and slighted in others. It behooves the teacher to begin by preparing a table of specifications, deciding in advance on the number of items for each category based on its relative importance. When the item-writing process is begun, it becomes a more purposeful activity. In addition, the test developer can have greater confidence that the test will be valid.

Logical Validity

Although written tests are used frequently in physical education and the exercise sciences, the tests most often used are those measuring physical skills and abilities. The concept of content validity does not make much sense for tests of motor performance. Instead of using clusters of items to measure various content areas, the test may consist of a single item or a repetition of the same item, usually referred to as trials of the test. However, the initial validation of these types of tests follows a set of rules similar in concept to content validity—logical validity. *Logical validity* is defined as the extent to which a test measures the most important components of skill necessary to perform a motor task adequately.

A test of motor skill is used to demonstrate how logical validity is evaluated. If the test incorporates and directly measures the important components of the skill being evaluated, logical validity can be claimed. Many tests in physical education measure only accuracy in performing a skill. While accuracy is undeniably important in the execution of many skills, it is not the only important factor. These limitations probably existed because tests were not being developed according to some logical plan, similar to the development of a good written test. Thus the idea of logical validity came into being. The general procedure to be followed in constructing a skills test is to define good performance in executing the skill, construct a test that measures the important components of skill in the definition, and score the test so that the best score represents a performance that approximates the definition of good performance.

Consider, for example, a test of the tennis forehand drive. Ms. Spencer, a physical education teacher, describes a good forehand drive as a ball hit so that it travels low over the net and deep into the backcourt. She decides to test her students on this skill using a test in which a target is place in the backcourt. The target is sectioned so that the areas with the higher scores are closer to the baseline of the tennis court. Is this a valid test? The test measures whether the ball is hit deep into the backcourt by giving more points to the ball landing close to the baseline, but it does not measure the height of the ball's flight over the net. Thus the evidence of logical validity is insufficient, and the test is not valid. Test validity could be increased by placing extensions on the standards holding the tennis nets and by stretching a rope across the middle of the court above the net. Then the examinee would attempt to hit the ball so that it passed between the rope and the top of the net.

Because logical validity is the degree to which the components of skill measured by a test correspond with those required to perform the skill adequately, the identification of important components of a skill is important. The previous section on logical validity dealt primarily with a single skills test. Although it is appropriate to measure specific skills when students are learning a sport, skills tests should not mistakenly be thought to measure playing ability. To measure playing ability, a battery of tests is often used. One of the first steps in validating a test battery of this type is to use logical validity. Logical validity in this context involves the definition of the important skills constituting playing ability. Tests are then selected to measure each of the skills identified as most important. Of course, each individual test must have logical validity as well.

Four major steps can be identified in assessing the logical validity of a skills test:

1. Review the test developer's statement on the purpose of the test and the components of skill the test is designed to measure. These components should be clearly stated in the test description. Make a list of these components.
2. Examine the test. List the components actually measured in the test.
3. Compare the two lists. Are the components identified and defined by the test developer actually measured by the test?
4. Examine the educational importance of the test:
   a. Are unimportant components of skill measured by the test?
   b. Are important components of skill omitted from the test?
   c. Do certain components of the skill receive inappropriate emphasis in the test?

Published tests of sports skills and playing ability frequently lack a statement identifying the important components of skill. In these cases, the test must be examined and the components being measured must be listed. Then the educational importance of the test must be analyzed. If developing your own test is necessary, start with a list of the important components of skill, which will provide the basis for the design of the test.

Criterion-Related Evidence of Validity

Criterion-related evidence of validity is demonstrated by comparing test scores with one or more external variables that are considered direct measures of the characteristic or behavior in question (known as the criterion). Two of the most common types of criterion-related validity are concurrent validity, which involves the comparison of a test with a criterion measure, and predictive validity, which deals with prediction of a behavior on a criterion test. Criterion-related evidence of validity is determined by statistical methods, although content and logical validity may play a part in the initial stages of constructing the test.

Concurrent validity is used when a test is proposed as a substitute for another test that is known to be valid. The latter test is called the criterion test, with *criterion* defined as a standard of behavior. More precisely, *concurrent validity* is defined as the degree to which a test correlates with (is related to) a criterion test, which has already been established as a valid test of the attribute of interest. Why would one search for a substitute test when a valid test is already available? Although the criterion test's validity has been established, it may be impractical. For example, administration of the test may require an excessive amount of time, trained personnel, or expensive equipment. Laboratory tests administered on a one-to-one basis are usually impractical in a school setting. Consider the wide variety of measures of cardiorespiratory (CR) function. It is well known that testing an examinee on the treadmill provides more valid indicators of CR function than a field test; however, trained physiologists, expensive laboratory equipment, and one-to-one testing are required. Therefore field tests are used most frequently in fitness clubs and physical education classes. Yet how is the adequacy of the field test determined? Usually a validity coefficient is reported for the test. This coefficient represents the correlation between scores on the field test (X) and the laboratory test (Y). This is the same correlation coefficient (r_{xy}) that was studied in Chapter 3, only now it is being used as an estimate of test validity. The higher the estimate, the stronger the relationship between the field test and the laboratory (criterion) test.

Three steps should be followed in evaluating the concurrent validity of a published test. To exemplify each step the 12-Minute Run Test is used as the field test of interest, and the maximal stress test on the treadmill is used as the laboratory (criterion) test.

1. Identify and examine the criterion test. Is it a logically valid measure of the attribute of interest?

   Although there are other valid indicators of CR function, the measure of maximum oxygen consumption (VO_2max) obtained from maximal stress testing on the treadmill is generally accepted as a valid criterion measure. (See Chapter 17 for additional information.)

2. Evaluate the correlation (validity coefficient) between the criterion test and the test you are interested in using. Is the correlation high enough to justify substituting the test you wish to use for the criterion test?

   The validity coefficient for the 12-Minute Run Test when compared with VO_2max is reported as .897 in one of Cooper's first published reports (Cooper, 1968). Thus, people who run longer distances tend to have higher VO_2max values, and vice versa. The validity coefficient is high enough to justify substituting the 12-Minute Run Test for the treadmill test. If you are developing the test yourself, you must calculate the validity coefficient. Use Formula 3-9 for calculating the Pearson product-moment correlation coefficient (r_{xy}).

3. If the criterion test is valid and the validity coefficient is .80 or above, use the test. If not, look for another test.

In general the Cooper test appears to be an excellent field test. However, several factors should be considered before using the test. Cooper's test group consisted of adult males who were well-trained and highly motivated. The test user should consider the examinee's sex, age, body fatness, and ability to pace properly and run efficiently during the test. (These elements are considered in more detail in Chapter 17.)

Predictive validity is defined as the degree to which a criterion behavior can be predicted using a score from a predictor test. Two uses of predictive validity are commonly observed in physical education and exercise science: as a description of the current status of an individual on the criterion behavior and as a predictor of future behavior on the criterion. (The criterion again refers to the standard against which the usefulness of the test is judged.) The predictors are tests or variables that predict criterion behavior.

Predictive validity used to describe the current status of an individual is essentially an extension of the concept of concurrent validity. Usually the test user is interested in estimating performance on an often complex criterion variable by obtaining a score on a simple predictor variable. To be reasonably accurate in the prediction, a relationship must exist between the predictor and criterion variables. In other words, the correlation between the two variables should be substantial. Consider a prediction study by Getchell and associates (1977) in which scores on the 1.5-mile run were used to predict CR function, specifically VO_2max as measured in a treadmill test. The relationship between the two measures was determined to be $-.915$. Since shorter times are associated with higher VO_2max values, the validity coefficient is expected to be negative. In this case the predictor measure, the 1.5-mile run, had high validity. This is essentially an estimate of concurrent validity.

Multiple Correlation

In many cases the use of only one predictor is not reasonable. In assessing body fatness using skinfold measures, for example, the use of more than one skinfold site is often recommended. When two or more predictors are used with one criterion measure (underwater weighing, for instance, in this example), multiple correlation procedures are used.

Regression

In addition to knowing that the 1.5-mile run test can be substituted for the treadmill test, one may also wish to predict or estimate the examinee's VO_2max value from his or her score on the 1.5-mile run. This can be done if a regression equation has been developed. The simple linear regression equation takes the following form:

$$Y' = a + bX$$ Formula 6-1

where Y' = predicted VO_2 max value
   a = intercept of the regression line
   b = slope of the regression line
   X = score on the 1.5-mile run expressed as minutes

The a and b values are presented by the test developer but can be calculated using simple formulas found in elementary statistics textbooks. The value for X, the examinee's score on the 1.5-mile run, is inserted in Formula 6-1, and Y', the estimated VO_2max, is then calculated. In the Getchell et al. (1977) report, the following regression equation was presented for college women:

$$Y' = 98.3 - 4.182X \qquad \text{Formula 6-2}$$

Suppose that a woman in a college conditioning course ran the 1.5-mile run in 12 minutes. Using Formula 6-2,

$$Y' = 98.3 - (4.182)(12)$$
$$= 48.1 \text{ (estimated } Vo_2 \text{max)}$$

How much faith can be placed in this estimated value? This depends on the care with which the test developer carried out the study. Factors such as sample size, standard error of estimate, and cross-validation must be considered.

The steps for conducting a predictive validity study are relatively straightforward:

1. Draw a random sample of approximately 200 subjects. Randomization is sometimes not possible; using the entire population is equally acceptable. If neither alternative is possible, the size of the sample should still be substantial.
2. Administer the predictor and criterion tests.
3. Correlate the predictor and criterion tests. If the validity coefficient is sizable, proceed with the next step.
4. Randomly divide the sample into two groups of equal size (100 in each group). Randomization is an essential process. Using group 1, calculate the intercept (a) and the slope (b) for the regression equation. These formulas are not included in this textbook but can be easily obtained in an elementary statistics book. Using the scores from group 2, apply the unknowns (a and b) from the first group's equation and estimate the Y values for group 2 (even though in reality these values are already known).
5. Since criterion test scores are available for group 2, these scores can be compared with the estimated criterion scores obtained in step 4. This process is known as cross-validation. The closer the two values, the more accurate the estimate. The use of a statistic known as the standard error of estimate provides a means of evaluating the accuracy of the estimate. The standard error of estimate can be calculated using Formula 6-3:

$$s_{y-x} = s_y\sqrt{1 - r_{xy}^2} \qquad \text{Formula 6-3}$$

where s_{y-x} = standard error of estimate
  s_y = standard deviation of the group on the criterion test
  r_{xy}^2 = square of the correlation coefficient between the predictor and the criterion test

If the standard error of estimate is sufficiently small, the estimate of the criterion score can be viewed as accurate.

The application of predictive validity in predicting future behavior uses one or more predictor variables to predict criterion behavior at some future point. Within this context, scores on the predictor and criterion variables are not obtained at the same time. Although this may initially seem strange, it actually is the only logical way to proceed. When future behavior is being predicted, the interest focuses on the person's future performance instead of present performance. For instance, one may want to predict the degree of success before the team members are selected; yet the success of the athlete would be unknown until the end of the season. Thus this is a more difficult type of predictive validity to determine. Fortunately, a test developer will handle the difficult part. The concern here is how well the predictor works.

Let's look at an example of predicting future behavior from the sports psychology literature. A number of studies have centered on the psychological factors that can be used to predict success in sport. For example, Morgan and Johnson (1978) studied the psychological characteristics of highly skilled oarsmen. For many years all entering freshmen at the University of Wisconsin were required to take the Minnesota Multiphasic Personality Inventory (MMPI). Using the scores on the MMPI, Morgan and Johnson evaluated the psychological profiles of successful and unsuccessful oarsmen on the University of Wisconsin teams. Successful oarsmen tended to be less anxious, depressed, angry, fatigued, confused, and neurotic, and more vigorous and extroverted. In 1974 at a training camp for potential Olympic oarsmen, the investigators administered a similar battery of psychological scales to all 57 candidates at the camp. No one, not even the investigators themselves, knew of the results of the psychological tests until the end of the training camp session. (Not until after the Olympic team members had been selected did Morgan and Johnson prepare the psychological profiles of the total group of candidates, since knowledge of these results might have influenced the coaches' decisions in making selections.)

After the team members had been selected, the psychological profiles were compared with the profiles of successful and unsuccessful oarsmen identified in Morgan and Johnson's earlier work. Based on these comparisons, each member of the group at the training camp was classified as successful (likely to be chosen for the Olympic team) or unsuccessful (unlikely to be chosen). Of course, at that point they knew who the actual team members were. Therefore Morgan and Johnson were able to compare their predictions with the actual results, as shown in Table 6-2. This is known as a contingency table.

Of the 57 candidates, 10 were accurately predicted for the Success category and 31 for the Fail category. The profiles accurately predicted 63% (10/16 = 0.625) of the oarsmen selected for the team and 76% (31/41 = 0.76) of those rejected. Thus psychological variables alone cannot be used to predict team membership, although knowledge of these variables can contribute to the accuracy of prediction.

Before proceeding to the next example, be sure you understand how to read a contingency table, since they are discussed in the next chapter. Do you under-

Table 6-2   Evaluation of the Clinical (a priori) Prediction Model's Accuracy

Actual Category	Predicted Category		Total
	Success	Fail	
Success	10	6	16
Fail	10	31	41
TOTAL	20	37	57

From Morgan, WP, Johnson RW.

stand how the 63% success rate in predicting team membership was determined? The 76% success rate in rejection?

In a more recent study, Morgan and Raven (1985) evaluated the effectiveness of trait anxiety in predicting respiratory distress during heavy physical work performed by subjects wearing an industrial respirator. The predictor test, the Spielberger State-Trait Anxiety Inventory, was administered to all subjects on the first day of the experiment. The criterion measure was a 7-point perceived exertion scale designed to assess respiratory distress. The subjects performed three submaximal exercise tests at light, moderate, and heavy work intensities. Of the 45 subjects, six were predicted to manifest respiratory distress and 5 actually did (Table 6-3). This represented a hit rate of 83% (5/6). Thirty-nine subjects were expected not to display respiratory distress, and 38 did not. The hit rate for this prediction was 97% (38/39). Thus this predictive validity study demonstrated that it is possible to identify individuals who are likely to experience respiratory distress when performing heavy work and wearing an industrial respirator.

Construct-Related Evidence of Validity

The last type of validity to be examined in this textbook is construct-related evidence of validity. *Construct validity* can be defined as the degree to which a test measures an attribute or trait that cannot be directly measured. Think about an attribute like athletic ability. Everyone assumes such an attribute exists, but it cannot be measured directly. Of course, certain aspects of athletic ability can be measured, but as a whole athletic ability defies precise measurement. Athletic ability can be thought of as a construct, a trait that cannot be directly measured.

Another example of a construct is anxiety, often an attribute of concern in athletics. Measuring the sweatiness of palms, administering an anxiety inventory, and checking heart rate or blood pressure are ways to determine if a person is anxious. However, these are merely indicators of anxiety. Anxiety cannot really be measured directly. Although a construct cannot be measured precisely, indicators of the construct behavior are often measured. How is this type of test validated, since no criterion test is available?

Table 6-3 Prediction of Distress for Individuals Wearing Industrial Respirators

	Predicted Respiratory Distress		
Actual Respiratory Distress	**Yes**	**No**	**Total**
Yes	5	1	6
No	1	38	39
TOTAL	6	39	45

From Morgan WP, Raven PB.

Group Differences Method

There are many ways of determining construct validity. One typical approach is the **group differences method.** Let's use Kenyon's Attitude Toward Physical Activity Inventory (Kenyon, 1968) as an example. One of the scales in the Kenyon inventory is labeled "vertigo." Essentially this scale is a measure of the risk-taking capacity of an individual in situations involving vigorous physical activity. How should this scale be validated? Logically, persons who participate in forms of vigorous physical activity involving risk taking would be more likely to obtain high scores on the scale than sedentary persons. For example, a group of mountain climbers should score significantly higher on the scale than a group of sedentary office workers. If not, the validity of the scale is questionable. Comparing two groups' scores, which are expected to differ, is one way of providing evidence of construct validity. This can be accomplished using a *t*-test, which was described in Chapter 4. The group difference method alone does not establish construct validity; many pieces of evidence are required for this purpose.

Another example of the use of the group-difference approach is to compare groups on scores on the health and fitness scale of the Kenyon inventory. Persons who are known to be highly fit should score higher than those who are not (e.g., sedentary office workers). If those with a high level of CR function do not score higher than those with low CR function, the construct validity of the scale would be open to question.

Convergent and Discriminant Validity

Another approach to determining construct validity is to compare the measuring instrument with other tests. Let's assume we wish to measure physical activity, and we would like to use a questionnaire rather than a more direct measure such as a heart rate monitor. [*Note:* There are now reasonably valid survey instruments that can be used to measure physical activity. (See Hensley, Ainsworth, and Ansorge, 1993, for more information.)] We would expect our questionnaire to correlate fairly well with other questionnaires measuring physical activity. This is referred to as **convergent validity.** On the other hand, we would expect the questionnaire to have a low correlation with another questionnaire measuring social activity. This is known as **discriminant validity.**

An example of convergent validity can be drawn from a study by Pate and colleagues (1993). As part of an investigation of the validity of upper-body measures of muscular strength, the authors correlated scores on five field tests (i.e., pull-ups, flexed-arm hang, push-ups, Vermont modified pull-ups, and New York modified pull-ups). The correlations ranged from .21 to .71, with over half reflecting moderate convergent validity.

Interpretation of the Validity Coefficient

When selecting a test, one of the factors to be evaluated is the size of the validity coefficient. How high should the coefficient be to be acceptable? If the test is being used as a substitute for a more sophisticated but impractical test, the validity coefficient should be high. Generally, coefficients of .90 and above are desirable, but those exceeding .80 are acceptable. Squaring the correlation coefficient demonstrates the amount of variance common to both tests, that is, the extent to which the two tests are measuring the same attribute. Thus a lower coefficient would not be acceptable. For a validity coefficient of .50, only 25% of the variance of the test and of the criterion measure overlap. For the most part these tests are measuring different qualities.

When a test is constructed for predictive purposes, a lower validity coefficient may sometimes be acceptable. Even tests with validity estimates of .50 or .60 may be retained. The key question is whether the test does a better job of predicting than any other method, that is, is the test superior to another test or a subjective method of making the prediction? The accuracy of the prediction increases as the size of the validity coefficient increases.

RELIABILITY

One of the most confusing points in measurement to the beginning student is the definition of test reliability. The reliability of a test refers to the dependability of scores, their relative freedom from error. *Reliability* is popularly defined as the consistency of an individual in performing a test. Suppose an examinee took a test once and then was able to go back in time as if the test had never been taken. Then suppose the same test was administered again. We would expect the scores on the two tests to be quite similar. If not, the test would be unreliable. If a test is administered at the end of a unit of instruction, we assume the scores will represent a stable level of achievement. In other words, if the test were administered again the next day, the test scores would be similar to those obtained on the first day.

The definition of reliability as consistency is both meaningful and appropriate; however, when reliability is estimated within a norm-referenced framework, a more complex definition is implied. The term *reliability* reflects the ability of the test to detect reliable differences between examinees; that is, given that the test was administered on two occasions to the same students, the same differences between students would be detected. Remember that a norm-referenced test is designed to reflect individual differences; thus this interpretation of reliability makes sense.

A test can be reliable without being valid, but a valid test has to be reliable. Reliability, then, refers to the consistency, not the general worthiness or validity, of the test. For example, suppose a physical education teacher administers a test of the football place kick from the 20-yard line. An assistant holds the ball in place on the tee, and the student taking the test kicks the ball 10 times to complete the test. The test may be highly reliable, but its validity might be questioned, especially if the examinees have had previous experience playing football. One way of improving the validity is to snap the ball to an assistant, who must place the ball on the tee before the kick. There is a tradeoff, however, in that the increased complexity of the test would probably reduce its reliability. The fewer variables associated with the test, the more reliable the test.

The same point can be exemplified using another test. A popular test in volleyball classes is the wall volley test, designed to measure volleying skill. Generally the test score is the number of times the ball hits the wall, with certain distance and height restrictions. A student might be able to perform the test reliably, yet use poor form, executing the skill poorly and perhaps illegally by game rules. Reliability does not ensure validity.

Types of Reliability

Most developers of motor performance tests do not provide much information about test reliability. Often a reliability coefficient is presented with little explanation. The coefficient will usually be symbolized by either $r_{xx'}$, the interclass correlation (or Pearson product-moment correlation) coefficient, or $R_{xx'}$, the intraclass correlation coefficient. Both of these symbols represent correlation coefficients, but the second represents a more informative estimate. Both reflect the ratio of true scores to obtained scores. A true score is the score a person would obtain on a test if there were no measurement error. An obtained score is the sum of true score plus error score. A true score is unknown but can be estimated by determining measurement error and subtracting it from the obtained score. The two reliability estimates mentioned represent the ratio of the true score to the obtained score.

The types of reliability described in the next sections are those most likely seen in the physical education field. These types, shown in Figure 6-2, are single-test administration, test-retest reliability, and precision of an individual test score.

Single-Test Administration

The reliability of a test can be estimated from a single administration of the test on any one occasion. The resultant interclass reliability coefficient estimates the reliability of the test at one point. There is no guarantee that an examinee's score on the test would be similar if the test were administered again the next

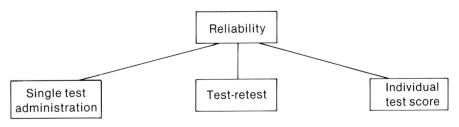

Figure 6-2   Types of reliability.

day. However, sometimes this does not matter. For instance, sports competition anxiety can be measured using an inventory developed by Martens (1977). Test users would not use this inventory unless it measured with consistency the anxiety level of an athlete before a game. However, the athlete would not be expected to obtain the same score the next day (even if another game was being played) or even after the game ended. Anxiety levels usually fluctuate, depending on the situation.

If a student is repeatedly tested during the time a skill is being learned, one might not expect his or her scores to be consistent from one day to the next. The student has been taught more about the skill before the second testing period. One point should be clarified before proceeding. Whenever test developers administer a test more than once to establish reliability, it does not mean that all tests users are expected to give the test twice. However, this information is important to know when selecting a test. If test reliability was established based on one administration of the test on a single occasion, the test is expected to elicit reliable performance only for that occasion. If test reliability was established based on two administrations of the test, each one on a different occasion, the test is expected to be reliable for that general period of time. If a test is used in a situation different from that proposed by the test developer, test reliability must be reestablished.

Now, how is the reliability of a test established when the test is administered on one occasion only? Either of two procedures for estimating reliability can be used. One is the Pearson product-moment correlation coefficient ($r_{xx'}$) (see Formula 3-9). The test must consist of at least two trials. If more than two trials are used, the trials must be reduced (usually by averaging) to two sets. You will recall that the correlation coefficient estimates the relationship between two sets of scores. In Chapter 3 the two sets of scores represented different variables, similar to the validity coefficients in this chapter. The reliability coefficient, however, represents two sets of scores on the same variable.

The second method is the intraclass correlation coefficient, known as $R_{xx'}$. This coefficient is estimated by calculating an analysis of variance. Generally, $r_{xx'}$ and $R_{xx'}$ are interpreted similarly. However, $R_{xx'}$ is a more accurate estimate of reliability for two reasons. First, it is not necessary to reduce the trials to two sets to calculate $R_{xx'}$. This is important because many tests of motor skill consist of more than two trials. A major portion of the test error could occur among

Table 6-4   Systematic Increase in Scores from Day 1 to Day 2

Student	Test 1, Day 1	Test 1, Day 2
A	2	20
B	4	40
C	6	60
D	8	80
E	10	100
	30	300
	$\overline{X} = 6$	$\overline{X} = 60$
	$s = 3.16$	$s = 31.62$

trials, but this would not be detected when $r_{xx'}$ is used. Second, if trial scores increase or decrease systematically, this should lower the reliability of the test. Yet these changes do not affect $r_{xx'}$. This fact can be verified by examining the scores in Table 6-4. Note that the scores on Test 2 are much higher than the Test 1 scores. However, $r_{xx'}$ equals + 1.00, reflecting perfect reliability. It is obvious that the examinees' performances were not consistent. Detailed information on the calculation of the intraclass correlation coefficient can be found in the instructor's manual accompanying this textbook.

Another way of estimating reliability on the basis of a single test administration is to divide the test into halves and correlate the two half-tests. This is referred to as a split-half reliability estimate. This procedure was originally devised for written tests but was subsequently used with tests in the exercise sciences. For example, the reliability of a 10-trial test of a sports skill could be determined by correlating the average of one set of five trial scores with the average of the scores on the remaining five trials. There are several ways the trials could be split. Two possibilities are a first half–second half split, where the two halves consist of trials 1 to 5 and trials 6 to 10, or an odd-even split, where the two halves consist of trials 1, 3, 5, 7, and 9 and trials 2, 4, 6, 8, and 10.

The odd-even split is used most frequently in tests of motor skill to guard against the possibility of fatigue or lack of motivation affecting performance on the last few trials of the test. To illustrate, let's use an extreme example. Suppose we were interested in the reliability of a 10-trial shuttle run test. If the division into halves was accomplished using a first half–second half split, the average of the first five trials is likely to be lower (better performance) than the average of the last five trials. This would result in a lower reliability estimate. If an odd-even split were used, the average of the odd-numbered trials would probably be similar to the average of the even-numbered trials. This comparison is demonstrated in Figure 6-3.

If a first half–second half split is used, the average of the last five trials (11.44

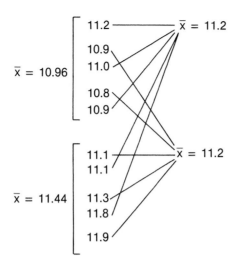

Figure 6-3   Comparison of odd-even split with first half–second half split using 10 shuttle run test scores (seconds).

seconds) clearly differs from the average of the first five trials (10.96 seconds), as shown in Figure 6-3. This is probably caused by the effect of fatigue. An odd-even split, on the other hand, yields identical averages for the odd-numbered and the even-numbered trials.

Once a test is split in halves and the averages of the halves determined, these scores can be correlated to yield $r_{xx'}$. However, since only half the test has been correlated with the other half, the resultant reliability coefficient represents an estimate for a five-trial test. We, of course, would like to know how reliable a 10-trial test would be. The formula used to estimate the reliability of the full length (in this case, 10-trial) test, called the Spearman-Brown prophecy formula, is shown in Formula 6-4.

$$r_{xx'}^* = \frac{n r_{xx'}}{1 + (n - 1) r_{xx'}}$$ Formula 6-4

where n = number of times the test length is increased
  $r_{xx'}$ = reliability of half of the test length
  $r_{xx'}^*$ = estimated reliability for the full test length

If the correlation between half-tests of a 10-trial test is .60, the estimated reliability of the full-length test would be .75. In this case, n = 2. Longer tests are expected to be more reliable than shorter ones.

The Spearman-Brown prophecy formula generally provides an overestimate of the actual reliability of the full-length test. Intraclass correlation procedures can also be used to estimate the reliability of a shortened or lengthened test.

Test-Retest Reliability

If a test is used to assess achievement on a skill at the end of a unit of instruction, obtaining a test score that reflects the examinee's skill level with precision would be desirable. The assessment would be inaccurate if some examinees who obtained high scores on the day testing took place would have received low scores if the test had been administered on a second day. To avoid this possibility the test user should look for a test with an acceptable reliability coefficient that has been established in a test-retest context. Test-retest reliability is also known as stability reliability.

Either of the two correlational procedures described in the previous section would be appropriate for estimating the reliability in a test-retest context. The split-half procedure, however, is not appropriate in this setting. See instructor's manual for details on calculating $R_{xx'}$.

Precision of an Individual Test Score

Thus far reliability estimates that are determined for groups have been discussed. In other words, the reliability coefficient is appropriate for a group of examinees, such as a class of students. Sometimes it is of greater interest to evaluate the reliability of an individual examinee's score. This can be done using the standard error of measurement. Any time a person takes a test, the test score will be subject to measurement error. If this error is small, we are confident that the person would receive a similar score if the test were taken again. A larger error, on the other hand, suggests we can have little confidence in the score because it could be vastly different if the test were taken again.

Let us assume we could administer a test to an examinee 1,000 times, with each administration completely independent of the others. We could plot a distribution of these 1,000 scores as described in Chapter 2. The standard deviation of this distribution of scores is the standard error of measurement for the examinee. As the examinee's scores become more similar, the standard error of measurement becomes smaller. Thus a smaller standard error of measurement is associated with a more precise score. This differs from other types of reliability discussed previously, where higher values of $r_{xx'}$ and $R_{xx'}$ represent greater consistency.

Since a test cannot be administered repeatedly, the standard error of measurement is estimated using Formula 6-5.

$$SE_m = s\sqrt{1 - r_{xx'}}$$ Formula 6-5

where SE_m = standard error of measurement
s = standard deviation of a group of examinees
$r_{xx'}$ = reliability coefficient

Suppose, for example, that the standard deviation of a set of Shuttle Run Test scores is 2 seconds and the test reliability is .84.

$$SE_m = 2\sqrt{1 - .84}$$
$$= 0.80 \text{ seconds}$$

How is an SE_m of .80 interpreted? First, it represents seconds in this case. In other words, the SE_m for the shuttle run test is 0.80 second. The SE_m is always presented in the actual score units of the test. Now, suppose Mary obtained a score of 9.8 seconds on the shuttle run test. How precise is her score? The SE_m can be used to form a band around the examinee's score. The smaller the band, the more precise the score. Remember that the SE_m is actually a standard deviation. Thus if a ± 1 SE_m band around Mary's score is used, it would be expected to span her true score 68% of the time. The SE_m is subtracted from Mary's score to obtain the lower bound of the band and added to obtain the upper bound. In this example Mary's band is 9.0 to 10.6 seconds. If Mary repeatedly took the shuttle run test, we would not necessarily expect her scores to be close to the original 9.8 seconds, since the SE_m band is relatively large. As the band decreases in size, we can have more faith in the precision of Mary's score.

The SE_m can also be used in comparing two persons' test scores. Assume two college men have taken a physical fitness test battery. John executes 60 sit-ups and Mark performs 55. John says he did better on the test than Mark. If only the two scores are considered, John is right. However, we know there was measurement error associated with each score. If we take this error into account, then we will be able to state with greater accuracy whether John's and Mark's scores differed. The SE_m for the sit-ups test for college men was found to be 7 sit-ups. The ± 1 SE_m band for John would be 53 to 67 sit-ups and for Mark, 48 to 62 sit-ups. Note that John's and Mark's SE_m bands overlap; therefore, we cannot say with certainty that their test performances were different. If the two men took the test again, Mark might even do more sit-ups than John!

Only when the two SE_m bands do not overlap can we be confident that two performances are indeed different. Let's take another example, this time using a test of aerobic capacity. Two high-school girls obtain VO_2max scores of 40 mL/kg/min and 47 mL/kg/min. The SE_m for this test is 3 mL/kg/min. Taking this error into account, the two ± 1 SE_m bands are 37 to 43 mL/kg/min and 44 to 50 mL/kg/min. Because these bands do not overlap, we can state with confidence that the aerobic capacity of the two girls is different.

To summarize, the SE_m provides an indicator of the precision of an individual's test score. The smaller the SE_m, the greater the reliability of the score. By forming a SE_m band around an examinee's score, the extent of the measurement error can be examined.

Factors Influencing the Reliability of a Test

Numerous factors influence the reliability of a test. Many of the factors are more important to test developers than test users, but knowledge of a few of these factors helps in selecting a test with acceptable reliability. See Figure 6-4 for an overview of the factors to be described in the next sections.

Type of Test

To expect the reliability of all tests in our field to be .90 or above is not reasonable. The type of test must be taken into account when interpreting the reliabil-

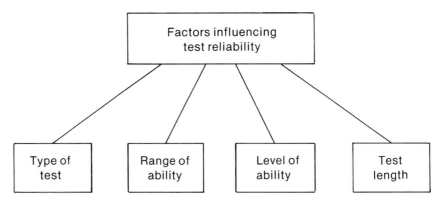

Figure 6-4   Factors influencing test reliability.

ity of a test. If performance on the test requires a maximum expenditure of effort, it is reasonable to expect reliabilities of around .80 or higher. For example, a grip strength test is taken by squeezing a hand dynamometer as hard as possible. This requires all-out physical effort. Performance on this test ought to be highly reliable. This is also true for measures of the long jump, vertical jump, dashes, distance throw, and similar abilities. The greater the force requirements (throw as hard as possible, jump as far as possible, squeeze the hand dynamometer as hard as possible), the higher the reliability coefficient should be.

As the accuracy demands of a test increase, reliability decreases. To expect reliability coefficients to be .80 or higher in most instances is not reasonable. In fact, a test primarily measuring accuracy, such as a test of the chip shot in golf or the short serve in badminton, might be acceptable with a reliability estimate of .70, assuming satisfactory validity. At the same time estimates below .70 are rarely acceptable, regardless of the type of test, even though reliability estimates theoretically range from .00 to 1.00. Negative reliability coefficients are uninterpretable. A test can be reliable or it can have little or no reliability.

Range of Ability

When reliability is estimated using test scores from a group with a wide range of ability, the estimate is artificially inflated. For example, assume that a test of the softball throw for distance is given to a group of children in grades 2 through 6. In this case, reliability is almost guaranteed to be high. The children in sixth grade will throw the ball farther than the second graders, primarily because sixth graders are bigger and stronger than second graders. This would be true as often as the test is repeated. In a relative sense the test is highly reliable. On the other hand, it is more informative to know whether the test is reliable for sixth graders—or second graders—and this suggests that reliability must be estimated for each grade separately. Although the scores will still fluctuate within each grade, the reliability estimate for each grade will not be an artifact of a wide range of ability. In short, when planning to test sixth graders, select a test with acceptable reliability for sixth-grade children.

Level of Ability

Closely related to range of ability is level of ability and its effect on reliability. In physical education there has been a tendency to expect skilled individuals to perform with more consistency than beginners. Therefore a specific skills test might be more reliable when administered to a highly skilled player. Interestingly enough, research in motor development has not totally verified this assumption. When a number of basic movement patterns are measured, poorly skilled individuals—presumably beginners in learning the pattern—tend to display highly reliable performances. They may not be very good, but they are consistent in their performance! As they learn more about the movement pattern—presumably moving up to intermediate level—their performances become less reliable. This may seem incongruous, but an intermediate-level performer is refining the movement pattern. At the advanced level these individuals become more consistent, with highly reliable performance. At this level the performer has begun to have control over the potential error and can perform with relative consistency.

Test Length

The reliability of a test can be increased by making it longer. This is a well-established fact. When measuring sports skills, increasing the number of trials will lead to a higher reliability estimate. Adding more items to a written test will have the same effect.

Significance of the Reliability Coefficient

As we discussed in Chapter 4, one way of interpreting the correlation coefficient is to test its significance. Essentially, the coefficient is tested to determine whether it is significantly different from zero. However, this type of interpretation does not readily extend to the reliability coefficient. The most meaningful interpretation of the reliability coefficient is to assess the practical significance of the coefficient.

When reliability is estimated for a small sample size (e.g., 10), the resultant reliability coefficient is likely to be highly unstable. Morrow and Jackson (1993) suggest 30 subjects are needed for a stable coefficient when the outcome is a very high coefficient (e.g., >.90). Larger sample sizes (e.g., 50) are needed to produce stable but smaller coefficients.

OBJECTIVITY OF SCORING

The degree of accuracy in scoring a test is often referred to as the objectivity of the test. If a test is labeled highly objective, this means there will be little error in scoring the test. Many persons could score the test and obtain the same result. A subjective test might be scored quite differently, depending upon the scorer. Variability among scorers increases when the scorer is required to make judgments that are more subjective, as in rating playing ability in a sport.

When a target is used to score a test or when a distance is measured, the test can be scored at a high level of objectivity. The objectivity is so obvious that an estimate of objectivity is rarely calculated. As the subjectivity of the test increases, the test developer is obligated to report an objectivity estimate. There are two types of objectivity, as depicted in Figure 6-5.

Intrajudge objectivity, the first type of objectivity, is the consistency in scoring when a test user scores the same test two or more times. If a written test is being considered, intrajudge objectivity can easily be determined. A set of tests can be graded once, put aside until a later date, and then graded again by the same person. Comparison of the two sets of scores would reflect the consistency of the scorer in scoring the test. In testing motor skills, estimates of intrajudge objectivity are more difficult to obtain because the same performance must be viewed twice. This is usually facilitated by recording the performance on film or videotape.

The second type of objectivity is *interjudge objectivity,* which is the consistency between two or more independent judgments of the same performance. Interjudge objectivity is an important part of rating events in gymnastics, diving, and figure skating, where several judges rate each performance.

Both types of objectivity can be estimated using correlational procedures similar to estimating reliability. The estimates are expected to be relatively high (.80 or above), because lower values suggest that the judges are weighting the various components of skill differently. When checklists are used to measure performance, the exact agreement method (Robertson, 1977; Langendorfer, 1987; Langendorfer and Bruya, 1994) is used. Langendorfer and Bruya (1994) describe the procedure for determining exact agreement between observers. First, using two observers, the decision rules are learned so that both observers are observing the same features of the behavior. Both observers independently observe the behavior, either live or on videotape, on two different occasions. The observations of the two observers are compared for each day. The total number of agreements between observers is divided by the total possible observations and multiplied by 100. The exact agreement index should be 80% or more. This same procedure can be used with one observer over two occasions to determine intrajudge exact agreement. Further training is necessary if the agreement index is below 80%.

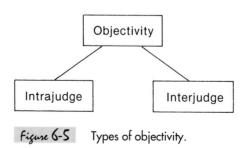

Figure 6-5   Types of objectivity.

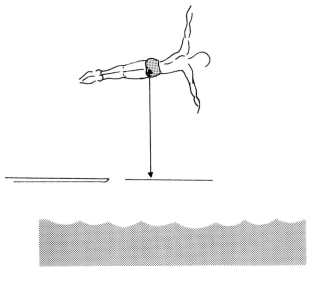

Figure 6-6   Measurement of maximum height of diver in front half-twist dive.

A method has been proposed to objectify judging of springboard diving (McCormick et al., 1982). For example, a videotape recording can be made of the front half-twist dive, and clear plastic grids are placed over the video monitor to measure various components of the dive, such as deviation of twist from 180 degrees. A total of four measures can be used to predict judges' scores—height of the diver above the board (see Figure 6-6), the distance out from the board, twist, and one or two angle measurements.

Efforts to identify the sources of biasing factors in judging motor performances have been numerous. Although knowing whether judges agree in their ratings is useful, knowing why they differ is more important. The possibility of reducing the bias and increasing the objectivity of ratings then exists.

SUMMARY

The characteristics of a test should be carefully evaluated before its administration to a group of examinees. Test validity, reliability, and objectivity are of major importance. Validity is the soundness of the interpretation of the test. It can be established on logical or statistical grounds or on both. Through a logical analysis evidence of content validity can be demonstrated for a written test, and evidence of logical validity can be demonstrated for a test of motor performance. Statistical evidence is used to determine criterion-related validity, and both logical and statistical information are needed to establish construct validity. Reliability is the consistency of performance on a test. Test reliability can be established for a single occasion or a general period of time. Either $r_{xx'}$ or $R_{xx'}$ can be used as reliability coefficients, although $R_{xx'}$ is generally viewed as the superior estimate. Objectivity is the accuracy of scoring a test. Statistical evidence of this characteristic should be provided when the scoring is subjective, as in gymnastics and diving. A good test will possess high levels of all three of these elements.

Learning Experiences

1. Select a test you might consider using in the future. (Examples of a wide variety of tests can be found in Chapters 18 to 21.) Carefully evaluate its evidence of validity, reliability, and objectivity. Suggest ways in which each of these test characteristics might be improved for the test you selected.
2. Develop a simple rating scale for a skill in a sport such as basketball. (See Chapter 15 for information on developing rating scales.) Attend a game with a friend who is also in your measurement and evaluation course, and use the scale to rate the skill. Do not try to rate more than one player. Each of you should independently rate the same person. Periodically compare ratings; if they are discrepant, discuss ways of improving the use of the scale or the scale itself.
3. Six trials of a basketball shooting test were administered to each of five students. Using this data set, answer the three questions below.

Student	Trial 1	Trial 2	Trial 3	Trial 4	Trial 5	Trial 6
A	10	11	11	12	11	12
B	14	13	14	14	15	14
C	12	12	12	13	12	13
D	9	8	8	9	9	8
E	7	9	8	8	9	9

   a. Calculate the split-half reliability coefficient for this six-trial test. Use an odd-even split.
   b. Use the Spearman-Brown formula to estimate the reliability coefficient for six trials.
   c. Briefly interpret this coefficient.

Answers to Learning Experiences

3a. The mean of the odd trials and the mean of the even trials should be determined for each person.

Student	Odd ($\bar{X}$)	Even ($\bar{X}'$)	$\overline{XX'}$
A	10.67	11.67	124.52
B	14.33	13.67	195.89
C	12.00	12.67	152.04
D	8.67	8.33	72.22
E	8.00	8.67	69.36

Use the Pearson product-moment correlation coefficient formula to determine the correlation between the odd (X) and even (X') means (Formula 3-9). The following values are needed for the formula:

$$\Sigma X = 53.67$$

$$\Sigma X' = 55.01$$

$$\Sigma XX' = 614.03$$

$$\Sigma X^2 = 602.37$$

$$\Sigma X'^2 = 628.14$$

$$(\Sigma X)^2 = 2880.47$$

$$(\Sigma X')^2 = 3026.10$$

$$r_{xx'} = \frac{5(614.03) - 2952.39}{\sqrt{[5(602.37) - 2880.47][5(628.16) - 3026.10]}}$$

$$= \frac{117.76}{122.76} = .959$$

3b. The answer to 3a is the reliability for a three-trial test, since the six-trial test was split into three halves to obtain the reliability coefficient. The reliability of the six-trial test must now be estimated using the Spearman-Brown prophecy formula (Formula 6-4):

$$r_{xx'}^* = \frac{2(.959)}{1 + (2 - 1)(.959)}$$

$$= \frac{117.76}{122.70} = .979$$

3c. The estimated reliability of the six-trial test (.979) is quite high, indicating that the basketball test is a reliable measure of performance. Since the three-trial test reliability (.959) is also high, this suggests that administering the full-length six-trial test to measure performance adequately is not necessary. A three-trial test would be adequate.

References

American Psychological Association (APA). 1985. Joint standards for educational and psychological tests. Washington, DC: American Psychological Association.

Cooper KH. 1968. A means of assessing maximal oxygen intake. Journal of the American Medical Association, **203**:201–204.

Getchell LH, Kirkendall D, Robbins G. 1977. Prediction of maximal oxygen uptake in young adult women joggers. Research Quarterly, **48**:61–67.

Hensley LD, Ainsworth BE, Ansorge CJ. 1993. Assessment of physical activity —Professional accountability is promoting active lifestyles. Journal of Physical Education, Recreation, and Dance, **64**(1):56–64.

Kenyon GS. 1968. Six scales for assessing attitude toward physical activity. Research Quarterly, **39**:566–574.

Langendorfer SJ. 1987. A prelongitudinal test of motor stage theory. Research Quarterly for Exercise and Sport, **58**:21–29.

Langendorfer SJ, Bruya LD. 1994. Aquatic readiness: Developing water competence in young children. Champaign, Ill: Human Kinetics.

Martens R. 1977. Sport Competition Anxiety Test. Champaign, Ill: Human Kinetics.

McCormick JH, Subbaiah P, Arnold HJ. 1982. A method for identification of some components of judging springboard diving. Research Quarterly for Exercise and Sport, **53**:313–322.

Morgan WP, Johnson RW. 1978. Personality characteristics of successful and unsuccessful oarsmen. International Journal of Sport Psychology, **9**:119–133.

Morgan WP, Raven PB. 1985. Prediction of distress for individuals wearing industrial respirators. American Industrial Hygiene Association Journal, **46**:363–368.

Morrow JR, Jackson AW. 1993. How "significant" is your reliability? Research Quarterly for Exercise and Sport, **64**:352–355.

Pate RR, Burgess ML, Woods JA, Ross JG, Baumgartner TA. 1993. Validity of fields tests of upper body muscular strength. Research Quarterly for Exercise and Sport, **64**:17–24.

Roberton MA. 1977. Stability of stage categorizations across trials: Implications for the "Stage Theory" of overarm throw development. Journal of Human Movement Studies, **3**:49–59.

Wood TM. 1989. The changing nature of norm-referenced validity. In: Safrit MJ, Wood TM, eds. Measurement concepts in physical education and exercise science. Champaign, Ill: Human Kinetics Publishers, Chapt. 2.

Annotated Readings

Brown FG. 1983. Principles of educational and psychological testing, ed 3. Lavallette, NJ: Holt, Rinehart & Winston.

Thorough coverage of both theory and techniques of educational and psychological testing: presents basic concepts in testing validity, reliability, and types of scores—and illustrates how to apply those principles in test construction, use, evaluation, and interpretation; explores rationale underlying educational and psychological testing.

Gronlund NE. 1985. Measurement and evaluation in teaching ed 5. New York: Macmillan.

Emphasizes principles and procedures of testing and evaluation important to elementary and secondary teachers; assumes no prior knowledge of measurement or statistics; illustrates both norm-referenced and criterion-referenced test specifications.

Mehrens WA, Lehrman IJ. 1984. Measurement and evaluation in education and psychology, ed 3. Lavallette, NJ: Holt, Rinehart & Winston.

Introduction to the construction, evaluation, interpretation, and uses of tests; offers a contemporary look at testing and some of its practical applications; includes updated discussion of criterion-referenced measurement; contains detailed information on the practical uses of assessment data; covers current issues in testing.

Noll VH, Scannell DP, Craig RC. 1979. Introduction to educational measurement, ed 4. Boston: Houghton Mifflin.

Nontechnical orientation to educational measurement; includes thorough coverage of criterion-referenced tests and national and state assessment programs.

Validity and Reliability of Criterion-Referenced Tests

Watch for these words as you read the following chapter

Contingency
  coefficient
Contrasting groups
  method
Criterion-referenced
  test
Decision validity
Domain

Instructed/
  uninstructed group
  comparison
Kappa coefficient
Mastery learning
Proportion of
  agreement
Reliability

Scores on a test can be meaningful interpreted in many ways. For example, a score can be converted to a percentile and thereby be compared with a normative group. This is an example of a norm-referenced measurement. When a criterion-referenced test is used, the score is compared with a standard reflecting a minimally acceptable level of behavior.

Although many published tests in physical education and exercise science are norm-referenced, a great deal of informal testing goes on in the field that is more similar to the criterion-referenced approach to testing (Safrit, 1981). A physical education teacher, for example, may set a standard that students are expected to achieve on a test. Those whose test scores equal or surpass the test standard are judged to have displayed the desired behavior. These students might be classified as "masters" on the test, while those whose scores fall below the standard are labeled "nonmasters." In a fitness center clients may be placed in a category reflecting their level of fitness based on the results of a test, or series of tests. People in the top category might be labeled "high fit" while those in the lowest category might be identified as "low fit."

In a situation where there are no constraints on the number of people who can meet the desired standard, a criterion-referenced test is appropriate. When only the top four or five examinees will be selected for a given purpose, a norm-referenced approach is more useful.

CRITERION-REFERENCED TESTS

A *criterion-referenced test* is defined as a test with a predetermined standard of performance, with the standard tied to a specified domain of behavior. There is more to a criterion-referenced test than setting a standard, although standard-setting is certainly important. The standard must be referenced to a criterion behavior. Suppose a fitness center staff member administers a battery of fitness tests to all new clients joining a fitness club. One of these tests is a modified sit-ups test of abdominal strength. A woman who is a new member of the club is classified "average" in abdominal strength based on the test results. The staff member suggests a series of exercises to increase abdominal strength and sets a goal of 45 sit-ups (in 1 minute) for her. How was this standard set? What does it mean? If this is a legitimate criterion-referenced test, the standard should have meaning in terms of criterion behavior. In this case, the criterion should be a minimally desirable amount of abdominal strength and endurance for good health. This means that 45 sit-ups (standard) should reflect adequate abdominal strength for good health (criterion) for women. Of course, there is no way of knowing this is true at the present time. A standard could be arbitrarily set for any test, but it might not be clearly interpretable in light of the criterion behavior.

Even though there are problems in developing a criterion-referenced test, it has certain advantages over a norm-referenced test. A norm-referenced test measures the status of the normative group, that is, "what is" rather than "what should be." For example, consider a measure of body fatness, the sum of a set of skinfold measures. Perhaps these measures are obtained from a large group of adult female examinees and used to estimate their percent body fat. The average percent fat for this group is 36%. Does this reflect a desirable standard for women to attain? This is legitimate normative data. However, it is well-known that many adult women tend to be overweight; therefore, normative data do not represent the most desirable standards in this case.

Furthermore, norm-referenced tests rarely provide extensive diagnostic feedback to the examinee. Think about the many tests you have taken in past years. How often did you receive meaningful feedback on your test score? In physical education few published tests provide specific feedback. All over the United States students are tested on the basketball free throw by taking a predetermined number of shots at the basket. The student who makes most of these

Measuring kicking skills in elementary physical education.

shots gets feedback on his or her skill level. The feedback is "I was successful in making 8 out of 10 free throws; therefore, I am competent in performing this skill." However, the student who misses the shot receives little systematic feedback. In this case, the feedback is "I wasn't successful in making free throws; however, I'm not sure about what to do to improve." If a criterion-referenced test is tied to a criterion behavior, it will provide needed feedback to the examinee.

Particularly notable are the problems tied to the use of norm-referenced standards in fitness testing. If the standard is too high (e.g., 85%), only a small proportion of children can meet the standard. This tends to discourage students with moderate or low fitness levels from attempting to improve their fitness levels, because they know their chances of ever meeting the standard are slim. The most important interpretation of a fitness test score is the information it provides about the student's health status. If a child takes a test of aerobic capacity, does the child's performance put him or her at a low, medium, or high level of risk for cardiac disease? While we cannot answer this question definitively, there is evidence from adult populations substantiating that people with higher levels of performance have lower risk of cardiac disease (Blair, 1993; Blair et al., 1992; Powell et al., 1987). Even young children can show signs of cardiac disease (Moller et al., 1994). One fitness test, the Prudential FITNESS-GRAM, refers to their fitness standards as health-referenced standards because the standard reflects the child's health state (Cooper Institute for Aerobics Research, 1994).

Setting a Criterion-Referenced Zone

In the Prudential FITNESSGRAM, a unique approach has been taken to standard setting. Rather than setting a specific standard for each fitness test, a Healthy Fitness Zone has been established. Test performance is classified in one of two ways: "Needs Improvement" and "Healthy Fitness Zone." For example, in measuring aerobic capacity (e.g., the One-Mile Walk/Run), the lower end of the Healthy Fitness Zone corresponds closely to a fitness level equal to the upper 60% of the population in terms of aerobic capacity (Cooper Institute for Aerobics Research, 1992). This range is justified on the grounds that there is a significant increase in the death rate of people who are in the lower 20% of the population on aerobic fitness level.

Let's look at the Healthy Fitness Zones for boys and girls on the One Mile Walk/Run. The zone for 12-year-old boys is 11:00 to 8:30; for 12-year-old girls, it is 12:00 to 9:00 (Cooper Institute for Aerobics Research, 1992, p. 46).

This is an innovative approach to standard-setting, and it emphasizes the fact that it is often not meaningful to identify one score as the standard. A range of scores is often more valid.

Measurement as an Integral Part of Learning

Criterion-referenced measurement is an integral part of mastery learning. Emphasis is placed on mastering the skill or consistently displaying the desired behavior.

MASTERY LEARNING

The normal distribution, as described in Chapter 3, can be used in determining norm-referenced grades. Regardless of the ability levels of students, some will receive A's, B's, and so forth, according to a predetermined set of percentages. In a mastery learning setting (Nitko, 1984) a student is expected to be a nonmaster before instruction or a training program. At this point, when tests are administered to the nonmasters, the distribution of scores will be skewed in a positive direction, since most examinees would receive low scores and only a small percentage would receive high scores. At the end of the unit of instruction or a training program, the majority of the group is expected to master the objective. In this case, test scores will be skewed negatively, since only a few people received low scores.

Criterion-referenced testing, then, is closely associated with the mastery model of instruction. Frequently, teachers care little about individual differences. If many students can master the test, so much the better. (Is not the objective of education for all or most students to learn?) Should not a large percentage of the students experience at least minimal success at the end of a unit of instruction? Along the same lines, in a fitness center it would be a positive feature if most of the clients displayed desirable health behaviors. It would defeat the goals of the club if only a small, highly fit group of clients adopted these behaviors. Thus, in many educational and worksite health promotion settings, the norm-referenced approach to testing is not quite appropriate. The criterion-referenced test is better suited to promoting behavior changes.

USES OF A CRITERION-REFERENCED TEST

Criterion-referenced tests have a variety of uses. Sometimes we seek information on a person's capabilities, even though we have no interest in comparing the test score to a standard. For example, a fitness center staff member might be interested in determining the strength of a client by administering one or more strength tests. In this case, only the current status of the person's strength is of interest. The individual is not classified according to some predetermined standard. However, it is much more typical to use a criterion-referenced test to compare scores with a standard of performance.

Several of the national physical fitness tests have attempted to use criterion-referenced standards instead of providing tables of norms in the test manual. In these tests, desirable levels of fitness are promoted rather than normative assessments. The Prudential FITNESSGRAM is a prominent example of these tests.

VALIDITY

The techniques for validating a criterion-referenced test are unique, although there are similarities conceptually to norm-referenced test validity methodology. The general definition of *validity* applies to both norm-referenced tests and criterion-referenced tests; that is, *validity* is the soundness of the interpretation of the test. However, just as specific types of validity have been identified for norm-referenced tests, there are several more specific definitions for types of validity for criterion-referenced tests. These definitions vary according to the type of validity of interest.

Types of Validity

Validity can be determined logically through domain-referenced validity or statistically, using decision validity methods. The focus is on the mastery test, where examinees are classified as masters or nonmasters on the basis of their test score (Safrit, 1989).

Domain-Referenced Validity

Remember that a *criterion-referenced test* has been defined as a measure of performance or behavior referenced to a criterion behavior. To develop a test of this type, the criterion behavior must be defined. Then the test is logically validated by showing that the tasks sampled by the test adequately represent the criterion behavior. This is called **domain-referenced validity,** with the term *domain* used to represent the criterion behavior. This has many parallels with both content and logical validity, which were described in Chapter 6. However, the focus of a criterion-referenced test is much narrower than its norm-referenced counterpart. A criterion-referenced test is usually designed to measure a single objective and is frequently used as a formative evaluation.

How might domain-referenced validity be established for a test of a sports skill? Let's use a test of the basketball jump shot as an example. The first steps in developing the test would be to analyze the skill, identify its most important elements, and devise a test to measure these elements. This is precisely how logical validity is determined, and it is equally appropriate in criterion-referenced testing. Suppose the test specifies that the student take 10 jump shots from a restraining line 15 ft away from the basket. In a physical education class of high-school boys, a standard of 7 out of 10 successful jump shots might be set. This is a typical approach to testing in the physical education field. How is the placement of the restraining line for the test chosen? Usually it is arbitrary, although the distance from the basket would be expected to be realistic. Yet any one of a number of realistic locations might be selected. Would it not be a better test of a boy's jump-shooting ability if he could make successful shots from several points on the court? This diversity would be necessary for the test to have domain-referenced validity. Of course, testing from every possible spot would be impossible. Instead, several spots on the court could be selected, and the test would include taking a jump shot from each of these spots. One way of selecting these spots would be to divide the basketball half-court into sections, as shown in Figure 7-1.

Think of each of the sections in Figure 7-1 as a test item. How many sections should be selected? For the sake of simplicity and practicality, let's use four sections. How should these sections be selected? Drawing a random sample from the entire set does not seem appropriate, because a player is much less likely to attempt a jump shot from certain sections of the court than others. Areas *O* through *S* represent sections seldom used for jump shots; therefore, the

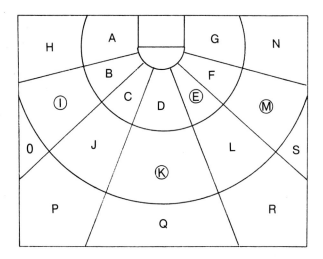

Figure 7-1   Sampling of basketball court areas to test jump shot.

sections to be sampled might reasonably be limited to *A* through *N*. From this set of letters, four can be randomly drawn. Let's say the letters *E, I, K,* and *M* are drawn. These letters are circled in Figure 7-1.

The number of trials to be taken from each area should also be determined. In many instances, more than one trial would be taken from each of the areas to have a reliable test.

Would this be a practical test to administer in a physical education class? Possibly not, in many school settings, but tests are not developed solely for use in classes. The jump-shot test, with several trials taken from four spots on the court, might be useful for a basketball camp or an all-school testing program. Actually, it is not as cumbersome as it might seem for use in a physical education class. If the students are divided into four groups, they could rotate from one testing station to the other. In this way more students would be active than if only one station was used.

Domain-referenced validity, then, requires a careful description of the criterion behavior, or domain, along with evidence that the test adequately represents this domain. Although this is a logical rather than a statistical analysis, it should not be viewed as an arbitrary process.

Decision Validity

In addition to evidence of the adequacy of the test as a measure of the criterion behavior, the accuracy of classification must be determined. The classification may be master/nonmaster, successful/not successful, meets standard/does not meet standard, or other variations. The accuracy of classifications is investigated using decision validity procedures, which typically require the use of statistical procedures. Does the test classify people accurately? Two approaches—empirical methods and judgmental-empirical methods—will be described.

EMPIRICAL METHODS

As the name implies, empirical methods require a database, and statistical procedures are used to estimate validity. One example of empirical procedures is a method that can be used to select a valid cutoff point for a criterion-referenced test. This is usually referred to as the instructed/uninstructed (or treatment/no treatment) approach. To use this approach, an objective is identified and a test is selected to measure the objective, but a performance standard has not been determined. The test is administered to two groups of students—one that has received no instruction on the objective and one that has received previous instruction. Then the two distributions of test scores are compared, as shown in Figure 7-2. A degree of overlap is expected between the distributions. The best students in the uninstructed group will probably have scores similar to the poorest in the instructed group. The point at which the two distributions overlap represents the cutoff score, which can be used to classify future students as masters or nonmasters.

This is a viable approach if the uninstructed group has had little previous experience with the activity. Students may have learned skills in past years or even outside of the school setting. If the uninstructed group does not consist only of nonmasters, the curves overlap too much. Then no meaningful cutoff point can be identified. This approach is probably most appropriate in units where more unusual activities are taught, such as self-defense or fencing, or when all students could be tested and the lower third of the distribution could be used to represent the uninstructed and the upper third, the instructed.

JUDGMENTAL-EMPIRICAL METHODS

The second type of decision validity is judgmental-empirical methods. These methods require judgment on the part of the test user as well as a database. One

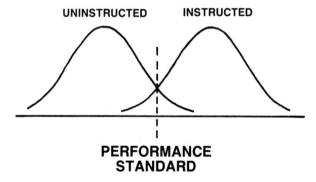

Figure 7-2 Setting standards using the instructed/uninstructed group approach.

type of judgmental-empirical method is known as the contrasting groups method. Although it can be used outside a school setting, the following example is relevant for physical education teachers in a school. To use the system properly, more than one physical education teacher must be knowledgeable about the physical capabilities of the students who will be tested. Assume again that an education objective has been set and ways of evaluating the objective have been determined, but no standard has been set. The only information the teacher needs is a list of names of the students involved. Based on his or her knowledge of the students' abilities, the teacher classifies each student as either a master or a nonmaster on the objective in question. Then the entire group of students is tested on the objective using the predetermined procedure. A distribution of scores is formed for those students who are expected to master the objective and one for those not expected to master it. These distributions are then compared for overlap, as shown in Figure 7-3. As in the previous approach, the point of overlap is the best estimate of the cutoff score.

COMPARISON OF METHODS

Note that both of the above methods use the comparison of distributions of scores to validate a cutoff score. An easier way to estimate test validity using these approaches is to set up a contingency table. An example of displaying the results of the instructed/uninstructed approach in a contingency table can be found in Figure 7-4. The examinees in the instructed and uninstructed groups have already been identified. The only factor that can be varied is the cutoff score used to identify masters and nonmasters. The master/nonmaster classifications are shown on the left of the table.

The test administrator's job is to select a cutoff score that seems reasonable. Then the examinees' scores are tallied in the table. For example, a student in the instructed group who is identified as a master by the test would be placed in the upper-left cell (*A*) of the table. A student in the uninstructed group who is classified as a master would be tallied in the upper-right cell (*B*) of the table.

Figure 7-3   Setting standards using the contrasting groups approach.

Criterion groups

	Instructed	Uninstructed
	A	B
Master	80[a] (.42)[b]	20 (.11)
	C	D
Nonmaster	15 (.08)	75 (.39)

Test classification

C = 0.81

[a]Number of students
[b]Proportion of students

Figure 7-4   Procedure for estimating test validity using the contingency coefficient C.

When all students have been tallied, the sum of the tallies in each cell is converted to a proportion. Each proportion is calculated by dividing the number of students within a cell by N, the total number of students. For example, in cell D the proportion of students is 75/190 or 0.39. The validity coefficient is calculated by summing the proportions in the upper-left cell (A) and the lower-right cell (D). The symbol for this coefficient is C, representing the contingency coefficient. Don't confuse this symbol with the letter C used to identify one of the cells in the contingency table in Figure 7-4. Different sizes of the coefficient C can be examined by changing the cutoff score. The highest C-value will represent the most valid cutoff score.

Review the numerical example in Figure 7-4. Note that the whole numbers in the cells of the table represent the number of examinees; the numbers in parentheses represent the proportion of examinees. Adding the proportion of examinees correctly classified ($A + D$) yields C, the contingency coefficient. In this case, C equals (.42 + .39) or .81. If a higher validity coefficient were desired, the test developer would set a different cutoff point and develop a new contingency table. In this way the cutoff score that maximizes the differences between groups is determined.

TENNIS SKILLS TEST EXAMPLE

A similar approach to standard-setting requires the teacher to classify students on a test as masters, borderline, or nonmasters. The median test score of the borderline is used as the performance standard for the skills test. This approach was taken with the Tennis Skills Test, published by the American Alliance for Health, Physical Education, Recreation, and Dance (AAHPERD) (Hensley, 1989). Students in tennis classes were classified as masters, borderline, or non-masters in tennis. They then were administered the AAHPERD Tennis Skills Test. Using this information, performance standards were identified for each test (Kalohn et al., 1992). The median scores for the borderline group were used to determine cutoff points (performance standards) for the individual tests.

In summary, a criterion-referenced test, like a norm-referenced test, can be validated both logically and statistically. If the test is to be used in an informal setting, logical validation of the test would probably suffice. If the test is used to make major decisions about examinees, both logical and statistical validity should be established. Since the test is used to classify students as masters or nonmasters, the accuracy of these classifications should be evident.

Interpretation of the Validity Coefficient

Since C, the validity coefficient, is the sum of two proportions, a high coefficient is desirable. In fact, if $C = 50$, this suggests that the classification may be no better than chance. Therefore when $C = .50$, the validity is essentially interpreted as zero. The meaningful interpretable range of C values is .50 to 1.00. Although no hard-and-fast rule has been set for evaluating the size of the validity coefficient, values of .80 or above are desirable.

RELIABILITY

Criterion-referenced reliability is defined somewhat differently from norm-referenced reliability, although the general concept of consistency applies to both types of reliability. In the criterion-referenced context, *reliability* is defined as consistency of classification. In other words, if the examinees were classified as masters or nonmasters (or successful/not successful) on one occasion, would they be classified the same way on a second occasion?

Procedures for Estimating Reliability

The simplest way to estimate reliability is to administer a criterion-referenced test on 2 days and tally the scores in a contingency table. The general layout of this contingency table is shown in Figure 7-5. To the left of the table, M (mastery) and NM (nonmastery) classifications for the first day (*Day 1*) of testing are displayed. Across the top of the table, M and NM classifications are identified for the second day of testing. If a person is classified as a master on both days, a tally is placed in the upper-left cell of the table. If a person is classified as a master on *Day 1* and a nonmaster on *Day 2*, the tally is placed in the upper-right cell. Locate the appropriate cell for the examinee who is a nonmaster on *Day 1* and a master on *Day 2*. This is the lower-left cell of the table. Once the scores have been tallied, the tallies in each cell are summed and converted to proportions.

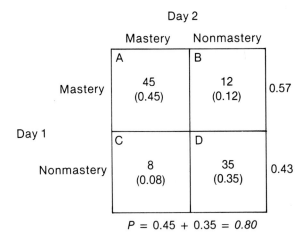

Day 2

Figure 7-5   Procedure for calculating P, the proportion agreement.

Proportion of Agreement

The most popular method for estimating reliability from a contingency table is to use P, which is the symbol for proportion of agreement. The coefficient P is calculated by summing the proportions in cells A and D. This should sound familiar because it is the same procedure used to estimate C, the validity coefficient. Of course, the two coefficients have different interpretations because the contingency tables are set up differently, but the calculation is identical. Look at the data in Figure 7-5. Of the 100 examinees taking this test, 45 were classified as masters on both days, and 35 were classified as nonmasters. There were errors in classification as well, with 12 examinees labeled masters on the first day and nonmasters on the second, while the remaining 8 students received the reverse classifications. Since N equals 100 in this case, the proportions will have the same numerical value as the number of students within cells preceded by a decimal point. In cell A, for example, the proportion is 45/100 or .45. The proportion of agreement P is (.45 + .35) or .80.

Kappa Coefficient

The coefficient P fails to take into account that some correct categorizations will be made purely by chance. If we tested a group of examinees and randomly placed their scores into the four cells of a contingency table, .25 of the sample would be placed in each cell purely by chance. A P of .50 could be obtained merely by chance. It would be of interest to know what degree of agreement has been obtained beyond the expectation of chance. One approach to this problem is to use κ, the kappa coefficient, to estimate reliability (Swaminathan et al., 1974). Formula 7-1 is used to calculate κ.

$$\kappa = \frac{P_0 - P_c}{1 - P_c}$$

Formula 7-1

where P_0 = proportion of agreement
P_c = proportion of agreement expected by chance

OR

$$P_c = \Sigma(P_i)(P_i)$$
where P_i = marginal proportion

To calculate P_c, follow this rule of thumb. Determine the marginal proportions by adding the proportions for each column and row of the contingency table. For example, in the first row of the table in Figure 7-5, the proportions for cells *A* and *B* are summed (.45 + .12) to equal the marginal proportion for this row (.57). Multiply the marginal proportions of the outermost row and column of the table [(.57) (.53), in this case] and add this product to the product of the marginal proportions of the innermost row and column [(.43) (.47), in this case]. The outermost row and column represent the first row and column of the contingency table, while the innermost row and column represent the second row and column. In the example in Figure 7-5, P_c = (.57) (.53) + (.43) (.47) = .3021 + .2021 = .5042.

$$\kappa = \frac{.80 - .5042}{1 - .5042} = \frac{.2958}{.4958} = .597$$

Not surprisingly, when chance is taken into account, the size of the proportion of agreement decreases.

Interpretation of the Reliability Coefficient

Since the proportion of agreement, P, can be affected by chance allocations, values of P below .50 are unacceptable. Thus the meaningful interpretable range of P is .50 to 1.00. In other words, a P of .50 is interpreted as a P of .00. Although values of κ can range from -1.00 to $+1.00$, the meaningful interpretable range of κ is 0.00 to 1.00. Negative values of κ have no meaning in the context of reliability, since test information either contributes positively to the consistency of classification or it does not.

When the group being tested consists of a large proportion of masters or nonmasters, P tends to be high. This is an expected characteristic of P, since it will be easier to classify people when they display low or high skill levels because their scores will be far below or above the cutoff point. Examinees who fall in between are more difficult to classify. When the test group consists primarily of this category of examinees, P typically drops, reflecting the difficulty of classifying people consistently as their scores approach the cutoff score.

Self-testing in elementary physical education.

SUMMARY

The criterion-referenced test offers an excellent option to norm-referenced testing when the identification of masters and nonmasters based on test performance or behavior is of interest. Yet the concept of criterion-referenced measurement is often not fully understood, often leading to oversimplified tests of mastery. Although a cutoff score can be determined with relative ease if set arbitrarily, this score, and thus the test, lacks validity unless the score can be interpreted in light of a criterion behavior. The validity and reliability of criterion-referenced tests are defined differently from the definitions of these concepts in a norm-referenced context. The *validity* of a mastery test is defined as the accuracy of classifications; *reliability* is the consistency of classifications.

Learning Experiences

1. This exercise is designed to give you some practical experience with criterion-referenced testing. Collect 15 pennies and a plastic container. Ask 10 people to try to toss the pennies in the container one at a time. Tell them that mastery on this task is successfully tossing 10 of the 15 pennies into the container. (Try it first yourself, so that the distance of the toss is realistic.) Record the number of successes out of 15 trials. Then ask each person to repeat the test, beginning again with all 15 pennies. After recording these successes, calculate P, the proportion of agreement. How reliable is this data set? Evaluate the size of this coefficient and indicate ways it might be increased.

2. An exercise specialist wishes to check the validity of a sit-ups test as a measure of abdominal strength. He compares the sit-ups test activity with a criterion test, electromyographic (EMG) readings of the abdominal muscles. Both tests are used in a criterion-referenced framework. On the EMG test a cutoff score of 27 or above reflects substantial activity in the abdominal muscles. The exercise specialist decides to try using a cutoff score of 55 or above on the sit-ups test to check the criterion-referenced test validity. He obtains the following test scores.

Subject	Sit-ups test	EMG test
1	73	32
2	42	20
3	51	19
4	63	25
5	59	27
6	39	18
7	57	33
8	70	36
9	65	29
10	69	28
11	46	19
12	51	21
13	52	30
14	56	31
15	64	27
16	71	17
17	42	19
18	50	25
19	50	23
20	60	29

a. Develop a contingency table for these scores.
b. Calculate C, the validity coefficient.
c. Is the sit-ups test valid? Explain.

Answers to Learning Experiences

2. a. Hint: To develop the contingency table, each of the scores must be converted to a 0 or 1 score. See Figure 7-6 for the answer to this problem.

EMG test

		M(1)	NM(0)
Sit-ups test	M(1)	(9)* .45†	(2) .10
	NM(0)	(1) .05	(8) .40

*Number of people

†Proportion of people (number in cell divided by total number; in this case, N = 20)

Figure 7-6   Contingency table; answer to Learning Experience 2a.

b. $C = .45 + .40 = .85$.
c. A C of .85 indicates a high degree of accuracy of classification; thus the validity of the sit-ups test is acceptable.

References

Blair SN. 1993. 1993 C.H. McCloy Research Lecture: Physical activity, physical fitness and health. Research Quarterly for Exercise and Sport, **64**:365–376.

Blair SN, Kohl HW, Gordon NF, Paffenbarger RF. 1992. How much physical activity is good for health? Annual Review of Public Health, **13**:99–126.

Cooper Institute for Aerobics Research. 1992. The Prudential FITNESSGRAM Test Administration Manual. Dallas: Cooper Institute for Aerobic Research.

Cooper Institute for Aerobics Research. 1994. The Prudential FITNESSGRAM Technical Reference Manual. Dallas: Cooper Institute for Aerobics Research.

Cureton KJ, Warren GL. 1990. Criterion referenced standards for youth health related fitness tests: A tutorial. Research Quarterly for Exercise and Sport, **61**:7–19.

Hensley L. 1989. Tennis Skills Test manual. Reston, VA: AAHPERD.

Kalohn JC, Wagoner K, Gao L, Safrit MJ, Getchell N. 1992. A comparison of two criterion-referenced standard setting procedures for sports skills testing. Research Quarterly for Exercise and Sport, **63**:1–10.

Looney MA. 1989. Criterion-referenced measurement: Reliability. In Safrit MJ, Wood TM, eds. Measurement concepts in physical education and exercise science. Champaign, Ill: Human Kinetics.

Moller JH, Taubert KA, Allen HD, Clark EB, Lauer RM. 1994. Cardiovascular health and disease in children: Current status. Circulation, **89**:923–930.

Nitko AJ. 1984. Defining "criterion-referenced test." In Berk RA, ed. A guide to criterion-referenced test construction. Baltimore: Johns Hopkins.

Powell KE, Thompson PD, Caspersen CJ, Kendrick JS. 1987. Physical activity and the incidence of coronary heart disease. Annual Review of Public Health, **8**:253–287.

Safrit MJ. 1981. Evaluation in physical education. Englewood Cliffs, NJ: Prentice Hall.

Safrit MJ. 1989. Criterion-referenced measurement: Validity. In Safrit MJ, Wood TM, eds. Measurement concepts in physical education and exercise science. Champaign, Ill: Human Kinetics.

Safrit MJ, Looney ML. 1992. Should the punishment fit the crime? A measurement dilemma. Research Quarterly for Exercise and Sport, **63**:124–127.

Swaminathan H, Hambleton RK, Algina JA. 1974. Reliability of criterion-referenced tests: a decision-theoretic formulation. Journal of Educational Measurement, **11**:263–268.

Annotated Readings

Educational Testing Service. 1982. Passing scores. Princeton, NJ: Educational Testing Service.

Focuses on setting standards of performance on tests; describes in clear, nontechnical language various methods of making decisions related to passing scores; provides advice for making fair and impartial decisions.

Feldt LS, Brennan RL. 1989. Reliability. In Linn RL, ed. Educational measurement, ed 3. New York: ACE/Macmillan, pp 105–146.

Describes techniques for estimating the reliability of criterion-referenced tests; includes estimates of the dependability of tests.

Linn RL. 1982. Two weak spots in the practice of criterion-referenced measurement. Educational Measurement, **1**:12–13, 25.

Discusses the terminology associated with criterion-referenced measurement; describes several of the problems associated with setting standards.

Looney MA. 1987. Threshhold loss agreement indices for criterion-referenced measurement: A review of applications and interpretations. Research Quarterly for Exercise and Sport, **58**:360–368.

An excellent discussion of kappa and modified kappa used as indices of agreement in criterion-referenced measurement; both statistics are interpreted as the proportion of consistent classifications between two administrations of a test when the influence of chance agreement has been removed; recommends modified kappa over kappa.

Nitko AJ. 1984. Defining "criterion-referenced test." In Berk RA, ed. A guide to criterion-referenced test construction. Baltimore: Johns Hopkins.

Differentiates between norm-referenced and criterion-referenced tests; reviews various definitions of criterion-referenced tests; proposes two categories for classifying criterion-referenced tests; provides guidelines for practitioners.

Safrit MJ, Baumgartner TA, Jackson AS, Stamm CL. 1980. Issues in setting motor performance standards. Quest, **32**:152–162.

Discusses issues in setting standards in physical education; provides a brief review of procedures for standard-setting; examines gender differences in motor performance and the impact of these differences on standard setting.

Measurement in a
School Setting

Assessing Students within a School Curriculum

Watch for these words as you read the following chapter

Accountability
Affective domain
Authentic assessment
Behavioral objectives
Cognitive domain
Curriculum objectives
Educational objectives
Evaluation objectives
Immediate objectives

Long-range goals
Needs assessment
Performance assessment
Psychomotor domain
Standards of performance
Taxonomy,

f you plan to teach physical education in the schools, you will be expected to evaluate your students' performance on a variety of tasks. If you plan to work in another type of setting (e.g., as an exercise specialist, or exercise scientist), move ahead to the next section of the book dealing with testing in a nonschool setting.

ACCOUNTABILITY

If you become a physical educator, you can expect to hear a great deal about **accountability** in the schools. Although emphasis may be placed on the so-called basic skills of reading, writing, and so forth, the physical educator is expected to be equally accountable for the learning outcomes of his or her students. Teaching students new skills and knowledge about physical activity is

Testing the basketball lay-up.

not enough; you must be able to demonstrate that your students have actually accomplished these abilities at the expected level. Perhaps physical fitness is one of your major goals, and you have stressed its importance throughout the year. The important question concerns your success in emphasizing this concept by changing student behavior. Remember—it's not what you do but what your students are able to do after instruction is completed. Thus to be accountable you must show how your students have changed behavior. To do so, an assessment program must be implemented. Of course, the tests you select must be feasible for a school setting. In the context of your fitness goal, although you realize a maximal stress test of cardiorespiratory function (shown in the illustration) is the most valid measure you could use, it is not realistic to consider using this test in a school. Instead, a battery of physical fitness tests might be administered at the end of the year so that changes in performance could be plotted. This information provides you with evidence that you are accountable for your work with students in their physical education classes.

The notion of accountability does not necessarily require traditional measures, such as skills tests. An accountability system might consist of regular record keeping and formative evaluation (Dunham, 1986). Three levels of accountability have been suggested by Tousignant and Siedentop (1983). Level 1 represents good behavior and managerial tasks; level 2, participation with effort; and level 3, evaluation of performance. While most measurement specialists in physical education recommend assessment at level 3, many teachers actually assess at levels 1 and 2. Some teachers believe that students may need a physical education program that focuses on enhancing self-esteem or increasing social responsibility. Research by Ennis and her colleagues (e.g., Ennis, 1992, 1994; Ennis and Zhu, 1991; Ennis et al., 1992) indicates that experienced teachers identify a variety of goals or value orientations for physical education programs in addition to the development of fitness and sport skills.

The accountability concept is not going to disappear, so expect to deal with it throughout your teaching career. Make it work for you rather than against you by planning ahead. It is difficult to demonstrate that you are accountable for your teaching when you do not think about it until the end of the year. Accountability is a sound educational concept and a reasonable job expectation. Even if communities did not demand accountability in school systems, good teachers and schools would still hold themselves accountable for their teaching.

FORMAL OR INFORMAL TESTING PROGRAM?

Most schools use several testing programs that have varying degrees of formality. The most formal program encompasses the administration of standardized achievement tests, although these will not make up a sizable part of the testing because not many standardized tests are available in the physical education field. Several organizations have published standardized tests of physical fitness for school children, described in Chapters 17 and 18. A series of test manuals for several sports can also be obtained through the American Alliance for Health, Physical Education, Recreation and Dance (AAHPERD). Certain types of standardized tests have been developed for special populations. Of the tests mentioned thus far, all are measures of motor behavior. Only one standardized knowledge test has been published in the field. In 1970 the Cooperative Knowledge Test was made available as a measure of the knowledge students in grades 4 through 12 have about physical education. The content of a knowledge test ought to be revised periodically, however, and this test has not been updated since its original development. This more formal part of the testing program is often the basis for informing people outside the school of the physical education program's effectiveness. Reports of test results and comparisons with national norms are prepared for parents, other schools in the district, the school board, and all tax-paying citizens in the community.

Testing also occurs at a less formal level in the schools. At this level the teacher selects or develops tests to be used in his or her classes. This differs from schoolwide testing in which all students at a given grade level are administered the same standardized test. For example, Mr. Moore, a physical education teacher, might use a specific health-related physical fitness test to measure the fitness of his students because it is a requirement in all physical education classes in the system. On the other hand, it might be Mr. Moore's responsibility to select additional tests to be administered to his students throughout a unit or at the end of a unit. These tests may or may not be used by any of the other physical education teachers in his school or school system. The fact that this level of testing is less formal is not meant to suggest that the tests are handled more casually. "Less formal" in this context means that the decision to use certain tests is made individually rather than on a schoolwide basis. One of the positive features of our society is that schools operate in various ways to achieve the goals of education. For instance, in some schools the entire staff of physical education teachers may decide that a certain series of tests will be used in all classes in the school. In others, each teacher makes these decisions; although this may result in different tests being used by each teacher, the objectives of the physical education program may be the same for all.

In this chapter some of the most basic decision-making processes in teaching will be reviewed. How do you decide what to test in your physical education classes? This decision can be made in a systematic manner if **behavioral objectives** have been properly prepared. This process is reviewed in the forthcoming sections after a discussion of the current status of testing in physical education.

DO PHYSICAL EDUCATION TEACHERS ASSESS?

When you accept your first teaching position, what sort of expectations should you have about the assessment program? The program may be excellent or virtually nonexistent. Probably most programs fall somewhere in between these extremes.

In the 1958 edition of a measurement textbook by Mathews, he referred to an informal survey of 50 student teachers on the grading practices in their cooperating schools. In 80% of the systems, the student's mark was based solely on being present and in uniform daily. In 1974 Cousins gave a keynote speech at a measurement symposium at Indiana University. He cited a number of incidents reflecting the misuse of tests in our field and suggested that the greatest misuse of tests was the lack of use by physical education teachers. In 1978 Morrow conducted a survey on the use of evaluation techniques and concluded that tests were simply not being used in the schools he sampled. Assessment of students was made on the basis of dress and participation. A 1982 survey of Florida physical education teachers (Imwold et al., 1982) provided further evi-

---

USE OF EVALUATION IN FLORIDA PUBLIC SCHOOL PHYSICAL EDUCATION PROGRAMS

USE OF TESTS

Skills tests	54%
Written tests	Less than 40%
Measurement model	Predominantly norm-referenced
Major users	Women teachers
	Junior high teachers
	Teachers with more experience
	Teachers with coaching responsibilities
Least frequent users	Elementary physical education teachers

DETERMINATION OF GRADES

Bases for grading	Performance scale (less than 50%)
	Subjective assessment
Type of grade	Letter (high school)
	P-F (elementary school)

Modified from Imwold CH, Rider RA, and Johnson DJ.

---

dence of the lack of testing in schools. A portion of their survey appears in the boxed material. These results were substantiated in a 1986 survey of physical education teachers in Iowa, Wyoming, Kansas, and Georgia (Hensley et al., 1988). Kneer (1986) and Veal (1988) further noted that many teachers do not believe formal assessment of student learning is necessary.

According to the results of the Florida survey, skills tests were used by only 54% of the teachers; less than 40% used knowledge tests. Skills tests were administered more frequently by female teachers, junior high teachers, and those with 4 or more years' experience. In general, norm-referenced tests were selected more frequently than criterion-referenced tests, with the latter being used primarily by senior high-school teachers with 4 or more years' experience. Few teachers graded on the curve. The most popular method of grading was a performance scale; however, this was used by less than 50% of the teachers. This survey clearly demonstrated that many teachers still use a subjective assessment of effort, sportmanship, class attendance, and assessment of behavior to determine grades. The subjective approach was most frequently used by elementary physical education teachers, the group most likely to use no tests at all. (However, elementary physical education classes often meet infrequently and for short durations.) Although it has been suggested that some coaches are too involved in athletics to be conscientious about their teaching, the Florida survey showed that teachers with coaching responsibilities used more skills tests than those without these responsibilities.

In a study of secondary school teachers by Veal (1988), when assessment was used, over half of the assessment took place at the end of the unit. The most commonly used type of assessment was performance testing (32%), followed by daily records or checklists (29%). Other forms of assessment used were written tests (22%) and subjective ratings (16%). Teachers felt effort was one of the most important indicators of student achievement. If they used skills tests, they gave credit for effort in interpreting the test scores. For some teachers, "motivating students to try harder has become an end in itself" (Veal, 1988, p. 333). The evidence points to an irrefutable conclusion: A sound testing program is not a strong feature of physical education programs in the United States.

Veal points out that some teachers do not understand the importance of testing, and this may be the result of unsatisfactory experiences with efforts to administer tests in their classes. Many teachers complain that test results are not taken seriously by students or their parents. This is especially true in schools where a pass-fail grading system is used. If the test is complicated, requiring unavailable equipment and lengthy testing time, teachers are not likely to use it. More recent approaches to assessment might be more palatable to teachers in today's schools. These approaches are discussed in the next section.

Where should the blame for this dilemma be placed? The likely culprit may appear to be the physical education teachers in the public schools. Perhaps some teachers are to blame, yet there are teachers who do use tests and use them very effectively. Before the total blame is placed hastily on teachers, the situation should be looked at from a broader perspective. King (1983) suggested that the tests available to physical education teachers are not being used because they are not appropriate for a school setting. He was not enthusiastic about these tests because most of them are norm-referenced, require too much time to administer, and often have an overly elaborate test setup. His solution to the problem is, at least in part, to develop new types of criterion-referenced tests that have satisfactory validity and reliability and yet are practical enough to be used in schools. While there is considerable merit in King's criticisms, tests are available that are appropriate for the school setting and feasible from an administrative standpoint. However, many of these tests require the use of a special test setup, such as a target. Taking a reasonable amount of time to prepare for testing should not be viewed as a burden but simply as a part of good teaching. Certainly teachers will come across tests that require expensive equipment their schools cannot afford. If a version of the equipment cannot be constructed or purchased by school personnel, then the test cannot be used. Also, some tests require so much time to set up that they may not be reasonable options. Yet this does not mean that all tests requiring setup time should not be used. A test requires planning, organization, and preparation time.

Veal (1990) has gone beyond the simple observation that many teachers do not formally assess their students to attempt to clarify the problems affecting the use of measurement. Socialization problems are a result of the context in which the teacher must function. These problems include lack of time, excessively large classes, and lack of collegial and administrative support. Teachers' beliefs are the crux of the second problem. Teachers often emphasize student behavior rather than learning outcomes, resulting in a lack of emphasis on assessment. Often the view of testing is a narrow one, in which assessment is regarded as testing and grading. Finally, Veal suggests that the process of learning to teach also poses problems for the novice teacher in learning to use assessment techniques in a physical education class. New teachers often do not know how to apply their measurement knowledge in their classes, and thus no longer incorporate this knowledge in their teaching as they become more experienced (Veal, 1990, pp. 36–37).

Of course, evaluating students by observing and rating their performance is always possible. This may be an effective approach if the rating scale is well-defined and can be demonstrated to be valid. Unfortunately, this approach is all too often used in the worst possible way—by merely looking at the student and jotting down a score, with no breakdown of the component of skill being rated and no assurance that the teacher is rating objectively. This is a form of subjective evaluation that is discussed more thoroughly later in this book. Now let us examine some of the more current approaches to evaluation in a school setting, in particular, authentic assessment.

AUTHENTIC ASSESSMENT

Authentic assessment is usually defined as a direct evaluation of student performance. The student not only completes or demonstrates the desired behavior but also does it in a real-life context. Authentic assessments are typically performance assessments in a specific context, although performance assessments are not necessarily authentic. **Performance assessment** refers to the kind of student response to be examined. In a physical education setting, a performance assessment might consist of the following: In a volleyball class, students are asked to develop and execute a play using three volleyball skills, culminating in striking the ball over the net. The first day each group of students is given up to 20 minutes to develop the play and practice it. The second day they are given the same amount of time to practice it. The third day they perform the play in front of their classmates and the teacher, who assesses the design and execution of the play. Students are asked to perform specific behaviors that are to be assessed, but the context is contrived. If this were an authentic assessment, performance would be assessed in a context more like real life—in this case, presumably a game setting. The students would be allowed to determine how long they would spend on play development and would determine the practice time they needed. Lund (1994) categorizes performance assessment and authentic assessment as components of alternative assessment, and describes authentic assessment as more realistic *and* as a terminal form of assessment.

Veal (1988) gives an example of authentic assessment in physical education. The successful serves of students in a volleyball game are counted and divided by the total number of serves attempted. If students are not performing successfully, the teacher then intervenes in some way to help them succeed. Presumably certain criteria are used to determine the success of each serve. If success is represented merely by serving the ball over the net, this is not a very discriminating measure. Authentic assessment may not be an easier way of evaluating students, but it is expected to be a better, more valid way.

While the notion of measuring performance directly is an admirable one, making every test gamelike does not necessarily reflect sound evaluation practice. If the first test students are exposed to in a sport unit is a test in a game setting, this may be unfair to them. Prior to being able to perform the skill well in a game setting, the student needs to learn to perform well in a practice setting. This may be done more validly by simulating the game situation without all the trappings of the game.

Validity and Reliability

Determining the validity of performance-based assessments has typically been handled through a logical approach. Often the term *face validity* is used as the indicator of validity for these assessments; however, this is not sufficient for accountability purposes. A more definitive approach to establishing the validity of performance measures has been to compare performance scores with the scores of relevant subtests of a standardized norm-referenced subtest (Burger and Burger, 1994). Estimating the reliability can be done through the examination of *interrater agreement,* that is, the extent that raters agree on their ratings of a performance assessment task (Linn and Burton, 1994). The reliability estimate is confounded, however, when different tasks (or standards for the same task) are used for a group of students. These differences typically have lowered the reliability estimates. It appears that there needs to be a relatively large number of tasks to make long-lasting decisions about students. For day-to-day decision-making in a physical education class, however, less stringent requirements would be necessary.

Characteristics of Authentic Assessment

Veal has identified several characteristics of authentic assessment in physical education. One is that it is regular and ongoing. This is the concept of formative evaluation, a very useful approach to tying testing to learning. It involves assessing on a continual basis, and using this information to assist students in improving their ability. A connection is established between daily instructional tasks and assessment. Each day students strive to achieve the goals designated by the teacher. Skills are also connected to real-life situations. This process typically involves various forms of physical activity that the student will be able to enjoy in real life. Finally, authentic assessment accounts for student effort, improvement, and participation. This thrust coincides with recent attempts to emphasize behavior rather than achievement, particularly in fitness testing. Involvement in class activities is a key factor. If students participate and stay on task, this is indicative of the appropriate attitude in the gymnasium.

Examples of Authentic Assessment

Lund (1994) has provided the following examples of authentic assessment (or, in her terminology, alternative assessment). These include written essays, oral discourse, exhibition and event tasks, and portfolios. In a *written essay,* students are expected to produce a product reflecting their knowledge of the subject. For example, a group of physical education students might write a paper on the exercise needs of residents in a retirement home, reflecting their knowledge of the benefits of exercise and exercise prescriptions. As Lund points out, *oral discourse* may not be practical in a physical education setting, but may have value for special purposes. A student might watch a video of a volleyball game and describe the strategies used (or not used) to the teacher. This would measure the student's ability to observe as well as his or her knowledge of offensive and defensive play. Oral discourse does not necessarily require one-on-one interaction between the student and the teacher. A student might read an article on physical fitness and analyze or synthesize the key points in the article for a small group of students. *Exhibitions and event tasks* are more readily understood in a physical education setting. Exhibitions typically involve some type of performance. Performing a sport or gymnastic activity at halftime of a basketball game could be used to demonstrate skill. Another form of an exhibition could be the demonstration of fitness activities on parents' night at school. As an example of an event task, the idea of developing a play for a game or sport and demonstrating it might be appropriate. *Portfolios* are collections of a student's work assembled over time (Feuer and Fulton, 1993). Students might be asked to keep records of their accomplishments in physical education throughout the year. Their portfolio could include short papers, examinations, scores on tests, journals recording their progress, and so forth. A covering letter must be included explaining why the material was selected for inclusion, and what the contents represent about the learning taking place throughout the year.

Authentic assessment may not be a truly new approach to measurement but rather a combination of a number of already existing approaches to assessment. It seems to encompass formative evaluation, objective-based evaluation, lifetime skills, and attitudinal factors. Whether this combination will produce truly new assessment practices in physical education remains to be seen. However, without doubt, deemphasizing testing as an isolated part of the curriculum and emphasizing testing as an integral part of instruction is sure to promote more desirable testing practices in the schools.

PLANNING A TESTING PROGRAM

What is the best way to begin planning your testing program once you arrive at your new school? First, review the objectives that have been agreed upon for the total school as well as the physical education program. Always keep in mind that you are a part of a total school system and that the physical education program should contribute to the objectives of the school. The physical education objectives may be written for the program as a whole. Then you may be expected to prepare the objectives specifically for your classes. After all, how will you know what to evaluate if you do not know what your objectives are?

REVIEW OF DOMAINS OF BEHAVIOR

Students enrolled in a measurement and evaluation course are expected to have had experience in preparing educational objectives. This book will not attempt to replicate this process; however, a brief review of the most pertinent information about behavioral objectives is appropriate.

In a school setting, the curriculum typically includes cognitive, affective, and psychomotor objectives. Each type of objective represents a domain of behavior.

Cognitive Domain

The classification of educational objectives for the **cognitive domain** is a result of the work of Bloom and his associates (1956). These were presented in the form of a **taxonomy**, that is, a classification scheme. The taxonomy represents levels of intellectual behavior ranging from a low level (memorization of facts) to a higher level (application of these facts). The levels of the taxonomy are hierarchical, with each one building on the other(s). It is assumed that mastery of a designated level of cognitive behavior must be preceded by mastery of all lower levels. For example, to apply facts, one must be able to recall them.

This taxonomy can be used in a physical education setting to develop knowledge tests. The teacher must decide on the levels of cognitive behavior that should be mastered by the class; then objectives can be written for each level.

Affective Domain

A taxonomy for the **affective domain** was developed by Krathwohl and associates (1964). An *affect* is defined as an emotional behavior. The affective domain encompasses levels of emotional behavior, including interests, attitudes, and personality characteristics. At a low level of affective behavior, an individual may display acceptable behavior because an authority figure (e.g., teacher or parent) is present. At higher levels of affective behavior, the individual's actions are based on personal beliefs about the value of a certain response. This belief is often strongly influenced by societal standards of affective behavior. In a sports setting players are expected to maintain acceptable levels of sportsmanship. If sportsmanlike behavior occurs only when an official is nearby, the player is operating at a low level of affective behavior. If the desired behaviors are displayed consistently, regardless of the situation, a higher level has been incorporated by the player.

Psychomotor Domain

The **psychomotor domain** is of greatest interest to the readers of this textbook. Several classification schemes for motor behavior have been proposed for physical education. An excellent example of one of these schemes is a taxonomy developed by Jewett (Nixon and Jewett, 1980). Jewett's taxonomy more closely parallels the cognitive and affective schemes than any other taxonomy of motor behavior. Her categories are hierarchical and deal with process rather than content.

At low levels of psychomotor behavior, the individual perceives the components of the movement and attempts to pattern the movement based on recall or observation of a demonstration of the movement. At higher levels, emphasis is placed on creating movement designed to fit a specific situation in sport, dance, or other form of physical activity.

Although criticisms of behavioral objectives have been numerous, emphasis on their tie to taxonomies has brought about a reexamination of teaching and learning in the classroom. As the motor domain is developed in a useful way for physical educators, a similar reexamination of what is being taught in the gymnasium should take place. This reexamination may show that a teacher spent an entire unit patterning basic skills, emphasizing a low level of motor behavior despite the fact that a number of students in the class should actually have been working at higher levels. If the objectives for this class had been written in behavioral terms, it would have been clear that either instruction ought to have been modified so that all students were learning patterning skills or that objectives ought to have been written to reflect actual student behavior. This type of information, when carefully analyzed, can lead to improved instruction.

PREPARING EDUCATIONAL OBJECTIVES

The process of preparing **educational objectives** is the first step in implementing the concept of accountability, that is, holding teachers in a school accountable for the results of their program. An *educational objective* can be defined as a statement of proposed change in the learner. This change will presumably take place as the result of planned learning experiences. When an objective is stated in terms of the performance or behavior that the student will exhibit upon successful attainment of the objective, it is referred to as a **behavioral objective.** Note that the objective refers to the behavior of the student. Objectives can be written in two ways: a description of the expected behavior of the teacher and a description of the expected behavior of the student. The latter type is of interest in a behavioral objective because the primary interest in education is the student's achievement. The assumption is that educators will teach in such a way that the desired results will be attained. Thus the following is the first rule of thumb in writing behavioral objectives: incorporate the behavior the student is expected to display when the objective has been successfully met. By stating objectives in terms of student response rather than teaching material, both the student and the teacher will know precisely what to expect. Also, stating objectives in behavioral terms helps to establish evaluation procedures that relate to student performance as it has been described.

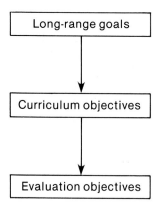

Figure 8-1   Relationship among levels of objectives.

In a school setting both long-range and immediate objectives are usually identified. **Long-range goals** specify the behavior of a fully educated person and are by nature general. Typically, these goals are first established within the school system. To learn whether students are moving toward the long-range goals, **immediate objectives** are determined that provide guidance for the selection of activities to be incorporated into a unit of instruction. These objectives can be attained in a relatively short period.

Many terms have been used to describe different types of behavioral objectives. In this book the terms *long-range goals, curriculum objectives,* and *evaluation objectives* are used to specify three levels of objectives that establish a link between long-range goals and immediate objectives. The relationship among these levels is shown in Figure 8-1.

The first level, long-range goals, represents the long-term general goals of education that describe the final product of a complete education. These goals might be a part of the overall objectives of the school or even the school system. New teachers' orientation will probably include a review of these long-range goals.

Once the long-range goals have been established, **curriculum objectives** are derived from these goals. This second level, curriculum objectives, is the reduction of the general goals into precise behaviors that reflect the terminal performance of students successfully completing an instructional unit during a course or following an entire course. Instead of stating expectations in general terms, curriculum objectives are written for specific courses or groups of courses. These objectives represent examples of ways in which the broad-based goals can be met.

At the third level **evaluation objectives** are used to describe at the unit or course level of specificity a step-by-step hierarchy, each step representing a behavior more sophisticated than the previous one. Evaluation objectives are derived from the curriculum objectives and specify the standards of performance that students are expected to meet after the objectives have been implemented. An essential part is the specification of a standard of performance. Usually the curriculum and evaluation objectives will have been written by the physical education staff. However, you may be responsible for writing the evaluation objectives. Note that the evaluation objectives may not specify exactly how the skills should be measured. This may be determined either by the physical education staff as a whole or by the individual teacher. In a large high school it is not unusual for the physical education teachers to work cooperatively to develop a testing program. In an elementary school where the physical education teacher often works on a part-time basis, the testing program is usually developed by the individual teacher. Behavioral objectives become increasingly specific and require different levels of decision-making.

Selecting Objectives

Covering all aspects of the physical education program within a school program is impossible; therefore, choices must be made before writing objectives. Before beginning, ask two important questions: What are the bases for the choices? Are the choices sound?

Curriculum developers often use the following information as a basis for making choices:

1. Data regarding the students themselves, their pretest abilities, knowledges, skills, interests, attitudes, and needs.
2. Data regarding the demands society is making on the graduates, opportunities and defects of contemporary society that have significance for education, and similar data.
3. Suggestions of specialists in various fields regarding the contribution they think their subjects can make to the education of students (Tyler, 1951, p. 50).

You may find these suggestions useful in writing objectives for your classes. Of course, considering this information could still lead to an excessive number of objectives, but the final choice should be based on a sound philosophy of physical education, the school's philosophy, and principles derived from motor learning. If other physical education teachers are members of the teaching staff in your school, a mutually agreeable approach to the formulation of objectives should be reached.

Decision-making based on the previous information may take place at the district level, but a number of choices are still left as the daily instructional program is planned. Certainly these choices will be influenced by personal interests and values. In a soccer unit, for example, an educator must decide which skills to teach, how much time to devote to learning skills, how much time to devote to playing the game, and so on. Most teachers and coaches would agree that several soccer skills are essential to the game. Beyond these, the teacher makes choices based on personal values, interests, knowledge of course content, and level of students, as considered in the perspective of the expectations of the physical education staff within a school and the school district as a whole.

Writing one's own objectives is not always necessary. Another teacher or a staff of teachers may have written behavioral objectives for specific units of instruction in physical education, and these objectives may be suitable for you, especially as a new teacher. However, you may wish to individualize those objectives, which requires writing your own. Even if you initially use someone else's objectives, you will probably want to modify these objectives after you become a more experienced teacher. Of course, this assumes that objectives have not been predetermined for physical education within your school.

CONDUCTING A NEEDS ASSESSMENT

Once your objectives have been written in behavioral form, your expectations of students are clearly defined by the **standards of performance.** Setting standards is, at best, an arbitrary procedure. What if your standards are inappropriate for your students? How will you know? If the standards have been used in the school for a number of years, the other teachers have probably established that they are reasonable for the students. If not, data can be collected to assist in the preparation of objectives. It might be wise to consider conducting a **needs assessment** before writing a set of objectives. This is a process for determining the appropriateness of the objectives for the targeted group of students. Each objective has a built-in evaluation procedure. In a needs assessment, students are evaluated on each objective at the beginning of the school year. This determines their actual status on each objective. These results are compared with the standards already specified in the objectives, referred to as their desired status. If the actual status is equal to or better than the desired status, the objective should be rewritten. In other words, students should be expected to improve beyond their actual status from the beginning of the year to the end. The definition of a *needs assessment,* then, is a comparison of actual and desired states. See Figure 8-2 for a flow chart of this process.

SUMMARY

New teachers of physical education face a formidable task in planning for their classes. This includes the formulation of behavioral objectives along with evaluation procedures for each objective. Even if a set of objectives has already been written for the physical education teachers in a school, writing more specific objectives for classes may be necessary. Of course, these must be in line with the broader objectives of physical education. A new set of objectives should be tested on students by first conducting a needs assessment. Objectives also serve as evidence of the accountability of a physical education teacher. Taxonomies of cognitive, affective, and psychomotor behavior can provide a firm basis for enhancing measurement practices as teaching experience is gained. New approaches to assessment in the schools, in particular performance assessment

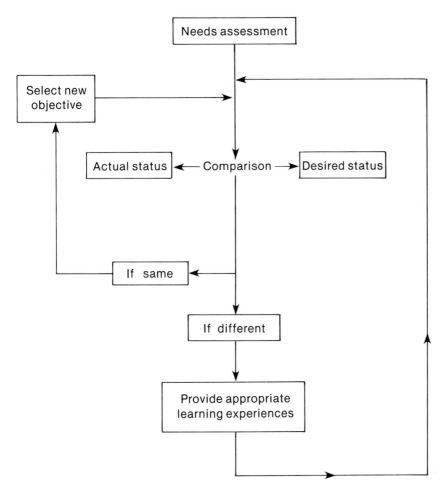

Figure 8-2   Flow chart of a needs assessment.

and authentic assessment, should assist physical education teachers in evaluating performances in a more real-life setting.

Learning Experiences

1. Choose one of your favorite sports. Select a skill and write a behavioral objective at a low level of motor behavior. Don't hesitate to use detailed descriptions. Most people are much too brief when they first begin writing behavioral objectives.
2. Form small groups in your class. Review the evaluation portion of the objectives written by members of your group. As changes are suggested, revise the objectives. Then pass your objective to someone else in another group and take someone else's objective. As a homework assignment carefully assess

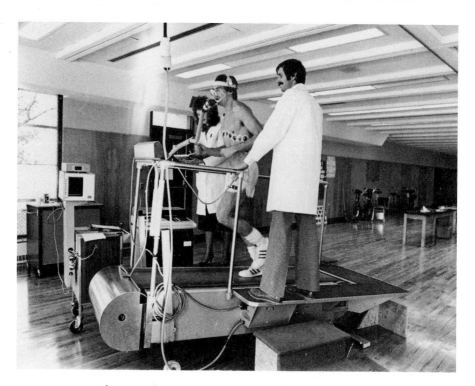

Administering maximum stress test on the treadmill.

the evaluation portion of the objective you received from someone else. Write suggestions for improving the objective, as well as the good points about it. Return the objective to the instructor at the beginning of the next class period.

3. Using the sport skill you selected in *1*, write an objective for a group operating at a high level of motor behavior. Be specific, especially in your description of the performance standard. Compare the standard with the one you described in *1*. Be sure both testing situations are clearly explained. On what basis did you determine the more difficult standard? How do you know it will not be *too* difficult? In other words, justify the standards you identified.

References

Bloom B, Ed. 1956. Taxonomy of educational objectives: Handbook I: the cognitive domain. New York: David McKay.

Burger SE, Burger DL. 1994. Determining the validity of performance-based assessment. Educational Measurement: Issues and Practices, **13**:9–15.

Dunham P. 1986. Evaluation for excellence: A systematic approach. Journal of Physical Education, Recreation and Dance, **57**(6):37–39, 60.

Ennis CD. 1992. The influence of value orientations in curricular decision making. Quest, **44**:317–329.

Ennis CD. 1994. Urban secondary teachers' value orientations: Delineating curricular goals for social responsibility. Journal of Teaching in Physical Education, **13**:163–179.

Ennis CD, Ross J, Chen A. 1992. The role of value orientations in curricular decision making: A rationale for teachers' goals and expectations. Research Quarterly for Exercise and Sport, **62**:33–40.

Ennis CD, Zhu W. 1991. Value orientations: A description of teachers' goals for student learning. Research Quarterly for Exercise and Sport, **62**:33–40.

Feuer M, Fulton K. 1993. The many faces of performance assessment. Phi Delta Kappan, **74**:478.

Hensley LD, Lambert LT, Baumgartner TA, Stillwell JL. 1988. Is evaluation worth the effort? Journal of Physical Education, Recreation and Dance, **59**(1):59–62.

Imwold CH, Rider RA, Johnson DJ. 1982. The use of evaluation in public school physical education programs. Journal of Teaching in Physical Education, **2**:13–18.

King HA. 1983. Measurement and evaluation as an area of study: a plea for new perspectives. In Tipton CH, Hay JG, eds. Specialization in physical education: the Alley legacy. Iowa City: University of Iowa.

Kneer M. 1986. A description of physical education instructional theory/practice gap in selected secondary schools. Journal of Teaching in Physical Education, **5**:91–106.

Krathwohl DR, Bloom BS, Masia B. 1964. Taxonomy of educational objectives: Handbook II: the affective domain. New York: David McKay.

Linn RL, Burton E. 1994. Performance-based assessment: Implications of task specificity. Educational Measurement: Issues and Practices, **13**:5–8, 15.

Lund J. 1994. Authentic assessment: Have we finally found user friendly assessment? Paper presented (June 1994) at the World Congress for the Association Internationale des Écoles Supérieures d'Éducation Physique, Berlin.

Nixon JE, Jewett AE. 1980. An introduction to physical education, ed 9. Philadelphia: WB Saunders.

Tousignant M, Siedentop D. 1983. A qualitative analysis of task structures in required secondary physical education classes. Journal of Teaching in Physical Education, **3**:47–57.

Tyler RW. 1951. The functions of measurement in improving instruction. In Lindquist EL, ed. Educational measurement. Washington, DC: American Council on Education.

Veal ML. 1988. Pupil assessment perceptions and practices of secondary teachers. Journal of Teaching in Physical Education, **7**:327–342.

Veal ML. 1990. Measurement and evaluation curricula in professional physical education preparation programs—a view from the practitioner. Journal of Physical Education, Recreation, and Dance, **61**(3):36–38.

Annotated Readings

Bain LL. 1980. Program evaluation. Journal of Physical Education and Recreation, **51**(2):67–69.

Proposes a framework for program evaluation that includes both an internal and external perspective; emphasizes criterion-referenced measurement for internal evaluation and either normative- or criterion-referenced measurement for external evaluation; includes an excellent summary of the total framework in chart form; discusses how to use the results to revise a physical education program.

Bayless JG. 1978. Conflicts and confusion over evaluation. Journal of Physical Education and Recreation, **49**(7):54–55.

Describes a study of the evaluation of physical education programs in Oklahoma and the success of the evaluation; shows that students and physical education teachers had different perspectives of the types of evaluation taking place in class; discusses the overemphasis on dress for class, attitude, and participation in determining grades; points to the need for tests appropriate for school-age children.

Dunham P Jr. 1986. Evaluation for excellence: a systematic approach. Journal of Physical Education, Recreation and Dance, **57**(6):34–36, 60.

Discusses evaluation as an integral aspect of the educational process; describes evaluation as the basis for determining the appropriateness of the curriculum, the effectiveness of instructional strategies, and the magnitude of student achievement; presents strategy for planning, evaluating, and implementing aspects of physical education instruction.

Gronlund NE. 1985. Stating objectives for classroom instruction, ed 3. New York: Macmillan.

Provides a practical guide for stating instructional objectives as intended learning outcomes, then defining the objectives by student performance; presents sample objectives for all three taxonomy domains—cognitive, affective, and psychomotor; includes sample specifications for computer banking of objectives.

Jewett AE, Bain LL, Ennis CD. 1995. The curriculum process in physical education. Dubuque, Iowa: Wm C Brown Group.

Presents an updated version of the Jewett Purpose–Process Curriculum Framework, which encompasses the Jewett taxonomy of motor behavior; includes examples of behavioral objectives written for various levels of the framework.

McCormick J. 1988. A field experience: enhancing instruction in measurement and evaluation. Journal of Physical Education, Recreation and Dance, **59**(6):27–29.

Discusses the relevance of measurement and evaluation courses in professional preparation programs in physical education; points to the need to bridge the gap between theory and practice in measurement; notes ways in which measurement and evaluation material can be made more acceptable to the practicing physical education teacher; describes a learning experience in which measurement and evaluation students administer a test battery to elementary school students.

Pflug J. 1980. Evaluating high school coaches. Journal of Physical Education and Recreation, **51**(4):76–77.

Describes a comprehensive, objective coaching evaluation program; provides a self-appraisal by the coach, evaluation by the head coach (if an assistant coach is present) and the building athletic administrator, and a conference with the building coordinator and the district athletic director; the program encompasses evaluation in five areas: administration, skills, relationships, performance, and self-improvement.

Vargas JS. 1982. Writing worthwhile behavioral objectives. New York: Harper & Row.

Self-instructional text; teaches students to recognize and classify behavioral objectives and to write quality objectives; presents fundamentals of writing behavioral objectives; includes examples from different subject areas and grade levels.

Grading

KEY WORDS

Watch for these words as you read the following chapter

Checklist of objectives
Grades
Pass-fail method
Percentage method
Percentage-correct method

Standard deviation method
Standard score method
Weight (of grade)

If you plan to teach physical education, you must be prepared to establish some sort of grading system as soon as you assume your first teaching position. This is not an easy task. In fact, even seasoned teachers often express dissatisfaction with the grading system they use. A **grade** is a permanent record of a student's achievement. It remains on record during and even after the lifetime of a student. Thus it is reasonable to expect teachers to think carefully about their approach to grading to make every effort to use the fairest and most objective system possible. Most prospective teachers would welcome straightforward recommendations from experienced teachers, administrators, and measurement specialists on the best grading system to use. Unfortunately, with all the advances in education, no one has developed a foolproof system of grading.

In this chapter several approaches to grading are examined, but no specific system is recommended. Each system has advantages and disadvantages that must be taken into account. Sometimes a teacher's choice of a grading system depends on his or her general philosophy about how students learn. It would be ideal if every teacher developed a grading system in this manner, but all too

© 1984 United Feature Syndicate, Inc.

Grading cartoon.

often an "armchair" approach (where the teacher merely sits in an armchair and determines grades subjectively) is taken in grading.

Why does grading present such a problem? Averaging a set of unit grades to calculate a final grade certainly is not difficult. It is the decision-making aspect of grading that presents the problem. What does the grade mean? Does it reflect achievement? Improvement? Attitude? How is a letter grade assigned? Is a normative approach to grading used or an approach involving mastery of a set of standards? If these questions are not carefully analyzed, inappropriate grading systems often result. Grades can vary from class to class and from teacher to teacher; for example, an A in one course may be the equivalent of a C in another course of the same type. Furthermore, the grades may not be based on objective evidence. Good grades may be used as a reward and poor grades as a punishment. The "halo effect" often operates in the determination of grades. Teachers are human beings and can succumb to a tendency to allow a student's personality to influence his or her grade. However, this is less likely to happen if the system is formulated as objectively as possible.

Unfortunately, testing has often been equated solely with grading by teachers, parents, and students. Determining grades is sometimes thought of as the only purpose for testing. This is one of the reasons for testing but certainly not the only one. In several other chapters measurement as an integral part of learning is discussed. Even if there were no grades, testing would be worthwhile as a means of improving performance and encouraging desired behaviors.

The student should be informed at the beginning of a unit how the unit grade is to be determined. For older students a handout describing the grading system is helpful. If some tests are to be weighted more heavily than others, this should be noted. At the end of a unit the student should receive no surprises regarding the prearranged grading system.

One final point should be emphasized: grades should always reflect the objectives of the course. Physical education teachers should be aware of the relationship between the initial objectives of a unit and the degree to which these objectives have been met in determining the grade. Otherwise, the basis for determining grades might be quite arbitrary. This is one of the most important concepts to remember about grading. In fact, it is one of the basic tenets of good teaching.

USE OF GRADES

Grades have many uses in the school system. They are used to inform the student of his or her status; inform parents, teachers, and administrators of the student's status; provide information for the student's permanent record; and motivate students. Even though many people dislike grades, they are a part of the American school system. Grading, although an imperfect aspect of education, can be acceptable if the system is carefully developed and refined.

Inform Students of Status

In a physical education class where the teaching and learning process is operating efficiently, students will continually receive feedback on perform-

Testing in physical education class.

ance. However, at the end of a unit most students would probably benefit from some type of summary information of their achievement. A unit grade can provide this kind of information.

Inform Parents of Student's Status

Although a student may receive feedback from day to day in a physical education class, the student's grade is the major method of communication between the school and the parents. As much information as possible should be given along with the grade. For example, the major objectives of the unit might be listed along with an indication of the student's progress toward meeting them. An excellent example of a well-developed procedure for informing students of their children's fitness state is the FITNESSGRAM program. The FITNESS-GRAM, described in Chapter 17, includes a student's fitness test scores and whether the scores fall in or out of the Health Fitness Zone, along with a brief exercise prescription for areas needing improvement. This information is printed on a computer and mailed to the child's parents.

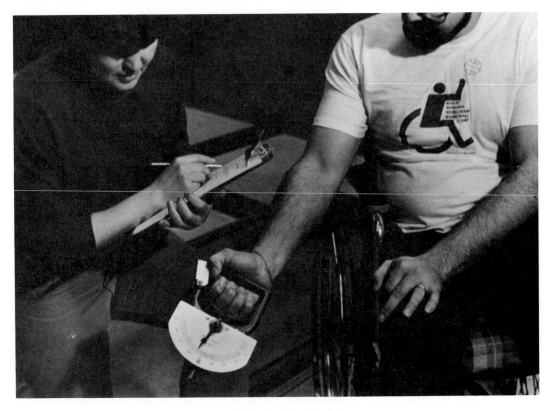

Testing grip strength of subject with disabilities.

Inform Teachers of Student's Status

Although all good teachers have a fairly concise view of the level of ability of each student, an overview of the ability of all students in the class may not be as clear. The class grades can be useful for providing this overview. They can be used to aid in the evaluation of teaching effectiveness, course content, and curriculum. A most valuable outcome of grading is to help the teacher gain a better overall understanding of the student's achievement. Information on grades can be valuable in providing future instruction to each student in the class as well as the class as a whole.

When a teacher begins a new year with a group of new students, grades from the previous year can be used in classifying the students into groups. Previous grades can also be used in planning units of instruction. However, teachers should avoid placing total reliance on previous grades, since there will always be a margin for error in grading.

Inform Administrators of Student's Status

The student's grades are used in many ways within a school system. Grades provide evidence that students are either meeting or not meeting stated objectives. Grades are also used for purposes of promotion, graduation, honors, athletic eligibility, and college entrance.

Add to a Student's Permanent Record

Grades are routinely added to a student's permanent record in the administrative office and retained indefinitely, often beyond a student's lifetime. This suggests that each grade has considerable importance to the student. Teachers must understand that a casually determined grade is not only unfair to the student at the time it is given but that it can also have a long-term negative impact.

Motivate Students

Grades are a motivational device for most students. Whether teachers like it or not, students' motivation is often to do whatever is needed to receive a satisfactory grade. If the process of grading improves learning in the desired direction, deriving motivation from grades is not necessarily bad. In this context, working for a grade may not be undesirable.

DETERMINING A FINAL UNIT GRADE

Measurement specialists in physical education agree that one important basis for determining a grade is achievement in one or more aspects of motor performance. These can include sports skills, playing ability, and physical fitness. Grading on improvement has also been considered, although this is a somewhat controversial issue. Specialists also agree that the achievement of cognitive skills (including knowledge and understanding of the principles and mechanics of movement, safety, conditioning, history, and so forth) should be graded, although perhaps to a lesser extent. The predominant area of disagreement is whether a physical education grade should be based, in part, on the student's affective behavior (including social behaviors such as effort, attitude, sportsmanship, and citizenship). Whether all three areas—motor, cognitive, and affective—should be considered in determining a grade is largely a matter of philosophy. Whether all three areas can be measured with sufficient objectivity to justify contributing to the determination of a grade is another matter.

Achievement in Motor Skills as a Basis for Grading

Many physical educators believe that the achievement of skill and ability in physical education should receive the greatest emphasis in grading. The type of achievement expected depends on the objectives of the unit. In a beginning class, emphasis may be placed on development of skills, whereas in an intermediate class, skill development and playing ability may be equally stressed.

One objective of many physical education programs is the development of physical fitness. Assessment of the level of fitness of students in these programs may be incorporated into their final grade. However, more recently it has been suggested that grading on physical fitness tests is inappropriate because grades detract from an important objective of the fitness curriculum, to bring about increased fitness behaviors. Yet, a grading system can be designed to reflect fitness behaviors rather than performance on a test, if this more accurately reflects the objective. Several criteria might be used rather than a single standard of fitness because there are individual differences in body build. These differences may be partially taken into account by using tables of scores adjusted for body weight, particularly for measures of muscular strength and endurance.

Another objective is the development of sports skills. An A in tennis should mean the student can play tennis well, considering the level of ability of the students in the course.

Improvement in Motor Skills as a Basis for Grading

When a student's performance improves over a given period of time, we assume that learning has taken place, although performance and learning are not synonymous. Intuitively, it seems highly desirable to use improvement as one means of determining a student's grade. After all, a teacher may reason, isn't the fact that improvement took place more important than the final level of achievement? This seems plausible to many physical education teachers. Obviously students hope to improve, and teachers want them to do so. The difficulty lies in attempting to use improvement as a basis for grading. Several problems are associated with the measurement of improvement—unreliability of improvement scores, inequality of scale units, and difficulty in motivating students during the first testing session.

In the first place, how is improvement usually determined? Usually a test is administered at the beginning and at the end of a unit. The pretest score is subtracted from the post-test score to yield an improvement score. Unfortunately, an improvement score calculated this way has been shown to be notably unreliable. This is a well-established fact. There is a degree of unreliability associated with both the pretest and post-test scores. The measurement error associated with each of these tests is compounded in the improvement score.

Furthermore, the amount of improvement a student can attain depends on his or her initial level of skill. This is referred to as inequality of scale units. The highly skilled person cannot be expected to improve as much as the poorly skilled because there is less room for improvement at higher levels of performance. For example, an improvement of 4 seconds on the 1-mile run has a different meaning for a world-class runner than it does for a novice runner, even though the numerical value of the improvement score (4 seconds) is the same for each performer. If the world-class runner's time improved from 4:11 to 4:07, it would represent a significant improvement. On the other hand, a change in the novice runner's time from 8:11 to 8:07 might have little or no practical significance. Decreasing one's running time by 4 seconds is easy if the time is initially slow. In addition, a child's performance on a test of physical performance may improve simply because he or she has grown older and become more mature physically during the time period between the pretest and the post-test. For example, as a child grows taller and heavier, throwing a ball farther or jumping a longer distance is possible as a result of the maturation factor. In other words, little or no actual improvement due to learning might have taken place.

One procedure developed for measuring improvement in physical education shows promise. Hale and Hale (1972) used a mathematical procedure to transform test scores so that improvement at a low level of performance is not weighted as heavily as the same amount of improvement at a higher level of performance. This procedure, in its simplest form, requires the standardization of initial and final test scores by converting them to T-scores. In some cases, tables of T-scores are published for skills tests; otherwise, the teacher can easily develop such a table. For a review of T-scores and the procedure for developing a table of T-scores, see Chapter 3. Once the raw scores have been transformed to T-scores, a conversion table (Table 9-1) is used to determine each student's progression score. The progression score representing the initial score is subtracted from the progression score for the final test score.

As an example, consider the pretest and the post-test scores of two students in a bowling class, as shown in Table 9-2. Student A bowled an average of 90 during the testing period at the beginning of the unit and an average of 120 during the post-test period. These scores were converted to T-scores of 30 and 50, respectively. Using these T-scores and referring to the conversion table in Table 9-1, subtract the progression score for a T-score of 30 (3.99) from the progression score for a T-score of 50 (10.05). The improvement score for student A was 6.06. Note that the raw gain was 30 points, the T-score gain was 20 units, and the actual improvement score was 6.06.

Student B, on the other hand, bowled an average of 170 during initial testing and 180 during final testing. In this case the raw gain was 10 points and the T-score gain (70–75) was 5 units. If these students had been graded on their raw gain scores, student A would receive a higher grade than student B; yet, in terms

Table 9-1   Conversion of T-Scores to Progression Scores

T-Score	Progression Score	T-Score	Progression Score	T-Score	Progression Score
20	2.52	40	6.34	60	15.94
21	2.64	41	6.65	61	16.70
22	2.76	42	6.95	62	17.48
23	2.89	43	7.27	63	18.31
24	3.03	44	7.62	64	19.16
25	3.17	45	7.98	65	20.09
26	3.32	46	8.35	66	21.03
27	3.48	47	8.75	67	22.02
28	3.64	48	9.16	68	23.07
29	3.81	49	9.60	69	24.14
30	3.99	50	10.05	70	25.29
31	4.18	51	10.52	71	26.46
32	4.38	52	11.03	72	27.72
33	4.59	53	11.54	73	29.09
34	4.80	54	12.09	74	30.42
35	5.03	55	12.66	75	31.86
36	5.26	56	13.25	76	33.37
37	5.51	57	13.87	77	34.92
38	5.77	58	14.53	78	36.58
39	6.05	59	15.23	79	38.31
				80	40.13

From Hale PW, Hale RM. 1972.

of actual performance, B's improvement may be equal to or better than A's. When the conversion table was used to calculate B's improvement score, the score was 6.57, slightly higher than A's score.

Even though the application of this procedure yields more valid improvement scores, there are problems with this approach. The exponential equations used to convert scores to progression scores are not necessarily an accurate reflection of actual changes in performance. Although the transformation represents a rough adjustment of scores that appears to be conceptually sound, there is no scientific evidence supporting this particular exponential equation over

Table 9-2   Example of Hale and Hale (1972) Method

Student	Pretest Score	T-Score	Post-Test Score	T-Score	Progression Score
A	90	30	120	50	6.06
B	170	70	180	75	6.57

others. On the other hand, it has not been disproved and it has considerable evidence of logical validity. For a more detailed analysis of the problems in measuring change, see Schutz (1989). PROGRAM CHANGE, a refinement of the Hale and Hale procedure, was programmed for the Apple IIe microcomputer by East (1985).

Another problem associated with grading on improvement is commonly known as "sandbagging." If it is common knowledge that final grades are to be based on improvement, some students may deliberately perform at a low level of skill on the pretest although they are capable of obtaining higher test scores. By obtaining a low pretest score, greater improvement will be reflected in the pretest–post-test score comparison at the end of the unit. This problem can be diminished by pretesting students BEFORE they are informed they will be graded on improvement.

If improvement is to occur, adequate time must be allowed for it. Some students need to practice over long periods to improve. Instructional units in physical education are often scheduled for 6 weeks or less; therefore, there may not be adequate time for improvement. For example, expecting students to hit 8 out of 10 free throws successfully after a 6-week basketball unit may be unrealistic.

Finally, emphasizing the student's improvement score does not conceal the true achievement level. If a student's performance is poor compared to others in class, it will be obvious. Grading on improvement, although desirable, should probably be minimized until more appropriate ways are developed to handle improvement scores.

Development of Cognitive Skills as a Basis for Grading

There is general agreement that knowledge of the course content of the instructional unit in physical education should be part of the final grade. Understanding the principles and mechanics of movement, along with the application of these principles to specific activities, are among the most important cognitive skills. Lower-level cognitive skills such as knowledge of rules and strategies of a sport can also be used in determining grades. Other cognitive skills that might be measured are safety factors, history of the sport, and principles of conditioning.

Development of Affective Skills as a Basis for Grading

The term *affect* has been loosely used in physical education to reflect factors such as attitude, attendance, sportsmanship, effort, dress, and, in some instances, whether a student showers after participating in a physical education class. These factors often constitute the major part of the grade in some physical education classes, even though their assessment is generally unreliable and frequently punitive. They are often considered a reflection of attitude; that is, if a student's attitude is good, he or she will attend class, be a good sport, try hard, wear the proper clothes, and shower after class. The measurement of some of these factors is highly subjective, often bringing into play the halo effect. Moreover, an overemphasis on affective behavior often leads to neglect of cognitive and motor skills. Furthermore, the presence of the desired affective behavior in no way guarantees achievement in motor skills or understanding movement. On the other hand, we must recognize that some physical education teachers use these factors in determining grades in an attempt to deal with student apathy or disciplinary problems. Although these are genuine concerns and must be dealt with in some way, grades may not be the best or most appropriate alternative. Of greater importance is that grades based only on these factors are not valid. Let us examine more closely a few of the affective behaviors that are often used in determining a grade.

Attendance

Even back in the middle of the twentieth century, grades were often based solely on students being present and in uniform daily (Mathews, 1958). Since that time, this observation has been verified in a number of surveys. Generally, the factors on which a grade is based depend on the course objectives. Is regular attendance a course objective, or is it a matter of school policy? Attendance is usually governed by school policy, and deviant behavior related to attendance is dealt with by the principal or other designated authorities.

The practice of grading has sometimes been justified by the view that a student cannot learn when not in class. If, however, the student is able to meet the course objectives satisfactorily, his or her grade should not be reduced because of poor attendance. Certainly disciplinary action should be taken against a student who is in school but does not attend class. Whether this action comes from the principal or the teacher, however, punishment should never take the form of reducing a grade.

As Cotten and Cotten (1985) aptly noted, grades should never be used as a weapon for dealing with behaviors and attitudes. Grades should be based on objectives. Does an A in history mean the student displayed a good attitude in the history class? Obviously, the answer is no.

Effort

Effort is extremely difficult to evaluate. Does a student who performs well with seemingly little effort work less than the student with less skill who obviously works hard? Can a teacher judge the amount of effort displayed by an individual based on facial expression or how tired he or she looks? If part of the grade is based on effort, it must be evaluated with a reasonable degree of objectivity. A physical education teacher may genuinely believe effort can be judged adequately using subjective judgment, but personal values will probably interfere.

Usually we assume that effort is reflected in achievement. However, if the achievement level is unchanged, is the effort meaningful? If effort is so important that it is part of the course objective, a procedure should be developed to objectively and systematically measure this affective skill.

Grading is a complex matter. Some teachers value effort over achievement, and grade accordingly. Students may even be asked to participate in the grading process. The following instructions were given to students in an elementary physical education class:

It is most important in physical education that each of you do the best that YOU can. It is not important to me that one of you can do more sit-ups than someone else. . . . Your grades in physical education are based upon HOW HARD YOU TRY—not on how good you are at a skill or in physical fitness. There is only ONE PERSON who knows how hard you try [YOU]. . . . I am asking each of you to give yourself a grade in physical education for the last nine weeks. . . . (Petray and Blazer, 1991, p. 68)

Dress and Showers

The need for gym clothes appropriate for physical education classes is obvious; however, the practice of grading on uniforms is questionable. In fact, few schools in the United States now require uniforms for physical education. However, most students are expected to change into clothing suitable for participation in physical activity. If the student has dirty gym clothes, or no gym clothes at all, a penalty is appropriate, although not in the form of lowering an achievement grade.

No longer do a majority of physical education programs require students to take a shower at the end of class. In settings where this is still a practice, the requirement should be controlled by departmental policy. What represents a satisfactory shower? A wet body? Wetness on some part of the body? Some teachers think that showering is a health habit important enough to be graded. Some believe that it reflects a positive attitude. Explaining the importance of showers to students and encouraging them to take showers regularly is not unreasonable, yet grading the student on showers is no assurance that the value will become ingrained. Whether showers are mandatory or not, grades should not be based on them.

Sportsmanship

Every physical education teacher hopes to implant in students values associated with good sportsmanship. The development and encouragement of habits reflecting good sportsmanship are basic to all physical education programs, yet this is a difficult affective trait to measure. The measurement of good sportsmanship is often haphazard and unreliable. If this affective skill is to be graded, the teacher should systematically record incidents of behavior for each student that reflect varying degrees of sportsmanship in a class situation. Although this process may be unrealistic because of the time involved, this is the only way to reduce the effect of the teacher's personal values on such judgments. (For more details, see Chapter 14.)

Comments

In a 1982 survey of the use of evaluation by physical education teachers, many teachers still used subjective assessment of effort, sportsmanship, class attendance, and assessment of behavior to determine grades (Imwold et al., 1982). The subjective approach was used most frequently by elementary physical education teachers, the group most likely to use no tests at all. While it might be desirable to include information on the child's behavior on the report form, an assessment of achievement should not be ignored. In fact, achievement of skills and abilities should be the primary focus of a report form. "If the teacher . . . has used the grade as a disciplinary tool, to enforce class policies, or to reflect anything other than final achievement in the course, the grade will be deceptive and misleading" (Cotten and Cotten, 1985, p. 53). Boyce (1990) compared three grading methods used in physical education classes: (1) 100% on motor skills; (2) 100% on participation; and (3) a combination of motor skills (50%), cognitive skills (30%), and participation (20%). She found that students in both the combination and skills grading methods groups performed better when tested than did the participation group. Participation was assessed on the basis of class attendance and the performance of assigned jobs associated with class organization. If skill development is a class objective, the combination grading method might be a viable option for the physical education teacher.

NORM-REFERENCED APPROACH TO GRADING

In general, a norm-referenced test (see Chapter 1) is used to detect individual differences among examinees. Grades can also be determined in a norm-referenced context by considering a student's performance relative to others in class. This system is based on the normal probability curve. If letter grades of A, B, C, D, and F are used, the curve is divided into five sections with each section representing a letter grade. As you know from reading the statistics chapters in this book, the entire area under the curve equals 100%. If the curve is divided into sections, the area in each section represents a certain percentage of the whole, and the sum of the percentages across all sections would equal 100%. When you use a norm-referenced system of grading, your primary task is to identify the areas under the curve that will represent each grade and their corresponding percentages.

In the following section, two methods of norm-referenced grading are described—the **standard deviation method** and the **percentage method**. Although all the examples use five grade categories (representing A, B, C, D, and F), any number of grade categories could be used in the same way. Note that this type of grading is sometimes referred to as "grading on the curve" and criticized as being unfair to students. The criticism need not be true if the grade categories are properly determined. They should, for example, be based on a large number of students, not merely on one or two classes. This issue is examined in the next section.

Standard Deviation Method

You have just given a test to a group of students, and now you wish to assign a grade to each test score. The standard deviation method is based on the standard deviation of the distribution of scores. Thus the first step is to calculate the mean and the standard deviation of the test scores, then divide the distribution into five sections using the standard deviation values. For example, in Table 9-3, note the area of the curve that is 1.5 standard deviations above the mean or higher. All scores falling in this area would receive a grade of A. Let's assume a test has a mean of 60 and a standard deviation of 8. Using Table 9-3, a score of 72 (mean plus 1.5 standard deviations = 60 + 12 = 72) or higher would receive an A. Scores ranging from 71 to 64 (mean plus 0.5 standard deviation = 60 + 4 = 64) would receive a B, and so forth.

The score ranges for each grade are given below:

A   72 and above
B   64–71
C -56–63
D   48–55
F   47 and below

Go through the calculations on your own for the C, D, and F grade ranges to verify these figures.

Now that you have an idea of how the standard deviation method works, it is important to understand what the results mean. First, this method is based on the assumption that the distribution of scores represents a normal curve. When the scores are normally distributed, the probabilities associated with the z-scores are known properties. This enables us to determine the percentage of students falling above or below a certain standard deviation (i.e., z-score associated with that standard deviation). Percentages such as those shown in Table 9-3 are based on the assumption of a normal distribution. When you have a large number of scores, you can expect to see similar percentages for the categories of scores developed for grades. With a smaller number of scores, however, the distribution of scores may not be at all normal, and the standard deviation method may not be the most appropriate procedure for determining grades in

Table 9-3   Example of the Standard Deviation Method of Grading

Grade	Standard(s) Deviation Range	Percent
A	1.5s or more above mean	7%
B	Between + 0.5s and + 1.5s	24%
C	Between + 0.5s and − 0.5s	38%
D	Between − 0.5s and − 1.5s	24%
F	1.5s or more below the mean	7%

this instance. Thus, when you are determining your own grading scale for one small class, use another grading system.

On the other hand, if you want to establish a grading system that you can use year after year in your classes, you can accumulate scores over several classes until you have sufficient scores to form a normal distribution. Then the standard deviation method would be an excellent choice for determining the grade scale. Keep in mind, however, that when you use the scale in the future, students in a given class will not necessarily receive all grades in the range. For example, in one class, there may be no students receiving an A while in another, the D and F grades might not be received by any of your students. This is due to the small sample size in each of your classes. Some classes will be better than others. In this case, the grading scale was appropriately developed based on a normal distribution, and can then be used with much smaller groups.

The following steps summarize the standard deviation method of determining grades:

1. Calculate the mean and standard deviation of a set of 500 test scores. Assume these values are obtained: $\overline{X} = 64$ and $s = 8$.
2. Using Table 9-3, determine the range for a grade of A. Using the mean + 1.5 standard deviations:

$$64 + 1.5(8) = 76$$

   A student scoring 76 or above would receive an A on the test.
3. Determine the range for a grade of B. To obtain the upper score in the range, subtract 1 from the lower score in the A range (76), $76 - 1 = 75$. For the lower score in the B range, calculate the mean + 0.5 standard deviation:

$$64 + 0.5(8) = 68$$

   Students scoring from 68 to 75 would receive a grade of B.
4. Determine the range for a grade of C. For the upper score in the range, subtract 1 from the lower score in the range for B (68), $68 - 1 = 67$. For the lower end of the C range, calculate the mean − 0.5 standard deviation:

$$64 - 0.5(8) = 60$$

   The range for a grade C is 60 to 67.
5. For a grade of D, calculate the scores for − 0.55 to − 1.5 s. For the upper score in the range, subtract 1 from the lower score in the C range (60), $60 - 1 = 59$. For the lower score, calculate the mean − 1.5 standard deviations:

$$64 - 1.5(8) = 52$$

   The range for a grade of D is 52−59.
6. A grade of F can be determined by subtracting 1 from the lower score in the D range (52), $52 - 1 = 51$. A student scoring 51 or below would receive an F on the test.
7. Lay out the entire scale for convenient usage:

A = 76 and above
B = 68–75
C = 60–67
D = 52–59
F = 51 and below

Note that we calculated the mean and standard deviation for a group of 500 students in the above example. However, the group of interest to you might consist of only 30 or 40 students. Remember that when the total number of scores is small, the distribution of scores might be badly distorted compared with the normal distribution.

This method is similar to the **standard score method.** In the standard score approach, the raw score is converted to a standard score; otherwise, the procedure is identical to the one described in this section. Actually, the example in Table 9-3 can be viewed as the standard score method. Consider the grade of A, for example. The number 1.5 preceding a score can be referred to as a z-score.

An advantage of this system is that scores for all tests are transformed to a common scale. For example, assume two tests are administered in a basketball unit. One test measures dribbling skill and is scored in seconds. The other is a shooting test, scored according to the number of successful shots in a given time period. By using standard score units, the same grading standard can be used for each test even though the actual score units are different. For each test a score falling at or above + 1.5 standard deviations would receive an A, following the example shown in Table 9-3. In this way scores can be directly compared from test to test, and then the grades can be averaged to determine a final grade.

A disadvantage of the system is that students set the standard. Not all classes are typical, yet some students in each class will receive As and some will receive Fs. This problem is reduced by using a large data set to determine the scale. This is the most reliable of any grading system. The standard deviation method can be used in physical education classes for grading cognitive skills, as well as sports skills and other forms of physical activity (Barrow and McGee, 1980).

When this approach to grading is used, the test with the greatest variability will automatically be weighted most heavily. For example, a test that is twice as variable as another is weighted twice as much. The variability of each test, then, must be taken into account when developing a system of weights.

Percentage Method

In the **percentage method** of grading, grade categories are assigned by designating the percentage of students who are to receive each grade. For instance, a teacher might decide to give As to the top 10% of the students, as shown in Example 2 in Table 9-4. If the percentages in this table are based on a large sample of students, this method is no different from the standard deviation method. The percentages in Example 1 will divide distributions of test scores at the same (or very close to) standard deviation points (z-scores), as shown in

Table 9-3. If the method is used with sets of test scores from one small class, comparing the grades of different tests may not be feasible because of fluctuations that can occur with small samples. Only three varieties of the percentage method of grading are presented in Table 9-4, although many other varieties are possible.

The following steps summarize the use of the percentage method of grading:

1. Determine the percentage of students who should receive each grade on a test. For example, consider the following grades and percentages:

A   10%
B   20%
C   40%
D   20%
F   10%

2. Rank the raw scores on a test from highest to lowest. Note the sample data set in Table 9-5.
3. Determine the number of students receiving each grade:

A   10% of 20 = 2
B   20% of 20 = 4
C   40% of 20 = 8
D   20% of 20 = 4
F   10% of 20 = 2

4. Assign grades to ranked scores, as shown in the right side of the table.

Which Method to Use?

Which method of norm-referenced grading is preferred—the standard deviation method or the percentage method? If the grade categories are determined using a large sample of students, either approach will lead to similar results. They merely approach the same problem from different directions. When the categories are used with small classes, the percentages of students in each category are not necessarily identical to those in Table 9-3 or 9-4. This is not a

Table 9-4 Examples of the Percentage Method of Grading			
Grade	**Example 1**	**Example 2**	**Example 3**
A	7	10	15
B	24	20	20
C	38	40	30
D	24	20	20
F	7	10	15

Student	No. of Pull-Ups	Grade
1	25	A
2	24	
3	23	
4	23	B
5	22	
6	21	
7	22	
8	21	
9	21	
10	20	C
11	17	
12	16	
13	15	
14	15	
15	14	
16	13	D
17	13	
18	12	
19	9	F
20	3	

Table 9-5   Modified Pull-Ups Scores

problem because we expect it to occur with small sample fluctuations. The major decision to be made is whether to use a norm-referenced or criterion-referenced approach to grading. Sometimes this is a policy dictated by the school, rather than a decision to be made by individual teachers.

CRITERION-REFERENCED APPROACH TO GRADING

How is a criterion-referenced approach to grading applied? First of all, recall that a criterion-referenced measure is a type of measure in which a standard of performance is identified that is referenced to a criterion behavior. This is a seemingly simple definition but defines a decidedly complex process. Once the performance standard is set, students scoring at or above the standard are given a grade (for instance, pass) and those scoring below the standard are given another grade (fail). However, as discussed earlier, most school systems use a five-point grading scale. Using the criterion-referenced approach, this means that we have to identify four cutoff points or performance standards to obtain five grade categories.

Percentage-Correct Method

In the section on norm-referenced grading, the determination of grade categories based on the percentage of students in a given category is discussed. Here we review a method where the percentage of items or trials successfully completed **(percentage-correct method)** is used to determine grade categories (Table 9-6). To receive an A on a test, the student would have to successfully complete 90% of the trials. In other words, for a 10-trial test, 9 out of 10 trials (or 18 out of 20 for a 20-trial test) must be properly executed. For a 100-item written test, 90 out of 100 items would have to be answered correctly.

It may be necessary to use a point system rather than percentages to designate grade categories, especially when there is no maximum score. For example, in a softball throw for distance, the maximum score for a given age group is unknown. In this case, a distance of n feet or greater could be set for the category for a grade of A. However, grades cannot be directly compared across tests, since the level of difficulty of each test will vary. This is readily apparent in testing muscular endurance, where different levels of endurance may be observed across muscle groups.

Setting Performance Standards for Grading

How are performance standards set? Let's go back to the definition of criterion-referenced measurement. It specifies that the performance standard must be referenced to a criterion behavior. In Chapter 7, the cutoff score of 45 sit-ups for women was discussed in terms of a criterion behavior. Does the ability to perform 45 sit-ups mean that a woman has adequate abdominal strength? Of course there is no evidence to support such a statement. We know that only a certain percentage of women can perform more than 45 sit-ups in 1 minute, but this is a norm-referenced rather than a criterion-referenced statement. As you can see, proper standard-setting is very difficult.

With this seemingly insoluble problem in determining a cutoff score, why discuss the criterion-referenced approach to grading? Primarily because teachers who use the mastery learning model of instruction believe it is a more appropriate method for establishing grades than the norm-referenced approach. In

Table 9-6   Example of Percentage-Correct Method of Grading

Grade	Percentage-Correct Score
A	90–100
B	80–89
C	70–79
D	60–69
F	Below 60

the mastery learning model, there are no constraints on the number of students who can satisfactorily meet an objective. Thus there are no limits on the number of students who receive As, Bs, and so forth. This means the grade distribution for a class is not determined in advance. This is not true when the normal distribution is used in determining norm-referenced grades. Regardless of the ability level of the students, some will receive As, some Bs, and so forth, according to a predetermined categorization of the distribution. Of course, as noted on p. 228, the grade distribution in an ordinary class is not necessarily the same as the distribution for a large sample used to determine the categories. Nonetheless, this approach is designed to reflect individual differences in ability, and it should be expected that the entire grade range will be represented in any class.

In a mastery learning setting, the teacher typically expects his or her class to consist of nonmasters at the beginning of the year. When students are measured on an objective at this point, the distribution of scores should be skewed in a positive direction, since most of the students should receive low scores and only a small percentage should receive high scores. At the end of the unit of instruction, the majority of the students are expected to master the skill. Now the students' scores on this objective are distributed negatively, since only a few students receive low scores. It is possible that many students would receive As and Bs. Once a letter grade has been determined for each test administered during the unit, the unit grade is calculated in the usual manner. Each letter grade is converted to a numerical value, weighted according to its importance, and the weighted grades are then averaged to yield a unit grade.

Another advantage of the criterion-referenced approach to grading is that repeated testing of the student in a formative evaluation context is encouraged. The disadvantages of criterion-referenced grading are associated with setting standards. First of all, it is an arbitrary process. However, this does not sanction careless standard-setting. Every effort must be made to reduce the degree of subjectivity in setting standards. Several solutions to this problem were discussed in Chapter 7. The second disadvantage of criterion-referenced grading is the problem of misclassifications. In classifying students in different grade categories, it is evident that sometimes we will be wrong. Sometimes a student will be given a C who should have been given a B, and vice versa. This is a measurement problem that may never be fully resolved, yet the probability of misclassifications can be reduced as the validity of the cutoff score is increased. (See Chapter 7 for more information on procedures for determining validity.)

CALCULATING FINAL GRADES

Once letter grades have been assigned to each test, they must be converted to numbers to calculate the final grade. The conversion table given in Table 9-7 exemplifies the finest breakdown a teacher could possibly need for grade conversion. If desired, the scale can easily be reduced to a smaller size. Some

Table 9-7   Table for Converting Letter Grades to Numbers

Grade	Number	Grade	Number
A +	12	C	5
A	11	C –	4
A –	10	D +	3
B +	9	D	2
B	8	D –	1
B –	7	F	0
C +	6		

teachers prefer to use a point system whereby test scores are not assigned to a letter grade. The total points for each test are accumulated and weighted accordingly; grade categories are then developed and a letter grade assigned to each. To use this approach, the test scales must be compatible. For example, it would be inappropriate to add time scores (in seconds) and distance scores (in inches). The point system is a valid way to determine a final grade and does not require a series of conversions from test score to letter grade to letter grade conversion, and so forth. Furthermore, averaging letter grades may result in a loss of precision compared with averaging raw test scores. On the other hand, raw scores often must be converted to standard scores, as test scales are frequently not compatible.

AVERAGING LETTER GRADES

Averaging letter grades is a simple way to determine a final grade. Some tests will be of greater importance than others in a given unit; therefore many teachers use a system of weighting the tests. If the scores of each test are averaged using a transformation and the tests are similar in level of difficulty, each test automatically receives the same **weight.** A teacher assigns higher weights to tests of greater importance. If one test is twice as important as another, a 2:1 ratio of weights might be used, as shown in Table 9-8. The knowledge test is given a weight of 2, while the test of playing ability is weighted 1. Note that skill development in badminton is weighted more heavily than any other ability. This is appropriate if skill development received the greatest emphasis in the instructional unit.

    Three letter grades are shown in Table 9-8. Using the conversion Table 9-7, we can determine the numerical value for each letter grade. For example, the numerical value for the skills grade of B − is 7. The weight for skill development (3) is multiplied by the numerical value for B − (7), yielding a total of 21. Follow

Table 9-8   Use of Weights in Determining Grades

BADMINTON UNIT FOR BEGINNERS

Test	Weight	Grade	Total

Skill development
  Short serve
  Long serve
  Overhead clear
	3	B −	$3 \times 7 = 21$

Development of knowledge
  Knowledge of rules
  Knowledge of principles
	2	C	$2 \times 5 = 10$

Playing ability	$\dfrac{1}{6}$	B +	$1 \times 9 = \underline{9}$ 40

Grade = 40/6 = 6.67 = B −

this procedure for each component to be used in determining the final grade, then add the total points for the components (40) and divide by the sum of the weights (6). In this case, the average numerical grade is 6.67, which should be rounded off to a 7. Referring to Table 9-7, note that the letter grade for a numerical grade of 7 is B −. (It is merely coincidental that the final grade is the same as the grade for the skill development test.)

AVERAGING T-SCORES

Test scores can also be converted to standard scores (e.g., T-scores) and averaged to determine final grades. The standard score method provides a finer distinction among students in calculating grades, as two students who receive the same grade on a test will not necessarily receive the same standard score. The standard scores can be weighted in the same way letter grades are weighted.

The following steps summarize the use of T-scores to determine a final grade:

1. Convert the raw scores on each test to T-scores. Tables can be developed to make these conversions, as described in Chapter 3.
2. Establish a grading scale for the averaged T-score values. For example:

> A   65 and above
> B   55–64
> C   45–54
> D   35–44
> F   34 and below

3. At the end of the grading period, sum the T-scores for each student and average them. Weights may be used, as shown below:

Test	T-score	Weight	Total
1	55	2	110
2	70	1	70
3	40	2	80
4	47	3	141
5	62	1	62
6	50	1	50
		10	513

$$\text{Grade} = \frac{513}{10} = 51.3 \text{ or C}$$

USING THE MICROCOMPUTER TO CALCULATE FINAL GRADES

In the previous edition of this textbook, a computer program for calculating grades was included. This program is not included in this textbook, because there are many programs now available for a variety of computers. We recommend using a spreadsheet (e.g., Quattro Pro; Excel; Lotus) or one of several commercially available grading programs (see Chapter 5) to set up your grading system. The weighting for each grade is input when the spreadsheet is set up, and test grades can be entered throughout the grading period. When it is time to determine final grades for your students, the computer handles the calculations and produces the grades.

OTHER SYSTEMS OF GRADING

Educators have used many other systems of grading, including **pass-fail grading** and a **checklist of objectives.**

Pass-Fail Method

Physical educators sometimes prefer the use of a two-grade category, such as pass-fail or mastery-nonmastery, so that the students' attempts to achieve for the sake of a grade will be reduced. In addition, this method is thought to reduce the error that occurs when attempting to classify students into a five-grade category. According to the literature, two-grade categories are less reliable than their five-grade category counterparts. This may be true if a norm-referenced approach is used to estimate reliability. However, when a criterion-referenced reliability estimate is computed, a two-category grade system can be quite reliable. On the other hand, the larger the number of grade categories, the more information there is available about the students in a class. A two-category system is simply not as discriminatory as a more elaborate system, although a more elaborate system will yield a larger number of misclassifications. When a misclassification occurs, it is more serious in the two-category case. In other words, giving a student a grade of C when the grade should have been a B is a serious matter, but not nearly as severe as giving the student a fail when he or she should have received a pass.

Checklist of Objectives

A grading system commonly used at the elementary school level is a system of symbols that can be used with a list of major objectives of the program (checklist of objectives). The following symbols might be used to rate each objective:

O   Outstanding
S   Satisfactory
N   Needs improvement

The appropriate symbol is placed next to each objective in the list. This system of marking is exemplified in Table 9-9.

The student's report card will probably not have adequate space to list the major objectives for each class; therefore, the physical education teacher may wish to send a letter containing more detailed information to the parents of each child or develop a special report card for physical education. An example of a complete report card used in elementary physical education in Madison, Wisconsin is shown in Figure 9-1. This report includes an evaluation of specific objectives as well as an overall assessment of the child's performance. Note that the child is not given a grade on the categories listed under *Movement Skills, Movement Understandings,* and *Work Habits.* Rather, a progress rating is used for these categories. An overall achievement grade is given. Both of these scales can be found in Figure 9-1.

An excellent way of reporting the student's fitness status is the use of the FITNESSGRAM, depicted in Chapter 17. A report can be prepared for children and youth 5 through 17 + years of age.

USE OF INSTITUTIONAL GRADES

Measurement specialists unanimously recommend the use of a common grading system throughout a school. When a common grading system is used, the grades will form a similar distribution, regardless of the area of instruction. In addition, the reliability of the grading system is somewhat increased. The same

Table 9-9   Sample Checklist of Objectives for Elementary School Physical Education

Symbol	Objective
S	Ability to move at different speeds, using different levels
S	Ability to handle various sizes of balls in a variety of ways
N	Ability to use a variety of locomotor patterns

NOTE TO PARENTS: Each skill listed can be performed at different levels of difficulty and with varying degrees of quality. Your child's progress is evaluated through skills and learning experiences considered developmentally appropriate at grade level.

MOVEMENT SKILLS
Progress

Semester
1 2

- Performs all types of foot locomotion (walk, hop, skip, etc.)
- Controls application of force in throwing, striking kicking
- Controls absorption of force in catching and fielding
- Uses space effectively
- Maintains balance and control in quick starts and stops
- Uses a variety of body parts to support, hold or transfer own body weight
- Maintains a steady even rhythm
- Responds to rhythmic patterns with appropriate body movements
- Uses movement to express ideas and feelings
- Creates combinations of movements and repeats them in order
- Shows control and flow in combining movements
- Sustains prolonged physical activity (endurance)
- Demonstrates muscle strength appropriate to movement task
- Demonstrates joint flexibility appropriate to movement task

Additional Information as needed:

M ADISON
ETROPOLITAN SCHOOL DISTRICT

PUPIL _____

TEACHER _____

SCHOOL _____

GRADE LEVEL _____

Physical Education

Semester
1   2

Achievement: ☐ ☐

EXPLANATION OF SYMBOLS

ACHIEVEMENT

E – EXCELLENT

V – VERY GOOD

S – SATISFACTORY

N – NEEDS IMPROVEMENT

PROGRESS

1 Consistent

2 Improving

3 Inconsistent

4 Having difficulty

X Does not apply at this time

MOVEMENT UNDERSTANDINGS
Progress

Semester
1 2

- Understands effects of exercise
- Understands simple strategies applied to game settings
- Understands basic movement concepts

Additional Information as needed:

WORK HABITS
Progress

Semester
1 2

- Listens and follows directions
- Works well independently
- Works well with others
- Participates readily (effort, enthusiasm)
- Respects rights and feelings of others
- Stays on task
- Makes appropriate decisions and choices
- Dresses appropriately for activity

Additional Information as needed:

Figure 9-1   Sample report form for elementary physical education. From Hafeman DA, PhD. Madison Metropolitan School District.

kind of information is provided for students in all areas of the curriculum. Special areas, such as physical education, should use grades to discriminate to the same degree as other parts of the curriculum so that excellence in performance is recognized in all areas.

REPORTING MULTIPLE GRADES

A procedure for reporting more than one grade for each curriculum area is often recommended so that one of the grades can be based purely on achievement. Frequently a second grade is classified as a "citizenship" grade. In physical education, separating motor skill grades from cognitive and affective grades would also provide useful information for all concerned. Although such a separation is somewhat artificial, the use of multiple grades will have more meaning than a single grade.

SUMMARY

Grades in physical education should represent the degree to which students have attained the objectives of the curriculum units. These often include the development of motor, cognitive, and affective skills within the physical education program. There is general agreement that the achievement of sports skills and other forms of physical activity should be given major emphasis in determining a physical education grade. Cognitive skills may be given less weight but nonetheless represent an important component of the grade. Although grading the affective behavior of students is intuitively appealing, it is difficult to measure these skills objectively and systematically.

Two systems of grading for physical education students are the norm-referenced method and the criterion-referenced method. The normal distribution is the basis for determining grade categories in the norm-referenced approach. Of primary interest is the student's performance relative to others in class. The criterion-referenced method of grading designates grade categories based on predetermined performance standards. This method is tied to the mastery learning instructional method, where many students are expected to meet minimal standards at the end of a unit. Either system can be used effectively in a school setting. The choice of a grading system is dependent on the philosophy of teaching and learning adopted by the instructional staff.

Learning Experiences

1. A test was administered to five beginning badminton classes. The mean for the set of test scores is 32 and the standard deviation is 4. Using Table 9-3, develop a table showing the range of test scores for each grade category. Then calculate the grades for the following five students:

Student	Test score
A	40
B	30
C	25
D	33
E	36

Using the information given below, calculate the final grades for five students.

Test	Weight
No. 1	1
No. 2	2
No. 3	1.5
No. 4	2.5

Student	Test no. 1	Test no. 2	Test no. 3	Test no. 4
A	A	C	B	D +
B	C	B	B −	C +
C	B	A	A −	A
D	B	D	C +	B +
E	B −	C	D	C

2. A bent-knee curl-ups test was administered to 20 high-school students. The number of sit-ups performed by each student is recorded below. Use the percentages in example 3 of Table 9-4 to determine the grade for each student.

Student	Curl-ups score
1	52
2	35
3	39
4	14
5	27
6	43
7	32
8	37
9	21
10	42
11	30
12	55
13	29
14	37

Continued

Student	Curl-ups score
15	26
16	40
17	35
18	44
19	17
20	46

References

Baumgartner TA, Jackson AS. 1991. Measurement for evaluation in physical education and exercise science. Dubuque, Iowa: Wm C Brown Group.

Barrow HM, McGee R. 1980. A practical approach to measurement in physical education, ed 3. Philadelphia: Lea & Febiger.

Boyce BA. 1990. Grading practices—how do they influence student skill performance? Journal of Physical Education, Recreation and Dance, **61**(6): 46–48.

Cotten DJ, Cotten MB. 1985. Grading: the ultimate weapon? Journal of Physical Education, Recreation and Dance, **56**(2):52–53.

East WB. 1985. PROGRAM CHANGE. Author.

Hale PW, Hale RM. 1972. Comparison of student improvement by experimental modification of test-retest scores. Research Quarterly, **43**:113–120.

Imwold CH, Rider RA, Johnson DJ. 1982. The use of evaluation in public school physical education. Journal of Teaching in Physical Education, **2**:13–18.

Mathews DK. 1958. Measurement in physical education. Philadelphia: WB Saunders.

Petray CK, Blazer SL. 1991. Health-related physical fitness: Concepts and activities for elementary school children, ed 3. Edina, Minn: Bellwether Press.

Schutz RW. 1989. Analyzing change. In Safrit MJ, Wood TM, eds. Measurement concepts in physical education and exercise science. Champaign, Ill: Human Kinetics.

Annotated Readings

Cotten DJ, Cotten MB. 1985. Grading: the ultimate weapon? Journal of Physical Education, Recreation and Dance, **56**(2):52–53.
   Emphasizes the importance of basing grades on objectives; identifies issues that should be considered when formulating a grading strategy; discusses the grading of group assignments.

Davis MW. 1983. Let's talk about Johnny's 'C' in P.E.! In Hensley L, East W, eds. Measurement and evaluation symposium proceedings. Cedar Falls, Iowa: University of Northern Iowa.
   Discusses the need for meaningful and effective evaluation in physical education; proposes a sports skill and physical fitness profile as the most desir-

able approach to an individualized evaluation summary; describes and illustrates the phases of profile development.

Hensley LD. 1990. Current measurement and evaluation practices in professional physical education. Journal of Physical Education, Recreation and Dance, **61**(3):32–33.

An overview of the status of grading practice in physical education; notes these practices have changed little in the past 25 years; characterizes the predominant grading model in physical education today as consisting of attitude, attendance, and effort combined with subjective ratings of motor performance.

Hensley LD, East WB. 1989. Testing and grading in the psychomotor domain. In Safrit MJ, Wood TM, eds. Measurement concepts in physical education and exercise science. Champaign, Ill: Human Kinetics.

An up-to-date treatise on literature dealing with testing in the psychomotor domain and evaluating student achievement in physical education; provides an interesting philosophical perspective on grading.

Laughlin N, Laughlin S. 1992. The myth of measurement in physical education. Journal of Physical Education, Recreation and Dance, **63**(4):83–85.

A critique of two grading plans used in physical education; supports four recommendations leading to more accurate estimates of student ability and motivation in grading.

Answers to Learning Experiences

1. The following table was developed showing the range of test scores for each grade category by using Table 9-3.

Grade	Range of test scores
A	38 and above
B	34–37
C	30–33
D	26–29
F	25 and below

A grade was determined for each of the students listed below:

Student	Test score	Grade
A	40	A
B	30	C
C	25	F
D	33	C
E	36	B

Table 9-7 was used to convert letter grades to numbers. The individual test grades (now numbers) were multiplied by the weighting for the respective test. These values were summed across all four tests and are shown below in column 2:

Student	Sum of grade by weight	Average of column 2	Grade
A	40.5	5.78	C+
B	46.5	6.64	B−
C	72.5	10.36	A−
D	43.5	6.21	C+
E	32.5	4.64	C

In the third column, the sums in the second column were divided by the sum of the weights for the four tests, in this case, 7. Then Table 9-7 was used to convert the numerical value in column 3 to a composite letter grade, shown in the fourth column.

2. Determine the number of students who will receive each grade:

> A   15% of 20 = 3
> B   20% of 20 = 4
> C   30% of 20 = 6
> D   20% of 20 = 4
> F   15% of 20 = 3

Rank the curl-ups test scores from highest to lowest. Assign grades to ordered scores.

Student	Ordered scores	Grade
12	55	A
1	52	A
20	46	A
18	44	B
6	43	B
10	42	B
16	40	B
3	39	C
8	37	C
14	37	C
2	35	C
17	35	C
7	32	C
11	30	D
13	29	D
5	27	D
15	26	D
9	21	F
19	17	F
4	14	F

Measurement in a Nonschool Setting

Assessment in a Nonschool Setting

Watch for these words as you read the following chapter

Bicycle ergometer
Body composition
Carotid artery
Circumference measure
Health risk appraisal
Maximal oxygen uptake (Vo₂ max)

METS (metabolic equivalents of oxygen consumption)
Pulse rate
Skinfold thickness
Step test

Many career options are available to the student who is interested in physical education and exercise science. Teacher preparation for the school setting represents only one of these options; others include fitness center instruction, sports center instruction, athletic training, sports management, sports medicine, exercise science, and administration. In this chapter the use of measurement and evaluation in several of these settings is discussed.

Formal instruction in many types of physical activity can take place outside the school setting. Even in the early part of the twentieth century, it was possible to take dance classes in private studios, receive private lessons in sports such as tennis and golf, learn a wide variety of skills in summer camps, and participate in activities at a YMCA or YWCA. Today many other opportunities are also available in private sports centers, fitness centers, and worksite health promotion programs. In this textbook the instructional aspects of these organizations are considered, as well as the managerial and assessment components.

Sound measurement practices are as important in nonschool settings as they are in the school setting. For example, the objectives of a private club may differ from those of a school, but a well-run organization will be accountable for its outcomes. While objectives vary from club to club, the bottom line for each club is to show a profit. This cannot be done unless members are recruited and retained. If a member chooses to enroll in a class, an additional fee may be charged. Once in class the member is presented with the opportunity to learn. It is assumed that a level of motivation initially exists, but often it is the instructor's responsibility to maintain this motivation. There is virtually no control over the "students" in these classes. They cannot be required to attend, study rules, practice skills, or take tests, for that matter. However, evaluation should not be ignored for these reasons. The club, not the client, sets the standards. If the client wishes to ignore the standards, it is his or her prerogative.

ASSESSMENT IN SPORTS CLUBS

Joining a sports club for recreational purposes only is not unusual. Advantages include the availability of court space when desired and the offering of instructional programs, which usually include private and group lessons. Undoubtedly, each instructor plans objectives for these classes. The objectives may be general or specific, including skills the instructor plans to introduce during the unit of instruction. In some instances these objectives may not be available in written form. Unless the instructional program is poor, the instructor has probably thought through the instructional plans and has loosely formed objectives in mind. If the club is part of a franchise, a set of objectives, able to be modified to meet the needs of each club, might be distributed by the home office. Regardless of the source, objectives should be prepared in writing. The small size of classes and the individualized nature of instruction create an ideal opportunity for tailoring objectives to clients' needs.

Writing objectives for class members in a private club is no different from preparing objectives for students in a school. The major difference is that, because of a smaller class size, the instructor in the private club often has the luxury of formulating objectives for each client. Individualized objectives also support the club as a business. The closer the class comes to meeting the client's needs, the more likely it is that others will enroll in future classes. If a client benefits from a class, the word will be passed on to other prospective clients; some of them will sign up for a future class. Word of mouth is a powerful factor in sustaining this type of private enterprise.

Although the process of writing objectives is the same in school and nonschool settings, the process of implementing them can differ. Although objectives have been set and the instructional process delineated, the client may not be concerned about meeting predetermined objectives. Clients' needs in a class setting may differ. Some sign up for a class simply to learn a little more about the sport; thus developing skills to a specified level may be of little interest to them. They may care little about specific objectives, as long as the basic skills needed for the game are covered. On the other hand, skill development may be important to others, who often respond positively to the use of objectives that include specific evaluation standards. For them, the setup materials for skills tests provide an excellent opportunity to practice their skills. Furthermore, the client can work toward a set of specific goals. Any published test of a skill can be used in a private club setting, as long as test validity and reliability are adequate for the situation and clientele. In fact, using tests requiring elaborate setup materials in a private club is far more feasible than it is in a school.

Since a private sports club is a business, the needs of the client must be met while ensuring a high-quality program. A multifaceted approach to preparing objectives is recommended. Objectives should be developed for the class as a whole. For example, in a beginning racquetball class, objectives could be written for the serve, forehand, and backhand drives; playing the game; and so forth. Each of these objectives should include specific evaluation standards. At the first meeting of the class, these objectives should be reviewed. Then the class members could be given choices regarding their own objectives. At the very least, the client should be encouraged to adapt the class objectives to his or her own needs. This allows testing to take place during the unit of instruction, as described in the objectives. Ideally the instructor would work closely with each client to tailor the class objectives to the individual. However, it should be made clear that all clients wishing to progress to a higher-level course must meet the class objectives at the current level. It is possible that individual modifications can be even more stringent than the class objectives. At the other extreme, some class members may not care about being evaluated and may object to taking any type of test and to any formalized rating by the instructor. In small clubs the number of members is often insufficient to allow several classes to take place at the same time, each with different objectives. Flexibility and individualization are the keys to success in the private club.

ASSESSING HEALTH-RELATED FITNESS IN FITNESS CENTERS

Many exercise specialists are being trained to assume jobs as instructors or directors of private fitness clubs, corporate fitness centers, and similar organizations. In these settings the objectives may be health-related rather than skill-oriented (or both). Also, objectives are usually individualized, since the fitness level of new clients can vary greatly. A typical objective is the reduction of body fat. The desired amount of weight loss is dependent on the client's distribution of fat and lean body mass at the time he or she joins the program. The client's body composition, consisting of bone, muscle mass, and fatty tissue, must be measured to determine his or her current status (Pollack, Schmidt, and Jackson, 1980). Types of measures of body composition vary from one organization to another; however, some methods, such as weighing the person, are not the best measure to use. (Valid measures of **body composition** are discussed in detail in

Chapter 17.) Once the client's body composition has been determined, a reasonable goal can be set for that person. Note that this is another example of needs assessment. The actual level of body fatness is compared with the desirable level.

The testing programs used in fitness centers vary widely, ranging from no tests at all to a relatively sophisticated series of measures. A review of the entrance tests used by several organizations follows. (Refer to Chapter 17 for specific information on the tests mentioned in these sections.)

Private Clubs

Private fitness centers in the United States have proliferated over the past 15 years. Although all clubs have as their goal the improvement of a client's fitness level, various methods are used to achieve this goal. Some clubs merely provide organized workouts for their clients, with no information on the effectiveness of the exercise sessions. Others test basic physiological and physical capacities of all new clients who join their club, and on the basis of these results prescribe an exercise program for each client. Obviously the latter approach is preferable. Not only is the program geared to the individual's needs but the client also becomes more knowledgeable about his or her health-related fitness status. The testing programs used in two private clubs are described first.

Vic Tanny Clubs

The Vic Tanny clubs (Vic Tanny International of Wisconsin, Inc.) offer two tests of health-related fitness to new members. The first is a Body Fat Analysis, in which percent body fat and ideal body weight are estimated from body **circumferences.** The rationale for using body circumference measures to estimate body composition has been discussed by Katch et al. (1991). Three body sites are used, although the sites differ with one's sex and age. For women less than 30 years old, circumferences are measured at the midabdomen, right thigh, and right forearm. The right calf is substituted for the right forearm for women over 30. For men under age 30, circumferences are measured at the right upper arm, midabdomen, and right forearm. The buttock is substituted for the right upper arm for men over 30. The second test is the Pulse Recovery Step Test, a modification of the step tests described in Chapter 17 (Figure 10-1). The client exercises for 3 minutes on a 12-inch bench, using a cadence of 24 steps per minute. The pulse rate is then measured for 10 seconds immediately after the end of the 3-minute period.

Figure 10-2 displays a portion of the form used to record fitness test information. This record is then used to plan an exercise program for the client.

Olympic Health and Racquet Club

The Olympic Health and Racquet Club uses the Kasch Pulse Recovery Test. This is another modification of the **step test,** in which the heart rate is measured during recovery. The bench height is 14 inches for women and 16 inches for men. The duration of the test is 3 minutes, with one step taken every 2 seconds. The heart rate is measured at the **carotid artery.** This rate is recorded in 10-

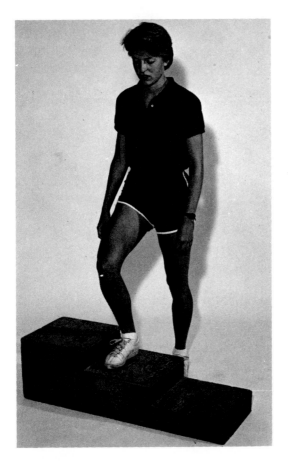

Figure 10-1   Administration of step test.

second increments during the first minute of recovery after the completion of exercise. The total score is the sum of the ten 10-second recordings. Body composition measures are made available through other sources.

The scoresheet for the Kasch test is shown in Figure 10-3. Note that suggested standards for men and women are included on the scoresheets used by both clubs.

Worksite Health Promotion Programs

Many large corporations and government agencies provide fitness centers or worksite health promotion programs to enable their employees to exercise during working hours was well as before and after work. These centers are often directed by a person with at least a master's degree in exercise physiology. Extensive assessment is usually available in these settings. These assessments often include a **health risk appraisal** (HRA).

CLUB TOUR   DR. PAUL WARD   3/16/82

□ Facilities   □ Workout Floor and Program Explanation

□ BODY FAT ANALYSIS

□ I.   INTRODUCTION: Body weight as shown on the scale is not a good indi-
        cator of body composition. One does not know what portion of their
        body is fat and or muscle. Therefore, it is necessary to determine
        an individual's % body fat and strive to reduce this percentage by
        proper diet and exercise programs. Percent fat determination using
        selected body circumferential measurements has been scientifically
        proven to give accurate estimates of body fat.

□ II. MEASUREMENTS: (measurements will be different for each sex and
        age group)

                              WOMEN

         Under 30   Over 30

    (A) Mid-Abdomen: _____   (A) Mid-Abdomen: _____
    (B) Right Thigh: _____   (B) Right Thigh: _____
    (C) Right Forearm:_____   (C) Right Calf: _____
    (D) Age Const: 19.6   (D) Age Const: 18.4

                              MEN

         Under 30   Over 30   BODY BUILDERS

    (A) Rt Upper Arm: _____   (A) Buttocks: _____   (A) WAIST: _____
    (B) Mid-Abdomen: _____   (B) Mid-Abdomen: _____ (B) BUTTOCKS: _____
    (C) Right Forearm:_____   (C) Right Forearm:_____ (C) WRIST: _____
    (D) Age Const: 10.2   (D) Age Const: 14.9   (D) NECK: _____

□   Locate the constant that corresponds to each of the three
        measurements on reference chart.

□ III. PERCENT FAT = _____ + _____ - _____ - _____ = [%   ]
                         A   B   C   D

□ IV. DETERMINATION OF IDEAL BODY WEIGHT

        1. % fat from formula = _____% Convert to a decimal = [   ]

        2. Fat Weight = Body Weight X % Fat (in decimal form) = [   ]

              = _____ X _____ = [lbs.   ]

        3. Lean Weight = Body Weight in lbs. - Fat Weight in lbs. = [   ]

              = _____ - _____ = [lbs.   ]

        4. STANDARDS Endurance Athletes 5-9% Suggested % fat for men = 12-15%

            Suggested % fat for women = 16-20%
            Optimal % fat used = 100 - _____ % = [   ]
            (change to a decimal)

Figure 10-2   Form used in exercise program planning. *From Vic Tanny International of Wisconsin Inc.*

5. Optimal Body Weight = Lean Weight ÷ Optimal % Fat (in decimal form)
    (assuming lean weight remains the same)

$$= \underline{\hspace{2cm}} \div \underline{\hspace{2cm}} = \boxed{\qquad\qquad \text{lbs.}}$$

6. Pounds of fat to lose = Body Weight - Optimal Body Weight =

$$= \underline{\hspace{2cm}} - \underline{\hspace{2cm}} = \boxed{\qquad\qquad \text{lbs.}}$$

□   V. These fat formulas are the exclusive property of Dr. Frank Katch and
        Dr. William McArdle and the Lea & Febiger Publishing Company,
        Philadelphia, Pa. Permission for their use has been exclusively
        given to the Health and Tennis Corporation of America. These formulas
        are protected by U.S. copyright regulations.

        Reproduced by permission
        FRANK I. KATCH and WILLIAM D. McARDLE
        Nutrition, Weight Control, and Exercise
        2nd Ed.
        Lea & Febiger Publishers
        Philadelphia, Pa.
        1983

□   PULSE RECOVERY STEP TEST

□   The three minute pulse recovery step test consists of a 12-inch
        bench, 24 per min. stepping rate for exactly three (3) minutes
        duration. Its purpose is to broadly determine the exercise
        tolerance or exercise classification of human subjects. It is not
        intended to be a diagnostic test, but for the screening and classi-
        fication of fitness as a means of prescribing an exercise program;
        (2) evaluating the subject's fitness in comparison to normals; and
        (3) to follow the progress of a person undergoing training or re-
        cuperating from a low fitness level or illness.

□   Resting pulse rate (beats per minute) _____

□   Number of heart beats exactly 0 to 10 seconds after the step-up
        exercise _____

□   "TENTATIVE" CLASSIFICATION OF HEART RATE RECOVERY

Classification	Men	Women
Excellent	17 or less	16 or less
Good	18 to 20	17 to 18
Average	21 to 23	19 to 22
Fair	24 to 26	23 to 25
Poor	27 or more	26 or more

Subsidiary of
HEALTH & TENNIS CORP.
OF AMERICA

Figure 10-2   **cont'd.** For legend see opposite page.

KASCH PULSE RECOVERY TEST

NAME _____

ADDRESS _____

	TEST 1 Date: _____	TEST 2 Date: _____	TEST 3 Date: _____
Resting heart rate	_____	_____	_____
Recovery	0-10 _____	0-10 _____	0-10 _____
Heart rate	11-20 _____	11-20 _____	11-20 _____
0-1 Min	21-30 _____	21-30 _____	21-30 _____
Post exercise	31-40 _____	31-40 _____	31-40 _____
	41-50 _____	41-50 _____	41-50 _____
	51-60 _____	51-60 _____	51-60 _____
	TOTAL _____	TOTAL _____	TOTAL _____

CLASSIFICATION: (Check one)

Superior	_____	_____	_____
Excellent	_____	_____	_____
Good	_____	_____	_____
Average	_____	_____	_____
Fair	_____	_____	_____
Poor	_____	_____	_____
Very poor	_____	_____	_____

SUGGESTED STANDARDS FOR MEN AND WOMEN

Men (over 30 yrs)	Men (18-30 yrs)	Classification	Women (18 yrs & over)
67	68	Superior	70
68-78	69-80	Excellent	71-82
79-90	81-90	Good	83-94
91-105	91-104	Average	95-109
106-115	105-114	Fair	110-119
116-125	115-124	Poor	120-129
126	125	Very poor	130

Figure 10-3   Kasch Test Score sheet. *From Olympic Health and Racquet Club.*

Because HRAs have been widely used during the past decade, a brief review of this assessment procedure is appropriate. An HRA is an instrument used to estimate a person's probability of dying from specific diseases over a period of time. Information about the person's health-related behaviors and personal characteristics is obtained through a questionnaire. This information, along with U.S. mortality statistics and epidemiological data, is used to calculate the person's probability of premature death. In addition, some HRAs include behavior modification programs.

There are advantages and disadvantages to using an HRA. The most obvious advantage is the early detection of risk factors. Another advantage is that the results can contribute to bringing about changes in health behaviors, particularly when followed up with an educational program designed to modify the high-risk behaviors. Disadvantages include the possibility of an undue emphasis on the risks of early death. Instead, emphasis should be placed on modifiable habits. Many users do not understand the limitations of probabilistic concepts (Terry, 1987). Another disadvantage is the questionable sensitivity of epidemiologic databases to specific populations, such as minority groups (Parr, 1989).

There have also been questions about the validity and reliability of HRAs. The database issue is a questionable aspect of validity. The validity of the statistical methodology used to calculate relative and absolute risks is also open to question (Parr, 1989). The impact that HRAs have on changing behavior is equivocal. For example, Dishman (1990) noted the HRAs have only a modest influence on participation in physical activity. The reliability of HRAs reflects the client's ability to provide an accurate self-report. The fact that the accuracy cannot be verified is a problem in the reproducibility of questionnaire results.

Many versions of HRAs exist, and they are not necessarily alike in their focus. All use national statistics to calculate the risk of dying; thus, all record information on age, race, sex, and health practices. Beyond these questions, the amount and quantity of information obtained can differ widely. One of the more comprehensive and widely used HRAs is the Health Risk Appraisal Program of the Carter Center of Emory University in Atlanta (Carter Center, 1991).

Now let's take a look at several examples of worksite health promotion programs.

Army Materiel Command Health Promotion Program

The Army Materiel Command's (AMC) health promotion program is located in Alexandria, Virginia. There are two main goals of this program: "to improve employee health and fitness using a comprehensive, individualized health/fitness program and to investigate the cost/benefit of an on-the-job wellness program" (USOPM, 1991). The health promotion program is offered free of charge to the 1,200 civilian employees at AMC.

The following six steps must be taken before an employee enters the program:

A

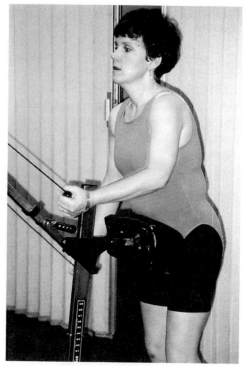

B

C

D

1. Applicants take a health risk appraisal, which includes questions about their lifestyle habits and medical history.
2. A preliminary assessment of their health status is obtained through measurements of height, weight, blood pressure, resting **pulse rate,** and a blood sample (used to determine levels of high-density lipoprotein [HDL], low-density lipoprotein [LDL], triglycerides, and fasting blood sugar).
3. A medical screening by a physician takes place involving an electrocardiogram (ECG) and a cardiovascular examination. This screening is provided free for employees over 40.
4. Applicants receive a fitness assessment, including measures of strength, flexibility, back fitness, body composition, and pulmonary function.
5. Each applicant meets with a health and fitness specialist to discuss the results of the medical screening and the fitness testing.
6. An exercise program is prescribed for each applicant. Applicants learn to monitor their own heart rates and to use exercise equipment safely. Instruction is also provided on the proper techniques for stretching, warm-up, and cool-down.

The AMC health promotion flow chart is shown in Figure 10-4. This chart provides more detail on the individualized health promotion program.

Participants who are accepted into the program can use the exercise facility to exercise on their own. They can also take advantage of the classes offered, including ones on cholesterol reduction, weight loss, smoking cessation, stress management, and preventive back strain.

A computerized database has been established to track participant progress in achieving specific health and fitness goals as well as facility usage. Productivity measures, sick leave data, and healthcare claims are recorded to be used in assessing the cost-effectiveness of the program.

The AMC program serves as a model for government worksite health promotion programs. It has been demonstrated that this program increased productivity, decreased absenteeism, and reduced healthcare costs at AMC.

CUNA Mutual Insurance Group

An example of a corporate health promotion program is the Exercise Resource Facility of the CUNA Mutual Insurance Group (Madison, Wisconsin), made available to all employees of CUNA Mutual. The test package includes measurement of body composition, functional capacity, strength, and flexibility. Body composition is assessed by measuring the **skinfold thicknesses** at three sites. The men's sites are pectoral, abdominal, and thigh; the women's, triceps, suprailiac, and thigh. The skinfold thickness values are used to estimate percent of body fat and lean body mass. To measure functional capacity, a **bicycle ergometer** test is used (Figure 10-5). A bicycle ergometer is a stationary bicycle that

---

A, Army Materiel Command (AMC) participant on rowing machine. **B,** AMC participant on Nordic track. **C,** AMC participant taking step class. **D,** AMC participant on stationary bicycle.

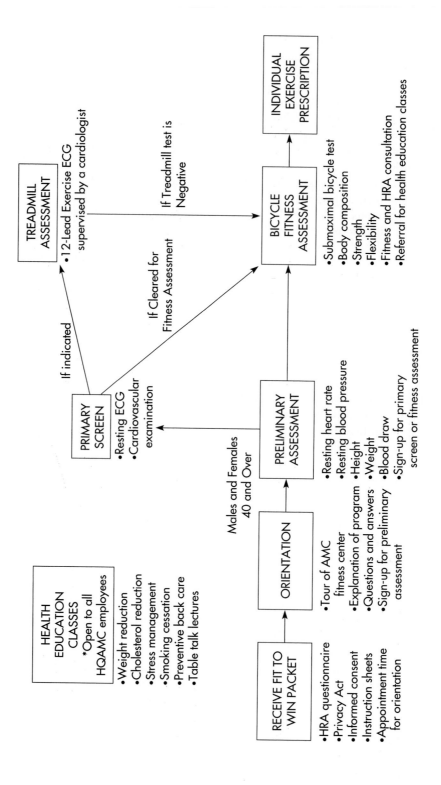

Figure 10-4 AMC health promotion flow chart. *HRA*, health risk appraisal.

* Please note: All phases through the Individual Exercise Prescription must be completed prior to use of the Fitness Center for exercise. Medical clearance is not necessary for participation in the nonphysical Health Education Classes.

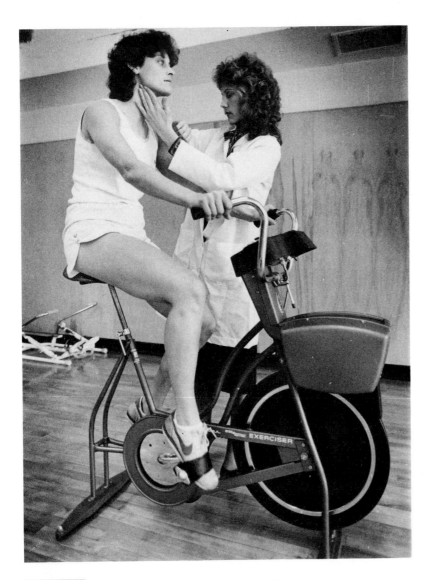

Figure 10-5 Administration of submaximal bicycle ergometer test.

can be used to measure physical work capacity. Since this is a submaximal stress test, the results provide an indirect measure of **maximal oxygen uptake (VO$_2$ max).** The score is also recorded in **METS (metabolic equivalents of oxygen consumption),** which is defined as an energy value, somewhat like a calorie, or, more specifically, the ratio of exercise metabolic rate to resting metabolic rate (1 MET = 3.5 mL/kg). Three measures of strength are administered: a leg press, a bench press, and a sit-ups test. To measure flexibility, the Sit and Reach Test is used.

EMPLOYEE TEST DATA

EXERCISE RESOURCE FACILITY

NAME _____ DATE _____/_____/_____

CHECK ONE: Original Test   Retest   Examiner _____

AGE _____ WEIGHT _____ lb _____ kg   OPTIMAL WEIGHT _____ HEIGHT _____
                                                (Estimate)

BODY COMPOSITION

(Circle one)

MEN   WOMEN

Pectoral   Triceps _____

Abdominal Suprailium _____

Thigh   Thigh _____

    Sum of three   _____

    % Fat   _____

    Lean body mass _____

16%   23%   _____

    Abdominal girth _____

    Other: 1.   _____

            2.   _____

            3.   _____

FUNCTIONAL CAPACITY

Original workload _____

Resting HR   _____

Resting BP   _____

Workload _____ kg@ _____ RPM= _____ KPM

EXERCISE   HR   BP

        Min. 1 _____ _____

            2 _____ _____

            3 _____ _____

            4 _____ _____

            5 _____ _____

            6 _____ _____

Steady State HR

STRENGTH DATA

1. Leg Press   _____
2. Bench Press   _____
3. Sit-Ups Test _____

FLEXIBILITY DATA

Sit and Reach Test _____

COMMENTS:

TRAINING DATA

METS Max   _____

METS Training   _____

Heart Rate Training _____/min

                    _____/15 sec

Figure 10-6 Employee record of training data. *From the Exercise Resource facility, CUNA Mutual Insurance Group, Madison, Wis.*

The results of this thorough testing program are used to prescribe an exercise program for the employee. Note the space provided for training data, the level at which the employee should be exercising, on the employee record shown in Figure 10-6.

Sentry World Headquarters

The Physical Fitness Center at the Sentry World Headquarters in Stevens Point, Wisconsin, is designed for the benefit of all Sentry Insurance employees. Physical fitness is viewed as a key element in maintaining personal health. The Sentry Wellness Program was developed to improve the quality of life of employees. It provides for an appraisal of the employee's current state of health as well as education regarding exercise, rest, nutrition, and other elements affecting one's health. Screening for potential problems such as high blood pressure is available on an ongoing basis. Assistance is provided for well and relatively well people, those with acute illness or injury, and those suffering from a chronic disability. A "flexible time" principle permits the employee to arrange

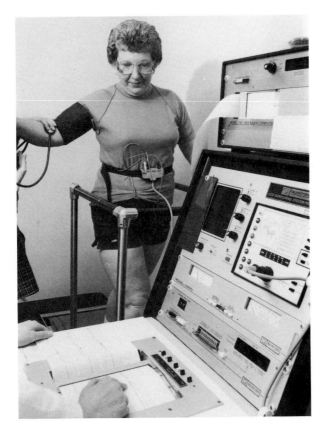

Employee taking treadmill test at Sentry
World Headquarters, Stevens Point, Wis.

FITNESS AND STRESS TEST PROTOCOL

Date_____

This form is to be completed and brought to the Medical Department prior to participating in an organized program in the Physical Fitness Center or a stress test.

1. Name _____ Address _____

2. Sentry employee _____ Spouse/Dependent (State employee's name) _____
   Other _____

3. Age _____ 4. Sex _____ 5. Phone: (Home) _____ (Bus.) _____
   Location _____

6. Exercise program interested in _____

7. Previous stress test? _____ If so, date: _____ A copy should be on file in the Medical Department.

8. **HABITS THAT AFFECT QUALITY AND QUANTITY OF LIFE:**

   PLEASE LIST TYPE OF EXERCISE

   A. **Exercise** _____ At least 3-5 times weekly for at least 15 minutes of vigorous exercise each time.

   _____ Less than above.

   _____ None

   _____
   _____
   _____
   _____

   B. **Rest:** Average number of hours of sleep per night_____

   C. **Smoker:** _____ If so, what? _____ For how long? _____

   How much have you been averaging per day? _____

   If you quit smoking, CONGRATULATIONS! How long ago? _____

   D. **Nutrition:** Do you eat breakfast? _____
   Do you eat at least three meals per day? _____
   Do you snack between meals? _____
   Average number of alcohol drinks per week? _____
   (1 drink = 1 can of beer, 1 glass of wine, 1 shot of hard liquor)

   Average number of cups of caffeinated coffee per week _____
   Average number of 8 oz. cola drinks per week _____

   E. **Stress:** Do you feel you take adequate relaxation time? _____
   Do you usually feel you are "in control" of how life is going? _____

9. Allergies to materials or drugs? _____ If so, what? _____
   _____

10. Use of medications, pills or shots? This would include either prescription drugs or "over the counter" prescriptions such as sleeping aids, tension-reducers, diet pills or vitamins. No _____ Yes _____ Please list: ____
    _____

11. Presently receiving care for any conditions? No _____ Yes _____

    Explain: _____

Figure 10-7   Fitness and stress protocol form.

12. If you have ever had problems with any of the following, please describe below:
Heart or blood vessels (blood clot, murmur, rheumatic fever, chest pain, irreg. heart beat) _____

_____

High blood pressure _____

Lungs, asthma, chronic bronchitis _____

Seizure disorder/epilepsy _____

Muscles, joints, or back _____

Thyroid gland or metabolism _____

Diabetes _____

Balance or dizziness _____

Any previous surgery/pregnancy _____

13. Have any blood relatives (parents, brothers, sisters) died before age 60 of any of the above
problems? Yes _____ No _____ Explain: _____

_____

14. Do any living blood relatives have any of the above health conditions? _____
Explain: _____

15. Have you ever had a cholesterol or triglyceride test? _____ If so, when and what were the results? _____

_____

I understand that the information on this form will be released to the Physical Fitness Center.
Signed_____

— —

THIS PORTION TO BE FILLED OUT BY MEDICAL DEPARTMENT STAFF

Height _____ Weight _____ Ideal Weight _____

Blood Pressure _____ Resting Heart Rate _____

Stress Test Date _____ Physical Condition _____

Age-Adjusted Maximum Heart Rate (220-Age) _____

65% _____ 75% _____ 85% _____

RECOMMENDED INITIAL TARGET HEART RATE _____

Conditions to be Aware of: _____

_____

_____

Restrictions: _____

_____

Reviewed by   _____
Date sent to PFC _____

Figure 10-7   **cont'd.** Fitness and stress protocol form.

NAME: _____   Target Heart Rate: _____ % _____ or _____ beats/10 sec.   8 weeks

_____ % _____ or _____ beats/10 sec.   12 weeks

_____ % _____ or _____ beats/10 sec.   Stay

Column headers: Weight | Resting H.R. | Warm Up & Stretching | Treadmill | Rowing | Ergometer (Cycle) | Jump Rope | Abdominal Boards (Sit-Ups) | Balance Beam | Cool Down | Recovery H.R.

For optimum cardiovascular benefits (those for your heart, lungs,
and blood vessels), three factors
must be incorporated:

FREQUENCY — exercising a
minimum of four times per week

INTENSITY — while exercising
achieve your target heart rate.

DURATION — Keeping your target
heart rate for 30 minutes of
continuous exercise.

*If at any time you are unsure about
any phase of your program, or if
you feel that you might need
additional help or guidance —
please — Contact ANY MEMBER
OF THE STAFF — AT ONCE!!*

57-3   (SWH)   2-80   *See Physical Fitness Assistant for New Card and Program Assessment*

Figure 10-8   Each participant keeps a daily record of personal activities.

working hours to allow scheduling of health promotion activities during a regular workday.

Three steps must be completed by an employee wishing to use the Physical
Fitness Center. First, an orientation program is undertaken to instruct the employee in identifying good health habits and taking control of his or her personal fitness program. Next, the employee receives a medical screening, completes the form shown in Figure 10-7 on pp 260 and 261, and takes the form to

LEGS: Progress to 20 repetitions then increase weight unit by one the next session while decreasing the repetitions.

ARMS: Progress to 15 repetitions then increase weight unit by one the next session and decrease repetitions.

Figure 10-8   **cont'd.** Each participant keeps a daily record of personal activities.

the medical department before participating in an organized program. This form is typical of the inventories designed to assess lifestyle, including both physical and mental health. Finally, a trained physical fitness specialist provides the employee with specific instructions for an individualized program consisting of two parts—cardiovascular and Nautilus strength and flexibility training (Sentry World Headquarters, 1990). Each participant keeps a daily record of personal activities using the form shown in Figure 10-8.

Employee using the Nautilus equipment for self-testing at Sentry World Headquarters.

OTHER ORGANIZATIONS

Many hospitals have their own fitness center which includes an exercise physiology laboratory. These facilities are frequently available only to patients with cardiac disease or hypertension and employees of the hospital. However, services are sometimes extended to special groups of patients such as pregnant women and elderly people. It is not unusual for hospitals to promote a wellness program, although exercise facilities may not be provided for those in reasonably good health. A physical education department in a university may provide fitness programs for faculty and staff. Basic assessments such as stress testing and skinfold measurement are often provided. If collaboration with a nearby hospital is established, a cardiac rehabilitation program may be established.

YMCA

The YMCA uses an extensive battery of tests in the *Y's Way to Physical Fitness* (Golding et al., 1989). Body composition is determined by measuring skinfold thicknesses at either four or six sites for men and three or five sites for women. The number of sites measured depends on the formula to be used in estimating percent fat. The measures of skinfold thickness are summed across the sites, and an estimate of percent body fat is calculated. Furthermore, percentile norms for each skinfold site are available. The Body Composition Rating Scale for males 35 years and younger is shown in Figure 10-9.

A physical work capacity (PWC) test is included as a measure of cardiorespiratory (CR) function. The male client begins exercising on a bicycle ergometer at

Y's WAY TO PHYSICAL FITNESS

Rating Scale

Norms Males 35 Years and Under

Name _____ Dates: _____ T$_1$ _____ T$_2$ _____ T$_3$ _____

Percentage ranking	Rating	Percent fat	Chest mm	Abdomen mm	Ilium mm	Axilla mm	Tricep mm	Back mm	Thigh mm
						Skinfolds			
95	Very lean	6	3	4	4	4	3	4	4
85	Lean	9	7	8	6	8	6	8	6
75	Leaner than ave.	14	12	16	11	13	10	12	10
50	Average	18	15	21	16	17	11	15	14
30	Fatter than ave.	22	18	27	20	21	13	19	16
15	Fat	25	22	34	26	25	16	24	21
5	Very fat	30	28	44	33	33	21	33	33
YOUR SCORE	T$_1$	___	___	___	___	___	___	___	___
	T$_2$	___	___	___	___	___	___	___	___
	T$_3$	___	___	___	___	___	___	___	___

Figure 10-9 Body Composition Rating Scale. (From Golding LA, Myers CR, Sinning WE, eds. 1982. Y's way to physical fitness. Chicago: National Board of YMCA of USA. Used by permission.)

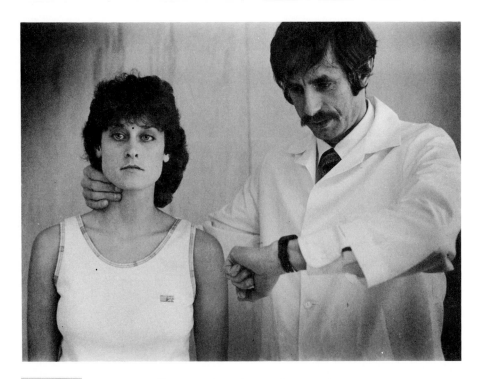

Figure 10-10   Estimation of heart rate by palpating the carotid artery.

300 kilometers per minute (kpm) (150 kpm for the female client), and the work-load is increased as dictated by the client's level of fitness (Figure 10-10). Two scores are calculated: VO_2 max and METS. To measure flexibility, a trunk flex-ion test is administered. Two measures of muscular strength and endurance are included: an 80-lb bench press and a 1-minute timed sit-ups test. These scores are recorded on the Physical Fitness Evaluation Form reproduced in Figure 10-11. This version of the form includes the norms for females 35 years and under. The YMCA has developed separate norms for males 35 years and under, females 35 years and under, males aged 36 to 45 years, and females aged 36 to 45 years.

At this point the steps used in determining fitness objectives for a client should be understood. The client's desired level of physical fitness is compared with his or her actual level. Then a program of physical activity is prescribed. The appropriate physiologic parameters are monitored on a regular basis to determine progress toward the desired level of fitness. Remember that the gen-eral procedure is no different in a private sports club or a school setting. The implementation of the objectives may differ because the client chooses to join a

Y'S WAY TO PHYSICAL FITNESS

Rating Scale

Norms   Females 35 Years and Under

Name _____

Dates: T₁ _____   T₂ _____   T₃ _____

Percentage ranking	Rating	PWC max kgm	Liters/min	ml/kg	Mets	Trunk flexion ins	Bench press repetitions	Sit-ups 1 min reps	3-Min step test post Ex. HR 1 min BPM	Resting HR BPM
95	Excellent	1700	3.32	55	15.	23	30	39	79	59
85	Good	1500	2.74	45	13.	21	24	34	94	63
75	Above Av.	1300	2.42	39	11.	20	20	30	109	68
50	Average	1100	2.09	34	10.	18	16	25	118	72
30	Below Av.	900	1.76	30	9.	15	13	20	122	80
15	Fair	700	1.44	26	7.	14	10	15	129	84
5	Poor	500	.86	20	6.	11	5	10	137	92

YOUR SCORE   T₁ ___ ___ ___   T₂ ___ ___ ___   T₃ ___ ___ ___

	Test 1	Test 2	Test 3
Target Weight	___	___	___
Actual Weight	___	___	___
Difference	___	___	___
% Body Fat (23% Target)	___	___	___
Blood Pressure	__/__	__/__	__/__

Your actual weight should be within 10% of your target weight.

Any values over 140/90 are considered high, and below 110/65 are considered low. Values exceeding 160/95 are labeled as hypertensive.

Figure 10-11   Physical Fitness Evaluation Form. (From Golding LA, Myers CR, Sinning WE, eds. 1982. Y's way of physical fitness. Chicago: National Board of YMCA of USA. Used by permission.)

```
┌─────────────────────────────────────────────────────────────────────────┐
│                     Y's WAY TO PHYSICAL FITNESS                           │
│                        SCORE SHEET FEMALES                                │
│                                                                           │
│  NAME _____    DATE _____              │
│                                              TIME _____              │
│  Temp. F°                                                                 │
│        Age _____ years    Weight _____ lbs _____ kg    Height _____ ins   │
│        Resting Blood Pressure ___/___ mm Hg    Resting Heart Rate ___ bpm │
└─────────────────────────────────────────────────────────────────────────┘
```

Y's WAY TO PHYSICAL FITNESS

SCORE SHEET FEMALES

NAME _____   DATE _____

TIME _____

Temp. F°

Age _____ years   Weight _____ lbs _____ kg   Height _____ ins

Resting Blood Pressure ___/___ mm Hg   Resting Heart Rate _____ bpm

1. SKINFOLDS

   Chest _____ mm
   Abdomen _____ mm
   Ilium _____ mm
   Axilla _____ mm
   Scapula _____ mm
   Tricep _____ mm
   Thigh _____ mm

2. PERCENT FAT

	Sum of 5	(or)	Sum of 3
Thigh	_____	Ilium	_____
Ilium	_____	Abdomen	_____
Abdomen	_____	Axilla	_____
Tricep	_____	Sum	_____
Scapula	_____		
Sum	_____		

   Percent fat ___ %   Percent fat ___ %

3. TARGET WEIGHT (23%) _____ lbs

4. PHYSICAL WORK CAPACITY TEST

   Seat Height _____ Predicted Max Heart Rate _____ B/M

   85% of Predicted Max Heart Rate _____ B/M _____ Seconds for 30 Beats

   WORKLOADS   HEART RATE

   1st Workload 150 kgm   _____ 2nd min
                                          _____ 3rd min
                                          _____ 4th min (if needed)

   2nd Workload _____ kgm   _____ 2nd min
                                          _____ 3rd min
                                          _____ 4th min (if needed)

   3rd Workload _____ kgm   _____ 2nd min
                                          _____ 3rd min
                                          _____ 4th min (if needed)

   NOTE: Transfer above results to the PWC Graph and Compute

5. FLEXIBILITY

   Trunk flexion _____ ins

6. MUSCULAR STRENGTH & ENDURANCE

   Bench Press (35 lbs) _____ reps

   1 min Timed Sit-ups _____ reps

   Transfer all results to Physical Fitness Profile

Figure 10-12 Master scoresheet. (From Golding LA, Myers CR, Sinning WE, eds. 1982. Y's way of physical fitness. Chicago: National Board of YMCA of USA. Used by permission.)

private club, while the student is required to be in school. Evaluation assumes an important role in instruction in school and nonschool settings.

Accountability is as important in a nonschool setting as it is in the schools. Because private clubs are profit-making organizations, they must gear their operation to attracting a large membership. To retain this appeal the club is often evaluated at several levels. For instance, the cleanliness and decor of the club are factors in retaining new members, as is the efficiency of the day-to-day operation. The nature of the publicity and the attractiveness of club member-ship packages affect the club's ability to secure new members. All these ele-ments must be evaluated periodically by the club manager. One of the best ways to retain members is to improve their skills. Theoretically, if people can play better, they will enjoy it more. This is why it is so important to attempt to individualize objectives in instructional settings in a private club. By creating a more personal atmosphere, the instructor is providing a rare opportunity for the member to receive individual attention from the club staff. Furthermore, the private club that is part of a franchise will be expected to demonstrate its ac-countability to the home office. Every effort should be made to satisfy the needs of the member while retaining high standards set by the club.

MEASURING HEALTH-RELATED FITNESS IN PROGRAMS FOR OLDER ADULTS

Measurement techniques developed for younger populations are not always suitable for older adults. In assessing the physical fitness of the older adult, the functional age of the examinee rather than the chronological age is of interest (Osness, 1986). Functional age is physiologic, although it is affected by genetics, the absence or presence of disease, lifestyle, and a person's day-to-day deci-sions.

Functional Fitness Assessment for Adults over 60 Years

A functional fitness test for adults more than 60 years old has been devel-oped. The test has not yet been published; data are being collected to establish norms. All test items have been administered to a small number of examinees. Evidence of reliability and validity has been obtained for some of the test items, but specific information is not available at the present time.

The following guidelines were used during the development of this test:

1. The test must relate to the full range of age among older people. Options may be used for subgroups.
2. The test would not relate to follow-up prescriptions at this point in time.
3. The test would be nondiagnostic from a pathological point of view.
4. The test is a physical function evaluation only.
5. The test would be drug independent.
6. The test will not need physician approval—no more risk than life itself.

7. The test will be prepared for paraprofessional use.
8. The test will require only normally available equipment.

(Osness et al., 1991, pp. vi–vii)

Before administering the test items, measurement of the examinee's weight and standing height is recommended. The test consists of five items, briefly described below:

Item 1: Trunk and Leg Flexibility

This item is often referred to as the V-sit and reach. The examinee sits on the floor with legs extended in a V position and reaches as far as possible along the top of a yardstick taped to the floor.

Item 2: Agility and Dynamic Balance

A chair is taped to the floor, and two cones (one to each side) are placed 6 feet to the side and 5 feet behind the chair. The examinee begins seated in the chair. He or she rises and moves to and around a cone and returns to a seated position in the chair. The same movement is repeated around the other cone. Another complete circuit is executed to complete a trial of the test.

Item 3: Soda Pop Coordination Test

A strip of tape is placed on a tabletop and marked at six 5-inch intervals. The examinee sits comfortably in front of the table. Three unopened (full) cans of soda pop are placed in squares 1, 3, and 5 on the table. When the test begins, the examinee turns each can upside down and places it in the adjacent square as rapidly as possible. The cans are then returned to their original placement.

Item 4: Strength and Endurance Test

The examinee sits in a chair with the nondominant hand resting in the lap and the dominant hand hanging to the side. A weighted milk bottle (plastic) is placed in the dominant hand. A 4-lb weight (quart container) is used for women and an 8-lb weight (gallon container) for men. The tester stands to the side of the examinee and places one hand on the dominant biceps and the other under the bottle to assist in supporting it. When the test begins, the examinee attempts to contract the biceps through the full range of motion. If this movement can be completed, the examinee is given a 1-minute rest and then asked to make as many repetitions as possible in 30 seconds.

Item 5: 880-Yard Walk

This is the usual timed walking test. Running is not permitted.

Rockport Fitness Walking Test

The Rockport Fitness Walking Test has been developed for both younger and older adults (ages 20–69 years). This test can be self-administered. Before taking the test, the examinee goes through a pretest warm-up. After walking in place for 30 seconds, the resting pulse rate is determined.

The test requires walking a mile as fast as possible. Time is recorded to the nearest second. The heart rate is recorded immediately after the end of the mile. The examinee should stretch for 5 to 10 minutes before beginning the test.

Refer to the Rockport Fitness Walking Test chart (Rockport Walking Institute, 1986) for the examinee's age and sex-appropriate fitness level. Use the chart to evaluate test performance. One strong point of this test is that, after the self-test has taken place, an exercise program is recommended that is designed for the examinee's age and sex. A 20-week walking program is recommended, followed by a repetition of the Rockport Fitness Walking Test.

MEASUREMENT IN OTHER CAREER OPTIONS

Earlier in this chapter, the uses of evaluation by instructors and managers in sports or fitness centers were discussed. The managerial role is only one of the career options a sports management major would be prepared to undertake. Other alternatives include a front-office position with a sports team, event organizer, athletic director, and similar administrative positions. Evaluation is an important part of these jobs. Programs must be evaluated as well as personnel. The needs and interests of those likely to attend the sports events might be surveyed. Instruments such as questionnaires or inventories are often employed in these settings. If rating scales are developed, they should possess valid content and be based on knowledge of the appropriate underlying measurement methodology.

In the National Athletic Trainer's Association handbook, many evaluation competencies are listed. Even the fledgling athletic trainer must know how to assess the extent of an injury and decide on a course of treatment. Most of the decisions made by an athletic trainer require the use of evaluation techniques. To be certified, the basic skills the trainer should possess are carefully evaluated. He or she must be evaluated on the ability to tape body parts properly. The ability to choose the best exercises to determine rehabilitation techniques must also be assessed. Extensive knowledge of measurement and evaluation are required of the athletic trainer.

There are many medical aspects of measurement, as, for example, in physical therapy and sports medicine. One of the most common types of measurement in these areas is the use of the goniometer to measure joint angles. Also frequently used is the Cybex machine to measure strength of specific parts of the body. These professionals are often called upon to assess the effectiveness of a rehabilitation program for a specific client, for instance, whether the program has been effective enough to allow the client to return to work. These types of decisions are critical both for the client and the hiring agency.

SUMMARY

Many instructional opportunities exist in nonschool settings. The process of writing objectives for these classes is similar to preparing objectives in a school setting. Individualizing objectives in a private club is often easier, however, and these objectives may be implemented differently in this setting. In a private-sports club the objectives might be tailored to the skill level of class members having similar skill levels. In a fitness center objectives are expected to be individualized, since the level of fitness of the clients typically varies markedly. Any test of sports skills or physical fitness can be adapted for the nonschool setting. In practice some organizations evaluate their clients' progress only in the most subjective manner, while others have instituted formal testing programs.

Learning Experiences

1. Visit a private fitness or sports club in your community and ask for information on entry-level testing for new clients. Secure the printed evaluation form from the club manager, if possible. Ask for clarification of any aspect of the testing you do not understand. Bring this information back to class, and report on it to your classmates.
2. Write one behavioral objective for a hypothetical new member of a private fitness club. Be sure to include all the important components of a behavioral objective as described in this chapter.
3. Write one behavioral objective for a beginning tennis class in a private club. Then modify the objective for a new member of the class who seems to have natural ability in tennis and is highly motivated.
4. Assume you are the manager of a fitness center. How many aspects of the club would you evaluate? List these aspects, and suggest one way of evaluating each one.

References

Carter Center of Emory University. 1991. Healthier People version 4.0: Health risk appraisal program. Atlanta: Carter Center of Emory University.

Dishman RK. 1990. Physical activity in medical care. In Torg JS et al., eds. Current therapy in sports medicine-2. Philadelphia: BC Decker.

Golding LA, Myers CR, Sinning WE. 1989. The Y's way to physical fitness. Chicago: National Board of YMCA.

Katch FI, Katch VL, McArdle WD. 1991. Exercise physiology: Energy, nutrition, and human performance. ed 3. Philadelphia: Lea & Febiger.

Osness WH. 1986. Physical assessment procedures—the use of functional profiles. Journal of Physical Education, Recreation, and Dance, **57**:35–38.

Osness WH. 1991. Functional fitness assessment for adults over 60 years (a field based assessment). Reston, Va: American Alliance for Health, Physical Education, Recreation and Dance.

Parr RB. 1989. Understanding health risk appraisals. Fitness in Business, April, pp 171–172.

Pollock ML, Schmidt DH, Jackson AS. 1980. Measurement of cardiorespiratory fitness and body composition in a clinical setting. Comprehensive Therapy, **6**:1227.

Rockport Walking Institute. 1986. The Rockport Fitness Walking Test. Marlboro, Mass: Rockport Walking Institute.

Sentry World Headquarters. 1990. Sentry physical fitness handbook. Stevens Point, Wis: Sentry World Headquarters.

Terry PE. 1987. The role of health risk appraisal in the workplace: Assessment versus behavior change. American Journal of Health Promotion, 1:18–21,36.

US Office of Personnel Management (USOPM). 1991. AMC promotes health and measures return investment. In Focus on Federal Employee Health and Assistance Programs. Washington, DC: US Office of Personnel Management.

Supplementary Readings

Heyward VH. 1984. Designs for fitness. Minneapolis: Burgess Co.

Pollock ML, Wilmore J, Fox SM. 1984. Exercise in health and disease: evaluation and prescription for prevention and rehabilitation. Philadelphia: WB Saunders.

Annotated Readings

Baun W, Baun M. 1984. A corporate health and fitness program. Journal of Physical Education, Recreation and Dance, 55(4):42–45.

Describes the use of a computer system to achieve objectives in a corporate fitness setting; discusses the use of initial screening of employees followed by daily assessments; provides immediate feedback to the participant as well as a monthly activity program; uses monthly statistics to evaluate the program continuously and to develop a database for longitudinal analysis.

Baun WB, Landgren MA. 1983. Tenneco health and fitness: a corporate program committed to evaluation. Journal of Physical Education, Recreation and Dance, 54(8):40–41.

Lists the objectives of the model fitness program at Tenneco Inc. in Houston; describes the program and program statistics; emphasizes the evaluation process, which includes four principal areas: (1) health and fitness monthly statistics, (2) fitness and wellness program evaluation, (3) special projects, and (4) longitudinal projects; uses information from the evaluation process to increase awareness of and commitment to positive health habits and improve the overall quality of life.

Cooper KH, Collingwood TR. 1984. Physical fitness: programming issues for total well-being. Journal of Physical Education, Recreation and Dance, 55(3):35–36,44.

Describes the involvement of the Institute for Aerobics Research in developing and evaluating employee health and fitness programs within the private and government sectors; notes that accountability is the major issue in program implementation; based on the authors' evaluations of many programs, identifies several factors contributing to the success of a program, thereby facilitating participant adherence to the program; describes several program models.

Crossley JC, Hudson SD. 1983. Assessing the effectiveness of employee recreation/fitness programs. Journal of Physical Education, Recreation and Dance, **54**(8):50–52.

Discusses a practical approach to assisting the effectiveness of employee recreation and fitness programs; labels this type of approach as controlled comparison: describes data collection to (1) construct an employee profile and (2) measure employee perceptions of program benefits; substitutes survey questions for objective data; data collection also includes employee perceptions of the effectiveness of a recreation and fitness program; discusses how the data can be used to improve the program.

Farley M. 1984. Program evaluation as a political tool. Journal of Physical Education, Recreation and Dance, **55**(4):65–67.

Examines program evaluation as it applies to public service agencies; suggests program evaluation can become a persuasive political tool if viewed as a communication device; proposes ways of using program evaluation as a political tool; discusses evaluation as a means of linking the agency and elected officials in the tasks of planning and delivering services and accounting for the use of public funds.

Howell, J. 1983. Wellness for the practitioners. Journal of Physical Education, Recreation and Dance, **54**(8):37,55.

Describes hospital wellness program for hospital employees; uses an aerobic circuit modeled after Kenneth Cooper's concept; discusses fitness advisor assisting participants in establishing personal goals and monitoring progress; uses two fitness assessments as a part of membership: initial testing and the Lifestyle-Health Audit; evaluates program using class evaluations and existing questionnaires.

Special Issues in Testing Motor Behavior

KEY WORDS

Watch for these words as you read the following chapter

Course evaluation
Instructor evaluation

Program evaluation

Measurement and evaluation do not occur in isolation. Scores must be interpreted in some meaningful way, and three major interpretive issues are examined in this chapter. The first issue focuses on testing minority students. In the second section, gender differences in motor performance and their impact on standard-setting are discussed. The third issue encompasses several evaluation topics, including objective assessments of instructional effectiveness, programs, and curricula.

TESTING DIFFERENT ETHNIC GROUPS

Testing different ethnic groups on motor skills is a little-discussed topic. Numerous discussions have been held on the appropriateness of certain cognitive and affective tests for persons coming from a variety of ethnic cultures. Studies of test bias provide information to be used in evaluating tests. A widely held view is that most tests are developed based on white middle-class values; therefore, whites score higher than African Americans (for example). On the surface, it would appear that tests of motor performance may be devoid of these concerns. However, this is largely an unexplored area. It is possible that, even if the tests themselves are not biased, the instructions for test administration may contain bias, and should be examined.

Certainly, when cognitive and affective tests are used in physical education and the exercise sciences, their usefulness with various ethnic groups should be analyzed. Many authors have proposed ways of dealing with potential bias in testing (e.g., Isen, 1986; Sharma, 1986). In addition to studying test bias, strategies include the use of multiple assessment procedures, an increase in motivation, a perception of learning difficulties as being culturally derived, use of a test administrator from the same ethnic group, and administration of the test in the student's native language. *Multiple assessment procedures* encompass both quantitative as well as qualitative assessments, along with assessing students in both individual and group settings. To accommodate differing views of assessment that might exist across ethnic groups, instructors might make available an array of assessment procedures, allowing students to choose the assessments they will take. To *increase motivation,* motivational techniques might be tailored to specific ethnic groups. Furthermore, the reward structure should be varied and be consistent with the values of the ethnic group. The *perception of learning difficulties as being culturally derived* may have its roots in language and other cultural differences rather than in learning disorders. The *use of a test administrator from the same ethnic group* would be beneficial; however, this is not a very practical notion. It might be possible, however, to have parents representing several ethnic groups present during the assessments. Parents may also be able to assist in the assessment procedure using their native language, when necessary.

The potential for test bias in physical education and exercise science has rarely been discussed, much less studied systematically. This is an especially important consideration for the more popular tests used across America, such as the major physical fitness tests.

GENDER DIFFERENCES IN MOTOR PERFORMANCE

That gender differences exist in motor performance cannot be denied. To what extent are these differences culturally induced or genuinely physiological? This question has been widely discussed for many years and remains controversial in the exercise science field.

Research has shown that, in general, boys have much more strength, height, weight, and cardiorespiratory (CR) endurance than girls. In addition, they tend to have a smaller percentage of body fat. The gender gap may be narrowing for some aspects of strength. While there is a clear difference in arm and shoulder girdle strength, performance on leg strength measures demonstrates considerable overlap. Even so, the strongest individuals are usually male and the weakest, female. Girls generally possess greater flexibility, rhythmic ability, and buoyancy. However, there are certainly exceptions to this delineation of gender differences, particularly among upper elementary school–age boys and girls and highly skilled vs. poorly skilled performers.

Gender differences have also been reported in sports skills. For example,

Stamm (1979) noted differences in the test scores of college men and women in tennis and bowling classes. This suggests the need to consider separate performance standards for men and women. However, separate standards are not always appropriate for all activities. At the United States Air Force Academy (USAF Academy, 1978), the same performance standards were used for both male and female cadets in swimming classes. In this situation, men and women were found to be equally capable. Drawing conclusions about gender differences in motor performance is difficult without a substantial, recent database for all ages, girls and boys.

Implications for Ability Grouping

Ability grouping is neither required nor prohibited by the Title IX regulation. However, if it is used, group membership cannot be determined on the basis of gender. On the other hand, the assignment of an equal number of boys and girls to a group does not necessarily yield a grouping that is fair to both genders. If the group consists of a wide range of skill levels, ability grouping should provide a more positive learning environment. Group membership must be established using predetermined standards.

There are factors to be considered in ability grouping when athletic competition takes place, particularly in contact sports such as football. During practice or in competition of contact sports, students must be separated by gender. However, this grouping may not be permissible during the instructional portion of the class.

What are the implications for ability grouping? In a report prepared by the state of Illinois, the use of sports skills tests was recommended for ability grouping when these skills were incorporated into unit objectives. If the objective involves physical fitness, a number of fitness tests are available to be used in grouping. Motor ability tests are not recommended to ability group students. "There is no evidence that a phenomenon such as motor ability is measurable or even that the phenomenon exists" (Illinois State Board of Education, 1982, p. 5). Random assignment to groups (heterogeneous grouping) is recommended when the objective is to help students learn to appreciate the level of skill of others.

When students of similar ability compete, the same standard should be used for ability grouping. When excellence in performance is the primary goal, separate standards should be used, particularly for fitness and sports skills objectives. With traditional mass instruction, a single standard is recommended. With an individualized approach, separate standards are recommended.

Research by Oakes (1992) has raised questions about the appropriateness of ability grouping in some situations. Oakes found that while ability grouping enhances the level of skill of highly skilled students, it may not have the same results with moderate or poorly skilled students. They may be more challenged and motivated when competing with students that are one ability group above their current level.

Implications for Performance Evaluations

The Illinois report also makes recommendations on sex-fair performance evaluation. Separate (higher) standards are proposed for boys when performance is based on strength, endurance, height, weight, or lean body mass. Separate (higher) standards for girls are recommended when performance is based on flexibility, buoyancy, or rhythm.

When an accuracy test is administered, where strength and power are not factors, a single standard should be used. A single standard is also proposed for wall volley tests not dependent on strength or power and for the assessment of form and game strategy.

EVALUATION TOPICS

You will recall from Chapter 1 that measurement involves the administration of a test and evaluation pertains to the interpretation of test scores. A test has many purposes, including assessment of the effectiveness of a course, teacher, curriculum, or program.

Formative Evaluation

The formative evaluation approach is emphasized in this chapter. When courses or programs dealing with sport or physical activity are evaluated, the traditional approach is to evaluate at the end of the designated period. If weaknesses are detected, plans are usually made to correct these weaknesses during the coming year. However, the next time the evaluation takes place, the same weaknesses may exist, thus an entire year has been consumed in applying ineffective solutions. If the evaluation had been of the formative type, determining that the proposed solutions were ineffective and in need of modification or replacement, this would have been possible early in the program. Keep in mind that the purpose of evaluation is to improve the course or program, not to judge it. Of course, evaluation techniques must be used to make judgments sometimes, but in most cases passing judgment should not be the primary reason for evaluation.

Accepting the premise that the use of formative evaluation is an appropriate method for improving effectiveness, what techniques can be used to obtain data over time? Essentially the evaluator must ask three basic questions:

1. Is the program, teacher, student, or administrator functioning successfully?
2. If not, how should one intervene?
3. Is the intervention successful?

Course and Instructor Evaluation

In the 1970s the emphasis on evaluating the effectiveness of courses and instructors increased a great deal, particularly in colleges and universities. Many institutions of higher learning required or strongly encouraged faculty members to obtain periodic evaluation of their courses and teaching. Much effort has been expended in the development of instruments that can be used for this purpose; the most popular type is an evaluation form using a Likert-type scale. Usually administered at the end of a unit or a year of instruction, this instrument represents the summative approach to evaluation. Although certain items on the scale would apply to any course, the evaluation forms are generally not applicable to activity courses in sports and physical activity. Efforts to develop a form for activity courses that would be usable nationwide have not been successful, probably because institutions have different missions and course objectives.

In the following sections a formative approach to course and instructor evaluation that may be used in elementary and secondary schools, private clubs, colleges, and universities is demonstrated. The underlying goal is to provide evidence of the effectiveness of a course or an instructor by monitoring behavior on a regular basis. When satisfactory progress is not being made, an intervention should take place. Three examples are used to illustrate this approach.

Example 1—Volleyball Unit

A physical education teacher establishes a goal for her students in learning the forearm pass or bump. The goal is to execute 10 consecutive, legal bumps within a given height range and area by the middle of the volleyball unit. Achievement of the goal would indicate that the students have developed adequate control and are ready for more refined work on the skill. Figure 11-1 shows the results obtained in a beginning class. The *straight line* is the criterion line, indicating a hypothetical line of improvement from 0 to 10 consecutive hits. The criterion line is used only as a guide, since the performance curve would not necessarily be expected to be linear. The *jagged line* connecting the dots is the actual performance curve for the class. Note that the performance line drops below the criterion line on day 5 and falls further away on days 6 and 7. Since we do not know the learning curve for students on this skill (perhaps research will show this drop to be expected), we must assume that the students are not going to reach the criterion unless the teacher intervenes in some way. The *dot* at day 7 represents a planned intervention, which might consist of additional instruction by the teacher, close supervision by a partner, use of instructional materials, or by varying teaching methods. In this case the performance line begins to move toward the criterion line again, revealing that the intervention was successful. By monitoring progress daily, the course itself or one aspect of it is evaluated on an ongoing basis.

Example 2—Class Management

A physical education teacher senses that he spends too much time in class talking to his students (e.g., giving directions and discussing mechanical principles). Although he believes the information he provides is important, he would like to impart it more efficiently, that is, in less time. He would like to increase the amount of learning time his students have in sport-, movement-,

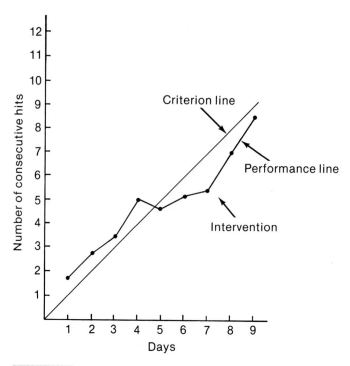

Figure 11-1   Performance on the volleyball forearm pass.

and fitness-related activity in class. First, he needs to know how much time he actually spends in class on verbal presentations. This information may be obtained in several ways—by audiotaping his classes or by having someone, perhaps a student from study hall, use a stopwatch to monitor the amount of time he spends talking in his class over a week. These results would provide him with a baseline from which to work. In this case the teacher spent an average of 40% of the total class time talking. This is shown in Figure 11-2 as the *solid horizontal baseline* at 40%. The teacher decides that 25% of class time should be adequate for class discussion. This is represented in Figure 11-2 by the *dashed line,* the criterion line set by the teacher. How can this designated criterion be met? Perhaps some of the material could be presented by preparing handouts and by using loopfilms on an individualized basis. If his talk time decreases to 25% and remains there, he has achieved his goal. If the percentage of time increases again, another method of intervening should be used. In Figure 11-2, the *jagged line* connecting dots represents the teacher's performance. Since talk time is being decreased in the desired direction and reaches the criterion line during class 8, no further intervention is necessary. The performance curve remains around the 25% level for the next seven sessions; therefore, the teacher has some assurance that he will be able to maintain this amount of

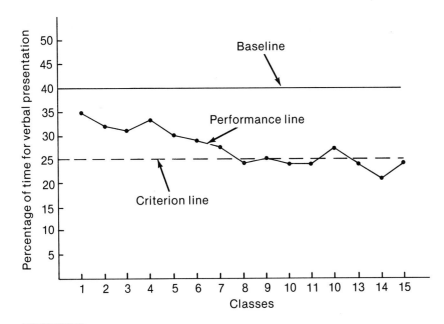

Figure 11-2   Time devoted to verbal presentation.

talk time. Using this approach, a teacher may monitor any aspect of instructional effectiveness on a continual basis. Problems can be identified and corrected before the end of the unit, course, or year, when modifying the teacher's behavior would essentially be ineffectual.

Example 3—Instructor Evaluation

A college instructor in a theory class administers a **course evaluation** form at the end of each semester and finds that the students consistently rate the clarity of her instruction from average to below average. If the material is not being presented clearly, the students cannot be expected to understand and apply it. The instructor does not want to wait until the end of the next semester to find out whether her presentations are improving in clarity. An evaluation procedure consisting of a rating scale (Figure 11-3) is devised. The students pick up the rating forms at the end of each class, circle the number best reflecting the perceived degree of clarity of instruction, and turn in the forms to a student who collects and returns them to the instructor. This process assures the students of an anonymous response.

The ratings are averaged each day and plotted, as in Figure 11-4. The *solid straight line* represents the baseline, the average end-of-semester rating the instructor has been receiving. She decides to strive for an average daily rating of 6 or higher, represented by the criterion (*dashed*) line. The *jagged line* connecting the dots is the teacher's performance curve, measured by the daily rating by students. By organizing the structure of the classes more carefully, the instruc-

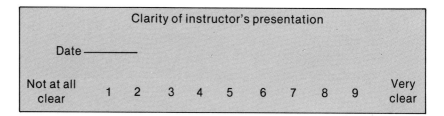

Figure 11-3   Rating scale to monitor clarity of instruction.

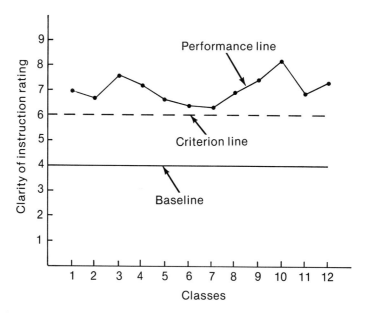

Figure 11-4   Ratings of clarity of instruction.

tor is able to maintain clarity ratings at a satisfactory level. If the performance curve had fallen below 6 for two or more consecutive classes, possibilities for intervention would have to be explored. One approach might be to ask the students why the presentation did not seem clear. Another approach would be to prepare at least two examples of each concept presented in class and discuss these examples. A low clarity rating might simply indicate that the instructor needs to present the same material again during the next class session. Unless experimental evidence on the best method of intervening is available, the instructor must intervene on the basis of a logical analysis.

Although the evaluation procedures described in the previous examples are useful, the measures used in all three examples are weak measures. For instance, a student rating of clarity of instruction may reflect something other than clarity, such as the instructor's personality. This effect can be controlled to some extent by obtaining two different measures of the same attribute. Student ratings of the clarity of instruction might be accompanied by an observer's rating of the clarity of instruction or a rating of tape recording of class sessions. Unobtrusive measures such as content analysis of lesson plans or instructional materials might also be used. This approach lacks the controls necessary in an experimental study. No control groups are used, only one teacher is involved, and factors other than the planned intervention might account for the desired performance.

Even with the foregoing limitations, if this informal approach assists a teacher or exercise scientist in achieving personal goals, it seems to be a worthwhile evaluation tool. It forces one to identify problems, work actively to alter behavior in the desired direction, and increase awareness of strengths and opportunities for improvement. It enables the professional to perform and somewhat control his or her self-evaluation in a nonthreatening environment.

In the arena of sports, the evaluation of coaching is a vital component of the assessment of an athletic department. Often this evaluation is based on the sole criterion of wins and losses. However, in an educational setting, placing such a heavy emphasis on a product-oriented goal has been widely criticized. A performance analysis system has been proposed as a means of evaluating a coach's role in enhancing the entire athletic program. The five-step process comprises: (1) a statement of departmental goals; (2) a review-of-position guide, (3) a review of performance criteria and development of performance standards, (4) a performance analysis, and (5) recognition of achievement.

Curriculum Evaluation

Although evaluating many aspects of the physical education curriculum is possible, this discussion is restricted to the evaluation of the overall merit of the curriculum. (The more familiar process of evaluating specific objectives within the curriculum receives extensive examination on pp. 205–208.) Let us assume that a staff of physical education teachers has decided to use the Purpose-Process Curriculum Framework (PPCF) as a guide for making curriculum decisions (Jewett et al., 1971). One approach to implementing this framework might be to use the gird shown in Table 11-1. Only one of the major categories of purposes for moving is included in Table 11-1 to exemplify this evaluative procedure. The first task of the physical education staff would be to select combinations of purposes and processes that are to receive emphasis in their physical education program. (The purposes for moving are represented across the top of the grid; the movement processes, along the side.) These purpose-process combinations can be viewed jointly by marking the appropriate cell in the grid. For example, in Table 11-1 an X has been placed in the cell representing a combination of cardiorespiratory (*CR*) endurance (purpose) and patterning (process). When all purpose-process combinations of interest have been recorded on the grid, the overall framework of the physical education curriculum has been identified.

However, the selections within the PPCF should be justifiable in the eyes of

Table 11-1 Portion of Grid for Evaluating Purpose-Process Curriculum Framework

| | **MAN MASTER OF HIMSELF** | | | | | | |
| | **Physiologic Efficiency** | | | **Psychic Equilibrium** | | | |
Process	CR Efficiency	Mechanical Efficiency	NM Efficiency	Joy	Self-knowledge	Catharsis	Challenge
Perceiving							
Patterning	X						
Adapting							
Refining							
Varying							
Improvising							
Composing							

CR, cardiorespiratory; NM, neuromuscular.

physical educators who are qualified to make such judgments. Otherwise, curriculum choices may be merely a reflection of the personal biases of the physical education staff. If, for example, a curriculum is considered too broad or too narrow by the physical education curriculum experts, the staff has not established sufficiently the merit of the curriculum.

How can physical education teachers evaluate the merit of a curriculum? First, a written rationale should be set forth for the choices made within the PPCF. This step provides the outside observer with the staff's philosophical orientation toward physical education. It also helps to ensure that curriculum choices are made on a logical basis. This rationale would provide input to the curriculum evaluator. One might disagree with the philosophical approach but at the same time judge the curriculum choices appropriate.

Bringing in outside evaluators to assess the physical education curriculum is not always possible. A team of teachers and administrators within a school system might be asked to review the rationale and subsequent curriculum choices. A needs assessment might be conducted to determine whether these choices meet the needs of students, parents, other community members, teachers, and administrators. It cannot be overemphasized that these curriculum choices are not arbitrary; they must be fully justifiable. Once the purpose-process combinations have been selected, the activities that will contribute to these

Sit-and-Reach Test.

combinations must be identified. Presumably different approaches could be taken at this stage. A variety of activities might be used to meet a given purpose at an identified process level. For example, if the purpose for moving is object projection, the student might experience throwing, striking, and kicking a variety of objects in a structured environment. As an alternative approach, a single sport might be selected as a means of emphasizing a purpose. Softball might be an appropriate sport for providing many opportunities for a variety of object projection tasks. Regardless of the approach to selecting activities, these activities must be justified as bona fide contributors to the designated purpose-process combinations.

The first step in the selection of activities is to review the literature to obtain data from research studies. Consider CR endurance as a purpose of interest. Evidence supports the selection of running as an activity that contributes to CR endurance, provided the run covers a reasonably long distance. If the distance is too short (e.g., half mile), running would no longer be an appropriate aerobic activity. The literature review may not be fruitful in many cases, because experimental studies have been conducted only on a small number of purposes. If this is the case, the next best source to use in the selection of activities is the content specialist in physical education. If the purpose is psychological (e.g., catharsis), the sports psychologist would be the appropriate content specialist to contact. The biomechanics specialist would be called on to deal with purposes such as object projection. If research data do not exist, at least the best possible judgment can be made.

Often the functional curriculum (i.e., what actually takes place in the gymnasium everyday) is not the same as the written curriculum (i.e., what teachers intend to do). Hellison (1993) suggests measuring the functional curriculum, and directs his comments specifically to the affective domain with the curriculum. What affective strategies are to be employed and how often were students engaged in these activities? Evidence relevant to these questions can be recorded by the teacher or an observer in class. On the matter of how often students were engaged in affective activities, an observer could use a stopwatch and time this activity. The strategies could be recorded on a daily basis.

In a curriculum evaluation the merit of the total curriculum as well as the worthiness of specific goals must be examined. Only then is it appropriate to assess the extent to which curriculum goals are being attained. However, even this assessment cannot be made in isolation but must be conducted in conjunction with other factors that the physical education staff views as important.

Program Evaluation

Program evaluation is essential in any setting where programs are offered to students, clients, club members, and so forth. The program evaluation techniques described here can be used both within and outside the schools. Two examples of evaluating program goals in the school setting are provided to emphasize important aspects of program evaluation and to describe approaches to the use of formative evaluation techniques. The first example was developed for a high-school physical education program and the second for a middle-school physical education program. A third example of program evaluation can be conducted in a worksite health promotion program.

Program Evaluation in Physical Education

A basic assumption is that all physical education teachers have a list of program goals stated in some fashion. If program goals are stated in general rather than behavorial terms, the evaluation of their effectiveness may be imprecise. For example, a high-school program goal might be stated as follows.

GOAL 1—GENERAL

To develop and maintain an optimal level of physical fitness needed to function in everyday life. To evaluate this goal, more specific information is needed. What is an optimal level of physical fitness? Also, what type of physical fitness is of concern? Let us assume that aerobic capacity was identified as an important component of fitness. A more explicit statement of this goal follows:

GOAL 1—SPECIFIC

High-school students will develop a level of aerobic capacity associated with good health by the end of the school year. An acceptable level of aerobic capacity is defined as achieving a 1-mile run score in the Healthy Fitness Zone identified in FITNESSGRAM for the appropriate age and gender. Eighty percent of the students are expected to achieve this goal. When the program goal is stated in behavorial terms, the procedure for evaluating the goal is described precisely.

Of course it seems logical to assume that the students cannot meet this goal at the outset, else it would not have been identified this way initially. Sometimes test users are not sure, however. A needs assessment can then be conducted, in which the actual status of the students is compared to the desired status. If no discrepancy exists, the goal should be rewritten. In this example, the 1-mile run test would be administered to all students. Their performance represents their actual status on aerobic capacity, and the FITNESSGRAM standard represents the desired status. Since FITNESSGRAM identifies separate standards for males and females, the actual status of boys and girls is recorded separately in Table 11-2 and compared with the desired status. (See Chapter 17 for more information on FITNESSGRAM.)

According to this comparison, the students' performance level is far from the desired status. Only 16% of the boys and 22% of the girls perform well enough to be classified in the FITNESSGRAM Healthy Fitness Zone. Using a formative evaluation approach, one can assess the students' average monthly performance in the 1-mile run and plot the results, as shown in Figure 11-5.

Now we can determine the monthly progress being made toward the desired status. If the average performance levels off in 2 or more months and it becomes clear that the desired status will not be reached at the present rate of improvement, the physical education teacher must intervene. Intervention may take the following forms: increasing the class time devoted to improving aerobic capacity, determining how the presently allocated time for improving aerobic endurance is being used, or using different ways to motivate students.

Once a program goal has been stated in behavorial terms, actual status can be determined and ways to monitor progress toward the desired status can be developed. However, the physical education teacher or fitness staff member may also wish to identify concomitant concerns that should not be sacrificed for the sake of achieving the goal. For example, it is reasonable to ask what kind of conditioning program is necessary to effectively improve aerobic capacity. Certainly the students must exercise regularly—at least three or four times a week.

Table 11-2   Discrepancy Between Actual and Desired Status on 1-Mile Run

	Actual status		Desired status	
	Boys	Girls	Boys	Girls
Within Healthy Fitness Zone	16%	22%	80%	80%
Outside Healthy Fitness Zone	86%	78%	20%	20%

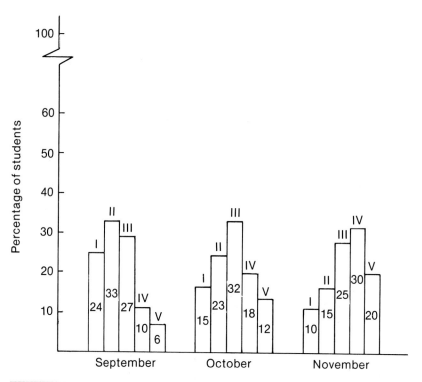

Figure 11-5   Monthly performance on 1-mile run.

If the activity is jogging, the jogging distance should be gradually increased within a given time limit. Thus the physical education teacher must commit a part of every class period to this goal, since the typical sport in class (even basketball and football) will not contribute to an aerobic capacity goal to any great extent. Is the teacher willing to spend the time necessary to develop aerobic capacity? How much class time is presently devoted to improving aerobic capacity? Plotting the way class time is allocated in physical education is possible. A student aide could easily record this information. After reviewing this chart, the teacher may decide that a goal involving improvement of aerobic capacity in class is not realistic because the achievement of this goal would require too much class time. The goal might be rewritten so that students are expected to understand the need for developing and maintaining aerobic capacity and be aware of ways of achieving an optimal level of endurance. On the other hand, the teacher may decide that this goal is so important that it warrants using whatever class time is necessary.

A second example of setting goals in a school setting deals with affective behavior, in particular, students' values. This goal, drawn from the proposed national standards for physical education programs (NASPE, 1994), is for middle-school physical education students:

GOAL 2—GENERAL

To appreciate the relationships with others that result from participation in physical activity (NASPE, 1994, p. 63). Again, more information is needed. What kind of relationships? How will appreciation be assessed? How many students are expected to meet the standard? A more specific statement of the goal follows:

GOAL 2—SPECIFIC

All middle-school students will demonstrate cooperation, sharing, respect, ethical behavior, and acceptance of others toward all members of the group. Students will outwardly support the abilities and limitations of others in game activity and play, as evidenced in student journals and teacher records. Eighty percent of the students are expected to meet this goal.

To write the specific goal in this way, the teacher would have to establish a means of recording these behaviors on a regular basis. Hellison (1993) suggested several ways of evaluating behaviors for program evaluation. One of these is a teacher self-report, where the teacher keeps a daily journal of his or her impressions of each day's classes. In this journal, specific affective goals can be noted, along with strategies attempted. Finally, how did these strategies work? Student journals can be used to support these observations, although they should not be the sole means of evaluation. Values expressed in writing do not always reflect actual behaviors. To monitor student progress toward this goal, daily performance could be plotted. The teacher might wish to review individual charts weekly or perhaps monthly.

Here again there may be concomitant factors that the teacher wishes not to forgo in achieving a goal. These factors should be noted in writing by the teacher. Some of these goals follow:

1. The student must have a positive attitude toward, and feel satisfied about, achieving the goal.
2. The teacher must have a positive attitude toward, and feel satisfied about, achieving the goal.
3. Opportunities should be provided for using varied instructional approaches focusing on values in classes.
4. Classes should be balanced, with some time devoted to affective behaviors such as acceptance of others, allowing the students to interact with the teacher about these behaviors. Formative evaluation procedures could be developed for each of these factors to monitor them throughout the year.

If there is more than one physical education teacher in a school, all must agree on the most important program goals. Usually this can be resolved informally. However, if citywide consensus is expected, more formal techniques can be adopted to aid the group in reaching an agreement. In the Delphi technique, each staff member ranks goals individually. These rankings are then summed for each goal and averaged. Each member is given the average rankings, and all members rank the goals again. If one member of the group ranks a goal very differently from the group ranking, a written rationale is submitted for retaining it. This process is continued until consensus is achieved. A second and perhaps more efficient technique in a school setting is the nominal group method. Using this method, the staff members form a group but work independently within that group. In other words, the individuals do not interact with one another in the early stages, even though they are physically together in a group. Again, feedback is given to the group, and gradually group interaction increases. Once a list of program goals has been generated, the group works toward agreeing on priorities. Although these techniques may be more effective if conducted by someone not on the physical education staff, good results can be obtained using a staff member who has had some experience in working with small groups.

By planning in advance how progress toward the achievement of program goals can be monitored, the chances of actually achieving the goals are greatly enhanced. Teachers evaluate to detect weaknesses and determine ways of correcting those weaknesses. Evaluation, then, becomes an integral part of the educational process.

Program Evaluation in a Worksite Health Promotion Program

According to the *Guidelines for Employee Health Promotion Programs* (AFB, 1992), several types of evaluation should take place in worksite health promotion programs. These include project evaluation, periodic reviews, and longitudinal data analysis. Project evaluation includes outcome evaluation (e.g., impact of the program on absenteeism), impact evaluation (e.g., impact of the program on exercise behaviors), and process evaluation (e.g., effectiveness of delivery methods). Periodic reviews include quality assurance (e.g., maintenance of high-quality operating standards), monthly reviews (e.g., weekly statistics on adherence), quarterly and semiannual reviews (e.g., the extent to which goals and objectives are being met), and an annual review (e.g., key accomplishments, results). Longitudinal data analysis includes program tracking (e.g., participants in the program), behavior change tracking (e.g., lifestyle changes), and cost-benefit analysis (e.g., program costs compared with benefits) (AFB, 1992, p. 75).

GOAL 1—GENERAL

To reduce the health risk factors of employees who are at risk in a worksite health promotion program. This general goal would be appropriate for most, if not all, health promotion programs. However, for any given risk factor, not every employee will be at risk. For example, not all employees have hypertension; those employees have no need to reduce their blood pressure.

GOAL 2—SPECIFIC

To decrease the incidence of functional low back pain in employees in the worksite after a healthy back awareness program. Fifty percent of the employees with low back pain will lower their absenteeism rate as well as their healthcare costs associated with low back problems.

Setting goals in a worksite health promotion program are often individualized more than in a physical education program, because of time constraints and crowded conditions in many schools. Let's use low back pain as an example. First of all, the employees with structural low back pain must be differentiated from those with functional low back pain, which can often be improved through a healthy back awareness program. Of the employees with functional low back pain, not all will improve after participation in the program. Thus, it is realistic to propose that 50% of the employees in the program will experience decreased low back pain. One indicator of improvement would be a decrease in absenteeism due to low back problems. It is important to separate these absences from those due to other health problems. Another indicator might be a reduction in the healthcare costs associated with low back pain. To determine this figure, the healthcare costs from the previous year could be compared with the healthcare costs for the current year, again focusing on those costs associated with low back problems.

One-Mile Run Test.

SURVEYS IN WORKSITE HEALTH PROMOTION PROGRAMS

In addition to the more quantitative measures, surveys are often useful tools to use in determining the extent to which employees feel program goals have been met. For example, employees in the healthy back awareness program might be asked to respond to a survey on their perceptions of the effectiveness of the program. The responses of employees who did not decrease their low back pain after participation in the program would be as useful as the responses of those who improved. Survey information would be especially important if the program had not produced the desired results.

SURVEYS IN A FITNESS CENTER

Surveys are often the primary tool used with members of a fitness center to determine if the center is meeting the needs of the membership. While the center can collect data on the attendance of members and the type of participation at each visit, the management knows little about a member's health status unless the member agrees to be tested (often at additional cost). Not only can a survey provide some of this information (although it must be viewed with caution because it is a self-report), it can also inform the management about the trappings of the club (e.g., cleanliness of the facility, expertise of the staff, friendliness of the staff). A survey can also provide information about behavior changes in the members, such as food choices, eating habits, and exercise habits. Interviews can also be helpful in providing additional information.

SUMMARY

To interpret scores on motor behavior tests, several factors should be taken into account, including course and program objectives and gender differences. Actual status of student ability as well as desired status must be considered in determining objectives. Typically, desired status is reflected in course and program objectives. Gender differences, particularly physiologic ones, may lead to a different interpretation of scores for males and females. In general, the process of interpreting test scores should be handled as conscientiously as the process of selecting and administering the test.

Learning Experiences

1. Assume one of the goals for female members of your fitness club is to increase arm and shoulder girdle strength. Your club owns a Universal machine (or something similar). Write a specific objective for this goal, including a performance standard. Note how you could monitor the progress in achieving the objective on an ongoing basis. If a client does not progress as expected, what type of intervention would you propose? Draw a hypothetical graph of your formative evaluation.

2. Assume you are a physical education teacher working with high-school

boys. Lately you have observed some problems with sportsmanship in your classes. You would like to monitor this behavior on an ongoing basis to determine its severity. Describe a simple procedure you might use to monitor sportsmanship on a daily basis. Propose several methods of intervening if the behavior problems become severe. Draw a hypothetical graph of this evaluation. Be specific in stating your evaluation objective, including a standard of performance for the class as a whole.

References

Hellison D. 1993. Evaluating the affective domain in physical education: Beyond measuring smiles. In Rink JE, ed. *Critical crossroads: Middle and secondary school physical education.* Reston, Va: National Association for Sport and Physical Education.

Illinois State Board of Education. 1982. *Tips and techniques: ability grouping and performance evaluation in physical education.* Springfield: Illinois State Board of Education.

Isen HG. 1986. Assessing the black child: a strategy. *Journal of Non-White Concerns,* **11**:47–58.

Jewett AJ, & others. 1971. Educational change through a taxonomy for writing physical education objectives. *Quest,* **15**:32–38.

National Association for Sport and Physical Education (NASPE). 1994. *Proposed national standards for physical education programs.* Unpublished paper. Reston, Va: National Association for Sport and Physical Education.

Sharma S. 1986. Assessment strategies for minority groups. *Journal of Black Studies,* **17**:111–124.

Stamm CL. 1979. The evaluation of coeducational physical education activity classes. *Journal of Health, Physical Education, and Recreation,* **50**:68–69.

Air Force Academy (USAF Academy). 1978. *Women's integration research project—phase III.* Colorado Springs, Colo: US Air Force Academy, Department of Athletics, April 10.

United States Department of Health, Education, and Welfare. 1975. *Federal Register,* **40** (June 4).

Annotated Readings

Finke CW. 1972. Use evaluation positively. *Journal of Health, Physical Education and Recreation,* **43**:16.
  Suggests that too many testing procedures in physical education produce anxiety; the author believes that evaluation should build the learner's self-reliance and increase desire and ability to move; supports the concept of continuous evaluation, using both teacher evaluations and self-evaluation.

Kneer ME. 1982. Ability grouping in physical education. *Journal of Physical Education, Recreation and Dance,* **53**(9):10–13, 68.
  Discusses the identification of performance standards to be used in grouping students in physical education on the basis of their ability; prescribes curricular and instructional approaches to accommodating these abilities.

Kosekoff J, Fink A. 1982. *Evaluation basics: a practitioner's manual.* Beverly Hills, Calif: Sage.

Provides a thorough introduction and overview of the techniques needed for a do-it-yourself evaluation; offers guidelines, checklists, and key points to watch at every stop of the evaluation process; uses almost 100 examples to illustrate its practical advice; invaluable to anyone who needs to know the basics of evaluating programs.

Howley ET, Franks BD. 1992. *Health fitness instructor's handbook,* ed 2. Champaign, Ill: Human Kinetics.

Written for people involved in the delivery of health and fitness programs; organized around the 1991 behavioral objectives developed by the American College of Sports Medicine; includes chapter on measurement and evaluation; how to select appropriate tests.

Loughrey TJ. 1988. Evaluation program effectiveness. *Journal of Physical Education, Recreation and Dance,* **59**(1):63–64.

Describes the goals of program evaluation identified by the Evaluation Research Council; lists program factors and products to evaluate in physical education.

McDonald D, Yeates ME. 1979. Measuring improvement in physical education. *Journal of Physical Education, Recreation and Dance,* **50**:79–80.

Discusses problems encountered in measuring improvement; reviews the Hale and Hale method for adjusting raw improvement scores so that the inequality of scale units is taken into account; presents a simplified procedure, in tabular form, for calculating the improvement score.

McGee R. 1989. Program evaluation. In Safrit MJ, Wood TM, eds. *Measurement concepts in physical education and exercise science.* Champaign, Ill: Human Kinetics.

Identifies and describes a variety of program evaluation models; provides numerous examples in physical education and exercise science settings.

Potter G, Wandzilak T. 1981. Youth sports: a program evaluation. *Journal of Physical Education and Recreation,* **53**(3):67–68.

Describes the evaluation of a basketball program for seventh- and eighth-grade boys; use of preseason and postseason questionnaires to determine whether program objectives are being met; includes a discussion of results.

Stringfellow ME. 1976. Competency-based instruction in measurement and evaluation. *Journal of Physical Education and Recreation.* **47**:50–51.

Describes the use of a competency-based approach to teaching a traditional undergraduate course in measurement and evaluation at the university level; prepares students to become critical test analyzers; includes samples of course outlines; general objectives, behavioral objectives, and grade criteria.

Zakrajsek DB. 1979. Student evaluations of teaching performance. *Journal of Physical Education and Recreation,* **49**:64–65.

Presents a method of collecting objective evidence to evaluate instruction; discusses the validity of student ratings; measures students' perceptions of effective instruction using an ''opinionnaire''; presents a 20-item example of a student opinionnaire.

Measuring Special Populations and Abilities

Measuring Motor Performance in Children

Watch for these words as you read the following chapter

Basic movement patterns
Component model of intratask development

Face validity
Intratask analysis
Motor ability

everal surveys in recent years have verified that less testing in physical education is done at the elementary school level than at any other level. Why is this true? One reason advanced is that the limited number of days and short class hours scheduled for physical education in most elementary schools prohibits testing in addition to teaching. Furthermore, physical education classes in the elementary schools are not always taught by trained specialists in physical education. In many schools, the regular classroom teacher may not be as knowledgeable about testing motor behavior as he or she is about testing cognitive skills. Another reason for the infrequent use of tests is that test development for this age group has been limited. The existing tests may not be the most useful ones in the elementary school setting. For instance, the teacher may be interested in the measurement of basic movement patterns, such as running, throwing, and jumping. Some may stress the outcome of the movement—how fast the child can run, how far the child can throw the ball, and so forth. Others may emphasize the execution of the movement—the form displayed in running, jumping, or batting, for example, as shown in Figure 12-1. Regardless of the approach used, the measuring instruments available to the teacher are lim-

Figure 12-1   Child taking batting test.

ited. Thus teachers often resort to subjective evaluation of performance based on a cursory judgment of the child's skills.

A third reason for not using tests is the notion that testing must be formal, with time set aside from instruction for this purpose. This point of view, discussed in Chapter 1, suggests that testing automatically takes time away from instruction. Implicit in this way of thinking is the assumption that testing is not desirable because it interferes with teaching. This, of course, does not have to be true. Rather than considering testing and teaching as separate activities, testing should be viewed as an integral part of teaching. In this context, testing is an ongoing activity. This is the concept of formative evaluation, previously described in Chapter 1. When this approach is used, children can take some responsibility for their own learning. They can keep records of their performance using charts posted on bulletin boards in the gymnasium. They can work independently on a task and then check with the teacher when ready to be evaluated. In other words, self-assessment can become an important part of the learning process.

In this chapter, examples of the types of tests that can be used in an elementary physical education program are discussed. This assumes that a well-rounded physical education program is implemented, including the following aspects of motor behavior: **basic movement patterns,** basic skills and games, physical fitness, perceptual motor behavior, and athletic competition. Affective tests for children are described in Chapter 14, and cognitive test development is discussed in Chapter 16.

NASPE STANDARDS AND ASSESSMENTS

In 1992, the National Association for Sport and Physical Education (NASPE) published a document on the outcomes of quality physical education programs. This landmark publication included a definition of the physically educated person, consisting of five focus areas expanded to 20 outcome statements. These statements were translated into benchmarks for selected grade levels. The benchmarks could be used by teachers in curriculum planning. For example, one of the focus areas is: "A physically educated person has learned skills necessary to perform a variety of physical activities" (NASPE, 1992, p. 5). An outcome statement in this area is: "Moves using concepts of body awareness, space awareness, effort and relationships" (NASPE, 1992, p. 5). Many examples of benchmarks were presented for this outcome statement. One of the examples for fourth-grade students is: "While traveling, avoid or catch an individual or object" (NASPE, 1992, p. 10).

NASPE is currently developing national standards for physical education programs (NASPE, 1994). For the above benchmark, several assessment options were proposed. One option is to videotape students traveling in different directions, and rate their ability to avoid running into other students. A five-point scale might be used, as exemplified in the box on p. 300.

In the NASPE publication, a skills test was proposed to measure the ability to catch an object on the move. It requires a student to slowly jog from a starting line to a 20-foot line and attempt to catch a ball thrown from the starting line beyond the 20 foot line. Four trials are taken, two to the left and two to the right. One point is given for a successful catch and one point if the ball is caught with no decrease in speed (NASPE, 1994, p. 4).

These are merely examples of assessment procedures that might be used to measure the benchmark. A more inclusive document will be published by NASPE on national standards.

Another example of an outcome, benchmark, and assessment developed by the NASPE team for fourth-grade children is the following:

> *Outcome:* "Assesses, achieves, and maintains fitness" (NASPE, 1992, p. 5).
> *Benchmark:* "Maintain continuous aerobic activity for a specified time" (NASPE, 1992, p. 10).
> *Example of assessment:* Students are asked to engage in an aerobic activity in their physical education class. The teacher identifies students who are unable to maintain the appropriate pace. Identify students who drop out at various time intervals (NASPE, 1994, p. 11).

The NASPE standards and assessments should be invaluable aids to physical education teachers. A set of prototype materials have been developed for the fourth and eighth grades, and similar packages are being prepared for kindergarten, second, and sixth grades.

RATING SCALE: AVOIDING CONTACT WITH OTHERS WHILE TRAVELING

4   Travels at a fast speed, changing directions sideways, backward, and forward at an angle without losing balance and avoids contacting others

3   Travels at a moderate speed, changing directions sideways and forward at an angle, without losing balance and avoids contacting others

2   Travels at a moderate speed, attempting to change directions, but tends to lose balance and sometimes contacts others

1   Travels at a slow speed, with few direction changes, while contacting others

0   Avoids contact by traveling very little

CALIFORNIA PHYSICAL EDUCATION FRAMEWORK

The NASPE outcomes and benchmarks have been reviewed as guidelines for physical education programs across the country. However, a number of states have moved ahead in developing their own framework for physical education. A notable example is the California public school system. Educators in California have proposed a comprehensive physical education program focusing on the holistic development of the physical, mental, emotional, and social well-being of every student (California Department of Education, 1992). The three major goals for the physical education curriculum are (1) movement skills and movement knowledge; (2) self-image, self-esteem, and self-realization; and (3) social development and social interaction.

This document addresses the assessment process with exceptional clarity and provides examples of assessment tools. The assessment tools can take a variety of forms. Cognitive learning in all three goal areas can be assessed through written tests; cooperative learning activities; individual, small-group, and class projects; problem-solving tasks; small-group and class discussions; task cards, worksheets and contracts; research projects; and homework. Psychomotor learning of skills and fitness development can be assessed through cooperative-learning activities; individual, small-group, and class projects; videotaped performances of skills; problem-solving tasks; written tests; performance tests; task cards; worksheets; contracts; and homework. Samples of different types of assessments are placed in a portfolio for each student. Product assessment emphasizes performance outcomes and demonstration of concepts learned. Process evaluation emphasizes correct movement patterns and technique. Both are important for assessment. (California Department of Education, 1992, p. 78)

This material provides extensive information on the disciplinary base of physical education, as well as the practical elements of goal-setting, teaching, and assessment. It is recommended reading for all physical educators who are involved in curriculum planning in their school districts, no matter where they reside.

DEVELOPMENTALLY APPROPRIATE PRACTICES

Elementary school physical education teachers can benefit from an association with the Council on Physical Education for Children (COPEC). This council is part of NASPE. Recently, COPEC developed a pamphlet on developmentally appropriate physical education for children (NASPE, n.d.). There are three underlying assumptions associated with physical education for children:

1. Physical education and athletic programs have different purposes.
2. Children are not miniature adults.
3. Children in school today will not be adults in today's world.

(NASPE, n.d., p. 4)

Developmentally appropriate physical education is designed for every child, not just skilled athletes. It is not a watered-down adult program. Furthermore, it must be a program that prepares the child to adapt to an ever-changing world. All physical education teaching majors who will be teaching in the elementary schools should review this pamphlet. Appropriate and inappropriate practices are delineated for a wide variety of components of a physical fitness program, such as curriculum, cognitive development, concepts of fitness, assessment, and gender-directed activities.

ASSESSING BASIC MOVEMENT PATTERNS

The area of motor development in the physical education field has encompassed the study of the development of **basic movement patterns** in children. Basic movement patterns are types of movement that emerge developmentally, usually at a young age, such as running, jumping, and throwing. In general, two models have been advanced to describe motor development in children. Seefeldt et al. (1972) advocate the intratask approach; Roberton (Roberton, 1978; Roberton and Halverson, 1984) promote **the component model of intratask development.** These two approaches are described in more detail below.

The assessment of movement patterns usually involves the use of a checklist. It must be carefully validated and have satisfactory reliability and objectivity just like any other test. Objectivity is extremely important when developing a checklist, since a highly valid instrument might be too complex for an observer to use. All too often, the development of a checklist is handled in a casual, offhand manner. This criticism also applies to the development of rating scales, perhaps because these measures seem to be so easy to compile. The checklist may be short and easy to use, but it should also include all appropriate test characteristics.

No matter how valid a checklist has been shown to be, it can easily be misused if the user does not have the ability to observe movement competently. Both Allison (1985) and Barrett (1983) have described the components of observational competence. The observer must have the ability to pick out the critical features of the movement designated in the checklist.

STAGES IN OVERARM THROWING

STAGE 1

The throwing motion is essentially posterior-anterior in direction. The feet usually remain stationary during the throw.

There is little or no trunk rotation in the most rudimentary pattern at this stage, but those at the point of transition between stages 1 and 2 may evoke a slight trunk rotation in preparation for the throw and extensive hip and trunk rotation in the follow-through.

The force of projection of the ball comes primarily from hip flexion, shoulder protraction, and elbow extension.

STAGE 2

The distinctive feature of this stage is the rotation of the body about an imaginary vertical axis, with the hips, spine, and shoulders rotating as one unit. The performer may step forward with either an ipsilateral or contralateral pattern, but the arm is brought forward in transverse plane.

The motion may resemble a sling rather than a throw because of the extended arm position during the course of the throw.

STAGE 3

The distinctive characteristic is the ipsilateral arm-leg action. The ball is placed into a throwing position above the shoulder by a vertical and posterior motion of the arm at the time the ipsilateral leg is moving forward. There is little or no rotation of the spine and hips in preparation for the throw.

The follow-through phase includes flexion at the hip joint and some trunk rotation toward the side opposite the throwing hand.

STAGE 4

The movement is contralateral, with the leg opposite the throwing arm striding forward as the throwing arm is moved in a vertical and posterior direction during the "wind-up phase." Thus, the motion of the trunk and arm closely resembles those of stages 1 and 3.

The stride forward with the contralateral leg provides for a wide base of support and greater stability during the force production phase.

STAGE 5

The shift of weight is entirely to the rear leg, as it pivots in response to the rotating joints above it.

The throwing hand moves in a downward arc and then backward as the opposite leg moves forward.

Concurrently, the hip and spine rotate into position for forceful derotation.

As the contralateral foot strikes the surface, the hips, spine, and shoulder begin to derotate in sequence.

The contralateral leg begins to extend at the knee as the shoulder protracts, the humerus rotates, and the elbow extends, thus providing an equal and opposite reaction to the throwing arm.

The opposite arm also moves forcefully toward the body to assist in the equal and opposite reaction to the throwing arm.

From Seefeldt V, Haulenstricker, J.

Intratask Analysis

The **intratask analysis** of a basic movement pattern is based on the identification of stages of the development of a task from the time it is first attempted to the time it is performed at a mature or adult level. Seefeldt and associates (1972) identify the stages of development of a number of motor tasks, based on the work of Wild (1938). An example of their description of stages is shown in the box on the previous page. The task is the overarm throw, and five developmental stages have been identified. The child is observed throwing a ball and is then placed in one of the five categories.

The throwing pattern should be observed several times on one or more days. On a given day, observing more than one stage in a child's performance is possible. If this happens, the stage represented most frequently should be used to classify the child. Also, the type of throw should be standardized for all children. Force should be emphasized, with accuracy viewed as secondary. If the child throws at a target, with the only force requirement being to project the ball to the target, a different movement pattern is elicited. Once the child is throwing at the level of stage 5, skills tests can be used to measure the force and accuracy.

Component Model of Intratask Development

The model used by Seefeldt and associates deals with the observation of the whole body in assessing the movement pattern of a child. Although the placement and movement of various body parts (e.g., throwing arm, position of the legs) is assessed, the movement pattern of the entire body is given one rating. The component model of intratask development differs from the Seefeldt approach. It is based on the identification of developmental characteristics of body parts within a task. This approach evolved from the work of Roberton (Roberton, 1978; Roberton and Halverson, 1984), whose innovative thinking about motor development led to the idea that changes in one body part in executing a task are not always associated with specified changes in another body part. For example, one child may display the trunk action of one stage and the arm action of another. Thus Roberton proposed analyzing the development of body parts as separate components. Her model can be used to generate checklists, as exemplified in the boxed material on p. 304. This checklist was developed to assess the child's level of ability in hopping.

Note that two different movement components have been identified for hopping—leg action and arm action. Under leg action four steps (somewhat like stages within a component) were delineated. In the example, the child being observed was placed in step 3 of the leg action. As the body projection was initiated, the swing leg (left leg in this case) was used to assist the movement. However, he was classified in step 5 of the arm action, which includes five steps altogether. The opposite arm was used to assist the movement. The movement profile recorded on the checklist is illustrated in Figure 12-2. Two other pieces of information are recorded—movement situation, which includes whether the child or teacher selected the movement to be observed, and the observation

OBSERVATION CHECKLIST FOR HOPPING

Child: *Jones, Randy*   Classroom: *S. Johnson*
Motor task: *Hopping*

Movement component:	Level observed		
leg action	Jan. 4		
Step 1. Momentary flight			
Step 2. Fall and catch; swing leg inactive			
Step 3. Projected takeoff; swing leg assists	✔		
Step 4. Projection delay; swing leg leads			
Movement component: *arm action*			
Step 1. Bilateral inactive			
Step 2. Bilateral reactive			
Step 3. Bilateral assist			
Step 4. Semiopposition			
Step 5. Opposing assist	✔		
Overall movement profile Legs	3		
Arms	5		
Movement situation Teacher selected			
Child selected	✔		
Observation type Direct	✔		
Videotape			
Film			
Comments:			

From Robertson MA, Halverson LE.

Figure 12-2   Hopping: leg action, step 3; arm action, step 5. *(Redrawn from Roberton MA, Halverson LE.)*

type, which determines whether the child was observed directly or on film or videotape. The hopping components and their associated steps have been partially validated, and the checklist is reliable and objective. For information on checklists to be used with other movement patterns, see Roberton and Halverson (1984).

ASSESSING PHYSICAL FITNESS

Physical fitness is important for a child's well-being. In the past 10 years, research has been published documenting the physiologic benefits of exercise in children. It has also been established that many of the risk factors associated with physical inactivity in adults are present in children. For example, evidence of atherosclerosis (hardening of the arteries) has been found in some children. The prevalence of overweight children has also been well documented. In Chapter 17, the major physical fitness tests used in the United States are described, with appropriate modifications for young children. However, many valuable aids can be found in the literature written for elementary school physical education teachers.

Petray and Blazer's (1991) book on health-related physical fitness for children includes policies and procedures for incorporating health-related physical fitness activities and concepts into the physical education program. A concept-based approach to the selection of fitness activities for children and tips for evaluating physical fitness are two primary features of the book. In the evaluation chapter, two descriptions of fitness evaluation are given, one for the classroom teacher and one for the physical education specialist. Grading is not based on fitness scores (Petray and Blazer, 1991, p. 66); rather, effort, participation, and self-improvement are emphasized. Children are asked to set goals for improvement. Many practical tips for fitness evaluation are given.

Another useful reference on fitness assessment (Safrit, 1995) consists of a detailed analysis of physical fitness tests used across the United States. Test administration tips are provided for the most widely used tests, and techniques for motivating children are described.

The YMCA Youth Fitness Program (Thomas et al., 1990) is a curriculum manual for teaching physical fitness to children. The first part of the manual provides background information on health-related youth fitness and its use in the curriculum. The second part includes lesson plans, with sets for grades 1 to 3 and 4 to 6. Each set contains four 10-week units, with 20 lessons for each unit. The format of each lesson consists of the presentation of a fitness concept, suggested fitness activities, and a health concept.

Assessing Level of Physical Activity in Children

Although physical educators have long observed that children are normally active, only in recent years have there been systematic efforts to accurately appraise the level of physical activity in elementary physical education. Pedometers, while easy to use, are not always accurate. A popular method of assessing activity is the use of a heart rate monitor (Hinson, 1994). However, this is often not the most practical approach. Physical activity questionnaires are frequently used to measure physical fitness. They are recommended as measures of change in self-reported physical activity behaviors and as a means of estimating the daily or weekly energy expenditure in various physical activity settings (Hensley et al., 1993).

Cognitive and Affective Components of Physical Fitness

One final point on assessing physical fitness in children: this assessment should not be limited to physical tests. NASPE's outcomes include both cognitive and affective goals for children. Young children, even first graders, can learn about physical fitness concepts. In the pulse power program (Hinson, 1994), a mastery learning approach is used to teach young children six phases of physical fitness knowledge. For example, phase I deals with the heart and uses charts, puzzles, and experiments to help students learn how the heart works. Phase IV deals with exercise and the heart, and covers (for example) the difference between resting heart rate and exercise heart rate.

TESTS OF SPORTS SKILLS

Few tests of sports skills have been developed specifically for children, especially in recent years. Although a great deal of informal skills testing may take place in the elementary schools, much of this work has not been published. Examples of tests of sports skills in this chapter are limited to those with published evidence of reliability and validity. Although they were developed many years ago, they represent the small number of sports skills tests for elementary school children that are available. Several of the recently published test batteries published by the American Alliance for Health, Physical Education, Recreation and Dance (AAHPERD) are appropriate for older children in an elementary school setting, but generally these tests were not designed for younger children. For examples of these tests, see Chapter 19.

The reliability and validity of the tests presented below may not be as satisfactory as desired and portions of some of these tests may be outdated. However, they serve as a useful framework for revising the tests in light of the skills as they are used today.

Basketball Wall Pass Test (Latchaw, 1954)

Test Objective   To measure passing skills of fourth-, fifth-, and sixth-grade students.

Description   The test layout is shown in Figure 12-3. The student stands behind the restraining line. On the signal "Ready, Go!," the ball is thrown at the target as many times as possible in 15 seconds. If a student loses control of the ball, he or she is responsible for recovering it. A 10-second practice period is allowed, followed by two 15-second trials.

Test Area   Floor area: 8 feet by 4 feet; wall area: 7 feet by 8 feet.

Equipment   Stopwatch, regulation basketballs, tape measure, floor tape, and scorecards.

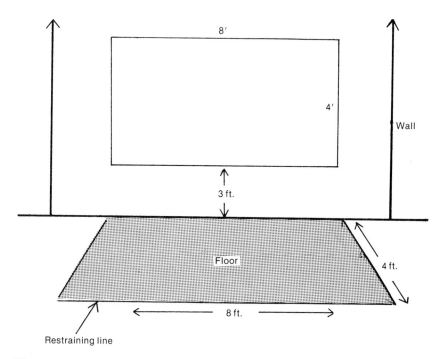

Figure 12-3   Test layout for the Basketball Wall Pass Test. *(Reprinted by permission of the American Alliance for Health, Physical Education, Recreation, and Dance.)*

Scoring The trial score is the number of correct hits in the 15-second period. The test score is the best of the two trials. Balls touching the target line do not count. If a student steps on or over the restraining line, the pass does not count.

Validity **Face validity.** (A test with face validity is one that appears to be valid but has not been formally validated.)

Table 12-1 Achievement scales: Basketball Wall Pass Test

T-Score	GIRLS Grade IV	Grade V	Grade VI	BOYS Grade IV	Grade V	Grade VI	Percentile
77				24	27		99
76	19						99
75			22	23	26	30	99
74					25		99
73		20		22	24		98
72	18				23	29	98
71				21	22	28	98
70						27	97
69						26	97
68	17		21		21	25	96
67		19				24	95
66				20			94
65						23	93
64		18	20				92
63	16	17		19	20		90
62						22	88
61				18			86
60	15		19		19		84
59		16		17			81
58						21	78
57	–		18		18		75
56	14	15		16			72
55							69
54			17			20	65
53					17		61
52	13	14					57
51			16			19	53

From Scott MG, French E.

Reliability Boys $r_{xx'}$ = .91 4th grade
$r_{xx'}$ = .84 5th grade
$r_{xx'}$ = .78 6th grade
Girls $r_{xx'}$ = .94 4th grade
$r_{xx'}$ = .89 5th grade
$r_{xx'}$ = .83 6th grade

Norms Norms are presented in Table 12-1.

Table 12-1 Achievement scales: Basketball Wall Pass Test—cont'd

	GIRLS			BOYS			
T-Score	Grade IV	Grade V	Grade VI	Grade IV	Grade V	Grade VI	Percentile
50	12				16		50
49						18	46
48			15	14			42
47	11	13			15		38
46						17	34
45	10		14				30
44		12		13	14		27
43	9						24
42			13			16	21
41		11		12	13		18
40	8						15
39		10			12	15	13
38			12				11
37				11	11		9
36	7	9				14	8
35			11				6
34		8		10	10		5
33			10				4
32	6	7				13	3
31				9	9		3
30			9				2
29					8		2
28		6			7		2
27				8			1
26	5						1
25			8		6	12	1

Table 12-2 Achievement scales: Volleyball Wall Volley Test

T-Score	GIRLS Grade IV	Grade V	Grade VI	BOYS Grade IV	Grade V	Grade VI	Percentile
77			21			29	99
76		18					99
75						28	99
74	13	17				27	99
73		15	20	20		26	98
72	12	14			20		98
71	11	13	19	18		25	98
70				16		24	97
69	10		18	15			97
68		12		14	19		96
67			17	13		23	95
66	9			12	18	22	94
65		11		11	17	21	93
64			16		16		92
63	8	10	15		15	20	90
62			14	10		19	88
61		9			14	18	86
60			13				84
59	7					17	81
58		8	12		13		78
57			11		12	16	75
56	6	7		8	11		72
55			10				69
54					10	15	65
53	5		9	7			61
52		6			9	14	57
51							53

From Scott MG, French E.

Comments   Use two assistants at each testing station, if possible. One should count the hits and the other, the faults. The ball must land inside the target, not on the line, to score a point.

Volleyball Wall Test (Latchaw, 1954)

Test Objective   To measure the ability of fourth-, fifth-, and sixth-grade students to strike objects.

Table 12-2 Achievement scales: Volleyball Wall Volley Test—cont'd

	GIRLS			BOYS			
T-Score	Grade IV	Grade V	Grade VI	Grade IV	Grade V	Grade VI	Percentile
50	4		8	6	8	13	50
49							46
48		5			7	12	42
47						11	38
46	3		7	5			34
45						10	30
44					6		27
43		4				9	24
42			6	4		8	21
41					5		18
40	2						15
39		3				7	13
38							11
37				3			9
36			5		4	6	8
35						5	6
34		2		2			5
33							4
32	1				3	4	3
31							3
30			3			3	2
29		1					2
28							2
27				1		2	1
26							1
25							1
24					2	1	1
23			2				0

Description   Use the test setup for the Basketball Wall Pass Test, shown in Figure 12-3. The student stands behind the restraining line. On the signal "Ready, Go!," the ball is thrown against the wall. As it bounces off the wall, the student attempts to hit the ball repeatedly against the target. Any type of hit may be used. Allow one 10-second practice trial and four 15-second test trials.

Test Area   Same as the Basketball Wall Pass Test.

Equipment   Volleyballs, stopwatch, tape measure, floor tape, and scorecards.

Scoring The trial score is the number of correct hits in the 15-second period. The test score is the best of four trials. The initial throw against the wall is not scored. Only balls that are hit count. If a student throws or carries the ball, it is not scored. If control of the ball is lost, it is the responsibility of the student to recover it. The ball must again be put into play with a throw against the target.

Validity Face validity.

Reliability Boys $r_{xx'}$ = .89 4th grade
$r_{xx'}$ = .89 5th grade
$r_{xx'}$ = .89 6th grade

Girls $r_{xx'}$ = .84 4th grade
$r_{xx'}$ = .85 5th grade
$r_{xx'}$ = .79 6th grade

Norms Norms are presented in Table 12-2 on pp. 310–311.

Comments Balls must land inside the target, not touching the line, to be scored.

Soccer Wall Volley Test (Latchaw, 1954)

Test Objective To measure the ability of fourth-, fifth-, and sixth-grade students to kick the ball.

Description Use the target layout shown in Figure 12-4. The student stands behind the restraining line. Place the ball anywhere in back of the line. On the

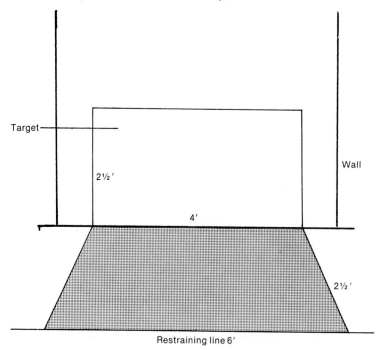

Figure 12-4 Test layout for the Soccer Wall Test. *(Reprinted by permission of the American Alliance for Health, Physical Education, Recreation and Dance.)*

signal "Ready, Go!," the student attempts to kick the ball into the target area of the wall as many times as possible in 15 seconds. If the student loses control of the ball, he or she must recover it. If the ball is within the 4-feet by 2½-feet floor area, the hands cannot be used for retrieval. If the ball is outside this area, the hands may be used. Allow one 15-second practice period and four test trials.

Test Area   Wall area: 4 feet by 2½ feet; floor area: 4 feet by 2½ feet, with a 6-foot restraining line.

Equipment   Soccer balls, stopwatch, tape measure, floor tape, and scoresheets.

Scoring   The trial score is the number of correct hits in 15 seconds. The test score is the best of four trials. Deduct a 1-point penalty whenever the ball is touched with the hands within the rectangular floor area.

Validity   Face validity.

Reliability   Boys $r_{xx'}$ = .82 4th grade
$r_{xx'}$ = .89 5th grade
$r_{xx'}$ = .88 6th grade

Girls $r_{xx'}$ = .77 4th grade
$r_{xx'}$ = .83 5th grade
$r_{xx'}$ = .77 6th grade

Norms   Norms are presented in Table 12-3.

Comments   The ball can be kicked from within the rectangular area, but the kick is not scored; however, this can be followed by a kick from behind the restraining line, which is legal.

Softball Repeated Throws Test (Latchaw, 1954)

Test Objective   To measure the ball-throwing ability of fourth-, fifth-, and sixth-grade students.

Description   The layout for this test is shown in Figure 12-5. The student stands anywhere within the 5½-foot-square throwing area. On the signal "Ready, Go!," the ball is thrown at the target using an overarm throw. The rebound is caught, either in the air or on the bounce, and the student continues throwing as many times as possible in 15 seconds. A 10-second practice trial is allowed, followed by two 15-second test trials.

Test Area   Floor area: 6 feet by 30 feet; wall area: 5½ feet by 10½ feet.

Equipment   Softballs, stopwatch, tape measure, floor tape, and scoresheets.

Scoring   The trial is the number of correct hits in 15 seconds. The test score is the best of two trials. A hit is not scored if the examinee steps on or over any one of the lines of the throwing area or if the ball lands on or outside one of the target lines.

Validity   Face validity.

Reliability   Boys $r_{xx'}$ = .82 4th grade
$r_{xx'}$ = .81 5th grade
$r_{xx'}$ = .85 6th grade

Girls $r_{xx'}$ = .80 4th grade
$r_{xx'}$ = .82 5th grade
$r_{xx'}$ = .85 6th grade

Table 12-3 Achievement scales: Soccer Wall Volley Test

	GIRLS			BOYS			
T-Score	Grade IV	Grade V	Grade VI	Grade IV	Grade V	Grade VI	Percentile
76		15		14	16		99
74	13					18	99
73		14			15		98
71				13		17	98
70		13	13				97
69	12					16	97
68					14		96
67						15	95
66	11	12	12				94
65				12			93
64		11			13	14	92
63	10						90
61			11		12		86
60		10		11		13	84
59	9						81
57			10		11		75
56		9		10		12	72
54	8						65
53			9	9	10	11	61
52		8					57
49	7					10	46
48			8	8	9		42
46		7				9	34
44	6						27
43			7	7	8		24
40		6				8	15
39					7		13
38			6	6			11
37	5						9
35						7	6
34		5					5
32			5				3
29	4					6	2
27		4		4			1
26			4				1
24			3	3	5	5	0

From Scott MG, French E.

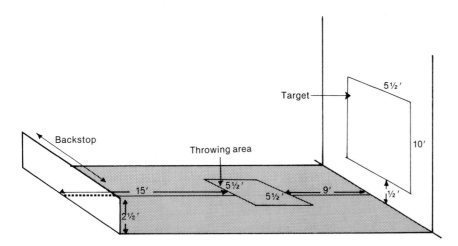

Figure 12-5   Test layout for the Softball Repeated Throws Test. *(Reprinted by permission of the American Alliance for Health, Physical Education, Recreation and Dance.)*

Norms   Norms are presented in Table 12-4.

Comments   If the student loses control of the ball, he or she is responsible for retrieving it. It is desirable to have on hand a dozen or more balls, since the impact of the ball hitting the wall may affect the shape of the ball. If construction of a backstop is not feasible, a rolled mat may be used.

Kicking Test (Johnson, 1962)

Test Objective   To measure the kicking skills (accuracy) of children in grades 1 through 6.

Description   Use the test setup depicted in Figure 12-6. Begin the test by placing a soccer ball behind the 10-foot line. The student kicks the ball against the wall, trying to hit the center of the target. Two practice kicks and three trials are taken. The same procedure is followed from behind the 20-foot and 30-foot lines.

Test Area   Wall area: 5 feet by 10 feet; floor area: 30 feet by 10 feet.

Equipment   Soccer balls, floor and wall tape, tape measure, and scoresheets.

Scoring   The score for each kick is the number of the target areas the ball hits. Add the total of the nine trials to obtain the total test score. A ball landing on a line between two target areas receives the higher point value of the two areas.

Validity   Concurrent validity, using a criterion measure of teachers' ratings of kicking performance.

Table 12-4 Achievement scales: Softball Repeated Throws Test

T-Score	GIRLS			BOYS			Percentile
	Grade IV	Grade V	Grade VI	Grade IV	Grade V	Grade VI	
78	9	10					99
76				12			99
74			12			15	99
73				11	14		98
72	8	9					98
68					13	14	96
66			11				94
65				10			93
64					12		92
63	7					13	90
61			10				86
60					11		84
58				9		12	78
55		8	9		10		69
54						11	65
51				8	9		53
49			8			10	46
48		7					42
47	6						38
46					8		34
45			7	7			30
44						9	27
41	5						18
40		6			7		15
39				6		8	13
38			6				11
35	4						6
33				5		7	4
32		5			6		3
29			5				2
28	3	4				6	2
27				4			1
24		3	4		5	5	1

From Scott MG, French E.

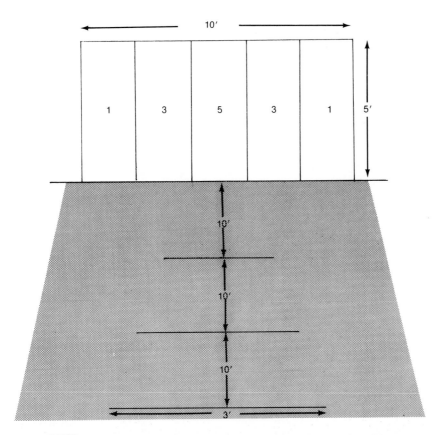

Figure 12-6 Test layout for the Kicking Test. *(Reprinted by permission of the American Alliance for Health, Physical Education, Recreation and Dance.)*

Grade	Boys*	Girls*
1	.29	.41
2	.66	.43
3	.34	.13
4	.38	.51
5	.04	.12
6	.17	.49

* Correlation coefficients.

Norm A table of percentiles is presented in Table 12-5.

Comments If the examinee steps on or over the restraining line, the trial is repeated.

Table 12-5 Percentiles for Kicking Test (points)

| | GRADES | | | | | | | | | | | |
| | 1 | | 2 | | 3 | | 4 | | 5 | | 6 | |
Percentile	Boys	Girls	Boys	Girls	Boys	Girls	Boys	Girls	Boys	Girls	Boys	Girls
100	34	30	36	35	40	36	42	39	43	40	44	42
95	28	27	33	33	37	34	38	37	40	38	41	40
90	27	26	31	31	36	32	37	35	39	36	40	38
85	26	25	30	30	34	31	36	34	38	35	39	36
80			28	29	33	30	35	33	37	34	37	35
75	25	24		28				32	36	33		34
70			27	27	32	29	34	31	35		36	
65	24	23		26	31	28				32	35	33
60		22	26		30	27	33	30	34	31		
55	23			25		26						32
50			25	24	29	25	32	29	33		34	
45						24	31			30		31
40	22	21	24	23	28				32		33	
35			23	22	27	23	30	28		29	32	30
30	21		21	20		22	29	27	31	28		
25		19	20		26	21		26		27	31	29
20	19	18	19	19	25	20	28	25	30	26	30	28
15	18	16	18	18	23	19	27	24	29	25	29	27
10	17	14	17	16	22	18	25	22	28	23	28	25
5	14	10	14	14	20	17	23	20	26	20	26	20
0	12	8	10	12	16	16	19	16	23	14	23	15

From Johnson RD.

Throw-and-Catch Test (Johnson, 1962)

Test Objective To measure the ability of first- through sixth-grade students to throw and catch.

Description Use the test setup shown in Figure 12-7. To begin the test the student stands in the first square and throws the ball at the wall target, using an underhand throw. Two practice trials are taken. The same sequence is repeated from each of the remaining four squares.

Test Area Wall area: 7 feet by 4 feet; floor area: 20 feet by 3 feet.

Equipment Playground balls (8½ inches in diameter) for the first through third grades; volleyballs for the fourth through sixth grades.

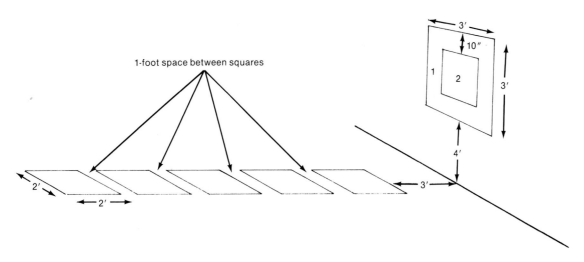

Figure 12-7   Test layout for the Throw-and-Catch Test. *(Reprinted by permission of the American Alliance for Health, Physical Education, Recreation and Dance.)*

Scoring   The total test score is the sum of 15 trials. The following scoring system is used:

1. Score 2 points for hitting the inner wall target.
2. Score 2 points for catching the rebound in the air while standing in the proper floor square.
3. Score 1 point for hitting the outer section of the wall target.
4. Score 1 point for catching the rebound in the air while standing on the line or outside the proper floor square.

Validity   Concurrent validity, using a criterion measure of teachers' ratings of throwing and catching performance.

Grade	Girls*	Boys*
1	.54	.47
2	.33	.54
3	.33	.54
4	.50	.45
5	.15	.38
6	.30	.47

* Correlation coefficients.

Reliability   Test-retest coefficients.

Table 12-6 Percentiles for Throw-and-Catch Test (points)

| | GRADES | | | | | | | | | | | |
| | 1 | | 2 | | 3 | | 4 | | 5 | | 6 | |
Percentile	Boys	Girls	Boys	Girls	Boys	Girls	Boys	Girls	Boys	Girls	Boys	Girls
100	34	29	39	35	41	38	50	43	57	53	59	55
95	26	23	38	31	40	34	47	40	54	50	56	51
90	24	21	34	28	39	33	45	39	52	45	54	49
85	23	20	32	27	38	32	43	38	50	44	53	47
80	22	19	31	26	37	30	42	37	48	43	52	46
75	21	18	30	25	36	29	41	36	47	42	51	45
70	20	17	29	24	35	28	40	35	46	41	50	44
65	19		28	23	34			34	45	40	49	43
60	18	16	27	22	33	27	39		44		48	
55		15	26	21		26	38	33		39	47	42
50	17		25		32	25		32	43	38	46	41
45		14	24	20	31		37		42	37		40
40	16	13		19	30	24	36		41		45	
35	15	12	23	18		23	35	30	40	36	44	39
30	14	11	22	17	29	22	34	29	39	35	43	38
25	13	10	21	16		21	33	28	38	34	42	37
20	12		20	15	28	20	32	27	37	33	41	36
15	11	9	19	14	27	19	31	26	36	32	40	35
10	10	8	17	12	25	18	30	24	34	31	39	33
5	9	5	13	10	21	16	27	21	33	29	37	31
0	6	3	8	7	17	13	23	16	29	24	34	28

From Johnson RD.

Grade	Girls*	Boys*
1	.94	.89
2	.79	.92
3	.90	.84
4	.78	.81
5	.65	.84
8	.93	.91

* Correlation coefficients.

Norms   A table of percentiles is presented in Table 12-6.

Comments
The trial is repeated if the student steps out of the square while throwing.

TESTS OF PHYSICAL FITNESS

The philosophy and foundation for incorporating physical fitness into the elementary physical education curriculum was discussed earlier in this chapter. A well-rounded curriculum for elementary school physical education should include physical fitness. Two types of fitness can be emphasized: one is the type needed for athletic performance; the other is tied to the individual's state of health, focusing on the relationship between physical activity and a positive state of health. Standardized tests available for each type of fitness are described in the following section.

AAHPERD Physical Best Test

The AAHPERD Physical Best Test (AAHPERD, 1988) is described in detail in Chapter 17. Although this test is not a part of the Physical Best Program any longer, the items may still be used. Five items are included in this test—each item measures a component of health-related physical fitness that is affected by

Physical education class taking the 1-Mile Run Test.

vigorous physical activity. This test is appropriate for any school-age child, including those of college age. Norms for children are presented in Chapter 17.

Prudential FITNESSGRAM

The FITNESSGRAM test is now recommended by the AAHPERD as well as the Cooper Institute for Aerobics Research. Three components of health-related fitness are measured, and the user is given a choice of tests for most of the components. For more information, see Chapter 17.

Several other national physical fitness test batteries are recommended for children of elementary school age. These include Fit Youth Today, Chrysler/

Testing curl-ups.

Dribbling task. *(Courtesy of Dale A. Ulrich.)*

AAU, and the President's Council on Physical Fitness and Sports. All these tests are described in Chapter 17.

TESTS OF PERCEPTUAL MOTOR BEHAVIOR

Educators and clinicians working with preschool- and early elementary school-age children are frequently interested in their perceptual motor behavior. Perceptual motor domains include spatial orientation, body image and differentiation, ocular control, form perception, perception of position in space, perceptual constancy, tactile discrimination, visual closure, and memory (Auxter and Pyfer, 1985). A number of well-known tests of this type are described in Chapter 13. Most of these tests are appropriate for children with or without handicaps, although many are used to screen children to identify those with perceptual motor deficiencies.

EXAMPLES OF GROWTH CHARTS

A number of procedures may be used to monitor the physical growth and development of children, but two of the most widely used growth charts are available from the American Medical Association (AMA) (discussed below) and Ross Laboratories (see Figures 12-8 and 12-9).

AMA Growth Charts (AMA, 1978)

Test Objective To plot the growth curves of children 4 to 18 years of age.

Description Two charts are available, one for boys and one for girls. The most recent version of the charts (AMA, 1978) was developed by H.V. Meredith and J.H. Spurgeon for the Joint Committee on Health Problems in Education of the National Education Association (NEA) and the AMA. To ensure accuracy in assessing students' weight, students should remove their shoes and wear minimal or lightweight clothing. Record weight to the nearest half-pound and height to the nearest one-quarter inch. Then find the age of the child on the appropriate chart. Plot and record the height and weight measurements in the respective portions of the chart. Repeat the assessment on an annual basis and connect the points within each portion (height and weight) of the chart. Both portions contain channels representing tall, heavy (upper 10%), average (next 20% and middle 40%), and short, light (next 20% and lower 10%). The child's growth is generally considered satisfactory if the plotted points remain within a channel.

Supplies Growth charts can be ordered from the American Medical Association, Order Department OP-311, 535 Dearborn Street, Chicago, IL 60610.

Validity The growth charts were developed after extensive study of the growth record of children at various age levels. They were based on height and weight measurements collected between 1960 and 1975 on boys and girls attending public schools in Iowa and South Carolina. The height and weight channels were obtained by subdividing height and weight distributions at different ages.

Reliability None reported for this specific test.

Comments When the child's growth curve moves from one channel to another, the underlying cause of this change should be determined and appropriate measures taken.

The Ross Laboratory Charts (Figures 12-8 and 12-9)

These charts provide similar procedures for charting physical growth. Channels representing height and weight were developed for both boys and girls from ages 2 to 18 years. The channels are based on percentiles including lines drawn at 5%, 10%, 25%, 50%, 75%, 90%, and 95%. Weight may be recorded in kilograms or pounds and height in centimeters or inches.

SUMMARY

Although informal testing may take place in elementary school physical education programs, few standardized tests of sport and physical activity were developed for this age group in the past. Now, however, the picture is changing. Since youth sports has become a viable area of study, a need has been generated for a wide variety of tests to measure different aspects of the sports environment. To test physical fitness, the Prudential FITNESSGRAM can be used in the lower as well as upper elementary grades. Other national tests are also available. Some of the more recently developed checklists used to assess basic movement patterns

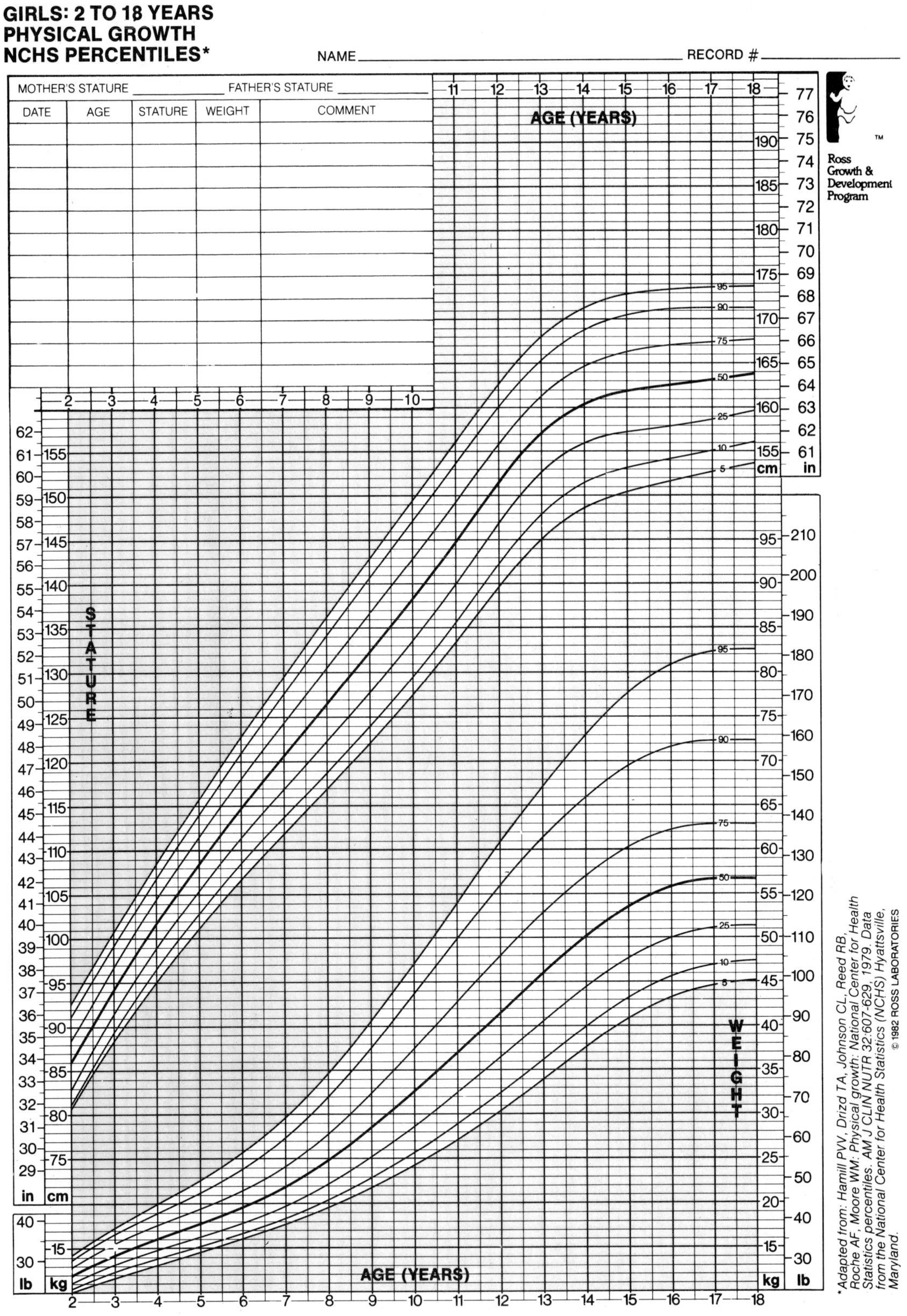

GIRLS: 2 TO 18 YEARS
PHYSICAL GROWTH
NCHS PERCENTILES*

Figure 12-8 Physical growth National Center for Health Statistics (NCHS) percentile chart for girls.

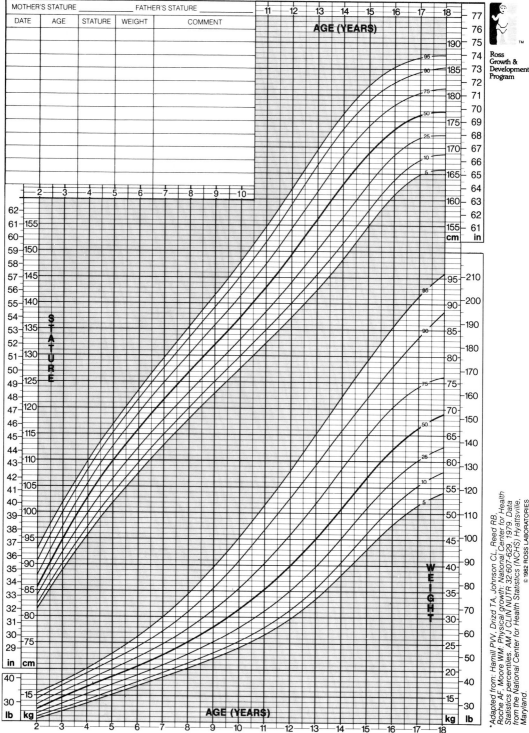

BOYS: 2 TO 18 YEARS
PHYSICAL GROWTH
NCHS PERCENTILES*

Figure 12-9 Physical growth NCHS percentile chart for boys.

are based on sound theory rather than armchair judgment. More tests with substantiated validity and reliability are needed that can be administered in a short period of time. The development of criterion-referenced tests for elementary school physical education would make a valuable contribution to a testing program for young children. Finally, any type of testing program is unlikely to be used with success in the elementary schools unless it is integrated into the instructional program in physical education.

Learning Experiences

1. Form a group with three other students in class. Study the checklist presented in the boxed material on p. 304. Take turns demonstrating each

---

DEVELOPMENTAL SEQUENCE FOR LEG ACTION IN HOPPING

STEP 1
Momentary flight. The support knee and hip quickly flex, pulling (instead of projecting) the foot from the floor. The flight is momentary. Only one or two hops can be achieved. The swing leg is lifted high and held in an inactive position to the side or in front of the body.

STEP 2
Fall and catch; the swing leg is inactive. Body leaning forward allows the minimal knee and ankle extension to help the body "fall" forward of the support foot and then quickly catch itself again. The swing leg is inactive. Repeat hops are now possible.

STEP 3
Projected takeoff; the swing leg assists. Perceptible pretakeoff extension occurs in the hip, knee, and ankle in the support leg. There is little or no delay in changing from knee and ankle flexion on landing to extension prior to takeoff. The swing leg now pumps up and down to assist in projection. The range of the swing is insufficient to carry it behind the support leg when viewed from the side.

STEP 4
Projection delay; the swing leg leads. The weight of the child on landing is now smoothly transferred along the foot to the ball before the knee and ankle extend to takeoff. The support leg nearly reaches full extension on takeoff. The swing leg now leads the upward-forward movement of the takeoff phase, while the support leg is still rotating over the ball of the foot. The range of the pumping action in the swing leg increases so that it passes behind the support leg when viewed from the side.

From Roberton MA, Halverson LE. 1984. Developing children—their changing movement. Philadelphia: Lea & Febiger. Used by permission.

DEVELOPMENTAL SEQUENCE FOR ARM ACTION IN HOPPING

STEP 1
Bilateral inactive. The arms are held bilaterally, usually high and out to the side, although other arm positions behind or in front of the body may be held. Any arm action is usually slight and inconsistent.

STEP 2
Bilateral reactive. Arms swing upward briefly, then medially rotated at the shoulder in a swinging movement prior to takeoff. It appears that this movement is a reaction to loss of balance.

STEP 3
Bilateral assist. The arms pump up and down together, usually in front of the line of the trunk. Any downward and backward motion of the arms occurs after takeoff. The arms may move parallel to each other or be held at different levels as they move up and down.

STEP 4
Semiopposition. The arm on the side opposite the swing leg swings forward with that leg and back as the leg moves down. The position of the other arm is variable, often staying in front of the body or to the side.

STEP 5
Opposing-assist. The arm opposite the swing leg moves forward and upward in synchrony with the forward and upward movement of that leg. The other arm moves in the direction opposite to the action of the swing leg. The range of movement in the arm action may be minimal unless the task requires speed or distance.

From Roberton MA, Halverson LE. 1984. Developing children—their changing movement. Philadelphia: Lea & Febiger. Used by permission.

level (step) of arm action and leg action in hopping. Then attempt to use the checklist by evaluating the children shown in Figures 12-10 and 12-11. Use the detailed description of leg and arm action in the two sections of boxed material on pp. 327–328. The correct classifications are included on p. 331. Finally, observe at least two children performing a hop and attempt to classify them, using the checklist. Check with the other members of the group to determine how closely you agreed on your classifications. If there is considerable disagreement, observe the children again and attempt to uncover the sources of disagreement.

2. Observe a group of elementary school–age children being tested on some aspect of their motor performance. Write a short paper on the problems that can be encountered in administering a test to young children. Suggest ways of avoiding these problems.

Figure 12-10   Arm and leg action in hopping. *(Redrawn from Roberton MA, Halverson LE.)*

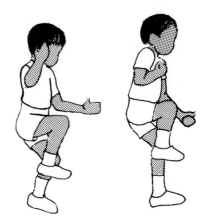

Figure 12-11   Arm and leg action in hopping. *(Redrawn from Roberton MA, Halverson LE.)*

References

Allison PC. 1985. Observing for competence. Journal of Physical Education, Recreation and Dance, **56**(7):50–51, 54.

American Alliance for Health, Physical Education, Recreation and Dance (AAHPERD). 1988. Physical best. Reston, Va: American Alliance for Health, Physical Education, Recreation and Dance.

American Medical Association (AMA). 1978. Height-weight interpretation folder for boys. Chicago: American Medical Association Medicine/Education Committee.

American Medical Association (AMA). 1978. Height-weight interpretation folder for girls. Chicago: American Medical Association Medicine/Education Committee.

Auxter D, Pyfer J. 1985. Adapted physical education and recreation. St Louis: Times Mirror/Mosby College.

Barrett KR. 1983. A hypothetical model of observing as a teaching skill. Journal of Teaching in Physical Education, **3**(1):22–31.

California Department of Education. 1992. Physical education framework for California public schools kindergarten through grade twelve. Sacramento: California Department of Education.

Hensley LD, Ainsworth BE, Ansorge CJ. 1993. Assessment of physical activity—professional accountability in promoting active lifestyles. Journal of Physical Education, Recreation and Dance, **64**(1):56–64.

Hinson C. 1994. Pulse power—a heart physiology program for children. Journal of Physical Education, Recreation and Dance, **65**(1):62–68.

Johnson RD. 1962. Measurements of achievement in fundamental skills. Research Quarterly, **33**:94–103.

Latchaw M. 1954. Measuring selected motor skills in fourth, fifth and sixth grades. Research Quarterly, **25**:439–449.

National Association for Sport and Physical Education (NASPE). (1992). The physically educated person. Reston, Va: National Association for Sport and Physical Education.

National Association for Sport and Physical Education (NASPE). (1994). Proposed national standards for physical education programs. Unpublished paper. Reston, Va: National Association for Sport and Physical Education.

National Association for Sport and Physical Education (NASPE). n.d. Developmentally appropriate physical education practices for children. Reston, Va: National Association for Sport and Physical Education.

Petray CK, Blazer SL. 1991. Health related physical fitness: Concepts and activities for elementary school children, Edina, Minn: Bellwether Press.

Roberton MA. 1978. Stages in motor development. In Ridenour M, ed. Motor development: issues and applications. Princeton, NJ: Princeton Book.

Roberton MA, Halverson LE 1984. Developing children—their changing movement. Philadelphia: Lea & Febiger.

Safrit MJ. 1995. Complete guide to youth fitness testing. Champaign, Ill: Human Kinetics.

Scott MG, French E. 1959. Measurement and evaluation in physical education. Dubuque, Iowa: Wm C Brown Group.

Seefeldt V, Reuschlein S, Vogel P. 1972. Sequencing motor skills within the physical education curriculum, Presented at the American Association for Health, Physical Education, and Recreation National Convention, Houston, March 27, 1972.

Thomas JR. 1983. Motor development during childhood and adolescence. Minneapolis: Burgess.

Thomas KT, Lee AM, Thomas JR. 1990. YMCA youth fitness program. Champaign, Ill: Human Kinetics.

Wild MR. 1938. The behavior pattern of throwing and some observations concerning its course of development in children. Research Quarterly, **9**:20–24.

Annotated Readings

Hardin DH, Garcia MJ. 1982. Diagnostic performance tests for elementary school children (grades 1–4). Journal of Physical Education, Recreation and Dance, **53**(2):48–49.
Recommends the use of four performance tests measuring running, jumping, throwing, and ball handling in elementary school physical education; norms are presented for children ages 6 through 9.

Melville S. 1985. Teaching and evaluating cognitive skills in elementary physical education. Journal of Physical Education, Recreation and Dance, **56**(2):26–28.
Describes the development of a written examination on cognitive skill acquisition for third and fourth graders; discusses the benefits of using written examinations in elementary school physical education.

Seefeldt V. 1984. Physical fitness in preschool and elementary school–aged children. Journal of Physical Education, Recreation and Dance, **55**(9):33–37, 40.

Describes the importance of enhancing children's physical fitness during their early years; discusses the relationship between fundamental motor skills and fitness in preschool years.

Siegel J. 1988. Children's target heart rate. Journal of Physical Education, Recreation and Dance, **59**(4):78–79.

Discusses the importance of using heart rate to control the intensity of children's vigorous physical activity; describes target heart rate range and presents a table of these ranges for children from ages 4 to 18.

Thomas JR, Lee AM, Thomas KT. 1988. Physical education for children: Concepts into practice. Champaign, Ill: Human Kinetics.

Discusses teaching quality physical education classes; includes sections on children's physical development, curriculum planning and organization, and curriculum planning and class organization; also deals with evaluating and improving teaching.

Thomas KT, Lee AM, Thomas JR. 1995. Physical education for children: Daily lesson plans, 2 vols. Champaign, Ill: Human Kinetics.

Lee AM, Thomas KT, Thomas JR. 1995. Physical education for children: Daily lesson plans, 2 vols. Champaign, Ill: Human Kinetics.

These volumes, covering levels 1 and 2 and 3 and 4 respectively, are companion pieces to Concepts into Practice; included are daily lesson plans for children in grades K to 8; and developing activities for fitness, games and sports, rhythmic activities, and gymnastics.

Thomas JR, Thomas KT. 1983. Strange kids and strange numbers: assessing children's motor development. Journal of Physical Education, Recreation and Dance, **54**(8):19–20.

Identifies important motor behaviors and characteristics to be measured in children; discusses the selection of appropriate tests of the movement performance of preschool and elementary school-age children; reviews the circumstances under which the assessments should be made.

Answers to Learning Experiences

Figure 12-10 represents leg action, step 2; arm action, step 2.

Figure 12-11 represents leg action, step 4; arm action, step 5.

Adapting Tests and Measurements for Special Populations

Watch for these words as you read the following chapter

Anomaly
Cerebral palsy
Cognitive disorders
Congenital
Deaf
Disabled
Educable mentally
 retarded
Eligibility
Hearing-impaired
Individualized
 Education Program
Least restrictive
 environment
Mental retardation

Motor ability
Multihandicapped
Needs assessment
Orthopedically
 impaired
Paraplegic
Placement
Reflexes
Screening
Seriously emotionally
 disturbed
Specific learning
 disability
Speech impairment
Visually impaired

ecent trends in the way services are delivered to persons with a disability require that physical educators constantly review their measurement and evaluation practices and keep abreast of changing philosophies. As a result of Public Law (PL) 94-142 passed in 1975, assessment has become an integral part of the **disabled** child's educational program. More recent legislation has focused on early intervention and emphasis on aiding persons with a disability to make the transition from the public school to vocational school, employment, post-secondary education, and effective community living. The focus is on testing environments with a high degree of ecological validity leading to assessment of how well the individual will be able to function successfully in the leisure and recreation, community, or employment setting. Moreover, the 1990 Americans with Disabilities Act (PL 101-476), which addresses discrimination and access to public and private accommodations, is forcing society to review treatment of the disabled population.

Measurement and evaluation techniques for persons with a disability are frequently used for purposes similar to those used for testing in regular physical education classes. For example, tests may be used to motivate students, to classify them, and for many other reasons (see Chapter 1). However, when students have physical, emotional, or mental impairments that lead to physical disabilities, assessments are typically used for **screening, placement,** developing curriculum, student evaluation, diagnosis, instructional planning, and program development (Auxter et al., 1993). Screening often takes place in the physical education setting and is used to identify students who are likely to have a motor delay and who might be eligible for adapted physical education services (Short, 1990). Screening is followed by more rigorous evaluation by adapted physical education specialists, physical therapists, school counselors, and other professionals to determine eligibility for adapted physical education services. Once the particular services and programs have been identified, decisions are made regarding the appropriate placement of the student to receive the services in the **least restrictive environment.** While the least restrictive environment is determined individually for each student according to the disabling condition, curriculum content, and teaching style, it is also necessary to consider delivering instruction in an environment which maximizes interaction with nondisabled children (Sherrill, 1993). Lastly, the child's program is periodically evaluated to determine the success of individualized instruction.

Several problems commonly surface when assessing the physical abilities of the person with a disability (Baumgartner and Horvat, 1988). One, a test battery is needed for each possible combination of disabling conditions. Each condition can create a different set of limitations in a test setting. Two, it is difficult to develop norms for tests used in disabled populations, since the size of each subgroup tends to be small and the individuals may not be readily accessible for testing. Three, persons with a disability may have problems typically associated with the testing of young children, such as short attention span, limited ability to understand complicated directions, and self-motivation. Additional factors that may influence the testing of children with a disability are the effects of medication, the child's understanding of the concept of "maximum effort," and the tester's rapport with the child. Indeed, the issue of testing persons with a disability has become so significant that entire books have been devoted to this topic (see, e.g., Werder and Kalakian, 1985).

Before initiating a program of physical activity for a person with a disability, a teacher must determine the person's level of physical functioning. Because of the wide variety of handicapping conditions, testing must often take place on an individualized basis. The physical education teacher, working with the appropriate specialists, tests the student to determine the level of psychomotor functioning. This information is used to plan a physical education program based on objectives developed specifically for the individual. The student is then evaluated in light of these objectives. In essence, before a student with impairments is allowed to participate in any form of physical activity in an educational setting, a two-stage approach to testing should take place. After the initial screening, a therapist often handles the first stage—determining the extent of the disability. Ideally, a specialist in adapted physical education assists the therapist in this assessment. The results are used to prepare individualized objectives, and the adequacy of these objectives is checked. Are they written at the appropriate level for the child? Are some of the objectives too easy? Too difficult? This analysis represents the second stage of planning, essentially a **needs** assessment—determining the extent to which the student is capable of meeting the individualized objectives. If the child can already meet an objective, it should be modified or rewritten. By this process the objectives are fine-tuned. After these assessments are completed, a program of physical activity can be initiated. The long-range goal of the program is to enhance performance in the non-impaired areas and to reduce the level of impairment as much as possible. Many textbooks on adapted physical education stress the importance of using formative evaluation to provide continuous monitoring of performance so that adjustments can be made in the program when necessary (Sherrill, 1993; Seaman and DePauw, 1989; Dunn and Fait, 1989). Although norm-referenced approaches to measurement are sometimes advocated, primary emphasis is placed on criterion-referenced testing.

As you might expect, there is no universal agreement on the factors related to motor performance that should be measured in this special population. Kirkendall et al. (1987) proposed testing 10 physical factors.

Basic areas

1. Strength
2. Endurance (muscular and cardiovascular)
3. Range of motion
4. Balance

Intermediate areas

5. Body awareness
6. Body sides awareness
7. Space awareness
8. Timing awareness

Advanced areas

9. Coordination
10. Agility

Seaman and DePauw (1989) refer to four broad levels of assessment, ranging from the basic to the complex:

1. Reflex behavior
2. Sensory systems
3. Motor patterns
4. Motor skills

Warm-up for bicycle ergometer test.

Examples of tests fitting several of these categories are presented later in this chapter. Several of these tests are also appropriate for nondisabled preschool children in a physical education setting. For example, it is not unusual to find the Denver Developmental Screening Test II described in textbooks on elementary physical education, motor development, and adapted physical education. However, whether the child is with or without a disability, many of these tests must be administered on an individualized basis, with, of course, certain exceptions. For example, when the disabling condition is mild, such as mild mental retardation, group testing is possible. When the American Alliance for Health, Physical Education, Recreation and Dance (AAHPERD) Motor Fitness Test for the Moderately Mentally Retarded is used, it can be administered to students as a group. As the extent of retardation becomes more severe, individualized testing is more effective. Most of the tests used to screen students for classification purposes require one-on-one testing, regardless of the extent of the disability.

LEGAL MANDATES AFFECTING EVALUATION

Although it is assumed that good instruction incorporates sound measurement and evaluation practices, the person with a disability has special needs and thus has been given unique protection by legal action. Passed in 1970 as Public Law (PL) 91-230 and most recently updated in 1990 as PL 101-476, the Individuals with Disabilities Education Act (IDEA) provides federal legislation dealing with educating persons with disabilities. Several significant updates and amendments to IDEA since 1970 have shaped the treatment of persons with disabilities in the educational system. The first significant change in IDEA occurred in 1975 with the passage of PL 94-142, the Education for All Handicapped Children Act (also known as IDEA-Part B). Winnick (1990, p. 9) summarizes the highlights of PL 94-142 as follows:

1. A right to a free and appropriate education
2. Physical education available to every handicapped student
3. Equal opportunity in athletics and intramurals
4. An individualized education program (IEP) designed to meet unique needs
5. A program developed by a planning committee including parents and, if appropriate, the student
6. A program conducted in the least restrictive environment
7. Nondiscriminatory testing and objective criteria for placement
8. Due process
9. Related services to assist in special education

Subsequent amendments to PL 94-142 focused on early intervention, extending services to children aged 3 to 5 years (1983, PL 98-199) and from birth through 2 years (1986, PL 99-457). In 1990 the most recent update of IDEA substituted the term *disability* for handicapped, expanded the definition of "disabilities," and added an emphasis on helping persons with disability to make the transition from the secondary educational system to vocational or post-secondary education, employment, and independent living, including the use of public recreations, health, and leisure resources (Sherrill, 1993).

Items 4 and 7 above have precise implications for evaluation in physical education. Although many aspects of education are affected by the law, the focus in this chapter is on measurement and evaluation in the physical education field.

Public Law 94-142 mandated an **Individualized Education Program (IEP)** for each disabled or handicapped person aged 3 to 21 years receiving special education services. A similar plan, called an individualized family service plan (IFSP), for infants and toddlers with disabilities is specified by PL 99-457 (see Sherrill, 1993, for a complete description of the IFSP). The IEP must include documentation about the child's educational program. It must be approved by a committee whose membership, which must include at least one parent, is determined under the law. Assessments must be completed within 30 days of the date of parental permission. Complete assessments are required by law every 3 years, and the results of assessment must be reported in a formal meeting. Although several adapted physical education textbooks (e.g., Sherrill, 1993) have thorough discussions of this law, the portions of the law affecting evaluation are especially well presented in Fait and Dunn (1989). A summary of part of their review follows.

Due Process

If the child is judged to have impairments requiring a special testing program, the school is required to inform the parents and child of their rights with the provision to challenge educational decisions they think are unfair. This requirement includes five components:

1. Permission before assessment. The school is required to inform the parents in writing in their native language of (a) the intent to refer the child for assessment, (b) the reasons for referral, (c) descriptions of tests and who will administer them, and (d) the parents' rights (Sherrill, 1993). The parents must give written permission to have their child evaluated.
2. Results of the assessment. The results must be interpreted in a meeting with the parents.
3. Outside evaluation. The parents may request that an independent evaluation be conducted outside the school. The parents must pay for these expenses unless the results differ from those reported by the school, in which case the school district must cover them.
4. Hearings. If the parents and the school system cannot agree on the evaluation findings, a special hearing must be held.
5. Confidentiality of records. Records of all evaluations must be kept confidential.

Standards for Evaluation

Public Law 94-142 also specifies standards for evaluation, including test selection, test administration, and test examiners. In addition, IDEA specifies that individual states develop a state plan outlining implementation of the law. State plans must be submitted to and reviewed by the U.S. Department of Education every 3 years (Sherrill, 1993).

1. Test selection. The school system must use tests to measure the achievement level rather than the impairment of the child. More than one test procedure must be used. All tests cannot be subjective (such as observational scales), nor can all be objective (like performance tests).
2. Test administration. Tests must be administered to test the student's ability rather than his or her communication skills. This is particularly critical for those with sensory impairments. If the child's native language is not English, the test instructions should be given in the native language, if necessary. If the child is **deaf,** sign language can be used.
3. Test examiners. A multidisciplinary team is required for the testing. Ideally, this team includes a specialist in adapted physical education. All testers must be trained and qualified to administer the measures.

The rest of this chapter contains examples of measures that are frequently recommended by specialists in the field. As you review each test, consider the feasibility of using it in a kindergarten or elementary physical education setting with children who have no disabling conditions.

OBSERVATIONAL TECHNIQUES

Checklists for assessing the child with impairments are available in adapted physical education textbooks, such as Auxter et al. (1993), Sherrill (1993), Seaman and DePauw (1989), and Fait and Dunn (1989). Some of these observational techniques were developed by physical educators who have had years of experience working with students having a variety of disabling conditions, including those with a special learning disability and those who are **seriously emotionally disturbed.** However, many of the observational tools are weak measures of the student's physical ability because they lack evidence of validity and reliability. Although logical validity may be self-evident to a certain extent, it does not substitute for the proper establishment of test characteristics. If the techniques are used as quick screening devices before making a thorough assessment, their use is more defensible. If the results of a weak measure are used to make temporary decisions that can be modified in the near future, the consequences of assessment are not as severe as those used to make decisions with long-term implications for the child.

Ulrich (1988) describes several approaches to assessing the quality of movement competence. These include product assessment, qualitative assessment, performance error assessment, developmental task analysis, and a comprehensive analysis. All but the first approach utilize observational techniques and checklists. Several methods (e.g., Roberton and Halverson, 1984; Ulrich, 1985) have sufficient evidence of validity and reliability. The use of criterion-referenced measurement to diagnose and improve student learning in adapted physical education and the virtues of criterion-referenced testing were explored by King and Aufsesser (1988).

PERFORMANCE TESTS

Reflex Testing

Generally, adapted physical education specialists are not expected to test **reflexes** (inborn, involuntary behaviors) (Figures 13-1 and 13-2), although the physical education teacher working in an adaptive setting needs to know the results of reflex testing to analyze the movement deficiencies of the student. This information should be a part of the student's records and is usually obtained by a therapist. Pyfer (1988) has developed a screening test for developmental delays that includes several reflex test items.

Sensorimotor Testing

Sensorimotor or perceptual motor testing samples the function of the underlying sensory system through observable motor performance (Seaman and DePauw, 1989). A description of one test in this category, the Purdue Perceptual Motor Survey, follows. (Sources for obtaining two other tests, the Quick Neurological Screening Test and the Frostig Developmental Test of Visual Perception, are included in Appendix F.)

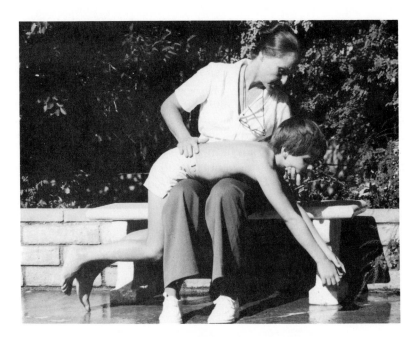

Figure 13-1   Test of the tonic labyrinthine reflex. *Courtesy of Janet A. Seaman.*

Purdue Perceptual Motor Survey (Roach and Kephart, 1966)

Test Objective   To sample the functions of the sensory systems as they support or contribute to efficient movement.

Description   The survey consists of 12 test items:

A. Balance and posture
   Test No. 1: Walking board
   Test No. 2: Hopping and jumping
B. Body image and right-left (R-L) discrimination
   Test No. 3: Identification of body parts
   Test No. 4: Imitation of movement
   Test No. 5: Obstacle course
   Test No. 6: Kraus-Weber Test
   Test No. 7: Angels in the snow
C. Perceptual-motor match
   Test No. 8: Chalkboard activities
   Test No. 9: Rhythmic writing
D. Test No. 10: Ocular control
   Test No. 11: Ocular pursuits
E. Test No. 12: Form reproduction (drawing simple geometric figures on blank paper)

Test Area   A multipurpose room or gymnasium is needed for several items; otherwise, a classroom can be used.

Equipment   Chalkboard, chalk, penlight, yardstick or dowel, and visual achievement forms.

Scoring   A 4-point rating scale is used.

Validity   A validity coefficient of .65 was reported between teachers and survey ratings.

Reliability   The test-retest reliability was .95, with 1 week intervening between test administrations.

Norms   Norms have been published for grades 1 through 4, based on the scores of 200 children with 50 children randomly selected from each grade.

Comments   The test manual should be purchased and reviewed before administering the survey. The survey can be administered in 45 minutes.

Motor Development Profiles

The current emphasis on early intervention and screening of preschool children at risk or with a developmental delay has placed greater responsibility on the public schools for testing and evaluation (Zittel, 1994). Many qualitative measures of the development of movement patterns have been published. These scales typically assess changes in whole-body configurations as the child grows

Figure 13-2   Assessment of asymmetrical tonic neck reflex in an upright position. *Courtesy of Janet A. Seaman.*

and develops. Zittel (1994) provides a critique of nine popular motor development tests using the following criteria: test purpose, technical adequacy, non-discriminatory, administrative ease, instructional link, and ecological validity. Table 13-1 presents a list of selected motor development tests. More complete descriptions of the Denver Development Screening Test II (Frankenburg and Dodds, 1967; Frankenburg et al., 1990, 1992) and the Test of Gross Motor Development (TGMD) (Ulrich, 1985) follow. (Sources for obtaining two other tests, the California State University Motor Development Checklist and the Bayley Scales of Motor Development, are presented in Appendix F.)

Table 13-1 Popular Tests of Motor Development

Test Name	Age (yr.)	No. of Items	Source
Battelle Developmental Inventory	Birth to 8	341 total 82 motor 44 gross motor	Newborg et al. (1984)
Brigance Inventory of Early Development	Below the developmental age of 7	98 total 13 gross motor	Brigance (1978)
Denver Developmental Screening Test II	Birth to 6	125 total 32 gross motor	Frankenburg et al. (1990)
Developmental Indicators for the Assessment of Learning–Revised	2–6	24 total 8 motor 2 gross motor	Mardell-Czudnowski and Goldenberg (1983)
I CAN Preprimary Motor and Play Skills	Preprimary	31 total 26 gross motor	Wessel (1980)
Miller Assessment for Preschoolers	2.9–5.8	27 total 8 motor 3 gross motor	Miller (1988)
Ohio State University Scale of Intra-Gross Motor Assessment	2.5–14	11	Loovis and Ersing (1979)
Peabody Developmental Scales	0–7	282 total 170 gross motor	Folio and Fewell (1983)
Test of Gross Motor Development	3–10	12	Ulrich (1985)

Adapted from Zittel LL. 1994. Gross motor assessment of preschool children with special needs: Instrument selection and considerations. Adapted Physical Activity Quarterly, 11(3):245–260. Used by permission.

Denver Developmental Screening Test II (Frankenburg et al., 1990, 1992)

Test Objective   To evaluate children aged 1 month to 6 years in fine motor-adaptive, gross motor, personal-social, and language skills.

Description   There are 125 tasks selected to identify developmental delays in the above four categories (32 tasks comprise the gross motor area). Test items are scored on a specially designed scoresheet using formal and informal observation. A subjective behavior rating scale which assesses compliance, interest in surroundings, fearfulness, and attention span is also included.

Test Area   A small room provides sufficient space.

Equipment   Small toy, rattle, piece of yarn, paper and pencil, box of raisins, eight small cubes, small bottle, pictures of familiar objects, and small ball.

Scoring   Each item is scored in one of four ways—pass, fail, refusal, or no opportunity for child to respond.

Validity   Validity of the Denver II was provided by (a) face validity based on stringent criteria for item selection including items which had low refusal rates, low "no opportunity" scores, high reliability, ease of administration, minimal test equipment, and small subgroup differences; and (b) evidence of the precision with which the test determined the ages at which 25%, 50%, 75%, and 90% of the standardization sample of 2,096 children could pass each item.

Reliability   Interrater reliability, 5 to 10 minutes' test-retest with different testers, and 7 to 10 days' test-retest with different testers and the same testers resulted in a mean percentage of agreement ranging from 80 to 100% for most items in each of the four categories (fine motor-adaptive, gross motor, personal-social, and language skills).

Norms   Charts have been developed showing the age level at which 25%, 50%, 75%, and 90% of the children can perform specific tasks. Data from over 2,000 children through age 6 were used to determine these standards.

Comments   Administration time varies, depending on the age and maturity of the child. Test items must be administered individually.

Test of Gross Motor Development (Ulrich, 1985; Ulrich and Wise, 1984)

The Test of Gross Motor Development (TGMD) is relatively easy to administer. The test consists of 12 gross motor skill patterns organized into two subtests—locomotion and object control. Nationally normed for children aged 3 to 10 years, the TGMD is primarily a measure of form or process and is useful for placement, instructional planning, and assessing student progress (Sherill, 1993).

Test Objective   To assess 12 gross motor skill patterns in children aged 3 to 10 years.

Description   The TGMD measures two subdomains of gross motor development—object control and locomotion. Object control tests include the two-handed strike, stationary bounce, catch, kick, and overhand throw. Locomotor tests include the run, gallop, hop, leap, horizontal jump, skip, and slide.

Test Area   A gymnasium or any open area measuring at least 60 feet by 30 feet.

Equipment   Chalk or masking tape for marking lines, 4- to 6-inch lightweight ball, plastic bat, 8- to 10-inch playground ball, 6- to 8-inch sponge ball, tennis ball, scoresheets, pencil.

Scoring   Testers judge the presence or absence of three to four behaviors for each of the 12 motor skills.

Validity   Content-related evidence for validity was presented via the judgment of content experts. Evidence for construct validity was presented by factor analysis, analysis of performance across age levels (group differences method), and by comparisons of performance between children with mental retardation and their nonretarded peers (group differences method).

Reliability   Test-retest reliability coefficients ranged from .84 to .99 for the 12 gross motor skills. Interrater reliability ranged from .79 to .98 over 10 raters. Internal consistency reliability using the split-half method yielded coefficients of .78 for the object control subtest and .85 for the locomotor subtest.

Norms   Nationally standardized scores and percentiles for the two subdomains are presented by age. In addition, a composite score called the Gross Motor Development Quotient can be computed.

Comments   Criterion-referenced interpretations of the TGMD are discussed by Ulrich (1984). See the TGMD test manual (Ulrich, 1985) for complete descriptions of each test.

Motor Ability Tests

Motor ability, a rather nebulous term, was originally used to represent innate ability to perform motor tasks. However, it was impossible to separate innate ability from learned skills. Motor ability has also been referred to as a predictor of athletic ability. Gradually the term took on a new meaning and is now thought to reflect motor educability, ability to learn motor skills. Although it seems intuitively reasonable that people possess an innate motor ability, there is no scientific evidence that the tests available at the present time tap this trait. This does not mean that these tests are not at all useful in an educational setting, but rather that labeling these tests as measures of motor ability is questionable. The Bruininks-Oseretsky Motor Development Scale, classified by Seaman and DePauw (1989) as a motor ability test often used with disabled students, follows. (Sources for obtaining two other motor ability tests, the Six Category Gross Motor Test and the Basic Motor Ability Test–Revised, are included in Appendix F.)

The Bruininks-Oseretsky Test of Motor Proficiency (Bruininks, 1978)

Test Objective   This is an individually administered test that assesses motor functioning in children from 4½ to 14½ years of age.

Description   Both a Complete Battery and a Short Form are available. The Complete Battery includes eight subtests, four to measure gross motor skills, three to measure fine motor skills, and one for both fine and gross motor skills.

SUBTEST NO. 1 Running speed and agility (one item)
SUBTEST NO. 2 Balance (eight items)

Assessment of running form. Item from Adapted Physical Education Assessment Scale. *Courtesy of Janet A. Seaman.*

SUBTEST NO. 3 Bilateral coordination (eight items)
SUBTEST NO. 4 Strength (three items)
SUBTEST NO. 5 Upper limb coordination (nine items)
SUBTEST NO. 6 Response speed (one item)
SUBTEST NO. 7 Visual-motor control (eight items)
SUBTEST NO. 8 Upper limb speed and dexterity (eight items)

The Short Form, consisting of 14 items from the Complete Battery, follows, along with the respective subtest numbers.

SUBTEST NO. 1 Item 1: Running speed and agility.
SUBTEST NO. 2 Item 2: Standing on preferred leg while making circles with the fingers.
Item 7: Walking forward heel to toe on a balance beam.
SUBTEST NO. 3 Item 1: Tapping feet alternatively while making circles with the fingers.
Item 6: Jumping up and clapping hands.
SUBTEST NO. 4 Item 1: Standing broad jump.
SUBTEST NO. 5 Item 3: Catching a tossed ball with both hands.
Item 5: Throwing a ball at a target with the preferred hand.

SUBTEST NO. 6 Item 1: Response speed.
SUBTEST NO. 7 Item 3: Drawing a line through a straight path with the preferred hand.
Item 5: Copying a circle on paper with the preferred hand.
Item 8: Copying overlapping pencils with the preferred hand.
SUBTEST NO. 8 Item 3: Sorting shape card with the preferred hand.
Item 7: Drawing dots in circles with the preferred hand.

Test Area   Room of any size, as long as space can be cleared for testing.

Equipment   All equipment needed for administration of the scale: ball, mazes, scissors, balance rod, matchbook, coins, small boxes, thread, playing cards, matchsticks, ballpoint pen, and paper. The kit can be purchased in a specially designed metal carrying case. In addition to the equipment, the kit includes an examiner's manual, individual record forms for the Complete Battery and the Short Form, and a package of 25 student booklets (for test items that require cutting or paper-and-pencil responses).

Scoring   Scale items are scored on a pass-fail basis. For the Complete Battery, there is a gross motor composite (Subtest nos. 6–8). For the Short Form a single score provides an index of motor proficiency.

Validity   Evidence of validity is primarily construct validity.

1. The relationship of test content to research findings in motor development was established.
2. A number of statistical properties of the test were reported: relationship of test scores to chronological age, internal consistency of subtests, and factor analysis of subtest items.
3. Comparisons were made between contrast groups: mildly retarded with normal subjects, moderately to severely retarded with normal subjects, and learning-disabled with normal subjects. The interrelationships between subtests were low to moderate, meaning that the subtests tapped different abilities.

Reliability   The test-retest reliability was high for composite scores (ranging from .68 to .86, with only the .68 estimate falling on the low side). The coefficients were lower for some of the subtests, where reliability estimates as low as .29 were reported; however, the range of estimates was from .29 to .89. Interrater reliability was generally quite satisfactory, ranging from .77 to .97. This type of reliability is quite important, since much of the scoring is subjective. The standard error of measurement was also reported for all age groups on each subtest.

Norms   Percentile norms were reported for boys and girls ranging from 6 to 14 years of age.

Comments   The Lincoln-Oseretsky version of this test is described in detail in Sloan (1955). The scale has undergone several revisions, the latest being the Bruininks-Oseretsky Test of Motor Proficiency (1978).* Approximately 45 min

---

* The Bruininks-Oseretsky Test of Motor Proficiency can be ordered from American Guidance Service, Circle Pines, MN 55014.

utes is required to administer the Complete Battery and 15 to 20 minutes to administer the Short Form. The Bruininks' revision was very well developed. Evidence of an item analysis and standardization of the test is included. Differences between individual standard scores are also reported.

Physical Fitness Tests

Sherrill (1993) notes that fitness practices are evolving and adapted physical activity personnel must keep up with changing trends. Current practice emphasizes a holistic health-related physical fitness approach focusing on lifetime physical activity, concepts of motivation to exercise, criterion-referenced standards, an ecological perspective, and an emphasis on reaching individual goals.

Previous philosophy concerning fitness testing of disabled populations resulted in the development of physical fitness tests and norms for various populations. For example, in the 1960s and 1970s, AAHPERD published tests for the educable mentally retarded, the trainable mentally retarded, and the **visually impaired.** Winnick (1988) discusses the classification of persons with handicapping conditions for physical fitness testing and sport participation. In Table 13-2, examples of various ways of classifying people are provided. Classifications for fitness testing are often based on the type and severity of the medical condition. More recent practice, however, focuses on adapting the same tests used in national tests such as FITNESSGRAM. Adjustments of this test may be

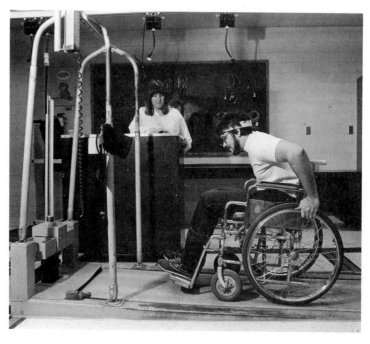

Warm-up for the treadmill test.

Table 13-2   Classifications in Selected Physical Fitness Tests

Test	Classification
Special physical fitness (AAHPERD, 1986)	Age, sex, type and severity of condition (mild mental retardation)
Project ACTIVE (Vodola, 1978)	Chronological and mental age, sex, type of condition (mental, emotional, learning disability)
Buell adaptation of the AAHPERD Health and Youth Fitness Test (Buell, 1982)	Age, sex, type and severity of condition (blind and partially sighted)
Motor Fitness Test for the Moderately Mentally Retarded (Johnson and Londeree, 1976)	Age, sex, type and severity of condition (moderate mental retardation)
UNIQUE Physical Fitness Test (Winnick and Short, 1985)	
Visual	· Age, sex, type of condition (visual), severity of condition (blind, partially sighted), level of assistance (unassisted, guidewires- or rope-assisted, partner-assisted)
Auditory	Age, sex, type of condition (auditory)
Orthopedic	Age, sex, type of condition (cerebral palsy, spinal neuromuscular, congenital anomaly/amputee), site of amputation or anomaly; mode of ambulation (unassisted; cane, crutch, or other assistive device; wheelchair), wheelchair propulsion (moved with arms, moved with feet forward or backward)

Reproduced by permission of the American Alliance for Health, Physical Education, Recreation and Dance.

necessary depending on the extent and type of disability. For example, if a student has severe **cognitive disorders,** a buddy system might be used effectively in administering distance run tests. If necessary, large muscle exercises such as swimming or a stationary bicycle test can be substituted and used as baseline data to measure progress. The FITNESSGRAM test manual (Institute for Aerobics Research, 1992) provides specific information concerning test modifications for special populations. In addition, adaptations to common health-related physical fitness test (HRPFT) items are reviewed by Eichstaedt and Lavay (1992, pp. 439–442).

The AAHPERD Motor Fitness Test for the Moderately Mentally Retarded is presented here in detail. The test for mentally retarded youth parallels two other tests for impaired youth published by AAHPERD: the AAHPERD Youth Fitness Test Adaptation for the Blind, and the Special Fitness Test for the Mentally Retarded. The second test—the Project UNIQUE Physical Fitness Test—is presented in less detail but is nevertheless an important contribution to the fitness test area because of its exceptionally sound psychometric underpinnings, adaptations for various disabled populations, and extensive norms. Other physical fitness tests for students with a disability have been described by Stein (1988) and Short (1990).

AAHPERD Motor Fitness Test for the Moderately Mentally Retarded (Johnson and Londeree, 1976)

The AAHPERD Motor Fitness Test for the Moderately Mentally Retarded is a modification of the AAHPERD Youth Fitness Test for **educable** (capable of learning) **mentally retarded** children. Persons with this level of retardation have intelligence quotients (IQs) ranging from 50 to 70. Included in the test manual are 13 items—flexed arm hang, sit-ups, standing long jump, softball throw for distance, 50-yard dash, 300-yard run-walk, height, sitting bob and reach, skipping, tumbling progression, and target throw. The first six items are recommended as sufficient for testing the motor fitness of the moderately mentally retarded; the other items are usable in local situations. In the test manual, norms are published for boys and girls, ages 6 through 20, although the norms are based on small sample sizes in many cases. An award system is also available for these age groups.

Flexed Arm Hang

Test Objective   Although the objective is not stated in the test manual, the Flexed Arm Hang is usually included in a fitness test battery as a measure of arm and shoulder girdle strength and endurance.

Description   Adjust the bar to approximately standing height. Instruct the student to grasp the bar with an overhand grip (palms away from the body). The student jumps (and is simultaneously lifted by a tester) to the flexed arm–hang position, with the chin above the bar and parallel to the floor. The elbows are held close to the sides, with the chin just above the bar. Once the student is in a motionless, hanging position and is no longer assisted by the tester, the stopwatch is started. The watch is stopped when "the chin touches the bar, the head tilts back to keep the chin above the bar, or the chin drops below the bar" (Johnson and Londeree, 1976, p. 16). One trial is administered. Do not allow the student to kick or swing the legs or lift the knees.

Test Area   A small indoor area, even a doorway, is adequate.

Equipment   In the test manual, a metal or wooden bar 1½ inches in diameter is recommended. However, a doorway gym bar or an angled or horizontal ladder would also be suitable. A stopwatch is used to time the test.

Scoring   The score is the amount of time, to the nearest tenth of a second, the proper position is held.

Validity   Although the manual includes a brief discussion of the validity of the total test battery, there is no reference to the validity of this specific test.

Reliability   Test-retest reliability coefficients of .90 were reported, with 6 months intervening between test administrations.

Norms   Norms are available for moderately mentally retarded boys and girls, ages 6 through 20. However, the norms are based on small sample sizes and should be used only as rough guidelines.

Comments   Evidence of validity and reliability for the population of educable mentally retarded youth needs to be obtained for future revisions of the manual. Reliability should be estimated with no more than 2 weeks elapsing between test periods. The most critical issue related to the Flexed Arm Hang Test is whether it can adequately measure differences in strength across all ages and both genders. In the table of norms for this test, more than 50% of the boys could not maintain the proper position for any recorded time. At least 50% of the girls were unable to obtain any score at all, regardless of age. The manual stated that children in this group had very low arm strength and endurance. Yet the results suggest that many have no strength in this area, which cannot be true. Stating that the test is not discriminating well is probably more accurate. It lacks a basic characteristic of measurement—that as ability changes, the test score changes correspondingly. Even in a normal population, too many 0 scores were obtained in the flexed arm hang. Other techniques measuring arm and shoulder girdle strength, such as the Baumgartner/Modified Pull-Ups Test, might be considered as substitutes. In cases of more severe impairments, a straight arm hang has been suggested as a reasonable substitute.

Sit-ups in 30 Seconds

Test Objective   Although no objective is stated in the manual, this test is usually used to measure abdominal strength and endurance.

Description   The starting is a back-lying position with knees flexed to less than 90 degrees, feet on the mat, and heels 12 inches from the buttocks. The hands are clasped behind the neck with fingers interlaced, with the elbows resting on the mat. The feet are held in contact with the mat throughout the test by a partner. To begin the test, use the command "Go!" The student curls to a starting position and touches one elbow to the opposite knee, curls back to the starting position, and curls up again, touching the other elbow and knee. This sequence is continued until a 30-second time period has elapsed.

Test Area   For group testing, a gymnasium or multipurpose room can be used; for individual testing a very small area will suffice.

Equipment   Tumbling mat and stopwatch.

Scoring   The number of sit-ups correctly executed in 30 seconds is the score. The sit-up is not counted if the student does not begin from the starting position, or if the elbow is not touched to the opposite knee. Also, the fingers must remain clasped behind the neck throughout the sit-up. One trial is administered.

Validity   There is no reference to the validity of this specific test.

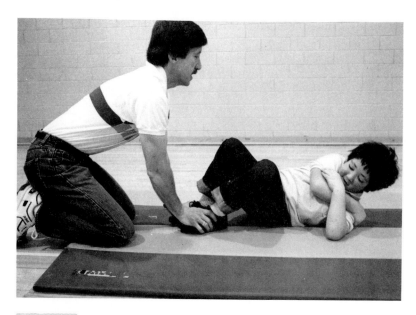

Figure 13-3   Testing sit-ups. *Courtesy of Dale A. Ulrich.*

Reliability   The test manual reports reliability estimates of .80 and above for a group of test items, presumably including the Sit-ups Test.

Norms   Norms are available for moderately mentally retarded boys and girls, ages 6 through 20. However, the norms are based on small sample sizes and should only be used as rough guidelines.

Comments   The position of the arms and hands should be altered to reflect currently recommended procedures. Therapists have noted that when the hands are clasped behind the neck, a tendency to use the arms in sitting up occurs. Furthermore, this position seems to encourage straight-back sit-ups. For these reasons, the Physical Best Test uses a modified position (Figure 13-3) with the arms crossed at chest level and hands placed on opposite shoulders.

Standing Long Jump Test

Test Objective   Although the objective of the Standing Long Jump Test is not stated in the test manual, it is usually used as a measure of explosive leg power.

Description   In the starting position, the student stands behind the restraining line. The toes must not touch the line, and the feet are several inches apart. Although any preliminary motions may be made as long as the feet are not moved, usually the examinee dips the body several times, swinging the arms backward with one dip and forward with the next. On the actual jump, the arms swing forward at the same time and land at the same time. The object of the test is to jump as far as possible.

Test Area   The test can be administered on a floor or a paved, outdoor surface. The manual recommends marking an open area with a restraining line and lines parallel to this line every inch, starting at 12 inches. A testing area of 120 inches is suggested, although this can be modified, if necessary. Each line should be 30 inches long, with the distance clearly marked. Another alternative is to tape a tape measure on the floor perpendicular to the restraining line.

Equipment Tape measure, if the alternate setup is used, and a yardstick to line up the distance on the tape with the student's heels.

Scoring Record the best of three trials to the nearest inch. "Measure the perpendicular distance from the restraining line to the heel or other body part that touches the floor nearest the takeoff line. Be sure to note carefully the point where the heels first contact the floor because there is a tendency for the feet to slide forward" (Johnson and Londeree, 1976, p. 19).

Validity There is no reference in the test manual to the validity of this specific test.

Reliability The test manual reports reliability estimates of .80 or higher for a group of test items, presumably including the Standing Long Jump.

Norms Norms are published for moderately mentally retarded boys and girls, ages 6 through 20. However, the sample sizes are small; thus the norms should be interpreted with caution.

Comments The test developers note that the best jump is often not attained in three trials. They recommend that the youngsters build up to a point they can perform 20 to 25 jumps with all-out effort. The tester should chart the students' performance over a number of days and determine when the best jump is made. On the actual testing day the student should be given as many practice trials as needed, as determined in previous weeks. The number of trials remains the same for all students, although the number of practice trials may vary. If one student achieved maximum distance on trial 12, he/she should be given 10 practice trials before testing.

Softball Throw for Distance Test

Test Objective Although there is no statement in the test manual on the objective of the Softball Throw for Distance Test, it is usually used to measure coordination.

Description The student throws overhand as far as possible, three times in succession. Mark the distance of the first throw. If the next throw is longer, remove the marking of the first throw and mark the better one. If not, leave the marking at the landing point of the first throw. Handle the third throw the same way. Use two or more students to retrieve balls after they hit the ground. Any type of approach may be used as long as the student does not cross the restraining line. The throw must be overhand. Students should warm up by playing catch.

Test Area An open field with a width of 50 feet and a length of 250 feet is recommended for administration of this test. Use agricultural lime to mark the field. Mark the restraining line first, then start 15 feet from the restraining line and mark lines at 5-foot intervals, up to 225 feet. This distance may be adjusted for different groups.

Equipment A minimum of three softballs (12-inch) in good condition are needed.

Scoring The test score is the best of three trials. The score is the perpendicular distance from the restraining line to the landing point. Record the distance to the nearest foot.

Validity There is no reference in the test manual to the validity of this specific test.

Reliability The test manual reports reliability estimates of .80 or higher for a group of test items, presumably including the Softball Throw for Distance Test.

Norms Norms are published for moderately mentally retarded boys and girls, ages 6 through 20. Because of the small sample sizes of the norm groups, the norms should be used only as rough guidelines.

Comments This test was eliminated from the AAHPER Youth Fitness Test in the 1976 manual because there was no evidence that coordination could be measured by a single item of this type. The softball throw seems to measure a specific skill rather than a general motor fitness trait. Whether it should be retained in this test battery is questionable. Other adapted physical education specialists (Winnick and Short, 1985) have suggested that the Softball Throw for Distance Test might be used as a substitute for a strength item in special cases. The test item probably measures a specific type of fitness required to perform a softball skill. It is unlikely that this ability generalizes to other sport skills. The most reliable indicator of the student's ability to throw the softball is the average of three trials rather than the best of three. This is a proven fact in measurement theory. Therefore the scoring procedure for this test should be reexamined.

50-Yard Dash

Test Objective Although there is no statement in the test manual on the objective of the 50-Yard Dash, this test is used as a measure of speed.

Description The manual recommends testing two students at the same time. The students take starting positions behind the starting line. The test administrator (at the finish line) raises both arms sideways to indicate the set position. The "Go" signal is given by rapidly lowering the arms to the side. The administrator has a stopwatch in each hand, and both watches are started when the arms reach the side of the body. The two students run as fast as possible to the finish line. The watch for a designated runner is stopped when the student's body (not head or arms) crosses the finish line. One trial is taken.

Test Area An outdoor space is usually preferred, although any smooth, solid surface of the appropriate distance may be used.

Equipment The test manual recommends using two stopwatches if students are to be tested in pairs. If only one watch is available, the students could be tested individually; however, they could still run in pairs for motivational purposes.

Scoring The score is the time between the "Go" signal and the moment the student's body crosses the finish line. The time is recorded to the nearest tenth of a second.

Validity There is no reference to the validity of this specific test.

Reliability   The test manual reports reliability coefficients of .80 or higher for a group of tests, presumably including the 50-Yard Dash.

Norms   Norms are published for moderately mentally retarded boys and girls, ages 6 through 20. These norms should be used with caution because of small sample sizes.

Comments   Does the visual signal provide a more accurate start then a verbal signal? Obviously a visual signal requires the examinee to watch the examiner closely. This may lead to slower start. Further study of these starts would be useful. The advantage of a visual start is that only one tester is needed to administer the test.

300-Yard Run-Walk

Test Objective   Although no statement of the objective of the 300-Yard Run-Walk was given in the test manual, it is usually used as a measure of cardiorespiratory (CR) function.

Description   The manual suggests testing 5 to 10 students at a time. Examinees should stand in a single row behind the starting line, using a standard start. On the signal "Ready, Go!" the students begin running. The 300-yard distance should be run as fast as possible. Walking is permitted but should not be encouraged. As the runner crosses the finish line, the timer calls out the time to the scorer.

Test Area   A track is ideal for testing the 300-Yard Run-Walk; however, any paved or smooth, solid surface, either indoors or outdoors, can be used.

Equipment   A stopwatch.

Scoring   The score should be recorded in seconds.

Validity   No evidence of the validity of this specific test is included in the test manual.

Reliability   No reliability estimates were reported for the 300-Yard Run-Walk.

Norms   Norms are published for moderately mentally retarded boys and girls, ages 6 through 20. These norms should be used as rough guidelines because of small sample sizes.

Comments   An abundance of scientific evidence now indicates that distances under 1 mile are not effective measures of CR function. Certainly a distance of 300 yards would not tap this parameter. Since CR function is such an important aspect of health-related fitness, strong consideration should be given to increasing the test distance to 1 mile for students with disabilities who have been properly trained to run this distance.

SUMMARY OF THE TEST BATTERY

The previous six items were presented in detail as an example of the type of fitness tests available for children with disabilities. For additional information on the test battery and the award system, refer to the AAHPERD Motor Fitness Testing Manual for the Moderately Mentally Retarded (Johnson and Londeree, 1976). In general, the test items in this battery measure fitness associated with athletic ability rather than health-related physical fitness. The objectives for using this test should be clearly in mind when it is used in a school setting. The normative data were collected during the spring of 1973. The norms should be updated using substantial sample sizes from a cross section of the United States rather than a single state. Finally the test items should be revised in light of sound measurement principles and scientific evidence on the measurement of physiological parameters. This fine contribution to the testing literature for children with disabilities should be continually modified so that it remains useful for teachers in school settings.

Project Unique Physical Fitness Test (Winnick and Short, 1985)

In an excellent study of the physical fitness of sensory and orthopedically impaired youth, Winnick and Short (1985) noted that the components of fitness are essentially the same for normal and sensory or orthopedically disabled children, but the performance of the impaired child generally falls below that of the normal child. Age, gender, educational setting, and type of severity of handicapping condition must be considered in interpreting the results of physical fitness tests. Based on a sound psychometric approach, the test battery identifies seven test items. Since all of the items are described elsewhere in this text, only a summary of the battery follows.

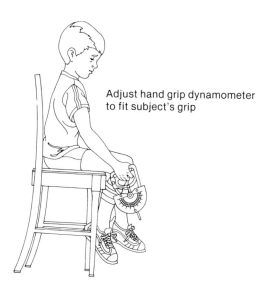

Adjust hand grip dynamometer
to fit subject's grip

Figure 13-4 Measurement of grip strength. *From Winnick JP, Short FX. 1985. Physical fitness testing of the disabled: Project UNIQUE. Champaign, Ill: Human Kinetics. Used by permission.*

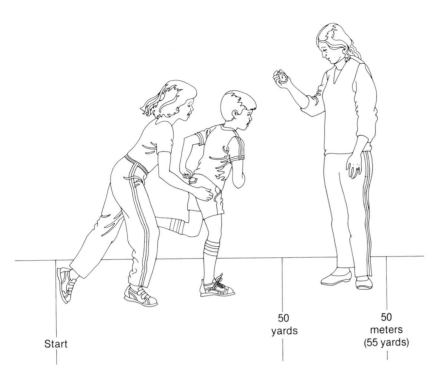

50 yards

50 meters (55 yards)

Start

Figure 13-5   The 50-yard/meter dash. *From Winnick JP, Short FX. 1985. Physical fitness testing of the disabled: Project UNIQUE. Champaign, Ill: Human Kinetics. Used by permission.*

Test Objective   The battery is designed to measure body composition, flexibility, CR endurance, and muscular strength and endurance.

Description   The test battery consists of seven items:

ITEM 1   Skinfold measures (triceps, subscapular, and sum of triceps and subscapular).

ITEM 2   Grip strength (Figure 13-4).

ITEM 3   50 yard/meter dash (Figure 13-5).

ITEM 4   Sit-ups (number in 60 seconds).

ITEM 5   Softball throw (distance).

ITEM 6   Sit and reach.

ITEM 7   Long distance run (1-mile/9-minute run or 1½-mile/12-minute run).

Test Area, Equipment, and Scoring   (See Chapters 17 and 18 on fitness testing.)

Validity   This test is exceptionally well validated. First, the logical validity of each test item is demonstrated. Second, evidence of criterion-related and construct validity is presented. In particular, the factorial validity of the instrument is stressed, forming the basis of this impressive study. Finally, scientific evidence supporting the validity of the test items is included where appropriate.

Reliability A number of reliability coefficients are presented for each test item. These estimates range from .49 to .975, although most coefficients are very high—in the .90s. Reliability data are presented for visually impaired, **hearing-impaired,** and **orthopedically impaired,** as well as mentally retarded persons. Anyone using these test items should refer to the Project UNIQUE report (Winnick and Short, 1985), which includes one of the best and most thorough tables of reliability estimates for fitness tests.

Norms Means, standard deviations, and percentiles are presented for each item by age and gender within each subject category with the exception of those with auditory impairment. Four major categories of subjects were identified: normal (nonimpaired), visually impaired, hearing-impaired, and orthopedically impaired.

Comments Since it is not possible for individuals with certain impairments to take some of the test items, Winnick and Short (1985) have recommended substitutions for specific situations. Although a rationale is not presented for the selection of these substitutions, it is apparent that the test developers do not necessarily view the substitute tests as measures of equivalent fitness parameters when compared to original measures. Rather, a testable area of fitness is selected, depending on the nature and extent of the disabling condition. Consider the following examples of substitute tests:

1. For boys with **cerebral palsy,** use an arm hang test instead of grip strength (Figure 13-6).
2. For **paraplegic** boys, wheelchair-bound with a spinal neuromuscular disorder, use an arm hang test instead of grip strength.

Overhand grip

Figure 13-6 Measurement of flexed arm hang. *From Winnick JP, Short FX. 1985. Physical fitness testing of the disabled: Project UNIQUE. Champaign, Ill: Human Kinetics. Used by permission.*

3. For boys classified as **congenital anomaly** or amputee, use an arm hang test instead of grip strength.
4. For paraplegic boys and girls, wheelchair-bound with a spinal neuromuscular disorder, the softball throw for distance can be used instead of grip strength (Figure 13-7).
5. For some boys and girls classified as congenital anomaly or amputee, the softball throw for distance may be substituted for sit-ups.
6. For boys and girls who have visual and hearing impairments, the broad jump may be substituted for grip strength.

SUMMARY OF TEST BATTERY

The soundness of the development of the Project UNIQUE Physical Fitness Test gives it an edge over other physical fitness tests for children with impairments. The test administrator should keep in mind, however, that the items in the battery measure different types of fitness. Several of the items test health-related physical fitness, and a few measure fitness in an athletic performance context. All in all, the physical fitness test batteries for impaired children do not differ markedly from those developed for the nonimpaired child. There is no need for the items to be different, except when a type of impairment prevents performance of an item. Of course, certain modifications of items may be necessary, and norms should be developed for different types of impairments.

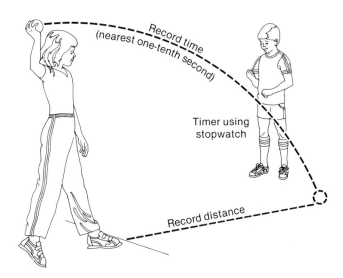

Figure 13-7   Softball throw for distance. *From Winnick JP, Short FX. 1985. Physical fitness testing of the disabled: Project UNIQUE. Champaign, Ill: Human Kinetics. Used by permission.*

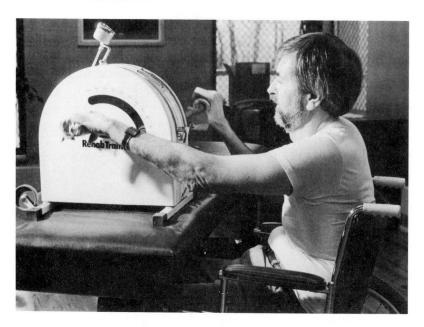

Warm-up for arm ergometer test.

MOTOR PERFORMANCE TESTING

Many strategies have been developed to provide initial screening of students in a physical education setting. This screening must be followed by a formal testing program. The Los Angeles Unified School District has developed a scale that can be used to determine appropriate placement of students in physical education. An overview of the Adaptive Physical Education Assessment Scale* follows.

The Adaptive Physical Education Assessment Scale (Seaman and Depauw, 1989)

Test Objective To place students appropriately in physical education. It measures five areas of motor performance: motor development, motor achievement, perceptual-motor function, posture, and physical fitness.

Description The scale includes 18 items measuring motor performance:

1. Agility run
2. Throwing accuracy
3. Hand preference
4. Kick stationary ball
5. Foot preference
6. Catching
7. Kicking rolling ball
8. Running
9. Posture
10. Vertical jump
11. Jumping form
12. Ocular control
13. Bent-knee curl-up
14. Imitation of postures
15. Standing balance
16. Alternate hopping
17. Arrhythmic hopping
18. Endurance

* For more information on the scale, test manual, and norms, write to Adapted Physical Education Consultant, Los Angeles Unified School District, 450 North Grand Avenue—Bldg. G, Los Angeles, CA 90012.

Figure 13-8   Catching task. *Courtesy of Dale A. Ulrich.*

A brief description of each of these items can be found in Seaman and DePauw (1989). Figures 13-8, 13-9, and 13-10 present the catching, standing balance, and alternate hopping tasks, respectively.

Test Area   The first eight items should be measured outdoors during a single testing session. The remaining items may be administered either indoors or outdoors during another testing session. The outdoor space requirements are a 4-foot by 18-foot wall target with at least 15 feet by 16 feet of free space in front for throwing, running, and kicking, and a 50-yard rectangular running course.

Equipment   In addition to the test manual and scoring materials, equipment needs include an 8½-inch rubber ball, an 18-inch ruler, five beanbags 6 inches by 6 inches, stopwatch, and chalk.

Scoring   Eight items are scored using ratios representing distance or repetitions, eight incorporate ratings, and two items yield categorical data. The objectivity of these scoring procedures ranges from .39 to .96.

Validity   The validity as reported in Seaman and DePauw (1989) is "face with literature" (p. 183). Evidence of factorial validity has also been presented by the Los Angeles Unified School District, as well as predictive validity based on a discriminant analysis showing that the scale correctly classifies students 89% of the time.

Reliability   Ten of the 18 items have reliability estimates of .70 or greater on a test-retest basis (Seaman and DePauw, 1989).

Figure 13-9   Standing balance task. *Courtesy of Dale A. Ulrich.*

Norms   Norms based on scores for 2,100 children, ages 5 through 18, from the Los Angeles area, including 1% trainably mentally retarded and 1% severe language-delayed children. Percentile ranks are available at 6-month intervals for 5 years through 7 years, 11 months, and 1-year intervals for 8 through 18 years. These norms were generated during the 1980 revision of the scale.

Comments   Testing time per student is approximately 20 minutes. The primary usefulness of this battery lies in its ability to place students in physical education with what appears to be an impressive degree of accuracy. Of course, the validity is defensible only for the Los Angeles area, but it would be a relatively straightforward matter to validate the procedure in other areas. Reducing the length of the test is highly desirable. If the test is to be used primarily for placement, are 18 items necessary? Despite several low reliability and objectivity estimates, the scale has many positive dimensions. Certainly it provides a useful model for placement in adaptive physical education.

Figure **13-10**   Alternate hopping item from the Adapted
Physical Education Assessment Scale.
Courtesy of Janet A. Seaman.

SUMMARY

It is not feasible to present all the motor performance tests developed for children with disabilities in a measurement and evaluation textbook. Observational
techniques are most frequently used on a daily basis in a field setting. Unless
these instruments have acceptable reliability and validity, they should not be
used in a more formal situation, as when a child's ability is assessed before
developing an individualized education program. Other types of tests, particularly performance measures, have been standardized and can be used with
greater confidence in their validity. Some examples of these types are motor
proficiency scales, developmental scales, and physical fitness tests. Few tests
are available to measure performance in a variety of sport skills. Excellent resources on this topic can be found in Seaman and DePauw (1989). Chapters 7
and 10 of their book are devoted to assessment, and Chapters 8 and 9 provide
descriptions of many tests. Furthermore, a quick reference to tests on the market
is included in Appendix D. The student interested in adaptive physical education is urged to review other sources of tests in this area.

Learning Experiences

1. Under the direction of your instructor, observe the administration of one or more motor performance tests to children with some type of disability. What aspects of test administration differ from testing in a physical education setting for the nondisabled child? Record these considerations and note how the tester handled them.

2. Assume you are working with a person with paraplegia who is confined to a wheelchair. How would you test this person on CR function, body fat, and low back and abdominal flexibility? First of all, are these important objectives for this person? If so, why? If not, what factors can you test? Why? How would the tests you select differ from those you would administer to a nondisabled person?

3. Visit an elementary or middle school and interview the principal or a physical education teacher concerning physical education programs and services for students with disabilities. Describe the programs and services with particular emphasis on purposes and procedures of assessment (e.g., screening, placement, tests used, etc.). Compare the school's program with the "ideal" program described in Chapter 13. What recommendations, if any, would you make concerning assessment in the adapted physical education program if you were hired to teach in the school?

References

Auxter D, Pyfer J, Huettig, C. 1993. Principles and methods of adapted physical education and recreation. ed. 7, St Louis: Mosby.

Baumgartner TA, Horvat MA. 1988. Problems in measuring the physical and motor performance of the handicapped. Journal of Physical Education, Recreation and Dance, **59**(1):48–52.

Brigance AH. 1978. Brigance diagnostic inventory of early development. North Billerica, Mass: Curriculum Associates.

Bruininks RH. 1978. The Bruininks-Oseretsky Test of Motor Proficiency. Circle Pines, Minn: American Guidance Service.

Buell CE. 1982. Physical education and recreation for the visually handicapped, rev ed. Washington DC: American Alliance for Health, Physical Education, Recreation and Dance.

Dunn J, Fait H. 1989. Special physical education: Adapted, individualized, developmental. ed 6. Dubuque, Iowa: Wm C Brown.

Eichstaedt CB, Lavay BW. 1992. Physical activity for individuals with mental retardation: Infancy through adulthood. Champaign, Ill: Human Kinetics.

Folio R, Fewell R. 1983. Peabody Developmental Motor Scales. Allen, Tex: DLM Teaching Resources.

Frankenburg WK, Dodds JB. 1967. Denver Developmental Screening Test. Journal of Pediatrics, **71**:181–191.

Frankenburg WK, Dodds JB, Archer P. 1990. Denver II technical manual. Denver, Col: Denver Developmental Materials.

Frankenburg WK, Dodds JB, Archer P, Shapiro H, Bresnick B. 1992. The Denver II: A major revision and restandardization of the Denver Developmental Screening Test. Pediatrics, **89**(1):91–97.

Institute for Aerobics Research 1992. The Prudential FITNESSGRAM Test Administration Manual. Dallas: Institute for Aerobics Research.

Johnson L, Londeree B. 1976. Motor fitness testing manual for the moderately mentally retarded. Reston, Va: American Alliance for Health, Physical Education, Recreation and Dance.

King HA, Aufsesser KS. 1988. Criterion-referenced testing—an ongoing process. Journal of Physical Education, Recreation and Dance. **59**(1):58–63.

Kirkendall DR, Gruber JJ, Johnson RE. 1987. Measurement and evaluation for physical educators. Champaign, Ill: Human Kinetics.

Loovis ME, Ersing WF. 1979. Assessing and programming gross motor development for children, ed 2. Bloomington, Ind: College Town Press.

Mardell-Czudnowski C, Goldenberg D. 1983. Developmental indicators for the assessment of learning—revised. Edison, NJ: Childcraft Education.

Miller LJ. 1988. Miller assessment for preschoolers: Manual revision. San Antonio: Harcourt Brace Jovanovich.

Newborg J, Stock JR, Wnek L, Guidubaldi J, Svinicki J. 1984. Battelle developmental inventory. Allen, Tex: DLM Teaching Resources.

Pyfer JL. 1988. Teachers, don't let your students grow up to be clumsy adults. Journal of Physical Education, Recreation and Dance, **59**(1):38–42.

Roach EG, Kephart NC. 1966. The Purdue Perceptual Motor Survey. Columbus, Ohio: Merrill.

Roberton MA, Halverson LE. 1984. Developing children—their changing movement. Philadelphia: Lea & Febiger.

Seaman JA, DePauw KP. 1989. The new adapted physical education: a developmental approach, ed 2, Palo Alto, Calif: Mayfield.

Sherrill C. 1993. Adapted physical activity, recreation and sport: Cross-disciplinary and lifespan, ed 4, Dubuque, Iowa: WC Brown.

Short FX. 1990. Measurement and appraisal. In Winnick JP, ed. 1990. Adapted physical education and sport. Champaign, Ill: Human Kinetics.

Sloan W. 1955. The Lincoln-Oseretsky Motor Development Scale. Chicago: CH Stoelting.

Stein JU. 1988. Physical fitness testing and rewards. Journal of Physical Education, Recreation and Dance, **59**(1):53–57.

Ulrich DA. 1985. The Test of Gross Motor Development. Austin, Tex: Pro-Ed.

Ulrich DA. 1988. Children with special needs assessing the quality of movement competence. Journal of Physical Education, Recreation and Dance, **59**(1):43–47.

Ulrich DA, Wise SL. 1984. The reliability of scores obtained with the objectives-based motor skill assessment instrument. Adapted Physical Activity Quarterly: **1**:230–239.

Vodoloa TM. 1978. Developmental and adaptive physical education. A.C.T.I.V.E. Motor ability and physical fitness norms: For normal, mentally retarded, learning disabled, and emotionally disturbed individuals. Oakhurst, NJ: Township of Ocean School District.

Werder JK, Kalakian LH. 1985. Assessment in Adapted Physical Education. Minneapolis: Burgess.

Wessel JA. 1980. I CAN pre-primary motor and play skills. East Lansing, Mich: Field Service Unit in Physical Education and Recreation for the Handicapped.

Winnick JP. 1988. Classifying individuals with handicapping conditions for testing. Journal of Physical Education, Recreation and Dance, **59**(1):34–37.

Winnick JP. 1990. Foundational topics in adapted physical education and sport. In Winnick JP, ed. 1990. Adapted physical education and sport. Champaign, Ill: Human Kinetics.

Winnick JP, Short FX. 1985. Physical fitness testing of the disabled: Project UNIQUE. Champaign, Ill: Human Kinetics.

Zittel LL. 1994. Gross motor assessment of preschool children with special needs: Instrument selection and considerations. Adapted Physical Activity Quarterly, **11**(3):245–260.

Annotated Readings

American Alliance for Health, Physical Education, Recreation and Dance. 1985. Testing for impaired, disabled, and handicapped individuals. Reston, Va: American Alliance for Health, Physical Education, Recreation and Dance.

Begins with a general introduction to a philosophy and rationale for testing; presents background information to aid in selecting tests: includes brief summaries of physical fitness tests, psychomotor (perceptual motor) scales, and developmental profiles; does not include information about sports skills tests, because the purpose of this publication is to assist others in selecting instruments for diagnostic and descriptive purposes.

Auxter D, Pyfer J, Huettig C. 1993. Principles and methods of adapted physical education and recreation. ed 7. St Louis: Mosby.

Includes chapter on types and purposes of assessment; describes purpose and appropriate usage of each test type; presents examples; also includes chapter on integrating evaluation and programming; provides chart of selected motor tests, including source, population, motor components, and norms.

Brunt D, Dearmond DA. 1981. Evaluating motor profiles of the hearing impaired. Journal of Physical Education, Recreation, and Dance, **52**(9):50–53.

Describes project in which the motor ability of approximately 150 upper elementary children with hearing impairments was assessed using the Bruininks Oseretsky Test, including a description of the eight subtests designed for children with severe or profound hearing loss.

Seaman JA, ed. 1988. Testing the handicapped: A challenge by law. Journal of Physical Education, Recreation and Dance, **59**(1):32–67.

A series of articles dealing with significant issues in measuring persons with disabilities; includes articles on classification of individuals, movement quality, measurement problems, physical fitness testing, and criterion-referenced testing.

Seaman JA, Baumgartner TA. 1983. Measurement implications of PL 94-142. In Hensley L, East W, eds. Measurement and evaluation symposium proceedings. Cedar Falls: University of Northern Iowa.

Summarizes the evaluation requirements mandated by Public Law 94-142; discusses efforts to develop a physical fitness test for special populations.

Ulrich DA. 1984. The reliability of classification decisions made with the Objectives-Based Motor Skill Assessment Instrument. Adapted Physical Education Quarterly, **1**(1):52–60.

Examines the reliability of classification decisions made with the Objectives-Based Motor Skill Assessment Instrument based on two different cutoff scores, using a mentally retarded group and a nondisabled group; concludes that the instrument consistently assigned examinees to the same mastery state in the fundamental motor skill domain for both mastery levels.

Winnick JP, ed. 1990. Adapted physical education and sport. Champaign, Ill: Human Kinetics.

A series of chapters focused on adapted physical education and sport by noted authors. Includes five major areas—foundational topics including measurement and appraisal, learning and teaching, descriptions of various disabled populations, developmental aspects, and physical education and sports activities.

FOURTEEN

14

Measures of Affective Behavior

KEY WORDS

Watch for these words as you read the following chapter

- Affect
- Attitude
- Forced-choice item
- Interests
- Likert scale
- Perceived exertion scale
- Testing effect
- Response distortion
- Response sets
- Semantic differential scale
- Social behavior
- Sportsmanship
- Weak measure

*E*xercise scientists and physical educators are not only interested in performance in physical activity and sport but also in the way participants feel about their performance. As William P. Morgan, a noted sports psychologist, put it—the body also has a head. It is well known that many factors have an impact on motor behavior. Only some of these factors are physical. Others, such as self-esteem, attitude, and psychological traits, also have a bearing on performance. These latter factors represent examples of affective behavior.

Affect refers to emotion, encompassing feelings such as anger, fear, sadness, and pleasure. However, educators have interpreted the term *affect* more broadly—as a sociological or psychological characteristic manifested in a feeling or behavior. Although this broader definition is not as accurate, it is commonly used in physical education. Hellison (1993, p. 27) provides an enlightening discussion of the affective domain:

While physical educations's heritage has been dotted with vague references to character development, self-esteem, fair play, cooperation, and so on . . . , attempts at conceptually clarifying the affective domain such as Hellison and Templin's (1991) discussion of "personal and social development models" are very recent.

Hellison (1993, p. 27) goes on to categorize affective goals in physical education as

1. Social conventions such as appropriate dress and language;
2. Appreciation and affection for physical activity and its benefits;
3. Psychological constructs such as self-esteem, self-efficacy, courage, motivation, and independence;
4. Moral qualities such as respect for the rights of others, compassion, and justice; and
5. Aesthetic qualities such as playfulness and gracefulness.

A sixth category, spirituality, may take shape as it has in health education (Seaward, 1991).

If you are in the exercise sciences, the more loosely defined concept will probably not be as useful. Affective behaviors of interest to the physical educator often include attitudes, interests, values, psychological traits, and emotional states. Physical educators have usually been interested in the development of inventories to measure the attitudes of individuals toward physical education or physical activity. Other inventories have been constructed to assess the psychological characteristics of an individual in a sport or physical activity; however, the majority of these instruments have been employed by researchers rather than by physical education teachers and exercise specialists.

An **attitude** is a feeling one has about a specific attitude object, such as a situation, a person, an activity, and so forth. Interest in the measurement of attitudes in physical education or exercise science is not surprising, since it is often assumed that a person with a positive attitude reflects desirable behavior. Although this line of reasoning is intuitively appealing, it is not always true that attitude reflects behavior. For example, when people are asked about their attitude toward physical activity in general, most will express a positive view, yet many of these people lead sedentary lifestyles. Although attitudes certainly have some bearing on behavior, the linkage between the two is complex. The relationship between attitude and behavior can be affected by intervening variables. For example, a smoker might express a negative attitude toward smoking because he or she knows that smoking is hazardous to one's health. In reality, the smoker's attitude may be positive, but knowledge (as an intervening variable) affects the *expressed* relationship. Even this example is simplistic as many intervening variables or their interaction may affect the attitude-behavior relationship.

In private fitness clubs as well as physical education classes, the belief that unfavorable attitudes toward physical activity can be altered with a good instructional program has provided a rationale for the measurement of attitudes. In view of the favorable attitudes generally expressed toward physical activity, this rationale loses much of its impact, and the practical significance of changing a person's expressed attitude from favorable to more favorable is minimal. However, if the real (not merely expressed) attitude can be tapped, interventions to alter attitudes may be productive.

Another affective behavior frequently measured in the physical education field is **interests,** which reflect one's likes and dislikes about various forms of physical activity, programming, scheduling, and so forth. In a school setting, **sportsmanship** is often stressed. In fact, some teachers grade each student on sportsmanship, although they may not measure this characteristic in a systematic, objective manner. (This is discussed in more detail later in the chapter.) Several instruments have been developed to measure social behavior, which encompasses the relationships among peers in a physical education setting. Of longstanding interest in the field are the measures of psychological characteristics, such as stress, anxiety, and a variety of elements of personality, which should be tested by a person trained in psychology.

Several shortcomings are associated with the use of affective inventories. Investigators may attempt to change affective behavior by imposing an intervention on the examinees during a designated period. A pretest of the affective behavior is administered before the intervention and a post-test afterward. However, the second administration of the inventory might be affected by a *reactive effect* from the first testing session. This is known as the **testing effect.** For instance, examinees may remember how they responded to the items during the first administration, or their affective behavior might change because of the first test session. For example, some may have given very little thought to their feelings about physical activity, especially in a broad context. Once they are exposed to new ideas, they may begin to examine their feelings carefully, leading to a solidification of attitudes. The next time the inventory is administered, they may change their response to certain items. In these cases, the score would reflect a change in affect, but it is not due to the planned intervention, as an investigator might conclude.

A secondary deficiency of many instruments measuring affective behavior is the possibility of **response sets** (Shaver, 1981, pp. 36–39). For example, examinees may not always respond with total honesty to these measures, faking good or bad responses, answering in a socially desirable way, or distorting responses in other ways. The more sophisticated inventories measuring affective behavior frequently include items designed to detect the tendency of examinees to distort items.

TYPES OF MEASURES

To construct a measure of affective behavior, the type of affect must be carefully defined so that a table of specifications can be developed, as described in Chapter 16. The number of items for each category is decided on the basis of the importance of each. (Remember that the number of items represents the weighting of each category.) At this stage a decision must be made on the type of item to use—generally, rating scales, **forced-choice** inventories, and questionnaires.

Likert Scale

The **Likert scale** requires an expression of the individual's degree of agreement or disagreement with a series of affective statements. Kenyon's Attitude Toward Physical Activity Inventory uses a Likert scale. One of the items on this inventory is the statement, "I would gladly put in the necessary years of daily hard training for the chance to try out for the U.S. Olympic team." Response choices are the following: very strongly agree, strongly agree, agree, undecided, disagree, strongly disagree, and very strongly disagree. The examinee responds by circling the desired response on the answer sheet. A five-step version of a Likert scale is shown below:

1	2	3	4	5
Strongly disagree	Disagree	Undecided	Agree	Strongly agree

If the statement is positively worded (as in the Kenyon statement in the above paragraph), the number circled by the examinee is the score for that item. If the statement is negatively worded, the scoring procedure must be reversed. The circled number must be subtracted from the highest possible number plus 1. For example, assume an examinee circles 4 in response to a negatively worded statement (e.g., "Only highly skilled athletes should participate in vigorous physical activity"). If an examinee circles 4, this indicates agreement with the statement but a negative view of vigorous physical activity. Thus, 4 is subtracted from 5 (the highest possible number) and added to 1. This calculation $(5 - 4 + 1)$ equals 2, accurately reflecting the examinee's negative perception.

Likert scales typically include five or seven steps. However, a two-step format (agree-disagree) may also be encountered, as well as scales including 10 or more steps. Increasing the number of scale steps increases the reliability of the item, up to a point. Most raters are not capable of using a large number of steps; therefore, it is probably best not to exceed seven categories.

Semantic Differential Scale

The **semantic differential scale** involves the rating of concepts using bipolar adjectives with scales anchored at the extremes. Bipolar adjectives represent opposite meanings, such as good-bad, strong-weak, and active-passive. An example of the semantic differential scale used to assess one's attitude toward physical activity is shown in the boxed material on p. 370. (Later in the chapter, the Children's Attitude Toward Physical Activity Scale, which uses the semantic differential scale, is described.)

The bipolar adjectives can readily be adapted to evaluate numerous concepts, and several different concepts can be easily evaluated using the same rating form. The examinee is asked to mark one of seven points best reflecting his or her feelings about the concept. The score for each item ranges from 1 to 7 if the positive adjective in the pair is listed to the right, and from 7 to 1 if the positive adjective is placed to the left.

SEMANTIC DIFFERENTIAL SCALE USED TO MEASURE ATTITUDES TOWARD PHYSICAL ACTIVITY

PHYSICAL ACTIVITY

Pleasant						Unpleasant	(E)
Relaxed						Tense	(A)
Passive						Active	(A)
Unsuccessful						Successful	(E)
Delicate						Rugged	(P)
Fast						Slow	(A)
Good						Bad	(E)
Weak						Strong	(P)
Heavy						Light	(P)

Note that a letter—E, A, or P—appears to the right of each item, representing the three dimensions of a concept that can be measured with a semantic differential scale. Evaluation represents the "goodness" of the concept. This dimension is often viewed as a reflection of attitude. Activity (A) reflects the action associated with the concept, while potency (P) involves the strength of the concept. The evaluation (E) dimension is best described by the good-bad adjective pair; the activity (A) dimension, by the fast-slow pair; and the potency (P) dimension by the strong-weak pair. At least three items should be included under each dimension. Both positive and negative items should be placed in each column. When more than one dimension is being measured, the adjective pairs should be randomly ordered so that pairs representing each dimension are dispersed throughout the instrument. When using the semantic differential with young children, adjectives should be selected that match their reading comprehension level. This can be determined by a reading specialist.

The letters representing dimensions are displayed in the boxed material for illustrative purposes only. Although the test user should know the correct dimension for each item, this information should not be included on the test form.

Other Types of Scales

When the Likert scale or the semantic differential scale is used, the respondent indicates agreement or disagreement with a statement or preference for specific meanings of a particular concept. Statements that must be answered true or false provide another example of agree-disagree scales. The Physical Estimation and Attraction Scale, described later in this chapter, uses true-false responses. This scale is similar in style to the forced-choice item. With scales of forced-choice items, the examinee is required to choose between two or more alternatives that appear equally favorable or unfavorable. Discrimination and preference values of the items are determined, and the alternatives are combined in such a manner as to equalize these values.

Rating scales such as the type described in Chapter 16 are also used to measure affective behavior. For example, a five-point scale could be used to measure sportsmanship, with a descriptor specifically dealing with sportsmanship listed under each point. The desired elements of sportsmanship would be included under point 5, and the undesirable elements under point 1. The points in between would reflect various stages of sportsmanship. Hellison (1993, p. 129) describes a rating scale that can be used to measure the affective goals of self-control, effort, self-direction, and service to others. The scale consists of the following five categories:

$$0 = \text{out of control/abusive}$$
$$1 = \text{off task}$$
$$2 = \text{extra effort}$$
$$3 = \text{self-directed activity}$$
$$4 = \text{took on a helping role}$$

Using this scale, the teacher can keep an ongoing record of student behaviors.

Another type of scale used in exercise science is the **perceived exertion scale** (Borg, 1973), which assesses the examinee's perception of his or her physical exertion during exercise. It is described later in this chapter.

Another method for measuring affective behavior is a questionnaire. Typically, the examinee responds to questions by selecting a response from a set of options. An example of this type of instrument is the Health-Related Physical Fitness Opinionnaire (Safrit and Wood, 1983). Users and nonusers of the AAHPERD (American Alliance for Health, Physical Exercise, Recreation, and Dance) Health-Related Physical Fitness Test are asked about their opinions of the test and how it compares with the Youth Fitness Test. Tests of psychological attributes (e.g., self-efficacy) might also be measured to assess the overall effectiveness of the physical education program in meeting its affective goals. Individual scores should probably not be used for student evaluations.

Weak Measures

Sometimes a well-developed standardized test is not available to measure an affect of interest. On the other hand, a suitable test may have been published, but it may be too technical or excessively time-consuming to administer in a practical setting. Sometimes it is desirable to develop a short test that can be administered quickly and easily. The test user may be interested in making a decision that will not have a long-term impact on the examinees. Thus, estimating the reliability and validity of the test may not be possible, although it would be desirable. This type of measure is often viewed as weak (although one-item instruments are not *always* weak). A **weak measure** is a measure with inadequate evidence of validity and reliability. When a measure is used to make a

WEAK MEASURE OF STUDENT ATTITUDE TOWARD JOGGING							
How did you feel about jogging today?							
Awful	1	2	3	4	5	6	7	Great

short-term decision about an examinee that could be readily modified, weak measures can be quite useful in the absence of a valid indicator. For example, a physical education teacher may include a goal of developing physical fitness. Time may be allotted for daily participation in jogging to meet an objective for cardiorespiratory function. Formative evaluation procedures may be used to monitor progress toward the predetermined standard. Since many teachers identify concomitant concerns associated with each major objective, testing attitudes toward this form of physical activity on a regular basis may be desirable. Although positive attitudes do not ensure participation in vigorous physical activity, a negative attitude would cause some concern, since it might reflect an unwillingness to engage in aerobic activities in the future.

A simple rating scale could be devised to obtain feedback on the students' attitudinal dispositions, as shown in the boxed material above. Although this is a weak measure, it can be justified if used on a continuing basis to provide a rough estimate of attitude. Students could be forced to run for 12 minutes during every class period; if they dislike this activity, however, they might develop negative attitudes toward physical fitness—even towards physical education—which may be retained.

Students would be asked to circle the number that best represents their feelings. Little time is required to obtain this information, since students can record a response as they leave class. They are asked not to mark the form in any other way, thus assuring anonymity. One word of caution: One should avoid collecting this type of data on only one day of the week. If the data were always collected on Fridays, the students' perceptions might be affected by the forthcoming weekend or by fatigue from the previous school week. A random selection of days is preferable. The averages of the responses for all students can be calculated every week and plotted, as in Figure 14-1.

Since a rating of 4 represents the neutral point on the scale, it is desirable if the average falls above that point. If more students felt awful about jogging than great, some type of intervention is necessary. Initially, the physical education staff might talk to them to find out why they have negative feelings.

Hellison proposed a similar means of obtaining student self-reports. He suggested asking students such questions as "What did you like and dislike about today's class?" (1993, p. 129). Journal entries would be equally useful. A journal provides an excellent means of learning of students' perceptions of their physical education class.

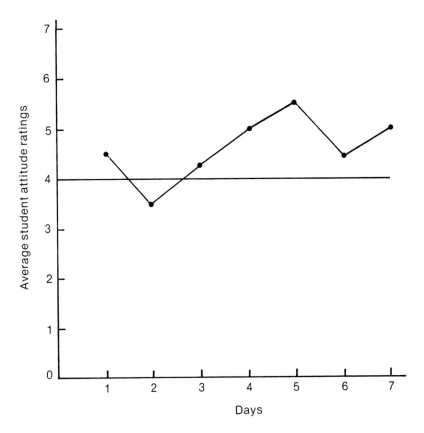

Figure 14-1   Attitude of Students Toward Jogging. See text.

USES OF AFFECTIVE MEASURES

Measures of affective behavior within the realm of sport and physical activity have been used in at least three ways: (1) to assess the affective behavior of individual students in physical education classes, (2) to assess the level of affective behavior for a class, and (3) to control or manipulate some aspect of affective behavior in conducting a research study.

Considering the affective behavior of an individual student first, educators most frequently express concerns about attitudes toward physical education, sportsmanship, and self-concept. Many physical education teachers feel a student's attitude should be an important component of his or her grade. Usually the teacher is most interested in the student's attitude toward participation in physical education classes, that is, the behavior of the student in class. Sometimes attitude is judged on the basis of the answers to these questions: Is an appropriate uniform worn? Does the student try in class? Does the student shower at the end of class? (See Chapter 9 for a discussion of whether factors such as these should be considered in determining a student's grade.)

Very few well-developed instruments are available to assess the affective behavior of an individual student in a physical education setting. Although a number of tests have been developed in the field, they were constructed years ago when the standards for test development were not as rigorous as today. Several affective measures used in the exercise science field are included at the end of this chapter to provide examples of this test market.

Most of the affective inventories in the field should be used only to examine group behavior. It would be appropriate to administer an attitude inventory to a physical education class, calculate the mean (or median) and standard deviation (or interpercentile range) of the class data, and use this information as part of the evaluation of the physical education program in the school. If, on average, the class attitude is negative, the physical education teacher could attempt to create a more positive environment. On the other hand, it would be inappropriate to use a student's score on the inventory to determine his or her grade on attitude toward physical education.

EXAMPLES OF AFFECTIVE MEASURES

While many instruments have been developed to measure the affective behavior of interest to the exercise scientist, few have been developed according to the rigorous standards set for the construction of educational and psychological tests (APA, 1985). In most cases, while reliabilities have been acceptable, content validity and construct validity have been inadequate and frequently overlooked. Examples of four types of instruments are included in this section: (1) stress and anxiety, (2) **social behavior,** (3) attitudes, and (4) sportsmanship and leadership.

Stress and Anxiety

Stress Inventory (Miller and Allen, 1982)
Test Objective   To measure an individual's level of stress.
Description   The inventory is presented in the box on p. 375.
Comments   The inventory provides information on a variety of stress indicators and, in this respect, would have logical validity. Obviously the examinee who marks "Yes" by many items would be viewed as having a high level of stress. A low-stress person would respond "No" to most of the items. It would be unusual for someone to mark "No" by all items, since everyone functions with a certain level of stress. For information on other aspects of this inventory, including reliability, validity, and scoring, refer to the original source.

Sport Competition Anxiety Test (Martens, 1977)
Test Objective   "To measure individual differences in the construct of competitive sport anxiety; to measure competitive A (anxiety) trait, which is defined as a

STRESS INVENTORY

Answer "Yes" or "No" to each of the following questions:

Yes   No

____ ____ 1. Do you often experience headaches or backaches?

____ ____ 2. When sitting in a chair and talking to someone, do you continually move in the chair to seek a comfortable position?

____ ____ 3. When retiring for the night, are you unable to fall asleep immediately?

____ ____ 4. Do you often grind your teeth when you are confronted with an unpleasant experience?

____ ____ 5. Do you easily become angry or frustrated when you are faced with a problem for which there is no immediate solution?

____ ____ 6. Do you often complain of being tired?

____ ____ 7. Does your face often hold expressions of intense concentration?

____ ____ 8. Do you often drum your fingers aimlessly or forcibly to express irritation?

____ ____ 9. Does your posture appear stiff when you sit or walk?

____ ____ 10. Are you unable to concentrate on one problem at a time?

____ ____ 11. Are you unable to relax voluntarily?

____ ____ 12. Do you often experience nervousness and uneasy feelings?

____ ____ 13. Do you become upset when your plans are interrupted or must be changed?

____ ____ 14. Are you highly competitive in sports, in your test grades, in your daily responsibilities?

____ ____ 15. Are you time-conscious?

____ ____ 16. Do you experience extreme dissatisfaction and anxiety when you fail to achieve success in your endeavors?

____ ____ 17. Are you an aggressive person?

____ ____ 18. Are you often too busy to allow time for physical activity?

____ ____ 19. Do you plan your day's activities and often budget your time?

____ ____ 20. Are you critical of yourself when you make a mistake?

____ ____ 21. Do you feel "uptight" at the end of the day?

____ ____ 22. Are you impatient when others are late for an appointment with you?

____ ____ 23. Do you often set high goals or levels of achievement for yourself?

____ ____ 24. Do you experience bad moods often?

____ ____ 25. Are you unyielding when others disagree with your beliefs or convictions?

From Miller DK, Allen TE.

construct that describes individual differences in the tendency to perceive competitive situations as threatening and to respond to these situations with A (anxiety) state reactions of varying intensity'' (Martens, 1977, p. 36).

Table 14-1 Sport Competition Anxiety Test for Children

ILLINOIS COMPETITION QUESTIONNAIRE
FORM C

Directions: We want to know how you feel about *competition.* You know what competition is. We all compete. We try to do better than our brother or sister or friend at something. We try to score more points in a game. We try to get the best grade in class or win a prize that we want. We all compete in sports and games. Below are some sentences about how boys and girls feel when they compete in sports and games. Read each statement below and decide if *you* HARDLY EVER, or SOMETIMES, or OFTEN feel this way when you compete in sports and games. Mark A if your choice is HARDLY EVER, mark B if you choose SOMETIMES, and mark C if you choose OFTEN. There are no right or wrong answers. Do not spend too much time on any one statement. *Remember:* choose the word that describes how you *usually* feel when competing in *sports and games.*

	Hardly ever	Some- times	Often
1. Competing against others is fun.	A ☐	B ☐	C ☐
2. Before I compete I feel uneasy.	A ☐	B ☐	C ☐
3. Before I compete I worry about not performing well.	A ☐	B ☐	C ☐
4. I am a good sportsman when I compete.	A ☐	B ☐	C ☐
5. When I compete I worry about making mistakes.	A ☐	B ☐	C ☐
6. Before I compete I am calm.	A ☐	B ☐	C ☐
7. Setting a goal is important when competing.	A ☐	B ☐	C ☐
8. Before I compete I get a funny feeling in my stomach.	A ☐	B ☐	C ☐
9. Just before competing I notice my heart beats faster than usual.	A ☐	B ☐	C ☐
10. I like rough games.	A ☐	B ☐	C ☐
11. Before I compete I feel relaxed.	A ☐	B ☐	C ☐
12. Before I compete I am nervous.	A ☐	B ☐	C ☐
13. Team sports are more exciting than individual sports.	A ☐	B ☐	C ☐
14. I get nervous wanting to start the game.	A ☐	B ☐	C ☐
15. Before I compete I usually get uptight.	A ☐	B ☐	C ☐

From Martens R.

Description   The Sport Competition Anxiety Test for Children (SCAT-C) is presented in Table 14-1.

Materials   Test forms and pencils.

Scoring   Items 2, 3, 5, 8, 9, 12, 14, and 15 are scored using the following key: 1 = hardly ever; 2 = sometimes; 3 = often. Items 6 and 11 are scored using the following key: 1 = often; 2 = sometimes; 3 = hardly ever. Items 1, 4, 7, 10, and 13, the remaining items, are not scored; they are included in the inventory as spurious items, to direct attention to elements of competition other than anxiety.

Validity   Content validity was claimed on the basis of an assessment by six judges of the content validity and grammatical clarity of the items. Extensive evidence of construct validity is presented in Martens's monograph. The details of these studies are beyond the scope of this book; however, the general approaches to construct validity included studies of group differences. High scorers on the SCAT-C were expected to manifest higher A states in stressful competitive situations than low scorers.

Reliability   Test-retest reliability was determined for both sexes of grades 5 and 6, and 8 and 9. Within-day reliability coefficients ranged from .85 to .93. Test-retest reliabilities ranged from .61 to .87. When $R_{xx'}$ was calculated to estimate reliability, the range of coefficients was .68 to .89.

Norms   Both standard scores and percentile norms for normal children, grades 4 to 6, and 7 to 9, are presented in Table 14-2.

Comments   This test is easy to administer in a group setting. However, the Martens monograph should be reviewed before using SCAT-C so that the theoretical framework generating this instrument is understood.

Social Behavior

Cowell Social Adjustment Index (Cowell, 1958)

Test Objective   To measure the extent of students' social adjustment, both positive and negative, within their social group.

Description   Forms A and B of the scale are shown in Table 14–3. Each student is rated by the teacher. A mark is placed in the cell that best reflects the degree to which the behavior is judged to be displayed.

Materials   Test forms and pencils.

Scoring   The total index score is the sum of the points for the 10 items in Form A minus the sum of the points for the 10 items in Form B.

Validity $r_{xy} = .63$, using the Pupil Who's Who Ratings as a criterion measure; $r_{xy} = .50$, using the Pupil Personal Distance Ballot.

Reliability $r_{xx'} = .82$.

Norms   Norms are available for junior high school boys in the original source.

Comments   This index was developed by Charles Cowell, a well-known physical educator and long-time faculty member at Purdue University. It can be used with boys and girls, ages 12 to 17.

Blanchard Behavior Rating Scale (Blanchard, 1936)

Test Objective   To measure the character and personality of the students.

Table 14-2 Normative Data for Sport Competion Anxiety Test

SCAT-C NORMS FOR NORMAL CHILDREN, GRADES 4–6

Raw score	Male		Female	
	Standard score	Percentile	Standard score	Percentile
30	744	99	734	99
29	722	99	711	99
28	700	99	688	98
27	678	97	666	97
26	656	95	643	92
25	634	90	620	88
24	612	87	597	85
23	590	84	575	80
22	568	77	552	74
21	546	71	529	67
20	524	63	507	56
19	502	56	484	48
18	480	46	461	39
17	458	41	438	31
16	436	33	416	24
15	415	28	393	16
14	393	21	370	14
13	371	13	347	10
12	349	9	325	6
11	327	2	302	2
10	305	1	279	1

From Martens R.

Description   The scale shown in Table 14-4 is used by the teacher to evaluate students in classes. For each item the teacher circles the item that best reflects his or her judgment of the student's behavior. A form is used for each student.
Materials   Test forms and pencils.
Scoring   The total score is the sum of the numbers that have been circled for all 24 items. The maximum number of points attainable is 120.

Table 14-2 Normative Data for Sport Competion Anxiety Test—cont'd

SCAT-C NORMS FOR NORMAL CHILDREN, GRADES 7–9

Raw score	Male Standard score	Percentile	Female Standard score	Percentile
30	730	99	688	99
29	709	99	669	97
28	687	99	649	96
27	665	97	630	91
26	644	93	610	88
25	622	90	591	84
24	601	85	571	76
23	579	79	552	70
22	558	73	532	63
21	536	66	513	53
20	515	59	493	49
19	493	51	473	42
18	472	43	454	35
17	450	37	434	30
16	429	30	415	26
15	407	24	395	19
14	386	18	376	17
13	364	12	356	12
12	342	8	337	9
11	321	4	317	5
10	299	2	298	2

Validity r_{xy} = .93, using the criterion of the average of the correlations of each item with the remainder of the items measuring the same trait.

Reliability $r_{xx'}$ = .71; this coefficient represents the correlation between the scores of teacher and student raters (interrater agreement).

Norms   No norms were reported. Local norms can easily be calculated for several classes, a school, or a school district. Norms developed at the local level are often the most useful, since the tests are more likely to measure the curricular goals of the school system.

Comments   This scale can be used with boys and girls, ages 12 to 17. The general

Table 14-3 Cowell Social Adjustment Index

FORM A

Instructions: Think carefully of the student's behavior in group situations; check each behavior trend according to its degree of descriptiveness.

Behavior trends	Descriptive of student			
	Markedly (+3)	Somewhat (+2)	Only slightly (+1)	Not at all (0)
1. Enters heartily and with enjoyment into the spirit of social intercourse				
2. Frank, talkative, and sociable; does not stand on ceremony				
3. Self-confident and self-reliant, tends to take success for granted; strong initiative, prefers to lead				
4. Quick and decisive in movement; pronounced or excessive energy output				
5. Prefers group activities, work or play; not easily satisfied with individual projects				
6. Adaptable to new situations, makes adjustments readily, welcomes change				
7. Is self-composed, seldom shows signs of embarrassment				
8. Tends to elation of spirits; seldom gloomy or moody				
9. Seeks a broad range of friendships; not selective or exclusive in games and the like				
10. Hearty and cordial, even to strangers, forms acquaintanceships very easily				

From Cowell CC.

Table 14-3 Cowell Social Adjustment Index—cont'd

FORM B

Instructions: Think carefully of the student's behavior in group situations; check each behavior trend according to its degree of descriptiveness.

Behavior trends	Descriptive of student			
	Markedly (−3)	Somewhat (−2)	Only slightly (−1)	Not at all (0)
1. Somewhat prudish, awkward, easily embarrassed in social contacts				
2. Secretive, seclusive, not inclined to talk unless spoken to				
3. Lacking in self-confidence and initiative; a follower				
4. Slow in movement, deliberative, or perhaps indecisive; energy output moderate or deficient				
5. Prefers to work and play alone, tends to avoid group activities				
6. Shrinks from making new adjustments, prefers the habitual to the stress of reorganization required by the new				
7. Is self-conscious, easily embarrassed, timid, or "bashful"				
8. Tends to depression; frequently gloomy or moody				
9. Shows preference for a narrow range of intimate friends and tends to exclude others from association				
10. Reserved and distant except to intimate friends; does not form acquaintanceships readily				

Table 14-4 Blanchard Behavior Frequency Rating Scale

Personal Information	No opportunity to observe	Never	Seldom	Fairly often	Frequently	Extremely often	Score
Leadership							
1. Popular with classmates		1	2	3	4	5	
2. Seeks responsibility in the classroom		1	2	3	4	5	
3. Shows intellectual leadership in the class-room		1	2	3	4	5	
Positive Active Qualities							
4. Quits on tasks requiring perseverance. . . .		5	4	3	2	1	
5. Exhibits aggressiveness in relationships with others		1	2	3	4	5	
6. Shows initiative in assuming responsibility in unfamiliar situations		1	2	3	4	5	
7. Alert to new opportunities		1	2	3	4	5	
Positive Mental Qualities							
8. Shows keenness of mind.		1	2	3	4	5	
9. Volunteers ideas		1	2	3	4	5	
Self-control							
10. Grumbles over decisions of classmates . . .		5	4	3	2	1	
11. Takes a justified criticism by teacher or classmate without showing anger or pouting		1	2	3	4	5	

From Blanchard BE.

nature of some of the test items may lead to considerable bias in the ratings. For example, note item 24: "Friendly." What behaviors would a teacher expect to observe for a rating of 5? A rating of 2? Would another teacher make identical judgments of the same student?

Attitudes

Attitude Toward Physical Activity Inventory (Kenyon, 1968a,b)
Test Objective   To measure six dimensions of the attitude construct of active and passive involvement in physical activity.
Description   The test items in the Health and Fitness Scale, one of the six dimen-

Table 14-4 Blanchard Behavior Frequency Rating Scale—cont'd

Personal Information	No opportunity to observe	Never	Seldom	Fairly often	Frequently	Extremely often	Score
Cooperation							
12. Loyal to group.		1	2	3	4	5	
13. Discharges group responsibilities well . . .		1	2	3	4	5	
14. Cooperative in his attitude toward the teacher.		1	2	3	4	5	
Social Action Standards							
15. Makes loud-mouthed criticisms and comments.		5	4	3	2	1	
16. Respects the rights of others		1	2	3	4	5	
Ethical Social Qualities							
17. Cheats		5	4	3	2	1	
18. Truthful		1	2	3	4	5	
Qualities of Efficiency							
19. Seems satisfied to "get by" with tasks assigned		5	4	3	2	1	
20. Dependable and trustworthy		1	2	3	4	5	
21. Has good study habits. . . . . , . . .		1	2	3	4	5	
Sociability							
22. Liked by others		1	2	3	4	5	
23. Makes a friendly approach to others in the group.		1	2	3	4	5	
23. Friendly.		1	2	3	4	5	

sions of involvement in physical activity, are shown in Table 14-5. Both the men's and women's versions of the Attitude Toward Physical Activity (ATPA) Inventory can be obtained by writing Dr. Kenyon at the address on p. 386. The six dimensions and a brief description of each are presented below:

1. *Social experience.* Physical activity is valued as medium for social relationships.
2. *Health and fitness.* Physical activity is valued because it contributes to the improvement of physical fitness and health.
3. *Pursuit of vertigo.* Physical activity is valued as a means of providing an element of risk to the participant.

Table 14-5 Health and Fitness Scale Items

VSA	SA	A	U	D	SD	VSD	Of all physical activities, those whose purpose is primarily to develop physical fitness would *not* be my first choice.
VSA	SA	A	U	D	SD	VSD	I would usually choose strenuous physical activity over light physical activity, if given the choice.
VSA	SA	A	U	D	SD	VSD	A large part of our daily lives must be committed to vigorous exercise.
VSA	SA	A	U	D	SD	VSD	Being strong and highly fit is *not* the most important thing in my life.
VSA	SA	A	U	D	SD	VSD	The time spent doing daily calisthenics could probably be used more profitably in other ways.
VSA	SA	A	U	D	SD	VSD	Strength and physical stamina are the most important prerequisites to a full life.
VSA	SA	A	U	D	SD	VSD	I believe calisthenics are among the less desirable forms of physical activity.
VSA	SA	A	U	D	SD	VSD	People should spend 20 to 30 minutes a day doing vigorous calisthenics.
VSA	SA	A	U	D	SD	VSD	Of all physical activities, my first choice would be those whose purpose is primarily to develop and maintain physical fitness.
VSA	SA	A	U	D	SD	VSD	Vigorous daily exercises are absolutely necessary to maintain one's general health.

Reprinted by permission of Kenyon GS, University of Lethbridge, Lethbridge, Alberta, Canada. VSA, *very strongly agree*; SA, *strongly agree*; A, *agree*; U, *undecided*; D, *disagree*; SD, *strongly disagree*; VSD, *very strongly disagree*.

4. *Aesthetic experience.* Physical activity is valued as a means of providing an artistic element to the participant, of experiencing the beauty of the movement.
5. *Catharsis.* Physical activity is valued for its cleansing nature, as a release of tension.
6. *Ascetic experience.* Physical activity is valued as means of self-sacrifice requiring dedication to strenuous training.

Materials   Tests forms, scoring key, and pencils.

Scoring   Each scale of the ATPA inventory is scored separately. Thus each examinee will receive six scores, one for each scale. The six scores should not be summed in an attempt to obtain a single indicator of attitude toward physical activity. Since the profile of six scores most accurately describes the examinee's attitude, a total of the scores is difficult to interpret.

A response to an item can range from very strongly disagree (VSD) to very strongly agree (VSA), using a seven-point scale. The maximum number of points that can be scored for each dimension is presented in Table 14-6.

Keep in mind that the scoring must be reversed on several items before summing the dimension score. Note, for example, one of the Health and Fitness Scale items: "Being strong and highly fit is not the most important thing in my life." An examinee who strongly agrees with this statement would record a score of 7 on the item. However, since the statement is worded negatively, his or her score should be converted to a score of 1 to convey the expression of a negative attitude toward physical fitness. Adhere to the scoring key when scoring the instrument.

Validity   The six dimensions of attitude toward physical activity as hypothesized by Kenyon were verified using factor analytic procedures. Expert opinion also confirmed that the six dimensions adequately represented attitude toward active and passive involvement in physical activity. Several studies of construct validity have been conducted, using the group differences approach. Generally, athletes and nonathletes differed on the scales, as did males and females.

Reliability   The within-day reliability coefficients for males and females on all six dimensions are given in Table 14-7.

Norms   Although means and standard deviations have been reported in studies too numerous to report in this textbook, no norms have been developed. However, an annotated bibliography by Kenyon and Andrews includes most of these studies up to 1981. References that became available after 1981 are included in

Table 14-6   Maximum Scores for ATPA Dimensions

	Men	**Women**
Social	70 (10 items)	56 (8 items)
Health and fitness	70 (10 items)	77 (11 items)
Vertigo	70 (10 items)	63 (9 items)
Aesthetic	70 (10 items)	63 (9 items)
Catharsis	63 (9 items)	63 (9 items)
Ascetic	70 (10 items)	56 (8 items)

Table 14-7   Within-Day Reliability Coefficients for ATPA

	Male	Female	*n*
Social			
United States	.782	.794	120
England	.783	.790	120
Health and fitness			
United States	.866	.883	120
England	.782	.840	120
Pursuit of vertigo			
United States	.910	.883	120
England	.867	.806	120
Aesthetic			
United States	.865	.915	120
England	.851	.839	120
Catharsis			
United States	.859	.873	120
England	.884	.868	120
Ascetic			
United States	.874	.892	120
England	.780	.789	120

From Pooley JC. 1971. The professionalism of physical education in the United States and England. Unpublished doctoral dissertation. University of Wisconsin, Madison. Used by permission.

the System of Information Retrieval for Leisure and Sport (SIRLS),* a retrieval system at the University of Waterloo, Ontario, Canada.

Comments   This is an excellent inventory, developed by an outstanding sport sociologist in the field. It can be used in a practical as well as a research setting and is appropriate for males and females of high-school through college age.

Children's Attitude Toward Physical Activity Inventory (Simon and Smoll, 1974)

Test Objective   To measure children's attitude toward vigorous physical activity.

Description   The Children's Attitude Toward Physical Activity (CATPA) was modeled after the ATPA. A semantic differential scale was used, with each dimension calculated on the basis of eight pairs of bipolar adjectives, which are used to assess the value of each domain. The items for the social dimension of CATPA are shown in the box on p. 387.

Materials   Test forms and pencils.

* The bibliography and more information on references available after 1981 may be obtained by writing to G.S. Kenyon, University of Lethbridge, Lethbridge, Alberta, Canada T1K 3M4.

ITEMS FOR SOCIAL DIMENSION OF CATPA

What does the idea in the box mean to you?

> PHYSICAL ACTIVITY AS A SOCIAL EXPERIENCE
> Physical activities that give you a chance to
> meet new people and be with your friends.

Always Think About the Idea in the Box.

1. Good ___ : ___ : ___ : ___ : ___ : ___ : ___ Bad
        1   2   3   4   5   6   7

2. Of no use ___ : ___ : ___ : ___ : ___ : ___ : ___ Useful
        1   2   3   4   5   6   7

3. Not pleasant ___ : ___ : ___ : ___ : ___ : ___ : ___ Pleasant
        1   2   3   4   5   6   7

4. Bitter ___ : ___ : ___ : ___ : ___ : ___ : ___ Sweet
        1   2   3   4   5   6   7

5. Nice ___ : ___ : ___ : ___ : ___ : ___ : ___ Awful
        1   2   3   4   5   6   7

6. Happy ___ : ___ : ___ : ___ : ___ : ___ : ___ Sad
        1   2   3   4   5   6   7

7. Dirty ___ : ___ : ___ : ___ : ___ : ___ : ___ Clean
        1   2   3   4   5   6   7

8. Steady ___ : ___ : ___ : ___ : ___ : ___ : ___ Nervous
        1   2   3   4   5   6   7

From Simon JA, Smoll FL.

Scoring   Each of the six CATPA scales is scored separately. The bipolar adjectives of each pair are separated by a seven-point continuum, and the numerical values assigned to each of the eight adjective pairs are summed for the score on a single dimension. The maximum score for each domain is 56.

Validity   It was assumed that the six ATPA dimensions were equally representative for young children. Except for the ascetic dimension, dimension names on the CATPA are the same as those used for the ATPA. The wording of the dimension descriptions was changed to be more appropriate for young children. In a study of construct validity, children's scores on the CATPA were significantly related to active involvement in physical activity but had no relationship to motor skill proficiency.

Reliability $R_{xx'} = .80 - .89$, within-day estimates; $R_{xx'} = .44 - .62$, test-retest estimates.

Norms   Not reported for this specific test.

Comments   This inventory is useful for program evaluation in the elementary and junior high schools.

Physical Estimation and Attraction Scale (Sonstroem, 1974)

Test Objective   To measure the motivational properties of physical self-esteem (estimation) and interest (attraction) in vigorous physical activity.

Description   The Physical Estimation and Attraction Scale (PEAS) consists of a random ordering of 11 neutral items, 50 attraction items, and 33 estimation items. Sample items are presented in the box below and the full-length test along with the scoring key may be obtained from Dr. Sonstroem at the University of Rhode Island, Kingston. There are two response choices: true, if the examinee agrees with the statement, and false, if not. Many of the items are of the forced-choice type, requiring the examinee to choose one activity over another.

Materials   Test forms, pencils, and scoring key.

Scoring   For each correct response 1 point is scored.

Validity   A number of studies of construct validity have been conducted (Sonstroem, 1978). Highly fit and poorly fit boys differed significantly in their scores on both the estimation and attraction dimensions of the PEAS. Moderate relationships were reported between estimation scores and a fitness index and between estimation scores and self-esteem. (Remember that the estimation dimension taps one's physical self-esteem.)

Reliability $r_{xx'} = .87$, attraction scale, within-day estimate; $r_{xx'} = .87$, estimation scale, within-day estimate; and $r_{xx'} = .90$, total scale, test-retest estimate.

Norms   No norms were reported. Summary data from Sonstroem's studies are given in Table 14-8.

Comments   Although the scale has been used with male and female adults and adolescent boys, validity has been determined primarily for the last sample.

SAMPLE ITEMS FROM PEAS

ESTIMATION ITEMS

Item 6.   My body is strong and muscular compared with other boys my age.

Item 26.   I am better coordinated than most people I know.

Item 33.   I am a good deal stronger than most of my friends.

ATTRACTION ITEMS

Item 4.   I would much rather play softball than go for a ride in a car.

Item 17.   I like to be in sports that don't require a great amount of running.

Item 34.   I would rather play poker than softball.

Reprinted by permission of Sonstroem RJ, University of Rhode Island, Kingston.

Table 14-8 Summary Statistics for PEAS

Group	Scale	n	Mean	Standard Deviation
Boys, grades 9–12	Estimation	187	20.40	6.60
	Attraction	187	35.52	8.99
Boys, high school	Estimation	106	22.2	5.75
Boys, junior high school	Estimation	112	21.96	6.29

Since responses to PEAS items can be distorted and the scores influenced by response sets, the use of a distortion scale is advisable. A scale for this purpose should be provided by the test developer. **Response distortion,** one of the key words in this chapter, was described in the introductory section. If a distortion scale is available, an examinee scoring below a predetermined score on the scale is perceived as distorting his or her responses to the test of affect. Because of the low score on the distortion scale, the score on the affective test is viewed as invalid.

Wear Attitude Scale (Wear, 1955)
Test Objective To measure attitudes toward physical education.
Description Two forms of the scale, A and B, were developed. Form A is shown on pp. 390–391. The students are instructed to respond to the scale according to their perceptions of physical education as an activity course taught during a regular class period. The five possible responses are strongly agree, agree, undecided, disagree, and strongly disagree. Students should answer anonymously, or they should be informed that their responses will not affect their physical education grades.
Materials Test forms and pencils.
Scoring The total score is the sum of the scores of the 30 items. Positively worded items are scored 5-4-3-2-1, and negatively worded items are scored 1-2-3-4-5. High scores reflect positive attitudes toward physical education.
Validity Face validity.
Reliability $r_{xx'} = .94$, Form A; and $r_{xx'} = .96$, Form B.
Comments The Wear Attitude Scale, one of the classic scales of attitudes toward physical education, has been widely used and cited. Although the psychometric properties could be strengthened by today's standards, the scale stood for many years as one of the best affective measures in physical education.

Sportsmanship and Leadership

Lakie Attitude Toward Athletic Competition Scale (Lakie, 1964)
Test Objective To measure player's attitudes toward competition.
Description Lakie's scale is shown in the boxed material on pp. 392–393. Examinees are instructed to read each item carefully and circle the number of the response best reflecting their judgment of the action described.

FORM A OF THE WEAR ATTITUDE SCALE

1. If for any reason a few subjects have to be dropped from the school program, physical education should be one of the subjects dropped.

2. Physical education activities provide no opportunities for learning to control the emotions.

3. Physical education is one of the more important subjects in helping to establish and maintain desirable social standards.

4. Vigorous physical activity works off harmful emotional tensions.

5. I would take physical education only if it were required.

6. Participation in physical education makes no contribution to the development of poise.

7. Because physical skills loom large in importance in youth, it is essential that a person be helped to acquire and improve such skills.

8. Calisthenics taken regularly are good for one's general health.

9. Skill in active games or sports is not necessary for leading the fullest kind of life.

10. Physical education does more harm physically than it does good.

11. Associating with others in some physical education activity is fun.

12. Physical education classes provide situations for the formulation of attitudes that make one a better citizen.

13. Physical education situations are among the poorest for making friends.

14. There is not enough value coming from physical education to justify the time consumed.

15. Physical education skills make worthwhile contributions to the enrichment of living.

From Wear CL.

Continued

Materials Test forms and pencils.

Scoring Total the scores for each item. Use the reverse order (5-4-3-2-1) to score negative items. The higher the score, the more competitive the player. A high score reflects a desire to win at any cost. The scale includes 22 items; thus, the highest possible score is 110 points.

Validity Face validity.

Reliability $r_{xx'} = .81$.

Norms Not reported for this specific test.

Comments The Lakie Attitude Scale is similar in type to a number of other measures, mostly unpublished, that have been developed in the field. Attitudes about competition have changed over the years, and some actions that are acceptable today were viewed as poor sportsmanship many years ago. It is diffi-

FORM A OF THE WEAR ATTITUDE SCALE—cont'd

16. People get all the physical exercise they need in just taking care of their daily work.

17. All who are physically able will profit from an hour of physical education each day.

18. Physical education makes a valuable contribution toward building up an adequate reserve of strength and endurance for everyday living.

19. Physical education tears down sociability by encouraging people to attempt to surpass one another in many of the activities.

20. Participation in physical education activities makes for a more wholesome outlook on life.

21. Physical education adds nothing to the improvement of social behavior.

22. Physical education class activities will help to relieve and relax physical tensions.

23. Participation in physical education activities helps a person to maintain a healthful emotional life.

24. Physical education is one of the more important subjects in the school program.

25. There is little value in physical education as far as physical well-being is concerned.

26. Physical education should be included in the program of every school.

27. Skills learned in physical education class do not benefit a person.

28. Physical education provides situations for developing character qualities.

29. Physical education makes for more enjoyable living.

30. Physical education has no place in modern education.

cult to develop this type of instrument without including items that seem to have quite obvious answers.

Nelson Sports Leadership Questionnaire (Nelson, 1966)

Test Objective   To measure leadership in athletic settings.

Description   Two questionnaires were designed, one for the coaches and one for members of athletic teams. (See both sections on pp. 394–396.) The coach's questionnaire has 14 items; the players', 20 items. On the team members' forms the examinee must list a first choice (under no. 1) and a second choice (under no. 2) of team members, excluding his or her own name. A team member's name can be used any number of times. Examinees are asked not to sign the questionnaire.

LAKIE ATTITUDE TOWARD ATHLETIC COMPETITION SCALE

The following situations describe behavior demonstrated in sports. Circle the category that indicates your feeling toward the behavior described in each of the situations.

1 = strongly approve; 2 = approve; 3 = undecided; 4 = disapprove;
5 = strongly disapprove

1 2 3 4 5   1. During a football game, team A has the ball on its own 45-yard line, fourth down and 1 yard to go for a first down. The coach of team A signals to the quarterback the play that he wants the team to run.

1 2 3 4 5   2. Team A is the visiting basketball team, and each time a member of the team is given a free shot, the home crowd sets up a continuous din of noise until the shot has been taken.

1 2 3 4 5   3. Tennis player A frequently calls out, throws up his arms, or otherwise tries to indicate that his opponent's serve is out of bounds when it is questionable.

1 2 3 4 5   4. In a track meet, team A enters a man in the mile run who is to set a fast pace for the first half of the race and then drop out.

1 2 3 4 5   5. In a football game, team B's quarterback was tackled repeatedly after handing off and after he was out of the play.

1 2 3 4 5   6. Sam, playing golf with his friends, hit a drive into the rough. He accidentally moved the ball with his foot; although not improving his position, he added a penalty stroke to his score.

1 2 3 4 5   7. A basketball player was caught out of position on defense, and rather than allow his opponent to attempt a field goal, he fouled him.

1 2 3 4 5   8. During a golf match player A made quick noises and movements when player B was getting ready to make a shot.

1 2 3 4 5   9. School A has a powerful but quite slow football team. The night before playing a smaller but faster team, they allowed the field sprinkling system to remain on, causing the field to be heavy and slow.

1 2 3 4 5   10. A basketball team used player A to draw the opponent's high scorer into fouling situations.

1 2 3 4 5   11. The alumni of college A pressured the board of trustees to lower the admission and eligibility requirements for athletes.

From Lakie WL.

Continued

LAKIE ATTITUDE TOWARD ATHLETIC COMPETITION SCALE—cont'd

1 2 3 4 5   12. Team A, by use of fake injuries, was able to stop the clock long enough to get off the play that resulted in the winning touchdown.

1 2 3 4 5   13. A tennis player was given the advantage of a bad call in a close match. He then "evened up" the call by intentionally hitting the ball out of bounds.

1 2 3 4 5   14. The coach of basketball team A removed his team from the floor in protest of an official's decision.

1 2 3 4 5   15. Between seasons a coach moved from college A to college B, and then persuaded three of college A's athletes to transfer to college B.

1 2 3 4 5   16. After losing a close football game, the coach of the losing team publicly accused the game officials of favoritism when the game movies showed the winning touchdown had been scored by using an illegal maneuver.

1 2 3 4 5   17. College C lowered the admission requirements for boys awarded athletic scholarships.

1 2 3 4 5   18. Team A's safety man returned a punt for a touchdown. Unseen by the officials, he had stepped out of bounds in front of his team's bench. His coach notified the officials of this fact.

1 2 3 4 5   19. A college with very few athletic scholarships to offer gives athletes preference on all types of campus jobs.

1 2 3 4 5   20. Several wealthy alumni of college C make a monthly gift to several athletes who are in need of financial assistance.

1 2 3 4 5   21. College K has a policy of not allowing any member of a varsity squad to associate with the visiting team until the contest or meet is completed.

1 2 3 4 5   22. The board of trustees of college C fired the football coach and gave as the reason for his dismissal his failure to win a conference championship during the past five years.

Materials   Test forms and pencils.

Scoring   List the names of team members appearing on a questionnaire. Allocate 5 points to a name appearing under no. 1 and 3 points to a name appearing under no. 2. Add the number of points for each player. These points can be summed by players, across all questionnaires. Players can then be ranked according to total points or average number of points.

Validity   Face validity; construct validity by comparing leaders and nonleaders.

NELSON SPORTS LEADERSHIP QUESTIONNAIRE

COACHES

The same names can be used any number of times, and in all cases give your first and second choice for each question.

1. Who are the most popular players on your squad?
   1. _____   2. _____

2. Which players on the team know the most basketball, in terms of strategy, team play, etc.?
   1. _____   2. _____

3. Of all the players on your team, who exhibits the most poise on the floor during the crucial parts of the game?
   1. _____   2. _____

4. Who are the take-charge players on your squad?
   1. _____   2. _____

5. Who are the most consistent ball handlers on your squad?
   1. _____   2. _____

6. Who are the most consistent shooters on your squad?
   1. _____   2. _____

7. Who are the most valuable players on your squad?
   1. _____   2. _____

8. Who are the two players who play "most for the team?"
   1. _____   2. _____

9. Which players have the most overall ability on the squad?
   1. _____   2. _____

10. Who are the most likeable players on the squad?
    1. _____   2. _____

11. Which players do you think would make the best coaches?
    1. _____   2. _____

12. If you were not present for practice, which players would you place in charge of the practice?
    1. _____   2. _____

13. Who are the players endowed with leadership qualities?
    1. _____   2. _____

14. Who are the players least endowed with leadership ability?
    1. _____   2. _____

From Nelson DO.

Continued

NELSON SPORTS LEADERSHIP QUESTIONNAIRE—cont'd

PLAYERS

Do not sign your name to the questionnaire. Fill in the name or names of the squad member who, in your opinion, best fits the question. Give your first and second choice in all cases. Do not use your own name on any of the answers. The names of the players can be used any number of times, and your answers will be kept confidential.

1. If you were on a trip and had a choice of the players you would share the hotel room with, who would they be?
   1. _____   2. _____

2. Who are the most popular players on the squad?
   1. _____   2. _____

3. Who are the best scholars on the squad?
   1. _____   2. _____

4. Which players on the team know the most basketball, in terms of strategy, team play, etc.?
   1. _____   2. _____

5. If the coach were not present for a workout, which players would be the most likely to take charge of the practice?
   1. _____   2. _____

6. Which players woud you listen to first if the team appeared to be disorganized during a crucial game?
   1. _____   2. _____

7. Your team is behind by 1 point with 10 seconds remaining in the game and you could pass to anyone on the squad. Who would it be?
   1. _____   2. _____

8. Of all the players on your team, who exhibits the most poise on the floor during the crucial parts of the game?
   1. _____   2. _____

Continued

Reliability $r_{xx'} = .96$, ninth-grade football players; $r_{xx'} = .78$, varsity college basketball players. Both of these estimates were reported in Johnson and Nelson (1974).

Norms   Not reported for this specific test.

Comments   Test directions should be typed onto the questionnaire. It can be used for males and females, junior high school through college level. A modified version of the player's questionnaire is presented in Johnson and Nelson (1974, p. 396). In this version the terms are not restricted to a specific sport; thus it has more widespread applicability.

NELSON SPORTS LEADERSHIP QUESTIONNAIRE (players)—cont'd

9. Who are the take-charge players on your team?

    1. _____   2. _____

10. Who are the most consistent ball handlers on your squad?

    1. _____   2. _____

11. Who are the most consistent shooters on your squad?

    1. _____   2. _____

12. Who are the most valuable players on your squad?

    1. _____   2. _____

13. Who are the most unselfish players who are interested most in the team as a whole and who play most "for the team?"

    1. _____   2. _____

14. Which players on the squad have the most overall ability?

    1. _____   2. _____

15. Who are the most likable players on the squad?

    1. _____   2. _____

16. Which players on your team have influenced you the most?

    1. _____   2. _____

17. Which players have actually helped you the most?

    1. _____   2. _____

18. Which players do you think would make the best coaches?

    1. _____   2. _____

19. Which players do you most often look to for leadership?

    1. _____   2. _____

20. Who are the hardest workers on the squad?

    1. _____   2. _____

Other Measures

Perceived Exertion (Borg, 1973)

Test Objective   To assess one's perception of his or her physical exertion during exercise.

Description   The scale is shown in the boxed material on p. 397. At regular intervals during exercise the examinee is asked to select a rating that reflects his or her perception of physical exertion. At some point the activity may be terminated when a certain rating is reached; this is dependent on the protocol being used. Typically, other data are also considered before terminating exercise. The

PERCEIVED EXERTION SCALE

6		14
7	Very, very light	15 Hard
8		16
9	Very light	17 Very hard
10		18
11	Fairly light	19 Very, very hard
12		20
13	Somewhat hard	

From Borg GAV.

photograph preceding the test description shows the perceived exertion scale being used in conjunction with a stress test on a treadmill.

Comments   Borg developed a version of the perceived exertion scale that has ratio properties (Borg, 1982). In a review of the study and application of perceived exertion, Pandolf (1983) discusses the scale and recommends that its use be limited to research. "Although this . . . scale may be more advantageous for studies requiring ratio scaling methods, Borg concluded that his old 15 point scale is still the best for applied studies" (Pandolf, 1983, p. 129).

SUMMARY

Measures of affective behavior are designed to measure attitudes, interests, values, psychological traits, social behavior, and emotional states. Many types of affective behavior are of interest to the physical educator, coach, and exercise specialist. Although a number of instruments have been developed to measure affective behavior in the field, many of these measures do not have strong psychometric underpinnings. However, they may have some usefulness if used as an indicator of a characteristic of a group of examinees rather than of an individual person. They might also be useful in a formative evaluation context. Few instruments are available that would be suitable in a research setting.

Learning Experiences

1. Analyze the Lakie Attitude Toward Athletic Competition Scale. First, take the test and determine your score. Identify the aspects of competition that are measured by this scale by naming each aspect of competition and listing the items falling under each. Are some aspects of competition overemphasized in this scale? If so, which ones? Are some aspects underemphasized? If so, which ones? Do you think this scale is useful in today's competitive settings? Give a thorough rationale for your answer.

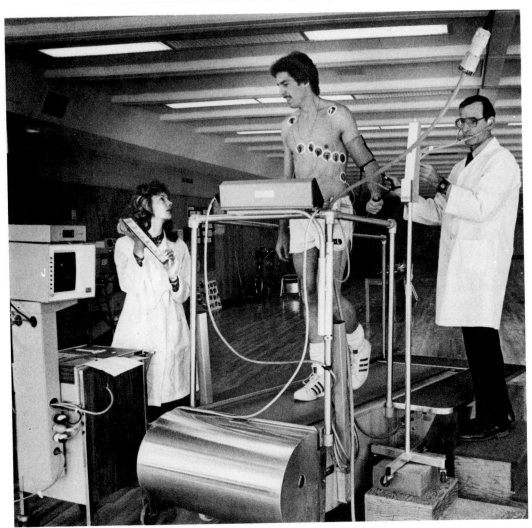

Use of Perceived Exertion Scale During Stress on Treadmill.

2. Develop a rating scale to measure attitudes toward an official in a game. Use a 5-4-3-2-1 rating scale and write a descriptor for each point value. Each descriptor should reflect behaviors rather than a general phrase, such as 5 = excellent attitude, 4 = good attitude, and so forth. What behaviors would you expect to see in a person who is given a rating of 5? A rating of 1? This means that you must write several short phrases for each descriptor.

References

American Psychological Association (APA). 1985. Standards for educational and psychological tests. Washington, DC: American Psychological Association.

Blanchard BE. 1936. A behavior frequency rating scale for the measurement of character and personality traits in a physical education classroom situation. Research Quarterly, **7**:56–66.

Borg GAV. 1973. Perceived exertion: A note on "history" and methods. Medicine and Science in Sports, **5**:90–93.

Borg GAV. 1982. Psychophysical bases of perceived exertion. Medicine and Science in Sports and Exercise, **14**:377–381.

Cowell CC. 1958. Validating an index of social adjustment for high school use. Research Quarterly, **29**:7–18.

Hellison D. 1993. Evaluating the affective domain. In Rink JE, ed. Critical crossroads: Middle and secondary school physical education. Reston, Va: National Association for Sport and Physical Education, pp 126–131.

Hellison D, Templin TR. 1991. A reflective approach to teaching physical education. Champaign, Ill: Human Kinetics.

Johnson BL, Nelson JK. 1974. Practical measurements for evaluation in physical education. Minneapolis: Burgess Co.

Kenyon GS. 1968a. A conceptual model for characterizing physical activity. Research Quarterly, **39**:96–105.

Kenyon GS. 1968b. Six scales for assessing attitudes toward physical activity. Research Quarterly, **39**:566–574.

Lakie WL. 1964. Expressed attitudes of various groups of athletes toward athletic competition. Research Quarterly, **35**:497–503.

Martens R. 1977. Sport competition anxiety test. Champaign, Ill: Human Kinetics.

Miller DK, Allen TE. 1982. Fitness: A lifetime commitment, ed 2. Minneapolis: Burgess Co.

Nelson DO. 1966. Nelson Sports Leadership Questionnaire. Research Quarterly, **37**:268–275.

Pandolf KB. 1983. Advances in the study and application of perceived exertion. In Terjung RL, ed. Exercise and sport science reviews. Philadelphia: Franklin Institute.

Pooley JC. 1971. The professionalism of physical education in the United States and England. Unpublished doctoral dissertation, University of Wisconsin, Madison.

Safrit MJ, Wood TM. 1983. The Health-Related Fitness Opinionnaire: A pilot survey. Research Quarterly for Exercise and Sport, **54**:204-207.

Seaward BL. 1991. Spiritual wellbeing: A health education model. Journal of Health Education, **22**:166–169.

Shaver KG. 1981. Principles of social psychology, Cambridge, Mass: Winthrop.

Simon JA, Smoll FL. 1974. An instrument for assessing children's attitude toward physical activity. Research Quarterly, **45**:21–27.

Sonstroem RJ. 1974. Attitude testing: Examining certain physiological correlates of physical activity. Research Quarterly, **45**:93–103.

Sonstroem RJ. 19798. Physical estimation and attraction scales: Rationale and research. Medicine and Science in Sports, **10**:97–102.

Wear CL. 1955. Construction of equivalent forms of an attitude scale. Research Quarterly, **26**:113–119.

Annotated Readings

Jones JG. 1975. An effective evaluation of an outdoor education experience. Journal of Physical Education and Recreation, **46**:54–55.

Describes the construction of two test forms to evaluate 10 outdoor activities in terms of student enjoyment, desire to continue the activity, and perceived learning; presents descriptive statistics for both forms of the test; concludes that the outdoor experience primarily emphasizes skill development and improved attitudes toward outdoor living.

Frye PA. 1983. Measurement of psychosocial aspects of physical education. Journal of Physical Education, Recreation and Dance, **54**(8):26–27.

Discusses the principles and practices of measurement and evaluation as applied to psychosocial characteristics; suggests using available tests to draw inferences about group rather than individual behavior.

McGee R. 1977. Measuring affective behavior in physical education. Journal of Physical Education and Recreation, **48**:29–30.

Notes that the affective domain deserves special attention by physical educators; recommends that affective measures such as self-concept, attitude, and social adjustment not be used for grading; should provide student with an opportunity to know self better; discusses four instruments and their current usage in the field.

Ostrow AC, ed. 1990. Directory of psychological tests in the sport and exercise sciences. Morgantown, WVa: Fitness Information Technology.

Identifies sport- and exercise-specific psychological tests published between 1975 and 1990; includes a review of each test, along with a reference; an excellent reference for measures of attitude, body image, motivation, and many other psychological attributes.

Seaward BL. 1994. Managing stress: Principles and strategies for health and wellbeing. Boston: Jones and Bartlett.

Includes samples of inventories and scales used to measure various attributes associated with stress, such as social readjustment, type A behavior, and locus of control; discusses theoretical frameworks for many of these measures.

Weise GE, Schick J. 1982. Affective measurement in physical education: doing well and feeling good. Journal of Physical Education, Recreation and Dance, **53**(2):15–25, 86.

Offers a series of articles on measuring affective behavior in physical education; discusses the pros and cons of evaluation in the affective domain; includes uses and abuses of affective measurement.

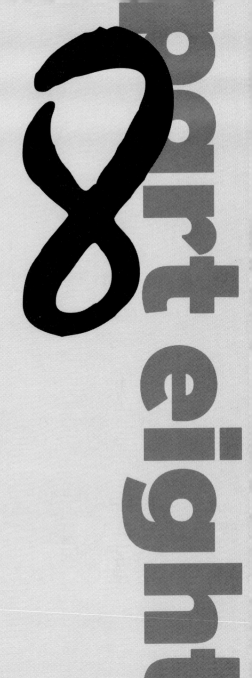

Principles of Test Construction

Constructing Sports Skills Tests

Watch for these words as you read the following chapter

Checklist
Components of skill
Game statistics
Observational analysis

Rating scale
Sport profile
Test battery

Whenever you need a test in physical education or exercise science, try to find an appropriate one from the many already available (see Chapter 19 for examples of sports skills tests and criteria for selecting sports skills tests). Test development is a time-consuming process that must be handled with care and thoroughness. There is nothing magical about the process, but full-time teachers and exercise specialists often do not have sufficient time for this purpose. If you work in a fitness club, you will already have at your fingertips a number of tests you can administer to your clients. In a school setting you may not always be able to find the type of test you need, partly because of the variety of physical activities taught. Consider the number of sports alone that are included in many physical education curricula. In each of these sports, many skills must be learned and, theoretically, tested; however, administering a great number of tests would not be very practical. Therefore a decision on what to test must be made, taking into consideration the most important skills and those that will receive the greatest emphasis.

The first step is to review the available tests of the skills that will be given the most emphasis. Looking through a variety of textbooks in measurement and evaluation is a cumbersome and time-consuming process. However, three available sources should provide a comprehensive overview of sports skills tests: the books by Collins and Hodges (1978) and Strand and Wilson (1993), which are devoted to descriptions of sports skills tests, and a series of manuals, published by the American Alliance for Health, Physical Education, Recreation, and Dance (AAHPERD), each dealing with skills tests for a specific sport (e.g., tennis, softball). These manuals are currently being revised, with greatly improved tests (see Chapter 19).

Developing a clear idea of the most appropriate type of test saves a lot of time when reviewing test literature. A test can be designed to measure a specific skill, a combination of skills, or playing ability. It may be developed as part of a battery of tests (e.g., the AAHPERD sports skills test batteries for tennis, softball, and basketball). Assume that a dribbling skill has been emphasized in a basketball class and that Mr. Masters, the teacher, is going to test the students on this skill. He finds a test that measures a combination of dribbling and shooting. This seems to be a legitimate basketball test, since the dribbling-shooting combination of skills occurs all the time in basketball. However, Mr. Masters reasons that a test measuring only dribbling would be more desirable. Using a test of dribbling alleviates any questions about interpreting the test score. It will reflect only dribbling ability. A test measuring both dribbling and shooting might yield a score that could have several interpretations. In another situation the dribbling-shooting combination test might be most appropriate. The test's appropriateness depends on the reason for using the test.

Perhaps after you have looked through the literature and have been unable to find a good, suitable test, you decide to develop your own test. The remainder of this chapter provides guidance in developing a test.

STEPS IN DEVELOPING A SPORTS SKILLS TEST

Be forewarned that test development is a lengthy process. Developing a good test takes, at best, several months. The following test-construction procedures are for a test of a sport skill such as the volleyball serve, baseball throw, or badminton short serve. Seven steps should be followed in developing this type of test:

1. Write the test objective.
2. Review the test literature.
3. Design the test.
4. Standardize test directions.
5. Administer the test on a pilot basis.
6. Determine validity and reliability.
7. Develop norms.

Obviously, following this process is not recommended, unless important decisions will be made on the basis of the test score and the test will be used on a regular basis. For simple testing during a class session (similar to a drill) where the test is used only in a practice setting and no major decision is made using the test score, strictly following these steps is not necessary. A quick-and-easy test can be developed for this purpose.

Let's construct a test of the tennis forehand groundstroke to illustrate the process of developing a sport skills test. Assume that Ms. Teasdale requires such a test to support her evaluation of students in an intermediate-level high-school recreational tennis class.

Test Objective

The first step in constructing a skills test is to write the objective(s) of the test. This process is not difficult, but it does require careful thought. Which critical elements of the skill have been emphasized in class? The test should be designed to measure these elements. During instruction of the skill Ms. Teasdale emphasized two components—the ability to accurately place the ball to the corner of the opponent's court with depth and velocity (i.e., speed of the ball). Therefore, the test should measure these components. Do not try to incorporate too many components of the skill in your objective. Remember that the test is supposed to measure each component. As the number of components increases, so does the complexity of the test. You may produce a test that is not practical for a school setting. A compromise is in order. Select only the most important components to be measured.

Review of Literature

After writing the test objective, review the test literature for the sport. Presumably you have already done this for the specific skill, since you would not develop a new test if a suitable one were already available. Familiarize yourself with tests of other skills used in the same sport, which may provide useful ideas for developing your own test. Review books and pamphlets on the sport written by experts, including successful teachers, coaches, and outstanding players. Their assessment of the important components of the skill you wish to test might be useful in designing the test. Journals might also be useful sources of tests. Three journals which occasionally publish tests are *Research Quarterly for Exercise and Sport, Journal of Physical Education, Recreation and Dance,* and *Journal of Teaching in Physical Education.* Textbooks dealing with measurement and evaluation in our field can provide additional information about available tests. See, for example, the list of sources for tests presented in Appendix D. In addition, several authors, including Strand and Wilson (1993), describe skills tests for a variety of sports and activities. For the purposes of this example, assume that Ms. Teasdale has reviewed the relevant literature on testing tennis skill and has determined that the Hewitt Tennis Achievement Test (see Chapter 19) can be adapted for use in her class.

Design of Test

Now Ms. Teasdale is ready to design the test. Each component of skill mentioned in the test objective should be measured in the test. For example, in the

Hewitt test a string is strung above the net to provide a rough estimate of velocity. Balls hit under the net and deep into the opponent's court must have sufficient velocity. Ms. Teasdale decides to place a string 2 feet above the net. To measure depth and accuracy of placement, Ms. Teasdale creates a target area similar to that shown in Figure 15-1. Note that higher point values are awarded to balls which land close to the baseline and in the corners. The test is designed so that the two components of the tennis forehand drive—velocity and accuracy with depth to the corners—are measured. Ms. Teasdale must determine ways of marking the court surface (e.g., chalk) so that the surface and permanent markings will not be damaged. She sets up the test and asks one or two students to try it. Their performance will help her decide if the test is too difficult or too easy. She makes the necessary modifications before proceeding to the next step. For example, when Ms. Teasdale administered her test to five volunteer students from her intermediate tennis class she discovered that no examinee was able to stroke the ball between the net and the string and hit a target area. She therefore raised the string to 3 feet above the net.

Standardization of Directions

Before administering the test, even on a trial basis, think through the instructions for administration of the test. These should be written as precisely as possible. Consistency in test administration is essential. Where should the examinee stand? How many practice trials are allowed? How many test trials does the test include? How will balls be delivered to the examinee, by the instructor or by a ball machine? What faults can occur during testing? How are the faults scored? The entire scoring process should be clearly delineated. For example,

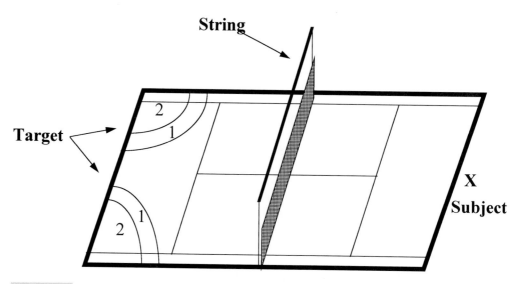

Figure 15-1   Court Markings for a Hypothetical Test of the Tennis Forehand Groundstroke.

Ms. Teasdale decided that after four warm-up attempts (two to each corner) each examinee should attempt 10 forehand drives (five consecutive attempts to each corner) from a position at the center of the baseline (the X marked on Figure 15-1). Balls were delivered at 7-second intervals by a ball machine set on medium speed such that balls traveled 3.5 feet above the net and landed 5 feet in front of the examinee. On each trial an accuracy score and a velocity score were recorded. For the velocity component a score of 2 was awarded if the ball traveled between the string and the net, while zero was recorded if the ball went over the string.

The accuracy component was scored according to where in the target area a ball landed. Balls that landed on a line received the score for the higher of the two target areas. Ms. Teasdale decided to record the sum of the 10 velocity scores and the sum of the 10 target scores separately to provide an indication of examinee proficiency in each of the two components.

Administration of Test

Try the test out first in a pilot study. Use your own students, if you wish, or a group that is similar to ones you will be testing in the future. This will allow you to work out any problems in advance of the actual testing. Although a test may appear to be straightforward and easy to administer, it may have deficiencies that do not show up until the test is administered to a group of examinees. The larger the number of students you can test, the better. If possible, administer the test to the same group of students on two different days (especially if your test consists of only one trial). This will allow you to estimate the test-retest reliability of the test. Be sure to follow the test instructions closely. Ms. Teasdale administered the test to the 20 students in her intermediate tennis class on Monday and again on Wednesday. As a result of the pilot study she discovered that the ball machine did not provide consistent velocity for more than 10 students. She therefore needed to reset the machine after groups of 10 examinees.

Validity and Reliability

The next step in test development is to provide evidence for the validity and reliability of the test. (The procedures recommended in this section are described in detail in Chapters 6 and 7. Refer to these chapters for additional information and examples.)

If the test is designed so that it measures each component of skill in the test objective, logical validity can be claimed for the test. However, this does not mean your test objective cannot be questioned by others. Maybe an important component of the skill was omitted from the test objective or a component is not necessary to include in the test. It could be argued that examinee form in executing a forehand drive is an important consideration and should be included in the test or that velocity is not a critical component in high-school recreational tennis classes and thus should be omitted. Your test objectives, then, must not only lead to a practical test but also should include the components that others would agree are essential. Since you are developing this test for the objectives of your school system or sports club only, you may think this does not matter. However, the basic **components of a skill** ought to be taught, and the objective should be rewritten to ensure that this actually happens. Establishing evidence of logical validity is essential in developing a test, either norm-referenced or criterion-referenced.

To provide evidence for logical validity, Ms. Teasdale gave a description of her test and a statement of the test's objectives to the school tennis coach.

She asked the coach to judge if the test measured the components of skill (i.e., velocity and depth or accuracy) stated in the test objective. She also asked the coach to judge if she had omitted any important components, included unimportant components, or had overemphasized or underemphasized components of the tennis forehand drive for intermediate-level tennis players in a high-school recreational tennis class. The tennis coach responded that the test description matched the stated test objectives; however, the velocity component was overemphasized. Because the velocity component was scored separately, Ms. Teasdale decided to maintain her scoring system.

Establishing concurrent validity as well as logical validity is useful if you are developing a norm-referenced test. To determine concurrent validity, the test scores are correlated with scores on a criterion test. For sport skills tests judges' ratings of skill are commonly used as the criterion test. Sometimes a measure of playing ability (e.g., ratings in a game setting or tournament ranking) is used as the criterion test for a test of skill. This is not a desirable criterion measure. Not surprisingly, the validity coefficients that result from this method of test development are often low.

Evidence of statistical validity is determined by correlating scores on the test being developed with criterion test scores. The higher the validity coefficient, the greater the validity of the test. The familiar Pearson product-moment correlation procedure is used to calculate the validity coefficient. The establishment of concurrent validity, while not always essential, is highly desirable, since it provides strong supportive evidence of test validity.

To provide evidence for concurrent validity, Ms. Teasdale asked the tennis coach to watch each of the 20 students in her class and rate them on their ability to execute the forehand drive. She provided the coach with a short rating form for this purpose so that there was agreement on the appropriate elements of skill to be evaluated. After the coach submitted his ratings, Ms. Teasdale administered her new forehand drive field test to each student. The Pearson correlation between the field test accuracy score and the coach's ratings was .85 ($r^2 = .72$) indicating an acceptable degree of concurrent validity. However, the concurrent validity coefficient for the velocity score was .60 ($r^2 = .36$) indicating that velocity may be a questionable element of skill for intermediate high-school recreational tennis players.

Next, the reliability of the test should be established. If you were able to administer the test twice, a test-retest reliability coefficient can be calculated using the intraclass correlation ($R_{xx'}$) (see Chapter 6). In addition, if your test consists of more than one trial, the internal consistency among trials can be calculated using the intraclass method.

To provide evidence for the test-retest reliability of the forehand drive test, Ms. Teasdale retested her students 2 days after the initial test. An intraclass coefficient of .91 for the accuracy score and .89 for the velocity score indicated a high degree of consistency across days.

Revise the Test

If the reliability, validity, or objectivity of the test is not satisfactory, it should be revised. Validity can be enhanced by developing a closer match between the components measured by the test and the ones identified in the test objective. Or, the criterion test might include extraneous elements. If so, a criterion test including the important components of skill should be sought. Reliability can be increased by increasing the number of trials or simplifying the test so that it is less affected by outside elements. Objectivity can be improved by simplifying the scoring system. If a subjective measurement is used, the rating scale might be scaled down so that it is more manageable. Or, the rater(s) might be trained more carefully.

After reviewing the evidence for validity and reliability, Ms. Teasdale decided to retain the velocity score even though the concurrent validity coefficient was low. The low coefficient for the velocity score may have been due to extraneous elements in the coach's ratings. Ms. Teasdale decided to reexamine the concurrent validity of the velocity component at a future date using the average score from the ratings of three independent judges.

Development of Norms

If the test is to be used as a norm-referenced measure, developing a table of norms is desirable. (The calculation of both percentiles and T-scores is described in Chapters 2 and 3.) A simple method for developing a table of T-scores is the constant-value method, which is described in Chapter 3. Test scores for several hundred students are needed for each table. That amount of test data may not be available from your pilot testing, but test scores for a year or two can be accumulated, if necessary. Developing separate norms for boys and girls may be necessary, depending on the nature of the particular skill. A federal law mandates that, when appropriate, separate performance standards must be set for boys and for girls.

DEVELOPMENT OF A BATTERY OF SKILLS TESTS

Often a battery of skills tests is developed to measure the most important skills in a sport. A good example of this type of **test battery** is the basketball skills test series (Hopkins et al., 1984) published by AAHPERD. (See Chapter 19; see also the hypothetical softball test battery described by Mood, 1980, and the battery of defensive softball skills tests of Shick, 1970.) Developing the individual tests in a battery is no different from the method described in the previous section. However, the validity is determined, in part, on logical grounds. A good, strong rationale should be presented for the inclusion of a specific set of skills in the battery. This logical appraisal can be substantiated using a statistical procedure known as factor analysis. Statistical validity can also be determined by comparing the combined tests with a criterion test of playing ability. This is beyond the scope of this book, since a multiple correlation coefficient must be calculated to estimate validity. The reliability of the test battery should also be estimated, but the appropriate procedures are also beyond the scope of this book, since they require knowledge of multivariate statistics.

DEVELOPMENT OF RATING SCALES AND CHECKLISTS

Observational analysis using checklists and rating scales is frequently used in the physical education field to measure skills that are difficult to measure in the more traditional manner. In contrast to the traditional motor skills tests, observational analysis tends to be subjective, measures process rather than product, and is relatively easy to use in a wide variety of settings (Hensley et al., 1990).

Checklists

Checklists are used to determine the presence or absence of critical elements during execution of a specific skill. They are commonly used to assess developmental stages of basic movement patterns such as walking, hopping, skipping, and throwing. However, checklists can be developed for assessing performance of the critical elements of more complex sport skills such as basketball shooting ability (Figure 15-2). Factors to consider when developing and using checklists are

1. The critical elements assessed by the checklist should reflect those critical elements stated in course objectives and delivered through instruction.
2. Each student should be observed on several occasions to ensure that poor performance is not due to external factors such as illness, injury, or having an "off day."
3. To maximize performance, students should be aware of the critical elements being examined.

Rating Scales

Rating scales (Figure 15-3) are similar to checklists. However, rating scales assess the degree to which specified elements of skill have been mastered, rather than simply the presence or absence of critical elements. Rating scales can be used to assess a specific sport skill such as the volleyball spike or more general characteristics such as volleyball playing ability. Like checklists, rating scales are usually associated with subjective measurement. They must be care-

Basketball 101 Shooting Checklist

Name: Sue Beck

Critical Elements	10/12/95	12/3/95
Body square with basket	✓	✓
Cradles ball on fingers of shooting hand with fingers spread		✓
Correct placement of non-shooting hand on ball	✓	✓
Shooting elbow near the body		✓
Bends knees and uses legs	✓	✓
Uses complete follow-through		✓

Figure 15-2   Sample Checklist for Basketball Shooting Skill.

fully developed so that the examinee clearly understands the basis of the ratings. For instance, suppose Ms. Miller, a physical education teacher, decides to measure her students' playing ability in badminton. She observes each of them as they play games and uses the following scale to rate them:

5 = Excellent
4 = Good
3 = Average
2 = Fair
1 = Poor

The problem with this scale is that no one except Ms. Miller knows what she means by "excellent," "good," and so forth, and perhaps Ms. Miller does not have a clear distinction between ratings. If John received a 4 and Mary a 5, in what way was John's performance inferior to Mary's? In an educational setting, test scores should have meaning to students as well as teachers. Granted, ex-

---

RATING SCALE FOR BADMINTON SHORT SERVE

5 = No faults*; serve close to net; serve close to short service line; placement appropriate for opponent's weaknesses or position

4 = No faults*; serve close to short service line; no evidence of placement

3 = No faults*; serve either close to net or close to short service line; no apparent placement†

2 = No faults*; serve neither close to net nor close to short service line; no apparent placement†

1 = One or more faults; serve neither close to net nor close to short service line; no apparent placement†

If one or more faults occur, lower the score by 1 point.
† If placement is considered satisfactory, raise the score by 1 point.

pecting a rating scale to incorporate every aspect of the ability being rated is unreasonable, but general descriptors should certainly be written for each category.

Review the rating scale for the badminton short serve, as shown in the boxed material above. A rating of 5, which could still be viewed as excellent, now has specific meaning to the player. A student receiving a rating of 4 knows that his or her ability to place the serve needs more work. Sometimes it is not possible to be this specific in rating more general abilities, since a combination of factors must be considered. However, if a rater is able to judge the examinee's ability by taking these factors into account, it should be possible to write descriptors for each rating used in the scale.

Rating scales do not necessarily have to be complex and elaborate. In beginning badminton a teacher may have few expectations of the student in a game setting, especially if the unit of instruction is short. However, the teacher has every right to expect the student to meet these expectations; thus, a rating scale could be devised to measure the aspects of playing ability deemed important. Figure 15-3 presents a rating scale for volleyball playing ability. This type of rating scale would be fairly simple to develop and use, and the players would know what is expected of them.

Of course, a rating scale, no matter how well developed, must be used by one or more raters. This introduces an element of subjectivity into the measurement process. However, subjectivity can be reduced by practicing the use of a rating scale before using it in an actual testing setting. If more than one rater is used, the ratings should be compared in a practice setting before actual testing. In Chapter 6 some of the problems associated with the use of rating skills and abilities in diving and gymnastics are discussed, along with procedures for determining the objectivity of raters.

Volleyball 101 Rating Scale

Name: _____

Date: _____

Scale Description:

5 points - Exceptional ability for the age and gender of the student
4 points - Above average ability for the age and gender of the student
3 points - Average ability for the age and gender of the student
2 points - Below average ability for the age and gender of the student
1 point - Inferior ability, far below average for a typical student

---

Critical Elements:

1.   Spiking
     a.   Approach   5 4 3 2 1
     b.   Jump   5 4 3 2 1
     c.   Spike placement   5 4 3 2 1

2.   Serve
     a.   Accuracy   5 4 3 2 1
     b.   Difficulty of return 5 4 3 2 1

3.   Passing
     a.   Proper use of hands   5 4 3 2 1
     b.   Accuracy   5 4 3 2 1

4.   Team Play
     a.   Hustle   5 4 3 2 1
     b.   Teamwork   5 4 3 2 1

                     TOTAL SCORE _____

Figure 15-3   Sample Rating Scale for Volleyball Playing Ability.

Rating scales constitute an important approach to measurement in the physical education field, especially when the form used by the participant in executing a skill is of primary concern. This is probably the most abused testing procedure in physical education because it can be misused so easily. If the scale is too subjective, the rating might be influenced by factors totally unrelated to the examinee's skill. For example, teachers have been known to be influenced in their ratings by students' personalities. Judges at Olympic events may modify their ratings depending on the nationality of the performer. However, rating scales should not be avoided; a properly developed and carefully used scale can be a valuable measurement tool.

To summarize, the following steps should be followed in developing a rating scale:

1. *Determine the purpose of the scale.* Why is the rating scale needed? A variety of reasons for measuring motor performance were delineated in Chapter 1, such as motivation, diagnosis of weaknesses, and grading. How important is the decision that will be made on the basis of the rating scale? If the decision is important, the rating scale should consist of at least five categories. Perhaps the scale is to be used to assess progress at one stage of learning, and the decision is not as major. Then a rating scale with three categories might suffice. Some attributes are well suited to a checklist. If a child is asked to demonstrate the ability to balance on two body parts in eight or more different combinations, a checklist might be adequate. However, if the quality of the balance is important, additional categories would probably be more suitable.

2. *Identify the most important components of the motor task.* It is rarely possible to rate every aspect of a sport skill, movement pattern, or some other motor task. This difficulty is magnified when attempting to rate overall performance, such as playing ability in a game. First, the most important skills in the sport should be identified. This is not an easy task, as the measurement of all skills in the game would be prohibitive. In basketball, for example, a long list of skills and combinations of skills could be generated, including passing, dribbling, shooting, defensive skills, and so forth. Subcategories of the rating scale might be developed for the skills identified as most important. Other aspects of the game, such as use of strategy, might form a separate subcategory.

   Even with the breakdown into subcategories, the rating scale will be rather general. Consider that each subcategory can be broken down even further by identifying the types of passes or shots emphasized most during the unit. The level of specificity of the scale depends on the purpose of the scale. In a school setting, it is difficult to use a rating scale with many subcategories owing to time constraints. A researcher, on the other hand, might videotape a performance and use a complicated rating scale to evaluate it.

3. *Weight the components to be rated.* All components of skill or playing ability may not be of equal importance. In badminton, the serves and the overhead

clear might be emphasized more than the drop shot. If so, the rating for the first two skills should be weighted more heavily than the last. One way of accomplishing this is to multiply the ratings of the serves and clear by 2 and the rating of the drop shot by 1. Another possibility is to assign higher values to the rating scale for the serves and the clear. In gymnastics and diving competition, the ratings of events are routinely weighted, although with much greater precision than in the examples given above.

4. *Identify the number of categories.* Several factors affect the selection of the number of categories in the rating scale. One is the importance of the decision to be made based on the scale. Another is the complexity of the skill or ability to be rated. A simple skill might be rated with fewer categories than a complex ability. However, it is difficult for a rater to effectively use more than seven or eight categories, especially in a practical setting. If a teacher wishes to rate all his/her students on their playing ability in basketball, the use of a large number of categories would not be feasible. This difficulty has sometimes led to the use of simplified (earlier identified as weak) versions of the rating scale that provide little or no information to the user or the examinee. Simply using good, average, fair, and poor (for example) with no descriptors provided for each category is poor practice. Rating scales are valuable methods of describing performance, but only if the ratings can be interpreted clearly. Why did one examinee receive a lower rating on shooting than another? This should be evident from the rating scale and its descriptors.

5. *Identify numerical values for the scale.* Although qualitative data are useful in some situations, it is often more convenient to assign a numerical value to each scale point. Then the scores can be analyzed descriptively. In Chapter 14, a variety of rating scales are described.

6. *Develop a rating sheet.* Development of the rating sheet is an extremely important step in preparing to use the rating scale. The rating sheet should be designed so that the rater can record ratings in the simplest possible way. A checklist in which the checks can later be converted to numerical scores is often the most practical version. A good rating sheet is clearly laid out and simple to use. The descriptors of each category should be printed on the rating sheet as an aid to the rater.

7. *Prepare raters.* Often, at least in practical settings, only one rater is available. The rater should practice using the scale on several occasions before using it in an actual rating situation. This will allow him or her to develop a consistent pattern of rating prior to the actual setting. Otherwise, the rater may be easier or harder on the first few examinees than on later examinees, resulting in a lack of objectivity in using the scale. When more than one rater will be used, the raters should use the scale in a practice setting and compare their ratings periodically. If there are discrepancies in the ratings, the raters should discuss the problems and continue practicing until reasonable agreement is attained. High levels of agreement between raters are expected for high levels of competition as well as in a research setting.

After the rating scale has been developed and used in an actual setting, information about the ratings should be conveyed to the examinees and other persons concerned. The results should be linked to the purpose of the scale, and the information should be analyzed and reported in a meaningful way.

OTHER APPROACHES TO MEASURING SKILL

Sometimes tournament rankings are used as an indicator of specific skills or playing ability in a sport. This is a much weaker measure than a well-developed rating scale. Tournament play incorporates not only skills and abilities but also elements of competition and dance factors that may not be of greatest concern in an educational setting. Note that the suggestions for a rating scale of playing ability in badminton described in the previous section did not take into account who won the game. Of primary interest was the student's ability to employ basic game strategy, even if this resulted in losing the game. At more advanced levels of skill, a rating scale may incorporate a won-loss component, but this would not be recommended as the sole indicator of playing ability. Tournaments in an educational setting should be educational, not simulations of the competitive circuit. **Game statistics** can also be used to supplement the rating of playing ability. If desired, this can be done at a very simplistic level. With the increasing popularity of microcomputers a student or teacher who is a computer buff could easily computerize a system for recording and summarizing data during a game that would make this type of data gathering much more feasible for the average physical educator. Simple microcomputer programs to record and summarize game statistics can be purchased from several commercial firms. Much more sophisticated systems are being developed for the coach. In addition to gathering game statistics, microcomputer programs are being written to assist coaches in making decisions by calculating the probability of success of a play after a specified sequence of events has occurred.

SPORT PROFILES

Assessment of sport performance is a difficult task. Yet, teachers are often required to assess student performance in a particular sport such as tennis. The complexity of sport performance, the questionable validity of sport skills tests, and the time required to administer sport skills tests complicate the assessment process (Hensley et al., 1990). A **sport profile** is an administrative tool for recording those components deemed necessary for successful performance in a sport. Sport profiles provide a list of the assessment instruments used to evaluate sport performance, a graphical profile of a student's performance relative to the rest of the class, and a composite score which indicates overall performance. Note that the assessment instruments should reflect the instructional objectives of the class. Figure 15-4 presents a sport profile for an intermediate basketball class. Note that raw scores are converted to T-scores for each test and then

Sport Profile for Basketball 101

	Test Score	20	30	40	50(AVG)	60	70	80	T-Score	Weight	Total
Name: John Doe											
Class: Basketball 101											
Date: 6/4/95											
Knowledge Tests											
Rules	20				x				50	1	50
Offensive Strategy	12			x					40	1	40
Defensive Strategy	25						x		70	1	70
Skills Tests											
Dribbling	10						x		70	2	140
Passing	23							x	80	2	160
Jump Shot	34							x	80	2	160
Foul Shot	21					x			60	2	120
Rebounding	12						x		70	2	140
								SUM		13	880
								Average			67.69

Figure 15-4   Sample Sport Profile for an Intermediate Basketball Class.

plotted to provide a profile for overall performance. T-scores for each test can be weighted and a composite score (the average T-score) computed. Use of an electronic spreadsheet greatly facilitates construction of sport profiles. Hensley et al. (1990, p. 44) list the following advantages of sport profiles:

1. Consistency between instructional objectives and student evaluation
2. A method for combining measurements for different evaluation components
3. A score that can be used to calculate unit grades
4. A cumulative student record for the instructor
5. Specific feedback for student and instructor concerning performance on each evaluation component.

SUMMARY

Test development is a time-consuming process. Whenever possible, a test should be selected from the existing test literature. If an appropriate test cannot be found, use the seven-step approach to develop the desired test. These steps include identifying the test objective, reviewing the test literature, designing the test, standardizing directions, administering the test on a pilot basis, determining test validity and reliability, and developing norms. As an alternative to traditional tests of sport skill, observational analysis using rating scales and checklists is also described. Finally, the construction and use of sport profiles is advocated as an administrative recording device for assessing sport performance.

Learning Experiences

1. Select your favorite sport. Choose one skill in this sport and review the literature to examine tests of this skill. Write an analysis of one of these tests. Is the test objective acceptable? Is the test valid? Reliable? Discuss ways in which the test could be improved.

2. Identify a sport skill for which no test is available. Carry out steps 1 through 4 of the process recommended for the development of a skill test. Also, discuss how validity and reliability could be determined. This can be done either as an individual or as a group project. If a group project is chosen, all members of the group should review the test literature.

3. Draw three targets that could be used to measure the accuracy of a volleyball serve. The first target should be drawn so that a beginner, at the end of a course, could hit it and obtain a high score. Do not oversimplify, however. The second target should be of medium difficulty and the third, very difficult (but not so difficult that even highly skilled volleyball players could not obtain a high score). Include the dimensions of each target in feet and inches. Describe the elements of targets 2 and 3, and discuss how these elements increase the difficulty level of the targets. Explain when you would use each of these three targets. Describe each situation specifically.

4. Choose a sport and (a) develop a checklist for a specific skill within the sport, (b) a rating scale for playing ability in the sport, and (c) a sport profile for a unit of instruction.

References

Collins DR, Hodges PB. 1978. A comprehensive guide to sports skills tests and measurement. Springfield, Ill: Thomas.

Hensley LD, Morrow JR, East WB. 1990. Practical measurement to solve practical problems. Journal of Physical Education, Recreation and Dance, **61**(3):42−44.

Hopkins DR, Shick J, Plack JJ. 1984. Basketball for boys and girls: skills test manual. Reston, Va: American Alliance for Health, Physical Education, Recreation, and Dance. [*Note:* This is a revision of one of the AAHPERD skills test series. Test manuals are also available for other sports; see Chapter 19.]

Mood DP. 1980. Numbers in motion. Palo Alto, Calif: Mayfield.

Shick J. 1970. Battery of defensive softball skills tests for college women. Research Quarterly, **41**:82−87.

Strand BN, Wilson R. (1993). Assessing sport skills. Champaign, Ill: Human Kinetics.

Annotated Readings

Bobo M, Bushong J. 1978. Skill testing—a positive step toward interpreting secondary school physical education. Journal of Physical Education and Recreation, **49**(1):45.

Discusses students' need for meaningful feedback from skills testing; stresses the importance of using valid and reliable skills tests to develop a positive attitude among students toward physical education; lists steps that can be taken by a teacher to provide functional, reliable, and enjoyable skills tests; recommends use of individual school norms for these tests.

Brown EW. 1982. Visual evaluation techniques for skill analysis. Journal of Physical Education, Recreation, and Dance, **53**(1):21–26,29.
Describes visual evaluation techniques for observing physical skills; techniques are grouped into five categories—vantage point, movement simplification, balance and stability, movement relationships, and range of movement; provides examples of the technique applied to the tennis serve, a wrestling takedown, batting, soccer instep kick, and other skills.

Davis MW, Hopkins VL. 1979. Improving evaluation of physical fitness and sport skill performance. Journal of Physical Education and Recreation, **50**(5):76–78.
Describes problems of evaluating student performance in physical education; stresses importance of improving performance in a variety of sports skills and physical fitness; recommends using profiles for feedback to students and parents; includes graphic example of a tennis student's profile representing performance on tests of skill in tennis.

Hensley LD. 1983. Biomechanical analysis. Journal of Physical Education, Recreation, and Dance, **54**(8):21–23.
Demonstrates how a rating scale can be developed through a biomechanical analysis; uses basic process evaluation techniques to identify the underlying components of a movement; presents an example of a kinesiogram, a biomechanical profile analysis.

Strand BN, Wilson R. 1993. Assessing sport skills. Champaign, Ill: Human Kinetics.
Includes description of 379 tests of 29 sports and activities; provides information on how to choose the appropriate test, proper testing procedures, and tables and diagrams.

Constructing Knowledge Tests

KEY WORDS

Watch for these words as you read the following chapter

Correction for guessing
Essay item
Halo effect
Index of discrimination
Item analysis

Item difficulty
Item function
Matching item
Multiple-choice item
Short-answer item
Table of specifications
True-false item

The motor performance and exercise behavior of an individual is often of primary concern to physical educators and exercise scientists; therefore, the major portion of this textbook is devoted to the measurement of various forms of sport and physical activity. However, educators also teach people the principles underlying the efficient use of their bodies as well as a knowledge of the relationship of physical activity to health and well-being. Educators teach rules that must be learned in order to participate in a sport, steps to be followed in carrying out lifesaving skills, and game strategies. Students are expected to learn these rules, skills, and strategies. It is hoped that clients in fitness clubs will do more than participate in physical activity—that they will learn more about the short-term and long-term effects of exercise and the scientific principles on which an exercise prescription is based. In private sports clubs members should be taught principles of conditioning for a specific sport as well as skills and rules. Thus, there is a need to develop and use knowledge tests. If knowledge tests are administered in a private club, they are often used in a self-testing capacity. However, in either setting, a knowledge test is a good way to reinforce learning.

In this chapter the development of various types of written test items is described. Items may be generated for norm-referenced or criterion-referenced tests (Roid, 1984). Most likely, you will have taken tests exemplifying all these types of items, so you will be familiar with them. As you might recall from the discussion of content validity in Chapter 6, developing a knowledge test must be undertaken in as careful a manner as any other type of test. A list of sources of physical education written tests can be found in Johnson and Nelson (1986). The best source of test items for various sports and other forms of physical activity is the book prepared by McGee and Farrow (1987).

TABLE OF SPECIFICATIONS

The first step in devising any type of knowledge test is to develop a **table of specifications,** in which the basic categories of knowledge are identified and a decision is made as to the relative importance of each. Without this plan the efforts of the test writer tend to be haphazard. Deciding how many items should be included to test memorization of facts and application of facts is also a good idea. The table of specifications is then set up as described in Chapter 6. The relative importance of each category is reflected in its weighting, which dictates the number of items to be written for the category. For example, in an exercise class the scientific principles of exercise might be viewed as twice as important as knowledge of basic exercise prescriptions. If so, twice as many items should be written on principles. In a basketball class rules may be more important or less important than knowledge of game strategies; the number of items should be adjusted accordingly.

Of course, other factors affect the length of the test. For example, an examinee should be able to answer the total number of items in the time available for testing. As a general rule of thumb, allow 45 seconds for each multiple-choice item and 30 seconds for each true-false item. However, practical experience with the test provides more definitive feedback on test length.

TEST ADMINISTRATION

The directions for test administration should be clearly stated. The most desirable method of presenting test directions is to print them on the test itself, which enables the test taker to read and reread them. At the beginning of the testing period, these directions should be read aloud by the administrator, since it is well known that some examinees do not read directions carefully. The following example of directions might be used for a written test:

DIRECTIONS: Read the following directions carefully before beginning the test. This is a six-page test consisting of 35 multiple-choice items. Be sure your test contains six pages and that all pages are in correct sequence. Circle the response that represents the best

Testing Knowledge in Physical Education and Exercise Science.

answer to the question or lead statement. Only one answer is correct for each item. Each item counts two points. Write your name at the top of this page and begin the test.

The administrator should also inform the examinee if a correction for guessing will be used. (The concept of correcting for guessing is explained later in this chapter.) The student should be notified if guessing will be penalized.

The test taker's attention should be called to anything else that will help him or her to interpret the test. For example, how much time will be allowed for the test? At periodic intervals the examinee should be informed of the amount of time remaining. Are there multiple pages of the test? If so, the group should be asked to count the number of pages to be sure no page is missing or blank. Are certain sections of the test weighted more heavily than others? If so, note this at the beginning of the test period so that the examinee can allocate time wisely. The number of points allocated to each section should also be printed on the test.

With the widespread availability of microcomputers, developing tests is easier using a test writer program. A number of these types of programs can now be purchased (see Chapter 5). Items are entered into the computer and then printed. Modification of test items is then a simple matter. Sometimes a test user might not realize an item is poor until it has been used once; thus the item must be either revised or discarded. This can be done by changing that item on the computer without retyping the whole test. Sometimes an educator does not teach every concept covered in the previous year's unit, so last year's tests may be inadequate this year. The items not covered can be eliminated on the computer, and a new version of the test can be printed. Better yet, a bank of items can be entered, and specific items can be requested. A random sample of items can also be drawn from each category of items (with the number of items designated by the teacher) that is different for each student's test. In other words, if the test is being administered to 20 people, 20 different versions of the test could be randomly generated. This facilitates monitoring an examination in a school setting, since copying someone else's answer to a different examination makes no sense.

The administration of a test, then, requires careful consideration before the actual testing period. Educators are primarily interested in how well the test taker can deal with the content of the test and not in the trappings of the test.

TYPES OF TEST ITEMS

Five types of knowledge test items are commonly used: true-false, multiple-choice, matching, short-answer, and essay. Generally the multiple-choice items are the hardest to write, since a number of choices must be prepared for each item. However, they are easy to score. The essay item, on the other hand, is often considered easy to write, yet it is difficult to grade because of the subjective nature of the test response. A review of each type follows.

True-False

Since the **true-false item** consists of a single statement, it seems relatively easy to write. It is a familiar type of test item and is widely used. Although there are several variations of the true-false item, none is appreciably different from the standard true-false version. Examples of several of these versions are presented in the boxed material. The correction variety, last in the box on p. 424, requires the test taker to correct the statement, with the correction limited to the underlined word(s).

The true-false item has been criticized in the past for several reasons. First, some teachers have developed true-false tests by merely taking complete sentences out of a textbook, either leaving them as they are or changing one or two words. This, of course, encourages students to study for these types of test by memorizing portions of the textbook, causing some to think that the true-false test has become associated with the lowest level of cognitive behavior (memorization). However, well-written test items can tap higher levels of cognitive behavior. (Refer to Chapter 8 for more information on levels of cognitive behavior.) Second, the true-false item is often ambiguous, since, with no standard of comparison, it must be judged in isolation. It must be clearly true or clearly false, rather than subject to multiple interpretations. A carefully written item leaves little or no room for ambiguity. A third objection to the true-false item is that it is less reliable than the multiple-choice item. However, more true-false items than multiple-choice items can be answered during a given time period. By increasing the number of true-false items, the reliability of the total test is improved.

Critics of the true-false test item often note that an examinee could receive a good score merely by guessing the answer. By guessing on every item, there is a

---

SAMPLES OF TRUE-FALSE ITEMS

THE TRUE-FALSE VARIETY
The mean is a measure of central tendency.   **T**   **F**

THE RIGHT-WRONG VARIETY
When aiming in field archery, the correct anchor point for the hand is
directly under the chin.   **R**   **W**

THE YES-NO VARIETY
Is "dunking" the ball legal in college basketball?   **Y**   **N**

THE CLUSTER VARIETY
A badminton serve that lands in the proper court is legal when the
shuttlecock is hit:

T   **F**   1. By the frame of the racket
T   **F**   2. Above the racket hand
T   **F**   3. Below the waist
T   **F**   4. While on one foot

THE CORRECTION VARIETY
The skill with which a tennis serve is executed can be measured by
determining the *accuracy* of the serve. (accuracy and force)

---

fifty-fifty chance of answering each item correctly. However, it is not likely that many test takers actually guess blindly on all questions. Think of your own test-taking behavior. You may not be certain you know the correct answer, but you can frequently take an educated guess. Based on your overall knowledge of the test content, you may make a plausible response, although you are not sure it is correct. Thus the probability of answering correctly is no longer fifty-fifty. Although a correction for guessing can be applied, as you will see later, it may not be desirable.

Suggestions for Writing True-False Items

As noted earlier, the process of writing a true-false item can seem deceptively simple. In reality, it is one of the more difficult items to write well. The following list summarizes a number of suggestions for writing good true-false items:

1. Avoid trivial items. Write items that measure meaningful content and that require application of concepts. Consider, for example, the following item from a volleyball test written for beginning players at the high-school level:

   T   F   The dimensions of a volleyball court are 20 feet by 50 feet. (F)

   How important is this content for a beginning volleyball player in a high-school physical education class? It is questionable whether a student at this level of skill needs to know this information at all. Of far greater value would be items dealing with skill execution and rules of the game, along with simple game strategies.

2. Avoid using sentences from textbooks or stereotyped phrases as items.
3. Avoid ambiguity.
4. Include an equal number of true and false items, or more false than true. (The tendency in constructing true-false tests is to include more true items than false, yet evidence shows that examinees tend to mark an item true when uncertain of the correct answer. False items discriminate better than true ones.)
5. Reorder the test items randomly after completing all of them. Otherwise, you might generate a pattern of responses that can be detected by the test-wise student.
6. Express only a single idea in each item statement. Examine, as an example, the following item from a badminton test:

> T   F   A serve is illegal if the shuttlecock touches the net before landing in the proper court or if the server steps over the service line.

This item refers to two rules affecting service. The first rule is false and the second is true. How should the test taker respond? This item should be divided into two separate items, so that a clear-cut, correct response is possible for each one.

7. Avoid negative statements. If an occasional item lends itself to the negative form, underline the negative term(s) in the statement. Consider the following example:

> T   F   The Kraus-Weber Test is no longer viewed as a valid test of the physical fitness of schoolchildren. (T)

In this case the negative form is justifiable because it accurately reflects a change in the way the test has been interpreted over the past 30 years. It was accepted (although erroneously) as a valid test of fitness for children, but now the test is correctly interpreted as a test of minimum strength associated with the absence of low back pain.

8. Avoid the use of words such as "sometimes," "usually," and "often" in true statements, and "always," "never," and "impossible" in false statements.
9. Make false statements plausible.
10. Make true statements clearly true.

Multiple-Choice

The **multiple-choice item** contains a stem—an introductory question or incomplete statement—and a set of alternatives—or suggested options, sometimes referred to as foils. The correct alternative is referred to as the answer; the incorrect alternatives are called distractors. Several varieties of the multiple-choice item are shown in the boxed material on p. 426. In the correct-answer variety only one alternative is correct. More than one answer is correct, but one answer is better than the other in the best-answer variety. In the multiple-answer variety more than one answer may be correct.

SAMPLES OF MULTIPLE CHOICE ITEMS

THE CORRECT-ANSWER VARIETY

When a fencer attacks to the high left side of an opponent's target area, the appropriate defensive action is

a. Parry 2   c. Parry 6
b. Parry 4   d. Parry 8

(b)

THE BEST-ANSWER VARIETY

To develop skill in shooting a basketball from a given distance, a player must learn to reproduce the correct

a. Vertical angle of projection   c. Trajectory
b. Horizontal angle of projection   d. Velocity

(c)

THE MULTIPLE-ANSWER VARIETY

The reliability of a written test can be raised by increasing the

a. Range of ability   c. Number being tested
b. Length of the test   d. Level of ability

(a,b)

The Stem

The stem is written either as a direct question or as an incomplete sentence. Usually the incomplete sentence consists of fewer words than the direct question and thus is more economical. However, the direct question is often easier to use effectively. When the stem is an incomplete sentence, each alternative must be written to conform satisfactorily to the stem. When the stem is a direct question, the task iş simplified somewhat because the alternatives are written only to conform with one another.

The stem should present the problem clearly and briefly. Be aware that if the stem is too long, the test taker may forget what he or she has read by the time the alternatives are reached. On the other hand, do not be so brief that no message is conveyed, as in the following:

Conscious relaxation is . . .

An exact, more meaningful statement follows:

The major characteristic of conscious relaxation is . . .

As is true with true-false statements, stereotyped phrases should be avoided. Generally, the stem should be written in the positive, not the negative, form.

The Alternatives

Usually between three and five alternatives are written for a multiple-choice item. Using the same number of alternatives with all items is not absolutely necessary. Writing five alternatives might be easy for one test item but difficult for another. Developing fewer, well-written alternatives is better than adding one or two poorly written ones for the sake of generating a predetermined number of alternatives for each item. As the number of alternatives increases, the reliability of the item increases and the chance level for getting an answer correct is reduced. Regardless of the number of alternatives used, plan to spend considerable time writing good ones.

Some test users find the distractors harder to write than the correct answer. It is only logical that the distractors should seem plausible to the test taker. One way of generating ideas about possible distractors is to administer a set of open-ended questions to a group similar to those who will be tested. There will, of course, be a number of correct answers, but there will also be a variety of incorrect responses. These can be used as a basis for developing good distractors.

The distractors should be parallel in grammatical form and of the same approximate length. Note the length of the alternatives in the following item from an archery knowledge test:

How may arrows are shot in a Columbia Round?
a. 12   c. 36
b. 24 at 50, 40, and 30 yards   d. 48

The difference in the length of *b* compared with the other three alternatives suggests that it might be the correct answer, which it is. The general format of all four alternatives should conform. Furthermore, the smallest and largest number of arrows in *a* and *d* do not appear to be as plausible as *b* and *c* are. A better version of this item follows:

How many arrows are shot in a Columbia Round?
a. 24 at 40, 30, and 20 yards   c. 36 at 40, 30, and 20 yards
b. 24 at 50, 40, and 30 yards   d. 36 at 50, 40, and 30 yards

As is true with true-false items, words such as "always" and "never" should be avoided. "None of the above" and "All of the above" should be used sparingly as distractors and not used as substitutes for the alternative that is difficult to write.

Be sure that no pattern to the correct responses exists. Sometimes a patterning occurs even though the test writer is unaware of it. An easy way to prevent this occurrence is to order the alternatives randomly. If an item has four alternatives, drop slips of paper numbered 1 through 4 into a container, and draw them out one by one. This represents the random ordering of the alternatives.

Multiple-choice items, like any other type of item, can easily be written in an ambiguous way. The only way ambiguity can be reduced is by writing and rewriting the item until there is a general agreement on the interpretation of the item and the feasibility of the alternatives.

Matching

A **matching item** consists of two columns of words or phrases, with the column on the right containing the alternatives. The examinee is instructed to select an alternative from the right column that corresponds with an item in the left column. Two examples of matching questions are given in the boxed material.

It is desirable to include a larger number of alternatives in the second column than the number of items in the first column, as depicted in the example in the boxed material below. If the number of alternatives is equal to the number of items, answering the last one or two items merely through the process of elimination may be possible. Between 5 and 15 items per test section is recommended.

Many variations of the matching item exist. A popular version in physical education is the use of a small number of alternatives, each of which can be used

---

SAMPLE MATCHING ITEMS

Directions: Place the letter of the appropriate organization in the space.

_____ 1. Organization governing amateur sports in America

_____ 2. Organization governing college athletics in America

_____ 3. National professional physical education association

_____ 4. Governed women's collegiate athletics

_____ 5. Rules governing body for golf

(a) AAHPERD
(b) AAU
(c) AIAW
(d) NCAA
(e) USGA
(f) USLTA

Directions: Place the letter of the appropriate person in the space provided to the left of each statement.

_____ 1. Grandfather of physical education

_____ 2. First president of physical education professional organization

_____ 3. Thought aim of education was happiness

_____ 4. Instrumental in growth of measurement in physical education

_____ 5. Developed athletic achievement tests with YMCA

_____ 6. Founded interpretive dancing

_____ 7. Gave first "modern dance" concert

_____ 8. Day's order of exercises in public schools

(a) Aristotle
(b) Catherine Beecher
(c) Isadora Duncan
(d) Martha Graham
(e) Luther Gulick
(f) Guts Muth
(g) Margaret H'Doubler
(h) Edward Hitchcock
(i) Dio Lewis
(j) Dudley Sargent
(k) Jesse F. Williams

From Haskins MJ.

more than once. See the boxed material below for two examples of this variation.

Short-Answer

The **short-answer item** is undoubtedly the easiest of all items to construct; however, there are drawbacks. More than one response may be correct. The test

---

SAMPLE OF VARIATION OF MATCHING ITEM

VOLLEYBALL

Directions: Indicate the official's decision in the following situations, using the key letters for your answers. There is only one best answer. Assume that no conditions exist other than those stated.

P—point   L—legal, or play continues
SO—side out   R—re-serve, or serve over

_____ 1. Server steps on the end line as the ball leaves hand.

_____ 2. On the service, the ball touches the top of the net and lands on the boundary line of the receiving team's court.

_____ 3. A player on the receiving team spikes the ball before it crosses to his or her side of the net. Player does not touch the net.

_____ 4. A front-line player on the serving team, in spiking the ball, returns to the floor across the center line. On the same play, a front-line player of the receiving team who attempts to block the ball steps on the center line.

_____ 5. As a player on the serving team attempts to contact the ball, it touches the upper arm.

SOCCER

Directions: Place the appropriate letter in the space provided.

A—Free kick for opposing team   E—Free kick on penalty circle
B—Kick-in for opposing team   F—Penalty kick
C—Roll-in   G—No penalty
D—Corner kick   H—Score

_____ 1. On a kick-in player A dribbles the ball rather than kicking it.

_____ 2. A team B player, taking a kick-in, sends the ball between the goal posts.

_____ 3. Player A is tackling player B who has the ball; it goes out of bounds off both players.

_____ 4. During play the ball is lofted into the air, and the left inner bounces it off the knee through the goal posts.

From Haskins MJ.

SAMPLES OF SHORT-ANSWER ITEMS

THE QUESTION VARIETY
If a bowler gets a strike in the first frame and six pins in the second frame, what is his second-frame score?

(22)

THE COMPLETION VARIETY
The extension of the foil arm in fencing is called the

(thrust)

THE INDENTIFICATION OR ASSOCIATION VARIETY
After each name write the sport in which he or she achieved fame.

Shaquille O'Neal   (Basketball)

Arnold Palmer   (Golf)

Joe Montana   (Football)

Steffi Graf   (Tennis)

Nancy Lopez   (Golf)

Mickey Mantle   (Baseball)

---

taker often has the difficult task of trying to think of the answer the test developer has in mind. Several words or phrases may be appropriate. Furthermore, this type of item often measures simple recall. Examples of three versions of short-answer items are shown in the boxed material above: the question variety, consisting of a direct question; the completion variety, written as an incomplete statement; and the identification or association variety, containing a list of words or phrases that the examinee must identify in the way that is designated.

Short-answer items should only be used when the desired answer is clear to experts and when the answer can be given in one or two words. These items are often used in tests of first-aid and cardiopulmonary resuscitation (CPR), where the series of steps that should be followed in an emergency setting has been established by experts.

Essay Items

An essay test usually contains a small number of **essay items,** each one requiring the examinee to construct a response at least several sentences long. Often an interpretation of facts is expected; therefore, no one response is correct, and a variety of responses might be acceptable.

One of the major limitations of an essay item is the lack of consistency that may occur in evaluating the answer. Various raters might assess the same response differently, and one rater might judge a response differently on two separate occasions. The lack of objectivity on the part of raters exists for several reasons. First, some raters are more severe than others and will always assign lower ratings. Second, some raters tend to give "middle-of-the-road" ratings, and others use the full range of ratings. If a rater predominantly uses the middle-of-the-road range, the best responses are penalized and the poorest ones are unduly rewarded. Third, raters may differ in the relative values they assign to different responses because each rater uses a separate criterion. One rater may emphasize writing form and style; another looks primarily for content.

Other factors also affect the consistency of ratings of essay items. The **halo effect,** where the rater is affected by the examinee's previous performance, can lower objectivity. For example, a good essay written by a usually poor student may receive a lower rating than a paper of the same quality written by a generally good student. One way of controlling this source of error is to ask that the examinee's name be placed only on the first page of the test. Then this page can be folded back out of sight until all examinations have been graded. Extraneous factors such as handwriting, spelling, and organization can contribute to less objective ratings. Carefully describe the degree to which these factors will be taken into account when the test is scored. Otherwise, the examinee may assume only content is being evaluated.

Because it is not possible to include a large number of items on an essay examination, the reliability of the test may be poor. Because of time limitations, sampling a wide range of content on an essay examination is usually not feasible. For this reason, students sometimes feel penalized by the particular set of questions included on an essay test.

Construction of Essay Items

At first glance, the essay test seems much easier to develop than an objective test. It is tempting to put together a few items in the shortest possible amount of time, but this often leads to a vague test that does not tap the desired knowledge. To avoid this, the objectives of the test should be carefully defined, and the items should be formulated based on these objectives. General questions, such as the following, should be avoided.

Discuss the mechanical principles of swimming.

There is no precise focus to this question; thus, it might be answered in a broad, superficial manner. The question should be narrowed, perhaps in the following way:

Discuss the principle of buoyancy as it applies to the breaststroke. Include the following points:
1. Definition of principle of buoyancy
2. Application with regard to coordination of body parts
3. Application with regard to position of body parts

Including from 10 to 15 questions that require relatively short answers is preferable to asking two or three questions needing longer responses. The greater the number of questions, the better the sampling of content will be.

After the items have been written but before the test is administered, a model answer should be constructed for each item. The model answer can be prepared in outline form, including all major points the student would be expected to make. These responses should be prepared in less than the amount of time the examinees will have to complete the test, since the student will have to compose an answer rather than merely formulate an outline. If problems arise in writing the model answer, perhaps the items need revision.

Sometimes the test taker is allowed to choose a number of items out of the total number available. If the test is tailor-made for a specific person, this is not unreasonable. However, if the test is being administered to a group, allowing a choice might not be as fair as it seems. When examinees select different sets of items, each with different levels of difficulty, comparing performances on the test is difficult. This is a problem especially when the tests are to be graded in a school setting.

Scoring Essay Items

Ebel (1972) has described six deficiencies that commonly occur in the response to an essay item:

1. Incorrect statements were included in the answer.
2. Important ideas necessary to an adequate answer were omitted.
3. Correct statements having little or no relation to the question were included.
4. Unsound conclusions were reached, either because of mistakes in reasoning or because of misapplication of principles.
5. Bad writing obscured the development and exposition of the student's ideas.
6. A number of errors occurred in spelling and in the mechanics of correct writing.

For maximum objectivity in scoring, evaluate one question for all examinees before moving to the next question. As discussed earlier, do not look at the examinee's name until the scoring of all tests is completed. Sometimes the rater's standards will change after scoring the first few items. Occasionally turning back and rechecking the first item on the tests initially scored is wise to be sure consistent standards have been applied. An even better approach is to skim through all answers to an item before scoring it to arrive at a feeling for the range of responses; this can lead to greater consistency in grading from the outset.

WEIGHTING TEST COMPONENTS

Earlier in this chapter the relationship of the number of items to the importance of the content area was discussed. In general, if more items are included on a given topic than on any other, this topic is automatically weighted more heavily. Although this may seem obvious, sometimes test developers neglect to examine the proportion of items per topic on a test.

Other factors also affect the weighting of test components. If a test item is answered correctly by all examinees, then it is essentially weighted zero. The item does not discriminate among examinees. The same effect occurs if no examinee can answer an item correctly. The weighting of test components, then, is affected not only by the number of items per component but also by the ability of the items to discriminate.

CORRECTION FOR GUESSING

When an objective knowledge test is used, it is possible to apply **a correction for guessing.** In some test settings, examinees are encouraged not to answer an item by guessing. If the answer is not known, the examinee is asked to leave the item unanswered. Then the total test score is corrected for guessing. For the true-false test, Formula 16-1 is used.

$$S = R - W$$ Formual 16-1

where S = corrected score
      R = number of right answers
      W = number of wrong answers

Clearly, when using this formula, one assumes that wrong answers are a function of guessing. This, of course, may not be true.

For multiple-choice tests, Formula 16-2 is used to correct for guessing:

$$S = R - \frac{W}{n - 1}$$ Formula 16-2

where n = number of alternatives per items

Note that Formula 16-1 is a special case of Formula 16-2 when $n = 2$.

When an objective knowledge test is developed so that all examinees should be able to finish in a given time period, a correction-for-guessing formula is often not necessary. This covers the majority of tests used in physical education and exercise science. However, when speed is an important part of the test, a correction formula should be used. Certain types of tests include so many items that the typical examinee is not expected to complete the test in the designated time period. In the physical education field these tests might be included in perceptual-motor learning test batteries and sport psychology test batteries. Here the use of a correction formula is recommended.

RELIABILITY AND VALIDITY

The reliability of a written test is sometimes determined by correlating scores on equivalent forms of the test. Although the items on the two tests differ, they cover the same content. The test-retest method is not appropriate because the examinee is likely to remember items from the first test.

Reliability

Perhaps the most frequently used method for determining the reliability of a written test is a measure of *internal consistency.* This can be calculated by administering the test on only one occasion. Then the test can be split into two halves, and the scores on the two halves can be correlated. If the two halves are highly correlated, what does this mean? It infers that an examinee would be likely to score similarly on each half of the test. This result would be particularly informative if it has been established that the two halves have been established as measuring the same content. However, it may not be possible to demonstrate that the two halves are comparable in content. Furthermore, there are many ways to split a test into two halves. The best way to proceed would be to use a method that averages all split-half correlations. This can be accomplished using the Kuder-Richardson method.

Kuder-Richardson Method

The Kuder-Richardson method was developed to provide a reliability estimate reflecting the average of the correlations of all possible pairings of halves of the test. The simplest of the Kuder-Richardson formulas is shown in Formula 16-3.

$$KR_{21} = \frac{k}{k-1}\left[1 - \frac{\overline{X}(k - \overline{X})}{k(s^2)}\right] \qquad \text{Formula 16-3}$$

where KR_{21} = Kuder-Richardson 21 reliability coefficient
k = number of items on the test
$\overline{X}$ = mean score on the test
s^2 = variance of the test scores (standard deviation squared)

Assume the following: $k = 20$, $s^2 = 8$, and $\overline{X} = 12$. Using Formula 16-3, the Kuder-Richardson 21 reliability coefficient is calculated as shown below:

$$KR_{21} = \frac{20}{20-1}\left[1 - \frac{12(20 - 12)}{20(8)}\right]$$

$$= 1.05\left[1 - \frac{12(8)}{160}\right]$$

$$= 1.05\left[1 - \frac{96}{160}\right] = 0.42$$

The interpretable range of the Kuder-Richardson 21 coefficient is .00 to 1.00. It is possible to have some reliability or no reliability (.00), but a negative coefficient lacks meaning. A negative reliability coefficient suggests that the test has less than no reliability. If all else is equal, the larger the standard deviation, the higher the reliability coefficient. The Kuder-Richardson formula is used for dichotomous scores, that is, when test items are scored as either right or wrong. When ordinal scores are used, other procedures are recommended. One of these is Cronbach's alpha coefficient.

Cronbach's Alpha Coefficient

Test scores are often ordinal (e.g., when a 5-4-3-2-1 scale is used), especially in questionnaires or surveys. In this case, Cronbach's alpha coefficient is more appropriate to use in estimating internal consistency. The most straightforward way of calculating this coefficient is to use the summary table for a two-way analysis of variance. (Review Chapter 4 for additional information on calculating and interpreting an analysis of variance.) Use Formula 16-4 to determine Cronbach's alpha:

$$\alpha = \frac{MS_s - MS_i}{MS_s} \qquad \text{Formula 16-4}$$

where α = Cronbach's alpha coefficient
MS_s = mean square for subjects (examinees)
MS_i = mean square for the interaction between subjects and items

An example is given in Table 16-1.

Validity

One procedure for determining the validity of a written test has already been discussed. This is the development of a table of specifications, which can be used as the basis for establishing content-related validity. Item analysis procedures can be used to provide information on the validity of the individual test items.

ITEM ANALYSIS

An **item analysis** is a procedure for determining the usefulness of each individual item as a part of the total test. It is applied after the test has been administered to a group of examinees. Overall, the results of an item analysis provide information on the effectiveness of the total test. It is a good idea to accumulate test scores for approximately 100 students before undertaking an item analysis. However, an informal analysis can be used with smaller numbers, especially if a rough indicator of how the items are working is needed. Two aspects of an item analysis are described—item difficulty and item discrimination.

Item Difficulty

How difficult was a particular item? **Item difficulty** can be determined quite easily by calculating the proportion of examinees answering the item correctly.

$$P = \frac{R}{N} \qquad \text{Formula 16-5}$$

where P = item difficulty
R = number answering correctly
N = total number in group

Overall the item should not be too easy or too difficult because neither extreme provides very much information on the achievement of the examinees. A gen-

Table 16-1 Hypothetical Data to Illustrate the Calculation of Coefficient Alpha

Examinees	Scores for 4 Items 1	2	3	4	Total
A	5	4	5	6	20
B	2	4	3	2	11
C	5	6	5	6	22
D	7	6	5	7	25
E	3	4	4	3	14
F	6	6	5	4	21
Total	28	30	27	28	113

SUMMARY TABLE

Source of Variation	df	SS	MS
Between examinees	5	34.71	6.94
Between items	3	.79	.26
Interaction	15	11.46	.76
Total	23		

Using Formula 16-4,

$$\alpha = \frac{6.94 - .76}{6.94} = \frac{6.18}{6.94} = 0.89$$

From Mood DP. 1989. Measurement methodology for knowledge tests. In Safrit MJ, Wood TM, eds. Measurement concepts in physical education and exercise science. Champaign, Ill: Human Kinetics, p 257. Used by permission.

eral range of .30 to .70 is recommended (Ebel, 1972). However, difficulty levels slightly above or below this range may be acceptable if the item discriminates well. It is not uncommon to observe one or two easy items at the beginning of a test, chosen to set the examinee at ease.

Knowing something about the level of difficulty of the item does not say anything about the students who answered correctly. Did students who answered the item correctly also receive higher scores on the test, and vice versa? This is unknown, based on P alone. The next step is to calculate D, the index of discrimination.

Item Discrimination

If an item discriminates well, more high scorers answer the item correctly than do low scorers. If the reverse occurs (i.e., if more low scorers answer the item correctly), the item is poorly constructed. The statistic used to determine item discrimination is known as the **index of discrimination.** The index of discrimination, D, compares the proportion of high scorers and low scorers who answer an item correctly.

The following steps are used to calculate the index of discrimination:

1. Separate two subgroups of test papers, an upper group (approximately 27% of the total group) that received the highest scores on the test and a lower group (27% of the total group) that received the lowest scores.
2. Count the number of times the correct response to each item was chosen on the papers of the upper group, then do the same for the lower group.
3. Tally these response counts on a copy of the test.
4. Subtract the lower group count of correct responses from the upper group count of correct responses. Divide this difference by the maximum possible difference, that is, the total number of people in the upper (or lower) group. Use Formula 16-6.

$$D = \frac{R_u - R_l}{N_u} \qquad \text{Formula 16-6}$$

where D = index of discrimination
R_u = number of correct responses in upper group
R_l = number of correct responses in lower group
N_u = total number in upper group

Although taking 27% of the upper and lower extremes is often recommended to maximize the differences between the extremes, any percentage between 25% and 33% is acceptable (Ebel, 1972). If the total group size is small, the top 9% and the bottom 9% may be counted twice.

Theoretically, the index of discrimination can be as high as 1.00. In reality, an index this high is rarely obtained. If D is greater than .40, the item discriminates well. Refer to Table 16-2 for an evaluation of the size of the index of discrimination.

Other Item Discrimination Methods

In a classroom setting there is a simpler way of obtaining the numbers of high and low scorers answering an item correctly. The teacher can identify the test

Table 16-2 Evaluation of the Size of the Index of Discrimination

Index of Discrimination	Item Evaluation
$\geq .40$	Very good items
$.20-.39$	Acceptable items (but may need revision at lower coefficients)
$\leq .19$	Poor items, to be rejected or rewritten

From Ebel, RL.

score that represents the cutoff score for the high group and the cutoff score identifying the low group. Then, for each item, the teacher asks those in the high group who answered the item correctly to raise their hands. The number is counted and recorded, and the same request is made of the low group. The groups can be labeled A and B instead of high and low to avoid possible embarrassment of the low scorers. The middle group could even be asked for a show of hands on each item to allow total class participation, although this information would not actually be used. The number of students in the low group who answered the item correctly should be subtracted from the number in the high group answering correctly and divided by the total number in either group, as shown in Formula 16-5. This procedure should be used with great care, taking into account the potential impact on students in the class. It may only be appropriate in selected, carefully controlled settings.

A computer can provide much more technical information, however. Many computer programs have been written to conduct an item analysis on a set of test scores (see Chapter 5). Although the results may be in more technical form, they nonetheless consist of item difficulty, item discrimination, and total test reliability. Coupled with an electronic scoring device (Figure 16-1), computerized item analysis provides a time-efficient method for test analysis.

Also of interest is the degree to which each alternative functions, referred to as item function. This is determined by the percentage of examinees choosing a given alternative. Tally the number of students who responded to each alternative. Each alternative should be plausible enough to be selected by 2% to 3% of the examinees. If not, it should be revised.

Figure 16-1   Scantron for Automated Test Scoring.

SUMMARY

Knowledge tests should be carefully constructed to ensure content validity. Before the test items are written, a table of specifications is prepared to provide the guidelines for test development. Test items are written according to this plan. The usefulness of individual items can be checked by conducting an item analysis. Additional validation techniques, as well as reliability estimation procedures, are described in Chapter 6.

Learning Experiences

1. Develop a table of specifications for a test of a sport or principles of exercise. Indicate content areas and levels of cognitive behavior on the table. Specify the number of items that should be written for each cell of the table.
2. Write 10 multiple-choice items, using the table of specifications you developed in 1 above. Exchange items with one of your classmates, and carefully analyze his or her items. Note ambiguous items that need rewriting. Revise your items according to his or her suggestions and give them to your instructor to be evaluated.
3. Use the 10-item test you developed in 2. Another revision may be necessary once the instructor has evaluated your items. Administer the test to 30 students on your campus (or in any appropriate setting). Group administration is not necessary; the test may be taken by one, two, or more students at a time. However, each student should have some knowledge of the sport or exercise principle measured by the test. When 30 students have completed the test, determine the score for each test and conduct an item analysis. Use the 10 top scores for the upper group and the 10 lowest scores for the lower group. Prepare a list of results as shown below.

Item number	Item difficulty	Item discrimination	Item function
1			
2			
3			
4			
5			
6			
7			
8			
9			
10			

Discuss any items that do not discriminate well. How might they be improved? Keep in mind, however, that a group of 30 people is too small for a definitive item analysis. Therefore, results should be interpreted somewhat tentatively.

References

Ebel RL. 1972. *Essentials of educational measurement.* Englewood Cliffs, NJ: Prentice-Hall.

Haskins MJ. 1971. *Evaluation in physical education.* Dubuque, Iowa: Wm C Brown Group.

Johnson BL, Nelson JK. 1986. *Practical measurements for evaluation in physical education.* Minneapolis: Burgess.

McGee R, Farrow A. 1987. *Test questions for physical education activities.* Champaign, Ill: Human Kinetics.

Mood DP. 1989. Measurement methodology for knowledge tests. In Safrit MJ, Wood TM, eds. *Measurement concepts in physical education and exercise science.* Champaign, Ill: Human Kinetics.

Roid GH. 1984. Generating the test items. In Berk RA, ed. *A guide to criterion-referenced test construction.* Baltimore: Johns Hopkins.

Annotated Readings

Hambleton RK. 1984. Using microcomputers to develop tests. *Educational Measurement,* **3**(2):10–14.

Discusses the advantages of item banking a collection of test items uniquely coded for easy retrieval; describes an item banking and test assembly system for microcomputers; points to the need to identify situations where computer testing enhances the quality of testing in appropriate and cost-effective ways.

Hopkins KD, Stanley JC. 1981. *Educational and psychological measurement and evaluation,* ed 6, Englewood Cliffs, NJ: Prentice-Hall.

Describes Bloom's taxonomy of educational objectives for the cognitive domain in simple, straightforward language; provides many practical suggestions for preparing a test, including the readability (reading difficulty) of the test, contains excellent illustrations of test items.

Melville S. 1985. Teaching and evaluating cognitive skills in elementary physical education. *Journal of Physical Education, Recreation and Dance,* **56**(2):26–28.

Describes efforts to measure cognitive skill acquisition of third and fourth graders using a written examination; discusses strategies for testing young children, such as reading questions and using pictures; delineates several benefits of written examinations in elementary school physical education; points to the need for an incremental, hierarchical list of cognitive skills for K-6 students from kindergarten and sixth grade.

Millman J, Green J. 1989. The specification and development of tests of achievement and ability. In Linn RL, ed. *Educational measurement.* New York: Macmillan.

Describes the process of developing a knowledge test, including the role of test purpose in test development, the test development plan, and external contextual factors, such as characteristics of the examinee population and time constraints; treats item development in detail, including format attributes, format importance, and item-writing schemes; concludes with sections on item evaluation, item selection, and test assembly.

Shick J. 1981. Written tests in activity classes. *Journal of Physical Education, Recreation and Dance,* **52**(4):21–22, 83.

Presents examples of various types of test items, including true-false, multiple-choice, multiple-response, rearrangement, and multiple-choice with constant alternatives; sample items are provided for bowling, golf, archery, badminton, and fencing.

Measures of
Physical Fitness

Measures of Health-Related Physical Fitness

Watch for these words as you read the following chapter

AAHPERD Physical Best Program
Body composition
Chrysler-AAU Physical Fitness Program
Field test
Health-related physical fitness
Hydrostatic weighing
Kraus-Weber Test

President's Challenge Physical Fitness Award Program
Prudential *FITNESSGRAM* Program
Skinfold caliper
Step test
Vo_2 max

Never in the history of the United States has so much attention been devoted to the status of physical fitness in children and youth as in the 1980s and 1990s. Several national surveys have been conducted, a number of nationally known fitness tests have been revised, the merits of health-related vs. motor performance–related fitness have been debated extensively, fitness tests have been incorporated into fitness programs, concepts and knowlege about fitness have been stressed, and criterion-referenced standards have been introduced into the realm of fitness testing.

IMPORTANCE OF PHYSICAL FITNESS

To what extent does physical fitness contribute to a healthy lifestyle? This question has been studied extensively in recent years by exercise scientists, including physicians, physical educators, exercise physiologists, health specialists, and others. The answer to this question is quite complex and not yet fully known. However, there is considerable evidence to support the value of maintaining an adequate state of physical fitness (AHA, 1992). How, then, can this state of fitness be assessed? The focus of this chapter is on tests developed to measure one or more components of health-related fitness. This type of fitness is related to one's positive state of health rather than one's athletic ability, although there is typically some overlap between the two.

In past years, school physical fitness programs consisted primarily of physical fitness assessment. Recently there has been a dramatic shift of emphasis to physical fitness programming. Within this context, more importance is attached to the delivery of educational programs that provide children and youth with the knowledge and understanding of fitness needed to make wise decisions about participation in physical activity. Students should be taught basic information about the body and its response to exercise. They should be able to identify the risk factors associated with disease and the importance of prevention of disease through the adoption of a healthy lifestyle. Physical fitness testing still plays a prominent role in the overall program, but major emphasis is given to the program. By refocusing our approach to physical fitness in the schools, perhaps tests will be used in more appropriate ways than sometimes observed in the past.

DEFINITION OF HEALTH-RELATED PHYSICAL FITNESS

Many definitions of physical fitness have been published. A common denominator across most of these definitions is that physical fitness is viewed as a multifaceted ability. Sometimes the multifaceted nature of fitness is explicit in the definition; in others it is implied by the types of tests included in the test battery. In several definitions, an attempt is made to separate **health-related physical fitness** from performance-related fitness. However, the tests used to measure physical fitness usually tap both health-related and performance-related abilities. In some cases the health-related element is predominant, while in others, the performance-related ability prevails.

Today the importance of defining *physical fitness* in terms of health rather than performance is generally accepted by health and fitness professionals, including physical educators. One frequently used definition describes physical fitness as "a physical state of well-being that allows people to perform daily activities with vigor, reduce their risk of health problems related to lack of exercise, and establish a fitness base for participation in a variety of physical activities" (McSwegin et al., 1989, p. 1). However, when fitness is associated with health, *fitness* is defined "by those components related to health. These components are [usually] identified as muscular strength and endurance, flexibility, aerobic capacity and body composition" (Safrit, 1995).

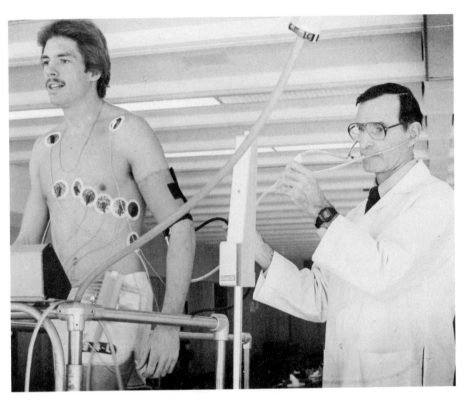

Administration of the Balke Treadmill Test.

Most physical educators and exercise scientists are not medical doctors and thus are not qualified to work independently with the physical activity needs of the person with a disease. Although exercise physiologists may be associated with cardiac rehabilitation programs, their work is under the supervision of a cardiologist. Generally, it is the job of the physical educator to work with the healthy person using physical activity as a medium for maintaining and improving that person's health and preventing disease. This global statement must be qualified by noting that lack of physical activity is only one of the risk factors associated with certain diseases. Certainly other factors such as smoking, high blood pressure, and obesity must be taken into account. At the same time, our unique function in physical education and exercise science is our training and background in sport and physical activity. Specialists in these areas should be qualified to provide exercise prescriptions for the healthy person.

To determine the level of physical fitness of an individual, a test that reflects an accurate definition of physical fitness should be used. In the context of health-related physical fitness, a test measuring short-distance runs (e.g., 100 yards) would not be valid, since it is the longer distances that affect one's capacity to use oxygen.

Although many physical fitness tests have been published in the United States, only a handful have been developed with an adequate concern for type of fitness, test validity, and test reliability. In addition to having these characteristics, a sound test should be accompanied by a table of norms that is useful on a national scale. The remainder of this chapter is devoted to an overview of tests of physical fitness that are typically used in school and laboratory settings. (For fitness testing in a nonschool setting, see Chapter 10.)

PHYSICAL FITNESS, PHYSICAL ACTIVITY, AND HEALTH

It has long been established that the health of the adult population is affected by several risk factors, such as smoking, obesity, high cholesterol levels, and high blood pressure, and that these risk factors could be reduced in many cases by regular participation in physical activity. In 1992, the relationship between physical activity and health in adults became much stronger as the American Heart Association identified physical inactivity as a risk factor. However, many physical educators questioned whether these results applied to children and youth. During the past decade, research on children's health and fitness became more prevalent. Several studies found evidence of risk factors in children. For example, evidence of atherosclerosis in young children was found. Widespread evidence of excessive body fatness in young children has been accumulated (Gortmaker et al., 1987; Ross et al., 1987). There is convincing evidence that children and youth can show early signs of risk factors.

Can these risk factors in children be reduced by participating in physical activity? Although the evidence is not extensive, there are studies demonstrating that aerobic activity has positive effects in reducing the risks associated with cardiac disease (Sallis et al., 1988; Taylor and Baranowski, 1991). Whether American children engage in sufficient amounts of physical activity is a controversial question. It appears that they do *not* exercise adequately in physical education classes. This has been demonstrated in junior high school (Lacy and LaMaster, 1990) as well as high school (McGing, 1989). In a middle-school setting, a heart rate monitor was used to monitor activity levels of students in physical education classes (Strand and Reeder, 1993a,b). No student was able to maintain the desired intensity level long enough to obtain an aerobic training effect. They exceeded a 60% maximum heart rate level for 15 minutes in only three sports (i.e., basketball, speedball, and football). However, merely by observing children—particularly preadolescents—it may seem obvious that a great deal of physical activity occurs after school and on weekends. Yet this is another controversial question. Is the activity sufficient to promote adequate levels of fitness? Some experts suggest it is not (Kuntzleman and Reiff, 1992). Others believe American children are, in general, fit. In examining performances of American children on health-related fitness items, only on body fatness is there evidence of lack of fitness (Corbin and Pangrazi, 1992). As more research on these issues is accumulated, better answers will be provided to these questions.

MEASURING HEALTH-RELATED FITNESS

In a laboratory setting fairly precise measures of health-related fitness can be made. Usually students are exposed to some of these measures in an exercise physiology course. Since using laboratory tests in a practical setting is not feasible, field tests are used. A good **field test** does not require expensive equipment that can only be used by highly trained personnel in controlled settings. There must be evidence that the test is a valid measure of some aspect of physical fitness, perhaps not as valid as the laboratory test but with acceptable validity nonetheless. The majority of the field tests of health-related physical fitness can be used in a variety of settings, including schools, private clubs, YMCAs, YWCAs, and so forth. Although this section focuses on measures that are appropriate in a school setting, their applicability extends beyond the schools.

Historical Perspective

Throughout most of the twentieth century, physical fitness has received its greatest emphasis during times of war. The focus on fitness was a result of the drafting of young men into the armed forces; inevitably a substantial number of men were not able to meet the physical requirements of the draft. Each time this occurred, government officials expressed dismay about the level of physical fitness of American citizens. After World War II, President Eisenhower became a strong advocate of the development of physical fitness throughout the United States. His support was largely due to the results of the **Kraus-Weber Test,** which was administered to elementary school children in the United States and Europe. President Eisenhower was distressed that American children fared poorly on the test in comparison with European children.

Although the presidential support of physical fitness was generated by poor results on the Kraus-Weber Test, this test was not designed as a measure of overall physical fitness. It was developed as a measure of minimal functioning of the low back area. Persons who could pass the test were considered unlikely candidates for developing low back problems but were not judged physically fit in a broader context. A brief examination of two of the six test items will verify the actual purpose of this test, which is still used today in clinical settings.

One item consists of a sit-up test with the examinee in a supine position, hands behind the neck. The feet are held down by an examiner. The objective of the test is to perform one sit-up. Another item requires the examinee to lie in a prone position with a pillow under the hips and lower abdomen. The hands are clasped behind the neck, and the feet are held down by the examiner. The examinee raises the chest, head, and shoulders and holds this position for 10 seconds. It is evident that these two tests are not valid indicators of health-related strength and endurance; however, this was not the intent of the test developers. Even though the Kraus-Weber Test was inappropriately used as a measure of overall physical fitness, it generated nationwide interest in fitness. Furthermore, it led to another positive outcome under the leadership of President Eisenhower—the initiation of a conference to consider ways of promoting physical fitness throughout the United States.

During the early 1950s the American Association (now Alliance) for Health, Physical Education, and Recreation (AAHPER, and now Dance, AAHPERD) began exploring tests that could be used to measure fitness on a broad scale in the public schools and that could be standardized, including tables of norms. The outcome of this exploration was the development of the AAHPER Youth Fitness Test, which is no longer sponsored by the AAHPERD. Although the developers of this test did not define physical fitness before developing the test, the last version of the test manual (AAHPER, 1976) stated that one criterion was that the test measure different components of fitness. The manual further noted that the test measured elements of strength, agility, and endurance as well as proficiency in running and jumping. This test became very popular in the United States. It was sponsored by the *FITNESS*GRAM program and the President's Council on Physical Fitness and Sports as well as the Alliance. The test items are familiar, require little or no equipment, can be administered to both boys and girls, can be administered to the entire range of grades 5 through 12, and allow self-testing by students (AAHPER, 1976, p. 10). On the other hand, the test has been criticized as a test of health-related physical fitness because of the types of items included. These criticisms became pronounced in the early 1970s when physical educators and exercise scientists became more concerned about the health-related fitness of Americans. During that time, a surge of interest in physical fitness was observed throughout the United States, only this time the emphasis was more closely tied to personal health and well-being than to fitness for fighting wars. The AAHPER Youth Fitness Test was generally viewed as a measure of physical performance related primarily to athletic ability. Furthermore, the test did not convey a definition of fitness that would be appropriate across the life span. In other words, a test measuring health-related fitness should be appropriate for persons of any age whether young, middle-aged, or elderly. The Youth Fitness Test included items such as the standing long jump and the 50-yard dash. Although these items are useful as measures of athletic performance-related fitness, they are not valid indicators of health-related fitness.

As a result of these concerns, the AAHPERD Health-Related Physical Fitness Test (HRPFT) was developed in 1980. This test was sponsored by the Alliance and the *FITNESS*GRAM program. Specific criteria were identified for choosing test items:

1. The physical fitness test should measure a range that extends from severely limiting dysfunction to high levels of functional capacity.

2. It should measure capacities that can be improved with appropriate physical activity.
3. It should accurately reflect an individual's physical fitness status as well as changes in functional capacity by corresponding test scores and changes in these scores (AAHPERD, 1980, pp. 4–5).

Three areas of physiological function appeared to be related to the above criteria: cardiorespiratory (CR) function, **body composition** (leaness/fatness), and abdominal and low back–hamstring musculoskeletal function. Recently, national tests of physical fitness have added a measure of arm and shoulder strength and endurance, using the rationale that fitness in this area may aid in the prevention of bone deterioration in later life. From a more practical standpoint, fitness in the arm and shoulder area is essential to participating effectively in many forms of physical activity.

In the mid-1980s, physical educators and exercise scientists around the country attempted to gain support for one national physical fitness test for children and youth. These efforts failed, and several organizations continued to revise and promote their own tests. However, negotiations continued between two of these organizations and, in 1993, **AAHPERD** established a strategic partnership with the **Cooper Institute for Aerobics Research** (CIAR) for the promotion of health-related fitness. The education component of the health-related fitness program was the responsibility of AAHPERD and was called **Physical Best.** The CIAR assumed the responsibility for the assessment component, which was the **Prudential *FITNESS*GRAM.** Each organization agreed to endorse and adopt the other's material and related products. The Physical Best test and its computer progam were phased out over the next year. The two organizations also agreed to work toward the formation of a National Coalition for the Promotion of Youth Health. This agreement is in effect for 5 years, until 1998.

Meanwhile other organizations continued to improve and promote their own tests. These include the **Chrysler-AAU Physical Fitness Program,** the **President's Challenge Physical Fitness Program,** and the **YMCA Youth Fitness Test and Program.** These tests, along with the Physical Best Program (not the test), the Prudential *FITNESS*GRAM, and the Fit Youth Today Test, have been selected for review in this chapter. Although there would be many advantages to a national fitness test for children and youth, the lack of such a test has promoted healthy competition among fitness developers. Thus, the major tests are continually being modified and improved. More sophisticated computer programs are available for fitness tests. New educational materials are being produced. Keep in mind that all information provided for the following tests should be supplemented by the latest information on their status from the test publisher. We have found test developers to be very eager to share information about their tests. Several of these developers have telephone hotlines operating every business day. Thus access to the latest developments in testing has been greatly simplified.

AAHPERD Physical Best Program

The AAHPERD Physical Best Program (McSwegin et al., 1989, p. 12) defines physical fitness as "a physical state of well being that allows people to perform daily activities with vigor, reduce their risk of health problems related to lack of exercise, and provide a fitness base for participation in a variety of physical activities." The major emphasis is on components of fitness that promote health: aerobic capacity, body composition, flexibility, and muscular strength and endurance. Each component is defined as follows:

1. Aerobic capacity is the ability to perform large-muscle, whole-body physical activity of moderate to high intensity over extended periods of time.
2. Body composition is the division of total body weight into two components: fat weight and lean weight.
3. Flexibility is the ability to move muscles and joints through their full range of motion.
4. Muscular strength and endurance is the ability of muscles to produce force at high intensities over short intervals of time (strength) and to sustain repeated products of force at low to moderate intensities over extended intervals of time (endurance) (AAPHERD, 1988, p. 12).

The Physical Best Program now consists of one dimension, an educational component. The Prudential *FITNESS*GRAM test will be used to assess fitness. Until AAHPERD and CIAR jointly adopt a new award and recognition system, either the existing Physical Best or the Prudental *FITNESS*GRAM system may be used.

The existing education materials consist of the instructor's guide, teaching idea cards, and instructional videos. The current version of the instructor's guide includes Physical Best test items as well as key program components. Because the Physical Best test items are no longer being used, the next version of the manual will probably not include this material. At the time this book was published, there was no information on whether the current *FITNESS*GRAM manual would be used in place of the Physical Best manual. The teaching idea cards contain information on health-related fitness concepts. The following content can be found on each card: the definition of a fitness concept, an activity to reinforce the concept, and additional suggestions for learning center activities. Different packets of cards are available for grades K through 6 and 6 through 12. Two videos can be purchased. One is *Physical Best: Integrating Concepts with Activities,* which provides examples of activities teachers can use to integrate fitness activities into sports and games. The other is *Measuring Body Fat Using Skinfolds,* which demonstrates techniques to use in taking skinfold measures.

The award system, called the American Alliance Physical Best Recognition System, consists of three types of awards. One is the Fitness Activity Award, which is a recognition for participation in appropriate physical activity beyond the requirement of physical education. The participant is required to maintain a log of activity related to physical fitness. The second is the Fitness Goals Award, which involves recognition for the attainment of individual goals developed by the student with the help of the physical education teacher. The third is the Health Fitness Award, which is recognition of mastery of health fitness standards. Mastery reflects achievement of a standard associated with minimal risk of health problems. To receive this award, the participant must attain a minimal level of fitness on all items in the Prudential *FITNESS*GRAM battery.

Although the Physical Best test items are no longer used, the work on the criterion-referenced standards for these items represented a significant contribution to fitness testing in the late 1980s (AAHPERD, 1988). Criterion-referenced standards are presented for each test. For those interested in exploring the historical aspect of fitness testing in more detail, the Physical Best test items along with the criterion-referenced standards are reproduced in Appendix F. Normative data from the National Children and Youth Fitness Studies (NCYFS) I and II are also included in the appendices. For more information, contact AAHPERD Physical Best Program, 1900 Association Drive, Reston, VA 22090, or AAHPERD Publications, P.O. Box 704, Waldorf, MD 20604.

The Chrysler Fund–AAU Physical Fitness Program

The AAU Physical Fitness Program is currently being cosponsored by the Chrysler Corporation. A test manual is available for test users. In the manual, a distinction is made between physical fitness and motor skill. "Unlike physical fitness, skill may be retained at reasonably high levels even without regular practice. Both physical fitness and motor skill are important in physical performance, but they are developed in different ways. In general, physical fitness is earned—skill is learned" (Chrysler Fund–AAU, 1992, p. 2). The Chrysler Fund–AAU test emphasizes physical fitness, not motor fitness.

This physical fitness program also stresses fitness literacy. "A child learns fitness literacy by experiencing change in his or her personal fitness and learning essential knowledge associated with physical fitness" (Updyke, 1987, p. 1). This knowledge includes the risk factors associated with disease, the importance of each component of fitness (i.e., CR endurance, flexibility, and muscular strength and endurance), the development of one's own exercise prescription, and how one's fitness status is affected by other factors, such as heredity.

The test battery, shown in Table 17-1, consists of four required items plus one optional item. Several variations should be noted in the test items. The distances used in the endurance run vary by age, with ¼ mile for ages 6 to 7, ½ mile for ages 8 to 9, ¾ mile for ages 10 to 11, and 1 mile for age 12 and over. The flexibility test is a V-sit reach. There are four required tests and one optional one.

Three awards are given in this program, each based on a normative standard. The Outstanding Award is given to students who score at the 80th percentile or higher. Students who score in the range of 45% to 79% are eligible for the Attainment Award. Those who score below the 45th percentile are given the Participation Award. In 1986–1987, 6% of the students taking the test received

Table 17-1 The Chrysler Fund–AAU Test	
Item	**Component of Fitness**
Required Tests	
Endurance run	Cardiorespiratory (CR) endurance
Bent-knee sit-ups	Trunk strength and endurance
Sit-and-reach	Flexibility in hamstrings and low back
Pull-ups (Boys)* Flexed arm hang (girls)	Upper body strength and endurance
Optional Tests	
Hoosier endurance run	CR endurance
Standing long jump	Leg strength; efficiency of body mass
Isometric push-up	Upper body static endurance
Push-ups, modified (girls)	Upper body strength and endurance
Phantom chair	Static leg endurance
Shuttle run	Agility and quickness
Sprints	Speed, quickness, and anaerobic ability

* Required for both boys and girls for Outstanding Performance certificate.

the Outstanding Award; 23%, the Attainment Award; and 71%, the Participation Award. An attractive feature of the AAU program is that all materials, including awards, are free with the exception of shipping and handling charges.

Several changes have been made in this test since the publication of the last edition of this book. One is the revision of the test battery, in particular in the set of optional items. The addition of the Hoosier endurance run is an example of a new item in the battery. Secondly, the development of educational materials has been emphasized. The long-standing testing packet has been joined by a brochure entitled *Special Test Tips* for students with special needs. A nutrition curriculum has been prepared for the classroom teacher and the physical education specialist (Benham, 1988). The fitness curriculum provides instructional materials, including activity cards, for the physical education teacher. The most recent publication is the *Home Fitness Curriculum,* which is used to promote the involvement of family members in physical fitness activities. A fitness testing video is also available. It is entitled *Fitness Fanfare,* an interesting portrayal of a group of students participating in a high-school band and their efforts to develop and maintain adequate fitness for the band's activities. Woven throughout the video is information on the Chrysler Fund–AAU test and how it should be used. Finally, the software has been upgraded and is reasonably user-friendly.

The computer software consists of one disk and a 1-page set of instructions. A software package is available for any Apple computer or compatible with 128K, an 80-column card, and a printer. A version is also available for the Macintosh. One can also be obtained for an IBM computer or compatible with 256K and a printer. As many as 50 records can be stored on the disk. The program is easy to use. For additional information, contact the Chrysler Fund–AAU Physical Fitness Program, Poplars Building, Bloomington, IN 47405.

The Fit Youth Today Program

The Fit Youth Today Program is sponsored by the American Health and Fitness Foundation. In the test manual (American Health and Fitness Foundation, 1988), physical fitness is not specifically defined, although four components of fitness are emphasized: CR endurance, muscular strength and endurance, flexibility, and body composition. These components are defined as follows:

1. Cardiorespiratory endurance is the ability of the heart, blood vessels, and lungs to respond effectively to the oxygen and energy demands of increasing muscular activity (p. 8).
2. Adequate strength refers to the level of muscular strength necessary to enable you to perform all normal daily activities in an efficient manner and maintain a sufficient reserve to confront emergencies (p. 11).
3. Muscular endurance refers to the ability of specific muscle groups to continue contracting for extended periods (p. 11).
4. Flexibility is the measure of the range of movement possible at each joint in the body (p. 14).
5. Body composition was not defined.

Four tests, listed in Table 17-2, are included in the Fit Youth Today (FYT) test. The test of CR endurance is called the steady-state jog, which is a measure of the distance an examinee can run in 20 minutes. Otherwise, the tests are comparable to those used in other testing programs.

The FYT awards program consists of three levels of awards. Level 1 is the All-Star Award, which requires participants to meet all four criterion standards. Level 2 is the FYT Star Award, given to the participant who achieves the crite-

Table 17-2 Fit Youth Today Test

Item	Component of Fitness
Steady-state jog	Cardiorespiratory endurance
Bent-knee curl-up	Muscular strength and endurance
Sit-and-reach	Flexibility
Body composition (triceps and calf)	Body composition

rion standard on the steady-state jog and one other test. Level 3 is the FYT Award, given for significant improvement toward the accomplishment of a participant's personal fitness goal.

The manual presents criterion-referenced standards but no tables of norms. The criterion-referenced standards are presented in Table 17-3. Suggestions are

Table 17-3 Fit Youth Today: Criterion-Referenced Standards

20-MINUTE STEADY-STATE JOG TEST

| Grade Level | Distance Covered in 20 Minutes | | | | | |
| | Males | | | Females | | |
	Miles	Yards	Meters	Miles	Yards	Meters
4	1.8	3,170	2,900	1.6	2,820	2,570
5	2.0	3,520	3,220	1.8	3,170	2,900
6	2.2	3,870	3,540	2.0	3,520	3,220
7–12	2.4	4,220	3,860	2.2	3,870	3,540

BENT-KNEE CURL-UP TEST—NUMBER OF CURL-UPS COMPLETED IN 2 MINUTES

| Sex | Grade Level | | | |
	4	5	6	7–12
Males and females	34	36	38	40

Sit-and-Reach Test
All grade levels and both sexes = 9.0 inches

BODY COMPOSITION—SUM OF CALF AND TRICEPS SKINFOLD

| Grade | Males | | Females | |
	Sum of Calf and Triceps	Approximate % body fat	Sum of Calf and Triceps	Approximate % body fat
4	23	19	32	26
5	26	21	32	26
6	29	23	33	27
7	29	23	34	28
8	29	23	34	28
9	27	22	34	28
10	25	20	34	28
11	23	19	34	28
12	23	19	34	28

From *American Health and Fitness Foundation. 1988. Fit youth today. Austin, Tex: American Health and Fitness Foundation, pp 61, 65, 69, 75. Used by permission.*

included for an FYT curriculum, and questions and answers are provided for teachers and students in various grade levels. Methods of conditioning are described.

The Prudential *FITNESS*GRAM Program

This program now includes the *FITNESS*GRAM test and the Physical Best educational materials. The test is characterized by a set of items continually revised and improved, updated criterion-referenced standards, and sophisticated computer software. The support staff at the Institute of Aerobics Research is excellent.

The Prudential *FITNESS*GRAM test manual identifies four components of physical fitness that are related to overall health status and optimal function: aerobic capacity, body composition, flexibility, abdominal strength and endurance, and upper body strength and endurance. Aerobic capacity relative to body weight is considered to be the best indicator of a person's overall CR capacity (Institute for Aerobics Research, 1992, p. 8). Body composition is vital in preventing the onset of obesity, which is associated with increased risk of coronary heart disease, stroke, and diabetes (Institute of Aerobics Research, 1992, p. 13). Musculoskeletal injuries are often the result of muscle imbalance at a specific joint; the muscles on one side may be much stronger than the opposing muscles or may have inadequate flexibility to allow complete motion or sudden motion to appear (Institute for Aerobics Research, 1992, p. 17).

The fitness tests used in the *FITNESS*GRAM program are shown in Table 17-4.

Table 17-4 Prudential *FITNESS*GRAM Test Battery

Item	Component of Fitness
Aerobic Capacity	
One-mile walk/run*	
The PACER	
Live up PACER with aerobic capacity	Aerobic capacity
Muscle Strength, Endurance, and Flexibility	
Curl-up test*	Abdominal strength
90 degree push-up*	
Pull-up	
Flexed arm hang	
Modified (Vermont) pull-up	Upper body strength
Trunk lift*	Trunk extensor strength and flexibility
Back-saver sit-and-reach*	
Shoulder stretch	Flexibility
Body Composition	
Percent fat*	
Body mass index	Body composition

* Item is recommended and used as the default choice on the software.

Criterion-referenced standards are presented in the manual, but no norms tables are given. [See Cureton and Warren (1990) for additional information on criterion-referenced standards.] The standards are reproduced in Table 17-5 on pp. 459–460. Modifications of the test battery are recommended for special populations. An extremely well-developed component of this program is its system of computerizing test results and sending a *Fitness*gram to parents. A sample *FITNESS*GRAM is shown in Figure 17-1 on pp. 461–462.

The national program model includes program delivery at three levels: (1) direct service, in which the Institute for Aerobics Research produces the fitness report cards for the school district; (2) development of microcomputer software for use by a school district to produce *FITNESS*GRAMs locally; and (3) availability of consultants to help selected districts program large computer systems to produce the cards and do statistical analyses locally (Institute for Aerobics Research, 1992).

The award system consists of four types of awards. The Get Fit Award is given to participants who complete a 6-week development program. An exercise log is maintained for this award. The Honor Award is given to students who meet fitness contracts that have been established with teachers. The I'm Fit Award can be obtained by meeting five of the six criterion-referenced standards. The Fit for Life Award is available for persons outside the school program who have displayed commendable exercise behavior. This award may be given to a child or an adult. A new recognition system called The Prudential SMART CHOICE has recently been developed and is now available.

THE NATIONAL CHILDREN AND YOUTH FITNESS STUDIES I AND II

The most recent studies of youth fitness, the National Children and Youth Fitness Studies (NCYFS) I and II, were published in 1985 and 1987 by the Department of Health and Human Services (Ross and Gilbert, 1985; Ross and Pate, 1987). The purposes of the studies were to describe the current fitness status of children and youth of the United States and the patterns of participation in physical activity and to evaluate the relationships between physical activity patterns and measured fitness. The HRPFT and a chin-ups test were used to measure health-related fitness.

The most recent studies of youth fitness, the National Children and Youth Fitness Studies (NCYFS) I and II, were published in 1985 and 1987 by the Department of Health and Human Services (Ross and Gilbert, 1985; Ross and Pate, 1987). The purposes of the studies were to describe the current fitness status of children and youth of the United States and the patterns of participation in physical activity and to evaluate the relationships between physical activity patterns and measured fitness. The HRPFT and a chin-ups test were used to measure health-related fitness.

Fitness test items were administered to 8,800 boys and girls ages 10 through
Continued on p. 463.

Table 17-5A The Prudential *FITNESSGRAM* Standards for Healthy Fitness Zone (HFZ)*

							BOYS						
Age (yr)	One Mile (min:sec)		PACER (no. of laps)		Vo₂ max (mL/kg/min)		Percent Fat		Body Mass Index		Curl-ups (no. completed)	

Age (yr)	One Mile (min:sec)		PACER (no. of laps)		Vo₂ max (mL/kg/min)		Percent Fat		Body Mass Index		Curl-ups (no. completed)	
5	Completion of distance. Time standards not recommended.		Participate in run. Lap count standards not recommended.				25	10	20	14.7	2	10
6							25	10	20	14.7	2	10
7							25	10	20	14.9	4	14
8							25	10	20	15.1	6	20
9							25	10	20	15.2	9	24
10	11:30	9:00	17	55	42	52	25	10	21	15.3	12	24
11	11:00	8:30	23	61	42	52	25	10	21	15.8	15	28
12	10:30	8:00	29	68	42	52	25	10	22	16.0	18	36
13	10:00	7:30	35	74	42	52	25	10	23	16.6	21	40
14	9:30	7:00	41	80	42	52	25	10	24.5	17.5	24	45
15	9:00	7:00	46	85	42	52	25	10	25	18.1	24	47
16	8:30	7:00	52	90	42	52	25	10	26.5	18.5	24	47
17	8:30	7:00	57	94	42	52	25	10	27	18.8	24	47
17+	8:30	7:00	57	94	42	52	25	10	27.8	19.0	24	47

Age (yr)	Trunk Lift (in.)	Push-ups (no. completed)		Modified Pull-ups (no. completed)		Pull-ups (no. completed)		Flexed Arm Hang (sec)		Back-Saver Sit-and-Reach† (in.)	Shoulder Stretch
5	6	12	3	8	2	7	1	2	2	8	8	
6	6	12	3	8	2	7	1	2	2	8	8	
7	6	12	4	10	3	9	1	2	3	8	8	
8	6	12	5	13	4	11	1	2	3	10	8	
9	6	12	6	15	5	11	1	2	4	10	8	
10	9	12	7	20	5	15	1	2	4	10	8	
11	9	12	8	20	6	17	1	3	6	13	8	
12	9	12	10	20	7	20	1	3	10	15	8	
13	9	12	12	25	8	22	1	4	12	17	8	
14	9	12	14	30	9	25	2	5	15	20	8	
15	9	12	16	35	10	27	3	7	15	20	8	
16	9	12	18	35	12	30	5	8	15	20	8	
17	9	12	18	35	14	30	5	8	15	20	8	
17+	9	12	18	35	14	30	5	8	15	20	8	

Shoulder Stretch column: Passing = touching the fingertips together behind the back.

From Institute for Aerobics Research. 1992. The Prudential FITNESSGRAM *test administration manual. Dallas: Institute for Aerobics Research.*

Vo₂max, *maximum oxygen consumption.*

* *Number on left is lower end of HFZ; number on right is upper end of HFZ.*

† *Test scored pass-fail; must reach this distance to pass.*

Continued

Table 17-5B   The Prudential *FITNESSGRAM* Standards for Healthy Fitness Zone (HFZ)*—cont'd

GIRLS

Age (yr)	One Mile (min:sec)		PACER (no. of laps)		Vo₂ max (mL/kg/min)		Percent Fat		Body Mass Index		Curl-ups (no. completed)	
5	Completion of distance. Time standards not recommended.		Participate in run. Lap count standards not recommended.				32	17	21	16.2	2	10
6							32	17	21	16.2	2	10
7							32	17	22	16.2	4	14
8							32	17	22	16.2	6	20
9							32	17	23	16.2	9	22
10	12:30	9:30	7	35	39	47	32	17	23.5	16.6	12	26
11	12:00	9:00	9	37	38	46	32	17	24	16.9	15	29
12	12:00	9:00	13	40	37	45	32	17	24.5	16.9	18	32
13	11:30	9:00	15	42	36	44	32	17	24.5	17.5	18	32
14	11:00	8:30	18	44	35	43	32	17	25	17.5	18	32
15	10:30	8:00	23	50	35	43	32	17	25	17.5	18	35
16	10:00	8:00	28	56	35	43	32	17	25	17.5	18	35
17	10:00	8:00	34	61	35	43	32	17	26	17.5	18	35
17+	10:00	8:00	34	61	35	43	32	17	27.3	18.0	18	35

Age (yr)	Trunk Lift (in.)		Push-ups (no. completed)		Modified Pull-ups (no. completed)		Pull-ups (no. completed)		Flexed Arm Hang (sec)		Back-Saver Sit-and-Reach† (in.)	Shoulder Stretch
5	6	12	3	8	2	7	1	2	2	8	9	Passing = touching the fingertips together behind the back.
6	6	12	3	8	2	7	1	2	2	8	9	
7	6	12	4	10	3	9	1	2	3	8	9	
8	6	12	5	13	4	11	1	2	3	10	9	
9	6	12	6	15	4	11	1	2	4	10	9	
10	9	12	7	15	4	13	1	2	4	10	9	
11	9	12	7	15	4	13	1	2	6	12	10	
12	9	12	7	15	4	13	1	2	7	12	10	
13	9	12	7	15	4	13	1	2	8	12	10	
14	9	12	7	15	4	13	1	2	8	12	10	
15	9	12	7	15	4	13	1	2	8	12	12	
16	9	12	7	15	4	13	1	2	8	12	12	
17	9	12	7	15	4	13	1	2	8	12	12	
17+	9	12	7	15	4	13	1	2	8	12	12	

From Institute for Aerobics Research. 1992. The Prudential FITNESSGRAM test administration manual. Dallas: Institute for Aerobics Research.

Vo₂max, *maximum oxygen consumption.*

* *Number on left is lower end of HFZ; number on right is upper end of HFZ.*

† *Test scored pass-fail; must reach this distance to pass.*

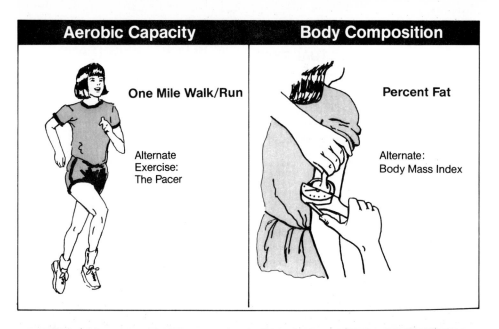

Aerobic Capacity

One Mile Walk/Run

Alternate
Exercise:
The Pacer

Body Composition

Percent Fat

Alternate:
Body Mass Index

Muscle Strength, Endurance & Flexibility

Curl-Up Test

Measures
Abdominal Strength

Push-Up

Alternate Exercises:
Pull-Up
Flexed Arm Hang
Vermont (Modified)
Pull-Up

Measures
Upper Body Strength

Trunk Lift

Measures
Trunk Extensor Strength
and Flexibility

Back-Saver Sit-and-Reach

Alternate Exercise:
Shoulder Stretch

Measures
Flexibility

Figure 17-1   Sample of *FITNESS*GRAM.   *Continued*

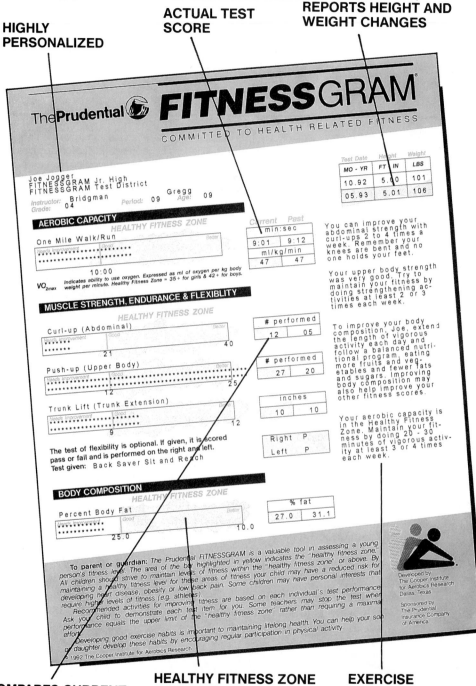

HIGHLY PERSONALIZED

ACTUAL TEST SCORE

REPORTS HEIGHT AND WEIGHT CHANGES

FITNESSGRAM

The Prudential

COMMITTED TO HEALTH RELATED FITNESS

Test Date	Height		Weight
MO - YR	FT	IN	LBS
10.92	5.00		101
05.93	5.01		106

Joe Jogger
FITNESSGRAM Jr. High
FITNESSGRAM Test District
Instructor: Bridgman   Period: 09   Age: 09   Gregg
Grade: 04

AEROBIC CAPACITY
HEALTHY FITNESS ZONE

One Mile Walk/Run

Needs Improvement _____ Better
****

10:00

VO_{2max} Indicates ability to use oxygen. Expressed as ml of oxygen per kg body weight per minute. Healthy Fitness Zone = 35+ for girls & 42+ for boys.

	Current	Past
	min:sec	
	9:01	9:12
	ml/kg/min	
	47	47

MUSCLE STRENGTH, ENDURANCE & FLEXIBLITY
HEALTHY FITNESS ZONE

Curl-up (Abdominal)
Needs Improvement | Good | Better
******* | 21 | 40

	# performed	
	12	05

Push-up (Upper Body)
Needs Improvement | Good | Better
************ 12 *************** 25

	# performed	
	27	20

Trunk Lift (Trunk Extension)
Needs Improvement | Better
************** 9 12

	inches	
	10	10

The test of flexibility is optional. If given, it is scored pass or fail and is performed on the right and left.
Test given: Back Saver Sit and Reach

	Right	P
	Left	P

You can improve your abdominal strength with curl-ups 2 to 4 times a week. Remember your knees are bent and no one holds your feet.

Your upper body strength was very good. Try to maintain your fitness by doing strengthening activities at least 2 or 3 times each week.

To improve your body composition, Joe, extend the length of vigorous activity each day and follow a balanced nutritional program, eating more fruits and vegetables and fewer fats and sugars. Improving body composition may also help improve your other fitness scores.

Your aerobic capacity is in the Healthy Fitness Zone. Maintain your fitness by doing 20 - 30 minutes of vigorous activity at least 3 or 4 times each week.

BODY COMPOSITION
HEALTHY FITNESS ZONE

Percent Body Fat
Needs Improvement | Good | Better
************ 25.0 10.0

	% fat	
	27.0	31.1

To parent or guardian: The Prudential FITNESSGRAM is a valuable tool in assessing a young person's fitness level. The area of the bar highlighted in yellow indicates the "healthy fitness zone." All children should strive to maintain levels of fitness within the "healthy fitness zone" or above. By maintaining a healthy fitness level for these areas of fitness your child may have a reduced risk for developing heart disease, obesity or low back pain. Some children may have personal interests that require higher levels of fitness (e.g. athletes).

Recommended activities for improving fitness are based on each individual's test performance. Ask your child to demonstrate each test item for you. Some teachers may stop the test when performance equals the upper limit of the "healthy fitness zone" rather than requiring a maximal effort.

Developing good exercise habits is important to maintaining lifelong health. You can help your son or daughter develop these habits by encouraging regular participation in physical activity.

© 1992 The Cooper Institute for Aerobics Research

Developed by
The Cooper Institute
for Aerobics Research
Dallas, Texas

Sponsored by
The Prudential
Insurance Company
of America

COMPARES CURRENT TEST SCORES TO PREVIOUS TEST

HEALTHY FITNESS ZONE IDENTIFIES ACCEPTABLE HEALTH FITNESS STANDARDS

EXERCISE RECOMMENDATIONS BASED ON TEST PERFORMANCE

Figure 17-1   cont'd

17 and 4,853 boys and girls ages 6 through 9 across the country. Excellent sampling techniques were used in that these children and youths were selected on a probability basis guaranteeing that they were representative of all American boys and girls in the 6- to 17-year-old age group. The fitness norms developed from the data of this national sample represent the most recent norms available for health-related physical fitness, although sound normative data for a variety of fitness tests are also available from Reiff et al. (1985). The sex and age norms for the NCYFS test items are reproduced later in this chapter.

In general, the NCYFS I data revealed that boys and girls showed continual improvement in most of the fitness test items as they advanced in age from 10 to 17. However, the sum of skinfold data demonstrated a tendency for all age groups to be fatter than comparable groups in the 1960s. Other results of the study pertained to the activity patterns of boys and girls. Over 80% of the students in this study were enrolled in physical education classes, which met an average of 3.6 times per week. Competitive sports were stressed for the older students; relays and informal games were emphasized for the younger students. This points to a deficiency in meeting one of the major national goals recently advocated for the public schools—developing physical skills needed for an active lifestyle throughout adulthood. Almost half of these students failed to engage in an adequate amount of vigorous physical activity to maintain a healthy cardiovascular system. The NCYFS was a landmark investigation of youth fitness in the 1980s.

Although test development was not one of the purposes of the NCYFS studies, the tests selected are of considerable interest in that they provide updated normative data on the fitness of younger age groups as well as information on other factors related to the level of fitness in the school-age population. The tests used in NCYFS II are included in Table 17-6. The NCYFS I test battery differed in that a regular pull-ups test was included and triceps and subscapular skinfold sites were measured. The half-mile walk/run was not an option in NCYFS I.

Table 17-6 NCYFS II Test

Item	Component of Fitness
Mile walk/run or half-mile walk/run (ages 6–7)	Cardiorespiratory endurance
Modified pull-ups	Upper body strength and endurance
Bent-knee sit-ups	Abdominal strength and endurance
Sit-and-reach	Low back flexibility
Sum of skinfolds (triceps, subscapular, and calf)	Body fatness

Valuable practical information on the administration of physical fitness tests was reported by the NCYFS personnel. This information cannot be found in comparable detail in any other source.

The Presidential Physical Fitness Award Program

The President's Council on Physical Fitness and Sports (PCPFS) is an organization based in Washington, DC. The primary mission of the council is to promote physical fitness and sports throughout the United States. The Presidential Physical Fitness Award Program is sponsored by the PCPFS, which is under the auspices of the Department of Health and Human Services. Two publications deal with the PCPFS program, a manual and a packet of materials (President's Council on Physical Fitness and Sports, 1991a,b) for the teacher or other test administrator and a monograph (Reiff et al., 1985) describing the results of a recent survey. Although physical fitness is not defined precisely, the components of fitness are identified as CR endurance, abdominal strength and endurance, arm and shoulder strength and endurance, flexibility of the lower back and posterior thighs, and leg strength, endurance, power, and agility.

The test items selected to measure each of the components are shown in Table 17-7. No norms tables are included in the manual, but a set of norm-referenced standards is reproduced in Table 17-8.

One award, the Presidential Physical Fitness Award, is designated for children and youth who participate in the program. They must score at or above the 85th percentile on all five items to qualify for the awards. A Presidential Instructor Emblem is available to instructors who qualify students for the award. A state champion program recognizes outstanding school achievement in physical fitness.

Comparison of Test Batteries

In general, the test batteries are more alike than different with regard to the components of physical fitness they measure. All the batteries include tests of aerobic capacity, flexibility, and abdominal muscular strength and endurance.

Table 17-7 Presidential Physical Fitness Test Battery

Item	Component of Fitness
Curl-ups	Abdominal strength and endurance
Pull-ups	Arm and shoulder strength and endurance
V-sit reach or sit-and-reach	Low back and posterior thigh flexibility
One-mile run/walk	Cardiorespiratory endurance
Shuttle run	Leg strength, endurance, power, agility

Body composition was identified as an important component of fitness in four of the six tests, and upper body strength was measured in five test batteries. Agility was measured in two of the batteries but was recommended only for young children in one battery. There is considerable similarity in the tests selected to measure the components of fitness as well. However, the tests are given different names, which is likely to be confusing to practitioners. All batteries include distance run tests of 1 mile or longer, with the exception of shorter distances for young children in two instances. The triceps and calf sites are measured in the sum of skin-fold tests in all batteries dealing with body composition. The body mass index is offered as an option to the skinfold measures in

Table 17-8A The Presidential Physical Fitness Award Qualifying Standards

	Age (yr)	Curl-ups (Timed 1 min)	Shuttle Run (sec)	V-Sit Reach or Sit-and-Reach (in.)	(cm)	One-mile Run (min:sec)	Pull-ups
Boys	6	33	12.1	+3.5	31	10:15	2
	7	36	11.5	+3.5	30	9:22	4
	8	40	11.1	+3.0	31	8:48	5
	9	41	10.9	+3.0	31	8:31	5
	10	45	10.3	+4.0	30	7:57	6
	11	47	10.0	+4.0	31	7:32	6
	12	50	9.8	+4.0	31	7:11	7
	13	53	9.5	+3.5	33	6:50	7
	14	56	9.1	+4.5	36	6:26	10
	15	57	9.0	+5.0	37	6:20	11
	16	56	8.7	+6.0	38	6:08	11
	17	55	8.7	+7.0	41	6:06	13
Girls	6	32	12.4	+5.5	32	11:20	2
	7	34	12.1	+5.0	32	10:36	2
	8	38	11.8	+4.5	33	10:02	2
	9	39	11.1	+5.5	33	9:30	2
	10	40	10.8	+6.0	33	9:19	3
	11	42	10.5	+6.5	34	9:02	3
	12	45	10.4	+7.0	36	8:23	2
	13	46	10.2	+7.0	38	8:13	2
	14	47	10.1	+8.0	40	7:59	2
	15	48	10.0	+8.0	43	8:08	2
	16	45	10.1	+9.0	42	8:23	1
	17	44	10.0	+8.0	42	8:15	1

Continued

Table 17-8B The National Physical Fitness Award Qualifying Standards—*cont'd*

	Age (yr)	Curl-ups (Timed 1 min)	Shuttle Run (sec)	V-Sit Reach or Sit-and-Reach (in.)	(cm)	One-mile Run (min:sec)	Pull-ups or Flexed-Arm Hang	(sec)
Boys	6	22	13.3	+1.0	26	12:36	1	6
	7	28	12.8	+1.0	25	11:40	1	8
	8	31	12.2	+0.5	25	11:05	1	10
	9	32	11.9	+1.0	25	10:30	2	10
	10	35	11.5	+1.0	25	9:48	2	12
	11	37	11.1	+1.0	25	9:20	2	11
	12	40	10.6	+1.0	26	8:40	2	12
	13	42	10.2	+0.5	26	8:06	3	14
	14	45	9.9	+1.0	28	7:44	5	20
	15	45	9.7	+2.0	30	7:30	6	30
	16	45	9.4	+3.0	30	7:10	7	28
	17	44	9.4	+3.0	34	7:04	8	30
Girls	6	23	13.8	+2.5	27	13:12	1	5
	7	25	13.2	+2.0	27	12:56	1	6
	8	29	12.9	+2.0	28	12:30	1	8
	9	30	12.5	+2.0	28	11:52	1	8
	10	30	12.1	+3.0	28	11:22	1	8
	11	32	11.5	+3.0	29	11:17	1	7
	12	35	11.3	+3.5	30	11:05	1	7
	13	37	11.1	+3.5	31	10:23	1	8
	14	37	11.2	+4.5	33	10:06	1	9
	15	36	11.0	+5.0	36	9:58	1	7
	16	35	10.9	+5.5	34	10:31	1	7
	17	34	11.0	+4.5	35	10:22	1	7

From President's Council on Physical Fitness and Sports. 1991b. The President's challenge physical fitness program packet. Washington, DC: President's Council on Physical Fitness and Sports, p 7. Used by permission.

two instances. Some variation is noted in the flexibility test. The sit-and-reach test is most frequently used, but the reach is measured in inches in some cases and centimeters in others. The V-sit reach is recommended in two of the batteries. The greatest variability occurs in the upper body strength measures. Variations include regular pull-ups, a pull-ups/flexed arm hang option, and a modified pull-ups test.

Instructions for Test Administration

Each test developer may have slight variations in the instructions for administering fitness tests. Instructions for the most popular tests are given below. They are modeled on the instructions given for the Health-Related Physical Fitness Test (AAHPERD, 1980). The pull-ups/flexed arm hang test options were not included in the health-related test. One or both of these options are not a part of all of the national fitness tests. Descriptions of these tests can be found in Chapter 18.

Distance Runs

Distance runs are included in the battery as measures of CR function. A person who possesses a satisfactory level of CR function is able to engage in sports or other physical activities that require sustained effort. A number of physiologic parameters reflect CR function; however, a person's maximum oxygen uptake (VO_2 max) is widely accepted as the best single indicator of CR function. VO_2 max is the maximum amount of oxygen an individual can transport and use during exercise (Astrand and Rodahl, 1970; see also Chapter 10). When the exercise continues to become more difficult yet the oxygen consumption fails to increase, this is referred to as the point of maximum oxygen uptake or maximum oxygen consumption. "Maximal oxygen consumption is one of the most important factors that determine a person's capacity to sustain high-intensity exercise for longer than 4 to 5 minutes" (Katch, Katch, and McArdle, 1991, p. 219).

Test Objective   The distance runs are used to measure maximal functional capacity and endurance of the CR system.

Description   The 1-mile run for time or the 9-minute run for distance may be administered, depending primarily on the teacher's personal preference. In addition, optional distance run tests may be used for students 13 years of age and older. These are the 1½-mile run for time or the 12-minute run for distance. The distance runs can be tested in a variety of settings. Examples of some of these are included in Figure 17-2.

Instructions   Regardless of whether the distance or the time of the run is fixed, students are instructed to run with maximal effort.

ONE-MILE RUN Instruct the students to run as fast as possible, beginning on the signal "Ready, start!" As the student crosses the finish line, call out the elapsed time, which should be recorded by the student or the student's partner. Walking, although permissible, should be discouraged since the purpose of the test is to measure maximal capacity. These instructions are also appropriate for the 1½-mile run.

NINE-MINUTE RUN Instruct the students to run as far as possible, beginning on the signal "Ready, start!" After 9 minutes, a whistle is blown and the student's partner records the distance run. These instructions are also appropriate for the 12-minute run test.

Test Area   The distance run tests can be administered on a 440-yard or 400-m track or on any other flat, measured surface. Examples of tests areas are displayed in Figure 17-2.

Equipment   Stopwatch, scorecards, and pencils.

Scoring   The 1-mile and 1½-mile runs are scored to the nearest second. The

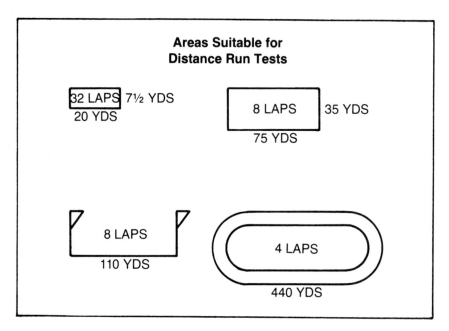

Figure 17-2   Schematic drawing of areas that can be used for distance run tests. From American Alliance for Health, Physical Education, Recreation, and Dance. 1980. AAHPERD health-related physical fitness test manual. Reston, Va: American Alliance for Health, Physical Education, Recreation, and Dance. Used by permission.

9-minute and 12-minute runs are scored to the nearest 10 yards or 10 m. Instructions on recording scores are typically included in the test manual.

Validity   Generally, the validity of distance run tests has been established by correlating the test scores with VO_2 max scores expressed in milliliters of oxygen per kilogram of body weight per minute (mL/kg/min). This expression is used to adjust for individual variations in body size. Validity coefficients of .81 for elementary school boys and .71 for girls at the same grade levels have been reported by Jackson and Coleman (1976) for the 9-minute run test. For the 12-minute run test, validity coefficients range from .65 to .90. The lower sizes of some of the coefficients may be attributable to a lack of motivation in the performance of the distance runs, body fatness, or running inefficiency. For example, if a student is not motivated to run as fast as possible, the distance run score will not be highly related to VO_2 max scores calculated directly from a treadmill test.

Reliability   Performance on distance run tests is usually highly reliable, with the reliability coefficients ranging from .75 to .94. In most cases the reliability estimates fall at the high end of this range. However, most of the reliability studies

Table 17-9   NCYFS II Norms by Age for the Distance Walk/Run (in Minutes and Seconds)

	Age							
	Boys				Girls			
	Half Mile		Mile		Half Mile		Mile	
Percentile	6	7	8	9	6	7	8	9
99	3:53	3:34	7:42	7:31	4:05	4:03	8:18	8:06
95	4:15	3:56	8:18	7:54	4:29	4:18	9:14	8:41
90	4:27	4:11	8:46	8:10	4:46	4:32	9:39	9:08
85	4:35	4:22	9:02	8:33	4:57	4:38	9:55	9:26
80	4:45	4:28	9:19	8:48	5:07	4:46	10:08	9:40
75	4:52	4:33	9:29	9:00	5:13	4:54	10:23	9:50
70	4:59	4:40	9:40	9:13	5:20	5:00	10:35	10:15
65	5:04	4:46	9:52	9:29	5:25	5:06	10:46	10:31
60	5:10	4:50	10:04	9:44	5:31	5:11	10:59	10:41
55	5:17	4:54	10:16	9:58	5:39	5:18	11:14	10:56
50	5:23	5:00	10:39	10:10	5:44	5:25	11:32	11:13
45	5:28	5:05	11:00	10:27	5:49	5:32	11:46	11:30
40	5:33	5:11	11:14	10:41	5:55	5:39	12:03	11:46
35	5:41	5:17	11:30	10:59	6:00	5:46	12:14	12:09
30	5:50	5:28	11:51	11:16	6:07	5:55	12:37	12:26
25	5:58	5:35	12:14	11:44	6:14	6:01	12:59	12:45
20	6:09	5:46	12:39	12:02	6:27	6:10	13:26	13:13
15	6:21	6:06	13:16	12:46	6:39	6:20	14:18	13:44
10	6:40	6:20	14:05	13:37	6:51	6:38	14:48	14:31
5	7:15	6:50	15:24	15:15	7:16	7:09	16:35	15:40

From the National Children and Youth Fitness Study II. Washington, DC: Department of Health and Human Services, 1987.

have been conducted using adults and adolescent children as subjects. Very few reliability coefficients have been reported for children in the lower elementary grades. Factors such as motivation, body fatness, and running efficiency can affect the reliability as well as the validity of distance runs.

Norms   Normative data are provided for each distance run test. Tables of norms from the NCYFS I and II are included in Tables 17-9 to 17-11.

Table 17-10 NCYFS Norms by Age for the One-Mile Walk/Run—Girls (in Minutes and Seconds)

Percentile	10	11	12	13	14	15	16	17	18
99	7:55	7:14	7:20	7:08	7:01	6:59	7:03	6:52	6:58
90	9:09	8:45	8:34	8:27	8:11	8:23	8:28	8:20	8:22
80	9:56	9:35	9:30	9:13	8:49	9:04	9:06	9:10	9:27
75	10:09	9:56	9:52	9:30	9:16	9:28	9:25	9:26	9:31
70	10:27	10:10	10:05	9:48	9:31	9:49	9:41	9:41	9:36
60	10:51	10:35	10:32	10:22	10:04	10:20	10:15	10:16	10:08
50	11:14	11:15	10:58	10:52	10:32	10:46	10:34	10:34	10:51
40	11:54	11:46	11:26	11:22	10:58	11:20	11:08	10:59	11:27
30	12:27	12:33	12:03	11:55	11:35	11:53	11:49	11:43	11:58
25	12:52	12:54	12:33	12:17	11:49	12:18	12:10	12:03	12:14
20	13:12	13:17	12:53	12:43	12:10	12:48	12:32	12:30	12:37
10	14:20	14:35	14:07	13:45	13:13	14:07	13:42	13:46	15:18

From the National Children and Youth Fitness Study I. Washington, DC: Department of Health and Human Services, 1985.

Comments Students should be taught to warm up with passive stretches and walking before participating in a distance run and to cool down in the same way afterward. Check to see that no medical reason exists to prevent a student from engaging in strenuous exercise of this nature. Prepare students in advance for the distance run by teaching them how to pace themselves throughout the run. Begin with shorter runs and gradually increase the distance of the run. Most test manuals now include explicit instructions on preparing examinees to be tested. These preparations should begin well in advance of the testing and should evolve out of a fitness education program. It is doubtful that runs shorter than 1 mile are valid measures of CR function (Jackson and Coleman, 1976). Thus, the use of shorter runs to accommodate young children may be viewed as a necessity from a motivational point of view but questionable as a sound fitness measure.

Several factors affect the distance run performance of children. Children display less economy of gait than adults when walking or running. For this reason, they experience a higher metabolic cost (Wells, 1986). The younger the child, the more difficult it is to predict Vo_2 max. Other factors that can have a negative impact on children's performance are experience, motor efficiency, environmental conditions, and motivation (Krahenbuhl et al., 1978).

Sum of Skinfold Fat

The body composition of a person consists of bone, muscle mass, and fatty tissue. Obesity is the result of an excess of fatty tissue and is associated with a

Table 17-11 NCYFS Norms by Age for the One-Mile Walk/Run—Boys (in Minutes and Seconds)

Percentile	10	11	12	13	14	15	16	17	18
99	6:55	6:21	6:21	5:59	5:43	5:40	5:31	5:14	5:33
90	8:13	7:25	7:13	6:48	6:27	6:23	6:13	6:08	6:10
80	8:35	7:52	7:41	7:07	6:58	6:43	6:31	6:31	6:33
75	8:48	8:02	7:53	7:14	7:08	6:52	6:39	6:40	6:42
70	9:02	8:12	8:03	7:24	7:18	7:00	6:50	6:46	6:57
60	9:26	8:38	8:23	6:46	7:34	7:13	7:07	7:10	7:15
50	9:52	9:03	8:48	8:04	7:51	7:30	7:27	7:31	7:35
40	10:15	9:25	9:17	8:26	8:14	7:50	7:48	7:59	7:53
30	10:44	10:17	9:57	8:54	8:46	8:18	8:04	8:24	8:12
25	11:00	10:32	10:13	9:06	9:10	8:30	8:18	8:37	8:34
20	11:25	10:55	10:38	9:20	9:28	8:50	8:34	8:55	9:10
10	12:27	12:07	11:48	10:38	10:34	10:13	9:36	10:43	10:50

From the National Children and Youth Fitness Study I. Washington, DC: Department of Health and Human Services, 1985.

number of disease states such as diabetes, hypertension, heart disease, and heat intolerance. Thus it is appropriate to include a measure of body composition in a health-related fitness battery.

Test Objective   This test is used to assess body composition, or more specifically, the level of fatness in an individual.

Description   Two skinfold sites are used to measure body fatness in recent revisions of fitness test batteries—the triceps and calf muscles. The subcutaneous adipose tissue can be lifted with the fingers to form a skinfold. A skinfold caliper is used to obtain the skinfold measure by measuring the thickness of a double layer of subcutaneous fat and skin at the designated site.

Instructions   To ensure accuracy and consistency across skinfold measures, the sites should be marked with a grease pencil. To obtain the triceps skinfold, mark the point halfway between the elbow and the acromial process of the scapula (Figure 17-3). The mark for the skinfold should be made parallel to the longitudinal axis of the upper arm (Figure 17-4). Mark the calf site "on the inside (medial side) of the right lower leg at the largest part of the calf girth. Grasp and gently lift the skin up slightly above the level of the largest part of the calf with the thumb and index finger so that the calipers may be placed at the level of the largest part of the calf. Have students place their right foot on a bench with the knee slightly flexed when taking the calf measurement" (Figure 17-5) (AAHPERD, 1988, p. 17). Both measurements are taken on the right side of the body. (Refer to the figures for examples of properly marked sites.)

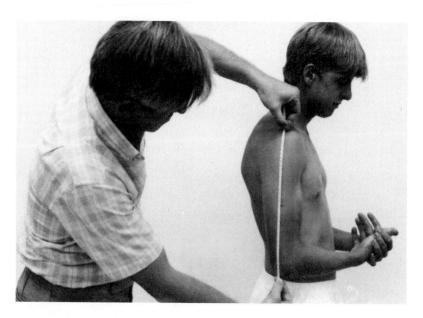

Figure 17-3 Determining triceps skinfold measurement. *Courtesy of Timothy Lohman, Tucson, Arizona.*

In one test manual (AAHPERD, 1980, p. 13) the following procedure is recommended for obtaining a skinfold measure:

1. Firmly grasp the skinfold between the thumb and forefinger and lift up.
2. Place the contact surface of the caliper 1 cm (0.4 inch) above or below the finger.
3. Slowly release the grip on the caliper enabling them (the jaws of the caliper) to exert their full tension on the skinfold.
4. Read skinfold to nearest .05 mm after needle stops (1–2 seconds after releasing grip on caliper).

Test Area A private testing area should be available for administering this test so that students will not suffer any embarassment resulting from the test.

Equipment A better constructed and more expensive caliper, such as the Harpenden or Lange skinfold caliper, is recommended for this test (Figure 17-6). These calipers are expensive, but they provide a constant pressure of 10 g/mm^2 throughout the range of skinfold thicknesses. Other less expensive calipers are now on the market and may be suitable for testing in a school setting. However, the pressure may not be constant throughout the lower portion of the range, thus yielding less accurate measures.

Scoring Three measures are taken at each site, and the median of each set of three measures is recorded to the nearest 0.5 mm. The median scores for the two sites are then summed, as in the following example:

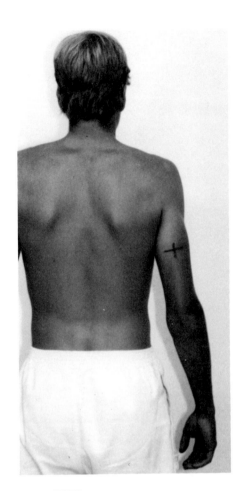
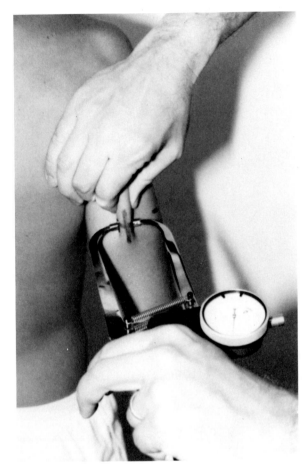

Figure 17-4   Measuring triceps skinfold. *Courtesy of Timothy Lohman.*

Triceps: 10, 7, 8   Median =   8
Calf: 6, 5, 7   Median =   6
TOTAL SCORE   14

Validity   The validity of the sum of skinfold fat is usually determined by correlating this sum with body fatness measured through hydrostatic weighting,
where the percent body fat and lean body mass are determined by submerging
the subject underwater. The validity coefficients range from .70 to .90 in both
children and adults (Baumgartner and Jackson, 1991), although far fewer studies have been conducted using children as subjects.

Reliability   The intertester reliability of skinfold measures is high, over .95 when
experienced testers measured adult subjects. Similar coefficients were obtained
for boys and girls of middle-school age.

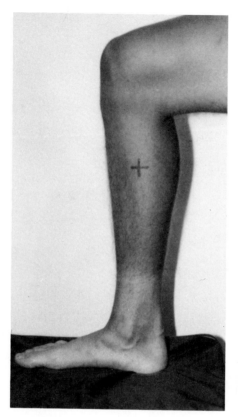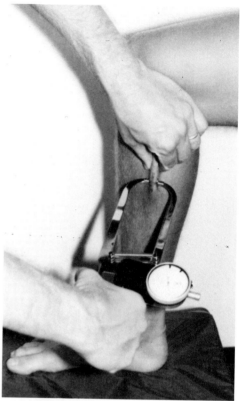

Figure 17-5 Measuring calf skinfold. *Courtesy of Timothy Lohman.*

Norms Norms for the triceps and subscapular skinfold measurements were reported in NCYFC I for 10- to 17-year-old children. The same sites plus the calf skinfold were measured in NCYFS II, where the subjects were 6 to 9 years of age. Norms are presented in Tables 17-12 to 17-19.

COMMENTS

Be careful to place the caliper properly. The correct location is midway between the crest and base of the skinfold, not at the base. Teachers who are inexperienced in using the caliper should practice measuring skinfolds with students as subjects. Measure each site a number of times and try to obtain the same reading within 1 or 2 mm.

Much is still unknown about the relationship of skinfold fat to body fatness in children, because of the occurrence of sex- and age-related changes. A specific skinfold thickness, then, does not represent the same amount of body fat in a young child as it does in an older child.

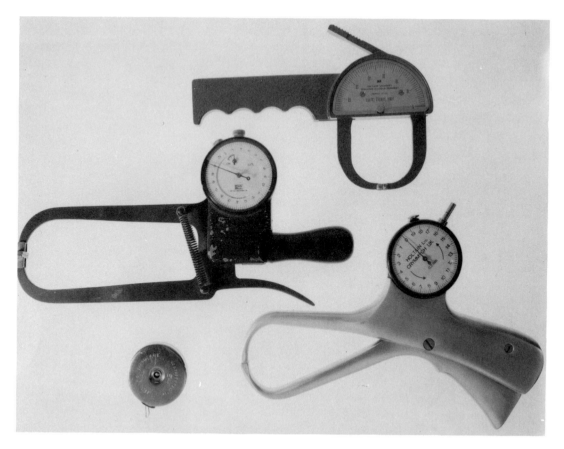

Figure 17-6   Some expensive skinfold calipers. *Courtesy of Timothy Lohman.*

Skinfold measures can be used to estimate percent body fat and ideal weight. Even more convenient is a set of nomograms developed by Lohman (1987) to convert the sum of triceps plus calf (or triceps plus subscapular) skinfolds to percent body fat merely by reading down the chart. Four of these nomograms, two for boys and two for girls (ages 6–17), are shown in Figure 17-7 on p. 483.

The *body mass index (BMI)* may be used as an optional item to measure body composition. *BMI* is defined as the ratio of body weight (measured in kilograms) and the square of height (measured in meters):

$$BMI = \frac{body\ weight\ (kg)}{height^2\ (m)}$$

Modified Sit-Ups

Two test items are included in a number of test batteries as measures of musculoskeletal function in the abdominal and low back area. The Modified Sit-Ups

Table 17-12 NCYFS II Norms by Age for the Medial Calf Skinfold (in Millimeters)

	Age							
	Boys				Girls			
Percentile	6	7	8	9	6	7	8	9
99	4	4	4	4	5	5	5	5
95	5	5	5	5	6	6	6	7
90	5	5	5	5	7	7	7	7
85	6	6	6	6	8	7	8	8
80	6	6	6	7	8	8	8	9
75	6	7	7	7	8	8	9	10
70	7	7	7	8	9	9	10	10
65	7	7	7	8	9	9	10	11
60	7	7	8	9	10	10	11	11
55	7	8	8	10	10	10	11	12
50	8	8	9	10	10	11	12	13
45	8	9	10	11	11	12	13	14
40	9	9	10	11	11	12	13	14
35	9	10	11	12	12	13	14	15
30	10	11	11	13	13	13	15	16
25	10	11	12	14	13	15	16	17
20	11	12	14	15	14	15	18	18
15	12	14	15	17	16	17	19	20
10	13	16	19	20	17	18	21	22
5	17	19	21	24	20	21	24	27

From the National Children and Youth Fitness Study II. Washington, DC: Department of Health and Human Services, 1987.

Test is characterized by a 1-minute time limit and a positioning of the arms in front of the chest.

Many Americans are affected by low back pain. This dysfunction can lead to a state of extreme discomfort, causing the sufferer to lose workdays, preventing him or her from leading a normal life. In a functional health context this syndrome is associated with weak abdominal muscles and excessively contracted muscles in the lower back. Many physicians recommend exercise to reduce low back pain.

Table 17-13 NCYFS II Norms by Age for the Triceps Skinfold (in Millimeters)

	Age							
	Boys				Girls			
Percentile	6	7	8	9	6	7	8	9
99	5	5	5	5	5	6	6	6
95	6	5	6	6	7	7	7	7
90	6	6	6	6	8	7	8	8
85	7	7	7	7	8	8	8	9
80	7	7	7	7	9	8	9	10
75	7	7	7	8	9	9	9	10
70	7	7	8	8	9	9	10	11
65	8	8	8	9	10	10	10	11
60	8	8	8	10	10	10	11	12
55	8	8	9	10	11	11	12	12
50	8	9	9	10	11	11	12	13
45	9	9	10	11	12	12	13	14
40	9	10	10	12	12	12	14	14
35	10	10	11	13	13	13	15	15
30	10	11	12	14	13	13	16	16
25	10	11	13	15	14	14	17	18
20	11	12	14	16	14	15	18	19
15	12	14	15	18	15	17	19	21
10	13	16	19	21	17	19	21	22
5	16	20	23	23	20	22	25	25

From the National Children and Youth Fitness Study II. Washington, DC: Department of Health and Human Services, 1987.

Test Objective   The Modified Sit-Ups Test is used to measure abdominal strength and endurance.

Description   The starting position of the test is the supine position with knees flexed, feet on floor, and heels between 12 and 18 inches from the buttocks. The arms are crossed on the chest with the hands on opposite shoulders. A partner holds the examinee's feet to keep them in contact with the testing surface. The examinee curls to a sitting position, maintaining arm contact with the chest.

Table 17-14 NCYFS II Norms by Age for the Subscapular Skinfold (in Millimeters)

	Age							
	Boys				Girls			
Percentile	6	7	8	9	6	7	8	9
99	4	4	4	4	4	4	4	4
95	4	4	4	4	4	4	5	5
90	4	4	4	5	5	5	5	5
85	4	5	5	5	5	5	5	5
80	5	5	5	5	5	5	5	6
75	5	5	5	5	5	5	6	6
70	5	5	5	5	5	5	6	6
65	5	5	5	6	6	6	6	6
60	5	5	5	6	6	6	6	7
55	5	5	6	6	6	6	7	7
50	5	5	6	6	6	6	7	8
45	5	6	6	7	6	7	7	8
40	6	6	6	7	7	7	8	9
35	6	6	6	7	7	7	8	9
30	6	6	7	8	7	8	9	10
25	6	7	7	9	8	9	10	12
20	7	7	8	10	8	10	12	15
15	7	8	10	12	10	11	15	17
10	8	10	14	15	12	13	17	21
5	12	16	19	20	16	19	21	25

From the National Children and Youth Fitness Study II. Washington, DC: Department of Health and Human Services, 1987.

The chin should be tucked on the chest and should remain in this position until the completion of the sit-up.

When the elbows touch the thighs, the sit-up is completed. The examinee curls back down to the floor until the midback contacts the testing surface. Another sit-up may then be attempted. (See photographs on p. 484.)

Instructions The examinee begins executing consecutive sit-ups on the word "Go!," using the signal "Ready, go!" At the end of 60 seconds, the test is ended with the word "Stop!" The score is the number of sit-ups executed correctly during this time. Pausing between sit-ups is permissible.

Table 17-15 NCYFS II Norms by Age for the Sum of Triceps and Medial Calf Skinfold (in Millimeters)

	Age							
	Boys				**Girls**			
Percentile	6	7	8	9	6	7	8	9
99	9	9	9	9	11	11	11	12
95	11	11	11	11	13	13	14	14
90	12	12	12	12	15	15	15	16
85	12	13	13	13	16	16	16	18
80	13	13	13	14	17	17	18	19
75	14	14	14	15	18	18	19	20
70	14	14	15	16	18	18	20	21
65	15	15	15	18	19	19	21	22
60	15	16	17	18	20	20	22	23
55	16	16	17	19	21	21	23	25
50	16	17	18	21	21	22	24	26
45	17	18	19	22	22	23	26	27
40	17	19	20	23	23	24	27	29
35	18	20	21	25	24	25	29	30
30	20	21	23	27	25	26	31	32
25	20	22	24	29	27	28	33	35
20	22	24	27	31	28	31	35	37
15	23	27	31	35	30	33	38	41
10	27	32	37	40	33	37	43	45
5	33	39	44	47	38	43	49	52

From the National Children and Youth Fitness Study II. Washington, DC: Department of Health and Human Services, 1987.

Test Area Any area with sufficient floor space may be used.

Equipment Mats are recommended for safety and comfort; a stopwatch.

Scoring The score is the number of sit-ups executed correctly during 60 seconds. Incorrect execution includes failure to curl up, pulling the arms away from the chest, failure to touch the thighs with the elbows, and failure to touch the midback to the testing surface in the down position.

Validity The validity of the sit-ups test has not been clearly established. Electromyographic studies of sit-ups have shown that the abdominal muscles are active during the execution of a sit-up. However, other muscles are active as well,

Table 17-16 NCYFS Norms by Age for the Triceps Skinfold—Boys (in Millimeters)

Percentile	10	11	12	13	14	15	16	17	18
99	5	4	4	4	4	4	4	4	4
90	7	7	6	6	5	5	5	5	5
80	8	7	8	7	6	6	6	6	6
75	8	8	8	7	7	7	6	6	6
70	9	9	9	8	7	7	7	7	7
60	10	10	10	9	8	8	7	7	8
50	11	11	11	10	9	9	8	8	8
40	13	12	12	11	10	10	9	9	10
30	14	14	14	13	11	11	11	11	11
25	15	15	15	14	12	12	11	12	12
20	16	16	17	15	13	13	12	13	13
10	20	20	21	20	18	18	16	15	16

From the National Children and Youth Fitness Study I. Washington, DC: Department of Health and Human Services, 1985.

Table 17-17 NCYFS Norms by Age for the Triceps Skinfold—Girls (in Millimeters)

Percentile	10	11	12	13	14	15	16	17	18
99	5	6	6	6	6	7	7	8	7
90	7	8	9	9	9	10	10	11	10
80	9	9	10	10	11	12	12	12	12
75	10	10	10	11	12	13	12	13	13
70	10	10	11	11	12	13	13	14	13
60	11	12	12	13	14	15	14	15	14
50	12	13	13	14	15	16	15	17	15
40	14	15	14	15	16	17	17	18	17
30	15	16	16	17	18	19	18	20	19
25	16	17	17	18	19	20	19	21	20
20	17	19	18	20	20	21	20	21	21
10	21	23	22	24	23	25	24	24	23

From the National Children and Youth Fitness Study I. Washington, DC: Department of Health and Human Services, 1985.

Table 17-18 NCYFS Norms by Age for the Sum of Triceps and Subscapular Skinfolds—Boys (in Millimeters)

Percentile	10	11	12	13	14	15	16	17	18
99	9	9	9	9	9	10	10	10	11
90	12	12	12	11	12	12	12	13	13
80	13	13	13	13	13	13	13	14	14
75	14	14	14	13	13	14	14	14	15
70	15	15	15	14	14	14	14	15	15
60	16	16	16	15	15	15	15	15	17
50	17	18	17	17	17	17	17	17	18
40	20	20	20	19	18	18	18	19	19
30	22	23	22	21	21	20	20	21	22
25	24	25	24	23	22	22	22	22	24
20	25	26	28	25	25	24	23	24	25
10	35	36	38	34	33	32	30	30	30

From the National Children and Youth Fitness Study I. Washington, DC: Department of Health and Human Services, 1985.

in particular the hip flexors. No evidence exists to justify a specified number of sit-ups as representative of a desirable amount of abdominal strength. Thus, the Modified Sit-Ups Test is validated on the basis of logical validity.

Robertson and Magnusdottir (1987) proposed a partial curl-up test that places the greatest demand on the abdominals and very little on the hip flexors. The test is highly reliable for adult men (.93) and women (.94). It requires a range of motion less than 45 degrees, which has been recommended for maximum involvement of the abdominals. Tests requiring a complete sit-up use a much larger range of motion.

Reliability   The reliability of this test is generally satisfactory. The range of test-retest reliability coefficients is .68 to .94; the lower coefficients are probably attributable to inconsistency in the level of motivation.

Norms   Normative data were obtained from NCYFS I and II. Norms tables are presented in Tables 17-20 to 17-22.

Comments   The position assumed by the examinee should be carefully checked before and during the execution of the sit-up. The distance between the heels and the buttocks (12–18 inches) should be monitored continuously, measuring if necessary. The use of partners to count and record scores is permissible; however, the execution of the sit-ups must be observed by the tester to be sure the partners are counting only correctly executed sit-ups. For example, as an examinee begins

Table 17-19 NCYFS Norms by Age for the Sum of Triceps and Subscapular Skinfolds—Girls (in Millimeters)

Percentile	10	11	12	13	14	15	16	17	18
99	10	11	11	12	12	13	13	16	14
90	13	14	15	15	17	19	19	20	19
80	15	16	17	18	19	21	21	22	21
75	16	17	18	19	20	23	22	23	22
70	17	18	18	20	21	24	23	24	23
60	18	19	21	22	24	26	24	26	25
50	20	21	22	24	26	28	26	28	27
40	22	24	24	26	28	30	28	31	28
30	25	28	27	29	31	33	32	34	32
25	27	30	29	31	33	34	33	36	34
20	29	33	31	34	35	37	35	37	36
10	36	40	40	43	40	43	42	42	42

From the National Children and Youth Fitness Study I. Washington, DC: Department of Health and Human Services, 1985.

to fatigue, sit-ups are often executed with a straight back rather than a curl-up. Partners should be instructed not to count the straight-back sit-ups.

Sit-and-Reach Test

The Sit-and-Reach Test is the second of the two tests often included as measures of abdominal and low back–hamstring musculoskeletal function. The abdominal area is tested by the Modified Sit-Ups Test, and the Sit-and-Reach Test is used to measure the low back–hamstring area.

Test Objective The Sit-and-Reach Test is designed to evaluate the flexibility of the low back and posterior thigh.

Description The examinees must remove their shoes to be tested. To begin the test, the examinee sits in front of the test apparatus with feet flat against the end board. The knees should be fully extended and the feet shoulder-width apart. To perform the test, the examinee extends the arms forward with one hand placed on top of the other.

Instructions In the actual test the examinee reaches forward, palms down, along the measuring scale of the testing apparatus. (See Figures 17-8 and 17-9 on p. 488 for drawings of the initial and final test positions.) The reach is repeated three consecutive times, and, on the fourth trial, the maximum reach is held

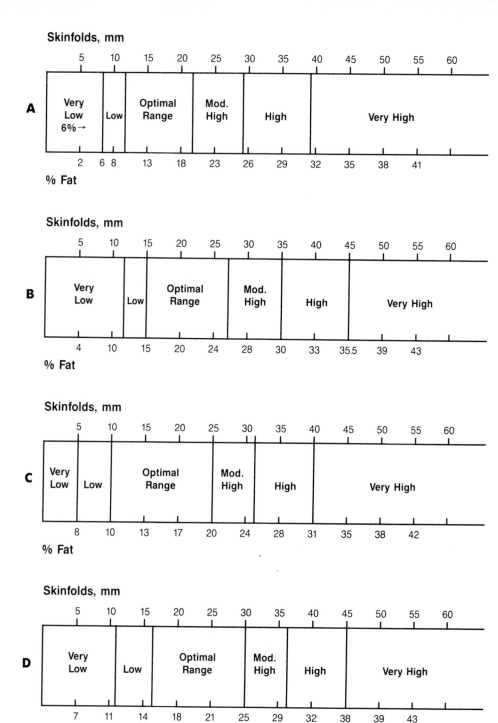

Figure 17-7   Body composition nomograms. **A,** Triceps plus subscapular skinfolds (boys). **B,** Triceps plus subscapular skinfolds (girls). **C,** Triceps plus calf skinfolds (boys). **D,** Triceps plus calf skinfolds (girls). *From Lohman TJ. 1987. The use of skinfold to estimate body fatness in children and youth. Journal of Physical Education, Recreation, and Dance, 58(9):98–102. Used by permission.*

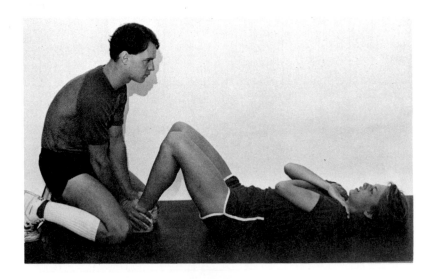

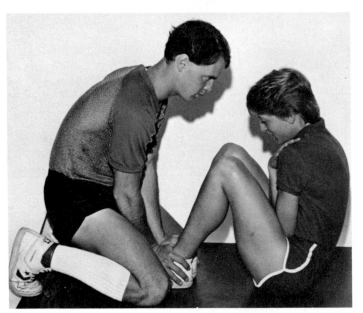

Initial and final test position for Sit-Ups Test.

for 1 second. The distance of the maximum reach is recorded as the test score.

Test Area Any small testing area with adequate floor space would be suitable.

Equipment The test apparatus is a specially constructed box with a measuring scale in which 23 cm is set at the level of the feet. A drawing of one version of

Table 17-20 NCYFS II Norms by Age for the Timed Bent-Knee Sit-Ups (Number in 60 Seconds)

	Age							
	Boys				Girls			
Percentile	6	7	8	9	6	7	8	9
99	36	42	43	48	36	40	44	43
95	31	35	38	42	31	35	37	39
90	28	32	35	39	28	33	34	36
85	26	30	33	36	26	30	32	34
80	25	29	32	35	24	28	30	32
75	24	28	30	33	23	27	29	31
70	22	27	29	32	22	26	28	30
65	21	26	28	31	21	24	27	29
60	20	25	27	30	20	23	26	28
55	19	24	26	29	19	22	25	26
50	19	23	26	28	18	21	25	26
45	18	22	25	27	17	21	24	25
40	17	21	24	26	17	20	23	24
35	16	20	23	25	16	19	21	23
30	15	19	21	24	15	17	20	22
25	14	18	20	23	14	16	19	21
20	12	16	19	22	12	15	17	19
15	11	14	17	19	10	13	16	17
10	9	12	15	16	6	11	13	15
5	4	7	11	13	1	7	9	10

From the National Children and Youth Fitness Study II. Washington, DC: Department of Health and Human Services, 1987.

the box is presented in Figure 17-10. Refer to the test manual (AAHPERD, 1988) for detailed instructions on constructing this version of the apparatus.

Score   The score, measured to the nearest centimeter, is the most distant point reached on the fourth trial. The fingertips of both hands should reach this point. If the reach of the two hands is uneven, the test should be readministered.

Validity   The Sit-and-Reach Test has been validated by comparing it with several other types of flexibility tests, with validity coefficients ranging between .80

Table 17-21 NCYFS Norms by Age for the Timed Bent-Knee Sit-Ups—Girls (Number in 60 Seconds)

Percentile	10	11	12	13	14	15	16	17	18
99	50	53	66	58	57	56	59	60	65
90	43	42	46	46	47	45	49	47	47
80	39	39	41	41	42	42	42	41	42
75	37	37	40	40	41	40	40	40	40
70	36	36	39	39	40	39	39	39	40
60	33	34	36	35	37	36	37	37	38
50	31	32	33	33	35	35	35	36	35
40	30	30	31	31	32	32	33	33	33
30	27	28	30	28	30	30	30	31	30
25	25	26	28	27	29	30	30	30	30
20	24	24	27	25	27	28	28	29	28
10	20	20	21	21	23	24	23	24	24

From the National Children and Youth Fitness Study I. Washington, DC: Department of Health and Human Services, 1985.

and .90. Logical validity has also been claimed for the test, since higher scores reflect better extensibility in the low back, hip, and posterior thigh.

A study by Jackson and Baker (1986) provides a thorough examination of this test. They compared the Sit-and-Reach Test with a test of back flexibility and a test of hamstring flexibility. The Sit-and-Reach Test had moderate validity. (.60–.73) when compared with hamstring flexibility but was not a valid measure (.27–.30) of low back flexibility.

Reliability This test has acceptable reliability, with reliability coefficients of .70 or higher.

Norms Normative data were reported in NCYFS I and II. Tables of norms are presented in Tables 17-23 to 17-25.

Comments The test must be repeated if the knees are flexed during the reach. To ensure that the knees remain extended, the tester should place one hand lightly across the knees. As with all measures of physical fitness, the accuracy and consistency of test scores are increased by adequately warming up before testing. In this case warm-ups should include passive stretching of the low back–hamstring area. If the recommended test apparatus cannot be secured, a bench with a metric ruler attached may be substituted for the V-sit reach, with the student seated on the floor. When preadolescent boys and girls as well as those

Table 17-22 NCYFS Norms by Age for the Timed Bent-Knee Sit-Ups—Boys (Number in 60 Seconds)

Percentile	10	11	12	13	14	15	16	17	18
99	60	60	61	62	64	65	65	68	67
90	47	48	50	52	52	53	55	56	54
80	43	43	46	48	49	50	51	51	50
75	40	41	44	46	47	48	49	50	50
70	38	40	43	45	45	46	48	49	48
60	36	38	40	41	43	44	45	46	44
50	34	36	38	40	41	42	43	43	43
40	32	34	35	37	39	40	41	41	40
30	30	31	33	34	37	37	39	39	38
25	28	30	32	32	35	36	38	37	36
20	26	28	30	31	34	35	36	35	35
10	22	22	25	28	30	31	32	31	31

From the National Children and Youth Fitness Study I. Washington, DC: Department of Health and Human Services, 1985.

in their adolescent growth spurt are tested, it is normal for many of them to be unable to reach 23. During this growth period the legs become proportionally longer than the trunk.

Pull-Ups   The pull-ups test and various modifications of this test are discussed in Chapter 18. All the recently revised physical fitness tests include a measure of arm and shoulder girdle strength. NCYFS norms for the pull-ups test (or chin-ups) and a modified (Vermont) pull-ups test are presented in Tables 17-26 and 17-27.

Overview of Health-Related Physical Fitness Test Items

Although health-related physical fitness tests are widely used, the test items are not without criticism. For example, questions have been raised about the validity of distance run tests as indicators of CR capacity.

Cureton (1982) discusses several factors other than CR capacity that might reflect individual differences in distance running performance—body fatness, running skill or efficiency, motivation, and use of proper pace. Cureton notes that distance run tests have usually been validated by using VO_2 max, expressed as milliliters per kilogram of body weight per minute (mL/kg BW/min) as a criterion measure. However, both variables (distance run score and VO_2 max as

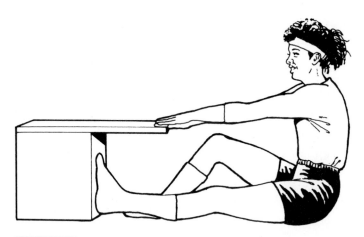

Figure 17-8   Initial test position for the Sit-and-Reach Test.

previously expressed) are negatively affected by the percentage of body fat. In other words, as percent fat increases, both distance run performance and V_{O_2} max would be more appropriately expressed by milliliters per kilogram of fat-free weight per minute (mL/kg FFW/min). He then demonstrates the accuracy of his analysis using data from a number of studies of adults and a single study of children. For example, he refers to a 1977 study (Cureton et al, 1977), which showed the following relationships for boys and girls ages 8 to 12.

Distance	V_{O_2} max (BW)	V_{O_2} max (FFW)
600 yards	− .62	− .32
1 mile	− .66	− .40

Figure 17-9   Final test position for the Sit-and-Reach Test.

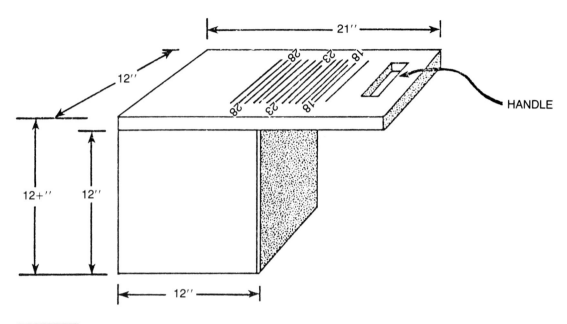

Figure 17-10   Apparatus for measuring the Sit-and-Reach Test.

In short, between 35% and 45% of the variance in distance runs can be accounted for by VO_2 max when total body weight is used to adjust the expression, but the percentage of variance accounted for drops to between 9% and 16% when fat-free weight is used. Thus, variability in body fatness accounts for almost half the relationship between VO_2 max and distance runs. For this reason, it is inappropriate to suggest that distance run tests measure only one physiologic variable. Cureton also notes that changes in distance run performance in children are often not paralleled by similar changes in VO_2 max. Changes are more likely to occur in running efficiency as well as percent fat and anaerobic capacity. Nonetheless, he supports the use of distance-run tests in the assessment of physical fitness in children. Such tests evaluate a unique physical ability not tapped in most other tests of physical performance. They reflect "the level of energy expenditure that a person can sustain over an extended period of time, or the physical work capacity in weight-bearing exercise" (Cureton, 1982, p. 66).

As a part of a fitness education program, children should be taught to use heart rate to monitor the intensity of activity. According to Siegel (1988, p. 78), most children from age 9 or 10, grade 3, can be taught to accurately count a 10-second carotid heart rate. If resting heart rate values are not available for a group of children, average heart rate (shown in Table 17-28) can be used to calculate the target heart rate range.

Table 17-23 NCYFS II Norms by Age for the Sit-and-Reach (in Inches)

	Age							
	Boys				Girls			
Percentile	**6**	**7**	**8**	**9**	**6**	**7**	**8**	**9**
99	17.5	18.0	18.0	17.5	18.5	18.0	19.0	19.0
95	16.5	16.5	16.5	16.0	17.5	17.5	17.5	18.0
90	16.0	16.0	16.0	15.5	16.5	17.5	17.0	17.0
85	15.5	16.0	15.5	15.0	16.0	16.5	16.5	16.5
80	15.0	15.5	15.0	14.5	16.0	16.0	16.0	16.0
75	15.0	15.0	14.5	14.5	15.5	16.0	16.0	16.0
70	14.5	14.5	14.5	14.0	15.0	15.5	15.5	15.5
65	14.0	14.0	14.0	14.0	15.0	15.0	15.0	15.0
60	14.0	14.0	14.0	13.5	15.0	15.0	15.0	15.0
55	13.5	13.5	13.5	13.0	14.5	15.0	14.5	14.5
50	13.5	13.5	13.5	13.0	14.0	14.5	14.0	14.0
45	13.0	13.0	13.0	12.5	14.0	14.5	14.0	14.0
40	12.5	12.5	12.5	12.0	14.0	14.0	13.5	14.0
35	12.5	12.5	12.5	12.0	13.5	14.0	13.5	13.5
30	12.0	12.0	12.0	11.5	13.0	13.5	13.0	13.0
25	12.0	11.5	11.5	11.0	12.5	13.0	12.5	12.5
20	11.5	11.5	11.0	10.5	12.0	12.5	12.0	12.0
15	11.0	11.0	10.5	10.0	12.0	12.0	11.5	11.5
10	10.5	10.0	9.5	9.5	11.5	11.5	11.0	11.0
5	10.0	9.0	8.5	8.0	10.5	10.5	10.0	9.0

From the National Children and Youth Fitness Study II. Washington, DC: Department of Health and Human Services, 1987.
NOTE: *The NCYFS set the zero point at 12 inches, whereas the 1980 AAHPERD norms employed a zero point of 23 cm. To translate the NCYFS inches into centimeters and to adjust the zero point to 23 cm, the following formula may be applied to the NCYFS norms: score in centimeters = (score in inches × 2.54) − 7.48.*

Problems in measuring the skinfold thicknesses of young children have been summarized by Lohman (1982). In laboratory settings investigators assume children are chemically mature with regard to such elements as potassium and water content. Under these assumptions, a mean fat content of 20% is usually found. In a field setting a different value for body fat is estimated using a regression equation. However, equations for predicting the percentage body fat for

Table 17-24 NCYFS Norms by Age for the Sit-and-Reach—Boys (in Inches)

Percentile	10	11	12	13	14	15	16	17	18
99	18.0	18.5	18.5	19.5	20.0	21.5	22.0	21.5	22.0
90	16.0	16.5	16.0	16.5	17.5	18.0	19.0	19.5	19.5
80	15.0	15.5	15.0	15.0	16.0	17.0	18.0	18.0	18.0
75	14.5	15.0	15.0	15.0	15.5	16.5	17.0	17.5	17.5
70	14.5	14.5	14.5	14.5	15.0	16.0	17.0	17.0	17.0
60	14.0	14.0	13.5	13.5	14.0	15.0	16.0	16.0	16.0
50	13.5	13.0	13.0	13.0	13.5	14.0	15.0	15.5	15.0
40	12.5	12.5	12.0	12.5	13.0	13.5	14.0	14.5	14.5
30	12.0	12.0	11.5	12.0	12.0	12.5	13.5	13.5	13.5
25	11.5	11.5	11.0	11.0	11.0	12.0	13.0	13.0	13.0
20	11.0	11.0	10.5	10.5	11.0	11.5	12.0	12.5	12.5
10	10.0	9.5	8.5	9.0	9.0	9.5	10.0	10.5	10.0

From the National Children and Youth Fitness Study I. Washington, DC: Department of Health and Human Services, 1985.
NOTE: *The 1980 AAHPERD norms used a zero point of 23 cm, but NCYFS used 12 inches. To adjust the zero point and to change inches to centimeters, use the following formula: score in centimeters = (score in inches × 2.54) − 7.48.*

adults are not appropriate for children. Furthermore, the relationship between anthropometric measures and body density varies between ages 8 and 15. For these reasons it is both logical and defensible to use the sum of skinfolds to measure body composition in elementary school children rather than applying invalid prediction equations in an effort to estimate percent body fat.

The expense of the skinfold caliper required to measure body composition has been viewed as problematic by some. The major criterion for a skinfold caliper is that it exert a constant force of 10 g/mm² at the skinfold site, regardless of the thickness of the skinfold. Large errors in skinfold measures occur at low pressures, that is, lower than 10 g/mm². In a study conducted by Lohman and Pollock (1981), three types of calipers were compared. A plastic caliper with neither spring nor tension required the tester to apply the appropriate amount of tension. A plastic caliper with a spring depended on the spring for the tension exerted. The third instrument was metal with a uniform tension independent of skinfold thickness. Both experienced and inexperienced testers measured a group of children at the triceps and subscapular sites. Differences between the scores of experienced and inexperienced testers occurred except when the expensive metal caliper was used. When the inexperienced testers were trained, the scores obtained using both pairs of calipers were closer. The less expensive

Table 17-25 NCYFS Norms by Age for the Sit-and-Reach—Girls (in Inches)

Percentile	10	11	12	13	14	15	16	17	18
99	20.5	20.5	21.0	22.0	22.0	23.0	23.0	23.0	22.5
90	17.5	18.0	19.0	20.0	19.5	20.0	20.5	20.5	20.5
80	16.5	17.0	18.0	19.0	19.0	19.0	19.5	19.5	19.5
75	16.5	16.5	17.0	18.0	18.5	19.0	19.0	19.0	19.0
70	16.0	16.5	17.0	17.5	18.0	18.5	19.0	19.0	18.5
60	15.0	15.5	16.0	17.0	17.5	18.0	18.0	18.0	18.0
50	14.5	15.0	15.5	16.0	17.0	17.0	17.5	18.0	17.5
40	14.0	14.0	15.0	15.5	16.0	17.0	17.0	17.0	17.0
30	13.0	13.5	14.5	14.5	15.0	16.0	16.5	16.0	16.0
25	13.0	13.0	14.0	14.0	15.0	15.5	16.0	15.5	15.5
20	12.0	13.0	13.5	13.5	14.0	15.0	15.5	15.0	15.0
10	10.5	11.5	12.0	12.0	12.5	13.5	14.0	13.5	13.0

From the National Children and Youth Fitness Study I. Washington, DC: Department of Health and Human Services, 1985.
NOTE: The 1980 AAHPERD norms used a zero point of 23 cm, but NCYFS used 12 inches. To adjust the zero point and to change inches to centimeters, use the following formula: score in centimeters = (score in inches × 2.54) − 7.48.

calipers may prove to be suitable for use in a field test setting, provided the tester is well trained. Several inexpensive skinfold calipers are shown in Figure 17-11.

Lohman and Pollock make several suggestions regarding the training of testers. At the very least, inexperienced testers should be trained above and beyond the required reading of the test manual. To attain proficiency in measuring skinfold thicknesses, testers should practice measuring between 50 and 100 people. Initially the sites should be marked with a grease pencil on the subject's skin. Testers within the same fitness club or school system should train together.

Several articles on health-related physical fitness testing that are useful for the practitioner have been published in recent years. For physical education teacher, Pate and Corbin (1981) discuss implications for curriculum. Program ideas are presented, including those in the cognitive and affective areas, as well as psychomotor performance. The article includes excellent suggestions for teachers that an innovative reader could apply in a nonschool setting as well. Their taxonomy of physical fitness objectives is shown in Table 17-29. The levels of the taxonomy range from the acquisition of physical fitness vocabulary to the development of physical fitness problem-solving ability. Another excellent article for teachers and exercise specialists is that of Pollock and Blair

Table 17-26 NCYFS Norms by Age for the Chin-Ups—Boys (Number Completed)

Percentile	10	11	12	13	14	15	16	17	18
99	13	12	13	17	18	18	20	20	21
90	8	8	8	10	12	14	14	15	16
80	5	5	6	8	9	11	12	13	14
75	4	5	5	7	8	10	12	12	13
70	4	4	5	7	8	10	11	12	12
60	2	3	4	5	6	8	10	10	11
50	1	2	3	4	5	7	9	9	10
40	1	1	2	3	4	6	8	8	9
30	0	0	1	1	3	5	6	6	7
25	0	0	0	1	2	4	6	5	6
20	0	0	0	0	1	3	5	4	5
10	0	0	0	0	0	1	2	2	3

From the National Children and Youth Fitness Study I. Washington, DC: Department of Health and Human Services, 1985.

Table 17-27 NCYFS Norms by Age for the Chin-Ups—Girls (Number Completed)

Percentile	10	11	12	13	14	15	16	17	18
99	8	8	8	5	8	6	8	7	6
90	3	3	2	2	2	2	2	2	2
80	2	1	1	1	1	1	1	1	1
75	1	1	1	1	1	1	1	1	1
70	1	1	1	0	1	1	1	1	1
60	0	0	0	0	0	0	0	0	0
50	0	0	0	0	0	0	0	0	0
40	0	0	0	0	0	0	0	0	0
30	0	0	0	0	0	0	0	0	0
25	0	0	0	0	0	0	0	0	0
20	0	0	0	0	0	0	0	0	0
10	0	0	0	0	0	0	0	0	0

From the National Children and Youth Fitness Study I. Washington, DC: Department of Health and Human Services, 1985.

Table 17-28 Children's Heart Data

Age (yr)	Average HRrest*	Normal Range*	Target HRR 60%–85% HRmax	20-Sec Values
4	100	80–120	170–199	56–66
6	100	75–115	168–197	56–64
8	90	70–110	163–194	54–64
10	90	70–110	162–192	54–64
		Girls (HRmax = 225)		
12	90	70–110	164–190	52–63
14	85	65–105	161–187	51–62
16	80	60–100	157–185	50–61
18	75	55–95	155–183	49–60
		Boys (HRmax = 220)		
12	85	65–105	159–190	52–63
14	80	60–100	156–187	51–62
16	75	55–95	152–185	50–61
18	70	50–90	149–182	49–60

From Siegel J. 1988. Children's target heart rate range. Journal of Physical Education, Recreation, and Dance, 59(4):78–79. Used by permission.
HRrest, *resting heart rate (beats per minute);* HRmax, *maximum heart rate.*
* *Data from Nelson WE, Behrman RE, Vaughan VC. 1987. Textbook of pediatrics. Philadelphia: WB Saunders.*

(1981). An overview of the state of the art of exercise prescription is presented, beginning with a discussion of the physiological and behavioral components of exercise prescription. This is followed by a review of the principles of overload, specificity, warm-up, initial levels of fitness, progressions, and individual differences. Finally, the effect of exercise on CR function is discussed, in particular, frequency, intensity, duration, and mode of exercise. A number of articles of this nature have appeared in the *Journal of Physical Education, Recreation and Dance,* published by AAHPERD.

STEP TESTS

Distance run tests, already described as measures of CR function, can be used as a part of a health-related physical fitness test or can be administered separately by physical education teachers and exercise specialists. Another practical test of

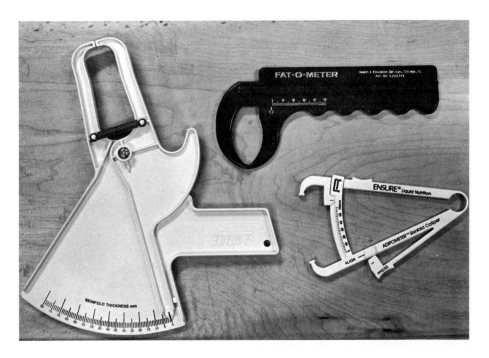

Figure 17-11   A variety of inexpensive skinfold calipers.

Table 17-29 Physical Fitness Objectives

Level	Objective
1	Physical fitness vocabulary (fitness components; distinction between health-related and skill-related components)
2	Exercising (teacher interacts and encourages students to exercise)
3	Achieving physical fitness (help children experience the satisfaction of being fit)
4	Establishing regular exercise patterns (objectives become learner-oriented rather than teacher-oriented)
5	Physical fitness evaluation
6	Physical fitness problem solving (interpret data and modify own exercise program)

From Pate R, Corbin C. 1981. Implications for curriculum. Journal of Physical Education, Recreation and Dance, 52(1):36–38. Used by permission.

CR function that can be used in a field setting is the **step test.** In this section the Harvard Step Test, the best-known step test, is described, followed by a description of several modifications of the Harvard test.

The Harvard Step Test

This test was developed at the Harvard Fatigue Laboratory in 1943. A landmark test in its day, it is no longer widely used because of its strenuousness. However, it still provides the standard for all step tests developed since that time and thus merits a thorough overview.

Test Objective The Harvard Step Test was designed to measure the CR function of adult males.

Description The examinee exercises on a 20-inch bench for as long a period as possible up to 5 minutes.

Instructions The stepping pattern is up with the left foot, up with the right foot, down with the left foot, and down with the right foot. Both of the examinee's legs should be straight when standing on the bench. The steps should be taken at a cadence of 30 steps per minute. The cadence can be easily established using a metronome, although a stopwatch can also be used. The test instructions and cadence can also be recorded on an audiotape for ease of administration. The test ends after the 5-minute period has elapsed, although examinees may stop at any time before the 5-minute limit.

Whenever the examinee stops exercising, a pulse count is taken during three recovery periods — from 1 to 1½ minutes, 2 to 2½, and 3 to 3½ minutes after exercise ceases. Two scores are recorded: the number of seconds the examinee exercised and the sum of the pulse counts in the three recovery periods.

Test Area One of the desirable features of a step test is that it can be administered in small areas.

Equipment Metronome or stopwatch and 20-inch bench.

Scoring Formula 17-1 is used to determine the index of physical efficiency:

$$\text{Index} = \frac{\text{duration of exercise in seconds} \times 100}{2 \times \text{sum of 3 recovery pulse counts}} \qquad \text{Formula 17-1}$$

Suppose an examinee stops exercising at the end of 4 minutes (240 seconds) and his recovery pulse rates are 80, 60, and 50, respectively. Using Formula 17-1, determine his index of physical efficiency.

$$\text{Index} = \frac{240 \times 100}{2(80 + 60 + 50)} = 63.2$$

What does a score of 63.2 mean? Is it a good score or a poor score? Mathews (1978, p. 269) at Ohio State University developed a set of standards for adult males based on a large data set accumulated over a period of several years.

Harvard Step Test Standards

Above 90	Excellent
80–89	Good
65–79	Average
55–64	Low average
Below 55	Poor

Validity The validity of the Harvard Step Test has been determined by correlating it with VO_2 max based on a maximal stress test, as a criterion measure. Validity coefficients ranging from $-.35$ to $.77$ have been reported, indicating that this step test is not a very precise indicator of CR function. Negative validity coefficients were obtained because several investigators used a modified scoring system where lower scores represented better performance on the step test.

Reliability Reliability coefficients ranging from .65 to .95 have been obtained for the Harvard Step Test of the test in modified form. Most of the these coefficients are higher than .80. The reproducibility or objectivity of the test, which is the ability to obtain the same heart rate using different testers, is high. Coefficients of .992 to .995 have been reported by Montoye (1978). Most of the reliability estimates are confounded (probably made lower) by the potential for error in obtaining the pulse rate. Sometimes the pulse rate is counted by a partner. On other occasions the same tester is not used for both testing sessions. Certainly, the lack of objectivity in obtaining a pulse rate is a problem, but the extent to which this problem affects the size of the reliability coefficient is unknown.

Comments The Harvard Step Test has been modified for young women and for boys and girls. Montoye (1978) has recommended specific bench heights, rates of stepping, and maximum durations for various age groups and both sexes.

AGES 8 TO 10 (BOYS AND GIRLS) Use a bench height of 8 inches, a stepping rate of 24 (4 counting cycles per minute), and a maximum duration of 3 minutes.

AGES 10 TO 12 (BOYS AND GIRLS) Use a bench height of 12 inches, a stepping rate of 24, and a maximum duration of 3 minutes.

AGES 12 TO 14 (BOYS AND GIRLS) Use a bench height of 18 inches, a stepping rate of 24, and a maximum duration of 3 minutes.

AGES 15 TO 22 (GIRLS) Use a bench height of 18 inches, a stepping rate of 24, and a maximum duration of 3 minutes. (These test specifications can also be used for women, ages 23–34.)

AGES 15 TO 22 (BOYS) Use a bench height of 20 inches, a stepping rate of 30, and a maximum duration of 5 minutes. (These test specifications can also be used for men, ages 23–34.)

The Ohio State University Step Test

Because of the strenuous nature of the Harvard Step Test, a more practical and less taxing step test was developed at Ohio State University (OSU) in 1969. This test can easily be used in a field setting.

Test Objective The purpose of this test is to measure CR function for males and females.

Description The OSU Step Test is divided into a series of 18 innings of exercise. Each inning is 30 seconds long and is followed by a 20-second rest period. Each 20-second rest period consists of 5 seconds to locate the pulse, 10 seconds to count the pulse, and 5 seconds to prepare for the beginning of the next inning. Therefore a new inning of exercise begins every 50 seconds. The 18 innings are divided into 3 phases:

  Phase I—6 innings at 24 steps/min on a 15-inch bench
  Phase II—6 innings at 30 steps/min on a 15-inch bench
  Phase III—6 innings at 30 steps/min on a 20-inch bench

During the 10-second interval of each rest period, the pulse rate is counted. If the pulse rate is less than 25 beats per 10 seconds, the examinee continues with the next inning. The first rest interval in which the pulse rate reaches or exceeds 25 is the inning that terminates the test. The test can also be terminated by completing all 18 innings without attaining a pulse rate of 25.

Instructions Before beginning the test, the examinee stands in front of the bench and grasps the handbar with both hands. The handbar should be level with the top of the examinee's head. The stepping pattern is initiated at the signal ''Ready, go!,'' and the examinee proceeds in cadence with the metronome. The up-up-down-down stepping pattern described for the Harvard Step Test is used, except either foot can initiate the first step up. The legs must be straight when both feet are on the bench, and the back should also be straight at this point. The examinee should be forewarned when the cadence changes at the beginning of a new phase.

Test Area A relatively small space is sufficient for administering the OSU Step Test.

Equipment A split-level bench with an adjustable handbar (lower level of the bench is 15 inches high; higher level, 20 inches) and a metronome and stopwatch, unless the cadence and time units are recorded on tape.

Scoring The score is the number of innings the subject is able to complete before reaching a heart rate of 25 in 10 seconds. The examinee may be permitted to count his or her own pulse, if able to do so fairly accurately. The tester should make arrangements before administering a step test to have additional help available for those who have difficulty detecting their pulse. Several students in class might assist in this capacity. The entire group of examinees should be informed that this type of assistance is available.

Validity The validity coefficient for the OSU Step Test when compared to a submaximal stress test is .94. VO_2 max values were estimated from the submaximal test. When the OSU Step Test scores were correlated with VO_2 max measured directly in a maximum stress test, the validity coefficients were considerably lower, ranging from .47 to .57. These latter coefficients correspond closely to those obtained for the Harvard Step Test.

Reliability The OSU Step Test has acceptable reliability, with reliability coefficients ranging from .69 to .94.

Comments The OSU Test has been modified for college women (Witten, 1973) and for elementary school boys (Callan, 1968).

COLLEGE WOMEN A trilevel bench is used with heights of 14, 17, and 20 inches. Twenty innings, divided into four phases, are used. In innings 1 to 5, a cadence of 24 steps per minute is used with a bench height of 14 inches. In innings 6 to 10, the cadence is 30 steps per minute using a bench height of 14 inches. In innings 11 to 15, the cadence is 30 steps per minute using a bench height of 17 inches. In innings 16 to 20, the cadence is 30 steps per minute with a bench height of 20 inches. Otherwise the test is similar to the OSU test for college males, except that the test is terminated when the pulse rate reaches 28 or higher.

ELEMENTARY SCHOOL BOYS This is an adaptation for boys in grades 4 through 6. The test is identical to the one used for college males, with two exceptions—the tester must count the heart rate using a stethoscope and the test is terminated when the heart rate reaches 29 beats during the 10-second period.

The Queens College Step Test

A simplified version of the step test, developed at Queens College in New York City (Katch, Katch, and McArdle, 1991), is useful for the quick screening of the CR function of college students. A bench height of 16¼ inches is used. This is the height of a bleacher step at Queens, thus allowing for mass testing. A metronome is used to monitor the stepping cadence, which is 88 steps per minute (22 complete step-ups) for women and 96 steps per minute (24 complete step-ups) for men. After a 15-second practice period, all examinees begin the test and continue for 3 minutes. At the end of 3 minutes the examinees are stopped. They are allowed 5 seconds to detect their pulse at the carotid artery. After 5 seconds examinees count their pulse rate for 15 seconds and multiply the value by 4. A table of percentile ranks and predicted VO_2 max for male and female students is shown in Table 17-30.

To determine test validity, scores on the Queens College Test were correlated with measures of VO_2 max obtained during treadmill testing. Validity coefficients are $-.75$ for college women and $-.72$ for college men. These coefficients are negative, since lower heart rates are associated with higher VO_2 max values. The test is highly reliable, with coefficients of .92 reported for women and .89 for men.

A number of fitness tests require the determination of heart rate through palpation of the carotid artery in the neck. The correct positioning of the fingers is shown in Figure 17-12. The pressure on the artery should be firm but light. Excessive pressure will distort the heart rate.

Table 17-30 Percentile Rankings for Recovery Heart Rate (HR) and Predicted Maximum Oxygen Consumption (VO_2 max) for Male and Female College Students

Percentile Ranking	Recovery HR, Female	Predicted VO_2 max (mL/kg · min)	Recovery HR, Male	Predicted VO_2 max (mL/kg · min)
100	128	42.2	120	60.9
95	140	40.0	124	59.3
90	148	38.5	128	57.6
85	152	37.7	136	54.2
80	156	37.0	140	52.5
75	158	36.6	144	50.9
70	160	36.3	148	49.2
65	162	35.9	149	48.8
60	163	35.7	152	47.5
55	164	35.5	154	46.7
50	166	35.1	156	45.8
45	168	34.8	160	44.1
40	170	34.4	162	43.3
35	171	34.2	164	42.5
30	172	34.0	166	41.6
25	176	33.3	168	40.8
20	180	32.6	172	39.1
15	182	32.2	176	37.4
10	184	31.8	178	36.6
5	196	29.6	184	34.1

From Katch FI, Katch VL, McArdle WD. 1991. Nutrition, weight control, and exercise, ed 3. Philadelphia: Lea & Febiger. Used by permission.

MEASURING HEALTH-RELATED FITNESS IN A LABORATORY SETTING

Cardiorespiratory Function

The most desirable approach to determining CR function is to measure it during exercise. With this approach, changes in physiologic parameters can be monitored throughout the exercise cycle.

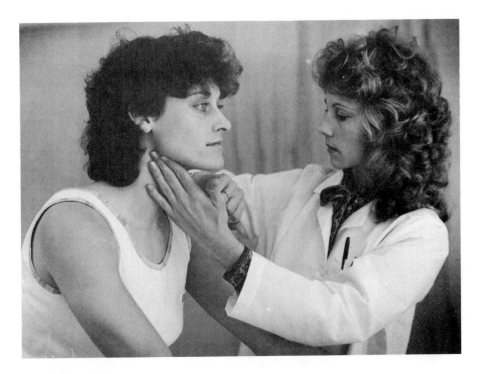

Figure 17-12   Palpation of carotid artery to determine heart rate.

Maximal Stress Testing

To assess VO_2 max directly, the subject's expired air is measured during exhaustive physical work. Typically, the examinee exercises on a bicycle ergometer or a motor-driven treadmill, as depicted in Figure 17-13, although a stepping bench may also be used. The workload is gradually increased. On the treadmill this is accomplished by increasing the speed, raising the slope, or both. On the bicycle ergometer the workload is increased by increasing the friction on the flywheel. As the workload increases, oxygen consumption also increases. Throughout the test period exhaled air is collected using a portable spirometer, Douglas bags, or computerized instrumentation. When the examinee can no longer continue, the test is stopped. VO_2 max is obtained when the increased workload is no longer accompanied by an increase in oxygen uptake.

Measuring time on the treadmill (between the initiation of the test to the point of exhaustion) can also be used to determine maximal stress. The time score is then used to predict oxygen uptake.

Submaximal Stress Testing

Indirect methods of measuring CR function are frequently used in a laboratory setting. Since heart rate and oxygen uptake increase linearly with increases in

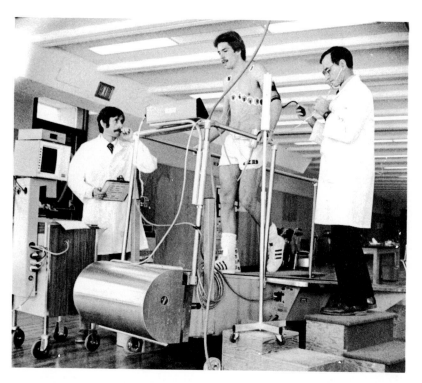

Figure 17-13   Balke Treadmill Test.

workload, heart rate can be used to predict oxygen uptake. While these tests are not as accurate as a direct measure, they do not require the examinee to exercise to exhaustion.

Bruce Protocol

This protocol is one of the most widely used treadmill stress tests. It consists of five stages, each lasting 3 minutes for a total testing period of 15 minutes. The fact that this test is relatively short in duration has contributed to its popularity. The test is based on changes in speed and treadmill grade within each 3-minute period. This protocol is designed for people at normal risk. The American College of Sports Medicine guidelines for exercise testing and prescription do not recommend this test for cardiac risk patients or post myocardial infarction pre-discharge exercise testing. The guidelines also report a 10% to 20% error rate in estimating VO_2 max from the Bruce Protocol. Rapid increase in speed and grade as well as excessive use of handrails for support are the factors that contribute to this error rate.

Balke Protocol

Balke (1952) devised a submaximal test that measures the duration of exercise required to produce a heart rate of 180 beats per minute. The examinee walks on a treadmill at a constant speed, approximately 3.5 miles per hour. At the end of each minute, the heart rate is taken and the slope of the treadmill is increased. Blood pressure is usually recorded as well, as shown in Figure 17-14. After the first minute and each succeeding minute of exercise, the slope is increased by a 1% grade. The equipment required to administer the test is a treadmill, stopwatch, and electrocardiograph. The test score is the number of minutes required to attain a heart rate of 180. The test is highly reliable and valid, although an individual's performance can be affected by several possible sources of error, such as time of most recent meal, time of day, temperature, and emotional state. One of the notable advantages of the Balke test is its safety. Since the work is increased at a gradual pace, the subject's physiological changes can be monitored on a continual basis and the test can be stopped when appropriate for an individual subject.

A classification scale has been devised to interpret test scores of adult men:

Minutes to heart rate of 180	Classification
22–above	Excellent
20–21	Very good
18–19	Good
17	Average
15–16	Fair
13–14	Poor
12–below	Very poor

Astrand and Rhyming Test

A submaximal stress test on the bicycle ergometer was developed by Astrand and Rhyming (1954). The examinee pedals for 6 or more minutes at a set cadence, with a heart rate between 125 and 170 beats per minute. Baumgartner and Jackson (1991) recommended workloads of 600 kpm/min for college women and 800 kpm/min for college men. The test score must be corrected for subjects 30 years of age or older. Validity coefficients ranging from .33 to .872 have been reported. In both cases the test scores were compared with a direct measure of CR function.

A maximal stress test can also be conducted on the bicycle ergometer. This procedure, with expired gas collected in Douglas bags, is shown in Figure 17-14.

PWC$_{170}$ Test

The PWC$_{170}$ Test is administered on a bicycle ergometer, with 4 to 10 minutes of exercise at each workload. The subject's PWC (physical work capacity) is the workload maintained up to a heart rate of 170 beats per minute. Heart rate is measured at each workload. Since PWC$_{170}$ is correlated with body size, a correction of the test score is necessary. The validity coefficients range from .57 to .88, when PWC$_{170}$ scores are correlated with VO$_2$ max values. This test is often recommended for testing the PWC of children.

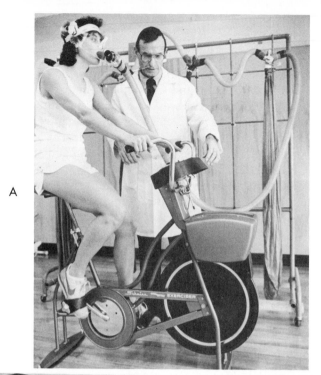

A

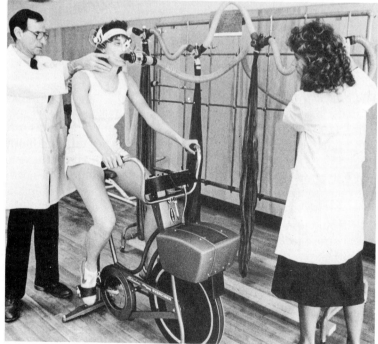

B

Figure 17-14   **A,** Maximal stress testing on the bicycle ergometer. **B,** Measuring heart rate and collecting expired gas during maximal stress testing on the bicycle ergometer.

Recommendations for Testing Cardiorespiratory Function

For purposes of mass screening, Montoye (1978) recommends administering some form of a step test to persons between the ages of 8 and 22. A step test may also be used to test healthy subjects ages 22 to 34. For people over 35 years of age, Montoye notes the potential medical risks and recommends that a physician be present when fitness tests are administered.

Body Composition

A direct measure of body composition can be made by chemical analysis. Until recently, making this analysis required a human cadaver. However, a new method of determining body composition using electrical waves passed through the wrists and ankles has now been developed. The most frequently used indirect measure in a laboratory setting is hydrostatic weighing.

Hydrostatic Weighing

Generally the assessment of body composition involves determining the relative percentage of fat and muscle. Specific gravity, which reflects body density, is a better indicator of body composition than weight alone. Specific gravity equals the ratio of the density of a body to that of an equal volume of water. Specific gravity is usually estimated by weighing the body in water. The subject

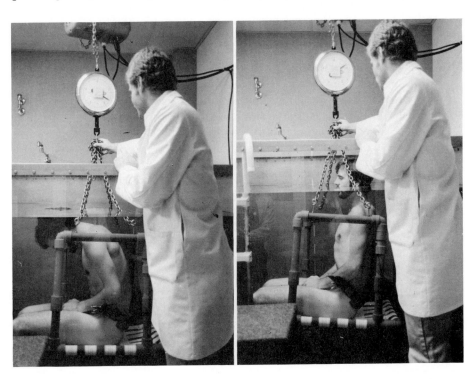

Figure 17-15   Assessment of body composition by underwater weighing. *From Pollock ML, Schmidt DH, Jackson AS.*

is immersed up to the neck in a specially built tank of water warmed to a comfortable temperature. The subject is instructed to hold his or her breath for 5 seconds, lower the head underwater, and expire the air forcefully, as depicted in Figure 17-15 on p. 505. At this point the underwater weight of the subject is recorded. To ensure accurate results, 10 to 12 repeated weighings are recommended.

After forceful expiration of air, some air remains in the lungs. This residual lung volume is measured before the underwater weighing; it must be used in calculating body density.

SUMMARY

An emphasis on health-related physical fitness is pervasive in both school and nonschool settings. A distinction should be made between health-related fitness and measures of athletic performance. Although tests of athletic performance are sometimes referred to as health-related physical fitness measures, this label is a misnomer. The 50-yard dash, for example, does not measure health-related physical fitness; rather, it measures a certain fitness for athletic performance, in this case, speed. However, the term *fitness* is used loosely in this context. Health-related physical fitness can be measured in both laboratory and field settings with an acceptable degree of validity and reliability.

Learning Experiences

1. Practice marking the site for triceps skinfold measurement. Use a grease pencil to mark the site. Measure the site five times using a skinfold caliper. Try to obtain the same reading to within 1 or 2 mm.
2. Visit a health club or fitness center in your community. Ask the manager or one of the instructors about the tests (if any) they administer to new clients. Request a copy of the form(s) used to record test results to take back to your measurement class. Evaluate the testing program in light of desirable physical fitness objectives.
3. Practice measuring your heart rate by palpating the carotid artery in your neck. Then practice on another person, both before and after exercise.
4. Administer the Prudential *FITNESS*GRAM test or a similar test to several of your fellow students. Study the instructions for test administration carefully before beginning. After you have completed the testing, write a short paper on the problems you encountered in administering the test and how you would alleviate these problems in future administrations of the test.

References
American Alliance for Health, Physical Education, Recreation and Dance (AAHPERD). 1980. AAHPERD health-related physical fitness test manual.

Reston, Va: American Alliance for Health, Physical Education, Recreation, and Dance.

American Alliance for Health, Physical Education, Recreation and Dance (AAHPERD). 1984. Technical manual. Reston, Va: American Alliance for Health, Physical Education, Recreation, and Dance.

American Alliance for Health, Physical Education, Recreation and Dance (AAHPERD). 1988. Physical Best. Reston, Va: American Alliance for Health, Physical Education, Recreation, and Dance.

American Association for Health, Physical Education and Recreation (AAHPER). 1976. AAHPER youth fitness test manual. Washington, DC. American Alliance for Health, Physical Education, Recreation, and Dance.

American Health and Fitness Foundation. 1988. Fit youth today. Austin, Tex: American Health and Fitness Foundation.

American Heart Association (AHA). 1992. Statement on exercise: Benefits and recommendations for physical activity programs for all Americans. Dallas: American Heart Association.

Astrand P, Rodahl K. 1970. Textbook of work physiology. New York: McGraw-Hill.

Astrand PO, Ryhming I. 1954. A nomogram for calculation of aerobic capacity (physical fitness) from pulse rate during submaximal work. Journal of Applied Physiology, **7:**218–235.

Balke B. 1952. Correlation of static and physical endurance. I. A test of physical performance based on the cardiovascular and respiratory response to gradually increased work. San Antonio, Texas: Air University, USAF School of Aviation Medicine. Project No. 21-32-004, Report no. 1, April.

Baumgartner TA, Jackson AS. 1991. Measurement for evaluation in physical education, ed 3. Dubuque, Iowa: Wm C Brown Group.

Benham TB. 1988. The A.A.U. developmental physical fitness curricular guide, grades 5–8: Instructor's manual. Bloomington, Ind: Amateur Athletic Union.

Chrysler Fund–Amateur Athletic Union (AAU). 1992. Physical fitness program. Bloomington, Ind: Chrysler–Amateur Athletic Union.

Corbin CB, Pangrazi RP. 1992. Are American children and youth fit? Research Quarterly for Exercise and Sport, **63:**96–106.

Cureton KJ. 1982. Distance running performance tests in children—what do they mean? Journal of Physical Education, Recreation and Dance, **53:**64–66.

Cureton KJ, Boileau RA, Lohman TC, Misner JE. 1977. Determinants of distance running performance in children: Analysis of a path model. Research Quarterly, **48:**270–279.

Cureton KJ, Warren GL. 1990. Criterion-referenced standards for youth health-related fitness tests: A tutuorial. Research Quarterly for Exercise and Sport, **61:**7–19.

Gortmaker SL, Dietz WH, Sobol AN, Wehler CA. 1987. Increasing pediatric obesity in the U.S. American Journal of Diseases in Children, **14:**535–540.

Institute for Aerobics Research. 1992. The Prudential *FITNESS*GRAM test administration manual. Dallas: Institute for Aerobic Research.

Jackson AE, Coleman AE. 1976. Validation of distance run tests for elementary school children. Research Quarterly, **47**:86–94.

Jackson AW, Baker AA. 1986. The relationship of the Sit and Reach Test to criterion measures of hamstring and back flexibility in young females. Research Quarterly for Exercise and Sport, **57**:183–186.

Katch FI, Katch VL, McArdle WD. 1991. Nutrition, weight control, and exercise, ed 3. Philadelphia: Lea & Febiger.

Krahenbuhl GS, Pangrazi RP, Peterson GW, Burkett LN, Schneider MJ. 1978. Field testing of cardiorespiratory fitness in primary school children. Medicine and Science in Sports, **10**:208–213.

Kuntzleman CT, Reiff GG. 1992. The decline in American children's fitness levels. Research Quarterly for Exercise and Sport, **63**:107–111.

Lacy AC, LaMaster KJ. 1990. Analysis of fitness activities in junior high school physical education. The Physical Educator, **47**:176–179.

Lohman TJ. 1982. Measurement of body composition in children. Journal of Physical Education, Recreation and Dance, **53**(7):67–70.

Lohman TJ. 1987. The use of skinfold to estimate body fatness on children and youth. Journal of Physical Education, Recreation and Dance, **58**(1):98–102.

Lohman TJ, Pollock ML. 1981. Which caliper? How much training? Journal of Physical Education, Recreation and Dance, **52**:(1):27–29.

Mathews DK. 1978. Measurement in physical education. Philadelphia: WB Saunders Company.

McGing E. 1989. Aerobic activity—Do physical education programs provide enough? Journal of Physical Education, Recreation and Dance, **60**(9):43–46.

McSwegin P, Pemberton C, Petray C, Going S. 1989. Physical best: The AAHPERD guide to physical fitness education and assessment. Reston, Va: American Alliance for Health, Physical Education, Recreation and Dance.

Montoye HJ. 1978. An introduction to measurement in physical education. Boston: Allyn & Bacon.

Pate RR, Corbin C. 1981. Implications for curriculum. Journal of Physical Education, Recreation and Dance, **52**(1):36–38.

Pollock ML, Blair SN. 1981. Exercise prescription. Journal of Physical Education, Recreation and Dance, **52**(1):30–35, 81.

President's Council on Physical Fitness and Sports. 1991a. Get fit: A handbook for youth ages 6–17. Washington, DC: President's Council on Physical Fitness and Sports.

President's Council on Physical Fitness and Sports. 1991b. The President's challenge physical fitness program packet. Washington, DC: President's Council on Physical Fitness and Sports.

Reiff GG, Dixon WR, Jacoby D, Ye GX, Spain CG, Hunsicker PA. 1985. National school population fitness survey. President's Council on Physical Fitness and Sports, Research Project 282-84-0086.

Robertson LD, Magnusdottir H. 1987. Evaluation of criteria associated with abdominal fitness testing. Research Quarterly for Exercise and Sport, **58**:355–359.

Ross JG, Gilbert GG. 1985. The national children and youth fitness study: A summary of findings. Journal of Physical Education, Recreation and Dance, **56**:45–50.

Ross JG, Pate RR. 1987. The national children and youth fitness study 11: A summary of findings. Journal of Physical Education, Recreation and Dance, **58**:51–61.

Ross JG, Pate RR, Lohman TG, Christenson GM. 1987. Changes in body composition in children. Journal of Physical Education, Recreation and Dance, **58**(9):74–77.

Safrit MJ. 1995. Complete guide to youth fitness testing. Champaign, Ill: Human Kinetics.

Sallis JF, Patterson TL, Buono MJ, Nader PR. 1988. Relation of cardiovascular fitness and physical activity to cardiorespiratory disease risk factors in children and adults. American Journal of Epidemiology, **127**:933–941.

Siegel J. 1988. Children's target heart rate range. Journal of Physical Education, Recreation and Dance, **59**:78–79.

Strand B, Reeder S. 1993a. Analysis of heart rate levels during middle school physical education activities. Journal of Physical Education, Recreation, and Dance, **64**:(3):85–91.

Strand B, Reeder S. 1993b. PE with a heartbeat—Hi-tech physical education. Journal of Physical Education, Recreation, and Dance, **64**(3):81–84.

Taylor W, Baranowski T. 1991. Physical activity, cardiovascular fitness, and adiposity in children. Research Quarterly for Exercise and Sport, **62**:157–163.

Updike. Chrysler Fund—Amateur Athletic Union (AAU). 1992. Physical fitness program. Bloomington, Ind: Chrysler—Amateur Athletic Union.

Wells CL. 1986. The effects of physical activity on cardiorespiratory fitness in children. In Stull G, Eckert H, eds. Effects of physical activity on children. Champaign, Ill: Human Kinetics, pp 114–126.

Witten C. 1973. Construction of a submaximal cardiovascular step test for college females. Research Quarterly, **44**:46–50.

Annotated Readings

Fox KR, Biddle SJH. 1988. The use of fitness tests: Educational and psychological considerations. Journal of Physical Education, Recreation, and Dance, **59**(4):47–53.

Stresses a focus on lifetime fitness, which places greater emphasis on the psychological orientation of students toward physical activity; identifies factors affecting fitness performance and discusses their impact on fitness test scores; encourages an emphasis on the process of regular exercise rather than the product of fitness (e.g., overuse of fitness norms); applies psychological principles to the fitness testing situation.

Koslow RE. 1988. Can physical fitness be a primary objective in a balanced PE program? Journal of Physical Education, Recreation and Dance, **59**(4):75–77.

Discusses the issue of the development and maintenance of physical fitness as a primary objective in physical education; reviews the principles and concepts pertaining to fitness development; describes the time requirements necessary to meet a fitness objective; points to the importance of setting objectives that are specific, measurable, and attainable within the restraints of the program.

Lacy E, Marshall B. 1984. *FITNESS*GRAM: An answer to physical fitness improvement for school children. Journal of Physical Education, Recreation, and Dance, **55**(1):18–19.

Describes the pilot program of *FITNESS*GRAM program in Tulsa, Oklahoma; discusses the unique aspects of the *FITNESS*GRAM program in promoting physical fitness in the community.

Pangrazi RP, Corbin CB. 1993. Physical fitness: Questions teachers ask. Journal of Physical Education, Recreation, and Dance, **64**(7):14–19.

Answers the 12 most frequently asked questions about physical fitness; questions deal with the fitness levels of American children and youth, the activity level of this population, and the impact of factors such as heredity and maturation on fitness test performance; focuses on the process of physical activity rather than the product; discusses the current fitness tests and the importance of teaching fitness concepts.

Pate RR, Ross JG. 1987. Factors associated with health-related fitness. Journal of Physical Education, Recreation, and Dance, **58**(1):93–95.

Reports on one phase of NCYFS II on the relationship between the physical activity patterns of 6- to 9-year-old children and their health-related fitness; emphasizes two key components of health-related fitness—CR endurance and body composition; children with higher levels of CR endurance tend to participate in more community-based physical activity, watch less television, and receive higher ratings on being physically active.

Pate RR, Ross JG, Dotson CO, Gilbert GG. 1985. The new norms: A comparison with the 1980 AAHPRED norms. Journal of Physical Education, Recreation, and Dance, **56**(1):70–72.

Compares norms developed from the NCYFS I data with the 1980 norms developed for the AAHPRED Health-Related Physical Fitness Test; discusses the sampling approaches used in both studies.

Ross JG, Dotson CO, Gilbert CC, Katz SJ. 1985. Maturation and fitness test performance. Journal of Physical Education, Recreation, and Dance, **56**(1):67–69.

Provides a new perspective on developmental trends in fitness by examining test performance on five different dimensions of fitness; the common beliefs about the effects of age on fitness test performance were not verified by the data from the NCYFS.

Ross JG, Dotson CO, Gilbert CC, Katz SJ. 1985. New standards for fitness measurement. Journal of Physical Education, Recreation, and Dance, **56**(1):62–66.

Discusses the development of fitness norms (included in this chapter) based on data from the NCYFS I; includes tables of percentiles by age and sex for five fitness tests, consisting of the Health-Related Physical Fitness Test items and a chin-ups test.

Siegel J. 1988. Children's target heart rate range. Journal of Physical Education, Recreation, and Dance, **59**(7):78–79.

Stresses the importance of using heart rate to control the intensity of activity; reviews the standard formula for deriving training heart rate and applies it to children; notes difficulty in obtaining resting heart rate in children; and presents table of average resting heart rate values for same-age children.

Tests of Performance-Related Physical Fitness

Watch for these words as you read the following chapter

50-Yard dash test
Flexed arm hang test
Individually based norms
Percentile norms

Performance-related physical fitness
Shuttle run test
Standing long jump test

Every physical education teacher, coach, and exercise scientist knows that physical fitness necessary to engage in sports and other forms of physical activity encompasses more than health-related physical fitness. Fitness specific to a sport is often referred to as performance-related physical fitness. (For a discussion of the distinction between health-related physical fitness and performance-related physical fitness, see Chapter 17.) The performance of most motor tasks probably involves some combination of health-related and performance-related fitness. Some aspects of performance-related fitness may be more important for a specific sport than health-related fitness. One example of performance-related fitness is agility. In teaching a variety of activities, physical education teachers recognize the need to enhance the level of agility in students. An optimal amount of agility may be needed so that a student can effectively move from one point to another, shifting weight properly, and using optimal speed. Agility is highly specific to a task; thus there is no valid measure of overall agility. The type of agility that enhances performance in basketball is different from the type benefiting performance in tennis. Furthermore, health-related physical fitness is not strongly reflected in agility.

Agility does not adequately meet the definition of health-related fitness (see Chapter 17). A one-to-one relationship between agility, for example, and a person's state of health has not been established. Nonetheless, a task-specific measure of agility might be used as a measure of performance-related physical fitness.

From a practical perspective, it is probably not essential for a physical education teacher to administer performance-related physical fitness tests in each unit of instruction. In a class setting, the student who meets standards of fitness associated with good health should be able to participate in normal school physical education activities. There may be exceptions in units such as gymnastics in which a minimal level of strength is necessary to perform some of the basic skills. Testing students on their performance-related strength (related to the specific gymnastics skills) would be useful in identifying students who need additional strength training. However, athletes who are members of teams, competing with other skilled athletes, should be properly conditioned to participate in the sport. The use of a sport-specific fitness test is appropriate for them.

The tests described in this chapter are primarily performance-related items that have been used on a large-scale basis for many years in the physical education field. It bears repeating that the examinee's medical record should be

Soccer test.

checked before administering any type of fitness test. In a school, these checks are usually made before participation in physical education classes. Because of this procedure, little risk exists in administering a fitness test to a school-age child. In a nonschool setting, care must be taken to see that the appropriate medical information is obtained for each client. If the client is over 35 years of age, a physician's permission should be obtained before the client is allowed to participate in vigorous physical activity. General medical information should be secured from a client who joins a health or fitness club.

HISTORICAL PERSPECTIVE

The earliest performance-related fitness tests in physical education and exercise science were anthropometric measures, used primarily by physicians in the late 1800s. In the first quarter of the twentieth century, interest in anthropometric measures lagged until the study of body types was initiated. As time passed, the emphasis gradually shifted from anthropometry to measures of strength. These strength measures (e.g., grip strength) were widely used, and many are still administered today. Posture grids and rating scales were popular through the 1950s. It was during this time that broad-based performance-related measures of fitness were developed. One of these tests was the AAHPER (American Association for Health, Physical Education and Recreation) youth fitness test.

The first version of the youth fitness test was published in 1958. Seven test items were included in the original battery, along with age and classification norms. These norms were revised (Hunsicker and Reiff, 1966) and published in the 1965 revision of the test manual. The classification norms were based on a combination of age, height, and weight. The normative data in the 1965 manual showed considerable improvement on most test items for boys and girls at almost every level. In 1975 the battery was again revised:

1. The sit-up was changed from a straight-leg to a bent-knee position to provide a more accurate measure of strength of the abdominal muscles.
2. The softball throw was eliminated because, to a large extent, it measured a specific skill whereas the primary purpose of the battery was to measure fitness.
3. The 600-yard walk/run was modified to include two optional runs: the 1-mile or 9-minute run for ages 10 to 12 or the 1.5-mile or 12-minute run for children aged 13 years or older. The optional runs were recommended as valid substitutes in schools where extensive running is a regular part of the physical education program.

In 1976, a revised set of age norms was published, and the use of classification norms was dropped. The organization of the test battery and the development of national norms represented a significant contribution to the physical education field. The test was popular in many parts of the United States for a variety of reasons—the items motivated students and the award system enabled them to receive national recognition for their performance on the test. Furthermore, many valued the measurement of a combination of health-related and athletic performance–related physical fitness. However, the test did not reflect a definition of health-related fitness that applies to all persons, as does the Prudential *FITNESS*GRAM test and several others. The youth fitness test was not a test that would appeal in its entirety to older age groups in general. Questions were also raised about the measurement characteristics of the test, in particular, its validity and reliability. In the test manual, no validation procedures were described for the individual test items, except for a general statement of expert opinion regarding the important components of fitness. Reliability estimates for the various age groups on the battery items were not reported in the manual. However, studies of the youth fitness test were subsequently published in a variety of journals, and an effort has been made to incorporate this information into the test descriptions presented in this chapter. Generally, these studies have reported that the items in the youth fitness test have satisfactory reliability.

Although the focus on fitness has largely shifted to health-related fitness, performance-related test items are still used frequently, although typically not in a battery of tests. These tests are often sport-specific, used to assess the status of athletes before and after preseason training. A few of these test items are still popular in school physical education programs, because they are items children enjoy and find motivating. Several of these items are described below.

PERFORMANCE-RELATED FITNESS TEST ITEMS

Three performance-related fitness items measure predominantly athletic **performance–related physical fitness:** the **standing long jump,** the **50-yard dash,** and the **shuttle run.** Three other items—sit-ups, distance run, and pull-ups (boys) and **flexed arm hang** (girls)—measure primarily health-related physical fitness. These items represent the final version of the youth fitness test, published by the American Alliance for Health, Physical Education, Recreation and Dance (AAHPERD). The test manual (AAHPER, 1976) contained test instructions and other information of historical interest.

The following test items are popular performance-related physical fitness items. The first item (pull-ups or flexed arm hang) is sometimes considered a health-related physical fitness item, especially for female examinees (i.e., related to bone density in the upper body; prevention of osteoporosis). However, it is frequently used as a performance-related item in activities with high upper body strength and endurance demands. This test is still included in the recently revised national fitness tests described in Chapter 17.

Pull-Ups (Boys) and Flexed Arm Hang (Girls) (AAHPER, 1976)
Test Objective To measure arm and shoulder girdle strength.
Description To perform the pull-ups test, the student begins by hanging from the bar by using an overhand (palms outward) grip (see Figures 18-1 and 18-2) with

Figure 18-1 Equipment options for pull-ups test. *From Youth Fitness Test Manual.*

Figure 18-2 Starting position for pull-ups test. *From Youth Fitness Test Manual.*

legs and arms fully extended. The feet should not touch the floor. From the hanging position, the student raises the body using the arms until the chin is positioned over the bar. The body is then lowered to a full hang, the starting position. This task is repeated as many times as possible. One trial is allowed. (Although the pull-ups test was originally recommended for boys only, it is now an option for both boys and girls in several national fitness tests.)

In the flexed arm hang test, two spotters should assist in administering the test, one in front and one in back of the student. The height of the bar should be adjusted so that it is approximately equal to the standing height of the examinee. The correct position of the hands is depicted in Figures 18-3 and 18-4. With the assistance of both spotters, the examinee lifts the student's body off the floor until the chin is positioned above the bar, elbows flexed, and chest close to the bar. This position should be held as long as possible. One trial is allowed. (This test item is now also an option for boys in several national tests.)

Test Area For the pull-ups test, only space adequate for the equipment is needed. A doorway, a small area for an inclined ladder, or a separate bar unit would suffice. The flexed arm hang test can be administered in the same space.

Equipment A metal or wooden bar roughly $1\frac{1}{2}$ inches in diameter (alternatives are a doorway gym bar, a piece of pipe, or an inclined ladder).

Scoring The score for the pull-ups test is the number of completed pull-ups to the nearest whole number. For the flexed arm hang test, the score is the number of seconds to the nearest second the student holds the hanging position. There is

Figure 18-3   Starting position for the flexed arm hang test. *From Youth Fitness Test Manual.*

Figure 18-4   Flexed arm hang. *From Youth Fitness Test Manual.*

no criterion time after which the test should be terminated. The student should maintain the position as long as possible.

Validity   There is limited validity evidence for both the pull-ups test and the flexed arm hang test. Several educators and therapists have suggested that pull-ups might not be an adequate measure of arm strength. The criterion measure was an isokinetic dynamometer pull, designed to determine the amount of force exerted in foot-pounds at any given point throughout the range of motion. The correlations between this measure and both the flexed arm hang and pull-ups were low, as were the relationships between the last two measures and lean body mass. The isokinetic measure, however, was related to lean body mass. This analysis demonstrated the inability of pull-ups and the flexed arm hang to provide an indicator of the full range of arm and shoulder girdle strength. It is also suggested that fatness, not total body weight, affected performance on both these test items.

Comments   The muscular strength and endurance of the arms and shoulder girdle involve the ability to move or support one's weight with the arms. Both strength and endurance are needed to execute the flexed arm hang or pull-up, but to varying degrees for different people. Performance on these tests is negatively correlated with body weight, presumably because of the relationship between the tests and body fats. Verifying that either test measures strength and endurance is difficult. When the endurance tests dips and bench press were used to evaluate performance in body conditioning courses at the University of Houston, the correlation between the two tests was low, only .32. This indicates that the two tests measure different abilities. When a repetition bench press was correlated with the maximum weight a student could lift (strength), the correlation was over .90 (Baumgartner and Jackson, 1970).

Reliability   Test-retest reliability coefficients were reported for children in grades 3 through 5. The reliability for girls was .95, and for boys, .94 (Engelman and Morrow, 1991).

MODIFIED PULL-UPS TESTS Baumgartner (1978) devised a modified pull-ups test for all ages and both sexes. This test appears to resolve many of the difficulties associated with other measures of arm and shoulder girdle strength and endurance, such as pull-ups and the flexed arm hang. A special piece of equipment, now marketed, is used. Baumgartner wrote that the parts required to construct the equipment cost about $50.

In the modified test, the examinee performs pull-ups on an inclined board. An overhand grip is used, with hands placed shoulder-width apart. Otherwise, the test is performed like the regular pull-ups test. All examinees, including

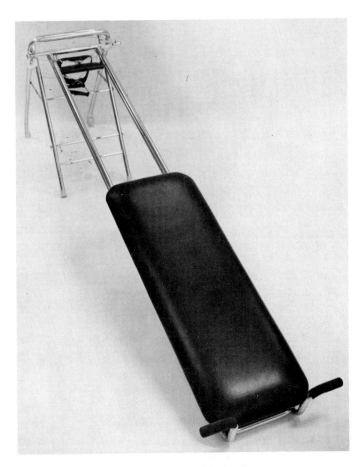

Equipment for the modified pull-ups test.

elementary school girls and college women, were able to execute at least one pull-up; most performed four or more. Logical validity was claimed for the test. Only the data set for the college women was substantial enough to estimate reliability and calculate norms. The intraclass correlation coefficient for one trial over 2 days was .91, reflecting highly acceptable test reliability.

The equipment for the modified pull-ups test was improved to make it safer (Baumgartner et al., 1984). Additional norms were also developed for the test. For example, the 50th percentile for college males is 30 modified pull-ups; for college females, 11 modified pull-ups. Scores below 2 and above 60 are rare.

Another modification of the pull-ups test was used in the National Children and Youth Fitness Study (NCYFS) II (Pate et al., 1987). This test is similar to an item in the Vermont physical fitness test.

Modified Pull-Ups Test (NCYFS II)

Test Objective   To measure upper body muscular strength and endurance.

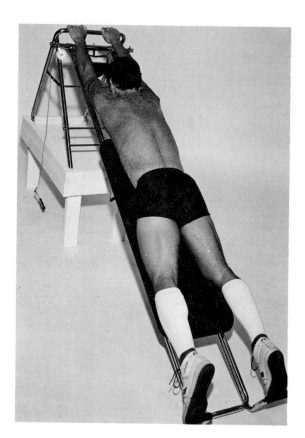

Starting position for the modified
pull-ups test.

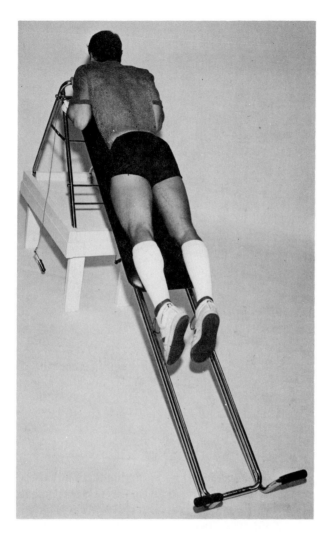

Up position for the modified pull-ups test.

Description   The examinee is positioned on his or her back with the shoulders directly below a bar that is set at a height 1 or 2 inches beyond reach. An elastic band is suspended across the uprights parallel to and about 7 to 8 inches below the bar. The examinee grasps the bar, which raises the buttocks off the floor. The arms and legs are straight, and only the heels are in contact with the floor. An overhand grip (palm away from body) is used, and thumbs are placed around the bar (Figure 18-5). To execute the pull-up, the examinee lifts the extended

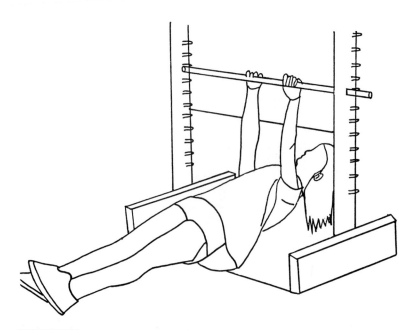

Figure 18-5   Starting position for the NCYFS II modified pull-ups test.

body until the chin is hooked over the elastic band (Figure 18-6). The movement should be accomplished using only the arms, and the body must be kept straight. The examinee executes as many pull-ups as possible (no time limit), keeping the hips and knees extended through each attempt (Pate et al., 1987, pp. 71–72).

Test Area   Only a small area is required for this test. A corner of the gymnasium will suffice.

Equipment   A specially constructed device, depicted in Figures 18-7 and 18-8, was used in the NCYFS II study. However, the NCYFS staff suggest that any low pull-up bar that can be adjusted for height will suffice. The apparatus can be built cheaply ($15–$35). The specifications may be obtained from Macro Systems, Silver Spring, Md.

Scoring   Each complete pull-up is given a score of 1. Partial pull-ups are not scored. The total score is the number of complete pull-ups executed by the examinee.

Validity   At the time this test was used in NCYFS II, it was validated on the basis of logical validity. Since then, Ross and Pate have concluded a validity study of the modified test. Satisfactory validity was established when the test was compared with tests of arm and shoulder girdle strength using weight machines.

Reliability   Pate (1988) reported a reliability coefficient of .80 for 94 elementary school children, higher than Erbaugh's test-retest coefficient of .52 for grades 1 through 3 (1990). Cotten (1990) studied the reliability using children in grades K through 6. The test-retest coefficients ranged from .72 to .90 for males and from

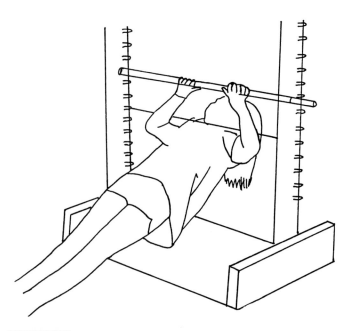

Figure 18-6   Up position for the NCYFS II modified pull-ups test.

.71 to .95 for females. Engleman and Morrow (1991) also studied the test-retest reliability of the modified pull-ups test. They reported reliability coefficients of .87 for boys and .89 for girls. Kollath and colleagues (1991) reported reliability coefficients of .91 for high-school boys and .72 for high-school girls for one trial on the modified test.

Objectivity   The objectivity of the modified pull-ups test was also studied (Kollath et al., 1991). When testers and raters counted the actual test scores, the percentage of interrater agreement was 68.6%. However, this percentage dropped to as low as 28.6% when the scores of the testers at the test site were compared with the scores of raters of videotapes of test performances. In other words, the on-site testers were not able to accurately identify an unacceptable pull-up in many cases. Thus, while the test has a relatively high reliability, the absolute objectivity is low.

Comments   The modified test is viewed as an improvement over the more traditional tests of upper body strength. Almost every child (boy or girl) can perform several pull-ups using the modified version of the test. On the other hand, it is not an easy test to administer. Some examinees experience difficulty in maintaining the hips in an extended position throughout the execution of the pull-up. According to the NCYFS II staff this problem can be alleviated somewhat by orienting the child properly prior to administering the test.

FLEXED ARM HANG   Cotten and Marwitz (1969) studied the validity of the flexed arm hang for girls by comparing performance on the AAHPER youth fitness test with a pull-ups test and a modified flexed arm hang test. Pull-ups

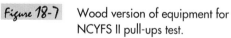 Wood version of equipment for NCYFS II pull-ups test.

Figure 18-8   Metal version of equipment for NCYFS II pull-ups test.

were measured using the overhand grip and partial scores were given, up to 1 (0.25, 0.50, 0.75). The reliability of the pull-ups test was .89. The correlation between this test and the AAHPER flexed arm hang was .72. In the modified flexed arm hang test developed by Cotten and Marwitz, the hanging position was identical to the AAHPER test, but the stopwatch was allowed to run until the angle at the elbow became greater than 90 degrees. The reliability for the modified test was .83. The correlation between the modified hang and the pull-ups was .93. The results of this study indicate that the modified flexed arm hang may be a better measure of the kind of arm strength measured by the pull-ups than the standard flexed arm hang test. This conclusion must be viewed with caution, however, because the results were based on test scores of only 14 college women.

Reliability   Reliability estimates ranging from .74 to .89 have been reported for the pull-ups and the flexed arm hang tests. A summary of the reliabilities of AAHPER youth fitness items is presented in Table 18-1 on pp. 524–525.

Table 18-1   Reliabilities for AAHPER Youth Fitness Test Items

Item	Source	Sample	Trials (t) and Days (d)	Reliability Coefficient
Pull-ups	Klesius (1968)	150 tenth-grade males	1t 2d	.89, .82
Flexed arm hang	Cotten and Marwitz (1969)	14 female physical education majors	2t 1d	.74
Standing long jump	Klesius (1968)	150 tenth-grade males	2t 1d	.94, .93
	Fleishman (1964)	Adult males	2t	.90
	Kane and Meredith (1952)	100 males, age 7	12t,* 1d	.97
		100 females, age 7	12t,* 1d	.98
		100 males, age 8	12t,* 1d	.98
		100 females, age 8	12t,* 1d	.98
		100 males, age 9	12t,* 1d	.99
		100 females, age 9	12t,* 1d	.98
		75 males, age 7	12t 2d†	.83
		75 females, age 7	12t 2d†	.86

* Best of 12 correlated with second-best.
† Best of 12 on one day correlated with best of 12 on second day.

(*Continued*)

Norms Norms are published in the test manual for ages 9 through 17+ and both sexes. An abbreviated form of the tables is presented in Tables 18-2 and 18-3.
Comments When administering the pull-ups test, carefully monitor the alignment and positioning of the student's body. The body must not swing during the execution of the movement. If the student begins swinging, the tester should check this by extending the arm across the front of the thighs. The examinee's body should remain vertical during the pull-up. Neither raising the knees nor kicking the legs is permitted. In the flexed arm hang test, the stopwatch should be started as soon as the student is fully supporting herself in the hanging position. The watch is stopped when the chin touches the bar or falls below the level of the bar.

Gabbard and associates (1983) studied the effects of grip and forearm position on flexed arm hang performance. Superior performance on the hang was obtained with the forearm supinated (palms turned inward) with the thumb over the bar. Their work demonstrates the need for standardizing both the thumb and forearm positions in the flexed arm hang test.

Table 18-1   Reliabilities for AAHPER Youth Fitness Test Items—cont'd

Item	Source	Sample	Trials (t) and Days (d)	Reliability Coefficient
50-yard dash	Baumgartner and Jackson (1970)	76 male physical education majors	2t 1d	.949‡
	Klesius (1968)	150 tenth-grade males	2t 1d	.86, .83
Softball throw	Klesius (1968)	150 tenth-grade males	2t 1d	.93, .90
	Fleishman (1964)	Adult males	2t	.93
600-yard run/ walk	Klesius (1968)	150 tenth-grade males	1t 2d	.80, .80
	Wilgoose et al. (1961)	70 junior high males	1t 2d	.92
		70 junior high fe-males	1t 2d	.92
	Askew (1966)	71 senior high males	1t 2d	.762
		46 senior high fe-males	1t 2d	.653
	Doolittle and Bigbee (1968)	9 ninth-grade males		.92
Sit-ups	Klesius (1968)	150 tenth-grade males	1t 2d	.57, .68
Shuttle run	Klesius (1968)	150 tenth-grade males	1t 2d	.68, .75

‡ *Intraclass correlation coefficient.*

Shuttle Run Test (AAHPER, 1976)

Test Objective   To measure speed and change of direction.

Description   For the shuttle run test place two parallel lines on the floor 30 feet apart. Place two wooden blocks behind one of the lines, as shown in Figure 18-9. The student starts from behind the other line. To start the test, use the signal "Ready, go!" On the word "go!" the student runs to the blocks, picks one up, runs back to the starting line, and places the block on the floor beyond the line. The student runs back, picks up the other block, and runs across the finish line as fast as possible. Start the stopwatch on the signal "go" and stop it as the student crosses the starting line. Two trials are administered, with a rest in between.

Table 18-2   Percentile Rank Norms for Girls on the AAHPER Flexed-Arm Hang Test (in Seconds)

Percentile	Age (yr)							
	9–10	11	12	13	14	15	16	17+
95	42	39	33	34	35	36	31	34
75	18	20	18	16	21	18	15	17
50	9	10	9	8	9	9	7	8
25	3	3	3	3	3	4	3	3
5	0	0	0	0	0	0	0	0

Modified from Youth Fitness Test Manual.

Test Area   An area equivalent to the width of a volleyball court is suitable.

Equipment   Two blocks of wood, 2 inches by 2 inches by 4 inches, and a stopwatch. If two stopwatches are available, or one with a split-second timer, two students can be tested at the same time.

Scores   The time of the better of two trials, recorded to the nearest tenth of a second, is the score.

Validity   No studies have been conducted on the validity of the shuttle run test; however, the nature of agility has been studied. Several investigators (Hilsendager et al., 1969) attempted to improve agility by increasing speed and strength. They found that students who practiced specific agility items increased their agility more than those who practiced either speed or strength. Their study also showed that the so-called agility tests that have been published do not measure the same underlying ability. The test directions for the shuttle run are more complex than those for other items in the battery. Furthermore, the test tends to be less familiar to students. If the student has not had sufficient

Table 18-3   Percentile Rank Norms for Boys on the AAHPER Pull-Ups Test (Number)

Percentile	Age (yr)							
	9–10	11	12	13	14	15	16	17+
95	9	8	9	10	12	15	14	15
75	3	4	4	5	7	9	10	10
50	1	2	2	3	4	6	7	7
25	0	0	0	1	2	3	4	4
5	0	0	0	0	0	0	1	0

Modified from Youth Fitness Test Manual.

Figure 18-9 Shuttle run test. *From Youth Fitness Test Manual.*

practice on this test, the score may represent performance on a novel task, rather than a test of agility.

Reliability Reliability estimates, based on test data, range from .68 to .75.

Norms Normative data have been published for boys and girls ages 9 to 10 through age 17+ in the AAHPER *Youth Fitness Test Manual* (AAHPER, 1976). An abbreviated form of the tables of norms is shown in Tables 18-4 and 18-5.

Comments To eliminate the necessity of returning the blocks after each trial, start the trials alternately, first from behind one line then from behind the other. Students should wear sneakers or run barefooted. Marmis and colleagues (1969) studied the number of trials needed for a reliable test and concluded that three instead of two trials of the shuttle run test should be administered.

Standing Long Jump (AAHPER, 1976)

Test Objective To measure explosive leg power.

Description In the standing long jump test the student stands behind the restraining line, with feet several inches apart and the toes pointed straight ahead, as shown in Figure 18-10. To get ready for the jump, the examinee swings the arms backward and bends the knees. To execute the jump, the student swings the arms forward, extends the knees, and jumps forward as far as possible, attempting to land on the feet and fall forward instead of backward if balance is lost. Three trials are taken.

Test Area The jump may be tested in an outdoor jumping pit or on a flat surface indoors or outdoors, with a clearance of 25 feet.

Equipment If testing takes place on a flat surface as opposed to a jumping pit, a mat is preferred; use a tape measure to determine the distance of the jump.

Scoring Measure the distance from the restraining line to the heel or other part of the body that touched the floor closest to the restraining line. If the student falls backward and touches the testing surface with the hand, the distance is measured from the part of the hand closest to the restraining line to the line itself. Record the best of three trials in feet and inches to the nearest inch.

Validity The standing long jump is generally accepted as an adequate measure of "explosive" power, although an element of timing exists in executing the jump

Table 18-4 Percentile Rank Norms for Girls on the Shuttle Run (in Seconds and Tenths)

Percentile	Age (yr)							
	9–10	11	12	13	14	15	16	17+
95	10.2	10.0	9.9	9.9	9.7	9.9	10.0	9.6
75	11.1	10.8	10.8	10.5	10.3	10.4	10.6	10.4
50	11.8	11.5	11.4	11.2	11.0	11.0	11.2	11.1
25	12.5	12.1	12.0	12.0	12.0	11.8	12.0	12.0
5	14.3	14.0	13.3	13.2	13.1	13.3	13.7	14.0

Modified from Youth Fitness Test Manual.

that does not exist to the same extent for other measures of explosive power such as the vertical jump. The validity of this test might be improved by standardizing the directions for executing the jump.

Reliability This item tends to be highly reliable, with reliability coefficients ranging from .83 to .99 in various studies.

Norms National norms have been published for boys and girls, ages 9 to 10 through 17+. An abbreviated form of the tables of norms is shown in Tables 18-6 and 18-7.

Comments Be sure the student knows how to jump off both feet and land on both feet. Children who are not familiar with this procedure have been tested, and their natural tendency is to jump off one foot. This invalidates the trial of course and valuable time must be spent in teaching the student how to jump properly. If the test is administered indoors, tape the tape measure to the floor and stand to the side, noting the distance to the nearest inch after each jump. Marmis and

Table 18-5 Percentile Rank Norms for Boys on the Shuttle Run (in Seconds and Tenths)

Percentile	Age (yr)							
	9–10	11	12	13	14	15	16	17+
95	10.0	9.7	9.6	9.3	8.9	8.9	8.6	8.6
75	10.6	10.4	10.2	10.0	9.6	9.4	9.3	9.2
50	11.2	10.9	10.7	10.4	10.1	9.9	9.9	9.8
25	12.0	11.5	11.4	11.0	10.7	10.4	10.5	10.4
5	13.1	12.9	12.4	12.4	11.9	11.7	11.9	11.7

Modified from Youth Fitness Test Manual.

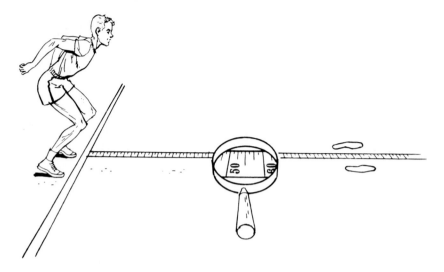

Figure 18-10   Standing long jump. *From Youth Fitness Test Manual.*

colleagues (1969) studied the number of trials recommended by the test manual and concluded that only two trials of the standing long jump are needed.

50-Yard Dash (AAHPER, 1976)

Test Objective   To measure speed.

Description   For the 50-yard dash test the student assumes a standing start behind the restraining line. Use the commands ''Are you ready?'' and ''Go!,'' timing the latter signal with a downward sweep of the arm. The student runs all out,

Table 18-6   Percentile Rank Norms for Boys on the Standing Long Jump (in Feet and Inches)

Percentile	Age (yr)							
	9–10	11	12	13	14	15	16	17+
95	6′ 0″	6′2″	6′ 6″	7′1″	7′6″	8′0″	8′2″	8′5″
75	5′ 4″	5′7″	5′11″	6′3″	6′8″	7′2″	7′6″	7′9″
50	4′11″	5′2″	5′ 5″	5′9″	6′2″	6′8″	7′0″	7′2″
25	4′ 6″	4′8″	5′ 0″	5′2″	5′6″	6′1″	6′6″	6′6″
5	3′10″	4′0″	4′ 2″	4′4″	4′8″	5′2″	5′5″	5′3″

Modified from Youth Fitness Test Manual.

Table 18-7   Percentile Rank Norms for Girls on the
Standing Long Jump (in Feet and Inches)

Percentile	Age (yr)							
	9–10	11	12	13	14	15	16	17+
95	5'10"	6' 0"	6' 2"	6'5"	6' 8"	6' 7"	6'6"	6' 9"
75	5' 2"	5' 4"	5' 6"	5'9"	5'11"	5'10"	5'9"	6' 0"
50	4' 8"	4'11"	5' 0"	5'3"	5' 4"	5' 5"	5'3"	5' 5"
25	4' 1"	4' 4"	4' 6"	4'9"	4'10"	4'11"	4'9"	4'11"
5	3' 5"	3' 8"	3'10"	4'0"	4' 0"	4' 2"	4'0"	4' 1"

Modified from Youth Fitness Test Manual.

without slowing down, to the finish line (Figure 18-11). The stopwatch is started as the starter's arm reaches the downward position and is stopped as the finish line is crossed. Two trials are taken.

Test Area   Usually administered outdoors, using any open area.

Equipment   One stopwatch is essential; using two watches or a split-second timer for simultaneous testing of two students is recommended.

Scoring   The time is recorded in seconds to the nearest tenth of a second.

Validity   Performance in the 50-yard dash is a function of running efficiency as well as speed. The student must clearly understand that slowing down before reaching the finish line will invalidate the test.

Reliability   Reliability coefficients ranging from .83 to .95 have been reported. The 50-yard dash is a very reliable measure, but the greatest source of error occurs during the first 20 yards. The student requires time to build up maximum speed. However, the test as a whole has satisfactory reliability. Only if finer discrimination is desired might the teacher consider timing only the last 30 yards of the dash test as the student's score. Norms must then be developed for the modified test.

Norms   Norms have been published for boys and girls, ages 9 to 10 through 17+. An abbreviated form of the tables of norms is presented in Tables 18-8 and 18-9.

Comments   Require the students to practice starting the test with the maximum possible speed and continuing at the fastest speed possible until past the finish line. Motivation is always important in test administration but especially in tests of short duration.

600-Yard Run (AAHPER, 1976)

Test Objective   To measure cardiorespiratory (CR) function.

Description   Instruct the student to use a standing start. Give the signal "Ready, go!," and start the stopwatch on the signal "go!" The student begins running and continues running all out until he or she crosses the finish line. Although

Figure 18-11   50-yard dash. *From Youth Fitness Test Manual.*

the examinee may walk during the test, it is not encouraged. One trial is taken.

Test Area   A variety of open spaces is suitable. See the examples presented in Figures 18-12 to 18-14.

Equipment   A stopwatch.

Scoring   The time is recorded in minutes and seconds. A partner should be identified for each runner. The partner either records the time or remembers it and reports it to the scorer.

Validity   When the 600-yard run has been correlated with a measure of maximum oxygen consumption (VO_2 max), moderate correlations have resulted, ranging from $-.27$ to $-.71$. This result means that there is some relationship between the test and criterion measure, but the relationship is not substantial. As the walk/run scores improve (i.e., the distance is run in a faster time), the VO_2 max scores also get better (i.e., higher) for some subjects. However, this does not happen in all cases; thus the relationship is not very strong. The 600-yard run, then, may not be an adequate predictor of CR endurance. (See Chapter 17 for a more detailed treatment of this topic.) The options available for this test (1 mile or 9 minutes; $1\frac{1}{2}$ mile or 12 minutes) have greater validity.

Reliability   Reliability coefficients ranging from .65 to .92 have been reported. In general, the estimates are high, suggesting that with proper motivation, the test can be properly administered.

Norms   Norms have been published for boys and girls, ages 9 to 10 through 17+. An abbreviated form of the tables is shown in Tables 18-10 and 18-11.

Comments   Before administering any of the distance run tests, warm-up prepara-

Table 18-8 Percentile Rank Norms for Girls on the 50-Yard Dash (in Seconds and Tenths of Seconds)

Percentile	Age (yr)							
	9–10	11	12	13	14	15	16	17+
95	7.4	7.3	7.0	6.9	6.8	6.9	7.0	6.8
75	8.0	7.9	7.6	7.4	7.3	7.4	7.5	7.4
50	8.6	8.3	8.1	8.0	7.8	7.8	7.9	7.9
25	9.1	9.0	8.7	8.5	8.3	8.2	8.3	8.4
5	10.3	10.0	10.0	10.0	9.6	9.2	9.3	9.5

Modified from Youth Fitness Test Manual.

tory training is essential. The student should be instructed about proper pacing and running efficiency. A group of students may be tested at one time, each working with a partner. The student should not attempt to run as fast as possible but should run at a pace that can be maintained throughout the entire distance. However, this pace should be maintained at as fast a rate as possible during the test. As discussed previously, the 600-yard run is not the best field test of CR function. The optional tests, which consist of the longer distance runs, are strongly recommended, even for young children. This test was included, nonetheless, for the benefit of those physical educators who believe that the only feasible distance runs for children should be shorter than a mile. Abbreviated forms of the tables for longer distances are included in Chapter 17.

Table 18-9 Percentile Rank Norms for Boys on the 50-Yard Dash (in Seconds and Tenths of Seconds)

Percentile	Age (yr)							
	9–10	11	12	13	14	15	16	17+
95	7.3	7.1	6.8	6.5	6.2	6.0	6.0	5.9
75	7.8	7.6	7.4	7.0	6.8	6.5	6.5	6.3
50	8.2	8.0	7.8	7.5	7.2	6.9	6.7	6.6
25	8.9	8.6	8.3	8.0	7.7	7.3	7.0	7.0
5	9.9	9.5	9.5	9.0	8.8	8.0	7.7	7.9

Modified from Youth Fitness Test Manual.

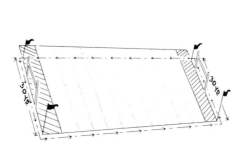

Figure 18-12 Using football field for 600-yard run test. *From Youth Fitness Test Manual.*

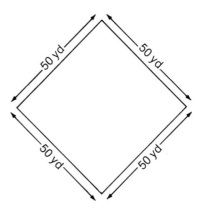

Figure 18-13 Using any open area for the 600-yard run test.

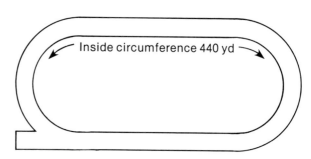

Figure 18-14 Using an inside track for the 600-yard run test.

Table 18-10 Percentile Rank Norms for Boys on the AAHPER 600-Yard Run (in Minutes and Seconds)

	Age (yr)							
Percentile	9–10	11	12	13	14	15	16	17+
95	2:05	2:02	1:52	1:45	1:39	1:36	1:34	1:32
75	2:17	2:15	2:06	1:59	1:52	1:46	1:44	1:43
50	2:33	2:27	2:19	2:10	2:03	1:56	1:52	1:52
25	2:53	2:47	2:37	2:27	2:16	2:08	2:01	2:02
5	3:22	3:29	3:06	3:00	2:51	2:30	2:31	2:38

Modified from Youth Fitness Test Manual.

Table 18-11 Percentile Rank Norms for Girls on the AAHPER 600-Yard Run (in Minutes and Seconds)

Percentile	Age (yr)							
	9–10	11	12	13	14	15	16	17+
95	2:20	2:14	2:06	2:04	2:02	2:00	2:08	2:02
75	2:39	2:35	2:26	2:23	2:19	2:22	2:26	2:24
50	2:56	2:53	2:47	2:41	2:40	2:37	2:43	2:41
25	3:15	3:16	3:13	3:06	3:01	3:00	3:03	3:02
5	4:00	4:15	3:59	3:49	3:49	3:28	3:49	3:45

Modified from Youth Fitness Test Manual.

ADMINISTRATION OF PHYSICAL FITNESS TESTS

Tests of motor performance are more complex to administer than most written tests. First, the examinee must understand the test instructions. Then he or she must be able to translate these instructions into the movements required by the test. Assume, for example, that John is taking a shuttle run test for the first time. On the first attempt he makes several errors. Perhaps he threw the block across the line instead of placing it on the floor, or maybe he forgot the number of times he should change directions. Did the errors occur because he did not understand the instructions or because he was unable to follow them? Before actual testing, John should see a demonstration of the test, first in slow motion and then at full speed. Then he should be allowed to move through the test slowly while the test administrator gives him cues on his movements. The test instructions can also be written on an index card and posted on a bulletin board in the gym. If a student has difficulty with the instructions, a review of the written instructions might be helpful. Finally, John should have the opportunity to practice the test at maximum speed. Now John is ready to be tested. Remember that if John cannot perform the test properly, the trial must be thrown out and another taken. This is time-consuming and inefficient. The time taken in preparing examinees for the test is time well spent.

Preparation for Testing

When fitness tests are administered, test users expect the student to perform at his or her maximum ability. If John had not received the preparation described previously, his agility would not be tested; rather, his ability to perform a novel task would be measured. This is not the purpose of administering the shuttle run test. Although proper preparation for testing should be emphasized, it can be carried to extremes. Requiring the student to practice the shuttle run

Test administrator.

test day after day as part of the regular physical education program makes no sense. If practicing the shuttle run increases the student's agility, some practice is justifiable. However, other means of improving agility are probably incorporated into the physical education program. This is an assumption, since no valid measure of overall agility has been developed. Furthermore, it is more likely that agility is highly task-specific. This means that one's performance on the shuttle run test might not reflect how well (or poorly) one would perform on another agility test. Yet it is still very popular in the physical education field to select a single test, such as the shuttle run, as a measure of a component of fitness (agility), assuming that this test measures one's "general" agility. This is not a fault of the test but rather of the test user who is making an erroneous assumption about the test.

Many practical matters should be considered in preparing examinees for a test. One such matter is the clothing worn for the test. In junior and senior high school, where students are often expected to bring appropriate clothes for their physical education class, this is not a problem. In the elementary school where special gym wear may not be required, the clothes worn on the day that fitness tests are to be administered can create problems. A wide variety of clothing is satisfactory, however, provided the student can move freely. Athletic shoes should always be worn, whether testing takes place indoors or outdoors. Without them it is unlikely that maximum performance can be achieved. No matter how hard one may try, running as fast as possible in leather-soled shoes is difficult, if not impossible. Although wearing various types of sport shoes is now quite common for students, these should not be worn in a gym because of the dirt collected on the soles. Even for outdoor testing, the sport shoes worn on a daily basis may not be preferred, especially if the shoes are in poor condition. Removing the shoes during testing does not solve the problem; it merely creates a new one. For example, if a shuttle run test is performed indoors with bare feet, the quick shift of direction can create enough friction between the floor and the bottoms of the feet to be painful and cause blisters. Simply be firm about having students bring proper shoes, instructing them well in advance of the testing day.

Because fitness testing is usually conducted on a mass testing basis, assistants are often needed. Students, teachers, parents, or other members of the community can be recruited as assistants. They should be thoroughly familiarized with the tests they will administer, which will not occur if they are simply given the test instructions to read. The following is a good rule of thumb to follow: preparing properly for testing always takes longer than you think it will! Do not assume anything. Bring assistants together for a practice session. Review and demonstrate the tests, giving each assistant experience in administering the tests or performing the assigned administrative task. Even when a test is administered year after year in a school, a brief review of procedures is essential. This is equally important in a nonschool setting where new clients are continually coming into the program and the same tests are administered frequently. A periodic check of testing procedures should take place. Provide all the materials needed to administer and score the test, and be sure the assistants know how to use them.

In addition to training assistants, frequently equipment must be gathered or lines and targets must be placed for testing. Adequate time must be allowed for setting up the test, which can be very time-consuming. In fact the amount of time required to set up the test is often the primary factor in deciding whether to use the test. This factor alone has prevented teachers from using some well-designed tests in physical education classes. If tape will be used for the lines or the target, take care of the taping ahead of time. If good-quality tape is used, it will not damage the gym floor and it is durable enough so that it can remain on the floor for several weeks. If a wall target is to be formed with tape, be sure that the texture of the wall will support the tape. Little problems like adhesive tape can ruin an entire testing session. Plan carefully for the testing session, and have an alternative plan ready for any possible problem.

Data Processing of Physical Fitness Test Results

The process of administering fitness tests to a large group of people is itself an enormous task. Once test scores have been recorded, the test user is faced with the job of analyzing them. There is no point in administering the tests if you do not use the results. Many school districts own a mainframe computer or a mini-computer or have access to one. Until recently, this provided the best mechanism for analyzing fitness data. It is still preferred when dealing with large data sets. For example, physical fitness teachers in Illinois have access to a computerized system for analyzing scores on a national physical fitness test. The results can be sent to Northern Illinois University, where the scores are fed into a computer and analyzed descriptively. The computer output containing the results of the analysis is then sent back to the school system. This procedure is also handled locally within a number of school systems around the country, generally when the system has access to a mainframe or minicomputer. Now the availability of the microcomputer opens up these services to virtually every professional in the country. Every teacher need not learn how to write programs, but well-written programs can easily be used by any teacher. (See Chapter 5 for more information on computers.)

Several computer programs are available for summarizing data from fitness tests and for determining norms. The following programs can be purchased at modest prices or at no cost:

To be used with the Prudential *FITNESS*GRAM Program:

The Prudential *FITNESS*GRAM Program
Institute for Aerobics Research
12330 Preston Road
Dallas, TX 75230

To be used with the Chrysler Fund–AAU test:

The Chrysler Fund-AAU Physical Fitness Program
Poplars Building
Bloomington, IN 47405

Number of Trials

When a test is developed, information is always included on the number of trials to be administered. In this way the motor performance test differs significantly from the written test. The written test contains a number of test items, all different. The motor performance test consists of one or more trials, all alike. There are reasons for this difference, of course. Repeating the same test item in a written test would make no sense. On the other hand, attempting to vary each trial on a motor performance test is nonsensical. Even though the examinee knows the next trial will be the same as the previous one, mental memory differs from motor memory in this context. This knowledge does not mean the trial will be performed in the same way as the previous one, despite the examinee's effort to do so (or change it if the previous performance was not satisfactory).

How, then, is the number of trials determined? The number is usually determined by finding out how many trials are needed for a reliable performance. Let us suppose that you are interested in developing a bowling test. You decide in advance that the test ought to have a reliability of at least .80. After completing the test, you decide to work with 10 trials as a starter. You administer the test to a group of students and determine that the reliability of the test is .92. This is above the target reliability, but you may decide to use the 10-trial test. However, maybe you could use fewer trials and still reach your target reliability. This has significant practical advantage in that the test would take less time to administer. After experimenting with different numbers of trials, which can be done with a formula (see the discussion of the Spearman-Brown prophecy formula in Chapter 6), you find that a five-test trial yields a reliability of .82. The test has been reduced by half, yet it still has acceptable reliability! The main point is that the number of trials of a test is not determined arbitrarily. One cannot casually decide to use a different number of trials than the number recommended by the test developer. Let us say that you are interested in a batting test for elementary school children. You find a test you like, but it requires 20 trials. You decide there is not sufficient time to administer a 20-trial test in class, but a 10-trial test could be administered. But wait! You cannot simply drop 10 trials because you have no idea whether a 10-trial test is reliable. Unless you have time to determine the reliability of the shorter version of the test, you should not use it.

A lot of time and effort goes into determining the number of trials to include in a test. Surprisingly, many test users record the best trial out of the total number for an examinee's score. This practice is acceptable in a competitive situation or when the individual's best performance is of primary interest. In most physical education classes, test users are interested in the student's true ability rather than the student's day-to-day fluctuations. In other words, teachers would like to assume that there is some stability (or reliability) to the student's level of ability. Except for a few tests measuring maximum performance, one trial of a test is usually not adequate to reflect reliable performance.

To obtain a stable representation of performance, the effects of practice, learning, and fatigue must be eliminated. One way practice and learning are eliminated is to prepare the examinee properly, as described in the previous section. Practice trials are usually administered before the actual test for this reason. A good test developer will also plot the trial scores and examine them closely. If the trial scores systematically increase or decrease, obviously a reliable performance has not been obtained. Note the example presented in Figure 18-15. Six trials of a test were plotted in this figure. Note that the scores increase from trials 1 to 2, 2 to 3, and 3 to 4; then the performance stabilizes. If this test were administered to a student, the test developer might recommend that six trials actually be administered but the average of only the last three trials be used for the student's score.

Baumgartner and Jackson (1970) computed reliabilities for tests having systematic increases or systematic decreases in trial scores. The trials causing the systematic changes were then dropped, and reliabilities were estimated for the remaining trials. The standing long jump was one of the tests they studied. When six trials were administered to junior high school boys, their performance was stable on the first three trials but dropped off systematically over the last three trials. Presumably, the boys in this age group began to fatigue after the

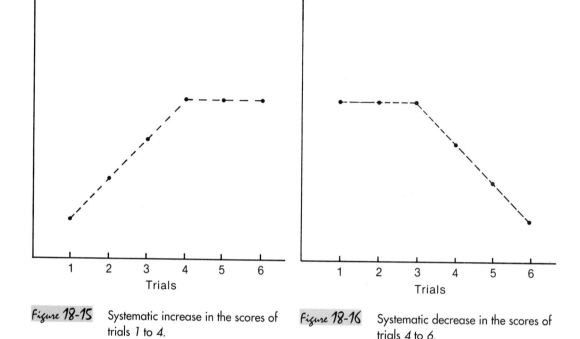

Figure *18-15*   Systematic increase in the scores of trials *1* to *4*.

Figure *18-16*   Systematic decrease in the scores of trials *4* to *6*.

third trial, as depicted in Figure 18-16. Baumgartner and Jackson recommend that the test score be represented by the average of the first three trials. In this case only three trials need be administered. The reliability of the test under these conditions was reported as .96. When six trials of the same test were administered to high-school boys, the scores increased systematically up to the fourth trial (as in Figure 18-15) and then leveled off. Apparently a practice effect caused the change in scores. In this case, administration of a six-trial test was recommended, using the average of the last three trials as the test score. The reliability of the three-trial test was .97. Of course, it would be best if enough practice trials could be administered before the test to obtain stable test trials. At the very least, when administering a test with more than one trial, plot the trials on a piece of paper. Examine the plot for systematic changes. If they exist, you will have some evidence that performance is being affected by practice, learning, or fatigue. Nothing can be done about the test scores at that point, but the test user may decide not to place much weight on the results.

Use of Norms

It is very helpful if norms have been published for the test you have administered, especially if you want to determine the effectiveness of your program. To be used properly, norms should be available for the same age and sex as the individuals tested. Then any score can be compared with the same score in the table of individually based norms. For example, the AAHPER *Youth Fitness*

Test Manual includes tables of percentile norms. A test score can be matched with the same score on the appropriate norms table, and the percentile corresponding with this score can be read from this table.

The tabled norms should be used to determine the percentile scores of individual students only. Using tables of norms to interpret group data, although appealing, is not appropriate. For example, assume a physical educator has administered the youth fitness test to a group of students. A mean and a standard deviation are calculated for each test. The teacher refers to the tables of norms and matches each mean with a score in the appropriate table. The percentile for each mean is then read from the table. The teacher would like to be able to say, for example, that performance in the long jump for a group of students falls at the 70th (or some other) percentile. This procedure is incorrect! The norms tables were developed on the basis of individually based norms. As Spray (1977) demonstrates, a group mean should not be compared with individually based norms, since the variability of individually based norms differs from the variability of group means. Thus, as shown in Figure 18-17, the norm for the group mean is an underestimate if the class is above average and an overestimate if the class is below average. The same situation applies if the median is used.

Spray (1977) describes several ways of interpreting group averages when only individually based norms tables are available. In one approach, the percentage of students receiving scores above the 50th percentile for the national norm group is identified for each test item. (For an example of this method, see Table 18-12.) This information could be very useful in evaluating a physical

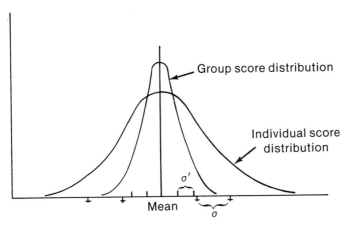

Figure 18-17   Distribution of individual scores vs. mean scores (σ = one standard deviation unit for individual score distribution; σ' = one standard deviation unit for group score distribution). *From Spray JA. 1977.*

Table 18-12 Seventh- and Eighth-Grade Boys' AAHPER Fitness Test Results	Percent of Students Above the National 50th Percentile
Eighth grade	
Shuttle run	88.6
600-yard run	77.5
Standing broad jump	72.3
Pull-ups	66.3
Sit-ups	65.2
50-yard dash	50.0
Seventh grade	
Shuttle run	87.6
Sit-ups	85.0
600-yard run	80.9
Standing broad jump	62.4
Pull-ups	58.0
50-yard dash	33.9

From Spray JA.

education program. Data for boys in all classes at each grade level were used in determining the percentages for the Waunakee (Wisconsin) group. Find the percentage of seventh-grade boys scoring at or above the 50th percentile on the sit-ups test in Table 18-12. Since 85% of the boys performed more than 38 sit-ups, the number representing the 50th percentile for the national group norm, one could conclude that they have above-average abdominal and leg flexor strength. On the other hand, only 33.9% performed above the 50th percentile on the 50-yard dash, suggesting a need for modifications in the physical education program.

A second alternative is to compare the distribution for the national norm group with the distribution of scores for a class. In Figure 18-18, the distribution of scores on the shuttle run test for all seventh-grade boys in a junior high school is compared with the distribution for the national norm group. A large portion of the distribution for the local group falls above the 50th percentile for the national group. In this case, lower times on the shuttle run reflect better performance; therefore, the higher percentiles are located to the left of the 50th percentile. The same information is shown in Table 18-12 in tabular form.

TESTS OF PHYSICAL FITNESS KNOWLEDGE

Few tests of physical fitness knowledge are available. A new physical fitness knowledge test has been developed for high-school students (Safrit et al., 1995).

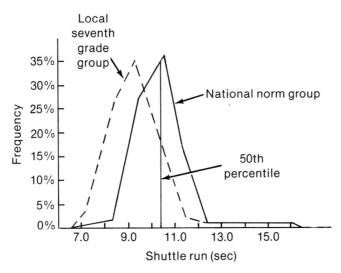

Figure 18-18   Thirteen-year-old boys national norm group vs. seventh-grade boys (Waunakee Junior High School, Waunakee, Wisconsin): shuttle run. The distributions appear to be positively skewed since a lower time implies a better performance on the shuttle run. *From Spray JA.*

The table of specifications for this test includes six content areas: (1) concept of fitness, (2) scientific principles of exercise, (3) components of physical fitness, (4) effects of exercise on chronic disease risk factors, (5) exercise prescription, and (6) other factors. The two content areas weighted most heavily are scientific principles of exercise and exercise prescription. The test items were evaluated by three nationally recognized experts in physical fitness for children and youth. Two 40-item forms were developed for the high-school level. Both classical test theory and item response theory were used to analyze responses to items. The items were refined as a result of three pilot tests. Content-related evidence of validity has been established for the test, and the reliability is satisfactory. Forms are also being developed for elementary and middle-school students.

SUMMARY

In this chapter, tests of performance-related physical fitness are discussed and differentiated from tests of health-related physical fitness, which are described in Chapter 17. A certain type of fitness only minimally related to the performer's positive health state is required for participation in athletic events. This does not mean that health-related fitness is unimportant to the athlete, but rather that another type of fitness is required as well. However, while health-related physical fitness applies to the entire population of healthy people, athletic performance–related fitness is relevant primarily to persons performing in athletic events, including recreational participation as well as organized teams.

Learning Experiences

1. Administer several performance-related fitness items in your class or to a class of children in a neighborhood school. Average the scores for each test. (If you are a female, use the test scores for the females in class. If you are a male, use only the male test scores. Do not combine male and female data.) Since you cannot convert the class averages to percentiles using the tables of norms (why can't you do this?) that have been published, how can you use the information in the tables to interpret your results? Interpret the results for all tests.
2. Using one of the above data sets, calculate the z-score and T-score for each raw score in the group. If you need to review the formulas, see Chapter 3.
3. Write a short paper on the problems you encountered in administering the youth fitness test. How could these problems be avoided in the future?

References

American Association for Health, Physical Education and Recreation (AAHPER). 1976. Youth fitness test manual. Washington, DC: American Association for Health, Physical Education and Recreation.

Askew NR. 1966. Reliability of the 600-yard run-walk at the secondary school level. Research Quarterly, **37**:451–454.

Baumgartner TA. 1978. Modified pull-up test. Research Quarterly, **49**:80–84.

Baumgartner TA, Jackson AS. 1970. Measurement schedules for tests of motor performance. Research Quarterly, **41**:10–14.

Baumgartner TA, and others. (1984). Equipment improvements and additional norms for the modified pull-up test. Research Quarterly for Exercise and Sport, **55**(1):64–68.

Berger RA, Medlin RL. 1969. Evaluation of Berger's I-RM chin test for junior high males. Research Quarterly, **40**:460–463.

Cotten DJ. 1990. An analysis of the NCYFS II modified pull-up test. Research Quarterly for Exercise and Sport, **61**:272–274.

Cotten DJ, Marwitz B. 1969. Relationship between two flexed arm hangs and pull-ups for college women. Research Quarterly, **40**:415–416.

Doolittle TL, Bigbee R. 1968. The twelve-minute run-walk: A test of cardiorespiratory fitness of adolescent boys. Research Quarterly, **39**:491–495.

Engleman ME, Morrow JR. 1991. Reliability and skinfold correlates for traditional and modified pull-ups in children grades 3–5. Research Quarterly for Exercise and Sport, **62**:88–91.

Erbaugh SJ. 1990. Reliability of physical fitness tests administered to young children. Perceptual Motor Skills, **71**:1123–1128.

Fleishman EA. 1964. The structure and measurement of physical fitness. Englewood Cliffs, NJ: Prentice-Hall.

Gabbard C, Gibbons E, Elledge J. 1983. Effects of grip and forearm position on flexed arm hang performance. Research Quarterly for Exercise and Sport, **54**(2):198–199.

Hilsendager DR, Strow MH, Ackerman KJ. 1969. Companion of speed, strength, and agility exercises in the development of agility. Research Quarterly, **37**:71–75.

Hunsicker P, Reiff G. 1966. A survey and comparison of youth fitness 1958–1965. Journal of Health, Physical Education and Recreation, **37**:22–25.

Jackson AS, Baumgartner TA. 1969. Measurement schedules of sprint running. Research Quarterly, **40**:708–711.

Kendall FP. 1965. A criticism of current tests and exercises for physical fitness. Journal of the American Physical Therapy Association, **45**:187–197.

Klesius SE. 1968. Reliability of the AAHPER youth fitness items and relative efficiency of the performance measures. Research Quarterly, **39**:801–811.

Kollath J, Safrit MJ, Zhu W, Gao L. 1991. Measurement errors in modified pull-ups testing. Research Quarterly for Exercise and Sport, **62**(4):432–435.

Manitoba Department of Education. 1977. Manitoba Physical Fitness Performance Test and fitness objectives. Manitoba, Canada: Department of Education.

Marmis C, et al. 1969. Reliability of the multi-trial items of the AAHPER youth fitness test. Research Quarterly, **40**:240–245.

Olree H, et al. 1965. Evaluation of the AAHPER youth fitness test. Journal of Sports Medicine and Physical Fitness, **5**:67–71.

Pate RR, Lonnett M. 1988. Validity of field tests of upper body muscular strength. Unpublished manuscript. University of South Carolina, Columbia.

Pate RR, Ross JG, Baumgartner TA, Sparks RE. 1987. The modified pull-up test. Journal of Physical Education, Recreation, and Dance, **58**(9):71–73.

Ross JG, Pate RR. 1987. The National Children and Youth Fitness Study II: A summary of findings. Journal of Physical Education, Recreation and Dance, **58**(9):51–56.

Safrit MJ. 1969. The physical performance of inner city children in Milwaukee, Wisconsin. Technical report. May 1969. University of Wisconsin, Milwaukee, Department of Physical Education.

Safrit MJ, Zhu W, Cohen AS. 1995. Physical Fitness Knowledge Test. Champaign, Ill: Human Kinetics Publishers, in press.

Sigerseth PO. 1978. Flexibility. In Montoye HJ, ed. An introduction to measurement in physical education. Boston: Allyn & Bacon.

Spray JA. 1977. Interpreting group or class performances using AAHPER youth fitness test norms. Journal of Physical Education and Recreation, **48**:56–57.

Wilgoose CE, Askew NR, Askew MP. 1961. Reliability of the 600-yard run at the junior high school level. Research Quarterly, **32**:264–266.

Annotated Readings

Dawson C, Croce R, Quinn T, Vroman N. 1992. Reliability of the Nicholas Manual Muscle Tester on upper body strength of children ages 8–10. Pediatric Exercise Science, **4**:340–350.

The Nicholas Manual Muscle Tester was used to measure maximum isometric strength of dominant and nondominant elbow flexors, elbow extensors, and shoulder abductors; test-retest reliability coefficients ranged from .72 to .90; the authors found significant differences between boys and girls on most of the muscle groups.

Faigenbaum AD, Zaichkowsky LD, Westcott WL, Micheli LJ, Fehlandt AF. 1993. The effects of a twice-a-week strength program on children. Pediatric Exercise Science, **5**:339–346.

Boys and girls approximately 10 years of age performed three sets of 10 to 15 repetitions on five exercises over an 8-week period; measures used were 10-repetition maximum, sit-and-reach test, vertical jump, seated ball squat, resting blood pressure, and body composition; the authors observed significant gains in strength and in sum of skinfolds.

Hunsicker P, Reiff G. 1977. Youth fitness report: 1958–1965–1975. Journal of Physical Education and Recreation, **48**:31–33.

Describes the large-scale studies of physical fitness using the youth fitness test; little or no improvement took place from 1965 to 1975; compares both boys and girls in grades 5 through 12; samples were selected from homerooms rather than physical education classes.

Shephard RJ, Lavallee H. 1994. Impact of enhanced physical education on muscle strength of the prepubescent child. Pediatric Exercise Science, **6**:75–87.

Describes the influence of daily physical education on prepubescent children over a 5-year period; measures were taken of height, weight, body circumferences, skinfolds, grip strength, shoulder flexion, elbow flexion, hip flexion, knee extension, and knee flexion; the authors concluded that daily physical education led to substantial increments of isometric strength without augmenting limb size.

Vincent WJ, Britten SD. 1980. Evaluation of the curl-up. Journal of Physical Education and Recreation, **51**(2):74–75.

Discusses the inappropriateness of the straight-leg sit-up based on scientific evidence; suggests that the bent-knee sit-up is also unacceptable and provides a rationale for this conclusion; reports low reliabilities for the curl-up test; and notes several possible reasons for this unreliability.

Other Measurements
of Physical Fitness

part ten

Tests of Sports Skills

Many examples of sports skills tests can be found in the literature. Books by Collins and Hodges (1978) and Strand and Wilson (1993) provide excellent overviews of a variety of these tests. Both books are devoted entirely to tests of skill in a variety of sports. A sampling of sports skills tests is included here to exemplify the types of tests that have been developed in the field of physical education. Describing all tests in each sport is unrealistic in a measurement and evaluation textbook. (See Chapter 12 for examples of skills tests for elementary school children. For information on other tests, refer to Strand and Wilson and the American Alliance for Health, Physical Education, Recreation, and Dance (AAHPERD) skills test series, which is undergoing revision.)

Although key words have been included at the beginning of all other chapters in this book, they are omitted here, since the primary purpose of this material is to provide examples of sports skills tests for 13 sports: archery, badminton, baseball, basketball, field hockey, football, golf, racquetball, soccer, softball, swimming, tennis, and volleyball.

One precaution should be kept in mind when reviewing the test setups. Many tests of sports skills require the use of a target on the floor or the wall of the gymnasium. The use of masking tape and fiber tape should be avoided, since they can pull the seal off the floor. Special tape can be purchased that does not damage the floor. Water paints can also be used on some floors.

TYPES OF MEASURES IN SPORTS SKILLS TESTS

Several types of measures can be used in testing a skill. These include time, distance, accuracy, and force. Measures of form (process) can also be included in skill assessment.

Measures of Time

When a time measure is used to measure a skill, the product rather than the process of skill execution is measured. The difference between process and product can be described using the example of measuring the speed of an ice hockey puck hit over a given distance. The product, the action of the puck, is being measured. The process, the force-producing actions of the player, is of indirect concern but is not directly measured. Time measures have also been used to measure the repeated executions of a skill.

Time measures are appropriate for speed events in such activities as swimming or track and for skills in which the projectile remains on the ground or floor, as in ice hockey or bowling. (The assumption is that minimal resistance will result from the object contacting the ground or floor.) If the object is projected into the air, a velocity rather than a time measure should be used to measure force.

When a given number of executions of a skill are timed, the use of time as a measure has questionable validity. First, the examinee is encouraged to hurry at the expense of accuracy. Second, when measuring ball skills in this way, the ball rebounds off the wall continually. There are very few sports in which the player is required to receive his or her own rebound. Thus, handling the rebound may add an unrealistic element of skill to the test. Third, the use of a single score in measuring repeated executions of a skill provides little diagnostic information on the skill itself. If throwing is being measured, for example, a ball rebounding off the wall may be poorly caught, resulting in a poor score. Thus the examinee's skill in catching affects the final score. Furthermore, this error might not occur on every execution of the skill. Measuring a single execution of a skill over several trials is preferable to measuring repeated executions within one trial.

Measures of Distance

Distance measures are frequently used to measure jumps and throws. A distance measure is probably adequate for measuring skill in jumping. However, when measuring skill in throwing, the distance measure is often inappropriate. Skill in throwing requires a combination of force and accuracy. If two objects are thrown, both might land at the same point, and yet the trajectories of the two objects might be quite different. In this case, both throws would be considered equally good if distance was used as the measure. However, only the accuracy of the two throws is identical; the force applied to each differs. Or, conversely, two objects might be projected with the same force and yet the distances of the two throws could vary owing to differences in the angle at which the ball is thrown. Thus skill in throwing should be measured by taking both the accuracy and force components of skill into account. This can best be done by utilizing both velocity and accuracy measures. The concept of measuring both force and accuracy does not apply to competitive situations in field events, where the skill is not a sport skill but rather a specific skill involving coordination and power. The latter skill requires maximum force and limited accuracy as opposed to a throw in softball, where the accuracy demands are high and optimal force is required.

Measures of Number of Executions in a Given Time

Another variety of motor skills tests measures the number of executions of a given skill that can be performed in a specified time period. A common example of this type of measure is a test of the number of repeated wall volleys executed in 30 seconds. The problems inherent in this type of test are similar to those described for measures of time: the examinee is required to receive his or her own rebound, the time limit stresses speed rather than accuracy, and the test has limited diagnostic value for the skill in question.

Measures of Velocity

Velocity measures take the speed, angle of projection, and distance components of the projectile skill into account. Thus, the force aspect of the skill is measured with a great deal of precision. Velocity is determined by dividing distance by time and is recorded in feet per second. Velocity should be used to measure any skill in which an object is projected into the air. The velocity score reflects the amount of force applied and should be accompanied by an accuracy measure.

Measures of velocity can be approximated in several ways. One method is to use ropes to measure the height of the trajectory. An early test in which a rope was used to measure force was the tennis drive test, developed by Broer and Miller (1950). In this test a rope was placed 4 feet above the net, and any drive where the ball passed between the net and the rope was given a higher score than an equally accurate drive in which the ball passed over the rope. By giving more points for a ball that passes between the rope and the net, the velocity (or force) of the ball is taken into account in a rough fashion. However, Glassow (1957) showed that a wide range of velocities could be obtained within any given scoring area for this particular test and suggested the need for reducing the area between the rope and the net. A refinement of this method was developed by Liba and Stauff (1963) in the volleyball pass test. Three ropes were used instead of one. The top rope was placed so that the trajectory of the volleyball would have a minimum high point of 15 feet in accordance with the definition of good performance. The remaining ropes defined scoring areas at lesser heights. Ropes are useful measures of force as long as their placement is such that the velocity scores within a given target area do not vary to a great extent. A 4-foot range in velocities within a given area should be acceptable. However, the use of the ropes will provide only an approximation of the force applied to the ball.

Another method of roughly assessing a component of velocity (vertical angle of projection) was described by West and Thorpe (1968). In measuring the short shot in golf using the eight iron, the authors used ratings of the vertical angle of projection to categorize the height of the trajectory. If the ball was hit at an angle of 290 degrees or more, 3 points were given for the flight score. If the angle was judged to be less than 290 degrees, 2 points were given. A topped ball received 1 point. Because of the subjectivity involved in making these judgments, the interjudge objectivity should be determined. (Intrarater objectivity was satisfactorily established for the West and Thorpe test.)

A rough approximation of velocity can be obtained by marking "power zones" on the test area. Both the AAHPERD tennis skills test and the AAHPERD softball skills test described later in this chapter use such zones. Power zones are based on the premise that a projectile must have sufficient velocity to bounce or roll a fixed distance. For example, for a tennis ball to bounce once in a target area and then land 20 feet beyond the target, it must be stroked with minimal velocity.

The most precise measure of velocity is electronic equipment such as the velocimeter currently in use at the University of Wisconsin. Less accurate but usable velocity scores can be obtained using a stopwatch and a wall target. This procedure was described by Safrit and Pavis (1969) for a measure of the force of the overarm softball throw. The velocity scores can be calculated using the method described in Cooper and Glassow (1976). This process is extremely time-consuming, and the use of velocity tables is recommended as a more expedient method. A velocity table for objects projected from a distance of 30 feet is presented in the appendix of the Cooper and Glassow (1963) book. Such tables can easily be developed through the use of a simple computer program.

Measures of Accuracy

Accuracy is one of the most frequently measured components of a skill and is generally measured using a target of some sort, which can range from the simple to the complex. In beginning badminton, for example, a useful target to aid in measuring the accuracy of the long serve might be a simple division of the long service court into three sections. Beginners should learn to hit the shuttlecock to the back section of the court.

It is assumed that the height of the trajectory is also being measured, as this is an important component of the badminton serve. The measurement of accuracy alone is insufficient for the assessment of this skill. Two shuttlecocks might land on the same section of the target and yet have different trajectories.

A more complicated target can be designed using arcs and rays for a more refined measure of accuracy. Deviations from the area with the greatest point value as well as distances from the net can be measured with this approach. Such a test is diagnostic in that both an accuracy and a deviation score can be obtained. Almost all attempted serves are scored, which is advantageous, because when many zero scores are obtained, no information is provided about the examinee's weaknesses.

Measures of Form

Often it is useful to measure form, the process by which the skill is executed. Measures of form are frequently carried out by means of a checklist or a rating scale. Both of these methods are discussed in Chapter 15.

If the product is satisfactory, there is some question regarding the need to measure the process. For example, if a player can execute a good place kick, does it matter if his or her form does not fit a typical pattern? Certainly a professional football coach would not consider changing a successful soccer-style place-kicker to the more traditional method of kicking off the toe. However, it may be desirable to measure beginners on some aspects of form, especially when deviations from the typical pattern of form are likely to hinder further development of the skill. As the learner develops a skill that is consistently satisfactory in terms of product, the instructor should no longer attempt to change idiosyncrasies in style. The measurement of form should probably be deemphasized after the players have advanced beyond the beginner's level in most sports activities, although this may not be true in such areas as movement education, dance, gymnastics, and swimming.

EXAMPLES OF TESTS

Archery Tests

AAHPER Archery Test (AAHPER, 1967)

Test Objective   To measure skill in archery.

Description   No more than four archers should be placed at each target. Two ends of six arrows each are shot at distances of 10, 20, and 30 yards for boys and 10 and 20 yards for girls. The test is started at the 10-yard distance. When all archers have completed two ends, the group moves back to the 20-yard line, and so forth. Any examinee not scoring at least 10 points at one distance is not permitted to shoot at the next distance.

Test Area   An archery range adequate to test a group of archers at distances of 10, 20, and 30 yards or a standard-size gymnasium with proper backstops.

Equipment   Standard 48-inch target faces; bows ranging from 15 to 40 lb in pull; matched arrows 24 to 28 inches long.

Scoring   Standard target scoring is used, with gold = 9, red = 7, blue = 5, black = 3, and white = 1. Arrows falling outside the white area are scored 0. Arrows bouncing off the target or passing completely through are awarded 7 points. The total test score is the sum of the total points at each distance.

Validity   Face validity (a test that appears to be valid but has not been formally validated).

Reliability   No reliability estimate is given in the test manual; the manual includes a statement that no test in the battery has a reliability of less than .70, the AAHPER minimum standard.

Comments   Abbreviated tables of norms of this test are included in Tables 19-1 and 19-2. Full-length tables are available in the manual. Four practice arrows are permitted at each distance. Generally, two class periods are required to administer the test to girls and three periods for boys.

Criterion-Referenced Archery Test (Shifflett and Shuman, 1982)

Test Objective   To measure ability in archery using the criterion-referenced testing approach.

Description   Examinees stand at a target line 20 yards from the target. Two ends (12 arrows) are shot at a 48-inch target face.

Test Area   Indoor or outdoor archery range.

Table 19-1 Percentile Ranks for Girls on the AAHPER
Archery Test: 20 Yards—12 Arrows

Percentile	Age (yr)				
	12–13	14	15	16	17–18
95	40	47	55	58	71
75	17	28	34	36	42
50	9	18	23	22	26
25	0	8	13	12	16
5	0	0	0	0	0

Abbreviated form of Table 6 of AAHPER.

Equipment   Bows (variety of weights), arrows (variety of lengths), targets, target faces, tripods, and scoresheets.

Scoring   Target scores of 1, 3, and 5 are converted to 0; scores of 7 and 9, to 1. The total test score is the sum of the converted scores for all 12 trials. A student with a test score of 5 or greater is classified as a master and with a test score of less than 5, a nonmaster.

Validity   The validity coefficient is .73, based on test scores of college men and women using the instructed/uninstructed approach to validation.

Reliability   P = .87, where P is the proportion of agreement between two administrations of the test; subjects—college women.

Comments   The same test standard is used for both males and females. The test developers suggest that this test could be used to exempt students from a beginning archery class or to grade students in physical education where a pass-fail grading system is used.

Table 19-2 Percentile Ranks for Boys on the AAHPER
Archery Test: 20 Yards—12 Arrows

Percentile	Age (yr)				
	12–13	14	15	16	17–18
95	53	61	77	78	78
75	31	38	58	59	59
50	22	26	39	46	43
25	12	16	24	33	29
5	3	6	9	14	11

Abbreviated form of Table 2 of AAHPER.

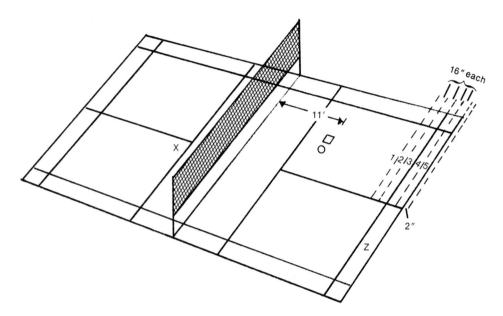

Figure 19-1   Court markings for the Poole long serve test. *(Redrawn from Johnson BL, Nelson JK.)*

Badminton Tests

Poole Long Serve Test (Poole and Nelson, 1970)

Test Objective   To measure the ability to serve high and deep into the opponent's backcourt.

Description   The examinee stands behind the short service line, anywhere in the service court diagonally opposite the target area. Twelve consecutive trials are taken, in which the examinee attempts to serve the shuttle over the extended racket of an assistant standing in a square 11 feet from the net, as shown in Figure 19-1.

Test Area   Regulation-size badminton court.

Equipment   Badminton rackets, 12 shuttlecocks, floor tape, and scoresheets.

Scoring   The scorer stands in the court adjacent to the target area. If the shuttlecock passes over the extended racket of the assistant, a check is recorded for height. The point value of the target area in which the shuttle lands is rescored for accuracy. If the shuttle does not pass over the racket, verified by the assistant calling "low," an X is recorded under "height" and one point is subtracted from the point value of the target area. The total test score is the sum of the best 10 of 12 trials.

Validity $r_{xy} = .51$, using the results of tournament play as a criterion measure.

Reliability $R_{xx'} = .81$, using the test-retest method; subjects—college men and women.

Comments   Although this test is simpler to set up than the Scott-Fox test (Scott and French, 1959), it is not as objective because an assistant with an extended racket is substituted for a rope. Poole and Nelson believe the use of an assistant is more realistic, but they agree that a rope could also be used to judge the height of the serve. The test developers suggest that the height of the assistant is immaterial, except in extreme cases. The target area is more appropriate, compared with the Scott-Fox target, for examinees of average ability. Note that the target extends beyond the baseline by a few inches. Generally, a shuttle dropping into this area would be returned by the receiver. If this test cannot be used because of its length requirements, the authors recommend shortening it to the best six of eight trials.

French Short Serve Test (Scott et al., 1941)

Test Objective   To measure the examinee's ability to serve accurately with a low and short placement.

Description   The examinee stands behind the short service line, anywhere in the right service area, and takes 20 short serves. Each serve that passes between the net and the rope and lands in the target area shown in Figure 19-2 is scored. The serve must be executed legally; for example, the examinee may not take a step while performing the serve.

Test Area   Regulation-size badminton court.

Equipment   Badminton rackets, 25 shuttlecocks, rope to stretch above net, tape, and scoresheets.

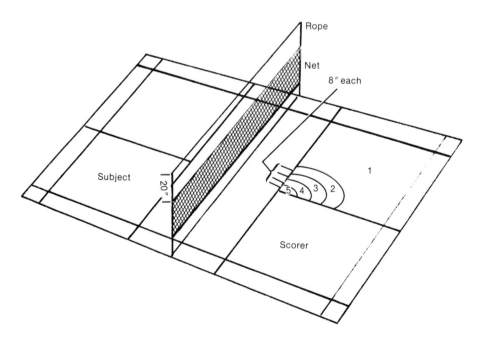

Figure 19-2   Court markings for the French short serve test. (From Scott MG, French E.)

Target area for the French short serve test.

Scoring A scorer stands in the court adjacent to the target area and records a check if the shuttle passes between the rope and net and an X if it does not. The target score (5, 4, 3, 2, or 1) is also recorded if the height was acceptable; otherwise, a 0 is recorded for the target score. If the shuttle lands on a target line, the score value of the higher area is given. If it hits the rope, the trial is retaken. The total test score is the sum of 20 trials.

Validity r_{xy} = .66, using a criterion measure of ladder tournament rankings.

Reliability $R_{xx'}$ = .51 to .89; subjects—college women (physical education majors).

Comments Two practice trials are permitted. Approximately 20 students can be tested in a 60-minute period at a single testing station. This test is also appropriate for junior high and high-school students. A version of the test adopted by the University of Wisconsin uses the same rope height but an easier target. Instead of a fan-shaped target, the Wisconsin version is a series of lines parallel to the short service line, with the highest point value given to the area closest to the service line.

Poole Forehand Clear Test (Poole and Nelson, 1970)

Test Objective To measure the ability to hit a forehand clear from the backcourt high and deep into the opponent's backcourt.

Description The examinee stands with one foot in the square marked X as in Figure 19-3. If the examinee is right-handed, the right foot should be in the

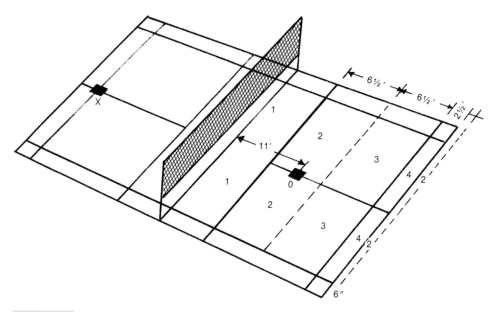

Figure 19-3   Court markings for the Poole forehand clear test. *(Redrawn from Johnson BL, Nelson JK.)*

square, and vice versa. Place the shuttle with the feather end down on the forehand side of the racket. The shuttle is tossed into the air by the examinee, who then hits an overhead forehand clear so that the shuttle passes over the extended racket of an assistant standing at point *0* as in Figure 19-3. The foot in contact with the square should remain so until the shuttle is hit; 12 trials are taken.

Test Area   Regulation-size badminton court.

Equipment   Badminton rackets, 12 shuttlecocks, floor tape, and scoresheets.

Scoring   Same as Poole long serve test.

Validity r_{xy} = .70, using tournament play as a criterion measure.

Reliability $R_{xx'}$ = .90, using the test-retest method; subjects—college men and women.

Comments   The test developers note that tossing the shuttle in the prescribed manner should be practiced on several occasions before actual testing. This test can also be used to measure the backhand clear, although it is not quite as valid and reliable as the forehand clear test. A shortened version of the test, consisting of the best six of eight trials, can be used.

Lockhart-McPherson Badminton Test (Lockhart and McPherson, 1949)

Test Objective   To measure badminton playing ability.

Description   The examinee assumes a service stance in back of the starting line on the floor 6½ feet from and parallel to the base of the wall. On the signal "Ready, go!'' the examinee serves the shuttle against the wall. The shuttle is then hit as many times as possible during a 30-second time period, as long as it is hit from behind the restraining line, which is 3 feet from and parallel to the base of the wall and above a 5-foot line on the wall. Three 30-second trials are taken. A 15-second practice session is permitted before testing.

Test Area   A smooth wall at least 10 feet by 10 feet and floor space of equal dimensions.

Equipment   Racket, six shuttlecocks, stopwatch, tape measure, floor and wall tape, and scoresheets.

Scoring   A point is scored each time the shuttle is hit from behind the restraining line and strikes the wall on or above the 5-foot wall line. If the shuttle falls to the floor during a trial, the examinee must pick it up and restart the wall volley with a legal serve. If, while taking consecutive hits, the examinee steps on or across the restraining line or strikes under the wall line, the trial continues, but no points are scored. The total test score is the sum of the legal hits in three 30-second trials.

Validity $r_{xy} = .71$ to .90, using criterion measures of judges' ratings and round robin tournament rankings.

Reliability $R_{xx'} = .90$, using the test-retest method; subjects—college women.

Comments   This test is appropriate for both males and females as young as junior high school age. It is easy to administer, and several testing stations can often be used with ease. However, the volleys are sometimes executed with poor form. In these cases proper form should immediately be stressed.

MILLER WALL VOLLEY TEST (Miller, 1951) This is another version of this test. The lines are set higher and farther from the wall so that the player must use an overhead clear to perform well on the test. The restraining line is 10 feet from the wall, and the wall height is 7½ feet from the floor. Although any type of stroke can be used in the Miller test, a definite advantage exists for the player who is able to hit repeated clears against the wall.

Baseball Tests

Kelson Baseball Classification Plan (Kelson, 1953)

Test Objective   To classify boys for baseball participation at the elementary school and Little League levels.

Description   This is a simple baseball throw for distance. The testing takes place outdoors. The examinee, holding a baseball, either stands behind the restraining line or runs up to the line, as long as the line is not stepped on or over. Three trials are taken, with instructions to throw the ball as far as possible.

Test Area   Level field 250 feet long and 50 feet wide; the throwing area is marked off from 50 to 200 feet with lines 5 feet apart.

Equipment   Baseballs, field-marking materials, tape measure, and scoresheets.

Scoring   The best of the three throws is the test score. Each of the three trial scores is recorded by the scorers. For the most effective scoring, it is recommended that scorers be positioned every 25 feet of the throwing area.

Validity r_{xy} = .85, using a criterion measure of a composite of baseball skills including batting averages and judges' ratings of throwing, catching, and fielding.

Reliability Not reported for this test.

Comments The strength of this test is purported to be its ability to classify boys in baseball quickly and easily. Kelson developed a classification chart that can be obtained from the original source (Kelson, 1953).

Basketball Tests

Speed Spot Shooting (Hopkins et al., 1984)*

Test Objective "To measure skill in rapidly shooting from specific positions and, to a certain extent, agility and ball handling" (p. 9).

Description The player begins the test with one foot behind any one of five markers, as shown in Figure 19-4. The 15-foot markers are appropriate for

_____

* The next four tests—speed spot shooting, passing, control dribble, and defensive movement—are part of a battery of basketball skills tests published by AAHPERD (Hopkins et al., 1984). Refer to the test manual for detailed information on this test battery. All four tests can be administered in two class periods.

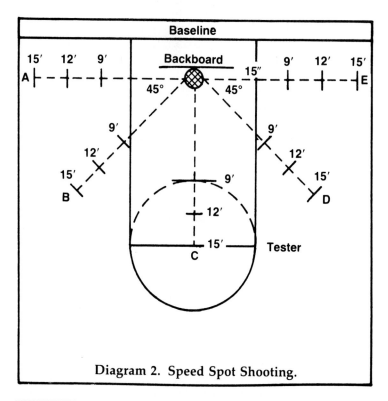

Diagram 2. Speed Spot Shooting.

Figure 19-4   Court markings for the speed shot shooting test. (From Hopkins DR, Shick J, Plack JJ.)

Performing the control dribble test.

grades 10, 11, and 12, and college. For upper elementary grades 5 and 6, the markers are placed 9 feet from the target; for grades 7, 8, and 9, markers are placed 12 feet from the target. On the signal "Ready, go!" the examinee takes the first of three 60-second trials. The ball is shot, retrieved, dribbled to the next marker, and shot again. At least one shot must be taken from each of the five markers. Although most shots must be taken from the marker, four lay-ups are permitted during the testing period, but no two may be taken in succession.

Test Area   Half of a regulation-size basketball court.

Equipment   Baseballs, stopwatch, floor tape, tape measure, and scoresheets.

Scoring   The first trial is a practice trial; the next two are recorded. Two points are awarded for each shot made. One point is given for each unsuccessful shot that hits the rim. The total test score is the sum of scores for the two trials.

Validity r_{xy} = .37 to .91 for all ages on individual test items, using a criterion measure of two subjective ratings of skill in shooting and game performance; r_{xy} = .65 to .95 for the test battery as a whole.

Reliability $R_{xx'}$ = .87 to .95 for females using the test-retest method; $R_{xx'}$ = .84 to .95 for males (test-retest).

Comments   Abbreviated tables of norms are shown in Tables 19-3 and 19-4. Full-length tables are provided in the test manual. The scoring is somewhat complicated, since the scorer must record the following: whether the examinee took at least one shot from each of the five markers ($A-E$); the number of lay-ups the student took; and the point value for each legal shot. Refer to the test manual for assistance in scoring.

No score is given when ball-handling infractions occur, that is, if more than four lay-ups are attempted, or if a lay-up is taken immediately following another one. If the examinee does not take a shot from each of the five markers, the trial must be retaken. Each floor marker should be 2 feet long and 1 inch wide.

Table 19-3 Percentile Norms—Speed Spot Shooting: Males

Percentile	Age (yr)							
	10	**11**	**12**	**13**	**14**	**15**	**16–17**	**College**
95	23	25	27	28	30	27	28	30
75	17	18	19	19	23	20	22	25
50	13	14	15	15	18	16	16	22
25	10	10	11	12	13	11	12	19
5	7	6	7	7	9	6	7	14

Abbreviated form of Table 6, p. 18, from Hopkins DR, Shick J, and Plack JJ.

Passing Test

Test Objective "To measure skill in passing and recovering the ball accurately while moving" (Hopkins et al., 1984, p. 11).

Description The examinee, holding a basketball, assumes a ready position behind the restraining line opposite the *A* target, as shown in Figure 19-5. On the signal "Ready, go!" the ball is passed to the first target (*A*), rebounds, and is recovered while moving in line with the second target (*B*). This sequence continues until the last target (*F*) is reached. The ball is passed twice to target *F*, and the examinee moves back toward target *A*, attempting to hit each target in succession. The trial is terminated at the end of 30 seconds. Three trials are taken, with the first used as a practice trial. Only the chest pass may be used throughout this test.

Test Area Smooth wall surface of 30 feet.

Equipment Basketballs, stopwatch, floor tape, wall tape or chalk, tape measure, and scoresheets.

Table 19-4 Percentile Norms—Speed Spot Shooting: Females

Percentile	Age (yr)							
	10	**11**	**12**	**13**	**14**	**15**	**16–17**	**College**
95	18	19	22	22	25	23	23	35
75	11	11	13	13	15	15	14	21
50	8	8	10	10	11	11	11	17
25	5	5	7	8	9	8	7	13
5	2	2	3	4	4	4	3	8

Abbreviated form of Table 5, p. 18, from Hopkins DR, Shick J, and Plack JJ.

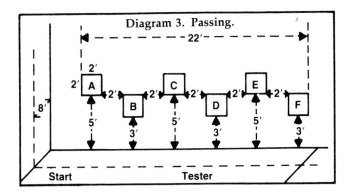

Figure 19-5   Wall markings for the passing test. *(From Hopkins DR, Shick J, Plack JJ.)*

Scoring   Each pass landing within the target or on a target line scores 2 points. Each pass hitting the wall between targets scores 1 point. The total test score is the sum of scores for the two trials.

Validity r_{xy} = .37 to .91, for individual tests and both sexes; r_{xy} = .65 to .95, for total test battery.

Passing test.

Table 19-5 Percentile Norms—Passing: Females

Percentile	Age (yr)							
	10	**11**	**12**	**13**	**14**	**15**	**16–17**	**College**
95	36	38	43	44	46	47	48	54
75	30	31	35	37	39	40	39	47
50	25	27	31	32	34	35	34	42
25	21	23	26	29	29	28	24	37
5	7	13	20	23	24	19	18	21

Abbreviated form of Table 7, p. 19, from Hopkins DR, Shick J, and Plack JJ.

Reliability $R_{xx'} = .82$ to $.91$, for females using the test-retest method; $R_{xx'} = .88$ to $.96$, for males (test-retest).

Comments Each pass must be taken from behind the restraining line. It is recommended that a student assistant be used to call out foot faults. No points are awarded if the examinee's foot is on or over the line, if a second pass is taken at the same target (except *A* and *F* when appropriate), or if a chest pass is not used. Abbreviated norms tables for males and females are given in Tables 19-5 and 19-6. See the test manual for full-length norms tables.

Control Dribble Test

Test Objective "To measure skill in handling the ball while the body is moving" (Hopkins et al., 1984, p. 13).

Description The player begins the test at cone *A* in Figure 19-6. Use the upper diagram for right-handed examinees and the lower one for left-handers. On the signal "Ready, go!" the ball is dribbled with the nondominant hand to the

Table 19-6 Percentile Norms—Passing: Males

Percentile	Age (yr)							
	10	**11**	**12**	**13**	**14**	**15**	**16–17**	**College**
95	41	43	48	54	55	55	57	70
75	35	36	40	43	45	48	49	58
50	31	32	35	39	40	39	41	53
25	25	28	30	35	35	23	25	47
5	8	18	22	23	23	18	21	35

Abbreviated form of Table 8, p. 19, from Hopkins DR, Shick J, and Plack JJ.

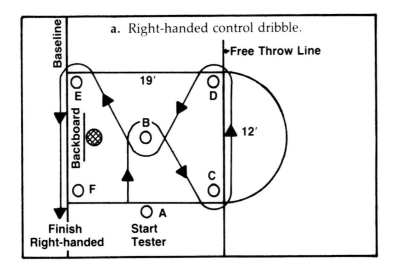

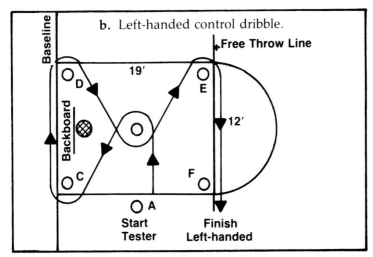

Figure 19-6   Court markings for the control dribble test. *(From Hopkins DR, Shick J, Plack JJ.)*

nondominant side of cone *B*. Thereafter the preferred hand may be used to dribble, and hands may be changed whenever appropriate. The watch is stopped as the examinee crosses the finish line. One practice and two test trials are administered.

Test Area   Half a regulation-size basketball court.

Equipment   Basketballs, six cones, stopwatch, and scoresheets.

Scoring   The trial score is the time required to complete the course legally. Record each trial score to the nearest tenth of a second. The total test score is the sum of the times for two trials.

Table 19-7 Percentile Norms—Control Dribble: Males

Percentile	Age (yr)							
	10	11	12	13	14	15	16–17	College
95	9.2	9.0	8.7	7.8	7.5	7.0	7.0	6.7
75	10.4	10.1	9.5	9.0	8.5	8.1	8.1	7.3
50	11.7	11.1	10.5	9.8	9.3	8.9	9.0	7.8
25	13.7	12.6	11.7	10.7	10.3	10.0	10.0	8.5
5	23.0	16.8	16.0	14.4	13.5	12.0	12.4	10.0

Abbreviated form of Table 10, p. 20, from Hopkins DR, Shick J, and Plack JJ.

Validity r_{xy} = .37 to .91, for individual tests and both sexes; r_{xy} = .65 to .95, for total test battery.

Reliability $R_{xx'}$ = .93 to .97, for females using the test-retest method; $R_{xx'}$ = .88 to .95, for males (test-retest).

Comments The trial must be retaken in the event of ball-handling infractions, failure to remain outside the cone (by either player or ball), and failure to continue the test from the proper spot when control of the ball has been lost. For abbreviated norms tables, see Tables 19-7 and 19-8. For the full-length tables, see the test manual.

Defensive Movement Test

Test Objective "To measure performance of basic defensive movements (Hopkins et al., 1984, p. 15).

Description Three trials are administered—one practice and two test. The test is begun at point A, as shown in Figure 19-7. The examinee faces away from the basket, slides to the left without crossing over the left foot, reaches point B, and

Table 19-8 Percentile Norms—Control Dribble: Females

Percentile	Age (yr)							
	10	11	12	13	14	15	16–17	College
95	10.8	10.3	8.8	8.7	8.4	8.2	8.2	7.6
75	12.3	11.8	10.6	10.0	9.6	9.7	9.8	8.5
50	14.3	13.2	11.9	11.0	10.7	10.7	10.7	9.3
25	16.6	15.0	13.3	12.4	12.0	12.0	12.2	10.4
5	21.7	20.5	19.0	17.8	18.1	15.8	15.0	13.8

Abbreviated form of Table 9, p. 20, from Hopkins DR, Shick J, and Plack JJ.

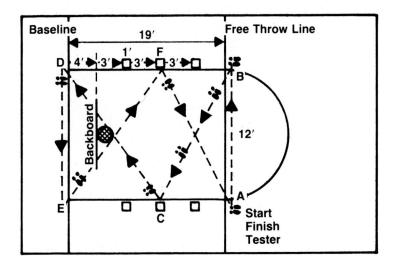

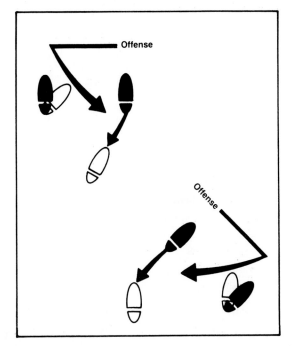

Figure 19-7   Court markings and foot positions for the defensive movement test. *(From Hopkins DR, Shick J, Plack JJ.)*

Table 19-9 Percentile Norms—Defensive Movement: Females

Percentile	Age (yr)							
	10	11	12	13	14	15	16–17	College
95	10.5	10.3	9.5	10.0	9.6	9.7	9.6	8.7
75	11.8	11.8	11.5	11.5	11.0	11.0	11.1	10.3
50	13.2	13.0	12.8	12.5	12.0	12.0	12.0	11.0
25	14.6	14.3	14.1	13.6	13.2	13.4	13.2	12.0
5	19.6	17.4	17.0	16.8	16.4	16.4	16.4	14.5

Abbreviated form of Table 11, p. 21, from Hopkins DR, Shick J, and Plack JJ.

touches the floor outside the lane with the left hand. The examinee then executes a dropstep (see Figure 19-7), slides to point *C*, and touches the floor outside the lane with the right hand. This continues until the course is completed back at point *A*. The stopwatch is started on the signal "Ready, go!" and stopped as the examinee crosses the finish line (*A*) with both feet.

Test Area   Half of a regulation-size basketball court.

Equipment   Basketballs, stopwatch, floor tape, tape measure, and scoresheets.

Scoring   A trial score is the time required to complete the course, measured to the nearest tenth of a second. The total test score is the sum of two trials.

Validity r_{xy} = .37 to .91, for individual tests, males and females; r_{xy} = .65 to .95, for total test battery, males and females.

Reliability $R_{xx'}$ = .95 to .96, for females using the test-retest method; $R_{xx'}$ = .90 to .97, for males (test-retest).

Comments   The trial is retaken if the feet cross during the slide or turn, if the examinee runs, or if the dropstep occurs before the hand touches the floor. Abbreviated tables of norms are presented in Tables 19-9 and 19-10. See the test manual for the full-length norms tables.

Table 19-10 Percentile Norms—Defensive Movement: Males

Percentile	Age (yr)							
	10	11	12	13	14	15	16–17	College
95	10.0	9.0	8.9	8.9	8.7	7.9	7.3	8.4
75	11.5	10.9	10.7	10.3	10.1	9.3	9.6	9.4
50	12.7	12.0	11.9	11.4	11.3	10.3	10.3	10.3
25	13.9	13.7	13.0	12.8	12.4	11.3	11.5	11.2
5	18.7	17.2	17.0	16.6	15.8	14.0	15.2	12.9

Abbreviated form of Table 12, p. 21, from Hopkins DR, Shick J, and Plack JJ.

Field Hockey Tests

Chapman Ball Control Test (Chapman, 1982)

Test Objective   To measure "the subject's ability to combine quickness in wrist and hand movements needed to manipulate the stick with ability to control the force element when contacting the ball" (p. 239).

Description   The ball is placed just beyond the outer circle of the target. On the signal "Ready, go!" the examinee taps the ball in and out of the center circle with a hockey stick. Three 15-second trials are administered. The two lower examples in Figure 19-8 depict legal hits. Before actual testing, the tester should demonstrate the procedures, and the examinees should be allowed to practice.

Test Area   Small indoor testing area; target on floor according to the dimensions shown in the upper portion of Figure 19-8; the outer circle of the target should be colored so that it contrasts with gymnasium floor (orange is suggested).

Equipment   Hockey sticks, several hockey balls, floor tape, stopwatch, and score-sheets.

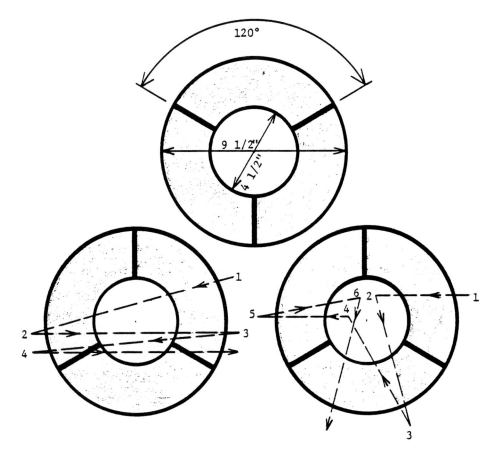

Figure 19-8   Target for the Chapman ball control test. *(From Chapman NL.)*

Scoring   Score 1 point whenever the ball is tapped (not pushed) either into or through the center circle. A point may also be scored when the ball is tapped from the center of the circle to the outside of the target area, if it passes through a segment other than the one from which it entered (*lower right*, Figure 19-8). To score a point, the ball must be tapped from either within the center circle or outside the outer circle. No points are scored when the ball is tapped on the orange area or with the rounded side of the stick. The total test score is the sum of points made on the three 15-second trials.

Validity   Logical validity; construct validity on the basis of significant differences between varsity and junior varsity teams' performances on the test; and concurrent validity (r_{xy} = .63 and .64), using a criterion measure of ratings of stickwork skills.

Reliability $R_{xx'}$ = .89, single test administration.

Comments   The use of three targets is recommended—two practice and one test. While two examinees practice, a third can be tested. If only one test administrator is available, the test can be timed using an audiotape of "Ready, go!" and "Stop!" recorded at 15-second intervals.

Football Tests

Ball-Changing Zigzag Run (AAHPER, 1966)

Test Objective   To measure speed of execution of zigzag movement as the football is changed from arm to arm.

Description   Place five chairs in a line 10 feet apart. The first chair is 10 feet from the starting line. To begin the test, the player assumes a ready position behind the starting line, with a football under his or her right arm. On the signal "Go!" the player runs to the right of the first chair, shifts the ball to the left arm as he or she passes to the left of the second chair, and continues in this manner, as shown in Figure 19-9. The ball must be under the outside arm each time a chair

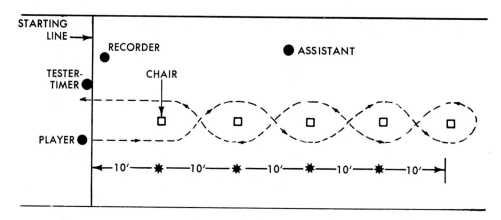

Figure 19-9   Field markings for the ball-changing zigzag run. *(From AAHPERD.)*

Table 19-11 Ball-Changing Zigzag Run (Test Scores in Seconds and Tenths)

Percentile	Age (yr)							
	10	11	12	13	14	15	16	17–18
95	9.9	7.7	7.8	8.0	8.7	7.7	7.7	8.4
75	10.7	9.3	8.8	9.0	9.5	8.6	8.7	9.0
50	11.5	10.3	9.6	9.7	10.0	9.1	9.3	9.6
25	12.5	11.3	10.5	10.3	10.7	9.9	10.1	10.3
5	15.8	14.2	12.3	12.1	12.0	11.5	12.2	12.1

From AAHPER.

is passed, and the inside arm must be extended (as in a stiff arm in football) toward the chair being passed. Two trials are taken.

Test Area   Football field or any grass field.

Equipment   Five chairs, footballs, stopwatch, and measuring tape.

Scoring   Each trial is timed to the nearest tenth of a second, starting with the signal "Go!" and stopping when the player crosses the starting line at the end of the run. The trial with the best time is the test score.

Validity   Not reported for this test.

Reliability   Not reported for this test.

Norms   An abbreviated table of norms is presented in Table 19-11. The full-length norms table can be found in the test manual.

Comments   One practice run is allowed before being tested. The prescribed position (ball under outside arm, inside arm extended) must be maintained when running to the side of a chair throughout the test. Touching a chair is illegal.

Golf Tests

Indoor Golf Skill Test for Junior High School Boys (Shick and Berg, 1983)

Test Objective   To measure golf skills, either indoors or outdoors, performed by junior high school boys.

Description   A target is placed on the floor of the testing area, as shown in Figure 19-10. Colored markers are recommended to identify the scoring areas. A mat is placed at the front edge of the target, where the student stands. A driving mat is placed 1 foot from the target line. The student hits a plastic ball off the driving mat with a five-iron as far as possible, aiming for an orange cone. Two practice and 20 test trials are taken.

Test Area   Small gymnasium or multipurpose room.

Equipment   At least two five-irons, one right-handed and one left-handed; 25 plastic balls; orange cone; floor tape; tape measure; scorecards; mat for examinee; and driving mat.

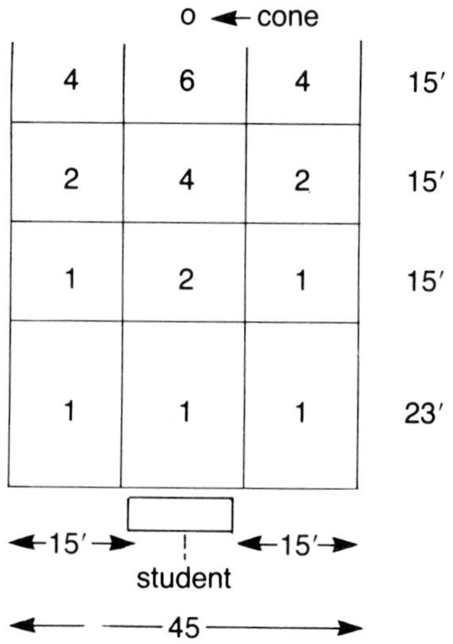

o ◄─ cone

4	6	4	15'
2	4	2	15'
1	2	1	15'
1	1	1	23'

◄─15'─► ┊ ◄─15'─►

student

◄─────── 45 ───────►

Figure 19-10   Target for indoor golf skill test for junior high school boys. *(From Shick J, Berg NG.)*

Scoring   Each trial score is the landing point of the ball on the target. If a ball lands beyond the target but is in line with the farthermost target areas (see *4, 6, 4* of Figure 19-10), the ball is assigned the point value of the closest area. In this case, assume the target lines are extended by imaginary lines. A topped ball that passes through the scoring area is given 1 point. A missed ball is given a score of 0. A ball landing on a target line is given the score of the highest adjacent target area. The total test score is the sum of the trial scores.

Validity $r_{xy} = -.84$, using a criterion measure of the best of three scores on a par 3, nine-hole golf course.

Reliability $R_{xx'} = .97$, for single test administration; $R_{xx'} = .91$, for test-retest administration.

Comments   This is a modification of a test developed for older examinees (Cotten et al., 1972). With two testing stations, 20 students can be tested in one 45-minute class period. Since test validity ($r_{xy} = -.80$) and reliability ($R_{xx'} = .90$) were also acceptable for 10 trials administered on 1 day, using a shortened (10-trial) version of the test would be appropriate.

Racquetball Tests

Racquetball Skills Test (Hensley et al., 1979)

Test Objective   To measure two fundamental components of racquetball speed and power; although accuracy is not emphasized, a gross accuracy component is measured.

Description   Two measures are administered—a short wall volley test and a long wall volley test. In the short wall volley test, the examinee, holding two racquetballs, stands behind the short line, drops a ball, and volleys it against the front wall for 30 seconds. All strokes must be made from behind the short line.

The ball may be hit in the air or after taking one or more bounces. If the ball does not return to the short line or if the examinee misses it, the ball may be retrieved or a new ball may be obtained from the scorer. The test consists of two 30-second trials, preceded by a 30-second practice period.

The testing procedures for the long wall volley test are essentially the same except that the ball is volleyed from behind a restraining line located 12 feet behind and parallel to the short line. In both tests any stroke may be used to keep the ball in play.

Test Area   Regulation-size racquetball court.

Equipment   Racquets, four new racquetballs, colored floor tape, stopwatch, score-sheets, and tape measure.

Scoring   The stopwatch should be started when the examinee releases the ball on the initial drop. The score in each test is the number of legal hits for two 30-second periods. In scoring the short wall volley test, it is recommended that the scorer stand inside the court; for the long wall volley test, standing outside the court, if possible, is recommended. No points are scored when the student steps on or over the restraining line or when the ball hits the floor or a side wall before reaching the front wall.

Validity   Content validity; concurrent validity: $r_{xy} = .79$ for the short test, and $r_{xy} = .86$ for the long test, using a criterion measure of instructor ratings of ability to sustain a rally.

Reliability   The following are test-retest coefficients: $R_{xx'} = .82$ for the long test, college women; $R_{xx'} = .85$ for the long test, college men; $R_{xx'} = .86$ for the short test, college women; and $R_{xx'} = .76$ for the short test, college men.

Comments   Refer to the original source for norms for college men and women. This test is easy to administer and requires about 3 minutes of testing time per student. Two extra balls should be available at all times during both tests. If the scorer is able to stand outside the court to score the long wall volley test, place the two extra balls in the crease at the back corner of the court.

Soccer Tests

McDonald Volleying Soccer Test (McDonald, 1951)

Test Objective   To measure general soccer ability.

Description   The soccer ball is kicked against the wall as many times as possible in 30 seconds. Any type of kick may be used. Both ground balls and fly balls hitting the target count if the ball is kicked from the ground behind the restraining line. Any part of the body, including the hands, may be used for retrieving a ball. If the player loses control of the ball, a spare ball may be used. This ball must be positioned behind the restraining line before being kicked. Four trials are taken.

Test Area   Wall 30 feet wide and 11½ feet high, with a restraining line 9 feet from the wall and parallel to it.

Equipment   Three soccer balls (the two spares are placed 9 feet behind the restraining line in the center of the area), stopwatch, and tape measure.

Scoring   The score is the number of legal kicks in a 30-second period.

Validity   The test scores were correlated with coaches' ratings of playing ability: r_{xy} = .94 varsity players; r_{xy} = .63 junior varsity players; r_{xy} = .76 freshman varsity players; and r_{xy} = .85 combined group.

Reliability   Not reported for this test.

Comments   This test can be used with younger age groups by reducing the size of the target and moving the restraining line closer to the wall.

Softball Tests

AAHPERD Softball Skills Test (Rikli, 1991)

The AAHPERD softball skills test consists of four tests—batting, fielding ground balls, overhand throwing, and baserunning. Percentile and T-score norms are provided for males and females in grades 9 through 12 and college. Brief descriptions of each test are presented below along with an abbreviated table of norms (Table 19-12). Refer to the test manual for more detailed test descriptions and tables of norms.

BATTING TEST

Test Objective   To measure power and placement in batting.

Test Area   Regulation-size softball field divided into three power zones and three placement areas (Figure 19-11).

Equipment   Batting tee, bats, cones, softballs, measuring tape.

Description   Using the batting tee, examinees hit the ball as far as possible. Two warm-up and six test trials are given.

Scoring   Sum of the target scores (Figure 19-11) for the six test trials.

Validity   Logical validity; concurrent validity coefficients using judges' ratings of skill as the criterion measure ranged from .54 to .85 for males and females in grades 5 through 8, high school, and college.

Reliability   Intraclass test-retest coefficients ranged from .69 to .91 for males and females in grades 5 through 8, high school, and college.

Comments   Students can be used to retrieve balls and assist with the scoring.

FIELDING GROUND BALLS TEST

Test Objective   "To measure skill involved in fielding ground balls" (Rikli, 1991, p. 14).

Test Area   A large grass area with dimensions and markings as shown in Figure 19-12.

Equipment   Cones, softballs, gloves, measuring tape.

Description   A thrower (position B in Figure 19-12) throws two practice and six test balls to the examinee (position A in Figure 19-12). Each thrown ball must hit the ground in front of the 30-foot line and be of sufficient velocity to roll to the velocity indicator (position C in Figure 19-12) for the grade level being tested.

Balls are thrown in a random order such that two balls are thrown directly to the examinee, two to the examinee's left, and two to the examinee's right.

Table 19-12 Selected Percentile Norms by Grade Level for the AAHPERD Softball Skills Test

Test	Percentile	Males					Females				
		5	7	9	11	College	5	7	9	11	College
Batting	99	36	36	36	36	36	26	32	28	32	34
	75	21	29	26	24	32	13	15	16	18	24
	50	14	23	20	20	26	8	9	10	11	19
	25	9	16	14	16	20	5	6	7	7	12
Fielding	99	24	24	24	24	24	24	24	24	24	24
	75	23	23	23	24	24	21	20	22	22	22
	50	20	20	20	20	21	18	17	18	18	18
	25	16	17	16	18	18	12	14	14	16	14
Throwing	99	129	195	218	238	268	111	112	132	161	180
	75	99	136	166	182	200	59	75	82	108	125
	50	85	118	141	160	180	46	62	67	86	104
	25	68	98	120	140	159	38	50	54	66	86
Running	99	6.5	6.1	5.9	5.6	5.7	7.0	6.6	6.8	6.3	6.5
	75	7.3	6.8	6.5	6.1	6.0	7.8	7.3	7.4	7.0	7.0
	50	7.8	7.3	6.9	6.4	6.3	8.2	7.8	7.9	7.5	7.3
	25	8.4	7.8	7.2	6.9	6.7	8.8	8.4	8.4	8.0	7.7

Modified from Rikli RE, ed. 1991. Softball skills test manual. Reston, Va: American Alliance for Health, Physical Education, Recreation and Dance. Used by permission.

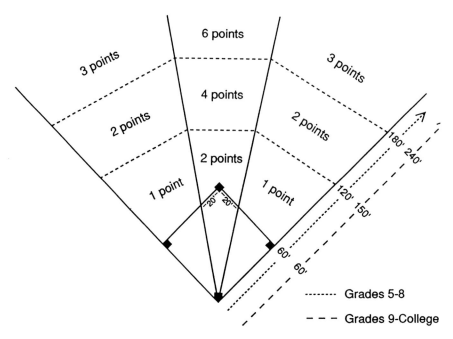

Figure 19-11 Field markings for the AAPHERD softball batting test. (From AAHPERD Softball Skills Test Manual.)

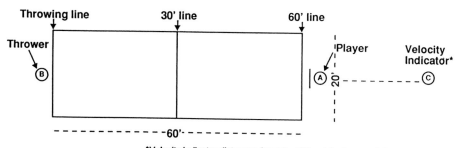

*Velocity indicator distances (past the 60' end line) are as follows:

65' - grades 5 & 6
75' - grades 7 & 8
90' - grades 9 - 12
100' - college

Figure 19-12 Field markings for the AAHPERD softball fielding test. (From AAHPERD Softball Skills Test Manual.)

Scoring   Four points are awarded for balls cleanly fielded in front of the 60-foot line and 2 points are awarded for bobbled balls. The score is reduced by 50% if the ball is fielded behind the 60-foot line. The final score is the sum of the six test trials.

Validity   Logical validity; concurrent validity coefficients using judges' ratings of skill as the criterion measure ranged from .60 to .85 for males and females in grades 5 through 8, high school, and college.

Reliability   Intraclass test-retest coefficients ranged from .75 to .89 for males and females in grades 5 through 8, high school, and college.

Comments   At least two trained testers are required to administer the fielding test.

OVERHAND THROWING TEST

Test Objective   To measure distance and placement in overhand throwing.

Test Area   A smooth grass field with dimensions and markings as illustrated in Figure 19-13.

Equipment   Measuring tapes, softballs, cones.

Description   The examinee (position X in Figure 19-13) is given two attempts to throw the ball as far as possible along the throwing line. Balls are marked where they first touch the ground.

Scoring   The longest of the two throws is scored. A "net throwing score," which consists of "the throwing distance, measured at the point on the throwing line straight across from (perpendicular to) the spot where the ball landed, minus the error distance—the number of feet the ball landed off target, away from the throwing line—is recorded" (Rikli, 1991, p. 16).

Validity   Logical validity; concurrent validity coefficients using judges' ratings of skill as the criterion measure ranged from .64 to .94 for males and females in grades 5 through 8, high school, and college.

Reliability   Intraclass test-retest coefficients ranged from .90 to .97 for males and females in grades 5 through 8, high school, and college.

BASERUNNING TEST

Test Objective   "To measure speed and skill involved in running two bases" (Rikli, 1991, p. 18).

Test Area   Field area with dimensions and markings illustrated in Figure 19-14.

Equipment   Stopwatch, bases.

Description   Examinees (position A in Figure 19-14) are timed as they run from position A, around first base, and into second base where the time is stopped. One warm-up and two test trials are administered.

Scoring   The time is measured to the nearest tenth of a second. Only the faster of the two trials is recorded.

Validity   Logical validity; concurrent validity coefficients using judges' ratings of skill as the criterion measure ranged from .79 to .92 for males and females in grades 5 through 8, high school, and college.

Reliability   Intraclass test-retest coefficients ranged from .89 to .95 for males and females in grades 5 through 8, high school, and college.

Comments   For safety, examinees must run through second base.

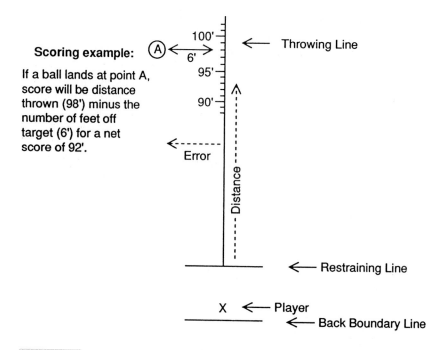

Figure 19-13   Field markings for the AAHPERD softball throwing test. *(From AAHPERD Softball Skills Test Manual.)*

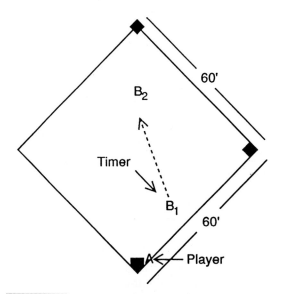

Figure 19-14   Field markings for the AAHPERD softball baserunning text. *(From AAHPERD Softball Skills Test Manual.)*

Shick Softball Test Battery (Shick, 1970)

Test Objective   To measure defensive softball skills in college women.

Description   Three tests are included in the test battery—repeated throws, fielding test, and target test. They can be used as a battery or as individual tests.

REPEATED THROWS TEST   The examinee stands behind a restraining line placed on the floor 23 feet from the wall. On the signal ''Ready, go!'' the examinee throws a softball at the wall and attempts to hit the wall above the 10-foot line, which is on the wall parallel to the floor. Either an overarm or a sidearm throw may be used. The rebounding ball may either be caught in the air or fielded from the floor. This is repeated as many times as possible in 30 seconds. Four trials are allowed. No penalty is given for a fumbled rebound, since this results in a loss of time. One practice throw is permitted before each trial.

The total test score is the sum of the number of times that the ball hit the wall in four trials. If the examinee steps on or over the restraining line or if the ball is thrown below the wall line, no hit is recorded. The validity of this test is $r_{xy} = .69$, using a criterion measure of judges' ratings of individual performance in game situations. Test reliability is $R_{xx'} = .86$.

FIELDING TEST   This test is similar to the repeated throws measure except that the primary objective is to field the ball on a bounce or from the floor rather than catching it in the air. The wall line is 4 feet from the floor, and the restraining line is 15 feet from the wall. Otherwise, the test is the same as the repeated throws measure in all respects but two: any type of throw may be used, and the ball should be thrown so that it hits the wall below the wall line.

The total test score is the sum of the number of times the ball is legally thrown and hits the wall below the line in four trials. Test validity is .48, using the same criterion measure. Test reliability is .89.

TARGET TEST   Wall and floor targets must be set up as shown in Figure 19-15. The wall target is 66 inches square with the center of the target 36 inches from the floor. The restraining line is 40 feet from the wall. It is recommended that the target areas be color-coded. The test consists of two trials of 10 throws each. The examinee stands behind the restraining line with a softball in hand. Two practice throws are permitted. Two scores are given for each test throw: the point value of the wall target area into which the ball is hit and the section of the floor target where the ball lands on its first bounce. No points are given for hits outside the two target areas. The scores are then summed across target areas and trials. Test validity is .63, using the same criterion measure. Test reliability is .88.

Test Area   Regulation-size gymnasium.

Equipment   Softballs, stopwatches, floor tape, tape measure, scoresheets, and softball gloves.

Comments   For the total test battery, test validity is .75 and test reliability is .88. The entire battery can be administered in two 40-minute class periods.

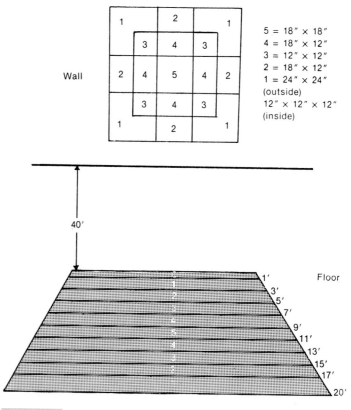

Figure 19-15 Wall and floor targets for the target test. (From Shick J.)

Swimming Tests

12-Minute Swim Test (Jackson et al., 1979)

Test Objective To provide a practical field test of swimming endurance using the crawl stroke.

Description Each examinee is assigned to swim in an individual lane. The poolside should be marked in 5-yard distances. The swimmer is instructed to start in the water with a pushoff from the side and to swim the crawl for 12 minutes, attempting to cover as much distance as possible. At the signal "Ready, go!" the stopwatch is started and the swimmers push off. A partner assigned to each swimmer counts the number of laps. On the signal "Stop!" the partner records the yardage closest to the swimmer's hand and the number of full laps the swimmer completes. The swimmer should continue swimming at a leisurely pace for another 2 to 3 minutes to unwind from the all-out effort.

Test Area Pool of 25 yards or longer, with lane dividers.

Equipment Stopwatch or other suitable timing device in pool; scoresheets.

Validity $r_{xy} = .89$, using a criterion measure of tethered swim, where the heart rate reached at least 172 beats per minute (concurrent validity); significant difference in test scores of competitive swimmers and noncompetitors (construct validity).

Reliability $R_{xx'}$ (α coefficient) = .99 for single administration of the test; subjects— college males; $R_{xx'}$ = .98 for test-retest administration; subjects—college men and women (Fried, 1983).

Comments   Before taking the test, swimmers should take a 5- to 10-minute warm-up in the water. It is assumed that the swimmers have had previous instruction and practice in pacing and stroke efficiency. If the swimmers are below average in swimming skills, it might be desirable to remove the effect of swimming skill using the residual score method described in Jackson et al. (1979).

Tennis Tests

AAHPERD Tennis Skills Test (Hensley, 1989)

The AAHPERD tennis skills test consists of a groundstroke test (forehand and backhand), serve test, and an optional volley test. Percentile and T-score norms are presented for males and females in grades 9 through 12 and college. Brief descriptions of each test are presented below along with an abbreviated table of norms (Table 19-13). Refer to the test manual for more detailed test descriptions and tables of norms.

GROUNDSTROKE TEST

Test Objective   To measure the accuracy and power of forehand and backhand groundstrokes.

Test Area   Regulation-size tennis court with markings as shown in Figure 19-16.

Equipment   Tennis racquet, tennis balls, chalk for marking court.

Description   Tester (position T in Figure 19-16) tosses 12 balls to the examinee's (position S in Figure 19-16) forehand side and 12 balls to the backhand side. The first two balls on each side are practice trials.

Scoring   Each trial is scored for both placement and power. Placement is scored according to the target area in which the ball lands. Power is scored according to which power zone the ball lands in after the first bounce. The total placement and power scores over 10 trials are summed for the total score.

Validity   Concurrent validity using judges' ratings as the criterion measure range from .76 to .86 for males and females of high-school and college age.

Reliability   Test-retest intraclass coefficients range from .80 to .88 for males and females of high-school and college age.

Comments   Students who are not being tested can be used as scorers, ball retrievers, and tossers.

SERVE TEST

Test Objective   To measure accuracy and placement of serving.

Test Area   Regulation-size tennis court with markings as shown in Figure 19-17.

Equipment   Racquet, tennis balls, chalk for marking court.

Description   Examinees serve eight balls from each of the two positions marked with an S in Figure 19-17. Four balls are directed to the outside target of the receiving court and four to the inside target.

Table 14-13 Selected Percentile Norms by Grade Level for the AAHPERD Tennis Skills Test

Test	Percentile	Males					Females				
		9	10	11	12	College	9	10	11	12	College
Groundstroke	99	97	108	107	109	124	94	92	108	104	105
	75	57	65	63	66	77	46	49	56	62	63
	50	45	53	51	54	63	32	37	41	50	50
	25	33	41	38	42	49	18	25	27	38	38
Serve	99	44	50	54	52	64	34	50	49	52	50
	75	21	26	31	33	37	16	26	26	31	28
	50	15	19	25	27	29	11	19	19	25	22
	25	8	12	18	21	21	6	12	13	19	16
Volley	99	32	39	39	47	45	29	26	37	36	38
	75	18	22	24	28	28	14	14	20	20	23
	50	14	17	20	23	23	10	10	16	16	19
	25	10	12	16	17	19	6	7	11	11	14

Modified from Hensley LD, ed. 1989 Tennis skills test manual. Reston, Va: American Alliance for Health, Physical Education, Recreation and Dance. Used by permission.

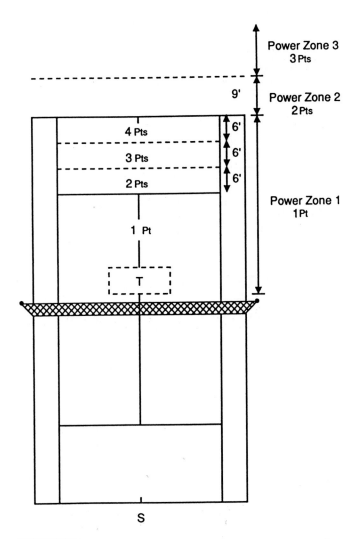

Power Zone 3
3 Pts

9'

Power Zone 2
2 Pts

4 Pts   6'

3 Pts   6'

2 Pts   6'

Power Zone 1
1 Pt

1 Pt

T

S

Figure 19-16   Court markings for the AAHPERD tennis ground-stroke test. *(From AAHPERD Tennis Skills Test Manual.)*

Scoring   Each trial is scored for both placement and power. Placement is scored according to the target area in which the ball lands. Two points are awarded for balls landing in the target area. One point is awarded for balls landing outside the target area. Power is scored according to which power zone the ball lands in after the second bounce for those balls landing in the target area. The total score is the sum of the placement and power scores over all trials.

Validity   Concurrent validity using judges' ratings as the criterion measure range from .78 to .91 for males and females of high-school and college age.

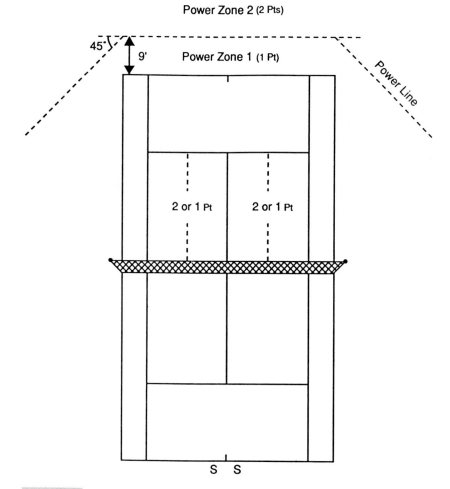

Figure 19-17   Court markings for the AAHPERD tennis serve test. *(From AAHPERD Tennis Skills Test Manual.)*

Reliability   Test-retest intraclass coefficients range from .79 to .95 for males and females of high-school and college age.

Comments   Students who are not being tested can be used as scorers and ball retrievers.

VOLLEY TEST (OPTIONAL)

Test Objective   To measure the accuracy of a volley.

Test Area   Regulation-size tennis court with markings as shown in Figure 19-18.

Equipment   Racquet, tennis balls, chalk for marking court.

Description   The tester (position T in Figure 19-18) strokes 10 balls to the forehand side and 10 balls to the backhand side of the examinee (position S in Figure 19-18). Only the last six trials on each side are scored.

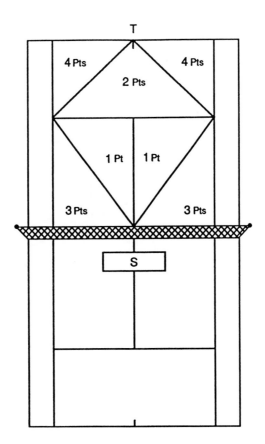

Figure 19-18   Court markings for the AAHPERD tennis volley test. *(From AAHPERD Tennis Skills Test Manual.)*

Scoring   Placement for each trial is scored according to where the ball lands in the target area. The trials are summed to obtain a total score.

Validity   Concurrent validity using judges' ratings as the criterion measure range from .65 to .76 for males and females of high-school and college age.

Reliability   Test-retest intraclass coefficients range from .69 to .79 for males and females of high-school and college age.

Comments   Students who are not being tested can be used as scorers, ball retrievers, and testers.

Hewitt Tennis Achievement Test (Hewitt, 1966)

Test Objective   To measure three basic tennis skills—forehand drive, backhand drive, and service; the service placement test, speed of service test, and forehand and backhand drive tests are used.

Test Area   Regulation-size tennis court.

Equipment   Tennis racquets, 25 tennis balls, and scoreboards.

SERVICE PLACEMENT TEST   A 10-minute warm-up is permitted. The examinee stands behind the baseline and serves 10 balls into the marked service court, as shown in Figure 19-19. The ball should pass between the net and the 7-foot-high

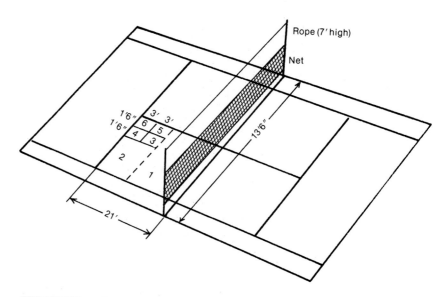

Figure 19-19   Court markings for the service placement test. *(From Hewitt JE.)*

rope. If this occurs, the trial score is the point value of the target area in which the ball lands. A ball traveling over the rope is scored 0.

The test score is the sum of 10 trials. The validity of the test ranges from .625 to .93, using a criterion measure of round robin tournament rankings. Test-retest reliability is .94.

SPEED OF SERVICE TEST   The court is divided into zones (Figure 19-20). The examinee serves the ball into the designated court, and the score is based on the zone in which the second bounce lands. The underlying assumption is that the distance the ball travels between the first and second bounce is a valid indicator of the speed of service. The zone number is the score for the trial.

The total test score is the sum of 10 trials. Test validity ranges from .723 to .89, using a criterion measure of round robin tournament rankings. Test-retest reliability is .84. This test can be given at the same time as the service placement test. Place both targets on the same side of the court; the placement score is the target value on the service court, and the speed score is the zone value.

FOREHAND AND BACKHAND DRIVE TESTS   The examinee stands at the center of the baseline, as shown in Figure 19-21. Five practice trials are allowed. The ball is hit to the examinee by the instructor or propelled by a ball machine and lands just beyond the service line. Using either a forehand or backhand drive, the examinee returns the ball. Then 20 test trials are administered in the same way. Although 10 test trials are given for each drive, the examinee is allowed to choose which 10 balls to hit forehand and backhand.

The ball should travel between the rope and the net to maximize the target score. If the ball passes over the rope, half the value of the regular target is awarded. The validity estimates range from .57 to .67 for the forehand trials and .52 to .62 for the backhand trials, using a criterion measure of round robin

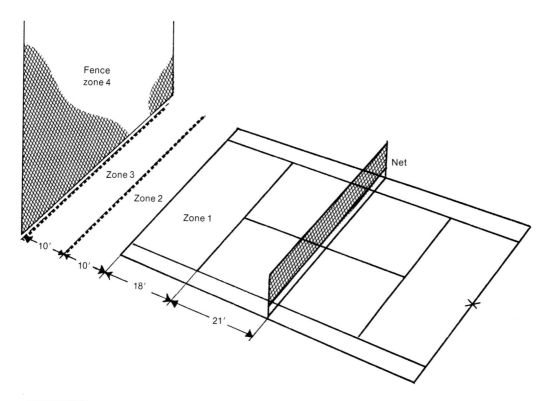

Figure 19-20   Court markings for the speed of service test. *(From Hewitt JE.)*

tournament rankings. The test-retest reliability is .75 for the forehand drive and .78 for the backhand.

Comments   A ball machine should be used whenever possible to test the drive. No information is given on recommended settings for the machine. A composite score for the three test items is not recommended. Each test item is scored separately.

Hewitt Revision of the Dyer Backboard Test (Hewitt, 1965)

Test Objective   To classify students by measuring rallying and serving ability.

Description   With two new tennis balls in hand, the examinee serves the ball against the wall from a restraining line 20 feet from the wall. The stopwatch is started when the ball hits the wall. On the rebound the player begins a rally by hitting the ball continually against the wall so that the ball hits on or above a wall line placed 3 feet above the testing surface. Three trials of 30 seconds each are taken.

Test Area   Smooth gymnasium wall or indoor or outdoor backboard 20 feet high and 20 feet wide and a 20-foot by 20-foot floor space.

Equipment   Tennis racket, two dozen balls, stopwatch (records to the nearest tenth of a second), tape measure, floor and wall tape, and scoresheets.

Scoring   One point is scored each time the ball hits on or above the wall line. If the examinee steps on or over the restraining line, the rally is continued, but no

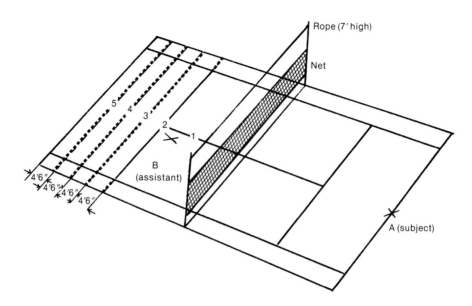

Figure 19-21 Court markings for the forehand and backhand drive test. *(From Hewitt JE.)*

point is scored and the player should be warned. The total score is the sum of three trials.

Validity r_{xy} = .68 to .73, for beginners; r_{xy} = .84 to .89, for intermediates.

Reliability $R_{xx'}$ = .82, for beginners using the test-retest method; $R_{xx'}$ = .93, for intermediates (test-retest).

Comments All lines should be 1 inch wide. Approximately 15 students can be tested at each station in 40 minutes. If the ball does not return to the examinee, another can be taken from the basket and served against the wall to initiate the rally again. No points are scored on the serve. The count should begin with the first wall hit after the serve.

Tennis Forehand and Backhand Drive Test (Purcell, 1981)

Test Objective To measure the forehand and backhand drives in a setting that closely resembles the actual game situation; to evaluate depth, direction, and speed of the drive by rewarding shots directed deep to the center of the court with sufficient speed.

Description The test examinee stands within 3 to 6 feet of the baseline of the court, facing the target area, as shown in Figure 19-22. A pneumatic ball-pitching machine is used to project the tennis ball to the examinee, who attempts to return the ball over the net and into the target area. Three practice and 10 test trials are administered for each drive, forehand and backhand. The ball flight is timed from the point of contact to the landing point.

The speed and angle of the ball machine are set so that the ball will pass approximately 2½ feet above the center of the net, land on or close to the service line, and bounce to its highest point about 3 feet from the baseline. With these

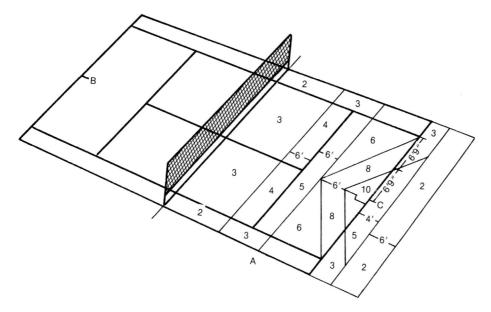

Figure 19-22   Court markings for the tennis forehand and backhand drive test. *(From Purcell K.)*

settings the maximum height of the bounce should be roughly 3 feet; the horizontal velocity should be approximately 59 ft/sec. The time of flight of the machine-projected ball should be approximately 1.02 seconds.

Test Area   Regulation-size tennis court, with target areas marked on the court using ordinary chalk.

Equipment   Ball machine, 40 balls, tennis racket, stopwatch, scoresheets, and tape measure.

Scoring   The target values for each set of 10 trials are summed, as well as the times for 10 trials. To determine the correction factor for the total time score, see Table 19-14. The total target score is multiplied by the correction factor to yield the test score. This is done for both the forehand and backhand drives. When a ball is clearly deflected by the net, the trial should be retaken. A typical let ball is scored in the regular manner.

Validity $r_{xy} = .83$, using a criterion measure of judges' ratings of the forehand and backhand stroke: $r_{xy} = .70$, for forehand trials alone; and $r_{xy} = .83$, for backhand trials alone.

Reliability   The following test-retest coefficients were calculated for college women: $R_{xx'} = .84$ total test; $R_{xx'} = .86$ forehand trials alone; and $R_{xx'} = .83$ backhand trials alone. For the criterion measure, the interjudge objectivity was $R_{j_1 j_2} = .87$.

Comments   Total testing time per examinee, including practice trials, is about 3½ minutes. Little time is lost between tests if the next examinee is ready to step up to the line as soon as the previous examinee has completed testing. For the group tested in the original study, the following descriptive statistics were reported for college women:

	Mean	Standard deviation
Forehand	30.3	9.4
Backhand	23.6	9.5
Total	53.9	17.7

Once the target lines have been marked on the court, the test should be relatively easy to administer, assuming that a ball machine is available.

Volleyball Tests

Brady Volleyball Test (Brady, 1945)

Test Objective   To measure general volleyball-playing ability.

Description   No restraining line is used. The examinee begins the test by throwing the ball against the wall and attempting to hit the ball into the target area on the wall repeatedly (Figure 19-23). One 60-second trial is administered. Only legal hits are allowed. If the examinee catches the ball or loses control of the ball, the test must be restarted by throwing the ball against the wall.

Test Area   Smooth wall space, 15 feet by 15 feet.

Equipment   Volleyballs, stopwatch, wall tape or chalk, tape measure, and scoresheets.

Scoring   The test score is the number of legal hits in 1 minute. Thrown balls are not scored, but balls landing on the target line are scored.

Validity $r_{xy} = .86$, using a criterion measure of subjective ratings of playing ability.

Table 19-14 Correction Factors for Converting Target Value Totals into Skill Test Scores Using Time in Flight (TF)

TF for 10 Trials (sec)	Correction Factor
5	1.35
6	1.30
7	1.25
8	1.20
9	1.15
10	1.10
11	1.05
12	1.00
13	.95
14	.90
15	.85
16	.80
17	.75
18	.70

From Purcell K.

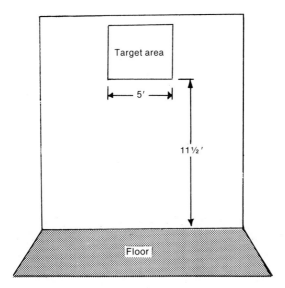

Figure 19-23   Wall target for the Brady volleyball test. *(From Brady CF.)*

Reliability $R_{xx'} = .93$ using the test-retest method.
Comments   Allow practice time before taking the test. Several students may be tested at the same time. Approximately 2 minutes per person are required to administer the test. This test is especially useful for making quick classifications of students in a class setting. The height of the target may be lowered for younger age groups, especially junior high or grade-school students.

Brumbach Volleyball Service Test (Brumbach, 1967)
Test Objective   To measure the ability to serve the volleyball low and deep into the opponent's court.
Description   The examinee stands behind the baseline and serves the ball, attempting to hit it between the net and the rope and deep into the backcourt on the opposite side (Figure 19-24). The test consists of 12 trials, in two sets of six.
Test Area   Regulation-size volleyball court.
Equipment   Volleyballs, standard extensions, rope, floor tape or chalk, tape measure, and scoresheets.
Scoring   A ball hit between the net and the rope and landing in the target area receives the higher of the two scores assigned to the target area. A ball passing over the rope and landing in the target area is given the lower of the two scores. The total test score is the sum of the 10 best trials. Foot faults, balls hitting the net, and balls landing outside the target area are scored 0.
Validity   Not reported for this test.
Reliability   Not reported for this test.
Comments   In one court 20 students can be tested in less than an hour. Only legal

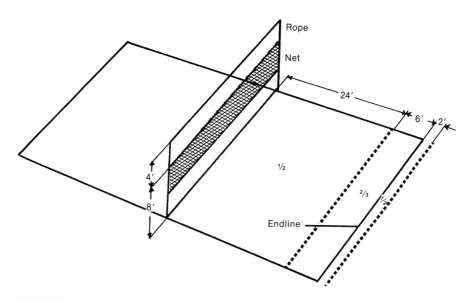

Figure 19-24   Court markings for the Brumbach volleyball service test. *(From Brumbach W.)*

serves should be scored. Although this test may be viewed as logically valid, the validity and reliability should be systematically studied. It appears to be appropriate for junior high, high-school, and college students.

North Carolina State University Volleyball Skills Test Battery (Bartlett et al., 1991)
Test Objective   To measure the basic volleyball skills of serve, forearm pass, and set in gamelike situations.
Test Area   A regulation-size volleyball court with net set at 7 feet 11⅝ inches.
Test Equipment   Standard inflated volleyballs, tape for court markings, two 8-foot and two 10-foot vertical poles, 30-inch-long string and 11-foot-long string.
Test Descriptions

SERVE TEST   The serve test is designed to measure consistency and accuracy. Examinees attempt 10 overhand or underhand serves from the serving area into the target area (Figure 19-25). Balls hitting a line are awarded the higher point value, while balls landing out of bounds or contacting the net or antennae are scored 0. The final score is the sum of all 10 trials (maximum score = 40).

FOREARM PASS TEST   This test measures passing accuracy, height, and consistency. Examinees receive a total of 10 trials, five trials from the right-back position and five from the left-back position (Figure 19-26). On each trial the examinee receives a two-handed overhead toss from a tosser located across the net on the attack line. Poor tosses result in a retrial. The examinee passes the ball over a string located 8 feet above the attack line and into a target area. Zero points are awarded for illegal contact, balls that contact or go under the string, or balls that contact or go over the net. Balls hitting a line are awarded the higher point value. The final score is the sum of all 10 trials (maximum score = 50).

SET TEST   This test measures consistency, height, and accuracy for the high

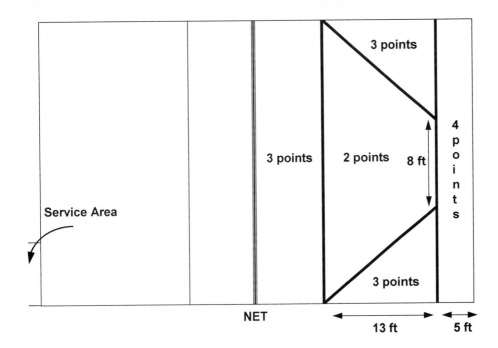

Figure 19-25 Court markings for the North Carolina State University Volleyball Serve Test. (Redrawn from Bartlett et al., 1991).

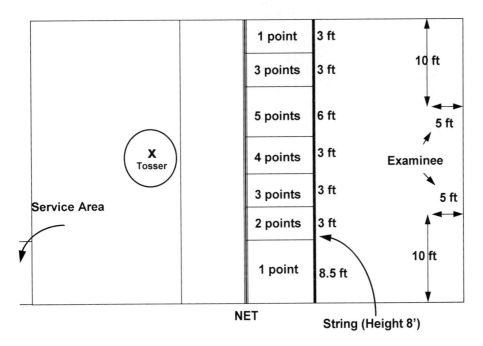

Figure 19-26 Court markings for the North Carolina State University Volleyball Forearm Pass Test. (Redrawn from Bartlett et al., 1991).

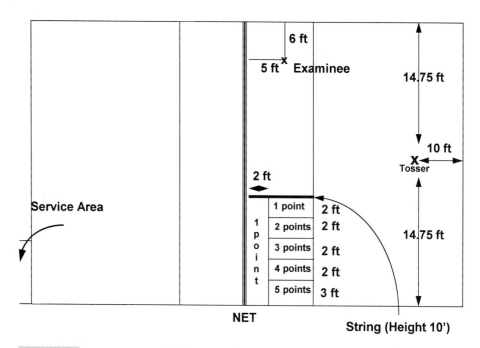

Figure 19-27 Court markings for the North Carolina State University Volleyball Set Test. *(Redrawn from Bartlett et al., 1991).*

set. Examinees receive 10 trials. On each trial a tosser located near the center of the court (Figure 19-27) tosses the ball underhanded to the examinee located in a starting position 6 feet from the right sideline and 5 feet from the net. Poor tosses result in a retrial. The examinee sets the tossed ball over a string positioned 10 feet above the court and into a target area. Zero points are awarded for illegal contact, balls that contact or go under the string, and balls that contact or go over the net. Balls hitting a line are awarded the higher point value. The final score is the sum of all 10 trials (maximum score = 50).

Validity   Face validity "because the ability to serve a ball, receive a ball with the forearm pass (coming across the net), and set a ball (coming from different angles) are basic volleyball skills . . ." (Bartlett et al., 1991, p. 20).

Reliability   Intraclass test-retest reliability coefficients (2 days between test administrations) for 313 college-age males and females in beginning volleyball classes were .65 for the serve, .73 for the forearm pass, and .88 for the set. Only one of the tests was administered during a single class and tests were administered by the physical education instructor.

Comments   Modifications in net height, string height, and court positions can be made to accommodate various age and ability groups.

SUMMARY

This chapter was designed to present a broad overview of the skills tests available in the physical education field. Other than the references already mentioned, the *Research Quarterly for Exercise and Sport* usually publishes the best of the recently developed tests.

Learning Experiences

1. This exercise will be most valuable for students who plan to teach physical education, but will also be useful for those who may work in a private sports club. Select one of the tests described in this chapter and administer it to the other students in class. Prepare carefully and well ahead of time for the testing. Plan how you will organize the group during the test administration. Take care of any court markings or targets before the actual testing session. Develop a scoresheet or scorecard for each examinee. Sometime after the testing has been completed, discuss the results with the examinees, telling them their scores and the summary data for the class.

2. Select one of the tests in this chapter in which a floor target is used. Determine two ways this target could be safely marked on a gymnasium floor. Experiment with both methods. Write a brief report of the two approaches, comparing them in terms of efficiency, cost, practicality, and so forth. Discuss your preference and give a rationale for your choice.

3. Select one of the tests in this chapter and determine the test-retest reliability of the test. Compare the reliability with the reliability reported in the test description and comment on similarities and differences in the coefficients.

4. Choose a sport skill test from the literature and critique the information provided for validity and reliability of the test. Comment on such factors as the methods used to determine validity and reliability, magnitude of the coefficients, and suitability of the test in physical education classes or research settings.

References

American Association for Health, Physical Education and Recreation (AAHPER). 1966. Football: Skills test manual. Washington, DC: American Association for Health, Physical Education and Recreation.

American Association for Health, Physical Education and Recreation (AAHPER). 1967. Archery for boys and girls: Skills test manual. Washington, DC: American Association for Health, Physical Education and Recreation.

Bartlett J, Smith L, Davis K, Peel J. 1991. Development of a valid volleyball skills test battery. Journal of Physical Education, Recreation and Dance, 62(2):19–21.

Brady CF. 1945. Preliminary investigations of volleyball playing ability. Research Quarterly, 16:14–17.

Broer MR, Miller DM. 1950. Achievement tests for beginning and intermediate tennis. Research Quarterly, 21:303–313.

Brumbach W. 1967. Beginning volleyball, a syllabus for teachers, revised edition. Eugene, Ore: Wayne Baker Brumbach (distributed by the University of Oregon).

Chapman NL. 1982. Chapman ball control test—field hockey. Research Quarterly for Exercise and Sport, 53(3):239–242.

Collins DR, Hodges PB. 1978. A comprehensive guide to sports skills tests and measurement. Springfield, Ill: Thomas.

Cooper JM, Glassow RB. 1963. Kinesiology, ed 1. St Louis: Mosby–Year Book.

Cooper JM, Glassow RB. 1976. Kinesiology, ed 4. St Louis: Mosby–Year Book.

Cotten D, Thomas JR, Plaster T. 1972. A plastic hall test for golf iron skill, Presented at the American Alliance for Health, Physical Education, Recreation and Dance National Convention, Houston, March 1972.

Fried CR. 1983. An examination of the test characteristics of the 12-minute swim test. Master's thesis, University of Wisconsin, Madison.

Glassow RB. 1957. Comments on the Miller-Broer tennis test. Unpublished paper, University of Wisconsin, Madison.

Hensley LD, ed. 1989. Tennis skills test manual. Reston, Va: American Alliance for Health, Physical Education, Recreation and Dance.

Hensley LD, East WB, Stillwell JL. 1979. A racquetball skills test. Research Quarterly for Exercise and Sport, 50(1):114–118.

Hewitt JE. 1965. Revision of the Dyer backboard tennis test. Research Quarterly, 37:231–240.

Hewitt JE. 1966. Hewitt's tennis achievement test. Research Quarterly, 37:231–237.

Hopkins DR, Shick J, Plack JJ. 1984. Basketball for boys and girls: Skills test manual. Reston, Va: American Alliance for Health, Physical Education, Recreation and Dance.

Jackson A, Jackson AS, Frankiewicz RG. 1979. The construct and concurrent validity of a 12-minute crawl stroke swim as a field test of swimming endurance. Research Quarterly for Exercise and Sport, 50(4):641–648.

Johnson BL, Nelson JK. 1979. Practical measurements for evaluation in physical education. Minneapolis: Burgess.

Kelson RE. 1953. Baseball classification plan for boys. Research Quarterly, 24:304–307.

Liba MR, Stauff M. 1963. A test for the volleyball pass. Research Quarterly, 34:56–63.

Lockhart A, McPherson FA. 1949. The development of a test of badminton playing ability. Research Quarterly, 20:402–405.

McDonald LG. 1951. The construction of a kicking skill test as an index of general soccer ability. Master's Thesis, Springfield College, Springfield, Mass.

Miller FA. 1951. A badminton wall volley test. Research Quarterly, 22:208–213.

Poole J, Nelson JK. 1970. Construction of a badminton skills test battery. Unpublished study. Louisiana State University, Baton Rouge.

Purcell K. 1981. A tennis forehand-backhand drive skill test which measures ball control and stroke firmness. Research Quarterly for Exercise and Sport, 52(2):238–245.

Rikli RE, ed. 1991. Softball skills test manual. Reston, Va: American Alliance for Health, Physical Education, Recreation and Dance.

Safrit MJ, Pavis A. 1969. Overarm throw skill testing. In Felshin J, O'Brien C, eds. Selected softball articles. Washington, DC: American Association of Health, Physical Education and Recreation.

Scott MG, French E. 1959. Measurement and evaluation in physical education. Dubuque, Iowa: Wm C Brown Group.

Scott MG. 1941. Achievement examinations in badminton. Research Quarterly, **12**:242–253.

Shick J. 1970. Battery of defensive softball skills tests for college women. Research Quarterly, **41**:82–87.

Shick J, Berg NG. 1983. Indoor golf skill test for junior high school boys. Research Quarterly for Exercise and Sport, **54**(1):75–78.

Shifflett B, Shuman BJ. 1982. A criterion-referenced test for archery. Research Quarterly for Exercise and Sport, **53**(4):330–335.

Strand BN, Wilson R. 1993. Assessing sport skills. Champaign, Ill: Human Kinetics.

West C, Thorpe J. 1968. Construction and validation of eight-iron approach test. Research Quarterly, **39**:1115–1120.

Annotated Readings

American Association for Health, Physical Education, and Recreation. 1966–1967; 1980–1995; Skills test series. Reston, Va: American Association for Health, Physical Education, Recreation and Dance.

Separate manual of skills tests for a variety of sports, including archery, basketball, football, softball, and volleyball; a revision is now available for basketball and tennis skills tests, and underway for soccer, tennis, and volleyball tests; although many tests are outdated, they can be modified by the teacher to provide valuable learning experiences.

Avery CA, Richardson PA, Jackson AW. 1979. A practical tennis serve test: Measurement of a skill under simulated game conditions. Research Quarterly for Exercise and Sport, **50**(4):554–564.

Good example of a more complex type of test that can be used in a class setting; describes a tennis serve test with a high degree of logical as well as statistical validity; an excellent test for intermediate and advanced players.

Collins, DR, Hodges PB. 1978. A comprehensive guide to sports skills tests and measurement. Springfield, IL: C Thomas.

A valuable reference for every physical education teacher; presents a wide variety of published and unpublished tests of sports skills; provides thorough descriptions of tests; includes more tests than can be found in any measurement and evaluation textbook in physical education.

Hopkins DR. 1979. Using the AAHPERD basketball skills test for women. Journal of Physical Education and Recreation, **50**:72–73.

Describes use of the test by coaches in selecting team members; evaluates a nine-item test battery primarily designed for instructional purposes; presents descriptive statistics; lists resources for other skills tests.

Strand BN, Wilson R. 1993. Assessing sport skills. Champaign, Ill: Human Kinetics. Includes descriptions of 379 tests of 29 sports and activities; information on how to choose the appropriate test, proper testing procedures, and tables and diagrams.

20

Tests of Muscular Strength, Endurance, and Power

Watch for these words as you read the following chapter

Cable tensiometer
Concentric action
Dynamic strength
Dynamometer
Eccentric action
Electromechanical device
Isokinetic resistance training
Isometric resistance training

Isotonic resistance training
Muscular endurance
Muscular power
Muscular strength
Specificity
Static strength
Vertical jump test
Weight-training machine

Assessment of muscular strength, endurance, and power is important in clinical, research, physical education, sport, and fitness club settings. Accurate assessment of strength, endurance, and power requirements for particular sports, followed by appropriate weight-training programs, can result in improved athletic performance. More important, muscular strength and endurance are recognized as components of health-related fitness. Adequate levels of strength and endurance can decrease the chances of low back pain, contribute to good posture, and provide people with the ability to cope effectively with life-threatening situations such as the capacity to pull another person away from a burning building. Moreover, the increasing popularity of strength training as a fitness activity places a greater emphasis on preassessment of strength for determining appropriate resistance training programs in both the fitness club and school settings.

Muscular strength, endurance, and power can be measured in many ways, ranging from practical tests requiring little or no equipment to expensive machines. Practical tests can be used in settings that have neither the space nor the money for gym machines. On the other hand, an isokinetic machine such as Cybex is expensive but provides the most accurate information about the strength of a particular muscle group. In this chapter the most expensive alternatives are dealt with only briefly. Examples of tests requiring use of weight-training machines such as Nautilus or Universal Gym equipment are included, as well as tests requiring the use of free weights or gymnastics equipment available in many schools.

BASIC CONCEPTS

Muscular strength is defined as "the maximum force or tension level that can be produced by a muscle group"; **muscular endurance** is "the ability of the muscle to maintain submaximal force levels for extended periods" (Heyward, 1984, pp. 4–5). In contrast, **muscular power** is the ability to generate maximum force in a minimum amount of time. Tests requiring continuous repetitions of a movement against moderate resistance measure endurance, not strength. A true measure of strength determines the maximum amount of weight that can be moved in a single effort. However, a high relationship does exist between strength and endurance measures. Correlations of .90 and higher have been reported between one maximum effort and the number of submaximal repetitions (Baumgartner and Jackson, 1982). Power is typically measured as the result of a single explosive movement such as a vertical jump or standing long jump. However, in clinical and research settings more precise measures of power provide a measure of power as force times distance per unit of time. In this chapter, examples of strength, endurance, and power tests are presented. Keep in mind the distinguishing factor between strength and endurance tests. When the test is used as a measure of strength, one repetition to maximum is executed. When it is used to measure endurance, a number of submaximum repetitions are performed.

Specificity is an important concept in resistance training and assessment. There is no individual test of overall body strength, endurance, or power. From a global perspective, strength, endurance, and power are specific to a muscle group. Thus a person may have strong legs and weak arms or strong abdominal muscles and a weak grip. Since muscle groups must be tested separately, choices about the most important muscle groups to be tested in a given setting must be made. From a more narrow perspective, task specificity also determines training and assessment procedures. **Isometric** or static **resistance training** involves no limb movement at the joint tested, thus no change in muscle length occurs. Pushing against a wall is an example of an isometric exercise. **Isotonic** or dynamic **resistance training** involves limb movement and concentric (i.e., muscle shortening) and eccentric (i.e., muscle lengthening) actions of muscle against a constant weight. **Isokinetic resistance training** is a type of isotonic movement requiring a machine that adjusts resistance throughout a range of motion at a preset fixed speed. Each training and assessment method has its advantages and disadvantages (see Corbin and Lindsey, 1985). From a measurement perspective it is important to remember that the type of assessment should correspond to the type of training employed. Therefore, strength increment as the result of isometric training should be measured isometrically, gains made through isotonic training should be measured with resistance lifting, while gains accrued through training on isokinetic devices are best measured with isokinetic machines.

Body weight is often a factor in strength and endurance testing. When an examinee must move (lift or lower) his or her body in executing a strength or endurance test, standards are varied according to weight. For instance, a higher score would be given to a lighter person who executes a given number of repetitions than to a heavier person executing the same number.

Several practical tests of strength and endurance may be found in Chapters 17 and 18. For example, the sit-ups test is a test of endurance of the abdominal muscles; the pull-ups test measures endurance of the arm and shoulder girdle; and the standing long jump test is a measure of explosive leg power.

TECHNIQUES FOR MEASURING MUSCULAR STRENGTH AND ENDURANCE

A wide range of methods are available for measuring muscular strength and endurance. In the clinical and therapeutic settings various functional tests (e.g., ability to walk up stairs with and without assistance, ability to get up from a chair with or without assistance) for patients with severe muscular impairment are used to assess the strength and endurance required to perform daily tasks (Amundsen, 1990). Practical tests of strength and endurance involve the use of free weights. When special equipment is required for strength and endurance testing, it is usually one of four types—**dynamometers, cable tensiometers, weight-training machines,** and **electromechanical devices.** Many colleges and universities have all four types of special equipment, but some public school systems do not have any. Weight-training machines are becoming common, however, in health and fitness clubs.

MEASURING ISOMETRIC STRENGTH AND ENDURANCE

Dynamometers

A dynamometer uses a nonelectronic spring or hydraulic system or an electronic load cell to measure static strength and endurance. Several types of dynamometers are available. In the clinical setting handheld dynamometers are portable devices used by clinicians to assess static strength at various body joints. The device is held perpendicular against a limb segment (e.g., the lower leg) and the patient pushes against the dynamometer. Modern handheld dynamometers use electronic strain gauges with digital readouts and can be interfaced with computers for data collection (e.g., Nicholas Manual Muscle Tester, Lafayette Instrument Co., Lafayette, Ind.). Although intra- and interrater reliability of handheld dynamometers is high (> .90) the criterion-related evidence for validity is equivocal depending on the joint tested and the strength of the subject. The primary drawback of handheld dynamometry is that the strength of the tester must exceed the capacity of the subject to exert force against the dynamometer in order to obtain an accurate reading.

Dynamometers for measuring **static strength** at specific muscle groups are the handgrip (not to be confused with the handheld dynamometer) and back and leg strength dynamometers. The most common type is the hand or grip dynamometer shown in Figure 20-1.

Figure 20-1   Handgrip dynamometer.

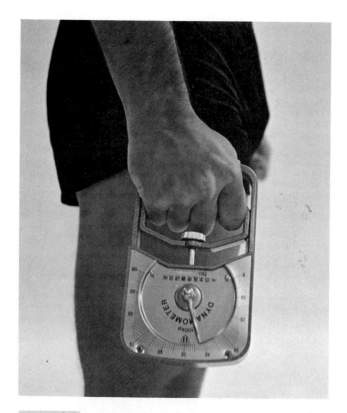

Figure 20-2   Use of the handgrip dynamometer.

To use the handgrip dynamometer, adjust the handgrip to fit the examinee's hand. The subject should stand, holding the dynamometer parallel to the side of the dial facing away from the body (Figure 20-2). To measure grip strength, the dynamometer should be squeezed as hard as possible without moving the arm. Three trials are recommended with a 1-minute rest between trials (Heyward, 1984).

When measuring grip endurance, the examinee should squeeze as hard as possible and continue squeezing for 60 seconds. Record the force in kilograms (kg) every 10 seconds. Relative endurance can be determined by dividing the final force by the initial force times 100. Instead of an all-out force, a submaximal force can be used, such as 50% of maximum. This is scored by the amount of time the submaximal force can be maintained.

The Jackson Strength Evaluation System (Lafayette Instrument) developed by Dr. Andrew Jackson at the University of Houston is designed to measure back strength for lifting and pulling tasks (Figure 20-3). Used as a preemployment screening device, it consists of a portable lifting platform, bar, and chain; 1,000-lb. capacity load cell with digital readout; and computer interface.

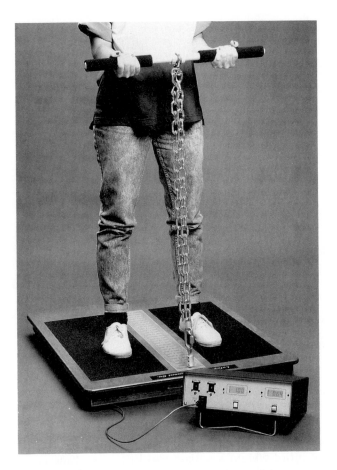

Figure 20-3   Preemployment isometric strength testing with the Jackson Strength Evaluation System. *Courtesy of Lafayette Instrument Co., Lafayette, Ind.*

Cable Tensiometer

A cable tensiometer is used to assess isometric strength. This technique was developed and refined by Harrison Clarke (1966a,b) at the University of Oregon and can be used to test 38 different muscle groups. A tensiometer is a device originally developed for measuring tension in steel cables. The technique requires a tensiometer, straps, cables, chains, a specially constructed table, and a goniometer. The goniometer is used to position the cable at the proper angle. The tensiometer yields a score in pounds of pressure exerted along the cable during a maximum muscular contraction, with possible scores ranging from 0 to 400. An example of the cable tensiometer is shown in Figure 20-4.

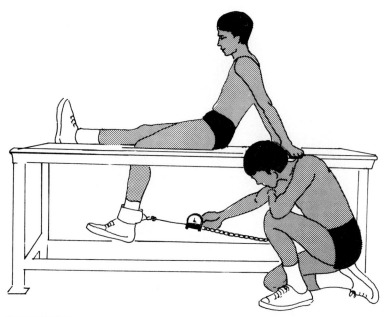

Figure 20-4   Cable tensiometer.

MEASURING ISOTONIC STRENGTH AND ENDURANCE

Measuring isotonic strength and endurance typically involves determining the maximum amount of weight a person can lift at one time (1-repetition maximum) or more (e.g., 10-repetition maximum). This technique can be used with free weights or with commercially available weight-training machines.

Weight-Training Machines

Weight-training machines are designed to measure isotonic muscle strength and endurance. The most useful of these machines offers both constant and variable resistance (Figure 20-5). The force varies throughout the movement, which is better for overall strength and endurance. Many tests of dynamic strength measure maximum strength at one point during the motion. A variable resistance machine such as the Nautilus or the Universal Gym Dynamic Variable Resistance machine can adjust load so that maximum strength is being measured during several phases of the movement; however, measuring maximum contraction throughout the movement on these machines is not possible.

Examples of Practical Dynamic Strength Tests

Measurement of 1-repetition maximum (1-RM) is used to test a variety of muscle groups, for example, those used in the bench press, standing press, arm

Figure 20-5 Cybex II.

curl, and leg press. It will be described first, followed by other techniques requiring less expensive equipment.

The 1-RM Test.

Test Objective To measure dynamic strength; to measure the maximum weight lifted in 1-RM.

Description Determine the 1-RM value by trial and error. Start with a weight the examinee can lift. After a successful trial, allow the examinee to rest for 3 minutes. Increase the weight by 5 to 10 lbs and take another trial. Allow for resting, then continue with the same pattern until the examinee can no longer execute a successful trial.

As an example, to test the leg extensors, seat the subject with hips and knees flexed, holding onto the chair rung with the hands (Figures 20-6 and 20-7). Adjust the seat to standardize the knee angle at approximately 120 degrees. The weights are lifted by fully extending the legs. To determine the maximum weight, refer to the previous paragraph.

Test Area A small, multipurpose room.

Equipment A weight-training machine and scoresheets.

Scoring A direct relationship exists between body weight and weight lifted. All other factors being equal, heavier people can lift heavier weights. Thus the test score—the maximum weight that can be lifted—should be interpreted considering the person's weight.

Figure 20-6   Leg press with knees flexed.

Figure 20-7   Leg press with legs fully extended.

Table 20-1 Optimal Strength Values for Various Body Weights (Based on the 1-RM Test)*

Body Weight	Bench Press Men	Bench Press Women	Standing Press Men	Standing Press Women	Curl Men	Curl Women	Leg Press Men	Leg Press Women
80	80	56	53	37	40	28	160	112
100	100	70	67	47	50	35	200	140
120	120	84	80	56	60	42	240	168
140	140	98	93	65	70	49	280	196
160	160	112	107	75	80	56	320	224
180	180	126	120	84	90	63	360	252
200	200	140	133	93	100	70	400	280
220	220	154	147	103	110	77	440	308
240	240	168	160	112	120	84	480	336

From Pollock ML, and others.
* Data collected on Universal Gym apparatus. Information collected on other apparatus could modify results. Data are expressed in pounds.

Validity   Logical and construct validity.
Reliability   Can be expected to be very high, since an all-out effort is being measured; verified by Jackson et al. (1980).
Norms   See Table 20-1 for norms on gender and body weight.
Comments   Several measurement experts (e.g., Jackson, 1986) have correctly noted that the assessment of isotonic strength is more accurate when individual differences are taken into account. Individual differences due to body weight are of particular concern because body weight and 1-RM performance are moderately correlated. Several methods have been proposed for evaluating isotonic strength while controlling individual differences in body weight.

One of these methods is to express 1-RM as a percentage of body weight. Table 20-2 is used to determine the score. For example, a 140-lb woman who bench-presses 100 lb has a strength-to-body weight of 0.71 (Figures 20-8 and 20-9). Referring to the closest ratio (0.70) in Table 20-2, the score on the bench test is 7.

If no weight-training machine is available, free weights can be used (Figures 20-10 and 20-11). Select a 5- to 6-foot-long weight bar and a variety of weight plates. A test-retest reliability coefficient of .93 was reported for the free weight version of the test (Johnson, 1966).

Bench Squat Test (Johnson, 1966)
Test Objective   To measure leg and back strength.
Description   Use two assistants to handle the weight bar. The examinee should sit near the edge of the chair or bench. The assistants should place the bar on the

Figure 20-8   Bench press with arms flexed.

Figure 20-9   Bench press with arms extended.

Table 20-2 Strength-to-Body Weight Ratios for Selected Dynamic Strength Tests*

			Men			
Bench Press	Arm Curl	Lateral Pull-Down	Leg Press	Leg Extension	Leg Curl	Points
1.50	0.70	1.20	3.00	0.80	0.70	10
1.40	0.65	1.15	2.80	0.75	0.65	9
1.30	0.60	1.10	2.60	0.70	0.60	8
1.20	0.55	1.05	2.40	0.65	0.55	7
1.10	0.50	1.00	2.20	0.60	0.50	6
1.00	0.45	0.95	2.00	0.55	0.45	5
0.90	0.40	0.90	1.80	0.50	0.40	4
0.80	0.35	0.85	1.60	0.45	0.35	3
0.70	0.30	0.80	1.40	0.40	0.30	2
0.60	0.25	0.75	1.20	0.35	0.25	1
			Women			
0.90	0.50	0.85	2.70	0.70	0.60	10
0.85	0.45	0.80	2.50	0.65	0.55	9
0.80	0.42	0.75	2.30	0.60	0.52	8
0.70	0.38	0.73	2.10	0.55	0.50	7
0.65	0.35	0.70	2.00	0.52	0.45	6
0.60	0.32	0.65	1.80	0.50	0.40	5
0.55	0.28	0.63	1.60	0.45	0.35	4
0.50	0.25	0.60	1.40	0.40	0.30	3
0.45	0.21	0.55	1.20	0.35	0.25	2
0.35	0.18	0.50	1.00	0.30	0.20	1

Total Points	Strength Fitness Category
48–60	Excellent
37–47	Good
25–36	Average
13–24	Fair
0–12	Poor

From Heyward VH.
* Based on data compiled by the author for 250 college-age men and women.

Figure 20-10   Bench press using free weights, with arms flexed.

Figure 20-11   Bench press using free weights, with arms extended.

shoulders and behind the neck of the subject. With feet a comfortable distance apart, the examinee should grasp the bar firmly and lower the body to a sitting position on the chair or bench. Using a smooth movement, the examinee stands again. Two trials may be taken. The weight can be adjusted before the second trial.

Test Area   A small, multipurpose room.

Equipment   Bench or chair, 15 to 17 inches in height; weight bar 5 to 6 feet long; sufficient assortment of weight plates; a thick towel to provide padding at the base of the neck where the bar will be placed.

Scoring   Total weight of the barbell lifted in the maximum repetition divided by body weight.

Validity   Face validity.

Reliability $r_{xx'} = .95$, using the test-retest method.

Norms   Norms have been developed for college men (see Johnson and Nelson, 1974).

Comments   This test can be used with females as well as males. Careful spotting is required by the two assistants in case the examinee loses control of the bar or begins to fall. Be sure the examinee sits on the edge of the chair or bench rather than farther back. Adjusting the height of the bench or chair may improve the testing conditions.

Although strength and endurance are highly correlated, the use of continuous repetitions of a leg movement is not recommended (Baumgartner and Jackson, 1987). Some subjects can continue indefinitely; thus, the development of a valid table of norms is a problem.

Because of the potential danger to the spine in executing a squat test requiring the examinee to sit down on a bench, use of the standard equipment shown in Figures 20-12 and 20-13 is recommended. The subject lifts the bar off the pins in the support poles, rests the bar on the shoulders, and lowers the body in the squat position until the tape adhering to the support poles is broken. The lower pins are a safety feature, in case the subject drops the bar.

Pull-Ups Test

The Pull-Ups Test (Figures 20-14 and 20-15) is used to measure arm and shoulder girdle endurance (see Chapter 18). It is recommended for males age 10 and older. Although it is often referred to as a strength test, it is more accurately classified as an endurance test.

Johnson (1966) developed a version of the pull-ups test measuring maximum effort on one repetition. In addition to the usual equipment, weight plates of $2\frac{1}{2}$, 5, 10, and 25 lbs must be available. A rope or strap should be used to secure the weight to the waist of the subject. Actually, the weight can hang in back of the subject, secured to a strap around the waist.

The examinee stands on a chair and grasps the chinning bar. The chair is removed, and the subject assumes a straight-arm hang. One pull-up is performed; the chair is replaced, and the subject lowers to the chair. A second trial is taken if desired. The weight may be adjusted before the second trial. The

Figure 20-12   Squat test—bar lifted off pins.

Figure 20-13   Squat test—body lowered.

 Pull-ups test—body extended.

Figure 20-15   Pull-ups test—elbows flexed.

score is the amount of extra weight lifted in the best of two trials divided by the body weight. A score of 0 is given to subjects who cannot complete the pull-up with more than their own body weight.

A reliability coefficient of .99 was reported (Johnson, 1966); otherwise, the test description is similar to that in Chapter 18.

Sit-Ups Test

This test is almost identical to a repeated sit-ups test, except only one repetition is executed. A weight plate should be held behind the neck. A dumbbell or barbell can also be used. The score is the maximum number of pounds lifted in a single repetition.

Figure 20-16 Lateral pull-down—bar properly grasped.

Figure 20-17 Lateral pull-down—bar touching upper back.

Examples of Practical Endurance Tests

Lateral Pull-Down (Jackson and Smith, 1974)

Test Objective To measure arm strength; to execute repeated lifts using arm flexors.

Description Select a weight that can be pulled down at least once by everyone in the group. The examinee assumes a kneeling position on the floor, grasping the bar on the handle grips, as shown in Figure 20-16. For one repetition, the examinee pulls the bar down behind the head until it touches the upper back at shoulder level (Figure 20-17). The weight is then returned to the starting position, avoiding jerky movements. The knees and lower legs must remain on the floor during the return movements. Use a 3-second cadence for each repetition. Note the way in which a spotter is used in this test. The examinee can be asked to touch the spotter's hands with the bar to complete the pulldown. The use of a spotter is especially important if a 1-RM test is being administered.

Test Area and Equipment Identical to those described in the bench-press test (see below).

Scoring, Validity, Reliability, and Norms Identical to those described in the bench-press test.

The bar can also be pulled down to the front of the body, as shown in Figures 20-18 and 20-19. Note the hands are placed much closer together on the bar. A different muscle group is used in this pull-down action.

Figure 20-18   Alternate pull-down—bar properly grasped.

Figure 20-19   Alternate pull-down—bar pulled in front of body.

Comments   Instead of using the same weight for everyone, the test can be individualized by using a weight that requires a percentage of maximum strength to be lifted. Pollock and associates (1978) recommended using a weight that is 70% of the 1-RM value for each exercise.

Bench-Press Test (Jackson and Smith, 1974)

Test Objective   To measure arm strength by lifting a constant weight load repeatedly until exhausted.

Description   The weight load is constant for everyone in the group. The examinee assumes a supine position on the bench, similar to the position shown in Figures 20-8 and 20-9, except that the feet must be flat on the floor. Use a weight load that can be lifted at least once by all examinees in the group. For example, a weight of 110 lbs is recommended for male college freshmen.

The back should rest flat on the bench. The handles are grasped with both hands, placed farther apart than the shoulders. The weight is lifted upward until the arms are fully extended, then lowered until the weights touch the weights beneath them. The weights should not be dropped or slammed. If free weights are used, the bar should be lowered to the chest.

Continue with repetitions of the same movement on a 3-second cadence. The examinee should not be allowed to begin a new repetition until the beginning of a new 3-second interval.

Test Area   A small, multipurpose room.

Equipment   A weight-training machine or free weights, a metronome or tape of a recording of cadence, and scoresheets.

Scoring   The score is the number of repetitions completed. The test is ended when an examinee can no longer execute a repetition correctly or maintain the proper cadence.

Validity   Logical, as an endurance measure; concurrent as a strength measure—high correlation with the maximum weight lifted with one repetition ($r_{xy} > .90$).

Reliability   None reported, but can be expected to be high if examinees are motivated to maximum performance.

Norms   Available for college men in original source.

Comments   Although this is a measure of muscular endurance, the authors believe the test can be used as a measure of strength since it is highly correlated with 1-RM.

Figure 20-20   Arm curl with arms extended.

Arm Curl (Jackson and Smith, 1974)

Test Objective   To measure arm strength; to execute repeated curls using arm flexors.

Description   Before beginning the test, the examinee must first be stabilized by standing with head, shoulders, and buttocks against the wall. The feet, placed 12 to 15 inches from the wall, are used to brace the back. To ensure that this position is maintained during exercise, the test developers recommend placing a sheet of paper behind the buttocks. The paper must remain pinned against the wall throughout the test. When the paper falls, the test is terminated.

To administer this test as described, the weight-training unit must be positioned close to a wall. Obviously, this may not be possible in many settings. If this is not possible, the standard curl shown in Figures 20-20 and 20-21 may be used. If the hips are thrust forward during the repetitions, the test should be terminated. Only the arms should move during this test.

Figure 20-21   Arm curl with arms flexed.

Figure 20-22   Arm curl using free weights, arms extended.

Figure 20-23   Arm curl using free weights, arms flexed.

The examinee should begin with arms fully extended. In this position, the exercise weight should be suspended slightly above the remaining weights. The examinee should flex the arms fully, touch the bar to the chin, and fully extend the arms again. A 3-second cadence for each repetition is used.

This test can also be administered using free weights, as shown in Figures 20-22 and 20-23. Note the equipment used to stabilize the examinee. This prevents any other body part from being used to assist in executing the curl.

Test Area and Equipment   Identical to those described in the bench-press test.

Scoring, Validity, Reliability, and Norm   Identical to those described in the bench-press test.

Squat Thrust Test (Burpee, 1976)

Test Objective   To measure the general muscular endurance of the body.

Description   The examinee stands erect, with arms hanging at the side. At the

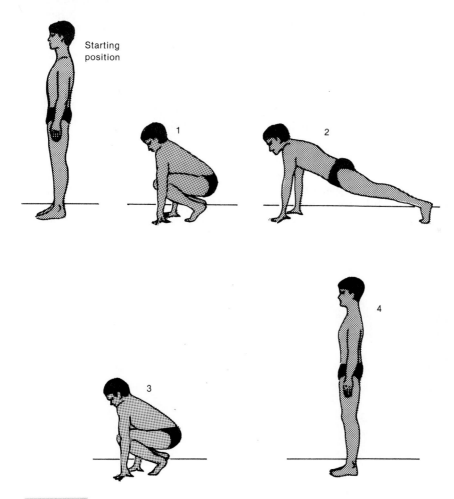

Figure 20-24   Squat thrust.

signal "Ready, go!" a squat position is assumed with the hands on the floor. Then the body is extended fully, as shown in Figure 20-24 on p. 617. The examinee returns to the squat position and then to the standing position. The procedure is repeated as rapidly as possible for 10 seconds. On the signal "Stop!" the test ends. Three trials are taken.

Test Area   A small room with smooth floor surface.

Equipment   Stopwatch and scoresheets.

Scoring   Score 1 point for each completed squat thrust. Each quarter movement is given 1/4 point. The test score is the best of three trials.

Validity $r_{xy} = .55$, reported by C.H. McCloy.

Reliability $r_{xx'} = .92$, reported by C.H. McCloy.

Comments   A large group of examinees can be tested at the same time. Each examinee should work with a partner, who counts the number of squat thrusts. Careful attention should be paid to the positions assumed in the squat thrusts. In particular, be sure that the body is fully extended at position *2* (see Figure 20-24). Instruct the examinees on the correct procedure for executing this movement before the actual test.

Other Approaches to Endurance Testing

A number of other practical approaches to endurance training have been reported in the literature. Among the more popular items are push-ups, used to measure arm and shoulder girdle endurance (Figures 20-25 and 20-26). The problem with this test is that, as with pull-ups, some examinees will not be able to execute even one. Thus it is not a discriminating measure for some groups.

Modified push-ups may be used as an alternative test for female examinees. These push-ups are performed with the knees instead of the feet, touching the floor, as in the full-length push-up. This test is depicted in Figures 20-27 and 20-28.

If gymnastics equipment is available, the parallel bars can be used to test repeated executions of the dip. The parallel bars on a weight-training machine

Figure 20-25   Push-ups with arms flexed.

Figure 20-26 Push-ups with arms extended.

can also be used for this purpose (Figures 20-29 and 20-30). The dip is performed by lowering the body until the elbow forms a 90-degree angle. A simpler version of endurance testing using the dip is a modified test using a single bar. The lower bar of the uneven bars can be used for this purpose. The body and arms are fully extended on the bar. The dip is performed by lowering the body on the bar until the elbows are at right angles. Then full extension takes place.

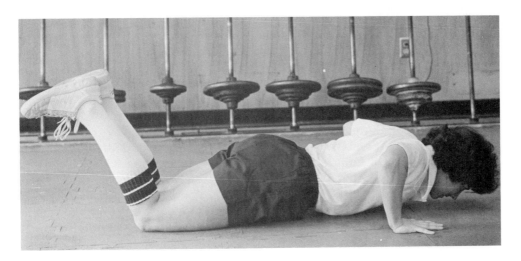

Figure 20-27 Modified push-up with arms flexed.

Figure 20-28   Modified push-up with arms extended.

MEASURING ISOKINETIC STRENGTH AND ENDURANCE

Isokinetics involves resisted exercise at a preset fixed speed (measured in degrees per second) such that the resistance accommodates to the individual throughout the range of motion (Wilk, 1990). By accommodating the resistance the muscle contracts maximally throughout the range of motion. This is in contrast to isotonic training where the resistance is fixed and the speed of contraction is variable resulting in variable force throughout the range of motion due to ballistic action of the muscle and changes in mechanical advantages of levers at different points during the movement.

Isokinetic training and testing requires expensive and sophisticated equipment. In 1968 the first commercially available isokinetic device was introduced under the brand name Cybex, followed by the Cybex II in 1975. The Cybex and Cybex II measured concentric contractions within a limited range of speed (0–50 degrees/sec). Currently, several computerized isokinetic devices for testing and rehabilitation are available including the Cybex 6000 Extremity System (Cybex Division of Lumex, Inc., Ronkonkoma, N.Y.) (Figure 20-31); Kinetic Communicator (Kin-Com, Chattanooga Group, Inc., Chattanooga, Tenn.) (Figure 20-32); Biodex (Biodex Corp., Shirley, N.Y.); and Lido Active (Loredan Biomedical, Inc., Davis, Calif.). These newer devices can measure isokinetic strength and endurance using either concentric or eccentric contractions at speeds up to 500 degrees/sec. Moreover, a computer interface provides instantaneous graphical feedback of results, control over preprogrammed exercise protocols, and data storage and reporting.

Figure 20-29   Dip—arms fully extended.

Figure 20-30   Dip—elbow at 90-degree angle.

POWER TESTING

Power is the ability to generate maximum force in a minimum amount of time. Athletic activities such as jumping and sprinting require power. Although the precise measurement of power is possible with sophisticated tests such as the Magaria-Kalamen test of leg power (see Fox and Mathews, 1981), several practi-

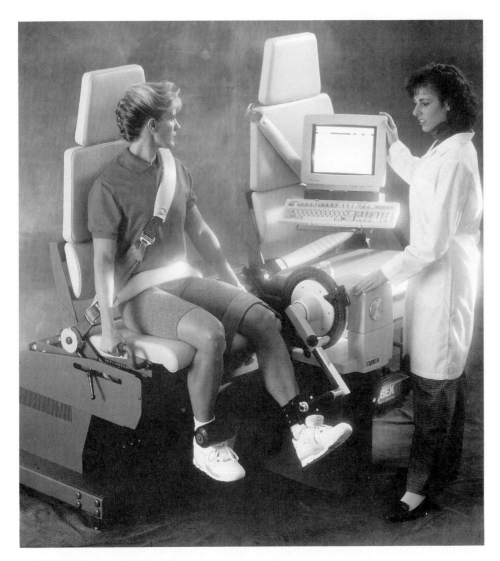

Figure 20-31   The Cybex 6000 Extremity Testing and Rehabilitation System. *(Courtesy of Cybex.)*

cal tests of explosive power are quite popular in the physical education field. Two examples are the standing long jump, described in Chapter 18, and the **vertical jump test,** described below. However, McArdle, and colleagues (1986) indicate that "any performance involving all-out exercise of 4 to 6 seconds duration can probably be considered indicative of the person's capacity for immediate power" (p. 169). Therefore, activities such as short sprints or brief periods of cycling can be used to estimate running and cycling power, respectively.

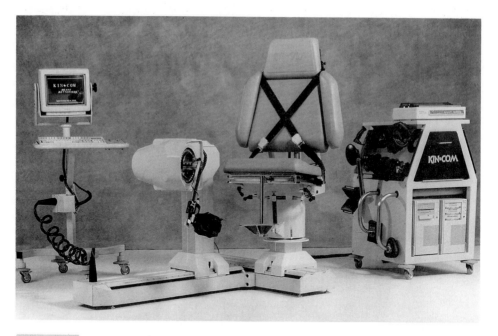

Figure 20-32   The Kinetic Communicator (Kin-Com). *(Courtesy of the Chattanooga Group, Inc.)*

Vertical Jump Test (Sargent, 1921)

Test Objective   To measure the explosive power of the leg extensors.

Description   For the vertical jump, the examinee stands with the dominant arm extended, as shown in Figure 20-33, holding a piece of chalk to mark the wall. The feet are flat on the floor. The examinee should reach as high as possible, making a mark on the measuring board. Then a preparatory position should be taken for the jump, which is a squat position with the feet still flat on the floor. The subject should jump as high as possible, touching the board again with the chalk at the height of the jump. Three trials are taken.

Test Area   Measuring board (self-constructed or purchased commercially), marked in half-inches, attached to the wall (if possible, the board should be attached 6 inches out from the wall so the examinee does not scrape the arm or side of the body while jumping); chalk and damp cloth (or eraser); yardstick; scoresheets.

Scoring   For each trial, the score is the distance between the two chalk marks, measured to the nearest half-inch. The test score is the best trial score.

Validity $r_{xy} = .78$, using a criterion test of four power events in track and field.

Reliability $r_{xx'} = .93$; objectivity coefficients greater than 0.90 have been reported.

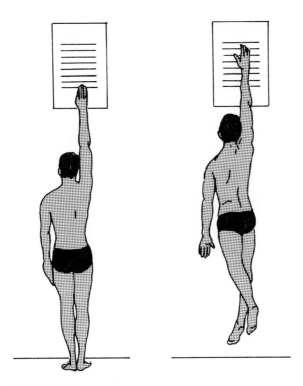

Figure 20-33   Vertical jump.

Norms   Norms for the vertical jump test are included in Table 20-3.

Comments   The following are four of the many versions of the test:

1. Instead of using a piece of chalk, magnesium chalk is placed on the fingertips of the hand on the wall side; or the fingertips are dipped in water; or a stepladder is placed adjacent to the measuring board, and an assistant measures the height from this position. If chalk is used, the chalk marks must be removed, preferably with a damp cloth, after each trial.
2. Instead of facing the wall to take the initial measurement, the subject stands with one side to the wall, with toes touching the wall.
3. Instead of standing flat-footed to take the initial measurement, the subject stands on tiptoes.
4. The measurement is taken to the nearest quarter of an inch instead of the nearest half-inch.

This test can be administered to 30 students in 45 minutes. If desired, the score can be adjusted so that body weight is taken into account.

Table 20-3 Vertical Jump Scoring Table*

	100	90	80	70	60	50	40	30	20	10	0
Boys and girls 9–11	16	15	14	12	11	10	9	7	4	2	0
Boys 12–14	20	18	17	16	14	13	11	9	5	2	0
Girls 12–14	16	15	14	13	12	11	10	8	4	2	0
Boys 15–17	25	24	23	21	19	16	12	8	5	2	0
Girls 15–17	17	16	15	14	13	11	8	6	3	2	0
Men 18–34	26	25	24	23	19	16	13	9	8	2	0
Women 18–34	14	13	13	12	10	8	6	4	2	1	0

From Friermood HT.
* Raw scores are located in the chart in accordance with age and gender, and percentile scores are located across the top.

SUMMARY

The measurement of muscular strength, endurance, and power requires careful attention to the position of the examinee and the execution of the movement. Serious injuries can occur if proper protocol is not followed. The spotters must be thoroughly trained and remain attentive throughout the testing. The safety of the examinee must receive top priority. Test selection depends on the type of equipment available. Several strength and endurance tests require little or no equipment. Although tests using sophisticated and expensive equipment may be more valid, the practical versions are satisfactory for field testing.

Learning Experiences

1. To understand strength and endurance testing more fully, enroll in a weight-training class. This will familiarize you with the proper positions, the safety considerations, and the use of appropriate equipment. If it is not possible to enroll in such a course, observe a class two or three times at your campus or at a private fitness club.
2. Ask a qualified classmate to administer an arm-press and a leg-press test to you. Be sure this person is thoroughly familiar with the protocol. Compare your scores to the norms in this chapter.
3. Administer the vertical jump test to everyone in your class. Obtain the weight of each classmate as well. Correlate vertical jump scores with weight. Is there a substantial enough relationship to warrant using body weight to adjust vertical jump scores? How might this sort of adjustment be made?

References

Amundsen LR. 1990. Measurement of skeletal muscle strength: An overview of instrumented and non-instrumented systems. In Amundsen LR, ed. Muscle strength testing: Instrumented and non-instrumented systems. New York: Churchill Livingstone, pp 1–23.

Baumgartner TA, Jackson AS. 1982. Measurement for evaluation in physical education. Dubuque, Iowa: Wm C Brown Group.

Clarke HH. 1966a. Muscular strength and endurance in man. Englewood Cliffs, NJ: Prentice Hall.

Clarke HH. 1966b. Application of measurement to health and physical education. Englewood Cliffs, NJ: Prentice Hall.

Corbin CB, Lindsey R. 1985. Concepts of physical fitness with laboratories. Dubuque, IA: Wm C Brown.

Fox EL, Mathews DK. 1981. The physiological basis of physical education and athletics, ed 3. Philadelphia: WB Saunders.

Heyward VH. 1984. Designs for fitness. Minneapolis: Burgess Co.

Jackson A. 1986. Strength measurement: Controlling for individual differences. Journal of Physical Education, Recreation and Dance, 57(6):82–84.

Jackson A, Watkins M, Patton R. 1980. A factor analysis of twelve selected maximal isotonic strength performances on the universal gym. Medicine and Science in Sports and Exercise, 12:274–277.

Jackson AS, Smith L. 1974. The validation of an evaluation system for weight training. Presented at the American Association for Health, Physical Education and Recreation Convention, Anaheim, Calif., March 1977.

Johnson BL. 1966. Isometric strength tests. Monroe: Northeast Louisiana University.

Johnson BL, Nelson JK. 1974. Practical measurements for evaluation in physical education. Minneapolis: Burgess Co.

McArdle WD, Katch FI, Katch VL. 1986. Exercise physiology: Energy, nutrition, and human performance. Philadelphia: Lea & Febiger.

Pollock ML, Wilmore JH, Fox SM. 1978. Health and fitness through physical activity. New York: Wiley.

Sargent DA. 1921. Physical test of a man. American Physical Education Review, 26(4):188–194.

Wilk K. 1990. Dynamic muscle strength testing. In Amundsen LR, ed. Muscle strength testing: Instrumented and non-instrumented systems. New York: Churchill Livingstone, pp 123–150.

Annotated Readings

Amundsen LR, ed. 1990. Muscle strength testing: Instrumented and non-instrumented systems. New York: Churchill Livingstone.
A complete and detailed description of strength testing aimed at physical therapists and others in the clinical setting.

Heyward VH. 1984. Assessment of muscular strength and endurance. Chapter in Designs for fitness. Minneapolis: Burgess.

Describes devices for measuring strength and muscular endurance; discusses problems associated with the assessment of static and dynamic muscle strength and endurance; analyzes calisthenic-type strength and endurance tests.

Katch FI, McArdle WD. 1983. Conditioning for muscular strength. Chapter in Nutrition, weight control and exercise, ed 2. Philadelphia: Lea & Febiger.
Describes three exercise systems for developing muscular strength—weight training, isometric training, and isokinetic training; includes sections on muscular adaptations with strength training, strength training for women, and circuit weight training; presents step-by-step procedure for planning a workout; provides instruction on selecting proper weights.

Leighton JR. 1983. Fitness, body development, and sports conditioning through weight training. Springfield, Ill: Thomas.
Provides beginning and advanced exercise programs for both men and women using free weights, multistation exercise machines, and variable resistance equipment; discusses conditioning for a variety of activities, such as golf, racquet sports, and soccer.

Sharkey BJ. 1984. Physiology of fitness, ed 2. Champaign, Ill: Human Kinetics.
Includes section on muscular fitness training; presents test for fitness training programs, in the appendix; covers the latest information on fitness.

Tests of Balance, Flexibility, and Posture

Watch for these words as you read the following chapter

Active stretching
Balance
Dynamic balance
Elgon
Flexibility
Flexometer
Goniometer
Inclinometer
Kyphosis

Lordosis
Passive stretching
Pendulum (gravity) devices
Posture
Scoliosis
Static balance
Task specificity

M otor skill performance and posture are dependent, to some extent, on **balance** and **flexibility.** While the contribution of balance and flexibility to motor skill performance is obvious (e.g., gymnastics and figure skating), the dynamic interplay between these psychomotor abilities and posture is significant, although less apparent.

Years ago, physical educators thought that people possessed a general ability to balance and another general ability reflecting overall flexibility. In other words, if a person could balance well on one body part, it was assumed that he or she could balance well on any body part. Based on this rationale, the development of practical tests of balance was quite straightforward. Only one balance test, for example, was needed to measure overall balance ability. Over the last two decades, however, research on both balance and flexibility has not substantiated the concept of general abilities. Rather, each of these abilities tends to be specific to a body part. This means that a person who is flexible at a hip joint is not necessarily flexible in a shoulder joint. Yet we have all seen gymnasts who are flexible in all joints. Does this not point to a general ability? Probably not. More likely, it reflects **task specificity,** a high level of flexibility in many specific abilities. Task specificity suggests that not only is the ability specific to a particular body part but also to a particular task. These research results complicate the measurement of balance and flexibility considerably, unless one's interest lies only with measurement at a specific site. Yet many tests of these two attributes have been developed in the physical education field. While none is valid as a test of general balance or flexibility, some are useful in more specific settings.

Historically, the assessment of **posture** in physical education has received decreasing emphasis. Yet, physical educators are in a unique position to screen children and the elderly for postural development leading to potentially harmful conditions such as chronic back pain and disability. While a detailed assessment of posture involves measurements of body segments such as leg length and pelvic angle, the primary method of assessment is observation. A relatively simple and practical posture rating scale is briefly described in this chapter.

MEASURING BALANCE

Balance is the ability to maintain equilibrium. Even before a great deal of research was conducted on the nature of balance, it was deduced that two types of balance exist—**static balance,** the ability to maintain equilibrium in a stationary position, and **dynamic balance,** the ability to maintain equilibrium while in motion.

A physical educator or exercise scientist might be interested in measuring balance for a variety of reasons. Achievement of minimal balance standards might be a goal in a physical education instructional unit, such as posture and body mechanics or gymnastics. Balance tests might be used to assess the movement patterns of young children and to evaluate the status of special education children. The measurement of balance is useful in assessing potential in gymnastics, diving, and other forms of physical activity that require balance skills. This topic is of great interest in the elderly population, where maintaining equilibrium is essential in the prevention of injury occurring as a result of falls. Several precise and practical tests are described for each type of balance.

Precise Measures of Static and Dynamic Balance

In therapeutic settings there are several populations for which maintaining balance is a significant challenge (e.g., the aged, persons with cerebral palsy or paralysis on one side of the body, and those with neural deficits leading to balance disorders). Recent advances in computer technology and the measurement of postural body sway using forceplates has led to the development of sophisticated rehabilitation tools for accurately monitoring, assessing, and training persons with balance deficits. One such device is the PRO Balance Master (Neurocom International, 1993) (Figure 21-1). The PRO Balance Master provides continuous visual feedback to patients regarding such attributes as center of gravity and postural alignment during static and dynamic balance testing on a dual movable forceplate platform surrounded by an overhead safety bar and straps. In addition, the apparatus is designed as a training device. Patient progress can be monitored during static and dynamic balance rehabilitative exercises under various conditions such as with eyes open or eyes closed. Moreover, the sophisticated computer interface permits storage and analysis of patient demographic and test data and control over therapeutic training and assessment.

An alternative strategy in the clinical assessment of balance is the development of functional tests of balance. The following are examples of such tests:

The balance scale (Berg et al., 1989) subjectively assesses elderly patients' videotaped performance on 14 common tasks such as the ability to change position from sitting to standing. Each task is rated on a 5-point scale.

The "get-up and go" test (Mathias et al., 1986) requires rating a videotape of patients standing up from a chair, walking a short distance, turning around, returning to the chair, and sitting down again. Overall performance is rated on a 5-point scale ranging from normal to severely abnormal. Additionally, the time it takes to complete the task can be recorded.

In a concurrent validity study comparing several functional balance tests with a laboratory test of postural sway using a forceplate apparatus, Berg et al. (1992) reported moderately strong correlations between the balance scale and the laboratory test.

Practical Measures of Static Balance

Bass Stick Test (lengthwise) (Bass, 1939)

Test Objective   To measure the ability to balance in a stationary, upright position using a small base of support.

Description   The examinee places the dominant foot lengthwise on a special stick, as shown in Figure 21-2. Both the ball of the foot and the heel should rest on the stick. The opposite foot is lifted from the floor and held in this position as long as possible. The stopwatch is started when the opposite foot leaves the floor and stopped when it touches the floor again, or when any part of the supporting foot touches the floor. Three trials are taken on each foot.

Test Area   Smooth, flat floor.

Equipment   A stick 1 inch wide, 1 inch high, and 12 inches long; stopwatch; and tape (to hold the stick to the floor).

Scoring   The test score is the time for the best of three trials.

Validity   Face validity.

Reliability $R_{xx'} = .90$.

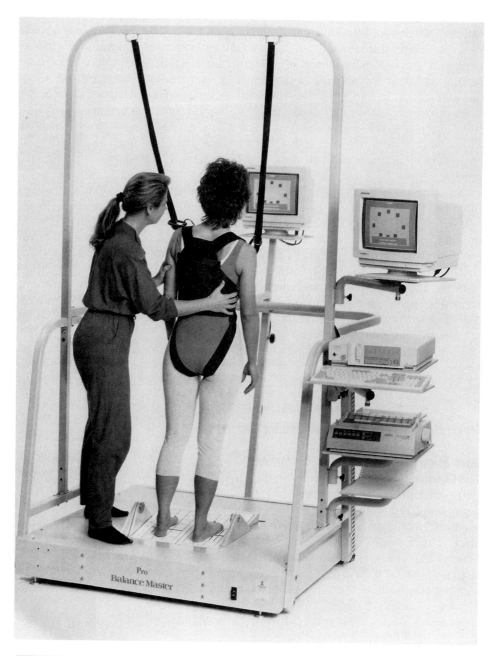

Figure 21-1   The PRO Balance Master balance testing and training device. Courtesy of Neurocom International.

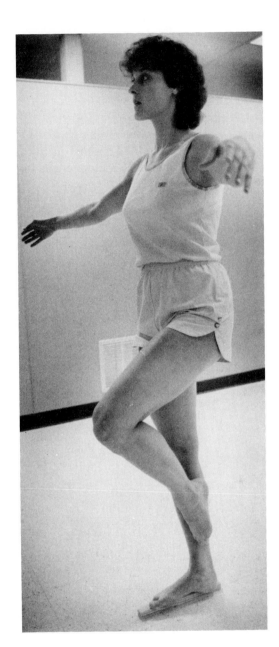

Figure 21-2   Bass stick test (length-wise).

Norms   Not reported for this test.

Comments   If an examinee loses balance during the first 3 seconds of the trial, the trial may be restarted. This is a popular test in the field and is usually very motivating to the examinee, although it measures only a specific type of balance.

Bass Stick Test (crosswise) (Bass, 1939)

Same as the Bass stick test (lengthwise) except that the foot is placed crosswise on the stick and the examinee balances on the ball of the foot (Figure 21-3).

Stork Stand

Test Objective To measure the ability to balance in a stationary, upright position using a small base of support.

Description The examinee stands on the dominant foot, flat on the floor. The other foot is held so that it touches the inside of the supporting knee, as shown in Figure 21-4. The hands are placed on the hips. As soon as the proper position has been established, the stopwatch is started. The examinee holds the position as long as possible. When the nondominant foot is moved away from the knee, the watch is stopped. This constitutes one trial; three trials are taken.

Test Area Smooth, flat floor.

Equipment Stopwatch.

Figure 21-3   Bass stick test (crosswise).   Figure 21-4   Stork stand test.

Scoring The best of three trials is the test score.

Validity Face validity.

Reliability $R_{xx'} = .85$, using the test-retest method (as reported by Jensen and Hirst, 1980); $R_{xx'} = .85$ (test-retest) (as reported by Johnson and Nelson, 1979).

Norms Available for college men and women in Johnson and Nelson (1979) for a slightly different version of the test in which the examinee balances on the ball of the foot.

Comments The lack of a time limit is a drawback in administering the test. An examinee who can balance well in this position can hold this position for a lengthy period. If a group of students is being tested, this could be too time-consuming.

Practical Measures of Dynamic Balance

Johnson Modification of the Bass Test of Dynamic Balance (Johnson and Leach, 1968)

Test Objective To measure dynamic balance.

Description Using the floor plan shown in Figure 21-5, the examinee begins with the right foot on the starting mark and leaps to the first tape mark, landing on the left foot and balancing on the ball of the foot as long as possible, up to 5 seconds. The examinee leaps to the next square, lands on the right foot, and tries to maintain balance for 5 seconds. This procedure is continued until the end of the floor pattern.

Test Area Smooth floor surface, 50 inches by 180 inches.

Equipment Stopwatch, tape measure, floor tape.

Scoring For each successful landing on the tape mark, 5 points are scored; 1 point is scored for each second the examinee remains balanced on the mark, up to 5 seconds. It is possible to score 10 points at each tape mark and 100 points on the total test. The examinee is penalized 5 points for any of the following landing errors: not stopping after landing on the tape mark, touching the floor with

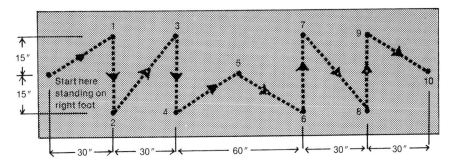

Figure 21-5 Floor markings for the Johnson modification of the Bass test of dynamic balance.

any body part other than the supporting foot, and not covering the tape mark with the ball of the foot. If the examinee makes a landing error, the correct position can be resumed for the 5-second balance.

An additional 1-point penalty is given for the following errors during the 5-second balance: touching the floor with the heel of the hand or any body part other than the supporting foot, and not holding the foot steady in the balance position. If the balance is lost, the examinee should return to the proper mark before leaping to the next mark.

Validity   Face validity; $r_{xy} = .46$ using as the criterion the original Bass test of dynamic balance (as reported by Kirkendall et al., 1987).

Reliability $R_{xx'} = .75$ using the test-retest method.

Norms   Norms are available for college women in Johnson and Nelson (1979).

Comments   While this is an interesting test, it is not a direct measure of dynamic balance. Usually, dynamic balance refers to balancing while the body (or body part) is moving. In this test, as in other tests of dynamic balance, the examinee moves but then stops and maintains a static balance.

Modified Sideward Leap (Scott and French, 1959)

Test Objective   To measure dynamic balance.

Description   The examinee begins on spot X, as shown in Figure 21-6, and places a small object on spots B and C. The starting position is assumed by standing on the left foot, with the right side toward spot A. The examinee takes a sideward

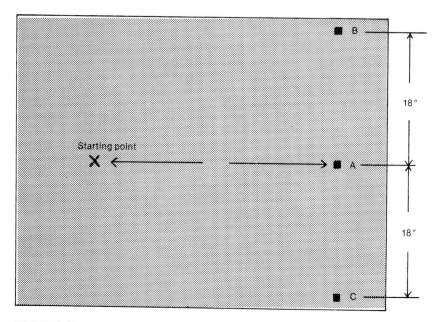

Figure 21-6   Floor markings for the modified sideward leap test. Spot A is the landing point; spots B and C mark the placement of a small object.

Figure 21-7 Balance beam walk test.

leap to spot *A*, landing on the ball of the right foot, leans to spot *B*, and brushes the object off, using one hand. Balance on the ball of the foot should then be maintained for 5 seconds. Four trials are taken, two to each side.

Test Area A smooth floor surface, 50 inches by 50 inches.

Equipment Stopwatch; tape measure, floor tape, and a small, light object, such as a badminton shuttlecock.

Scoring The maximum number of points for each trial is 20: 5 points for landing correctly on spot *A*; 1 point for each second that balance is held on spot *A*, up to 5 seconds; 5 points for leaning and pushing object off spot *B* or *C*; 1 point for each second that balance is held on spot *B* or *C*, up to 5 seconds.

Validity Face validity.

Reliability $R_{xx'}$ = .66 to .88.

Norms Not reported for this test.

Comments Like the original version, this modification measures the ability to balance while performing other movements.

Balance Beam Walk (Jensen and Hirst, 1980)*

Test Objective To measure dynamic balance.

* Although this test is described in Jensen and Hirst (1980), various versions of it have been in use for many years.

Description   The examinee should stand on one end of the balance beam, slowly walk the full length of the beam (see Figure 21-7 on p. 637), pause for 5 seconds, turn around, and return to the starting position. Three trials are taken.

Test Area   Smooth floor surface, 5 feet by 15 feet.

Equipment   Balance beam and stopwatch.

Scoring   Pass-fail.

Validity   Face validity.

Reliability   Not reported for this test.

Norms   Not reported for this test.

Comments   There should be a time limit for this test; otherwise, the examinee could move at an excessively slow pace, consuming an unreasonable amount of time. Also, penalties should be identified for errors that occur throughout the test.

MEASURING FLEXIBILITY

Flexibility is the range of motion around a joint, specifically from a position of extension to flexion or the opposite movement. The degree of flexibility is a result of the interplay between such factors as the stretch of muscles, ligament length, and the shape of bones at the joint. In addition, flexibility can measure the range of motion resulting from an active stretch or a passive stretch. **Active stretching** results from the forceful contraction of opposing muscles (e.g., lying on your back and lifting your extended right leg as high as possible). **Passive stretching** most often results from an assist from gravity or another person while the subject is relaxing the muscles around the joint (e.g., lying on your back and having another person gently lift your relaxed and extended right leg as high as possible). Flexibility measured as the result of passive stretching is most commonly used in the clinical and therapeutic settings. As noted previously, there is ample evidence that flexibility is specific to a given joint.

A flexibility test is included in all the recently revised national physical fitness tests. Low back flexibility is identified in these tests as an important factor in preventing low back pain. Many activities have a significant flexibility element, and flexibility is maintained and improved on a regular basis by persons engaged in these activities. Flexibility tests are useful for monitoring the level of flexibility on a regular basis. Sufficient flexibility for the prevention of injury is essential, especially in the elderly population. Flexibility tests are widely used in today's society. Factors to consider when measuring flexibility are motivation, warm-up, presence of muscular soreness, pain tolerance, room temperature, and ability to relax (Corbin and Lindsey, 1985). In this chapter, both precise and practical measures of flexibility are discussed.

Precise Measures of Flexibility

Precise measures of flexibility can be categorized as **pendulum or gravity devices** (Figures 21-8 and 21-9) or as **goniometers** (Figures 21-10 and 21-11).

Figure 21-8 The Leighton flexometer. *Courtesy of Lafayette Instrument Co.*

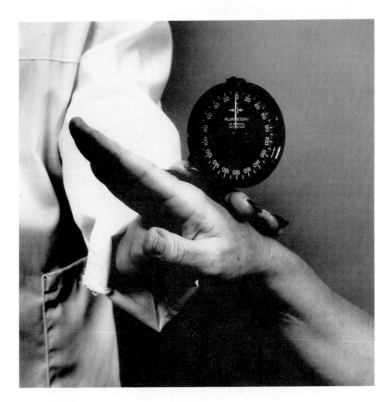

Figure 21-9 Measuring spinal range of motion with an inclinometer. *Courtesy of Lafayette Instrument Co.*

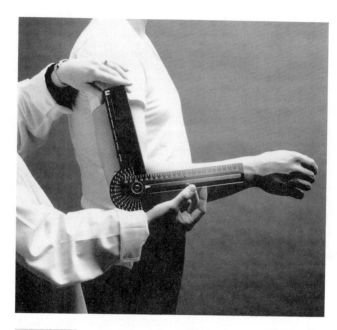

Figure 21-10   A manual goniometer. *Courtesy of Lafayette Instrument Co.*

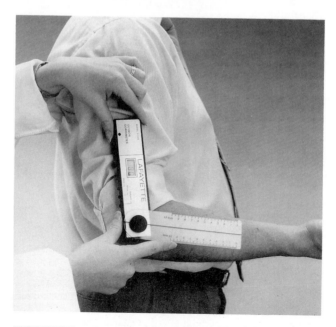

Figure 21-11   The Guymon electric goniometer. *Courtesy of Lafayette Instrument Co.*

Goniometers are protractor-like devices with extended arms that measure joint angles in degrees. Range of motion is measured by recording the starting position in degrees (typically the anatomical position), moving the body part through the range of motion either actively or passively, and recording the ending position in degrees. Subtracting the starting position from the ending position provides a measure of the arc or range of motion. Detailed descriptions of proper techniques for measuring with goniometer can be found in Duesterhaus-Minor and Duesterhaus-Minor (1985). Goniometers are available in several sizes (e.g., 6-inch finger goniometer or 14-inch goniometer for measuring angles at the knee), materials (commonly plastic or metal), and with 180-degree or 360-degree protractors. The electric goniometer (also known as an **elgon**) substitutes a potentiometer for the protractor, and provides a continuous digital display of degrees throughout the range of motion. Recent models of electric goniometers such as the Guymon goniometer (Lafayette Instrument Co., Lafayette, Ind.) can store multiple data points for multiple subjects. The data can subsequently be downloaded to a microcomputer.

Gravity devices include the **flexometer** and the **inclinometer.** The flexometer is a pendulum instrument with a weighted 360-degree dial and a weighted pointer (Leighton, 1942, 1955). Both the dial and the pointer move independently and are affected by gravity. The flexometer is strapped onto an appropriate body segment such as the lower arm. The limb is placed in the starting position so that the zero marks on the dial are in a vertical position. The dial is locked in place. The subject moves the body segment through the range of motion to the extreme position. During the movement the locked dial moves with the segment while the free-swinging pointer remains pointed down due to gravity. At the extreme position the pointer is locked and the reading is taken. Sigerseth (1978) provides detailed descriptions for measuring range of motion of the primary body segments with the flexometer. The reliability of the flexometer has ranged from .90 to .98. The inclinometer is a popular instrument in medical and clinical settings for measuring joint angle and range of motion, particularly spinal range of motion.

Practical Tests of Flexibility

Because of the specific nature of flexibility tests, not may of the practical tests have a high degree of validity as measures of general flexibility, but some have a certain usefulness as measures of the flexibility of specific segments. Caution must be used in the selection of flexibility tests, since certain measures require positioning the body in ways that might cause physical injury to some examinees.

Sit and Reach Tests

The Sit and Reach Test, described in detail in Chapter 17, was designed to measure flexibility of the low back and posterior thigh muscles. However, research has shown that for girls (Jackson and Baker, 1986) and women (Jackson and Langford, 1989) sit-and-reach flexibility scores do not correlate well with an independent measure of low back flexibility and only moderately with hamstring extensibility. Although this is a reasonably practical test, it is not without problems. Flexibility is measured in centimeters (or, more recently, inches) rather than degrees. Performance on the test is somewhat dependent on the ratio of trunk length to lower body length. Hoeger and Hopkins (1992) offered a modification of the sit-and-reach test using a sliding sit-and-reach scale to adjust for varying arm-to-length ratios and shoulder girdle mobility. Examinees sit with their back against a wall and reach forward with their arms toward the modified sit-and-reach box. The sliding top of the box is then adjusted so that the fingers can just touch the edge of the top, providing the 0 point. Examinees then perform the sit-and-reach test. Other modifications of the test have been suggested. In the current version of the *FITNESS*GRAM a bent-leg sit-and-reach test is employed to reduce compression in the disks in the low back (Plowman and Corbin, 1994). Examinees perform the test twice—four trials with the left knee bent, and four trials with the right knee bent. Despite these problems, the sit-and-reach test does provide comparative measurement. Furthermore, it requires little equipment, is inexpensive and easy to administer, and requires little time to administer. Students can learn to give the test to one another. (See Chapter 17 for more information on this test, including abbreviated tables of norms.)

Kraus-Weber Floor Touch Test (Kraus and Hirschland, 1954)*

Test Objective To measure trunk flexibility or the length of the back and hamstring muscles.

Description The examinee assumes an erect standing position in bare or stocking feet, with the feet together. The arms should hang by the sides. With no prior warm-up bounces, the examinee slowly leans downward, attempting to touch the floor with the fingertips (Figure 21-12), and holds the floor-touch position for 3 seconds. The knees must be straight throughout the test.

Test Area A small room.

Equipment Stopwatch.

Scoring As the test battery was originally devised, all test items were scored on a pass-fail basis. Using this procedure, if the floor touch is held for 3 seconds, the examinee passes the test. Otherwise, the examinee receives a fail. This system of scoring appears to be the one most frequently used. Another scoring option uses numerical scores ranging from 0 to 10. If the floor-touch position is held for 3 seconds, the examinee receives a score of 10. If the floor is not touched, 1 point is subtracted for every inch between the floor and the fingertips. If this distance is 10 inches or more, the score is 0.

Validity The validity of the Kraus-Weber tests of minimum muscular fitness is based on clinical evidence that patients with low back pain were unable to pass one or more of the Kraus-Weber test items. As their back conditions improved, their test results also improved.

---

* This test is a part of the Kraus-Weber tests of minimum muscular fitness described in Chapter 17. The test battery includes six items.

Figure 21-12 Kraus-Weber floor-touch test.

Reliability Not reported for this test.

Norms Since the scoring is usually pass-fail, the use of norms is irrelevant.

Comments The test administrator might wish to hold the knees of the examinee being tested to ensure that they remain straight throughout the test.

Trunk Extension (Cureton, 1941)

Test Objective To measure the ability to hyperextend the trunk.

Description To assume the starting position of this test, the examinee lies in a prone position on the mat. Both hands are placed on the lower back. A partner holds the hips against the mat (Figure 21-13). Using a tape measure, determine the distance from the mat to the suprasternal notch, the pronounced depression at the upper end of the sternum, at the base of the neck. Measure to the nearest quarter of an inch.

Test Area A small room.

Equipment Mat and tape measure.

Scoring To determine the test score, a standard measure of trunk length must first be taken. The examinee should sit with his or her back against the wall. Using a tape measure, determine the distance between the suprasternal notch and the floor or bench where the examinee is seated. Measure to the nearest quarter of an inch. Then, multiply the test measurement by 100 and divide by the standard

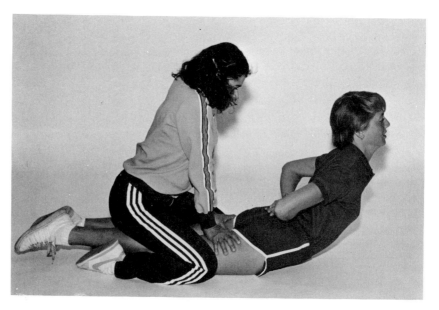

Figure 21-13   Trunk extension test.

measurement of trunk length to determine the test score (Jensen and Hirst, 1980).

Norms   No national norms have been reported. In a local setting, the 50th percentile for college men was a score of 40; the 50th percentile for college women, a score of 38 (Johnson and Nelson, 1979).

Comments   This test can be administered to an entire class of students in one class period.

Forward Bend of Trunk Test (Jensen and Hirst, 1980)

Test Objective   To measure the flexion of the trunk and hips.

Description   This test can be administered either on the floor or on a table. The examinee assumes a sitting position with feet against the wall, hips-width apart. The knees must remain straight throughout the test. The hands are placed palms down on the mat, next to the upper thighs. The examinee leans forward and downward as far as possible, reaching toward the heels of the feet (Figure 21-14). Measure the vertical distance from the suprasternal notch to the floor and record the distance to the nearest quarter of an inch.

Test Area   A small room with a smooth wall surface.

Equipment   Mat (preferred) and tape measure.

Scoring   The test score is the distance measured to the nearest quarter of an inch.

Validity   Not reported for this test.

Reliability   Not reported for this test.

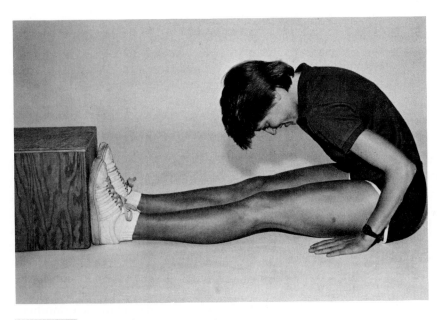

Figure 21-14   Forward bend of the trunk test.

Norms   None available. Setting up a table of norms for one's own students is advisable.

Comments   Keep in mind that lower scores (shorter distances) represent greater flexibility.

MEASURING POSTURE

Posture is defined as the alignment of the body and its segments at any one moment. Since the human body is a dynamic organism there is no single posture. Instead we can describe many static postures such as sitting posture and standing posture, and many dynamic postures such as walking posture and running posture. In addition, there are no absolute or correct postures. Individuals exhibit a rather wide range of functional posture and posture tends to change over the life span. However, experts agree that good posture minimizes stress to joints while poor posture increases stress on joints. Flexibility and balance are related to posture. Poor posture can lead to shortened muscle and potential loss of mobility, while increased flexibility can result in improved posture and reduced chronic pain such as in the lower back. Similarly, severe postural abnormalities can result in loss of balance and resultant postural adjustments.

Posture assessment in physical education primarily serves a monitoring function. Physical educators are in a unique position to identify persons at risk for common spinal deformities such as **lordosis** (excessive anterior curvature of the spine), **kyphosis** (excessive posterior curvature of the spine), and **scoliosis** (lateral curvature of the spine). The New York State posture rating test described below is a relatively easy test for such monitoring. An alternative posture test, which includes measures of dynamic posture, was developed at the University of Iowa and is described by Scott and French (1959) and Barrow and McGee (1968).

New York State Posture Rating Test (New York State Education Department, 1966)

Test Objective   To evaluate the posture of public school students in grades 4 through 12.

Description   The posture rating chart in Figure 21-15 is used to assess 13 areas of the body. Three profiles are shown for each area: the correct position, a slight deviation, and a pronounced deviation from the correct position. The examinee stands on a line in front of a screen. A plumb line is suspended just in front of the line. Another line is placed at right angles to the first line, extending 10 feet in front of the screen and perpendicular to it. The total distance from the screen to the line is 13 feet. The 13-foot point marks the location of the examiner. The first six areas of the body are rated while the examinee stands facing the screen, with the plumb line bisecting the back of the head, the spine, and the legs and feet. The remaining seven areas are rated with the examinee's left side to the screen. The plumb line should fall along the ear, shoulder, hip, knee, and ankle.

Test Area   An area 15 feet by 10 feet.

Equipment   Screen, rating chart, and plumb line.

Scoring   For the correct position, 5 points are scored; for a slight deviation, 3 points are scored; for a pronounced deviation, 1 point is scored. The total point value is the student's score. Space to record the student's posture ratings in grades 4 through 12 is provided on the chart.

Validity   Logical validity.

Reliability   Ranges from .93 to .98, for boys and girls at various grade levels.

Norms   Norms are reported by sex and grade in the original source.

Comments   This test has been in use in the physical education field for many years. It is fairly easy to administer, although prior training in using the chart is necessary. If a teacher administers the test, it can be quite time-consuming, since individual testing is necessary. For a rough screening of the students' posture, older students can be trained to use the chart. Having students test one another is an effective way of making them aware of good posture.

SUMMARY

Although it is evident that balance and flexibility are important attributes in the performance of a motor skill and the maintenance of good posture, the task-specific nature of each prohibits the use of one measure for each attribute. Because

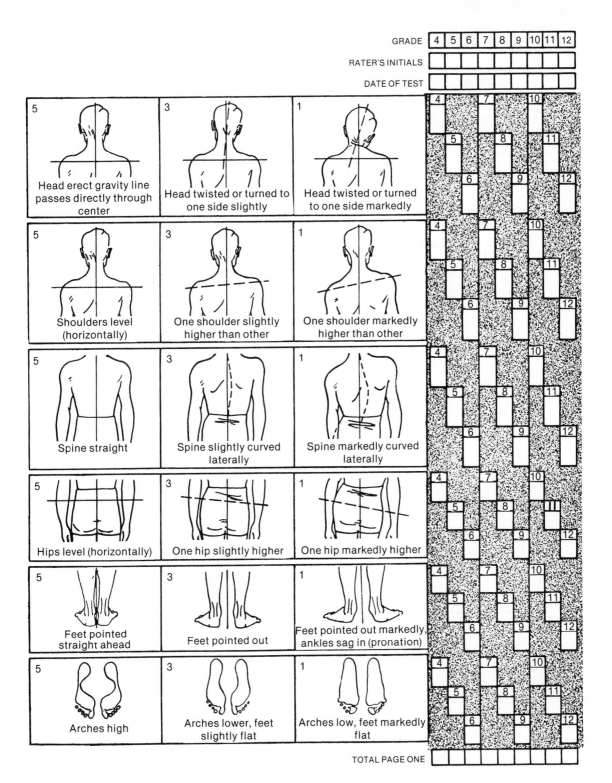

5	3	1
Head erect gravity line passes directly through center	Head twisted or turned to one side slightly	Head twisted or turned to one side markedly
Shoulders level (horizontally)	One shoulder slightly higher than other	One shoulder markedly higher than other
Spine straight	Spine slightly curved laterally	Spine markedly curved laterally
Hips level (horizontally)	One hip slightly higher	One hip markedly higher
Feet pointed straight ahead	Feet pointed out	Feet pointed out markedly, ankles sag in (pronation)
Arches high	Arches lower, feet slightly flat	Arches low, feet markedly flat

TOTAL PAGE ONE

Figure 21-15   Posture chart. *By permission of the State Education Department, State University of New York, Albany.*

Continued

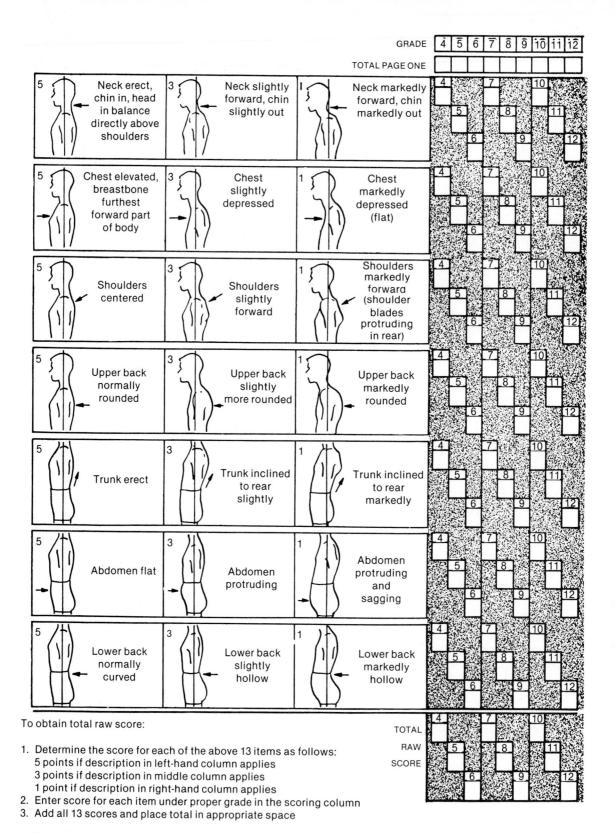

GRADE | 4 | 5 | 6 | 7 | 8 | 9 | 10 | 11 | 12

TOTAL PAGE ONE

| 5 | Neck erect, chin in, head in balance directly above shoulders | 3 | Neck slightly forward, chin slightly out | 1 | Neck markedly forward, chin markedly out |

| 5 | Chest elevated, breastbone furthest forward part of body | 3 | Chest slightly depressed | 1 | Chest markedly depressed (flat) |

| 5 | Shoulders centered | 3 | Shoulders slightly forward | 1 | Shoulders markedly forward (shoulder blades protruding in rear) |

| 5 | Upper back normally rounded | 3 | Upper back slightly more rounded | 1 | Upper back markedly rounded |

| 5 | Trunk erect | 3 | Trunk inclined to rear slightly | 1 | Trunk inclined to rear markedly |

| 5 | Abdomen flat | 3 | Abdomen protruding | 1 | Abdomen protruding and sagging |

| 5 | Lower back normally curved | 3 | Lower back slightly hollow | 1 | Lower back markedly hollow |

To obtain total raw score:

TOTAL RAW SCORE

1. Determine the score for each of the above 13 items as follows:
   5 points if description in left-hand column applies
   3 points if description in middle column applies
   1 point if description in right-hand column applies
2. Enter score for each item under proper grade in the scoring column
3. Add all 13 scores and place total in appropriate space

Figure 21-15 **cont'd.** *For legend see opposite page.*

an individual may be flexible in one joint and not in another, each joint must be measured separately to determine flexibility. The most valid measures are those requiring expensive equipment, trained personnel, and individual testing that is usually time-consuming. Practical tests of balance and flexibility have several drawbacks, but some of them can be useful to measure a specific segment of the body if carefully selected.

Learning Experiences

1. Administer the Stork stand test to at least 10 people. This can be done outside class, as long as you have a stopwatch or a watch with a secondhand. Plot the trials for each person. Does each person improve as the number of trials increases? Analyze this test in terms of logical validity.
2. Take the sit-and-reach test and the bent-knee sit-and-reach test in your class or laboratory session. Summarize the data for males and females separately, including the means and standard deviations or medians and interpercentile ranges. Plot a frequency distribution for each sex, then compute the correlation between the standard sit-and-reach test scores and the bent-knee test scores. For each gender compare the test scores for the two tests. Do the two tests tend to similarly rank-order the examinees? Do males and females tend to have the same degree of flexibility?
3. Select a partner and review the posture chart in Figure 21-10. Use the chart to evaluate the posture of at least two other people. Ask each one to assume his or her normal posture at first, then his or her best posture. Rate both postures independently. Discuss the ratings with your partner after the assessment has been completed. Where discrepancies exist between ratings, discuss the differences. If there are major differences between ratings, rate the same examinees again.
4. Imagine that you have developed a new test of low back flexibility. Describe how you would provide evidence for the validity and reliability of the test.

References

Barrow HM, McGee R. 1968. A practical approach to measurement in physical education. Philadelphia: Lea & Febiger.

Bass RI. 1939. An analysis of the components of semi-circular canal function and of static and dynamic balance. Research Quarterly, **10**:33–42.

Berg KO, Maki BE, Williams JI, Holliday PJ, Wood-Dauphinee SL. 1992. Clinical and laboratory measures of postural balance in an elderly population. Archives of Physical Medicine and Rehabilitation, **73**:1073–1080.

Berg KO, Wood-Dauphinee SL, Williams JI, Gayton D. 1989. Measuring balance in the elderly: Preliminary development of an instrument. Physiotherapy Canada, **41**:304–311.

Corbin CB, Linsey R. 1985. Concepts of physical fitness with laboratories. Dubuque, Iowa: Wm C Brown Group.

Cureton TK. 1941. Flexibility as an aspect of physical fitness. Research Quarterly **12**(Suppl):388–389.

Duesterhaus-Minor MA, Duesterhaus-Minor S. 1985. Patient evaluation methods for the health professional. Reston, Va: Reston Publishing.

Hoeger WW, Hopkins DR. 1992. A comparison of the sit and reach and the modified sit and reach in the measurement of flexibility in women. Research Quarterly for Exercise and Sport, **63**:191–195.

Jackson AW, Baker AA. 1986. The relationship of the sit and reach test to criterion measures of hamstring and back flexibility in young females. Research Quarterly for Exercise and Sport. **57**:183–186.

Jackson AW, Langford NJ. 1989. The criterion-related validity of the sit and reach test: Replication and extension of previous findings. Research Quarterly for Exercise and Sport, **60**:384–387.

Jensen CR, Hirst CC. 1980. Measurement in physical education and athletics. New York: Macmillan.

Johnson BL, Leach J. 1968. A modification of the Bass test of dynamic balance. Unpublished study. Commerce: East Texas State University.

Johnson BL, Nelson JK. 1979. Practical measurements for evaluation in physical education. Minneapolis: Burgess.

Kirkendall DR, Gruber JJ, Johnson RE. 1987. Measurement of evaluation for physical educators. Champaign, Ill: Human Kinetics.

Kraus H, Hirschland RP. 1954. Minimum muscular fitness tests in school children. Research Quarterly, **25**:177–188.

Leighton JR. 1942. A simple objective and reliable measure of flexibility. Research Quarterly, **13**:205–216.

Leighton JR. 1955. An instrument and technique for the measurement of range and joint motion. Archives of Physical Medicine and Rehabilitation, **36**:571–578.

Mathias S, Nayak USL. 1986. Balance in elderly patients: The "get-up and go" test. Archives of Physical Medicine and Rehabilitation, **67**:387–389.

New York State Education Department. 1966. New York State physical fitness test for boys and girls grades 4–12. New York: New York State Education Department.

Neurocom International. 1993. PRO Balance Master operator's manual. Neurocom International.

Plowman S, Corbin C. 1994. Muscular strength, endurance, and flexibility. In Morrow JR, Falls HB, Kohl HW III, eds. The Prudential *FITNESS*GRAM technical reference manual. Dallas: Cooper Institute for Aerobics Research.

Scott MG, French E. 1959. Measurement and evaluation in physical education. Dubuque, Iowa: Wm C Brown Group.

Sigerseth PO. 1978. Flexibility. In Montoye HJ, ed. An introduction to measurement in physical education and exercise science. Boston: Allyn & Bacon.

Annotated Readings

American Alliance for Health, Physical Education, Recreation and Dance. 1980. Health-related physical fitness test manual. Reston, Va: American Alliance for Health, Physical Education, Recreation and Dance.

Reviews exercises for improving the flexibility of the low back region; presents exercises in terms of progressive difficulty; can be used as an aid to diagnosis, as well as the basis for development of flexibility; provides excellent photographs of starting and exercise positions.

Corbin CB, Noble L. 1985. Flexibility—a major component of physical fitness. In Cundiff DE, ed. Implementation of health fitness exercise programs. Reston, Va: American Alliance for Health, Physical Education, Recreation and Dance.

Defines static and dynamic flexibility: discusses the joint specificity of flexibility; reviews measurement techniques; analyzes the relationship between flexibility and good health and flexibility and performance in sport; recommends techniques for improving flexibility.

Gerhardt JJ. 1993. Documentation of joint motion, ed 3. Portland, Ore: Omedic. Describes the technique for using goniometers, inclinometers, and calipers with special emphasis on the neutral zero measuring method.

Sigerseth PO. 1978. Flexibility. In Montoye HJ, ed. An introduction to measurement in physical education. Boston: Allyn & Bacon.

Required reading for physical educators interested in precise measures of flexibility at each joint; describes the use of the Leighton flexometer to measure 30 joint movements at the neck, trunk, shoulder joint, elbow joint, radial-ulnar wrist joint, hip joint, knee and ankle joints; recommends exercises for improving flexibility.

Simri U. 1974. Assessment procedures for human performance. In Larson LA, ed. Fitness, health, and work capacity: International standards for assessment. New York: Macmillan.

Presents international standards for measuring flexibility, recommends a test of forward flexion of the trunk (for a practical setting), as this movement is one of greatest importance in human movement; in a clinical setting, Simri recommends that the flexibility of each joint should be treated separately.

appendixes

Critical Values of the Correlation Coefficient

$df = n - 2$	$\alpha = .10$	.05	.02	.01
1	.988	.997	.9995	.9999
2	.900	.950	.980	.990
3	.805	.878	.934	.959
4	.729	.811	.882	.917
5	.669	.754	.833	.874
6	.622	.707	.789	.834
7	.582	.666	.750	.798
8	.549	.632	.716	.765
9	.521	.602	.685	.735
10	.497	.576	.658	.708
11	.476	.553	.634	.684
12	.458	.532	.612	.661
13	.441	.514	.592	.641
14	.426	.497	.574	.623
15	.412	.482	.558	.606
16	.400	.468	.542	.590
17	.389	.456	.528	.575
18	.378	.444	.516	.561
19	.369	.433	.503	.549
20	.360	.423	.492	.537
21	.352	.413	.482	.526
22	.344	.404	.472	.515

Continued

$df = n - 2$	$\alpha = .10$	.05	.02	.01
23	.337	.396	.462	.505
24	.330	.388	.453	.496
25	.323	.381	.445	.487
26	.317	.374	.437	.479
27	.311	.367	.430	.471
28	.306	.361	.423	.463
29	.301	.355	.416	.456
30	.296	.349	.409	.449
35	.275	.325	.381	.418
40	.257	.304	.358	.393
45	.243	.288	.338	.372
50	.231	.273	.322	.354
60	.211	.250	.295	.325
70	.195	.232	.274	.302
80	.183	.217	.256	.283
90	.173	.205	.242	.267
100	.164	.195	.230	.254

Units of Measure

Distance	
1 inch	= 2.54 centimeters (cm) = 25.4 millimeters (mm) = 0.0254 meters (m)
1 foot	= 30.48 cm = 304.8 mm = 0.304 m
1 yard	= 91.44 cm = 914.4 mm = 0.914 m
1 mile	= 5280 ft = 1760 yd = 1609.35 m = 1.61 kilometers (km)
1 cm	= 0.3937 in
1 m	= 39.37 in = 3.28 ft = 1.09 yd = 100 cm = 1000 mm
1 km	= 0.62 mi = 1000 m
Weights	
1 ounce (oz)	= 0.0625 lb = 28.35 grams (g) = 0.028 kg
1 pound (lb)	= 16 oz = 454 g = 0.454 kg
1 g	= 0.035 oz = 0.0022 lb = 0.001 kg
1 kg	= 35.27 oz = 2.2 lb = 1000 g

The F Distribution

$\alpha = .05$									
$V_1 = df$ of numerator $V_2 = df$ of denominator									

V_2 \ V_1	1	2	3	4	5	6	7	8	9	10
1	161.4	199.5	215.7	224.6	230.2	234.0	236.8	238.9	240.5	241.9
2	18.51	19.00	19.16	19.25	19.30	19.33	19.35	19.37	19.38	19.40
3	10.13	9.55	9.28	9.12	9.01	8.94	8.89	8.85	8.81	8.79
4	7.71	6.94	6.59	6.39	6.26	6.16	6.09	6.04	6.00	5.96
5	6.61	5.79	5.41	5.19	5.05	4.95	4.88	4.82	4.77	4.74
6	5.99	5.14	4.76	4.53	4.39	4.28	4.21	4.15	4.10	4.06
7	5.59	4.74	4.35	4.12	3.97	3.87	3.79	3.73	3.68	3.64
8	5.32	4.46	4.07	3.84	3.69	3.58	3.50	3.44	3.39	3.35
9	5.12	4.26	3.86	3.63	3.48	3.37	3.29	3.23	3.18	3.14
10	4.96	4.10	3.71	3.48	3.33	3.22	3.14	3.07	3.20	2.98
11	4.84	3.98	3.59	3.36	3.20	3.09	3.01	2.95	2.90	2.85
12	4.75	3.89	3.49	3.26	3.11	3.00	2.91	2.85	2.80	2.75
13	4.67	3.81	3.41	3.18	3.03	2.92	2.83	2.77	2.71	2.67
14	4.60	3.74	3.34	3.11	2.96	2.85	2.76	2.70	2.65	2.60
15	4.54	3.68	3.29	3.06	2.90	2.79	2.71	2.64	2.59	2.54
16	4.49	3.63	3.24	3.01	2.85	2.74	2.66	2.59	2.54	2.49
17	4.45	3.59	3.20	2.96	2.81	2.70	2.61	2.55	2.49	2.45
18	4.41	3.55	3.16	2.93	2.77	2.66	2.58	2.51	2.46	2.41
19	4.38	3.52	3.13	2.90	2.74	2.63	2.54	2.48	2.42	2.38
20	4.35	3.49	3.10	2.87	2.71	2.60	2.51	2.45	2.39	2.35
21	4.32	3.47	3.07	2.84	2.68	2.57	2.49	2.42	2.37	2.32
22	4.30	3.44	3.05	2.82	2.66	2.55	2.46	2.40	2.34	2.30

$\alpha = .05$

$V_1 = df$ of numerator $V_2 = df$ of denominator

V_2 \ V_1	1	2	3	4	5	6	7	8	9	10
23	4.28	3.42	3.03	2.80	2.64	2.53	2.44	2.37	2.32	2.27
24	4.26	3.40	3.01	2.78	2.62	2.51	2.42	2.36	2.30	2.25
25	4.24	3.39	2.99	2.76	2.60	2.49	2.40	2.34	2.28	2.24
26	4.23	3.37	2.98	2.74	2.59	2.47	2.39	2.32	2.27	2.22
27	4.21	3.35	2.96	2.73	2.57	2.46	2.37	2.31	2.25	2.20
28	4.20	3.34	2.95	2.71	2.56	2.45	2.36	2.29	2.24	2.19
29	4.18	3.33	2.93	2.70	2.55	2.43	2.35	2.28	2.22	2.18
30	4.17	3.32	2.92	2.69	2.53	2.42	2.33	2.27	2.21	2.16
40	4.08	3.23	2.84	2.61	2.45	2.34	2.25	2.18	2.12	2.08
60	4.00	3.15	2.76	2.53	2.37	2.25	2.17	2.10	2.04	1.99
120	3.92	3.07	2.68	2.45	2.29	2.17	2.09	2.02	1.96	1.91
∞	3.84	3.00	2.60	2.37	2.21	2.10	2.01	1.94	1.88	1.83

Pearson ES and Hartley HO. Biometrika tables for statisticians, New York: Cambridge University Press, 1966. Vol. 1. By permission of the authors and publisher.

$\alpha = .05$

V_2 \ V_1	12	15	20	24	30	40	60	120	∞
1	243.9	245.9	248.0	249.1	250.1	251.1	252.2	253.3	254.3
2	19.41	19.43	19.45	19.45	19.46	19.47	19.48	19.49	19.50
3	8.74	8.70	8.66	8.64	8.62	8.59	8.57	8.55	8.53
4	5.91	5.86	5.80	5.77	5.75	5.72	5.69	5.66	5.63
5	4.68	4.62	4.56	4.53	4.50	4.46	4.43	4.40	4.36
6	4.00	3.94	3.87	3.84	3.81	3.77	3.74	3.70	3.67
7	3.57	3.51	3.44	3.41	3.38	3.34	3.30	3.27	3.23
8	3.28	3.22	3.15	3.12	3.08	3.04	3.01	2.97	2.93
9	3.07	3.01	2.94	2.90	2.86	2.83	2.79	2.75	2.71
10	2.91	2.85	2.77	2.74	2.70	2.66	2.62	2.58	2.54
11	2.79	2.72	2.65	2.61	2.57	2.53	2.49	2.45	2.40

Continued

$\alpha = .05$									
V_1 V_2	12	15	20	24	30	40	60	120	∞
12	2.69	2.62	2.54	2.51	2.47	2.43	2.38	2.34	2.30
13	2.60	2.53	2.46	2.42	2.38	2.34	2.30	2.25	2.21
14	2.53	2.46	2.39	2.35	2.31	2.27	2.22	2.18	2.13
15	2.48	2.40	2.33	2.29	2.25	2.20	2.16	2.11	2.07
16	2.42	2.35	2.28	2.24	2.19	2.15	2.11	2.06	2.01
17	2.38	2.31	2.23	2.19	2.15	2.10	2.06	2.01	1.96
18	2.34	2.27	2.19	2.15	2.11	2.06	2.02	1.97	1.92
19	2.31	2.23	2.16	2.11	2.07	2.03	1.98	1.93	1.88
20	2.28	2.20	2.12	2.08	2.04	1.99	1.95	1.90	1.84
21	2.25	2.18	2.10	2.05	2.01	1.96	1.92	1.87	1.81
22	2.23	2.15	2.07	2.03	1.98	1.94	1.89	1.84	1.78
23	2.20	2.13	2.05	2.01	1.96	1.91	1.86	1.81	1.76
24	2.18	2.11	2.03	1.98	1.94	1.89	1.84	1.79	1.73
25	2.16	2.09	2.01	1.96	1.92	1.87	1.82	1.77	1.71
26	2.15	2.07	1.99	1.95	1.90	1.85	1.80	1.75	1.69
27	2.13	2.06	1.97	1.93	1.88	1.84	1.79	1.73	1.67
28	2.12	2.04	1.96	1.91	1.87	1.82	1.77	1.71	1.65
29	2.10	2.03	1.94	1.90	1.85	1.81	1.75	1.70	1.64
30	2.09	2.01	1.93	1.89	1.84	1.79	1.74	1.68	1.62
40	2.00	1.92	1.84	1.79	1.74	1.69	1.64	1.58	1.51
60	1.92	1.84	1.75	1.70	1.65	1.59	1.53	1.47	1.39
120	1.83	1.75	1.66	1.61	1.55	1.50	1.43	1.35	1.25
∞	1.75	1.67	1.57	1.52	1.46	1.39	1.32	1.22	1.00

$\alpha = .01$									
V_1 V_2	1	2	3	4	5	6	7	8	9	10
1	4052	4999.5	5403	5652	5764	5859	5928	5981	6022	6056
2	98.50	99.00	99.17	99.25	99.30	99.33	99.36	99.37	99.39	99.40
3	34.12	30.82	29.46	28.71	28.24	27.91	27.67	27.49	27.35	27.23

V_1 V_2	1	2	3	4	5	6	7	8	9	10
					$\alpha = .01$					
4	21.20	18.00	16.69	15.98	15.52	15.21	14.98	14.80	14.66	14.55
5	16.26	13.27	12.06	11.39	10.97	10.67	10.46	10.29	10.16	10.05
6	13.75	10.92	9.78	9.15	8.75	8.47	8.26	8.10	7.98	7.87
7	12.25	9.55	8.45	7.85	7.46	7.19	6.99	6.84	6.72	6.62
8	11.26	8.65	7.59	7.01	6.63	6.37	6.18	6.03	5.91	5.81
9	10.56	8.02	6.99	6.42	6.06	5.80	5.61	5.47	5.35	5.26
10	10.04	7.56	6.55	5.99	5.64	5.39	5.20	5.06	4.94	4.85
11	9.65	7.21	6.22	5.67	5.32	5.07	4.89	4.74	4.63	4.54
12	9.33	6.93	5.95	5.41	5.06	4.82	4.64	4.50	4.39	4.30
13	9.07	6.70	5.74	5.21	4.86	4.62	4.44	4.30	4.19	4.10
14	8.86	6.51	5.56	5.04	4.69	4.46	4.28	4.14	4.03	3.94
15	8.68	6.36	5.42	4.89	4.56	4.32	4.14	4.00	3.89	3.80
16	8.53	6.23	5.29	4.77	4.44	4.20	4.03	3.89	3.78	3.69
17	8.40	6.11	5.18	4.67	4.34	4.10	3.93	3.79	3.68	3.59
18	8.29	6.01	5.09	4.58	4.25	4.01	3.84	3.71	3.60	3.51
19	8.18	5.93	5.01	4.50	4.17	3.94	3.77	3.63	3.52	3.43
20	8.10	5.85	4.94	4.43	4.10	3.87	3.70	3.56	3.46	3.37
21	8.02	5.78	4.87	4.37	4.04	3.81	3.64	3.51	3.40	3.31
22	7.95	5.72	4.82	4.31	3.99	3.76	3.59	3.45	3.35	3.26
23	7.88	5.66	4.76	4.26	3.94	3.71	3.54	3.41	3.30	3.21
24	7.82	5.61	4.72	4.22	3.90	3.67	3.50	3.36	3.26	3.17
25	7.77	5.57	4.68	4.18	3.85	3.63	3.46	3.32	3.22	3.13
26	7.72	5.53	4.64	4.14	3.82	3.59	3.42	3.29	3.18	3.09
27	7.68	5.49	4.60	4.11	3.78	3.56	3.39	3.26	3.15	3.06
28	7.64	5.45	4.57	4.07	3.75	3.53	3.36	3.23	3.12	3.03
29	7.60	5.42	4.54	4.04	3.73	3.50	3.33	3.20	3.09	3.00
30	7.56	5.39	4.51	4.02	3.70	3.47	3.30	3.17	3.07	2.98
40	7.31	5.18	4.31	3.83	3.51	3.29	3.12	2.99	2.89	2.80
60	7.08	4.98	4.13	3.65	3.34	3.12	2.95	2.82	2.72	2.63
120	6.85	4.79	3.95	3.48	3.17	2.96	2.79	2.66	2.56	2.47
∞	6.63	4.61	3.78	3.32	3.02	2.80	2.64	2.51	2.41	2.32

					$\alpha = .01$				
V_1 / V_2	12	15	20	24	30	40	60	120	∞
1	6106	6157	6209	6235	6261	6287	6313	6339	6366
2	99.42	99.43	99.45	99.46	99.47	99.47	99.48	99.49	99.50
3	27.05	26.87	26.69	26.60	26.50	26.41	26.32	26.22	26.13
4	14.37	14.20	14.02	13.93	13.84	13.75	13.65	13.56	13.46
5	9.89	9.72	9.55	9.47	9.38	9.29	9.20	9.11	9.02
6	7.72	7.56	7.40	7.31	7.23	7.14	7.06	6.97	6.88
7	6.47	6.31	6.16	6.07	5.99	5.91	5.82	5.74	5.65
8	5.67	5.52	5.36	5.28	5.20	5.12	5.03	4.95	4.86
9	5.11	4.96	4.81	4.73	4.65	4.57	4.48	4.40	4.31
10	4.71	4.56	4.41	4.33	4.25	4.17	4.08	4.00	3.91
11	4.40	4.25	4.10	4.02	3.94	3.86	3.78	3.69	3.60
12	4.16	4.01	3.86	3.78	3.70	3.62	3.54	3.45	3.36
13	3.96	3.82	3.66	3.59	3.51	3.43	3.34	3.25	3.17
14	3.80	3.66	3.51	3.43	3.35	3.27	3.18	3.09	3.00
15	3.67	3.52	3.37	3.29	3.21	3.13	3.05	2.96	2.87
16	3.55	3.41	3.26	3.18	3.10	3.02	2.93	2.84	2.75
17	3.46	3.31	3.16	3.08	3.00	2.92	2.83	2.75	2.65
18	3.37	3.23	3.08	3.00	2.92	2.84	2.75	2.66	2.57
19	3.30	3.15	3.00	2.92	2.84	2.76	2.67	2.58	2.49
20	3.23	3.09	2.94	2.86	2.78	2.69	2.61	2.52	2.42
21	3.17	3.03	2.88	2.80	2.72	2.64	2.55	2.46	2.36
22	3.12	2.98	2.83	2.75	2.67	2.58	2.50	2.40	2.31
23	3.07	2.93	2.78	2.70	2.62	2.54	2.45	2.35	2.26
24	3.03	2.89	2.74	2.66	2.58	2.49	2.40	2.31	2.21
25	2.99	2.85	2.70	2.62	2.54	2.45	2.36	2.27	2.17
26	2.96	2.81	2.66	2.58	2.50	2.42	2.33	2.23	2.13
27	2.93	2.78	2.63	2.55	2.47	2.38	2.29	2.20	2.10
28	2.90	2.75	2.60	2.52	2.44	2.35	2.26	2.17	2.06
29	2.87	2.73	2.57	2.49	2.41	2.33	2.23	2.14	2.03
30	2.84	2.70	2.55	2.47	2.39	2.30	2.21	2.11	2.01

				$\alpha = .01$					
V_1 V_2	12	15	20	24	30	40	60	120	∞
40	2.66	2.52	2.37	2.29	2.20	2.11	2.02	1.92	1.80
60	2.50	2.35	2.20	2.12	2.03	1.94	1.84	1.73	1.60
120	2.34	2.19	2.03	1.95	1.86	1.76	1.66	1.53	1.38
∞	2.18	2.04	1.88	1.79	1.70	1.59	1.47	1.32	1.00

CRITICAL VALUES OF t

	Level of Significance for One-Tailed Test					
df	.10	.05	.025	.01	.005	.0005
	Level of Significance for Two-Tailed Test					
	.20	.10	.05	.02	.01	.001
1	3.078	6.314	12.706	31.821	63.657	636.619
2	1.886	2.920	4.303	6.965	9.925	31.598
3	1.638	2.353	3.182	4.541	5.481	12.941
4	1.533	2.132	2.776	3.747	4.604	8.610
5	1.476	2.015	2.571	3.365	4.032	6.859
6	1.440	1.943	2.447	3.143	3.707	5.959
7	1.415	1.895	2.365	2.998	3.499	5.405
8	1.397	1.860	2.306	2.896	3.355	5.041
9	1.383	1.833	2.262	2.821	3.250	4.781
10	1.372	1.812	2.228	2.764	3.169	4.587
11	1.363	1.796	2.201	2.718	3.106	4.437
12	1.356	1.782	2.179	2.681	3.055	4.318
13	1.350	1.771	2.160	2.650	3.012	4.221
14	1.345	1.761	2.145	2.624	2.977	4.140
15	1.341	1.753	2.131	2.602	2.947	4.073
16	1.337	1.746	2.120	2.583	2.921	4.015
17	1.333	1.740	2.110	2.567	2.898	3.965
18	1.330	1.734	2.101	2.552	2.878	3.992
19	1.328	1.729	2.093	2.539	2.861	3.883

Continued

df	Level of Significance for One-Tailed Test					
	.10	.05	.025	.01	.005	.0005
	Level of Significance for Two-Tailed Test					
	.20	.10	.05	.02	.01	.001
20	1.325	1.725	2.086	2.528	2.845	3.850
21	1.323	1.721	2.080	2.518	2.831	3.819
22	1.321	1.717	2.074	2.508	2.819	3.792
23	1.319	1.714	2.069	2.500	2.807	3.767
24	1.318	1.711	2.064	2.492	2.797	3.745
25	1.316	1.708	2.060	2.485	2.787	3.725
26	1.315	1.706	2.056	2.479	2.779	3.707
27	1.314	1.703	2.052	2.473	2.771	3.690
28	1.313	1.701	2.048	2.467	2.763	3.674
29	1.311	1.699	2.045	2.462	2.756	3.659
30	1.310	1.697	2.042	2.457	2.750	3.646
40	1.303	1.684	2.021	2.423	2.704	3.551
60	1.296	1.671	2.000	2.390	2.660	3.460
120	1.289	1.658	1.980	2.358	2.617	3.373
	1.282	1.645	1.960	2.326	2.576	3.291

Abridged from Table III of Fisher. Statistical methods for research workers, *published by Oliver and Boyd, Ltd., Edinburgh. By permission of the author and the pubisher.*

Sources for Selected Sports Skills Tests

Archery

American Association for Health, Physical Education and Recreation. 1967. Archery skills test manual. Washington, DC: American Association for Health, Physical Education and Recreation.

Bohn RW. 1962. An achievement test in archery. Master's thesis, University of Wisconsin, Madison.

Hyde EI. 1937. An achievement scale in archery. Research Quarterly, **8**:109–116.

Shifflett B, Schuman B. 1982. A criterion-referenced test for archery. Research Quarterly for Exercise and Sport, **53**:330–335.

Zabick RM, Jackson AS. 1969. Reliability of archery achievement. Research Quarterly, **40**:254–255.

Badminton

French E, Stalter E. 1949. Study of skill tests in badminton for college women. Research Quarterly, **20**:257–272.

Greiner MR. 1964. Construction of a short serve test for beginning badminton players. Master's thesis, University of Wisconsin, Madison. (Microcard PE 670, University of Oregon, Eugene.)

Hale PA. 1970. Construction of a long serve test for beginning badminton players (singles). Master's thesis, University of Wisconsin, Madison. (Microcard PE 1133, University of Oregon, Eugene.)

Hicks JV. 1967. The construction and evaluation of a battery of five badminton skill tests. Doctoral dissertation, Texas Women's University, Denton, Tex.

Johnson BL, Nelson JK. 1979. Badminton smash test. In Practical measurements for evaluation in physical education. Minneapolis: Burgess Co.

Lockhart A, McPherson FA. 1949. The development of a test of badminton playing ability. Research Quarterly, **20**:402–405.

McDonald ED. 1968. The development of a skill test for the badminton high clear. Master's thesis, Southern Illinois University, Carbondale, Ill. (Microcard PE 1083, University of Oregon, Eugene.)

Miller FA. 1951. A badminton wall volley test. Research Quarterly, **22**:208–213.

Poole J, Nelson J. 1970. Construction of a badminton skills test battery. Unpublished manuscript, Louisiana State University, Baton Rouge.

Scott MG. 1941. Achievement examinations in badminton. Research Quarterly, **12**:242–253.

Scott MG, Fox M. 1959. Long serve test. In Measurement and evaluation in physical education. Dubuque, Iowa: Wm C Brown Group.

Thorpe J, West C. 1969. A test game sense in badminton. Perceptual and Motor Skills, **28**:159–169.

Baseball

Kelson RE. 1953. Baseball classification plan for boys. Research Quarterly, **24**:304–309.

Rodgers EG, Heath ML. 1931. An experiment in the use of knowledge and skill tests in playground baseball. Research Quarterly, **2**:113–131.

Basketball

Barrow HM. 1959. Basketball skill test. The Physical Educator, **16**:26.

Dyer JT, Schurig JC, Apgar SL. 1939. A basketball motor ability test for college women and secondary school girls. Research Quarterly, **10**:128–147.

Edgren HD. 1932. An experiment in the testing of ability and progress in basketball. Research Quarterly, **3**:159–171.

Glassow RB, Colvin V, Schwartz MM. 1938. Studies measuring basketball playing ability of college women. Research Quarterly, **9**:60–68.

Hopkins DR. 1977. Factor analysis of selected basketball skill test. Research Quarterly, **48**:535–540.

Hopkins DR, Shick J, Plack JJ. 1984. Basketball for boys and girls: skills test manual. Reston, Va.: American Alliance for Health, Physical Education, Recreation and Dance.

Johnson LW. 1976. Objective tests in basketball for high school boys. In Clarke HH, ed. Application of measurement to health and physical education. Englewood Cliffs, NJ: Prentice-Hall.

Kay HK. 1966. A statistical analysis of the profile technique for the evaluation of competitive basketball performance. Master's thesis, University of Alberta, Edmonton, Canada.

Knox RK. 1947. Basketball ability tests. Scholastic Coach, **17**:45.

Lambert AT. 1969. A basketball skill test for college women. Master's thesis, University of North Carolina, Greensboro.

Latchaw M. 1954. Measuring selected motor skills in fourth, fifth, and sixth grades. Research Quarterly, **25**:439–499.

Lehsten N. 1948. A measure of basketball skills in high school boys. The Physical Educator, **4**:103–106.

Leilich A. 1980. Leilich basketball test. In Barrow HM, McGee R, eds. A practical approach to measurement in physical education, ed 3, Philadelphia: Lea & Febiger.

Miller WK. 1954. Achievement levels in basketball skills for women physical education majors. Research Quarterly, **25**:450–455.

Schwartz H. 1937. Knowledge and achievement tests in girls' basketball on the senior high school level. Research Quarterly, **8**:152–156.

Stroup F. 1955. Game results as a criterion for validating basketball skill tests. Research Quarterly, **26**:353–357.

Thornes MB. 1963. An analysis of a basketball shooting test and its relation to other basketball skill tests. Master's thesis, University of Wisconsin, Madison. (Microcard PE 694, University of Oregon, Eugene.)

Young G, Moser H. 1934. A short battery of tests to measure playing ability in women's basketball. Research Quarterly, **5**:3–23.

Bowling

Martin JL. 1960. Bowling norms for college men and women. Research Quarterly, **31**:113–116.

Martin J, Koegh J. 1964. Bowling norms for college students in elective physical education classes. Research Quarterly, **35**:325–327.

Olson JK, Liba MR. 1967. A device for evaluating spot bowling ability. Research Quarterly, **38**:193–210.

Phillips M, Summers D. 1950. Bowling norms and learning curves for college women. Research Quarterly, **21**:377–385.

Schunk C. 1969. Test questions for bowling. Philadelphia: WB Saunders.

Fencing

Bowar MG. 1961. A test of general fencing ability. Master's thesis, University of Southern California, Los Angeles.

Cooper CK. 1968. The development of a fencing skill test for measuring achievement of beginning collegiate women fencers in using the advance, beat, and lunge. Master's thesis, Western Illinois University, Macomb.

Fein JT. 1964. Construction of skill tests for beginning collegiate women fencers. Master's thesis, University of Iowa, Iowa City.

Safrit MJ. 1962. Construction of a skill test for beginning fencers. Master's thesis, University of Wisconsin, Madison.

Schultz JK. 1940. Construction of an achievement scale in fencing for women. Master's thesis, University of Washington, Seattle.

Wyrick W. 1958. A comparison of the effectiveness of two methods of teaching beginning fencing to college women. Master's thesis, Woman's College of the University of North Carolina, Greensboro.

Field Hockey

Chapman NL. 1982. Chapman ball control test—field hockey. Research Quarterly for Exercise and Sport, **53**:239–242.

Friedel JW. 1956. The development of a field hockey skill test for high school girls. Master's thesis, Illinois State University, Normal. (Microcard PE 289, University of Oregon, Eugene.)

Illner JA. 1968. The construction and validation of a skill test for the drive in field hockey. Master's thesis, Southern Illinois University, Carbondale. (Microcard PE 1075, University of Oregon, Eugene.)

Perry EL. 1969. An investigation of field hockey skill tests for college women. Master's thesis, Pennsylvania State University, University Park.

Schmithals M, French E. 1940. Achievement tests in field hockey for college women. Research Quarterly, **11**:84–92.

Strait CJ. 1960. The construction and evaluation of a field hockey skills test. Master's thesis, Smith College, Northampton, Mass.

Football

American Association for Health, Physical Education and Recreation. 1960. Football skills test manual. Washington, DC: American Association for Health, Physical Education and Recreation.

Borleske SE. 1937. Achievement of college men in touch football. In Cozens FW, ed. Ninth annual report of the committee on curriculum research of the college physical education association. Research Quarterly, **8**:73–78.

McElroy HN. 1938. A report on some experimentation with a skill test. Research Quarterly, **9**:83–88.

Golf

Brown HS. 1969. A test battery for evaluating golf skills. Texas Association for Health, Physical Education and Recreation Journal, October–November, 28–29.

Clevett MA. 1931. An experiment in teaching methods of golf. Research Quarterly, **2**:104–112.

Cochrane JF. 1960. The construction of indoor golf skills test as a measure of golfing ability. Master's thesis, University of Minnesota, Minneapolis.

Cotten D, Thomas JR, Plaster T. 1972. A plastic ball test for golf iron skill. Presented at the American Association for Health, Physical Education and Recreation convention, Houston, March 23, 1972.

McKee ME. 1950. A test for the full swinging shot in golf. Research Quarterly, **21**:40–46.

Nelson JK. 1979. An achievement test in golf. In Johnson BL, Nelson JK, eds. Practical measurements for evaluation in physical education. Minneapolis: Burgess.

Shick J, Berg N. 1983. Indoor golf skill test for junior high boys. Research Quarterly for Exercise and Sport, **54**:75–78.

Vanderhoof ER. 1956. Beginning golf achievement tests. Master's thesis, State University of Iowa, Iowa City. (Microcard PE 306, University of Oregon, Eugene.)

Watts H. 1942. Construction and evaluation of a target on testing the approach shot in golf. Master's thesis, University of Wisconsin, Madison.

West C, Thorpe J. 1968. Construction and validation of an eight-iron approach test. Research Quarterly, **39**:1115–1120.

Gymnastics

Bowers CO. 1965. Gymnastics skill test for beginning to low intermediate girls and women. Master's thesis, Ohio State University, Columbus. (Microcard PE 734, University of Oregon, Eugene.)

Faulkner J, Loken N. 1962. Objectivity of judging at the national collegiate athletic association gymnastic meet: A ten-year follow-up study. Research Quarterly, **33**:485–486.

Handball

Cornish C. 1949. A study of measurement of ability in handball. Research Quarterly, **20**:215–222.

Griffith MA. 1960. An objective method of evaluating ability in handball singles. Master's thesis, Ohio State University, Columbus.

Montoye HJ, Brotzmann J. 1951. An investigation of the validity of using the results of a doubles tournament as a measure of handball ability. Research Quarterly, **22**:214–218.

Pennington GG, et al. (1967). A measure of handball ability. Research Quarterly, **38**:247–253.

Ice Hockey

Merrifield HH, Walford GA. 1969. Battery of ice hockey skill tests. Research Quarterly, **40**:146–152.

Ice Skating

Carriere DL. 1969. An objective figure skating test for use in beginning classes. Master's thesis, University of Illinois, Urbana.

Leaming TW. 1959. A measure of endurance of young speed skaters. Master's thesis, University of Illinois, Urbana.

Recknagel D. 1945. A test for beginners in skating. Journal of Health and Physical Education, **26**:91–92.

Lacrosse

Hodges CV. 1967. Construction of an objective knowledge test and skill tests in lacrosse for college women. Master's thesis, University of North Carolina, Greensboro. (Microcard PE 1974, University of Oregon, Eugene.)

Lutze MC. 1963. Achievement tests in beginning lacrosse for women. Master's thesis, State University of Iowa, Iowa City.

Wilke BJ. 1967. Achievement tests for selected lacrosse skills of college women. Master's thesis, University of North Carolina, Greensboro.

Racquetball

Hensley LD, East WB, Stillwell JL. 1979. A racquetball skills test. Research Quarterly, **50**:114–118.

Karpman M, Isaacs LD. 1979. An improved racquetball skills test. Research Quarterly, **50**:526–527.

Skiing

Rogers HM. 1960. Construction of objectively scored skill tests for beginning skiers. Master's thesis, University of Colorado, Boulder.

Wolfe JE, Merrifield HH. 1971. Predictability of beginning skiing success from basic skill tests in college age females. Presented at the National American Association for Health, Physical Education and Recreation convention, Detroit, April 6, 1971.

Soccer

Bailey CI, Teller FL. 1969. Test questions for soccer. Philadelphia: WB Saunders.

Bontz J. 1942. An experiment in the construction of a test for measuring ability in some of the fundamental skills used by fifth and sixth grade children in soccer. Master's thesis, State University of Iowa, Iowa City.

Heath ML, Rodgers EG. 1932. A study in the use of knowledge and skill tests in soccer. Research Quarterly, **3**:33–43.

Johnson JR. 1963. The development of a single-item test as a measure of soccer skill. Microcarded master's thesis, University of British Columbia, Vancouver.

McDonald LG. 1951. The construction of a kicking skill test as an index of general soccer ability. Master's thesis, Springfield College, Springfield, Mass.

McElroy HN. 1938. A report on some experimentation with a skill test. Research Quarterly, **9**:82–88.

Mitchell JR. 1980. Mitchell modification of the McDonald soccer skill test. In Barrow HM, McGee R, eds. A practical approach to measurement in physical education, ed 3. Philadelphia: Lea & Febiger.

Schaufele EF. 1980. Schaufele soccer volleying test. In Barrow HM, McGee R, eds. A practical approach to measurement in physical education, ed 3. Philadelphia: Lea & Febiger.

Tomlinson R. 1964. Soccer skill test. Soccer-speedball guide—July 1964–July 1966. Washington, DC: Division of Girls' and Women's Sports, American Association for Health, Physical Education and Recreation.

Warner GFH. 1950. Warner soccer test. Newsletter of the National Soccer Coaches Association of America, **6**:13–22.

Whitney AH, Chapin H. 1946. Soccer skill testing for girls. Soccer-speedball guide—July 1946–July 1948. Washington DC: National Section on Women's Athletics, American Association for Health, Physical Education and Recreation.

Softball

American Association for Health, Physical Education and Recreation. 1967. Softball skills test manual for boys. Washington, DC: American Association for Health, Physical Education and Recreation.

American Association for Health, Physical Education and Recreation. 1967. Softball skills test manual for girls. Washington, DC: American Association for Health, Physical Education and Recreation.

Broer MR. 1958. Reliability of certain skill tests for junior high school girls. Research Quarterly, **29**:139–143.

Davis R. 1959. The development of an objective softball batting test for college women. In Scott MG, French E, eds. Measurement and evaluation in physical education. Dubuque, Iowa: Wm C Brown Group.

Dexter G. 1957. Checklist for rating softball batting skills. Teachers guide to physical education for girls in high school. Sacramento, Calif.: California State Department of Education.

Elrod JM. 1969. Construction of a softball skill test battery for high school boys, Unpublished master's thesis, Louisiana State University, Baton Rouge.

Fox, MG, Young OG. 1954. A test of softball batting ability. Research Quarterly, **25**:26–27.

Fringer MN. 1980. Fringer softball battery. In Barrow HM, McGee R, eds. A practical approach to measurement in physical education, ed 2. Philadelphia: Lea & Febiger.

Kehtel CH. 1958. The development of a test to measure the ability of a softball player to field a ground ball and successfully throw it at a target. Master's thesis, University of Colorado, Boulder.

O'Donnell DJ. 1960. Validation of softball skill tests for high school girls. Master's thesis, Indiana University, Bloomington.

Research Committee, Central Association for Physical Education of College Women. 1959. Fielding test. In Scott MG, French E, eds. Measurement and evaluation in physical education. Dubuque, Iowa: Wm C Brown Group.

Rikle RE, editor. 1991. Softball skills test manual. Reston, Va: American Alliance for Health, Physical Education, Recreation and Dance.

Safrit MJ. 1974. Wisconsin softball pitching test: Summative evaluation. Softball guide: January, 1974–January, 1976. Washington, DC: Division of Girls' and Women's Sports, American Association for Health, Physical Education and Recreation.

Safrit MJ, Pavis A. 1969. Overarm throw skill testing. In Felshin J, O'Brien C, eds. Selected softball articles. Washington, DC: Division of Girls' and Women's Sports, American Association for Health, Physical Education and Recreation.

Scott MG, French E. 1959. Softball repeated throws test. In Scott MG, French E, eds. Measurement and evaluation in physical education. Dubuque, Iowa: Wm C Brown Group.

Shick J. 1970. Battery of defensive softball skills tests for college women. Research Quarterly, **41**:82–87.

Sopa A. 1967. Construction of an indoor batting skills test for junior high school girls. Master's thesis, University of Wisconsin, Madison.

Thomas J. 1947. Skill tests. In Softball-volleyball guide—July 1947–July 1949. Washington, DC: National Section on Women's Athletics, American Association for Health, Physical Education and Recreation.

Speedball

Buchanan RE. 1942. A study of achievement tests in speedball for high school girls. Master's thesis, State University of Iowa, Iowa City.

Smith G. 1980. Speedball skills test for college women. In Barrow HM, McGee R, eds. A practical approach to measurement in physical education, ed 3. Philadelphia: Lea & Febiger.

Stunts and Tumbling

Cotteral B, Cotteral D. 1936. Scale for judging quality of performance in stunts and tumbling. The teaching of stunts and tumbling. New York: Ronald Press.

Edwards VM. 1969. Test questions for tumbling. Philadelphia: WB Saunders.

Swimming and Diving

Bennett LM. 1942. A test of diving for use in beginning classes. Research Quarterly, **13**:109–115.

Chapman PA. 1965. A comparison of three methods of measuring swimming stroke proficiency. Master's thesis, University of Wisconsin, Madison. (Microcard PE 738, University of Oregon, Eugene.)

Fox MG. 1957. Swimming power test. Research Quarterly, **28**:233–237.

Fried CR. 1983. An examination of the test characteristics of the 12-minute aerobic swim test. Master's thesis, University of Wisconsin, Madison.

Hewitt JE. 1948. Swimming achievement scales for college men. Research Quarterly, **19**:282–289.

Hewitt JE. 1949. Swimming achievement scale scores for high school swimming. Research Quarterly, **20**:170–179.

Jackson A, Jackson AS, Frankiewiez RG. 1979. The construct and concurrent validity of a 12-minute crawl stroke swim as a field test of swimming endurance. Research Quarterly for Exercise and Sport, **50**:641–648.

Jackson AS, Pettinger J. 1969. The development and discriminant analysis of swimming profiles of college men. Proceedings of the 72nd Annual Meeting, National College Physical Education Association for Men.

Munt MR. 1964. Development of an objective test to measure the efficiency of the front crawl for college women. Master's thesis, University of Michigan, Ann Arbor.

Rosentswieg JA. 1968. A revision of the power swimming test. Research Quarterly, **39**:818–819.

Wilson CT. 1934. Coordination tests in swimming. Research Quarterly, **5**:81–88.

Wilson MR. 1971. Wilson achievement test for intermediate swimming. In Barrow HM, McGee R, eds. A practical approach to measurement in physical education. ed 2, Philadelphia: Lea & Febiger.

Table Tennis

Mott JA, Lockhart A. 1946. Table tennis backboard test. Journal of Health and Physical Education, **17**:550–552.

Tennis

Avery CA, Richardson PA, Jackson AW. 1979. A practical tennis serve test: measurement of skill under simulated game conditions. Research Quarterly for Exercise and Sport, **50**:554–564.

Avery C, Richardson P, Jackson A. 1981. Response to McGhee's discussion. Research Quarterly for Exercise and Sport, **52**:296–297.

Benton R. 1963. Teaching tennis by testing. In Davis D, ed. Selected tennis and badminton articles. Washington, DC: Division of Girls' and Women's Sports, American Association for Health, Physical Education and Recreation.

Broer MR, Miller DM. 1950. Achievement tests for beginning and intermediate tennis. Research Quarterly, **21**:301–313.

Cobane E. 1962. Test for the service. In Tennis and badminton guide—June 1962–June 1964. Washington, DC: Division of Girls' and Women's Sports, American Association for Health, Physical Education and Recreation.

DiGennaro J. 1969. Construction of forehand drive, backhand drive, and service tennis tests. Research Quarterly, **40**:496–501.

Dyer JT. 1938. Revision of the backboard test of tennis ability. Research Quarterly, **9**:25–31.

Edwards J. 1965. A study of three measures of the tennis serve. Master's thesis, University of Wisconsin, Madison. (Microcard PE 746, University of Oregon, Eugene.)

Felshin J, Spencer E. 1963. Evaluation procedures for tennis. In Davis D, ed. Selected tennis and badminton articles. Washington, DC: Division of Girls' and Women's Sports, American Association for Health, Physical Education and Recreation.

Fox K. 1953. A study of the validity of the Dyer backboard test and the Miller forehand-backhand test for beginning tennis players. Research Quarterly, **24**:1–8.

Hewitt JE. 1965. Revision of the Dyer backboard tennis test. Research Quarterly, **36**:153–157.

Hewitt JE. 1966. Hewitt's tennis achievement test. Research Quarterly, **37**:231–236.

Hewitt JE. 1968. Classification tests in tennis. Research Quarterly, **39**:552–555.

Hubbell NC. 1960. A battery of tennis skill tests for college women. Master's thesis, Texas Women's University, Denton.

Hulac GM. 1971. Hulac rating scale for the tennis serve. In Barrow HM, McGee R, eds. A practical approach to measurement in physical education, ed 2. Philadelphia: Lea & Febiger.

Hulbert BA. 1966. A study of tests for the forehand drive in tennis. Master's thesis, University of Wisconsin, Madison. (Microcard PE 818, University of Oregon, Eugene.)

Johnson J. 1957. Tennis serve of advanced women players. Research Quarterly, **28**:123–131.

Johnson J. 1963. Tennis knowledge test. In Davis D, ed. Selected tennis and badminton articles. Washington, DC: Division of Girls' and Women's Sports, American Association for Health, Physical Education and Recreation.

Kemp J, Vincent MF. 1968. Kemp-Vincent rally test of tennis skill. Research Quarterly, **39**:1000–1004.

Malinak NR. 1961. The construction of an objective measure of accuracy in the performance of the tennis serve. Master's thesis, University of Illinois, Urbana.

McGhee R. 1981. Discussion of: A practical tennis serve test: measurement of skill under simulated game conditions. Research Quarterly for Exercise and Sport, **52**:294–295.

Purcell K. 1981. A tennis forehand-backhand drive skill test which measures ball control and stroke firmness. Research Quarterly for Exercise and Sport, **52**:238–245.

Ronning HE. 1959. Wall tests for evaluating tennis ability. Master's thesis, Washington State University, Pullman. (Microcard PE 441, University of Oregon, Eugene.)

Scott MG. 1941. Achievement examinations for elementary and intermediate tennis classes. Research Quarterly, **7**:40–49.

Scott MG, French E. 1959. Scott-French revision of the Dyer wallboard test. In Scott MG, French E, eds. Measurement and evaluation in physical education. Dubuque, Iowa: Wm C Brown Group.

Shepard GJ. 1972. The tennis drive skills test. Tennis-badminton-squash guide. Washington, DC: Division of Girls' and Women's Sports, American Association for Health, Physical Education and Recreation.

Volleyball

American Association for Health, Physical Education and Recreation. 1967. Volleyball skills test manual. Washington, DC: American Association for Health, Physical Education and Recreation.

Bartlett J, Smith L, Davis K, Peel J. 1991. Development of a valid volleyball skills test battery. Journal of Physical Education, Recreation and Dance, **62**(2):19–21.

Bassett G, Glassow RB, Locke M. 1937. Studies in testing volleyball skills. Research Quarterly, **8**:60–72.

Blackman CJ. 1968. The development of a volleyball test for the spike. Master's thesis, Southern Illinois University, Carbondale.

Brady CF. 1945. Preliminary investigation of volleyball playing ability. Research Quarterly, **16**:14–17.

Broer MA. 1958. Reliability of certain skill tests for junior high school girls. Research Quarterly, **29**:139–145.

Brumbach WB. 1979. Brumbach service test. In Johnson BL, Nelson JK, eds. Practical measurements for evaluation in physical education. Minneapolis: Burgess.

Clifton M. 1962. Single hit volley test for women's volleyball. Research Quarterly, **33**:208–211.

Crogan C. 1943. A simple volleyball classification test for high school girls. The Physical Educator, **4**:34–37.

Cunningham P, Garrison J. 1968. High wall volley test for women. Research Quarterly, **39**:486–490.

French EL, Cooper BI. 1937. Achievement tests in volleyball for high school girls. Research Quarterly, **8**:150–157.

Helman RM. 1971. Development of power volleyball skill tests for college women. Presented at the Research Section of the 1971 American Association for Health, Physical Education and Recreation National Convention, Detroit, March, 1971.

Jackson PL. 1966. A rating scale for discriminating relative playing performance of skilled female volleyball players. Master's thesis, University of Alberta, Edmonton, Canada. (Microcard PE 931. University of Oregon, Eugene.)

Kessler A. 1968. The validity and reliability of the Sandefur volleyball spiking test. Master's thesis, California State College, Long Beach.

Kronqvist RA, Brumbach WB. 1968. A modification of the Brady volleyball skill test for high school boys. Research Quarterly, **39**:116–120.

Latchaw M. 1954. Measuring selected motor skills in fourth, fifth, and sixth grades. Research Quarterly, **25**:439–449.

Liba MR, Stauff MR. 1963. A test for the volleyball pass. Research Quarterly, **34**:56–63.

Londeree BR, Eicholtz EC. 1970. Reliabilities of selected volleyball skill tests. Presented at the Research Section of the 1970 American Association for Health, Physical Education and Recreation National Convention, Seattle.

Lopez D. 1957. Serve test. In Volleyball guide—July 1957–July 1959. Washington, DC: Division of Girls' and Women's Sports, American Association for Health, Physical Education and Recreation.

Mohr DR, Haverstick MJ. 1955. Repeated volleys tests for women's volleyball. Research Quarterly, **26**:179–184.

Russell N, Lange E. 1940. Achievement tests in volleyball for junior high school girls. Research Quarterly, **11**:33–41.

Ryan MF. 1969. A study of tests for the volleyball serve. Master's thesis, University of Wisconsin, Madison. (Microcard PE 1040, University of Oregon, Eugene.)

Slaymaker T, Brown VH. 1969. Test questions for power volleyball. Philadelphia: WB Saunders.

Snavely M. 1960. Volleyball skill tests for girls. In Lockhart A, ed. Selected volleyball articles. Washington, DC: Division of Girls' and Women's Sports, American Association for Health, Physical Education and Recreation.

Thorpe J, West C. 1967. A volleyball skills chart with attainment levels for selected skills. Volleyball guide—July 1967–July 1969. Washington, DC: Division of Girls' and Women's Sports, American Association for Health, Physical Education and Recreation.

Watkins A. 1960. Skill testing for large groups. In Lockhart A, ed. Selected volleyball articles. Washington, DC: Division of Girls' and Women's Sports, American Association for Health, Physical Education and Recreation.

West C. 1957. A comparative study between height and wall volley test scores as related to volleyball playing ability of girls and women. Master's thesis, Women's College of the University of North Carolina, Greensboro.

Wrestling

Sickels WL. 1980. Sickels amateur wrestling ability rating form. In Barrow HM, McGee R, eds. A practical approach to measurement in physical education, ed 3. Philadelphia: Lea & Febiger.

Yetter H. 1963. A test of wrestling aptitude: A preliminary explanation. Master's thesis, University of Wisconsin, Madison.

NCYFS Norms

Table A-1	NCYFS Norms By Age For the One-Mile Walk/Run— Boys (In Minutes and Seconds)								
Percentile	10	11	12	13	14	15	16	17	18
99	6:55	6:21	6:21	5:59	5:43	5:40	5:31	5:14	5:33
90	8:13	7:25	7:13	6:48	6:27	6:23	6:13	6:08	6:10
80	8:35	7:52	7:41	7:07	6:58	6:43	6:31	6:31	6:33
75	8:48	8:02	7:53	7:14	7:08	6:52	6:39	6:40	6:42
70	9:02	8:12	8:03	7:24	7:18	7:00	6:50	6:46	6:57
60	9:26	8:38	8:23	7:46	7:34	7:13	7:07	7:10	7:15
50	9:52	9:03	8:48	8:04	7:51	7:30	7:27	7:31	7:35
40	10:15	9:25	9:17	8:26	8:14	7:50	7:48	7:59	7:53
30	10:44	10:17	9:57	8:54	8:46	8:18	8:04	8:24	8:12
25	11:00	10:32	10:13	9:06	9:10	8:30	8:18	8:37	8:34
20	11:25	10:55	10:38	9:20	9:28	8:50	8:34	8:55	9:10
10	12:27	12:07	11:48	10:38	10:34	10:13	9:36	10:43	10:50

Table A-2	NCYFS Norms By Age For the One-Mile Walk/Run— Girls (In Minutes and Seconds)								
Percentile	10	11	12	13	14	15	16	17	18
99	7:55	7:14	7:20	7:08	7:01	6:59	7:03	6:52	6:58
90	9:09	8:45	8:34	8:27	8:11	8:23	8:28	8:20	8:22
80	9:56	9:35	9:30	9:13	8:49	9:04	9:06	9:10	9:27

Tables A-1 to A-12 are from Ross JG, Gilbert GG. 1985. The national children and youth fitness study: a summary of findings. Journal of Physical Education, Recreation and Dance, **56**:45–50.

Continued

Table A-2 NCYFS Norms By Age For the One-Mile Walk/Run—Girls (In Minutes and Seconds) cont'd

Percentile	10	11	12	13	14	15	16	17	18
75	10:09	9:56	9:52	9:30	9:16	9:28	9:25	9:26	9:31
70	10:27	10:10	10:05	9:48	9:31	9:49	9:41	9:41	9:36
60	10:51	10:35	10:32	10:22	10:04	10:20	10:15	10:16	10:08
50	11:14	11:15	10:58	10:52	10:32	10:46	10:34	10:34	10:51
40	11:54	11:46	11:26	11:22	10:58	11:20	11:08	10:59	11:27
30	12:27	12:33	12:03	11:55	11:35	11:53	11:49	11:43	11:58
25	12:52	12:54	12:33	12:17	11:49	12:18	12:10	12:03	12:14
20	13:12	13:17	12:53	12:43	12:10	12:48	12:32	12:30	12:37
10	14:20	14:35	14:07	13:45	13:13	14:07	13:42	13:46	15:18

Table A-3 NCYFS Norms By Age For the Timed Bent-Knee Sit-ups—Boys (Number in 60 Seconds)

Percentile	10	11	12	13	14	15	16	17	18
99	60	60	61	62	64	65	65	68	67
90	47	48	50	52	52	53	55	56	54
80	43	43	46	48	49	50	51	51	50
75	40	41	44	46	47	48	49	50	50
70	38	40	43	45	45	46	48	49	48
60	36	38	40	41	43	44	45	46	44
50	34	36	38	40	41	42	43	43	43
40	32	34	35	37	39	40	41	41	40
30	30	31	33	34	37	37	39	39	38
25	28	30	32	32	35	36	38	37	36
20	26	28	30	31	34	35	36	35	35
10	22	22	25	28	30	31	32	31	31

Table A-4   NCYFS Norms By Age For the Timed Bent-Knee Sit-ups—
Girls (Number in 60 Seconds)

Percentile	10	11	12	13	14	15	16	17	18
99	50	53	66	58	57	56	59	60	65
90	43	42	46	46	47	45	49	47	47
80	39	39	41	41	42	42	42	41	42
75	37	37	40	40	41	40	40	40	40
70	36	36	39	39	40	39	39	39	40
60	33	34	36	35	37	36	37	37	38
50	31	32	33	33	35	35	35	36	35
40	30	30	31	31	32	32	33	33	33
30	27	28	30	28	30	30	30	31	30
25	25	26	28	27	29	30	30	30	30
20	24	24	27	25	27	28	28	29	28
10	20	20	21	21	23	24	23	24	24

Table A-5   NCYFS Norms By Age For the Sit-and-Reach—Boys (In Inches)*

Percentile	10	11	12	13	14	15	16	17	18
99	18.0	18.5	18.5	19.5	20.0	21.5	22.0	21.5	22.0
90	16.0	16.5	16.0	16.5	17.5	18.0	19.0	19.5	19.5
80	15.0	15.5	15.0	15.0	16.0	17.0	18.0	18.0	18.0
75	14.5	15.0	15.0	15.0	15.5	16.5	17.0	17.5	17.5
70	14.5	14.5	14.5	14.5	15.0	16.0	17.0	17.0	17.0
60	14.0	14.0	13.5	13.5	14.0	15.0	16.0	16.0	16.0
50	13.5	13.0	13.0	13.0	13.5	14.0	15.0	15.5	15.0
40	12.5	12.5	12.0	12.5	13.0	13.5	14.0	14.5	14.5
30	12.0	12.0	11.5	12.0	12.0	12.5	13.5	13.5	13.5
25	11.5	11.5	11.0	11.0	11.0	12.0	13.0	13.0	13.0
20	11.0	11.0	10.5	10.5	11.0	11.5	12.0	12.5	12.5
10	10.0	9.5	8.5	9.0	9.0	9.5	10.0	10.5	10.0

*The 1980 AAHPERD norms used a 0 point of 23 cm, but NCYFS used 12 inches. To adjust the 0 point and to change inches to centimeters, use the following formula: score in centimeters = (score in inches × 2.54) − 7.48.

Table A-6 NCYFS Norms By Age For the Sit-and-Reach—Girls (In Inches)*

Percentile	10	11	12	13	14	15	16	17	18
99	20.5	20.5	21.0	22.0	22.0	23.0	23.0	23.0	22.5
90	17.5	18.0	19.0	20.0	19.5	20.0	20.5	20.5	20.5
80	16.5	17.0	18.0	19.0	19.0	19.0	19.5	19.5	19.5
75	16.5	16.5	17.0	18.0	18.5	19.0	19.0	19.0	19.0
70	16.0	16.5	17.0	17.5	18.0	18.5	19.0	19.0	18.5
60	15.0	15.5	16.0	17.0	17.5	18.0	18.0	18.0	18.0
50	14.5	15.0	15.5	16.0	17.0	17.0	17.5	18.0	17.5
40	14.0	14.0	15.0	15.5	16.0	17.0	17.0	17.0	17.0
30	13.0	13.5	14.5	14.5	15.0	16.0	16.5	16.0	16.0
25	13.0	13.0	14.0	14.0	15.0	15.5	16.0	15.5	15.5
20	12.0	13.0	13.5	13.5	14.0	15.0	15.5	15.0	15.0
10	10.5	11.5	12.0	12.0	12.5	13.5	14.0	13.5	13.0

*The 1980 AAHPERD norms used a 0 point of 23 cm, but NCYFS used 12 inches. To adjust the 0 point and to change inches to centimeters, use the following formula: score in centimeters = (score in inches × 2.54) − 7.48.

Table A-7 NCYFS Norms By Age For the Triceps Skinfold—Boys (In Millimeters)

Percentile	10	11	12	13	14	15	16	17	18
99	5	4	4	4	4	4	4	4	4
90	7	7	6	6	5	5	5	5	5
80	8	7	8	7	6	6	6	6	6
75	8	8	8	7	7	7	6	6	6
70	9	9	9	8	7	7	7	7	7
60	10	10	10	9	8	8	7	7	8
50	11	11	11	10	9	9	8	8	8
40	13	12	12	11	10	10	9	9	10
30	14	14	14	13	11	11	11	11	11
25	15	15	15	14	12	12	11	12	12
20	16	16	17	15	13	13	12	13	13
10	20	20	21	20	18	18	16	15	16

Table A-8 NCYFS Norms By Age For the Triceps Skinfold—Girls (In Millimeters)

Percentile	10	11	12	13	14	15	16	17	18
99	5	6	6	6	6	7	7	8	7
90	7	8	9	9	9	10	10	11	10
80	9	9	10	10	11	12	12	12	12
75	10	10	10	11	12	13	12	13	13
70	10	10	11	11	12	13	13	14	13
60	11	12	12	13	14	15	14	15	14
50	12	13	13	14	15	16	15	17	15
40	14	15	14	15	16	17	17	18	17
30	15	16	16	17	18	19	18	20	19
25	16	17	17	18	19	20	19	21	20
20	17	19	18	20	20	21	20	21	21
10	21	23	22	24	23	25	24	24	23

Table A-9 NCYFS Norms By Age For the Sum of Triceps and Subscapular Skinfolds—Boys (In Millimeters)

Percentile	10	11	12	13	14	15	16	17	18
99	9	9	9	9	9	10	10	10	11
90	12	12	12	11	12	12	12	13	13
80	13	13	13	13	13	13	13	14	14
75	14	14	14	13	13	14	14	14	15
70	15	15	15	14	14	14	14	15	15
60	16	16	16	15	15	15	15	16	17
50	17	18	17	17	17	17	17	17	18
40	20	20	20	19	18	18	18	19	19
30	22	23	22	21	21	20	20	21	22
25	24	25	24	23	22	22	22	22	24
20	25	26	28	25	25	24	23	24	25
10	35	36	38	34	33	32	30	30	30

Table A-10 NCYFS Norms By Age For The Sum of Triceps and Subscapular Skinfolds—Girls (In Millimeters)

Percentile	10	11	12	13	14	15	16	17	18
99	10	11	11	12	12	13	13	16	14
90	13	14	15	15	17	19	19	20	19
80	15	16	17	18	19	21	21	22	21
75	16	17	18	19	20	23	22	23	22
70	17	18	18	20	21	24	23	24	23
60	18	19	21	22	24	26	24	26	25
50	20	21	22	24	26	28	26	28	27
40	22	24	24	26	28	30	28	31	28
30	25	28	27	29	31	33	32	34	32
25	27	30	29	31	33	34	33	36	34
20	29	33	31	34	35	37	35	37	36
10	36	40	40	43	40	43	42	42	42

Table A-11 NCYFS Norms By Age For the Chin-Up—Boys (Number Completed)

Percentile	10	11	12	13	14	15	16	17	18
99	13	12	13	17	18	18	20	20	21
90	8	8	8	10	12	14	14	15	16
80	5	5	6	8	9	11	12	13	14
75	4	5	5	7	8	10	12	12	13
70	4	4	5	7	8	10	11	12	12
60	2	3	4	5	6	8	10	10	11
50	1	2	3	4	5	7	9	9	10
40	1	1	2	3	4	6	8	8	9
30	0	0	1	1	3	5	6	6	7
25	0	0	0	1	2	4	6	5	6
20	0	0	0	0	1	3	5	4	5
10	0	0	0	0	0	1	2	2	3

Table A-12 NCYFS Norms By Age For the Chin-Up—Girls (Number Completed)

Percentile	10	11	12	13	14	15	16	17	18
99	8	8	8	5	8	6	8	7	6
90	3	3	2	2	2	2	2	2	2
80	2	1	1	1	1	1	1	1	1
75	1	1	1	1	1	1	1	1	1
70	1	1	1	0	1	1	1	1	1
60	0	0	0	0	0	0	0	0	0
50	0	0	0	0	0	0	0	0	0
40	0	0	0	0	0	0	0	0	0
30	0	0	0	0	0	0	0	0	0
25	0	0	0	0	0	0	0	0	0
20	0	0	0	0	0	0	0	0	0
10	0	0	0	0	0	0	0	0	0

Sources of Tests and Skinfold Calipers

CHAPTER 12

The following references are excellent sources of additional tests of motor behavior for children. Each reference includes an analytical critique of selected tests to assist the teacher in identifying appropriate tests.

Haubenstricker JL. 1977. A critical review of selected perceptual-motor tests and scales currently used in the assessment of motor behavior. In Landers D, Christina R, eds. Psychology of motor behavior and sport—1977. Champaign, Ill: Human Kinetics.

Herkowitz J. 1977. Instruments which assess the efficiency/maturity of children's fundamental motor pattern performance. In Landers D, Christina R, eds. Psychology of motor behavior and sport—1977. Champaign, Ill: Human Kinetics.

Herkowitz J. 1978. Assessing the motor development of children: presentation and critique of tests. In Ridenour M, ed. Motor development: Issues and applications. Princeton, NJ: Princeton Book.

McGee R. 1984. Evaluation of processes and products. In Logsden B, ed. Physical education for children: A focus on the teaching process. Philadelphia: Lea & Febiger.

CHAPTER 13

Sensorimotor Tests

Quick Neurological Screening Test
Academic Therapy Publications
20 Commerical Boulevard
Novato, CA 94949

Frostig Developmental Test of Visual Perception
Consulting Psychologist Press, Inc.
577 College Avenue
Palo Alto, CA 94360

Motor Development Tests

California State University Motor Development Checklist
Janet A. Seaman
California State University
5151 State University Drive
Los Angeles, CA 90032

Bayley Scales of Motor Development
Psychological Corporation
757 Third Avenue
New York, NY 10017

Motor Ability Tests

Six Category Gross Motor Test
B.J. Cratty
Perceptual Motor Behavior and Educational Processes
Springfield, Ill.:
Charles C Thomas, Publisher, 1969

Basic Motor Ability Test—Revised
D. Arnheim and A. Sinclair
The Clumsy Child
St. Louis: Mosby–Year Book, Inc., 1979

CHAPTER 17

Fat-O-Meter:
Health Education Services Corp., 7N015 York Road, Bensenville, IL 60106

Slim Guide
Creative Health Products, 9135 General Ct., Plymouth, MI 48170

Physique Meter
Dr. H. Co., P.O. Box 266, Chesterfield, MO 63017

Harpenden
Quinton Instrument Co., 2121 Terry Avenue, Seattle, WA 98121

Lange
J.A. Preston Corp., 71 Fifth Ave., New York, NY 10013

Areas Under the Normal Curve Between the Mean and z

z	Area from mean to z	z	Area from mean to z	z	Area from mean to z
0.00	.0000	0.19	.0753	0.38	.1480
0.01	.0040	0.20	.0793	0.39	.1517
0.02	.0080	0.21	.0832	0.40	.1554
0.03	.0120	0.22	.0871	0.41	.1591
0.04	.0160	0.23	.0910	0.42	.1628
0.05	.0199	0.24	.0948	0.43	.1664
0.06	.0239	0.25	.0987	0.44	.1700
0.07	.0279	0.26	.1026	0.45	.1736
0.08	.0319	0.27	.1064	0.46	.1772
0.09	.0359	0.28	.1103	0.47	.1808
0.10	.0398	0.29	.1141	0.48	.1844
0.11	.0438	0.30	.1179	0.49	.1879
0.12	.0478	0.31	.1217	0.50	.1915
0.13	.0517	0.32	.1255	0.51	.1950
0.14	.0557	0.33	.1293	0.52	.1985
0.15	.0596	0.34	.1331	0.53	.2019
0.16	.0636	0.35	.1368	0.54	.2054
0.17	.0675	0.36	.1406	0.55	.2088
0.18	.0714	0.37	.1443	0.56	.2123

z	Area from mean to z	z	Area from mean to z	z	Area from mean to z
0.57	.2157	0.88	.3106	1.19	.3830
0.58	.2190	0.89	.3133	1.20	.3849
0.59	.2224	0.90	.3159	1.21	.3869
0.60	.2257	0.91	.3186	1.22	.3888
0.61	.2291	0.92	.3212	1.23	.3907
0.62	.2324	0.93	.3238	1.24	.3925
0.63	.2357	0.94	.3264	1.25	.3944
0.64	.2389	0.95	.3289	1.26	.3962
0.65	.2422	0.96	.3315	1.27	.3980
0.66	.2454	0.97	.3340	1.28	.3997
0.67	.2486	0.98	.3365	1.29	.4015
0.68	.2517	0.99	.3389	1.30	.4032
0.69	.2549	1.00	.3413	1.31	.4049
0.70	.2580	1.01	.3438	1.32	.4066
0.71	.2611	1.02	.3461	1.33	.4082
0.72	.2642	1.03	.3485	1.34	.4099
0.73	.2673	1.04	.3508	1.35	.4115
0.74	.2704	1.05	.3531	1.36	.4131
0.75	.2734	1.06	.3554	1.37	.4147
0.76	.2764	1.07	.3577	1.38	.4162
0.77	.2794	1.08	.3599	1.39	.4177
0.78	.2823	1.09	.3621	1.40	.4192
0.79	.2852	1.10	.3643	1.41	.4207
0.80	.2881	1.11	.3665	1.42	.4222
0.81	.2910	1.12	.3686	1.43	.4236
0.82	.2939	1.13	.3708	1.44	.4251
0.83	.2967	1.14	.3729	1.45	.4265
0.84	.2995	1.15	.3749	1.46	.4279
0.85	.3023	1.16	.3770	1.47	.4292
0.86	.3051	1.17	.3790	1.48	.4306
0.87	.3078	1.18	.3810	1.49	.4319

Continued

z	Area from mean to z	z	Area from mean to z	z	Area from mean to z
1.50	.4332	1.81	.4649	2.12	.4830
1.51	.4345	1.82	.4656	2.13	.4834
1.52	.4357	1.83	.4664	2.14	.4838
1.53	.4370	1.84	.4671	2.15	.4842
1.54	.4382	1.85	.4678	2.16	.4846
1.55	.4394	1.86	.4686	2.17	.4850
1.56	.4406	1.87	.4693	2.18	.4854
1.57	.4418	1.88	.4699	2.19	.4857
1.58	.4429	1.89	.4706	2.20	.4861
1.59	.4441	1.90	.4713	2.21	.4864
1.60	.4452	1.91	.4719	2.22	.4868
1.61	.4463	1.92	.4726	2.23	.4871
1.62	.4474	1.93	.4732	2.24	.4875
1.63	.4484	1.94	.4738	2.25	.4878
1.64	.4495	1.95	.4744	2.26	.4881
1.65	.4505	1.96	.4750	2.27	.4884
1.66	.4515	1.97	.4756	2.28	.4887
1.67	.4525	1.98	.4761	2.29	.4890
1.68	.4535	1.99	.4767	2.30	.4893
1.69	.4545	2.00	.4772	2.31	.4896
1.70	.4554	2.01	.4778	2.32	.4898
1.71	.4564	2.02	.4783	2.33	.4901
1.72	.4573	2.03	.4788	2.34	.4904
1.73	.4582	2.04	.4793	2.35	.4906
1.74	.4591	2.05	.4798	2.36	.4909
1.75	.4599	2.06	.4803	2.37	.4911
1.76	.4608	2.07	.4808	2.38	.4913
1.77	.4616	2.08	.4812	2.39	.4916
1.78	.4625	2.09	.4187	2.40	.4918
1.79	.4633	2.10	.4821	2.41	.4920
1.80	.4641	2.11	.4826	2.42	.4922

z	Area from mean to z	z	Area from mean to z	z	Area from mean to z
2.43	.4925	2.74	.4969	3.05	.4989
2.44	.4927	2.75	.4970	3.06	.4989
2.45	.4929	2.76	.4971	3.07	.4989
2.46	.4931	2.77	.4972	3.08	.4990
2.47	.4932	2.78	.4973	3.09	.4990
2.48	.4934	2.79	.4974	3.10	.4990
2.49	.4936	2.80	.4974	3.11	.4991
2.50	.4938	2.81	.4975	3.12	.4991
2.51	.4940	2.82	.4976	3.13	.4991
2.52	.4941	2.83	.4977	3.14	.4992
2.53	.4943	2.84	.4977	3.15	.4992
2.54	.4945	2.85	.4978	3.16	.4992
2.55	.4946	2.86	.4979	3.17	.4992
2.56	.4948	2.87	.4979	3.18	.4993
2.57	.4949	2.88	.4980	3.19	.4993
2.58	.4951	2.89	.4981	3.20	.4993
2.59	.4952	2.90	.4981	3.21	.4993
2.60	.4953	2.91	.4982	3.22	.4994
2.61	.4955	2.92	.4982	3.23	.4994
2.62	.4956	2.93	.4983	3.24	.4994
2.63	.4957	2.94	.4984	3.25	.4994
2.64	.4959	2.95	.4984	3.26	.4994
2.65	.4960	2.96	.4985	3.27	.4995
2.66	.4961	2.97	.4985	3.28	.4995
2.67	.4962	2.98	.4986	3.29	.4995
2.68	.4963	2.99	.4986	3.30	.4995
2.69	.4964	3.00	.4987	3.40	.4997
2.70	.4965	3.01	.4987	3.50	.4998
2.71	.4966	3.02	.4987	3.60	.4998
2.72	.4967	3.03	.4988	3.70	.4999
2.73	.4968	3.04	.4988		

Critical Values of the Studentized Range Statistic q

df for Denominator	a	\multicolumn{9}{c}{k (Number of Means)}
		2	3	4	5	6	7	8	9	10
1	.05	18.0	27.0	32.8	37.1	40.4	43.1	45.4	47.4	49.1
	.01	90.0	135	164	186	202	216	227	237	246
2	.05	6.09	8.3	9.8	10.9	11.7	12.4	13.0	13.5	14.0
	.01	14.0	19.0	22.3	24.7	26.6	28.2	29.5	30.7	31.7
3	.05	4.50	5.91	6.82	7.50	8.04	8.48	8.85	9.18	9.46
	.01	8.26	10.6	12.2	13.3	14.2	15.0	15.6	16.2	16.7
4	.05	3.93	5.04	5.76	6.29	6.71	7.05	7.35	7.60	7.83
	.01	6.51	8.12	9.17	9.96	10.6	11.1	11.5	11.9	12.3
5	.05	3.64	4.60	5.22	5.67	6.03	6.33	6.58	6.80	6.99
	.01	5.70	6.97	7.80	8.42	8.91	9.32	9.67	9.97	10.2
6	.05	3.46	4.34	4.90	5.31	5.63	5.89	6.12	6.32	6.49
	.01	5.24	6.33	7.03	7.56	7.97	8.32	8.61	8.87	9.10
7	.05	3.34	4.16	4.69	5.06	5.36	5.61	5.82	6.00	6.16
	.01	4.95	5.92	6.54	7.01	7.37	7.68	7.94	8.17	8.37
8	.05	3.26	4.04	4.53	4.89	5.17	5.40	5.60	5.77	5.92
	.01	4.74	5.63	6.20	6.63	6.96	7.24	7.47	7.68	7.78
9	.05	3.20	3.95	4.42	4.76	5.02	5.24	5.43	5.60	5.74
	.01	4.60	5.43	5.96	6.35	6.66	6.91	7.13	7.32	7.49
10	.05	3.15	3.88	4.33	4.65	4.91	5.12	5.30	5.46	5.60
	.01	4.48	5.27	5.77	6.14	6.43	6.67	6.87	7.05	7.21
11	.05	3.11	3.82	4.26	4.57	4.82	5.03	5.20	5.35	5.49
	.01	4.39	5.14	5.62	5.97	6.25	6.48	6.67	6.84	6.99

df for Denominator	a	\multicolumn{9}{c}{k (Number of Means)}
		2	3	4	5	6	7	8	9	10
12	.05	3.08	3.77	4.20	4.51	4.75	4.95	5.12	5.27	5.40
	.01	4.32	5.04	5.50	5.84	6.10	6.32	6.51	6.67	6.81
13	.05	3.06	3.73	4.15	4.45	4.69	4.88	5.05	5.19	5.32
	.01	4.26	4.96	5.40	5.73	5.98	6.19	6.37	6.53	6.67
14	.05	3.03	3.70	4.11	4.41	4.64	4.83	4.99	5.13	5.25
	.01	4.21	4.89	5.32	5.63	5.88	6.08	6.26	6.41	6.54
16	.05	3.00	3.65	4.05	4.33	4.56	4.74	4.90	5.03	5.15
	.01	4.13	4.78	5.19	5.49	5.72	5.92	6.08	6.22	6.35
18	.05	2.97	3.61	4.00	4.28	4.49	4.67	4.82	4.96	5.07
	.01	4.07	4.70	5.09	5.38	5.60	5.79	5.94	6.08	6.20
20	.05	2.95	3.58	3.96	4.23	4.45	4.62	4.77	4.90	5.01
	.01	4.02	4.64	5.02	5.29	5.51	5.69	5.84	5.97	6.09
24	.05	2.92	3.53	3.90	4.17	4.37	4.54	4.68	4.81	4.92
	.01	3.96	4.54	4.91	5.17	5.37	5.54	5.69	5.81	5.92
30	.05	2.89	3.49	3.84	4.10	4.30	4.46	4.60	4.72	4.83
	.01	3.89	4.45	4.80	5.05	5.24	5.40	5.54	5.56	5.76
40	.05	2.86	3.44	3.79	4.04	4.23	4.39	4.52	4.63	4.74
	.01	3.82	4.37	4.70	4.93	5.11	5.27	5.39	5.50	5.60
60	.05	2.83	3.40	3.74	3.98	4.16	4.31	4.44	4.55	4.65
	.01	3.76	4.28	4.60	4.82	4.99	5.13	5.25	5.36	5.45
120	.05	2.80	3.36	3.69	3.92	4.10	4.24	4.36	4.48	4.56
	.01	3.70	4.20	4.50	4.71	4.87	5.01	5.12	5.21	5.30
∞	.05	2.77	3.31	3.63	3.86	4.03	4.17	4.29	4.39	4.47
	.01	3.64	4.12	4.40	4.60	4.76	4.88	4.99	5.08	5.16

Glossary

AAHPER youth fitness test: Battery of six test items measuring primarily performance-related physical fitness, although two of the items are measures of health-related fitness

AAHPERD physical best test: Five-item test battery designed to measure physical performance, particularly health-related physical fitness

accountability: Provision of evidence that predetermined goals and objectives have been met

achievement: Ability level of an examinee at a designated point

active stretching: Muscle stretching resulting from the voluntary forceful contraction of opposing muscles

affect: Sociological or psychological characteristic manifested in a feeling or behavior, such as attitude, interest, and sportsmanship

affective domain: Levels of emotional behavior, including attitudes, interests, and various personality characteristics

alternatives: Set of responses in a multiple-choice item; correct alternative is the *answer;* incorrect alternatives are *distractors*

anomaly: Unusual; irregular; contrary to general rule

applications programs: Computer programs designed to aid users in solving specific problems (e.g., word processing, spreadsheets)

athletic performance–related physical fitness: Type of physical fitness that enhances performance in sports and other forms of physical activity; different from health-related physical fitness, although health-related fitness may also benefit performance

attitude: Feelings about a specific attitude object, such as a situation, a person, or an activity

balance: Ability to maintain equilibrium

basic movement patterns: Types of movement that emerge developmentally, usually at a young age, such as running, jumping, and throwing

behavioral objective: Objective stated in terms of the behavior the student will exhibit when the objective is successfully attained

bicycle ergometer: Stationary bicycle that can be operated at a variety of workloads; used to measure physical work capacity

bit: Smallest amount of information that can be identified by a computer; can specify either of two alternatives, 1 or 0

body composition: Combination of bone, muscle mass, and fatty tissue

booting: Loading a program into the computer's memory

The definitions of words marked with an asterisk (*) are taken from the Rules and Regulations for PL 94-192 published in the Federal Register.

The definitions of words marked with a dagger are taken from the American Alliance for Health, Physical Education, Recreation and Dance. 1980. AAHPERD health-related physical fitness test manual. Reston, VA: AAHPERD.

bus: Communication links between the components of a computer system

byte: Equals one character, which is a letter, number, or punctuation mark; made up of eight bits or two nibbles

cable tensiometer: Device used to measure static strength; cable tension is determined "from the force needed to create offset on a riser in a cable stretched between two points" (Clarke, 1976:124)

carotid artery: Either of two arteries on the sides of the neck that carry blood to the head; often used to measure pulse rate

CATALOG: BASIC command to list the files on a disk

central processing unit (CPU): Component of a computer that performs mathematical calculations and coordinates the flow of information through the computer

central tendency: Center of distribution of test scores

cerebral palsy: Neuromuscular disability resulting from brain damage

checklist: An observational analysis instrument that records the presence or absence of critical elements of behavior

checklist of objectives: Set of symbols to rate major objectives; often used in elementary schools

circumference measure: Measure of the outer surface of a body part, such as the upper arm; sometimes used to estimate body fatness

cognitive domain: Intellectual behavior ranging from a low level (memorization of facts) to a higher level (application of these facts) in some way

compact disk read only memory (CD-ROM): Laser disk used as a computer storage device

competency-based evaluation: Approach to evaluation in which a desired level of competency is identified, and examinees designated as competent must be able to meet or exceed this level

component model of intratask development: Identification of developmental characteristics of body parts in performing a task

components of skill: Elements of the skill that are essential to its correct execution

computer program: A set of instructions directing the computer to perform a task

concentric action: Muscle action that results in a shortening of the muscle

concurrent validity: Degree to which a predictor test correlates with a criterion test

condition (in an objective): Situation in which behavior is expected to occur

congenital: Condition present at birth

construct validity: Degree to which a test measures an attribute or a trait that cannot be directly measured

content (in an objective): Material or skill the student is expected to learn

content validity: Degree to which the sample of test items, tasks, or questions on a test are representative of some defined universe or "domain" of content (American Psychological Association, 1985)

contingency coefficient: Method of determining the validity of a mastery test

contingency table: Table with numbers in each cell determined by jointly considering the two joint categories

contrasting groups method: Determination of valid cutoff point by comparing students expected to master an objective with those not expected to master it

correction for guessing: Alteration of test score based on number of items answered incorrectly

correlation: Relationship between two variables

correlation coefficient: Statistical procedure for estimating the relationship between two variables, x and y

criterion: Standard of behavior

criterion-referenced test: Test with a predetermined standard of performance that is tied to a specified domain of behavior

criterion-related validity: Extent to which a test measures the true or criterion behavior of examinees, usually determined by correlational procedures

criterion test: Highly valid test of the attribute to be measured; cannot be used in a practical setting because of its complexity, expense, and need for specially trained testers; standard against which a practical test is compared

cumulative frequency (cf): Column in frequency distribution table obtained by summing the frequencies from the bottom to the top of the column; the number at the top of the column equals N, the number of scores; represents the number of examinees scoring at or below a given interval

cumulative percent (c%): Column in frequency distribution table obtained by dividing the cumulative frequency by N and multiplying by 100; represents the percentage of examinees scoring at or below a given interval

curriculum objective: Translation of long-term objective into specific behavior expected after exposure to a curriculum

database: Information organized into records and fields and used as a filing system; computerized database management systems provide an electronic means for inputting, organizing, and managing a database

deaf: Severe lacking in sense of hearing

decision validity: Accuracy of classification of masters and nonmasters

descriptive statistics: Statistics used to describe a set of data

desktop computers: Computers that fit comfortably on a desk

disabled: Because of an impairment, the disabled individual is limited or restricted in executing some skills, performing specific jobs or tasks, or participating in certain activities (American Alliance for Health, Physical Education, Recreation and Dance)

disk: Magnetic media on which the computer stores information; also known as floppy disk or diskette

disk drive: Device for storing data; means of communication between disk and central processor

disk operating system (DOS): Operating system for microcomputers; controls communication between the disk drives and the central operating system (see operating system)

display: Information appearing on screen of monitor

domain: Range of all possible criterion behaviors

domain-referenced validity: Extent to which the tasks sampled by the test adequately represent the total domain of tasks

dot-matrix printer: A printer that employs an array of dots (e.g., metal pins) to create images on paper

dynamic balance: Ability to maintain equilibrium while in motion

dynamic strength: Force exerted by a muscle group as a body part moves through space

dynamometer: Device used to measure static strength and endurance

eccentric action: Muscle action that results in a lengthening of the muscle

educable: Capable of learning or being educated, as in educable mentally retarded

electromechanical device: A device (such as Cybex II) used to measure static and dynamic strength, endurance, and power

electronic bulletin board: A computer used to store messages; users access the bulletin board via a modem and post and retrieve messages much like a paper bulletin board

electronic mail (e-mail): Mail sent directly from computer to computer along a computer network or via a modem

elgon: Goniometer with a potentiometer substituted for the protractor; also known as electrogoniometer; used to measure flexibility

eligibility: In special education, the process of verifying if a significant impairment exists; used to develop additional services for the student

enter key: Key on the keyboard used to enter commands into the computer

essay item: Item requiring examinee to construct a response at least several sentences long

evaluation: Interpretation of a test score

evaluation objective: Short-term objective reflecting a change in behavior that has occured over a short period

face validity: Having the appearance of validity, but not formally validated

field test: Practical but valid substitute for a more complex laboratory test

Flexed-arm hang test: Measures arm and shoulder girdle strength; usually designated for girls

flexibility: Range of movement about a joint, from a position of extension to flexion or the opposite movement

flexometer: Instrument with a weighted 360-degree dial and a weighted pointer, used to measure flexibility; both the dial and the pointer move independently as affected by gravity

forced-choice item: Item requiring examinee to choose between two or more alternatives that appear equally favorable or unfavorable

formative evaluation: Evaluation that occurs throughout a training period or instructional unit

formatting a disk: Preparing a disk for use; must be applied to new disks before using

freeware: Computer software obtained for the price of a blank disk

frequency (f): Number of scores in an interval; sum of tallies in an interval

frequency distribution: Method of organizing test scores into mutually exclusive intervals

frequency polygon: Line graph of the frequency distribution, with score limits on the horizontal axis and frequency of cases on the vertical axis

game statistics: Record of events occurring during a game, such as number of shots attempted, percentage of successful shots, and so forth

gates: Pictorial representation of bits; open gate represents a "yes" choice; closed gate represents a "no" choice

gigabyte: Unit of computer memory storage representing approximately 1 billion bytes or typed characters

goniometer: Protractor of 180 degrees with extended arms; used to measure flexibility

grade: Mark assigned to a student based on his or her performance on one or more tests

graphical-user interface (GUI): A computer program that provides a visual or pictorial mode of communication between the user and the computer; GUI is characterized by use of a mouse, icons, and windows

halo effect: Rater bias that can occur when the rater is unduly influenced by previous performance of the examinee

handicapped†: Because of an impairment or disability, the handicapped individual is adversely affected psychologically, emotionally, or socially

hard disk: A rigid magnetic disk encased in an airtight box; used to store data and programs

hardware: Physical components of the computer, such as keyboard and monitor

health-related physical fitness: See **Physical fitness (health-related)**

histogram: Bar graph of the frequency distribution, with score limits on the horizontal axis and frequency of cases on the vertical axis

HOME: BASIC command to clear the screen

hydrostatic weighing: Assessment of body composition by weighing a person underwater

impaired†: An impaired individual has an identifiable organic or functional condition; some part of the body or a portion of an anatomical structure is actually missing; one or more parts of the body do not function properly; may be temporary or permanent

improvement: Change in behavior occurring between an initial and a final testing period

inclinometer: A clinical device for measuring joint angle and range of motion, particularly of the spine

index of discrimination: Ratio of high to low scorers on the total test who answer a given item correctly

Individualized Education Program (IEP): Written plan of instruction, including evaluation procedures, developed for each student receiving special education

individually based norms: Norms based on the distribution of scores of individual examinees; type of norms used in the AAHPER youth fitness test

initializing a disk: Preparing a disk for use, specifically on an Apple computer

ink-jet printer: A printer that uses ink sprayed through nozzles to form characters on paper

instructed/uninstructed approach: Determination of valid cutoff point by comparing an instructed group with an uninstructed group

integrated software: Computer programs that include two or more application programs in a single package; provide the capacity to easily transfer data between applications

interclass reliability coefficient: Method of estimating reliability ($R_{xx'}$) using correlation procedures

interests: Affect reflecting one's likes and dislikes about various matters, such as physical activity, programming, and scheduling

interface card: Element of a bus that provides communication between the computer circuit board and a hardware component

interjudge objectivity: Consistency in scoring between two or more independent judgments of the same performance

interpercentile range: Measure of variability used in conjunction with the median; can be represented by a variety of ranges as long as equal portions of each end of the distribution are eliminated

interval (i): Range of scores identified to form categories of a frequency distribution

intraclass reliability coefficient: Method of estimating reliability ($R_{xx'}$) using analysis of variance

intrajudge objectivity: Consistency in scoring when one person scores the same test two or more times

intratask analysis: Identification of stages of development of a task from the time the task is first attempted to the time it is performed at a mature or an adult level

isokinetic resistance training: Resistance training that requires a machine that adjusts resistance throughout the range of motion at a preset fixed speed

isometric resistance training: Resistance training that involves no limb movement at the joint being exercised

isotonic resistance training: Resistance training that involves concentric and eccentric contractions against a constant weight

item analysis: Method for determining the usefulness of each individual item as a part of the total test

item difficulty: Proportion of examinees answering the item correctly

item function: Percentage of examinees selecting an alternative as the correct response, whether it is correct or not

kappa coefficient (κ): Method of determining the reliability of a mastery test where change is taken into account

keyboard: Used to transmit information to computer; similar to keyboard of typewriter

kilobyte (K): 1,024 bytes

Kraus-Weber test: Test of minimal functioning of the low back area

kyphosis: A postural defect characterized by excessive posterior curvature of the spine

laptop computer: A small (usually under 10 lb) computer that fits comfortably in an attaché case

laser printer: A printer that uses a laser beam much like a dot-matrix printer to create high resolution images on paper

least restrictive environment: The learning environment that enables persons with a disability to perform to their fullest capacity

level of behavior: Level of the process (cognitive, affective, or psychomotor) the learner uses in attaining an objective

Likert scale: Scale measuring degree of agreement or disagreement with a series of affective statements

LIST: BASIC command to list each line of the program in random access memory (RAM)

LOAD (program): A BASIC command to take a specified program from the disk and put it into RAM

logical validity: Extent to which a test measures the most important components of skill required to perform the motor task adequately

long-range goals: Long-term global goals that describe the end product of a complete education

lordosis: A postural defect characterized by excessive anterior curvature of the spine

mastery learning: Model of instruction whereby frequent feedback is given to the learner and a large percentage of learners can attain at least minimal success in a unit of instruction

mastery test: Type of criterion-referenced test in which examinees are classified as masters or nonmasters

matching item: Item containing two columns of words or phases, with the right-hand column used as alternatives to match with the material in the left-hand column

maximum oxygen uptake (VO$_2$ max): Maximum amount of oxygen an individual can transport and use during exercise, expressed as milliliters per kilogram of body weight per minute (ml/kg/min)

mean: Arithmetic average of a set of scores; a measure of central tendency

measure: When used as a noun, refers to an instrument or technique used to obtain information (usually a score) about an attribute of a person or an object; when used as a verb, refers to the process of obtaining the score

measurement: Process of assigning a number to an attribute of a person or an object; the process of obtaining test scores

median: Score dividing the distribution such that 50% of the scores fall above that point and 50% fall below; the 50th percentile

megabyte: Unit of computer memory storage representing approximately 1 million bytes or typed characters

mentally retarded*: Significantly subaverage, general intellectual functioning existing concurrently with deficits in adaptive behavior and manifested in the developmental period, which adversely affects a child's education performance

MET: Metabolic equivalent; the oxygen cost of energy expenditure at rest; 1 MET = 3−4 mL/kg/min

microcomputer: A computer that employs a microprocessor as a central processing unit; laptop, desktop, and palmtop computers are types of microcomputers

mode: Most frequently occurring score in the distribution; a measure of central tendency

modem: Device allowing a computer to communicate over telephone lines and other communication media

motor ability: Originally, the innate ability to perform motor skills; more commonly, the ability to perform motor skills

motor capacity: Individual's capacity to perform motor skills

motor educability: Individual's ability to learn new motor skills

mouse: A handheld pointing device used to direct the movement of the cursor on a computer screen

multiple-choice item: Test item that is answered using one of three or more alternatives

muscular endurance: "The ability of the muscle to maintain submaximum force levels for extended periods" (Heyward, 1984:5)

muscular strength: "The maximum force or tension that can be produced by the muscle group" (Heyward, 1984:4)

needs assessment: Comparison of actual status of target group with desired status on some attribute to determine program needs

network: Two or more computers connected for purposes of sharing resources and communication

normal curve: Bell-shaped curve with known properties

norm-referenced test: Test used to compare an examinee's score with the scores of other similar examinees

objective test: Test with highly precise scoring system, yielding little error

objectivity: Precision with which test is scored

observational analysis: Analysis of performance that involves recording subjective observations of behavior

operating system: A series of computer programs that control the flow of information and overall operation of the computer (see disk operating system)

orthopedic impairment*: A severe orthopedic impairment adversely affecting a child's educational performance; includes impairments caused by a congenital anomaly (e.g., clubfoot, absence of some member), impairments caused by disease (e.g., poliomyelitis), and impairments from other causes (e.g., cerebral palsy, leukemia)

palmtop computer: A computer that will fit comfortably in the palm of the hand

parallel communication: Communication between computer components that transmits information on parallel paths (e.g., 8 bits are transmitted at one time along parallel paths)

paraplegia: Paralysis of the legs and lower part of the body

pass-fail method: Method of grading using two grade categories

passive stretching: Muscle stretching that is largely involuntary and results from an assist from gravity or from another person while the subject relaxes the muscles around the joint

Pearson product-moment correlation coefficient: Statistical technique used to determine the relationship between two sets of measures of the same persons

perceived exertion scale: Scale used to assess the examinee's perception of his or her physical exertion during exercise

percentage method: Method of grading based on the assignment of a percentage to each grade category; a norm-referenced approach to grading

percentage-correct method: Method of grading based on the percentage of test items or trials successfully completed; a criterion-referenced approach to grading

percentile: Score value for a specified percentage of cases in a distribution of scores

percentile norms: Norms calculated by converting raw scores to percentiles

percentile rank: Percentage of cases falling at or below a specified score in a distribution

peripheral: Device that can send information to the computer as well as receive information from it

physical fitness (health-related)†: Multifaceted continuum extending from birth to death; affected by physical activity; ranges from optimal abilities in all aspects of life to severely limiting disease and dysfunction

placement: In special education, the process to determine the least restrictive environment for the student

posture: Alignment of the body and its segments

power: Ability to generate maximum force in a minimum amount of time

predictive validity: Appropriateness of a test as a predictor of behavior

predictor: Test or variable that predicts a criterion behavior

program evaluation: Assessment of the extent to which a program has met predetermined objectives

proportion of agreement (P): Method of determining the reliability of a criterion-referenced test

psychomotor domain: Motor behavior ranging from a low level, reproducing a skill, to higher levels in which the skill is used creatively in a game setting

Pull-ups test: Measures arm and shoulder girdle strength; usually designated for boys

pulse rate: Estimation of heart rate; often made by placing the tips of two or three fingers on the skin above an artery and counting the beats

qualitative measurement: Predominantly judgmental approach to measurement

quantitative measurement: Objective approach to measurement in which a number is assigned to the attribute of interest

range: Spread of scores; in a distribution, the bottom score subtracted from the top score plus 1

random access memory (RAM): Primary memory of a computer; information can be stored in RAM as well as retrieved and modified

rank difference correlation coefficient: Statistical technique used to calculate the correlation coefficient when the scores are ranked

rating scale: Scale used to subjectively assess performance

raw score: Score obtained by an examinee on a test

reactive effect: Change in affect resulting from heightened awareness because of the experience of taking an inventory measuring the affective behavior

read only memory (ROM): Computer memory in which information is stored once, usually by the manufacturer; cannot be changed

real limits: Upper and lower limits of intervals in a frequency distribution representing the entire area between intervals; do not represent score units actually obtained on the test

reflexes: Inborn, genetically endowed, involuntary behaviors

reliability: Dependability of scores, their relative freedom from error; the consistency of an individual's performance on a test

reliability (criterion-referenced): Consistency of classification of masters and non-masters

response distortion: Invalid response because of failure to respone to an item, usually an affective measure, with total honesty

scoliosis: A postural defect characterized by lateral curvature of the spine

score limits: Upper and lower limits of intervals in a frequency distribution represented in raw score units, i.e., the actual scores obtained on the test

screening: In special education, the process to determine if a student is likely to require special assistance

semantic differential scale: Rating of concepts with scales anchored at the extremes with bipolar adjectives

serial communication: Communication between computer components that transmits information one bit at a time along a single path

shareware: Computer software that is distributed for free; users are asked to make a donation if they intend to use the software

short-answer item: Test item including a statement with one or more blank spaces to be filled in by the examinee

Shuttle run test: Measures speed and change of direction

Sit-ups test: Measures abdominal strength

skewness: Shape of the curve when the majority of the scores fall at one end of the distribution, with the remainder of the scores tapering off as reflected in the long tail of the distribution

skinfold caliper: Device for measuring skinfold thickness

skinfold thickness: Thickness of a fold of skin when lifted away from the muscle; used to estimate body fat

social behavior: Behavior displayed in dealing with others, such as relationships among peers

software: Encompasses the instructions used to run a computer (i.e., programs), the media on which the instructions are stored (e.g., disks), and the documentation required to effectively use the program (i.e., computer manuals)

specificity: A concept in resistance training that asserts that muscle strength, endurance, and power are specific to muscles and groups of muscles

speech impairment*: Communication disorder, such as stuttering, impaired articulation, language impairment, or voice impairment, which adversely affects a child's educational performance

split-half reliability estimate: Reliability estimate determined by dividing the test into halves and correlating scores on the two half-tests

sport profile: An administrative tool used for recording test scores associated with the cognitive, affective, and psychomotor components deemed necessary for successful performance in a particular sport or activity

sportsmanship: Behaviors considered appropriate for sports participants and spectators; e.g., fair play, following rules, and showing respect for officials

spreadsheet: A matrix of columns and rows into which data are entered for mathematical analysis; computerized spreadsheet application programs provide the capacity for sophisticated calculation and forecasting using numerical data

standard deviation: Square root of the average of the squared deviations of scores from the mean; a measure of variability

standard deviation method: Method of grading based on the standard deviation of the distribution of scores; a norm-referenced approach to grading

standard error of measurement: Estimate of the absolute error of an individual's score

standard of performance: Degree to which the student is expected to meet the objective

standard score: Score standardized by taking the deviation of the score from the mean and dividing it by the standard deviation

standard score method: Same as the standard deviation method of grading; use of z-scores

Standing long jump test: Measures explosive leg power

static balance: Ability to maintain equilibrium in a stationary position

static strength: Force exerted against an immovable resistance

statistics: Methodology for analyzing a set of test scores

stem: Introductory question or statement in a multiple-choice item

step test: Field test of cardiorespiratory function in which the examinee steps up and down on a bench until a predetermined heart rate is reached

subjective test: Test with imprecise scoring system, usually because of differences in the judgment of scorers

subjectivity: Use of individual judgment in evaluating motor performance

summative evaluation: Evaluation that takes place at the end of a training period or instructional unit

systematic decrease in scores: Gradual decrease in test scores from trial to trial, often because of fatigue or loss of motivation

systematic increase in scores: Gradual increase in test scores from trial to trial, often because of practice or learning

table of specifications: Table of the categories of cognitive behavior (knowledge) to be tested; categories are weighed according to their importance

tally: Mark placed adjacent to an interval in a frequency distribution representing a score in the interval

task specificity: Concept that ability to perform a task is specific to the task

taxonomy: Classification scheme

terminal behavior: Behavior a student is expected to display upon successful attainment of the objective

test: Instrument or technique used to obtain information (usually a score) about an attribute of a person or object

test battery: Two or more tests administered together to measure separate dimensions of a single characteristic or single sport or activity (e.g., *FITNESS*GRAM is a test battery of several tests which together measure health-related physical fitness)

test user: Person who selects or administers the test

Title IX: Legislation providing for equality by gender in many areas, including physical education programs

trait: Enduring and unchanging characteristic

true-false item: Test item that is answered using one of two alternatives

T-scores: Distribution of standard scores with a mean of 50 and a standard deviation of 10; a conversion of the z-score distribution

user-friendly: Describes computer programs that are easy to learn, easy to use, and self-instructing

validity: Soundness of the interpretations of a test; the extent to which a test measures what it is supposed to measure

validity coefficient: Correlation coefficient representing the relationship between a test and a criterion measure

variability: Spread of scores in a distribution

variance: Squared deviations of scores from the mean; indicator of the variability or spread of a set of scores

vertical jump: Jump executed as high as possible in a vertical direction; reflects explosive power of leg extensor muscles

virus: A destructive computer program secretly attached to an existing program that alters and deletes data and causes other malfunctions

visual impairment*: A visual impairment, even with correction, adversely affecting a child's educational performance; includes both partially seeing and blind children

weak measure: Measure lacking adequate evidence of validity and reliability

weight (of grade): Number designating the importance of a grade; higher number reflects greater importance

weight-training machine: Device used to measure muscular strength and endurance

Windows: A popular graphical user interface developed by Microsoft Corporation

word processor: A computer application program designed for editing, storing, formatting, and printing documents

50-yard dash test: Measures speed

600-yard run: Measures cardiorespiratory function

z-scores: Most basic of standard score distributions, with a mean of 0 and a standard deviation of 1; used as the basis for many other standard score transformations

Credits and Acknowledgments

Chapter 2 Summarizing a Set of Test Scores
P. 26—Courtesy Midvale Elementary School, Madison, Wis.
37—Courtesy Measurement Laboratory, Department of Physical Education and Dance, University of Wisconsin, Madison.

Chapter 3 Describing a Distribution of Test Scores
P. 59—From Test Service Notebook 148, 1980. p 1: The Psychological Corporation.
71—Courtesy Midvale Elementary School, Madison, Wis.

Chapter 5 Computers in Measurement and Evaluation
P. 111—Courtesy Intel.
112,113,118,119,120—Courtesy Hewlett-Packard Company.
126—Reprinted by permission: Tribune Media Services.
137—Courtesy Chattanooga Group, Inc.
138—Courtesy PEAK systems.

Chapter 6 Validity and Reliability of Norm-Referenced Tests
P. 146—Courtesy Measurement Laboratory, Department of Physical Education and Dance, University of Wisconsin, Madison.

157—From Morgan WP, Johnson RW, 1978. Personality characteristics of successful and unsuccessful oarsmen. Internat J Sports Psychol 9:119-133. By permission of the publisher.
158—From Morgan WP, Raven PB. 1985. Prediction of distress for individuals wearing industrial respirators. Am Ind Hyg Assoc J 46(7):363-368.

Chapter 7 Validity and Reliability of Criterion-Referenced Tests
Pp. 176,188—Courtesy Midvale Elementary School, Madison, Wis.

Chapter 8 Assessment in a School Curriculum
P. 196—Courtesy Measurement Laboratory, Department of Physical Education and Dance, University of Wisconsin, Madison.
199—Modified from Imwold CH, Rider RA, Johnson DJ. 1982. J Teaching in Phys Ed 2:13-18.
210—Courtesy Biodynamics Laboratory, Department of Physical Education and Dance, University of Wisconsin, Madison.

Chapter 9 Grading
P. 215—Reprinted by permission of United Feature Syndicate, Inc.
221—Hale PW, Hale RM. 1972. Comparison of student improvement by experimental

modification of test-retest scores. Research Quarterly 43:113-120.
237—Reprinted by permission of Hafeman, DA, PhD, Superintendent, Madison Metropolitan School District, Madison, Wis.

Chapter 10 Assessment in a Nonschool Setting
Pp. 249,257,266—Courtesy Biodynamics Laboratory, Department of Physical Education and Dance, University of Wisconsin, Madison.
250–251—From Vic Tanny International of Wisconsin. By permission of Dr. Paul Ward, Dr. Frank I Katch, and Mr. Bernard F Palluck, Vice President and Area Director; procedures were formulated by Dr. Ward; percentage of fat regression equation was developed by Drs. Katch and McArdle.
252—From the Olympic Health and Racquet Club. By permission of Ray Fraley.
254—From Department of the Army Materiel Command.
258—From the Exercise Resource Facility, CUNA Mutual Insurance Group, Madison, Wisconsin. By permission of Katie Munns.
264,259,260,261,262,263, 264—Courtesy Sentry World Headquarters, Stevens Point, Wis.

265,267,268—Golding LA, Myers CR, Sinning WE, eds. 1982. National Board of YMCA of the USA. Chicago. Copies available YMCA of the USA, Program Resources, 6400 Shafer Court, Rosemont, IL 60018. By permission of the YMCA.

Chapter 12 Measuring Motor Performance in Children
P. 302—From Seefeldt V, Haubenstricker J. 1982. Patterns, phases, or stages: an analytical model for the study of developmental movement. In Kelso JAS, Clark JE, eds. The development of movement control and coordination. London: John Wiley & Sons, Ltd. By permission of the publisher.
304,305,329—Redrawn from Roberson MA, Halverson LE. 1984. Courtesy Motor Development and Child Study Laboratory, University of Wisconsin, Madison.
307,309,310,311,312,314,315, 317,319—Reprinted by permission of the American Alliance for Health, Physical Education, Recreation, and Dance, 1900 Association Drive, Reston, VA 22091.
308–309,310–311,316,317— From Scott MG, French E. 1959. Measurement and evaluation in physical education. Dubuque, Iowa: Wm C Brown Group. By permission of Scott MG, PhD.
318,320,321—From Johnson RD. 1962. Measurements of achievement in fundamental skills of elementary school children. Res Quart 33:94-103. Reprinted by permission of the American Alliance for Health, Physical Education, Recreation, and Dance, 1900 Association Drive, Reston, VA.
322—Courtesy American Medical Association. Copyright 1978.
323—Courtesy of Dale A. Ulrich, 1989.
325–326—Reprinted by permission of Ross Laboratories. Adapted from Hamill PVV, Driżd TA, Johnson CL, et al:

Physical growth: National Center for Health Statistics percentiles. Am J Clin Nurtr 32:607-629, 1979. Data from the National Center for Health Statistics (NCHS), Hyattsville, Md.
327,330—Roberson MA, Halverson LE. 1984. Developing children—their changing movement. Philadelphia: Lea & Febiger. Used by permission.

Chapter 13 Adapting Tests and Measurements for Special Populations
Pp. 335,346,358—Courtesy Measurement and Biodynamics Laboratories. Department of Physical Education and Dance, University of Wisconsin, Madison.
339,340,344,361—Courtesy Janet A Seaman, Professor, California State University, Los Angeles.
341—Adapted from Zittel LL. 1994. Gross motor assessment of preschool children with special needs: Instrument selection and considerations. Adapted Physical Activity Quarterly, 11(3):245–260. Used by permission.
347—Reproduced by permission of the American Alliance for Health, Physical Education, Recreation and Dance.
354,355,356,357—From Winnick JP, Short FX. 1985. Physical fitness testing of the disabled: Project UNIQUE. Champaign, Ill: Human Kinetics. Used by permission.
350,359,360—Courtesy Dale A Ulrich, 1989.

Chapter 14 Measures of Affective Behavior
375—From Miller DK, Allen TE. 1982. Fitness: a lifetime commitment, ed. 2. Minneapolis: Burgess Publishing Co. Reprinted by permission of the publisher.
376,378–379—From Martens R. 1977. Sport Competition Anxiety Test. Champaign, Ill: Human Kinetics Publishers. By

permission of the publisher.
380–381—From Cowell CC. 1958. Validity: an index of social adjustment for high school use. Res Quart 29:7-18. Reprinted by permission of the American Alliance for Health, Physical Education, Research, and Dance, 1900 Association Drive, Reston, VA 22091.
382–383—From Blanchard BE. 1936. A behavior frequency rating scale for the measurement of character and personality traits in physical education classroom situations. Res Quart 7:56-66. Reprinted by permission of the American Alliance for Health, Physical Education, Research, and Dance, 1900 Association Drive, Reston, VA 22091.
384—Reprinted by permission of Kenyon GS, University of Lethbridge, Lethbridge, Alberta, Canada.
386—From Pooley JC. 1971. The professional socialization of physical education students in the United States and England. Unpublished doctoral dissertation, The University of Wisconsin, Madison. By permission of the author.
387—From Simon JA, Smoll FL. 1974. An instrument for assessing children's attitudes toward physical activity. Res Quart 45:21-27. By permission of the author.
388—From Sonstroem RJ. 1974. Attitude testing: examining certain psychological correlates of physical activity. Res Quart 39:566-574. Reprinted by permission of the author, University of Rhode Island, Kingston.
390–391—From Wear CL. 1955. Construction of equivalent forms of an attitude scale. Res Quart 26:113-119. Reprinted by permission of the American Alliance for Health, Physical Education, Recreation, and Dance, 1900 Association Drive, Reston, VA 22091.
392–393—From Lakie WL. 1964. Expressed attitudes of various groups of athletes

toward athletic competition. Res Quart 35:497-503. Reprinted by permission of the American Alliance for Health, Physical Education, Recreation, and Dance, 1900 Association Drive, Reston, VA 22091.
394–396—From Nelson DO. 1966. Nelson Sports Leadership Questionnaire. Res Quart 37:268-275. Reprinted by permission of the author.
397—From Borg GAV. 1973. Perceived exertion: a note on "history" and methods. Med Sci Sports 5:90-93. Reproduced by permission of the publisher.
398—Courtesy Biodynamics Laboratory, Department of Physical Education and Dance, University of Wisconsin, Madison.

Chapter 16 Constructing Knowledge Tests
Pp. 428,429—From Haskins MJ. 1971. Evaluation in physical education. Dubuque, Iowa. Wm C Brown Group. By permission of the author.
437—From Ebel RL. 1965. Measuring educational achievement. Englewood Cliffs, NJ: Prentice-Hall, Inc. By permission of the publisher.
436—From Mood DP. Measurement Methodology for Knowledge Tests. In: Safrit MJ, Wood TM, eds. Measurement Concepts in Physical Education and Exercise Science (p 275). Champaign, Ill. Human Kinetics Publishers. Copyright 1989 by Margaret J Safrit and Terry M Wood. Reprinted by permission.

Chapter 17 Measures of Health-Related Physical Fitness
P. 447—Courtesy Biodynamics Laboratory, University of Wisconsin, Madison.
454—From The Chrysler Fund-AAU Physical Fitness Program. 1987. The Chrysler Fund-Amateur Athletic Union: Bloomington, Ind.
455,456—Reproduced from Fit Youth Today Program Manual. 1988. Austin, Tex. American Health and Fitness Foundation.

By permission of the publisher.
459,460—From Institute for Aerobics Research. 1992. The Prudential *FITNESS*GRAM test administration manual. Dallas: Institute for Aerobics Research.
461–462 Fig. 17-1—From Cooper Institute for Aerobic Research, Prudential *FITNESS*GRAM.
465—Reproduced from the Presidential Physical Fitness Award Program: Instructor's Guide. 1987. Washington, DC, President's Council on Physical Fitness and Sports. By permission of the publisher.
466—From President's Council on Physical Fitness and Sports. 1991b. The President's Challenge physical fitness program packet. Washington, DC. President's Council on Physical Fitness and Sports; p 7. Used by permission.
472–475—Reproduced by permission of Timothy Lohman.
483—Reprinted with permission from the J Phys Ed Recreation Dance, 58(9):100, 1987. The Journal is a publication of the American Alliance for Health, Physical Education, Recreation, and Dance, 1900 Association Drive, Reston, VA 22091.
468,488–489—From Health-Related Physical Fitness Test Manual. Reston, Virginia. AAHPERD, 1980. By permission of the AAHPERD.
470,471,480,481,482,486,487, 491,492,493—From the National Children and Youth Fitness Study I. 1985. Public Health Service, Office of Disease Prevention and Health Promotion, US Department of Health and Human Services: Washington, DC 20201.
463,469,476,477,478,479,485, 490—From the National Children and Youth Fitness Study II, 1987. US Department of Health and Human Services: Washington, DC 20201.
494,495—Reprinted with permission from the J Phys Ed Recreation Dance, 59(4):79, 1988. The journal is a

publication of the American Alliance for Health, Physical Education, Recreation, and Dance, 1900 Association Drive, Reston, VA 22091; From Pate R, Corbin C. 1981. A taxonomy of physical fitness objectives. Implications for curriculum, J Phys Ed Recreation 52(1):36. Reprinted by permission of the American Alliance for Health, Physical Education, Recreation, and Dance, 1900 Association Drive, Reston, VA 22091.
500—From Nutrition Weight Control and Exercise, by Katch FI, McArdle WD. 1983. ed 2. By permission of Lea & Febiger.
504—Courtesy Pollock ML and the WB Saunders Co. From Pollock ML, Wilmore JM, Fox SM. 1984. Exercise in health and disease: evaluation and prescription for prevention and rehabilitation. Philadelphia: WB Saunders Co.
505—From Pollack ML, Schmidt DH, Jackson AS. 1980. Measurement of cardiorespiratory fitness and body composition in the clinical setting. Comprehen Ther 6(9):12-27. By permission of the Laux Co, Inc, Harvard, Mass.

Chapter 18 Tests of Performance-Related Physical Fitness
Pp. 512,517,518,519,534—Courtesy Measurement Laboratory, Department of Physical Education and Dance, University of Wisconsin, Madison.
515,516,526,528,530,532—From Youth Fitness Test Manual. Washington, DC. AAHPER, 1976. Used by permission.
523,524—Reprinted by permission of the American Alliance for Health, Physical Education, Recreation, and Dance, 1900 Association Drive, Reston, VA 22091.
525,527,529,531,532,533—Modified from Youth Fitness Test Manual. Washington, DC: AAHPERD, 1976. Reprinted by permission of the American

Alliance for Health, Physical Education, Recreation, and Dance, 1900 Association Drive, Reston, VA 22091.
539,541—From Spray JA. 1977. Interpreting group or class performances using AAHPER Youth Fitness Test Norms. J Phys Ed Recreation, 48:56-57. By permission of the publisher;
540—From Table 1 in Spray JA. 1977. Interpreting group or class performances using AAHPER Youth Fitness Test Norms. J Phys Ed Recreation, 48:56-57. Reprinted by permission of the American Alliance for Health, Physical Education, Research, and Dance, 1900 Association Drive, Reston, VA 22091.

Chapter 19 Tests of Sports Skills
P. 552—From Archery for boys and girls: Skills test manual. 1967. Washington, DC: AAHPER. Reprinted by permission of the American Alliance for Health, Physical Education, Research, and Dance, 1900 Association Drive, Reston, VA 22091.
553,556—Redrawn from Johnson BL, Nelson JK. 1979. Practical measurements for evaluation in physical education. Minneapolis: Burgess Publishing Co. By permission of Nelson JK, PhD.
554—In Scott MG, French E. 1959. Measurement and evaluation in physical education. Dubuque, Iowa: Wm C Brown Group. By permission of Scott MG, PhD.
558,560,561,562,563,564,565, 566—From Hopkins DR, Shick J, Plack JJ. 1984. Basketball for boys and girls: skills test manual. Reston, VA. AAHPERD. Reprinted by permission of the American Alliance for Health, Physical Education, Recreation, and Dance, 1900 Association Drive, Reston, VA 22091.
567—From Chapman NL. 1982. Chapman ball control test-field hockey. Res Quart Exercise Sport 53(3):239-242. Reprinted by permission of the American Alliance for Health, Physical

Education, Recreation, and Dance, 1900 Association Drive, Reston VA 22091.
568,569—From AAHPER. 1966. Football: skills test manual. Washington, DC: AAHPER. Reprinted by permission of the American Alliance for Health, Physical Education, Recreation, and Dance, 1900 Association Drive, Reston, VA 22091.
570—From Shick J, Berg NG. 1983. Indoor golf skill test for junior high school boys. Res Quart Exercise Sport 54(1):75-78. Reprinted by permission of the American Alliance for Health, Physical Education, Recreation, and Dance, 1900 Association Drive, Reston, VA 22091.
578—From Shick J. 1970. Battery of softball skills tests for college women. Res Quart 42:82-87. Reprinted by permission of the American Alliance for Health, Physical Education, Recreation, and Dance, 1900 Association Drive, Reston, VA 22091.
584,585,586—From Hewitt JE. 1966. Hewitt's tennis achievement test. Res Quart 31:231-237. Reprinted by permission of the American Alliance for Health, Physical Education, Recreation, and Dance, 1900 Association Drive, Reston, VA 22091.
587,588—From Purcell K. 1981. A tennis forehand-backhand drive skill test which measures ball control and stroke firmness. Res Quart Exercise Sport 52(2):238-245. Reprinted by permission of the American Alliance for Health, Physical Education, Recreation, and Dance, 1900 Association Drive, Reston, VA 22091.
589—From Brady GF. 1945. Preliminary investigation of volleyball playing ability. Res Quart 16:14-17. Reprinted by permission of the American Alliance for Health, Physical Education, Recreation, and Dance, 1900 Association Drive, Reston, VA 22091.
590—From Brumbach WB.

1967. Beginning volleyball, a syllabus for teachers, revised edition. Eugene, Ore: Wayne Baker Brumbach. By permission of the author.

Chapter 20 Tests of Muscular Strength, Endurance, and Power
P. 601—Courtesy Lafayette Instrument.
605—Pollock ML, and others. 1978. Health and fitness through physical activity. New York: John Wiley & Sons. By permission of the publisher.
607—Heyward VH. 1984. Designs for Fitness. Minneapolis: Burgess Publishing Co. By permission of the publisher.
623—Courtesy Cybex.
624—Courtesy Chattanooga Group, Inc.
626—Friermood HT. 1967. "Volleyball Skills Contest for Olympic Development," in US Volleyball Association, Annual Official Volleyball Rules and Reference Guide of the US Volleyball Association, Berne, Ind: USVBA Printer, pp 134-135. By permission of HT Friermood and the US Volleyball Association.
†Raw scores are located in the chart in accordance with age and sex, and percentile scores are located across the top.

Chapter 21 Tests of Balance, Flexibility, and Posture
P 632—Courtesy Neurocom International
639,640—Courtesy Lafayette Co., Lafayette, Ind.
647-648—By permission of the State Education Department, State University of New York, Albany.

Appendix E NCYFS Norms
Tables A-1 to A-12—From Ross JG, Gilbert GG. 1985. The national children and youth fitness study: a summary of findings. Journal of Physical Education, Recreation, and Dance, **56**:45-50.

Index